THOMAS CRANMER

Portrait by Fliccius. The inscription 'Anno aetate 57. Julij 20'
indicates that it was painted in July 1545, and not in the year 1546
which is usually given as the date.

THOMAS CRANMER

BY

JASPER RIDLEY

OXFORD
AT THE CLARENDON PRESS

Oxford University Press, Ely House, London W.1

GLASGOW   NEW YORK   TORONTO   MELBOURNE   WELLINGTON
CAPE TOWN   SALISBURY   IBADAN   NAIROBI   LUSAKA   ADDIS ABABA
BOMBAY   CALCUTTA   MADRAS   KARACHI   LAHORE   DACCA
KUALA LUMPUR   HONG KONG

*For copyright reasons
this book may not be issued on loan
or otherwise except in its original
soft cover*

*First published 1962
Reprinted 1962*

First issued in OXFORD PAPERBACKS
1966

REPRINTED LITHOGRAPHICALLY IN GREAT BRITAIN
AT THE UNIVERSITY PRESS, OXFORD
BY VIVIAN RIDLER
PRINTER TO THE UNIVERSITY

CONTENTS

CRANMER AND HIS BIOGRAPHERS

FEW characters in history have aroused as much controversy as Thomas Cranmer. For four hundred years he has been bitterly attacked and ardently defended by biographers and historians as if the righteousness of the English Reformation and the justification of the Church of England depended on the moral probity of the man who was its first Archbishop. The Roman Catholics have hardly troubled to waste their ammunition on so easy a target as Henry VIII, and the Protestants have not been particularly concerned to defend the reputation of Thomas Cromwell; but the character of Cranmer has been a bitterly contested issue between Foxe and Sanders, between Burnet and Bossuet, between Todd and Lingard, between Pollard and Belloc.

Nearly every important action in Cranmer's life has been interpreted both favourably and unfavourably. His remarks to his secretary about his ill-treatment at school have been put forward as an excuse for his weaknesses and as an example of his tendency to put the blame for his failings on to others. His undistinguished career at Cambridge is cited either as proof of his innate intellectual mediocrity or of his commendable dissatisfaction with the University syllabus in the old, Papist days. His protestation at his consecration has been denounced as perjury and praised as an outstanding example of moral rectitude. His letters after the arrest of Anne Boleyn and Cromwell have been seen both as courageous intercessions and as cowardly betrayals of fallen patrons. To the Catholics, his changes of opinion in questions of religious doctrine suggest unscrupulous opportunism; to the Protestants, they show his broad-minded approach and his readiness to admit that he had been mistaken. His first and second marriages, his conduct at the time of the Six Articles, and his attitude during the *coup d'état* against Somerset, have been vigorously attacked and defended. Even his recantations at Oxford have been excused, if not condoned, as resolutely as they have been condemned.

At the same time, his admirers have pursued a subsidiary controversy amongst themselves as to the nature of Cranmer's theological doctrines, particularly on the question of the Eucharist. Men holding different opinions on the Sacrament have been eager to prove that Cranmer agreed with them, and have cited passages from his books and disputations to show that his doctrine was as high or as low as their own.

In 1548, the Protestant writer John Bale—who had been at Jesus College, Cambridge, with Cranmer—published his *Centuries*, which consisted of short biographical notices of five hundred eminent Britons of the past and present. Bale naturally included Cranmer among the five hundred, and his comment was fulsome. 'In the midst of Babylon, he always acted as the upright leader of the people of Israel, and among the Papist tyrants he guided, with unheard of wisdom, the people of God to the truth of Christ, lest they should become the prey of the foxes.'[1] Eight years later, Cranmer was burned as a heretic by the English government. While his triumphant enemy Stephen Gardiner was laid to rest in a splendid tomb in Winchester Cathedral after the honours of a great state funeral, Cranmer's ashes were left in a ditch outside the walls of Oxford, and his memory was subjected to an intensive campaign of vilification. Within a few months of his death, some official publicist—it was probably Alan Cope—had written the book which either then or subsequently was named *Bishop Cranmer's Recantacyons*, with the object of blackening Cranmer's memory. Before the end of Mary's reign, Nicholas Harpsfield, who had replaced Cranmer's brother as Archdeacon of Canterbury, and was one of the most active and pitiless judges in heresy trials, wrote *The Pretended Divorce of Catherine of Aragon*, in which he attacked Cranmer at considerable length.

But the burning of Cranmer had made him a hero and a martyr in the eyes of the Protestant refugees. Men who had previously been strongly opposed to Cranmer's policies, and who certainly scoffed at Bale's panegyric in 1548, now believed that Cranmer had atoned, by his death, for the sins which he had committed in his life. At some time between 1556 and 1559, two English Protestants wrote a short biography of Cranmer. Strype thought that the second part of this manu-

[1] Bale's *Centuries*, f. 238 b.

script, which consists of a description of Cranmer's death, was written by either Becon or Scory, both of whom had been Cranmer's chaplains; but no one has made any conjecture as to who was the author of the first part, which is written in a different hand, and is an account of Cranmer's early life. This account was incorporated by Foxe into the second Latin edition of his *Book of Martyrs* in 1559, and afterwards in his first English edition of 1563. In 1560, a Hungarian Protestant used it as the basis of his pamphlet in Hungarian on 'Thomas Cranmer the Martyr', and a German version was published in the following year. Meanwhile the new Queen of England, after preserving a tactical silence for a year on the subject of her sister's victims, had in 1560 sanctioned a propaganda campaign which glorified Cranmer and his fellows as martyrs. Elizabeth ordered her officials to deliver up, for Parker's use, all Cranmer's writings in their possession, 'forasmuch as such a rare and precious a treasure we think is not to be kept in secret oblivion, as a candle under a bushel'; and her Secretary, William Cecil, added a directive in which he referred to Cranmer as 'the late most reverend and godly father Thomas Archbishop of Canterbury'.[1]

Cranmer's old secretary Ralph Morice had returned from exile when Mary died. Morice remembered Cranmer as a most considerate master as well as revering him as a Protestant martyr. After the publication of Foxe's first English edition, Morice told Matthew Parker, the Archbishop of Canterbury, that he knew many facts about Cranmer which had not appeared in Foxe's book, and at Parker's request he wrote his reminiscences of his old master. It is certain that Foxe not only read Morice's manuscripts, but also met him, and learned new facts which Morice had not written down for Parker. Foxe included all this information in the second English edition of the *Book of Martyrs* in 1570. Two years later, Parker himself

[1] For the authorship and the title of *Bishop Cranmer's Recantacyons*, see Gairdner's Preface, *Bishop Cranmer's Recantacyons*, p. v–xiii. The work of the two English Protestants is entitled 'The Lyfe and Death of Thomas Cranmer, late Archebushope of Caunterbury'; it is printed in Nichols, *Narratives of the Days of the Reformation*, pp. 218–33. It is referred to hereafter as the work of the anonymous biographer. See also Sztárai, *Historia Cranmerus Thamas Erseknek*, which was first published in 1582, but was written in 1560; *Historia von Thoma Cranmero dem Ertzbischoff zu Cantuaria inn Engelland*; Elizabeth I and Cecil to Herd, 14 April 1563 (Cranmer's *Works*, ii. 459); Parker to Cecil, 22 August 1563; Cecil to Parker, 25 August 1563 (Parker's *Correspondence*, pp. 186–7).

published, in his *De Antiquitate Britannica*, biographies of his
seventy predecessors in the see of Canterbury. His chapter on
Cranmer is of great interest, for although, like Foxe's work, it
contains some errors, Parker had been personally acquainted
with Cranmer, as well as being in contact with Morice and
Foxe.[1]

Meanwhile Cranmer's enemies had not been idle. When
Cope and his friends in their turn went into exile, they continued their polemics against Cranmer with undiminished
bitterness. Cranmer is attacked in Harpsfield's *Six Dialogues*,
which Cope published under his own name at Antwerp in 1566
when Harpsfield was a prisoner in the Tower. In 1576, Sanders
singled out Cranmer for criticism in his book on the *Anglican
Schism*, which had not yet been published when Sanders left
Madrid to join the Spanish expedition to Ireland, where he
died as a fugitive in the bogs. In 1584, the future Cardinal
Allen denounced Cranmer in the *Defence of English Catholics*.
Next year, Briegerus published at Naples his *Flowers of
Calvinism, as shown in the lives of Robert Dudley Earl of Leicester, John Calvin, Thomas Cranmer, John Knox and other
protectors and apostles of the Zwinglian sect*; it was dedicated to
Alexander Farnese of Parma, the commander of the Spanish
forces fighting the English in the Netherlands. Twenty years
later, Robert Parsons, the English Jesuit leader in Rome,
joined the attack on Cranmer in the *Three Conversions of England*.

The Protestant and Catholic attitude on the subject of
Cranmer which was laid down in these publications has been
followed with very little variation for four hundred years. To
the Protestants, Cranmer was an honest man who began life
under the disadvantage of having been educated as a Papist; he
therefore expounded Papist doctrines, and burned and persecuted Protestants, until the truth was gradually revealed to
him. Once he had seen the light, he did not falter until his final
ordeal at Oxford; and his recantations, which were extracted
from him by a fraudulent promise of life, brought more discredit on the Papists than on him. From the very beginning, the
recantations and other incidents placed the Protestants to some

---

[1] Morice, 'A declaration concernyng the Progeny, with the maner and trade of
the lif and bryngyng upp, of that most Reverent Father in God, Thomas Cranmer'
(in *Nar. Ref.*, pp. 238–72); Parker, *De Antiquitate Britannicae Ecclesiae*, pp.
374–6, 381–404.

extent on the defensive where Cranmer was concerned; but everything was excused him because of his martyrdom, and Foxe, who was not blind to Cranmer's faults, nevertheless felt able to declare that he was 'much more worthy the name of St. Thomas of Canterbury than he whom the Pope falsely before did canonize'.[1]

The Catholics saw Cranmer, not merely as a heretic and the heresiarch who had led England into heresy, but also as a lascivious hypocrite and careerist who was not even sincere in his heresy. This line was put forward by the counsel for the prosecution at Cranmer's trial in 1555. The author of *Bishop Cranmer's Recantacyons* wrote that Cranmer had deserted 'his Luther' at the time of the Six Articles. 'If his doctrine were good,' wrote Harpsfield, 'why did he give it over?' Sanders wrote that 'Cranmer himself had been a Henrician, that is a follower of Henry VIII, from whose instructions he never dared to depart even a hair's breath in anything. . . . But when the King died, Cranmer ceased to be a Henrician and became wholly a Lutheran, knowing at the same time that Henry had been a most earnest opponent of Luther', and published a Lutheran catechism. 'But a few months had hardly gone by when the miserable man found out that the Protector of the King, the Duke of Somerset, was a Calvinist, not a Lutheran. What was he to do? He recasts the catechism, changes his language, and he who was once a Henrician, then a Lutheran, becomes a Calvinist.' And Parsons wrote that it 'was his nature, then and ever after, to run after the time'.[2]

In the Catholic interpretation, Cranmer was a man who, being chaplain to the Boleyns, suggested to them that Anne could marry Henry and become Queen if Papal supremacy was overthrown. As a reward, he was granted the see of Canterbury, committing perjury in his consecration oath to the Pope. He repeatedly changed his doctrines to curry favour with the authorities, while he showed his lecherous nature by his two marriages and his advocacy of the marriage of priests. After committing high treason by supporting Jane Grey, he was called to account for his heresy; he then pretended to recant in

[1] Foxe, *Acts and Monuments*, viii. 90.
[2] Report of Cranmer's trial (Foxe, viii. 56–57); *Bishop Cranmer's Recantacyons*, pp. 8–9; Harpsfield, *The Pretended Divorce of Catherine of Aragon*, p. 290; Sanders, *The Anglican Schism*, pp. 180–2; Parsons, *Three Conversions of England*, ii. 373.

order to save his life, but he repudiated his recantations and
adhered to his heresies, out of inveterate malice, when he knew
that his ruse had failed and that he would be burned in any case.

The Protestant view of Cranmer was again put forward by
Bishop Godwin at the beginning of the seventeenth century,
and by Lord Herbert in 1649, while Fuller in 1655 defended
Cranmer from the criticism of Prynne. Prynne attacked Cranmer
because he was a Bishop. After his release from the Tower, he
published in 1641 his *Antipathy of the English Lordly Prelacy
both to Regal Monarchy and Civil Unity*, in the course of which
he attacked Cranmer, using many of the Catholic arguments.
He referred to the perjury in the consecration oath, to Cranmer's part in the persecution of Lambert, to his recantations and
his treason against his Queen, and ultimately fell back on the
curious argument that Cranmer's case did not prove that a
Bishop could be a martyr, because he had been degraded from
the episcopal order before he suffered martyrdom, though he
was still an Archbishop when he committed high treason.
Fuller replied with the traditional defences of Foxe and the
other Protestant writers.[1] Charles I's chaplain Heylin, who at
least on the subject of Cranmer could agree with Fuller, was
equally laudatory in his *Ecclesia Restaurata* in 1661.

At the end of the seventeenth century, two divines of the
Church of England pursued extensive researches into the history
of the Reformation, and produced works which for the next
hundred and fifty years ranked in Protestant eyes second only
to Foxe's book. John Strype, in his quiet retirement at Hackney,
augmented the historical labours in which Gilbert Burnet had
engaged amid the excitements of revolutionary politics. Burnet
did not have so high an opinion as Strype did of Cranmer; but
in the first volume of the *History of the Reformation* in 1679,
for which he received the thanks of a Whig Parliament, he
wrote that Cranmer had 'as eminent virtues, and as few faults
in him, as in any prelate that has been in the Christian Church
for many ages'. In his third volume in 1715, Burnet made the
more qualified comment that 'if it had not been for Cranmer's
too feeble compliance in King Henry's time, and this last in-

---

[1] Godwin, *De Praesulibus Angliae Commentarius*, pp. 137–44; and his *Annals of
England*, pp. 120–2, 171, 280, 301, 318–22; Prynne, *Antipathy of Prelacy to
Monarchy*, pp. 131–4; Fuller, *Church History of Britain*, ii. 42–46. See also
Fuller's short biography of Cranmer in his *Abel Redevivus*, i. 262–70.

excusable slip, he might well be proposed as one of the greatest patterns in history'. Strype, who began his historical writings with his biography of Cranmer in 1694, called Cranmer 'the first Protestant Archbishop of this Kingdom, and the greatest instrument under God of the happy Reformation of this Church of England'; he repeatedly referred to Cranmer as 'the good Archbishop', and stated that he was 'one of the holiest Bishops and one of the best men that age produced'. The Catholic criticism of this line could only be expressed by foreign writers —above all by Bossuet and by Joachim Le Grand; in England, the views of Burnet and Strype were unchallenged for a century, though the nonjuring Collier in 1714 was a trifle cool towards Cranmer. Cranmer was seen by the world of squire and parson as the model servant of God and the King. His Protestantism and his royalism endeared him to both Whigs and Tories; his weakness and subservience were excused as submission to what Archdeacon Todd called 'the command of his sovereign'.[1]

But controversy was revived in the nineteenth century. In 1820, the Roman Catholic attitude was ably expounded by Lingard. Lingard was strongly criticized by some of his coreligionists for the moderation with which he expressed his views; but though his style was very different from that of the Papist tractarians of Cranmer's time, his interpretation of Cranmer's character was basically the same as that of Harpsfield and Sanders. In the long controversy between Lingard and Todd, both sides used the old arguments on the consecration oath, the burning of Lambert, and the recantations and all other questions.[2] But Cranmer was now attacked from a new quarter —from the liberal and humanist historians who had come to realize that Cranmer's Protestantism was not enough to place him among the ranks of the heroes of English freedom. These writers were shocked at Cranmer's subservience to an autocratic monarch.

[1] Burnet, *History of the Reformation of the Church of England*, i. 18; iii. 432; Strype, *Memorials of the Most Reverend Father in God Thomas Cranmer*, pp. 1, 671; Bossuet, *Histoire des variations des Églises protestantes*, i. 361–79, 382–4, 388–97, 415–19, 437–44, 451–2; Le Grand, *Lettres à M. Burnet touchant l'Histoire des variations*, pp. 24–26, 30–38, 64–69, 73–75, 178; Collier, *Ecclesiastical History of Great Britain*; Todd, *Life of Archbishop Cranmer*, i. 55–56.

[2] Lingard, *History of England*, vol. v; and his *Vindication of the 'History of England'*; Todd, *Archbishop Cranmer*; and his *Vindication of the Most Reverend Thomas Cranmer*; and his *Reply to Lingard's Vindication*.

In 1827, Hallam roused the indignation of the Church of England with his comments on Cranmer in his *Constitutional History of England*. His aloof impartiality was deeply shocking to many Protestants; but his summary is probably the most accurate of all the statements which have been made about Cranmer in the last four centuries. 'If, casting away all prejudice on either side, we weigh the character of this prelate in an equal balance, he will appear far indeed removed from the turpitude imputed to him by his enemies, yet not entitled to any extraordinary veneration. Though it is most eminently true of Cranmer that his faults were always the effect of circumstances, and not of intention, yet this palliating consideration is rather weakened when we recollect that he consented to place himself in a station where those circumstances occurred.' Hallam's opinion was expressed more brilliantly and provocatively in the review of his book which Macaulay wrote during the next year. Macaulay agreed that 'if we consider Cranmer merely as a statesman, he will not appear a much worse man than Wolsey, Gardiner, Cromwell or Somerset. But when an attempt is made to set him up as a saint, it is scarcely possible for any man of sense who knows the history of the time to preserve his gravity'. He was not 'a monster of wickedness', but 'merely a supple, timid, interested courtier'. As for Cranmer's readiness to forgive his opponents, Macaulay considered that it was comparable to the attitude of the slave who feels neither gratitude for kindness nor resentment of injuries, and was a proof that a man may not only be above revenge, but also below it.[1]

These criticisms, however, were mild compared to that which William Cobbett hurled at Cranmer in 1829. He wrote in the *History of the Protestant Reformation* that Thomas Cranmer was 'a name which deserves to be held in everlasting execration; a name which we could not pronounce without almost doubting of the justice of God, were it not for our knowledge of the fact that the cold-blooded, most perfidious, most impious, most blasphemous caitiff expired at last amidst those flames which he himself had been the chief cause of kindling . . . the progress of this man in the paths of infamy need incontestable proof to

---

[1] Hallam, *Constitutional History of England,* i. 95–96; Macaulay, 'Essay on Hallam's "English Constitutional History" ' (Macaulay's *Works*, vii. 235, 239).

reconcile the human mind to a belief in it', as Cranmer's acts 'can be surpassed by nothing of which human depravity is capable.'[1]

The controversy continued throughout the nineteenth century, during which thirty biographies and biographical essays were published about Cranmer. His admirers rallied to his defence under the leadership of the Swiss Protestant Merle d'Aubigné, who answered the criticisms of Macaulay in a letter to the Marquis of Cholmondeley. He admitted that he much preferred the character of a Luther, a Calvin or a Knox; but 'God employs for the mysterious accomplishment of His purposes a great variety of character . . . if this God of sovereign wisdom gave a Cranmer and not a Luther as reformer to the Church of England, it was because, in His unanswerable counsel, He had given as King to your people not a Frederick the Wise but a Henry VIII. The extreme prudence of Cranmer, his timidity, his want of decision, his pliability, deplorable in certain cases, preserved him under the government of the despotic Tudor from the scaffold to which that bloody Prince sent many of his Bishops and his statesmen, and thus saved, with his own life, the work for which he was required. . . . He was the instrument employed by God for a work which, while it has saved, during the last three centuries, thousands and thousands of souls, and has served as a torch to illumine the most distant nations, has at the same time created and preserved the most powerful and illustrious nationality which modern times have witnessed'. But Dr. Littledale, who whatever his views on ritual was a clergyman of the Church of England and an opponent of the Church of Rome, called Cranmer a liar and a thief, and could not understand 'how anyone with any sense of religion, of honour, of manly feeling, can look on him with any sentiments save those of disgust and indignation'; and on the assumption that courage in a man was the equivalent of purity in a woman, he reached the surprising conclusion that 'Cranmer must take his stand with Lais and Messalina, nay with the nameless depravities which we associate with Faustina and Sappho'.[2]

---

[1] Cobbett, *History of the Protestant Reformation in England and Ireland*, paras. 64, 104, 105 (unpaginated).

[2] Merle d'Aubigné, *Vindication of Cranmer's character from the attack of Mr. Macaulay*, pp. 8–10; Littledale, *Innovations*, p. 37; and his letter to Cazenove, 16 September 1869, cited in Ashton, *The Father of the English Reformation*, p. 28.

The time had come when the study of the history of the Reformation was being lifted on to an altogether higher plane. Writers like Froude, Gairdner and Pollard—who almost alone among the historians of the Reformation were not in holy orders—along with Canon Dixon and Cardinal Gasquet, made a far deeper study of the period than any of the earlier authors had done, and they were followed by the more specialized researches of the leading historians of the twentieth century. But this great output of scholarship has produced only one biography of Cranmer; and Pollard's *Thomas Cranmer and the Reformation* is not his best work. It leaves a great deal unsaid, and is much less impartial than it appears at first sight. Pollard in effect takes the traditional Protestant line about Cranmer. His most useful contribution was to impress on his readers in 1905 that freedom of speech and conscience have not always been accepted in all ages as a sacred right of the individual; but the facts which weigh against Cranmer are too often ignored.

In the fifty-five years since Pollard's book was first published, there have been nineteen books and pamphlets about Cranmer. Six of these are full-length biographies; but one of the six must be classified as semi-fictional, and the other five are more in the nature of biographical essays than a complete biography.[1] The most interesting is that which Hilaire Belloc wrote in 1931. He put forward, for the first time for several centuries, a new interpretation of Cranmer's character, though Gairdner in one of his books had suggested that he was thinking along the same lines. Whereas all the previous Roman Catholic writers had seen Cranmer as a time-server, as opposed to the sincere convert of the Protestant biographers, Belloc's Cranmer is a secret agent. Belloc argued that men do not change their fundamental opinions when they are aged sixty, but form their opinions in their youth; he believed that when Cranmer became Archbishop of Canterbury, he had already adopted the Protestant doctrines which he openly proclaimed in Edward's reign, and dissimulated his opinions, burning men who believed as he did himself, in order to retain a position of power from

<hr/>

[1] Deane, *Life of Thomas Cranmer* (1927); Belloc, *Cranmer* (1931); Hutchinson, *Cranmer and the English Reformation* (1951); Bromiley, *Thomas Cranmer, Archbishop and Martyr* (1956); Theodore Maynard, *Life of Thomas Cranmer* (1956). The semi-fictional work is Styron, *The Three Pelicans: Archbishop Cranmer and the Tudor Juggernaut* (New York, 1932).

which he could one day make England a Protestant state. The fact that Cranmer, by yielding to Henry's wishes, survived till 1547 was for Merle d'Aubigné a proof that the hand of God was at work; for Belloc, it was a cunning and calculated policy. In Belloc's version, Cranmer—whom Canon Mason in 1898 had called 'as artless as a child'—was an unscrupulous and supremely successful exponent of the tactic of political infiltration. This theory, though entertaining, is hardly credible. It is difficult to believe that anyone who was not a disciplined member of an organized espionage service would devote sixteen years of his life to enforcing a policy in which he did not believe, and such an action would have been even less likely in the sixteenth than in the twentieth century. Cranmer would not knowingly have committed the folly against which Calvin warned him, and allowed the years to slip by as he advanced into old age oppressed with the fear that he might die before he had done what God required of him.[1]

But it is also impossible to accept the traditional Catholic and Protestant analyses of Cranmer. The Catholic picture of Cranmer as an unprincipled opportunist and a tool of royal tyranny, which became increasingly popular as British society moved farther away from the age of absolute monarchy, will not stand the test if Cranmer's record is compared with that of his contemporaries. If the life of almost any other leading churchman or politician of the sixteenth century were to be subjected to the same detailed examination and criticism, he would emerge from the ordeal more discredited than Cranmer. Gardiner has a worse record than Cranmer as an instrument of royal dictatorship, both under Henry and under Mary, who was as much a despot as her father and sister; and as far as time-serving is concerned, a stronger case can be made out against Gardiner, Bonner and all the other Bishops, to say nothing of the nobles and gentlemen of the Court. The Protestant interpretation of Cranmer as an honest Papist who gradually saw the light is a little nearer the truth; but it is not the whole truth. Its weakest point is its treatment of Cranmer's conduct during the Henrician reaction which followed the Six Articles.

[1] Mason, *Thomas Cranmer*, p. 200; Calvin to Cranmer (1551) ('Calvini Epistolae', p. 62, in *Calvini Opera*, vol. ix; Gorham, *Gleanings*, p. 279). Pollard refers to 'Cranmer's simple, transparent honesty' (*Thomas Cranmer and the Reformation*, p. 339).

There is no doubt that in 1539, in 1540 and above all in 1543, Cranmer betrayed his principles and retreated from Protestant doctrines to a much greater extent than his admirers admit.

If the known facts of Cranmer's life are impartially examined, nearly all the apparent contradictions disappear and a consistent personality emerges. Like most of his contemporaries—but by no means all of them—Cranmer believed in royal absolutism. He believed that his primary duty as a Christian was to strengthen the power of the King, and was prepared if necessary to sacrifice all his other doctrines to accomplish this. There was only one circumstance in which he considered that he was justified in opposing the royal policy—if he were ordered to sin. Then he must refuse to obey, as God must be served rather than man. When Cranmer was ordered to support a religious policy of which he disapproved, he had to decide, on this basis, whether to obey or resist. In the twentieth century, few people will deny that men are influenced by unconscious motives; and Cranmer, when he repeatedly faced this problem in Henry's reign, was obviously aware that obedience meant continued residence at Lambeth, and that resistance would bring him to the stake. But this is not the same thing as deliberate time-serving; and when in 1553 the issue was too plain for mental evasion, Cranmer was prepared to choose the hard road.

Cranmer was greatly influenced by another factor—his dread of revolution and disorder. He spent six months in Germany in 1532, and married a German wife, and may have been even more conscious than other English statesmen that the popular excitement which Luther had aroused in Germany had led to the Peasants War and the Anabaptists at Münster. Cranmer believed that Protestantism must be introduced by the Prince, not by the people, and it was fortunate for him that he died just in time before Protestantism became a revolutionary movement. He was always looking over his shoulder at the extremists behind him, and showed more resolution against Joan Bocher than against the Lady Mary. The English Zwinglians were right in 1548 in regarding him as 'lukewarm' towards the Reformation; but in the next few years, like many other leaders of great reforming movements, he was carried forward much farther than he really wished to go, and after 21st March 1556 there was no more criticism of Cranmer in Protestant circles.

CHAPTER I

THE FIRST FORTY YEARS

CRANMER was born at Aslockton in Nottinghamshire on 2nd July 1489. The only authority for the date is the statement of the anonymous biographer who wrote a few months after Cranmer's death. This writer makes several mistakes about Cranmer's early life, and he also states that Cranmer was thirty-four when he became a Doctor of Divinity, though we know that this was in 1526. But the fact that he gives the date of Cranmer's birth with such precision suggests that it is correct. Cranmer's father Thomas was the squire of the village of Aslockton. The family had moved there sixty years before from Lincolnshire, and had married the daughters of the Nottinghamshire gentry. It could boast of its Norman origin, and it bore the same arms, the three cranes, as did a French gentleman named Cranmer who was entertained by the Archbishop when he came to London, probably in 1546, on a diplomatic mission. By this time, Cranmer no longer wore the three cranes, for some seven years before, Henry VIII had granted him a new coat of arms of three pelicans, to signify Cranmer's readiness to shed his blood for the benefit of his spiritual children. As gentlemen, the Cranmers did not hold that great position in society which the gentlemen of England were to occupy in later centuries; they were not the equals of the nobility. In a society in which there were infinite graduations of rank rather than rigid class divisions, Cranmer was a long way from the top—as Bishop Brooks pointed out to him at his trial for heresy—and very conscious that he had superiors as well as inferiors.[1]

Cranmer had an elder and a younger brother, and at least five sisters, and possibly more, apart from the children who

---

[1] Anon. Biogr.; Morice (*Nar. Ref.*, pp. 218–19, 238, 250–1); Parker, p. 400; Foxe, viii. 46. Cranmer still bore the cranes on his seal in November 1538, but had adopted the pelicans by April 1540 (see Gorham, *Gleanings*, pp. 13–14; Waters, *Chesters of Chicheley*, p. 383; but Gorham is wrong in stating (pp. 9–10 n.) that Cranmer first adopted the cranes as his arms after he became Archbishop; see Morice, in *Nar. Ref.*, p. 238).

doubtless died in infancy. His younger brother Edmund followed him to Cambridge; in 1534, Cranmer made him Archdeacon of Canterbury. His sister Alice became a nun, and in
1534, thanks probably to Cranmer's influence, she was chosen
to be Prioress of a nunnery in Sheppey for a year or so before
its dissolution. Another sister married a miller, and was supposed to have been married bigamously to another man at the
same time. The lives of these sisters are very obscure, but we
get a strange glimpse of two of them in the pages of *Bishop
Cranmer's Recantacyons*—a glimpse of them contending together
for Cranmer's soul in the last few weeks of his life.[1]

In due course Cranmer was sent to school, probably at the
usual age of seven. According to the anonymous biographer,
his teacher was a 'rude parish clerk'; but Ralph Morice,
Cranmer's secretary, states that Cranmer went to a grammar
school, where his schoolmaster was 'marvellous severe and
cruel'. In any case, it is clear that his teacher was one of those
ignorant and brutal schoolmasters who were so strongly condemned by Erasmus and Cranmer's colleague Sir Thomas
Elyot and the modern school of educationalists. It was an age
in which religious leaders impressed upon their flock that their
chief duty as parents was to punish their children, because
Scripture taught that by striking their child with a rod they
would deliver his soul from Hell. Not only were the children
beaten for trivial offences; they were sometimes flogged when
they had committed no offence at all in order to mortify and
humble them. Cranmer told Morice in after life that the schoolmaster had dulled the wits of the scholars in his charge, and
had made them hate, rather than appreciate, good literature;
and he said that in his own case, the treatment which he had
received at school had permanently damaged both the good
memory and the natural audacity with which he had been endowed as a small child. Here Cranmer is using almost the
identical words with which Erasmus and Elyot condemn bad
teaching and brutality in schools. He was probably not so much

[1] Waters, *Chesters of Chicheley*, pp. 369–72, 396–7; Baskerville, 'A Sister of
Archbishop Cranmer' (*English Historical Review*, li. 287–8); Strype, *Cranmer*,
p. 602; Depositions in the Prebendaries' Case (*Letters and Papers of Henry VIII*,
xviii [ii]. 546, pp. 329–30, 359); *Bishop Cranmer's Recantacyons*, pp. 51, 93.
Edmund Cranmer was appointed Archdeacon of Canterbury on 9 March 1533/4
(Le Neve, *Fasti*, i. 43); Cooper (*Athenae Cantabrigienses*, i. 173) and Waters
wrongly give the year as 1534/5.

making an accurate statement as to what had happened in his own case as expressing the accepted views of his circle. Many of Cranmer's biographers have held the schoolmaster responsible for the defects in Cranmer's character; but Cranmer's statement to Morice probably indicates nothing more than that he held advanced views on education.[1]

Thomas Cranmer the father, though he left his son in the hands of this ignorant wretch, was kind to the boy, and tried to relieve his misery whenever he came home. We are told that it was in order to prevent him from becoming utterly disgusted with his studies that his father gave him the opportunity to live the healthy outdoor life appropriate to the son of a country gentleman. His father evidently agreed with the experts that the boy should learn to ride large and unruly horses at an early age, before the brawns and sinews of his thighs were fully consolidated. Cranmer learned early, and throughout his life was a splendid horseman. He also learned the national sport of shooting with the longbow. He grew up to be a healthy man—short in stature, but with a dignified presence, and a clear, ruddy complexion; his only physical ailment, his shortsightedness, did not interfere either with his reading or with his archery. It was obviously a tragedy for the unhappy schoolboy—he was to have many during his life— when his father died in May 1501; but his mother took an interest in his education. After two more years in the clutches of the schoolmaster, he was sent to Jesus College, Cambridge, when he was fourteen. The College had only been founded seven years before, when the monastery of St. Radegonde's was converted into a new College in 1496.[2]

During Cranmer's first eight years at Cambridge, we are told that he was 'nosseled in the grossest kind of sophistry, logic, philosophy moral and natural, not in the text of the old philosophers, but chiefly in the dark riddles and quidities of Duns and

---

[1] Anon. Biogr.; Morice (*Nar. Ref.*, pp. 218, 239); Erasmus, 'De Pueris Instituendis' (in Woodward, *Desiderius Erasmus concerning the Aim and Method of Education*, pp. 198, 203–10); Elyot, *The Boke named the Governour*, pp. 25, 33, 69–70. See the Bishops' Book and the King's Book (in Lloyd, *Formularies of Faith*, pp. 150, 314) for the reference to the text from Prov. xxiii.14.

[2] Anon. Biogr.; Morice (*Nar. Ref.*, pp. 218, 239–40); Parker, pp. 386–7; Elyot, *The Boke named the Governour*, p. 79; Foxe, viii. 43; *Bishop Cranmer's Recantacyons*, p. 3; memorial to Thomas Cranmer the father in Whatton Church; Probate of the will of Thomas Cranmer the father, 1 October 1501 (Waters, *Chesters of Chicheley*, p. 369).

other subtle questionists' till he was twenty-two years old. This was written by Cranmer's anonymous biographer at some time between 1556 and 1559—long after Duns had been driven out of Cambridge as well as 'set in Bocardo' in Oxford—and his criticism of scholastic philosophy is the prejudice of fifty years after. The period to which the biographer refers was the eight years during which Cranmer was working for his B.A. degree, which he took in July 1511. His name stands thirty-second in the list of the forty-two successful candidates. Latimer was eighth in that year's list; John Nicholson, later to be known as Lambert, was seventeenth, George Day was twenty-second, and Thomas Goodrich, near the bottom of the list, was thirty-first, one place above Cranmer. Cranmer then spent three years reading for his M.A. degree studying Erasmus, Faber and good Latin authors, and also Greek and Hebrew, and was awarded the degree in July 1514. Either before or soon after this, he became a Fellow of Jesus College.[1] He was twenty-five, and almost certainly intending to enter the Church when he abandoned his career, as well as his Fellowship, by marrying his first wife.

Cranmer's first marriage has exercised a peculiar fascination for his more modern biographers; but we know very little about it. In 1515 or 1516, he married a young woman who was called 'Black Joan of the Dolphin' in the articles against Cranmer at his trial forty years later.[2] In the same articles, Cranmer's second wife is called Anne, though in fact her name was Margaret, and the articles may also be wrong as to the name of his first wife. But it is as Black Joan that she has become famous. There is nothing to distinguish her story from that of all the other young women of her generation who married young and died in childbirth. But twenty years after her death an event occurred of which Joan did not have the slightest foreboding: her

---

[1] Anon. Biogr. (*Nar. Ref.*, p. 219); *Cambridge University Grace Book* B(i). 255; *Grace Book Γ*, p. 115. Cranmer may have become a Fellow before or after he took his M.A. degree, because (at least in the years 1535–51) some of the Fellows were Masters, and some Bachelors, of Arts (see Gray and Brittain, *Jesus College Cambridge*, p. 35). For the reference to Duns being 'set in Bocardo', see Layton to Cromwell, 12 September 1535 (Wright, *Letters relating to the Suppression of the Monasteries*, p. 71).

[2] The date of Cranmer's first marriage is uncertain. Cranmer said at his trial that it was some twenty years before his second marriage in 1532; but he was often inaccurate about dates. Morice states that it was after Cranmer became a M.A., which was in July 1514. It was certainly before 1520, when Cranmer was already a priest (see 'Processus contra Thomam Cranmer', in Cranmer's *Works*, ii. 545, 557); Morice (*Nar. Ref.*, p. 240).

husband became the first Protestant Archbishop of Canterbury. So for four hundred years historians have been arguing about Joan's social position and her morals.

Foxe and his colleagues tell us that she was a gentleman's daughter, but was related to the wife of the proprietor of the Dolphin Inn at Cambridge. When Cranmer married her, he became ineligible for his Fellowship at Jesus, which was limited to celibates. He was therefore obliged to find some other means of livelihood, and became the common reader at the monastic establishment of Buckingham College. Joan's relatives at the 'Dolphin' offered to allow her to live there for the time being, and Cranmer gratefully accepted the offer, because he had barely enough money to maintain his wife and the child she was expecting; his father had only left him an annuity of twenty shillings in his will. He himself did not live at the 'Dolphin'. Foxe attributes Cranmer's decision to live under a different roof from his wife to his desire to pursue his studies without disturbance, and obviously considered that this was a right and proper attitude for a future Archbishop; but Parker, who is at least as reliable an authority as Foxe with regard to Cranmer's life, says that it was because of Cranmer's poverty. Later, Cranmer apparently sent Joan to St. Ives to have her child, for it was there that she died.[1]

Cranmer often visited Joan when she was living at the 'Dolphin'. It was this which caused people to say that Cranmer was an ostler at the inn, and his wife the tapster. The rumour that Cranmer was an ostler was still being circulated twenty years later by the rebels of the Pilgrimage of Grace; and Nicholas Harpsfield, spitting out his venom in Mary's reign, wrote that Cranmer's first wife was 'a wanton maid at the sign of the Dolphin that was wont to sell young scholars their breakfasts'. As no one now believes that Cranmer was ever an ostler, it is curious that it is still so often said that his first wife was a barmaid. In view of the great emphasis on distinction in class and rank at the time, it is much more likely that she was at least the daughter of a tradesman, if not of a gentleman.[2]

[1] Foxe, viii. 4–5; Parker, p. 387; Probate of Cranmer's father's will, 1 October 1501 (Waters, *Chesters of Chicheley*, p. 369); Harpsfield's Latin MS. (Bémont, *Le Premier Divorce de Henri VIII*, p. 54). Fellows were required to be celibates by Bishop Stanley's statutes of 1514–15, if not since the foundation of the College (see Gray and Brittain, *Jesus College Cambridge*, p. 38).

[2] Morice (*Nar. Ref.*, p. 269); Foxe, viii. 4–5; Harpsfield, *The Pretended Divorce*, p. 289.

At the time of his first marriage, Cranmer had not yet taken holy orders or any vow of celibacy. His action in marrying was therefore not a crime, or in any way more reprehensible than the marriage of any other young man. But it appeared in a very different light when Cranmer became an Archbishop, and especially when he became a heretical Archbishop who had openly announced that he had married for the second time after taking orders. The men who burned Cranmer in 1556, and the mass of the English people, thought that marriage was not so worthy a state as celibacy, and expected their priests to attain this high moral state to which they themselves had no intention of aspiring. The fact that Cranmer had satisfied his lust, even within the bounds of matrimony, before he became a priest, was discreditable in an Archbishop. Thus Harpsfield would write that Cranmer became inured to the sins of the flesh when he married Joan at Cambridge; and at his trial in 1555 a perfectly lawful marriage which he had contracted as a young layman forty years before was made the basis of an article in the charge against him. The first marriage was important for another reason. The reformers who advocated the lawfulness of the marriage of the clergy relied above all on Paul's directive to Timothy that a Bishop should be the husband of one wife; and though this was often interpreted as meaning that a Bishop should not commit bigamy by having two wives simultaneously, Chrysostom and Jerome had stated that it meant that a Bishop should not marry more than once. This interpretation was unequivocally accepted by the reformers' spokesman, Redman, when he persuaded Convocation to approve of the marriage of priests in 1547. It was therefore well worth while for Cranmer's enemies to mention his first marriage to Joan when they were denouncing his second, illegal marriage as a priest.[1]

Cranmer's first marriage, entailing as it did the loss of his Fellowship, the sacrifice of his career in the priesthood, and immediately plunging him into poverty, had very serious consequences for him, and it has sometimes been hinted that Cranmer was forced into the marriage because Joan was

[1] Harpsfield, op. cit., p. 290; 1 Tim. iii.2; Tit. i.6; Chrysostom, 10th Homily on 1 Tim. and 2nd Homily on Tit. (Chrysostom, *Homilies on Epistles to Timothy, Titus and Philemon*, pp. 76–77, 283); Jerome, Commentary on Epistle to Titus (Hieronymi, *Opera*, xi. 895); Records of Convocation, November–December 1547 (Wilkins, *Concilia*, iv. 16–17).

pregnant by him before the marriage. If this is the true explanation, it shows that Cranmer at the age of twenty-five had
a higher standard of honour and morality in such matters than
many of his contemporaries; but there is no reason at all to
believe that he was forced into the marriage in this way. It is
more likely that he had fallen in love, and decided that the right
course was to marry and abandon his training for the priesthood. If Cranmer had fallen in love, he obviously could not
resist the temptations of the flesh and was unable to follow
chastity; he must therefore irrevocably abandon his intention of
taking orders by marrying at once. Many young scholars in
1515 would cheerfully have taken holy orders and a concubine
at the same time; but Cranmer was not one of those cynical
priests whom we meet in the writings of Erasmus and More.

Within less than a year, the marriage ended in tragedy.
After an unhappy childhood, Cranmer had fallen deeply in love,
and sacrificed his whole career for a happy married life; and
before he could set up a home with his wife, he had lost both
wife and child. He had sacrificed his career for nothing. It was
soon after this, according to the date given by the anonymous
biographer, that Cranmer began to study the Bible. More than
twenty years later, in his Preface to the English Bible of 1540,
Cranmer quoted the words of St. John Chrysostom: 'The loss
of thy dear and well-beloved causeth thee to mourn. . . .
Where canst thou have armour or fortress against thine
assaults? Where canst thou have salves for thy sores, but of
holy Scripture?' [1] These words had perhaps a personal significance for Cranmer, although when he wrote them he had more
recent griefs in mind than the death of his first wife. The
bloody statute of the Six Articles had just forced him to separate
from his second wife.

The death of Joan and the child was certainly the greatest
turning point in Cranmer's life. If Joan had lived, he would
presumably have settled down to an ordinary life with her, and
have avoided all the honours and agonies which were in store
for him. As it was, he was not required to lose his career as
well as his wife. He was re-admitted as a Fellow of Jesus
College. The College authorities seem to have extended an
altogether exceptional indulgence to Cranmer, for there is no

[1] Cranmer, Preface to the Bible of 1540 (Cranmer's *Works*, ii. 120).

other record of a Fellowship having been given to a widower during the next two hundred years. Soon afterwards—within three years at the most of his wife's death—Cranmer took holy orders. He had certainly done so before 1520, when he was one of the University preachers. The University had been permitted by a Papal Bull of 1503 to grant preaching licenses to twelve preachers which would enable them to preach anywhere in England, except in the presence of a Bishop or his Ordinary, without a license from the diocesan Bishop. All these preachers were required to be priests. We do not know when Cranmer was appointed, but he was already a University preacher by July 1520. On some Saturday between 1516 and 1520, when Cranmer was about thirty years of age, he was ordained a priest. He did not swear a vow of chastity at his ordination; this practice had been obsolete for many years. In 1521, having studied divinity for six years since he had incepted in Arts, and having preached two sermons, one to the clergy in Cambridge and one to the people at Paul's Cross in London, he was granted his B.D. degree.[1]

By this time, heresy had begun to infect the University and cause serious alarm to the authorities. The five years while Cranmer completed his studies in divinity before taking his doctor's degree were the years of the official fulminations against Lutheranism at Cambridge, of the secret meetings at the White Horse Inn, of the campaign of Bilney and Arthur, of Barnes and Latimer, against Purgatory, masses for the dead, prayers to the Saints and the great festivities of the Church. But Cranmer did not play any part in this. When the Lutheran controversy first began in Germany, he decided to make a thorough study of the issues involved before committing himself. He began by studying Scripture for three years, reading with pen in hand and taking copious notes; then he turned to other authors, both new and old, whose doctrines could throw light on the validity of the Lutheran doctrines.[2] There is a real indication here of Cranmer's character and temperament. While Wolsey and Fisher were

---

[1] Fuller, *University of Cambridge*, p. 203; Bass-Mullinger, *University of Cambridge*, i. 612 n.; Pilkington, 'On the Burning of Paul's Church' (Pilkington's *Works*, p. 581); Collier, *Ecclesiastical History*, vi. 69; Fisher's license, 31 May 1522 (Strype, *Life of Parker*, iii. 121-2); *Grace Book* B (ii). 77 (where the names of thirteen preachers are given); *Grace Book Γ*, p. 193.

[2] Anon. Biogr. (*Nar. Ref.*, p. 219).

intensifying their drive against the growing number of 'Lutherans' who were openly or secretly defying them at the risk of victimization, imprisonment and burning, Cranmer was spending not months but years in quietly studying both sides of the question.

It is true that the fact that Cranmer approached the problem in this way shows that he was already an incipient heretic. After 1520, all Lutheran books were banned in Cambridge, and unless Cranmer obtained a license to read heretical tracts—such licenses were not readily granted—he must have read, illegally and secretly, the Lutheran works which were being surreptitiously circulated in the University. In any case, Cranmer, as an orthodox priest, ought to have condemned Luther, not on the basis of his own reason, but because the authority of the Church had condemned him. If Cranmer was judging between the Church and Luther on the basis of his private interpretation of the Bible, he was already a heretic in his heart, even if he did not know it. But he did not join the heretics in the White Horse Inn, or engage in open resistance to the established religion. Thirty years later, when he was on trial for heresy, Brooks told him that though people might suspect that he had always been a heretic, there was absolutely no evidence of this. There is no reason to believe that Cranmer had any contact with Barnes or Bilney; on the contrary, he seems to have been greatly influenced by Robert Ridley when he was at Cambridge. Robert Ridley, who was the uncle of Cranmer's future colleague Nicholas Ridley, was a very orthodox divine, and was actively engaged at this time in persecuting heretics; but Cranmer apparently told Cochlaeus in 1532 that he regarded Robert Ridley as his teacher and inspirer in philosophy.[1]

Nor is there any reason to believe that Cranmer held any strong views at this time about Papal supremacy. The Papacy had become very unpopular in England, particularly among the clergy, on account of its financial exactions, and this unpopularity increased when Wolsey became the Papal Legate; but while Cranmer obviously shared the national hostility to Rome, there is no reliable evidence that he went beyond this.

[1] Foxe, viii. 46; Cochlaeus, *Beati Isidori . . . de Officiis Ecclesiasticis* (Pref., 1534 ed.).

It has often been said that by about 1525 he was secretly praying for the overthrow of Papal power in England; but this theory is not borne out by the two statements which are quoted in support of it. In 1536, Cranmer wrote to Henry VIII an account of a sermon which he had preached at Canterbury the year before, in which he had said that for many years he had prayed for the overthrow of Papal power in England. We do not know what Cranmer meant by 'many years' in 1535 and 1536; but he may have meant no earlier than 1529, when he was already working for Henry in connexion with the divorce. The other statement is far less reliable. When Cranmer was investigating the conspiracy of the Prebendaries of Canterbury in 1543, he was informed that a bricklayer had said that Cranmer had said that he had prayed for the overthrow of Papal authority in England seven years before the authority was cast off.[1] This takes us back to the end of 1526; but it would be difficult to imagine a less trustworthy witness than this Canterbury bricklayer as to what Cranmer was praying for at Cambridge seventeen years before. These statements probably indicate nothing more than that in 1526 Cranmer was as anti-Papist as were most of his compatriots, and remembered and exaggerated this after Papal supremacy had been overthrown.

Of all the ideas which Cranmer held in later life, there is only one which can clearly be traced back to his Cambridge days. Before he left Cambridge, he had already come to the conclusion that it was much more important to study the Bible than Duns Scotus; on the question of the superiority of Scripture, Cranmer was indeed an old truant.[2] After he became a Doctor of Divinity in 1526, he was appointed as the University examiner in divinity, and as an examiner he refused to allow students to take their degree if they were ignorant of Scripture. This caused great indignation among some monks and friars who had studied the doctrines of the schoolmen but knew very little about the Bible; but the authorities could not complain if he tried to ensure that his students did not share the deplorable ignorance of Scripture which was so widespread among

[1] Cranmer to Henry VIII, 26 August 1536 (Cranmer's *Works*, ii. 327); Depositions in the Prebendaries' Case (*L.P.* xviii [ii]. 546, p. 303).
[2] It was in connexion with Cranmer's arguments as to the superiority of the four Gospels over the Apostolic Canons that Henry VIII said to Gardiner: 'My Lord of Canterbury is too old a truant for us twain' (Morice, *Nar. Ref.*, p. 250).

parish priests; and he did succeed in inducing at least some of the students to study the Bible.[1]

There is no doubt that Cranmer's career at Cambridge was surprisingly undistinguished. After more than twenty-five years of residence, he had not risen to any important position in the University. In this he is in striking contrast to almost all those of his contemporaries who later played an important part in the struggles of the Reformation. Gardiner was Master of his College at the age of twenty-eight. His subsequent appointment as Chancellor of the University was a political reward after he had attained high office in the State; but Heynes, Day, Thomas Smith, Parker, Sandys and Haddon all became Vice-Chancellors while they were still in residence at Cambridge. Ridley, Goodrich and John Taylor were Proctors; Latimer and Heath became Chaplain to the University. Cranmer attained none of these offices, though it was certainly a mark of some distinction to be one of the twelve University preachers, as it was to be selected as a tutor for Cardinal College at Oxford. In 1525, when Wolsey was searching both Oxford and Cambridge to find the best tutors for his new College, his chaplain Capon, the Master of Jesus, chose Cranmer as one of the Cambridge men who should go there. Apparently Cranmer definitely decided to accept, and actually set out on the journey to Oxford; but on the road he met a friend, who warned him that now that he was a student of divinity he would do better to study quietly and humbly at Jesus rather than seek glory and self-advancement at Cardinal's College. Cranmer was convinced by his friend's argument; he decided to refuse the post, and returned to Cambridge, where he was appointed Reader in Divinity at Jesus.[2] He was not one of the keen young Cambridge men who went to the Cardinal's College, carrying with them the virus of heresy which they had caught at Cambridge and infecting the more conservative University. He preferred the quieter, less adventurous course.

Cranmer was in residence at Cambridge for nearly twenty-six years—as long a period of time, all but a few months, as that which was to elapse between his departure from Jesus in

[1] *Grace Book Γ*, p. 225; Foxe, viii. 5. For Cranmer's attitude to Scripture, see Bromiley, *Thomas Cranmer Theologian*, pp. 12–27.
[2] Parker, p. 387; Morice (*Nar. Ref.*, p. 240); Foxe, viii. 5.

the summer of 1529 and the kindling of the fire at Oxford on 21st March 1556. The desultory references to him during these twenty-six years show that he was honest and respected rather than distinguished. For four years he acts as one of the auditors of the Proctors' accounts and of other University expenditure; he is available to preach a sermon to the University on Ash Wednesday when the appointed preacher is absent; he is chosen by his College to visit Cromwell, who was Wolsey's solicitor and agent, to discuss the price of some wheat which has risen to eleven shillings a quarter, and the reversion of some lands of the College in Southwark; he is appointed as an executor by one of the other Fellows at Jesus. He was still in contact with his native village of Aslockton and owned some property there. After the dreadful summer and autumn of 1527, when it rained almost continuously, the authorities sent Commissioners all over England to ascertain the wheat which was available; and in January 1528 they reported that Cranmer was one of six landowners at Aslockton who had wheat for sale. But these were incidental activities; most of the time he was engaged in his studies of divinity. He was so busy with his studies in the spring of 1527 or 1528 that he found it difficult to find-time to prepare for a disputation with Henry Gold, when Gold had to dispute for his B.D. degree. Cranmer found time enough to argue with Gold in grimmer circumstances in 1533.[1]

[1] *Grace Book B* (ii). 120, 139, 146, 147, 153; *Grace Book Γ*, pp. 226, 236, 237; Report of the Commissioners at Bingham, 18 January 1528; Capon to Cromwell, 24 October 1528; Longforth to Henry Gold, 25 March (1527 or 1528) (*L.P.* iv. 3819, 4872; v. 1700); *Collectanea Topographica et Genealogica*, viii. 410–11.

CHAPTER II

THE WALTHAM MEETING
AND THE MISSION TO ITALY

In the spring and summer of 1529, there was once again an outbreak of plague at Cambridge. Cranmer was at that time acting as a tutor to two sons of a Master Cressey of Waltham, whose wife was related to Cranmer; and owing to the plague, Cranmer moved with the boys to their father's house at Waltham. By the beginning of July, the plague had subsided sufficiently to allow the University to re-assemble, and Cranmer was again in Cambridge, where he once more audited the proctorial accounts; but he evidently returned to Waltham soon afterwards, for he was there at the beginning of August, when the King came to Waltham Abbey. Stephen Gardiner, the King's Secretary, and Edward Fox, the King's Almoner, were billeted on Cressey. Cranmer had known both Gardiner and Fox at Cambridge, and when they met on the first night at supper on 2nd August 1529, they spoke first about the affairs of the University. Then the conversation turned to the subject that everyone in England was discussing—the King's divorce. A month before, Cardinal Campeggio had suddenly adjourned the trial at Blackfriars when everyone had thought that he was on the point of giving judgment that Henry's marriage to Catherine was invalid. Since then the Pope, in breach of his promise to Henry, had advoked the proceedings to his Court in Rome.[1]

John Foxe is almost certainly wrong when he says that Cranmer suggested to Gardiner and Edward Fox that Henry should appeal from the Pope to the English and foreign Universities. Morice, from whom Foxe derived his information, tells the story differently. He says that Cranmer told Fox and Gardiner that he had not studied the question of the King's divorce, but he felt that they were going the wrong way about

[1] Cooper, *Annals of Cambridge*, i. 330; *Grace Book B* (ii). 153; Morice (*Nar. Ref.* pp. 240–2); Foxe, viii. 6–7; Parker, p. 374. Morice says that the meeting at Waltham took place 'the firste night at supper'. The Court arrived at Waltham on 2 August 1529 (Note on the King's Progress, *L.P.*, iv. 5965).

it. The legal proceedings in the ecclesiastical Courts would lead to endless delays; but in fact there was only one truth in the matter, and it was for the divines to decide what it was. If the King referred the question to theologians, he could act on their advice with a clear conscience without troubling himself about the verdict of the Courts.

Cranmer was right in saying that the issue in the divorce was a theological one. The validity of Henry's marriage to his brother's widow depended on a Papal dispensation, and the issue in the case was whether the prohibition on the marriage of a man to his brother's widow was merely a rule of canon law, from which the Pope could dispense, or whether it was the law of God, and therefore indispensable—unless the Pope could dispense from the observance even of the divine law. But to suggest that the King could set aside an existing marriage on the advice of theologians without any decree of a competent ecclesiastical Court was a very unorthodox suggestion. It was the suggestion of a theologian who was opposed to canonists, and of an Englishman who was hostile to Rome. Cranmer, though he had to learn and administer the canon law when he was Archbishop of Canterbury, was always a theologian and not a canonist. The theologians were not overfond of the canonists, who controlled the whole government of Church and State; and Cranmer showed his feelings about them when, in his controversy about the Eucharist with Gardiner in 1551, he repeatedly abused his opponent as an 'ignorant lawyer'.[1] Both as a theologian and as an Englishman, Cranmer had reason to mistrust divorce proceedings in the Papal Courts, where theology had much less weight than corruption and political intrigue. He believed that there was only one truth in the divorce question, and that it was for the divines to decide what it was; and it is clear enough that he believed that this truth must be discovered, not by a study of the doctors of the schools, or even primarily of the Fathers, but from Scripture.

Fox and Gardiner were obviously interested in Cranmer's suggestion; but John Foxe's story of how Fox told the King next day, and how Henry, declaring that Cranmer 'hath the sow by the right ear', forced Cranmer to come reluctantly to his presence at Greenwich, is almost certainly wrong. If Foxe

[1] Cranmer, *Answer to Gardiner* (Cranmer's *Works*, i. 157, 185, 235).

and Morice are right when they say that Cranmer's interview with the King was at Greenwich, it cannot have taken place until nearly three months after the conversation at Waltham; but apart from this, their story is probably not quite accurate. It would really be very surprising if Cranmer had been summoned to an interview with the King merely because he made a clever suggestion to the King's ministers at a supper party, especially as there was nothing new in the idea. The proposal that the Universities, and the theologians there and elsewhere, should be consulted about the divorce, had already been under consideration for more than two years. But something certainly came of the meeting at Waltham. Fox and Gardiner probably persuaded Cranmer to study the King's great matter, for some time after the meeting at Waltham, Cranmer was arguing the case for Henry with his colleagues at Cambridge. Henry arranged for a discussion on the divorce to be held at Cambridge between six divines from Cambridge and six other divines from Oxford. Cranmer was chosen to be one of the six Cambridge men; but as he was, for some reason, absent from Cambridge at the time, he was replaced by another of his Cambridge colleagues. The twelve divines agreed, as a result of their discussions, that the King's marriage was valid; but soon after, Cranmer returned to Cambridge, and argued with the divines that the marriage was unlawful with such effect that five of the six—or perhaps the anonymous biographer means five of the twelve—were converted to this view, and repudiated their former opinion in favour of the marriage. Cranmer's success was reported to the King, who decided to enlist his services in working for the divorce. This discussion at Cambridge probably took place between August and October 1529. If Cranmer had distinguished himself as a propagandist for the King at Cambridge, it is much more likely that he would have been summoned to an interview with Henry than if he had merely made intelligent suggestions to Fox and Gardiner at supper.[1]

[1] Foxe, viii. 7–8; Anon. Biogr.; Morice (*Nar. Ref.*, pp. 219–20, 242). Henry did not return to Greenwich until 23 October 1529 (see Chapuys to Charles V, 25 October 1529, in Bradford, *Correspondence of Charles V*, p. 268 and n.). Even if Morice is wrong in stating that it was at Greenwich that Cranmer first met Henry, it is unlikely to have been as far afield as Windsor, which was the nearest place to Greenwich and London where Henry resided between the beginning of August and the end of October. The last week of October 1529 is much the most

Cranmer may have been at Aslockton, as Foxe states, when he received word that the King wished to see him; but the rest of Foxe's story of how he tried to avoid the interview is less likely. He first met Henry at Greenwich—probably towards the end of October 1529. Henry ordered him to write a book on the divorce. According to Foxe, the King told Cranmer that he loved and respected Queen Catherine, but that he was troubled in his conscience as to the lawfulness of his marriage to her; and he stressed the need for Cranmer to consider the question of the validity of his marriage with complete impartiality.[1] Henry may well have said this to Cranmer, for he frequently expressed these hypocritical sentiments when he spoke about the divorce; but he would not have asked Cranmer to write a book about his marriage unless he had known the conclusions which Cranmer would reach. He arranged for Cranmer to reach his impartial conclusions in the house of the father of Anne Boleyn. Cranmer was sent to stay at Durham House, the Earl of Wiltshire's house in the Strand, while he wrote his book. Anne herself was not living there; she had taken up residence at Court a few months before.

On 2nd August, Cranmer had told Fox and Gardiner that he had not studied the divorce issue; by the end of October, he had become recognized as one of the King's leading advocates, and was being given special facilities for writing his propaganda, and brought into close association with the Boleyns. In August, he had not yet decided whether Henry's marriage was lawful; he merely thought that the question should be settled by theologians, and not by canonists in the Courts. By October, he had decided that the marriage was unlawful by the law of God, and that consequently the Pope could not permit it by dispensation. He had considered Leviticus and Deuteronomy, and preferred Leviticus:[2] and the decision opened the door

likely date of his meeting with Cranmer. For the earlier suggestions of an appeal to the Universities, see Wakefield to Henry VIII, 5 July 1527 (Blunt, *The Reformation of the Church of England*, i. 130); du Bellay to Montmorency, 23 August and 18 September 1529 (Le Grand, *Histoire du Divorce de Henry VIII et Catherine d'Arragon*, iii. 339, 355); Cavendish, *Life of Wolsey*, p. 102; Collier, iv. 150 (where the date of the judgment of Orleans University of 5 April 1530 is wrongly given as 1529). Morice is wrong in placing the discussion at Cambridge as being at the time when the University was asked for its opinion on the divorce in February–March 1530, for by that date Cranmer had already left for Italy (see infra).

[1] Foxe, viii. 7–8.
[2] Lev. xviii.16; xx.21; Deut. xxv.5.

to fame and fortune. Cranmer is not the only scholar who has been required to solve an intellectual problem fully conscious that his own material interests would be vitally affected by his decision; for he knew, as he examined the two conflicting passages, that if he preferred Deuteronomy, as the Pope's doctors did, he would never emerge from the obscurity of Cambridge. The temptation was all the greater because the way of escape from obscurity was disguised to look like the path of duty. By preferring Leviticus, he would serve his King, he would help to thwart the Papacy which everyone resented, and he would further the supremacy of the Bible over the institutions of the Church and the canon law. Four years before, Cranmer had resisted the lure of the road to Cardinal's College; he could not resist the lure of the road to Durham House.

He stayed at Durham House for two months, and wrote his book. It was written primarily with the intention of influencing the doctors of Cambridge University, who were soon to be asked to give an opinion on the validity of Henry's marriage, and it had been distributed and read in Cambridge before February 1530, when the question was submitted to the University. Cambridge would have been the obvious place to use the services of Cranmer; but the King and his advisers realized that he was too well known as one of the King's partisans for him to do anything there. When the twenty-nine delegates were chosen to decide the question on behalf of the University, the Queen's supporters objected to the selection of Salcott, Repps and Crome, because they had publicly declared that they agreed with the views which Cranmer had expressed in his book. There would obviously have been even more criticism if the author of the book had himself been chosen. So Cranmer was not sent to Cambridge. By the time that the King's question was submitted to Cambridge, he had already left England for Italy in the embassy of the Earl of Wiltshire, who was sent to attend the coronation of Charles V as Holy Roman Emperor at Bologna. Before his departure, Cranmer had another interview with Henry, who praised his book, and asked him if he was prepared to defend the doctrines which he had put forward in it before the Pope himself in the Rotta in Rome. Cranmer said that he was ready to do so; but he was never given the opportunity. The Pope was determined that the divorce case should be decided in his Court by the canon law, and not by theologians. When Cranmer challenged his opponents to dispute before the Rotta, the disputation was repeatedly put off, and in the end it was never held.[1]

Wiltshire and his retinue, including Cranmer, left London very early in the morning on 21st January 1530. The envoys went first to Paris, and then rode slowly across France to Bologna. They did not reach Bologna until 14th March—nearly eight weeks after leaving London. It is not clear whether Cranmer travelled all the way to Bologna with Wiltshire, or whether he went straight to Rome. He was not accredited as an envoy to the Emperor, and does not seem to have been presented to him at Bologna; but Wiltshire had received instructions from Henry to tell Charles about Cranmer's learned arguments in favour of the divorce. Wiltshire was to say that Henry was now being advised by a 'wonderful and grave wise man' who was urging him to obey God's law and put away Catherine. This 'wonderful and grave wise man' was almost certainly Cranmer, for it is difficult to see who else was unknown by name to Charles, and could therefore be referred to in this way, and yet was sufficiently learned and active in Henry's cause to qualify for the description. Cranmer's book had obviously made a very favourable impression on Henry.[2]

By the middle of April, Cranmer was in Rome, and the Pope had returned there from Bologna. The Pope then proceeded to appoint Cranmer as Grand Penitentiary for England. There is no record of the date of the appointment, but it was probably 18th April 1530; for when Cranmer returned to England in October, and his expense allowance during his mission was computed, he was allowed six shillings and eightpence a day for the period from 20th January to 18th April, and twenty shillings a day from 18th April to 23rd October. This sudden triplication of his expense allowance is almost certainly to be explained

---

[1] Gardiner and Fox to Henry VIII (February 1530) (Burnet, iv. 130–1); Foxe, viii. 9–10. Anon. Biogr. (*Nar. Ref.*, p. 221) says that the disputation was actually held in the Rotta, and that Cranmer worsted his opponents there; but this is less likely.
[2] Chapuys to Charles V, 25 January 1530 (*Span. Cal.* iv. [i]. 255); Household Book of Henry VIII (*Trevelyan Papers prior to 1558*, pp. 167, 172); Friedmann, *Anne Boleyn*, i. 106; Instructions to Wiltshire, (January 1530), (*L.P.*, iv. 6111, where the original 'ung merbvilleux et serieulx sage homme' is translated as 'a wonderfully virtuous and wise man'; cf. Record Office, S.P.1, f.148).

by the fact that on 18th April Cranmer received a promotion in rank, and this was probably when he was appointed Penitentiary.[1]

The significance of this appointment as Penitentiary was misunderstood by Foxe and his contemporaries, as well as by later historians. They imply that Cranmer was appointed Penitentiary at the end, not the beginning, of his visit to Rome, and interpret it either as a recognition of his great abilities which even a grudging Pope was unable to withhold, or as an attempt by the Pope to bribe Cranmer to join his side. In fact, the office was one held by an English representative resident in Rome, and the duties were to act in connexion with the granting and drafting of Papal dispensations—or rather, to represent English interests in this department. The appointment was probably always made on the recommendation of the King of England, and the Pope no doubt appointed Cranmer as Penitentiary merely because Henry had requested this; for when Cranmer left Rome in September, Henry asked the Pope to appoint Brother Dionysius, an Italian friar in English pay, to succeed Cranmer as Penitentiary.[2]

The most important duty which Cranmer was required to perform in Italy was to obtain the opinions of the Universities in favour of Henry's divorce. This was a difficult, but by no means impossible, task. In England and France, Henry and Francis had virtually forced the Universities to give judgment that Henry's marriage was invalid; in the Emperor's territories, the Universities were afraid to discuss the question at all. But the Emperor's control of Italy was only indirect, and the rivalries of local Italian politics made it possible for the Universities to show some independence. This gave great opportunities for bribery and intrigue, and the English agents resorted to bribery on a large scale. The bribes were supposed to be the price paid to induce the doctors to deliver the official opinions of the Universities—as respectable as the modern practice of paying an arbitrator for his opinion. But though Cranmer and his colleagues referred to these bribes by the polite name of 'retainers' paid on the King's behalf, they made very little

[1] Household Book of Henry VIII (op. cit., pp. 167, 172). Another entry in the Household Book gives the date as the 17 not 18 April.
[2] Benet to Henry VIII, 30 January 1530/1 (State Papers of Henry VIII, vii. 281); Foxe, viii. 10; Parker, p. 376.

attempt to conceal from themselves what they were doing.

In March 1530, Cambridge gave its decision that Henry's marriage was against the divine law; by the beginning of May, Oxford, Orleans and Angers had followed suit. When the news reached Rome, Clement, after his usual period of hesitation, issued a brief on 21st May prohibiting the Universities from discussing the matter, on the grounds that it was *sub judice* in his Court in Rome.[1] This was a serious obstacle in the way of the attempts of the English agents to obtain similar opinions from the Italian Universities, and they set about persuading the Pope to revoke his ban. They asked him to grant a brief which, without revoking his general prohibition on the discussion of the divorce, would permit the matter to be discussed at each of the Italian Universities where the English had made sure of obtaining a favourable verdict. Clement as usual was vacillating and equivocal, and on 12th July Cranmer wrote from Rome to his colleague Croke, the eminent Greek scholar, in Venice, complaining of the Pope's dishonesty. He told him how his attempts to obtain the desired brief were continually being frustrated by the Emperor's Ambassador and by Cardinal St. Quatuor, who some years before had refused a large bribe to become an English agent; but though Cranmer did not think that they would ever get a really satisfactory brief, he was hopeful about obtaining a reasonably useful one. There is a revealing passage in this letter. One of the agents in English pay was the aged friar Francis, a scion of the Venetian aristocracy, who was supposed to be persuading the Pope to grant Henry a divorce; but Francis did not seem to be carrying out this duty. When Cranmer raised the matter with him the friar explained that when he spoke to the Pope, he pretended to be impartial in the divorce question in the hopes of inducing the Pope to reveal his plans and those of Catherine's supporters. Cranmer approved of this tactic, and was sure that they could trust Francis, though on Croke's advice he decided, while continuing to employ Francis as an agent, to confide in him as little as possible.[2] This is less than a year after the supper party at

---

[1] Brief of 21 May 1530 (Pocock, *Records of the Reformation*, ii. 633–4).

[2] Cranmer to Croke (12 July 1530) (Pocock, i. 409–10). The date of this letter is given in Croke to Henry VIII, 28 July 1530 (*L.P.*, iv. 6531). It is somewhat incorrectly summarized in *L.P.*, iv. 6543, which led Pollard to imagine that it was Cranmer, and not Francis, who was ill in Rome (see Pollard, *Thomas Cranmer*, p. 45).

Waltham; but the Cambridge theologian has become a skilful foreign agent of his King. At Waltham, he had urged that the divorce question should be decided by theologians; now he was working to ensure that it was decided by bribing Italian canonists, and had learned how to use suspect characters in dishonest enterprises without trusting them too far. He was acting on the principle that all means are justified where the King's service is concerned.

Cranmer had been right in his optimism when he wrote to Croke that he thought that he would get a reasonably satisfactory brief. It was issued on 4th August. It declared that the Pope had never intended, by his brief of 21st May, to deprive learned men of the right to discuss the issues involved in the divorce case between Henry and Catherine, and that canonists and theologians were free to do so provided that they were influenced only by their conscience, and not by money or other remuneration.[1] It is easy to see why Cranmer regarded this brief as being only moderately satisfactory, for he can hardly have relished the fact that the Pope had thought it necessary to insert an express statement that the opinions were not to be obtained by bribery.

At the beginning of September, Cranmer left Rome to return to England. On his way, he passed through Bologna, and visited Croke. Croke had been having a great deal of trouble in Bologna. The town was in the Papal territories, and was governed for the Pope by Cardinal de Gambara. Stokesley, the new Bishop of London, had been there in June, and had spent sixteen hundred crowns in bribing the canonists of the University to support Henry; but one of the friars whom Stokesley had bribed had immediately told the Cardinal-Governor about it, and Gambara thereupon strongly reprimanded Croke, and refused to permit the University to deliver its opinion about the divorce.[2] It was at this very embarrassing juncture that Cranmer arrived in Bologna, and he immediately went with Croke to see the Governor.

Cranmer seems to have handled the situation skilfully. Gambara's attitude had completely changed since his interview

[1] Brief of 4 August 1530 (Pocock, ii. 645–6).
[2] Pallavicini to Stokesley, 8 September 1530; Croke to Cranmer, 12 September 1530; Croke to Henry VIII, two letters both dated 16 September 1530 (Pocock, i. 418, 421, 423–6; L.P., iv. 6622).

with Croke a few days before; he was now most co-operative. He was well aware of the object of Papal diplomacy. He had no particular interest in Catherine's cause; he wished to maintain to the full the Pope's authority, and not to irritate the Emperor, and subject to these considerations to do everything possible to gratify the King of England. He therefore ordered the faculty of canonists to meet and give an opinion in favour of Henry which did not contain anything derogatory of the Pope's power. This meant that the canonists were to say that Henry's marriage was unlawful, but were not to add that the Pope had no power to grant a dispensation in this or any other case. It was a most welcome surprise for Croke and Cranmer. Finding the Governor so friendly, they pressed him to tell them which of the friars whom Stokesley had bribed had betrayed them to him; but Gambara resolutely refused to give the name of his informant, and refused to allow any of the suspected friars to swear that it was not he.[1]

Cranmer left Bologna for England soon afterwards—probably before the end of September. Meanwhile Croke, who was conscious that he had not been very successful in obtaining the opinions of the Italian Universities, was attempting to throw the blame for his failure on to Cranmer and his other colleagues. On 17th September, the day after he and Cranmer had had their successful interview with Gambara, Croke wrote to Stokesley that all his difficulties with Gambara had been caused by what Cranmer had said to Gambara, and not by anything which he himself had said. This was obviously untrue, for it is clear that, whether through a coincidence or not, Gambara's attitude became friendly as soon as Cranmer arrived in Bologna. On 28th September, Croke again wrote to Stokesley accusing Cranmer of disloyalty; but within ten days of writing this letter to Stokesley about Cranmer, Croke was writing to Cranmer accusing Stokesley of being responsible for his troubles at Ferrara. Realizing that Cranmer would soon be seeing the King, Croke wrote him a succession of letters, which were obviously meant to overtake him on the road to England, in which he asked Cranmer to use his influence with Henry, Wiltshire and Anne to prevent Stokesley from intriguing

---

[1] Croke to Henry VIII; Croke to Stokesley, both 17 September 1530 (Pocock, i. 427; *L.P.*, iv. 6624).

against him. The repercussions of these intrigues continued for a long time. More than three years later, Sir Gregory de Casale, one of Henry's Italian agents, wrote to the Council in London, requesting that Cranmer, now Archbishop of Canterbury, should be examined on oath, together with Stokesley and others, to prove that it was Croke, not Casale himself, who had betrayed them to the Governor of Bologna in 1530.[1] Cranmer did not stoop to engage in intrigues of this kind. He was prepared to use unscrupulous tactics to further the King's interests; but he did not plot against his colleagues for personal advancement.

Cranmer travelled home by way of Lyons, and reached London on 23rd October 1530. After this, we know very little about his activities for the next fifteen months; but it was probably during this time that he developed that intimate association with the Boleyn family which was commented upon by all his Papist opponents. This intimacy must have been based on something more than his two months' stay at Durham House at the end of 1529. There has been a great controversy as to whether he was ever Anne Boleyn's chaplain. The suggestion that he was emanates from his enemies. When he became Archbishop of Canterbury in 1533, it was believed at the Emperor's Court in Bologna that one of Anne's chaplains had been appointed Archbishop. Later in the year, when Catherine protested to the Pope against Cranmer's sentence of divorce against her, she pointed out the injustice of her being judged by the chaplain of Anne Boleyn. All these were prejudiced witnesses, but they would never have mentioned the matter unless Cranmer's connexion with the Boleyns had at one time been very close; and there is no doubt that whether or not he held the position of chaplain to Anne, he attached himself firmly to the fortunes of Wiltshire and his daughter, and almost certainly lived under their roof after his return from Italy.[2]

[1] Croke to Stokesley, 17 and 28 September 1530; Croke to Cranmer, 8, 17, 19 and two letters of 23 October 1530; Gregory de Casale to the Council (January 1534) (*L.P.*, iv. 6624, 6639, 6669; Pocock, ii. 12–15, 23–24, 32–33, 38–41, 519, where Croke's letter of 8 October is printed as two separate letters).

[2] Cranmer visited Stokesley, who was at Lyons, on his journey to England (see Croke to Stokesley, 29 September 1530, *L.P.*, iv. 6644). His expense account for his visit to Italy runs from 20 January to 23 October 1530 (Household Book of Henry VIII (*Trevelyan Papers prior to 1558*, pp. 167, 172)). As for Cranmer being Anne Boleyn's chaplain, see Ortiz to the Empress Isabella, 22 February 1533 (*Span. Cal.*, iv. [ii]. 1051; *L.P.*, vi. 178); Friedmann, *Anne Boleyn*, i. 174.

On 13th June 1531, Cranmer wrote to Wiltshire from Hampton Court, analysing a document which Reginald Pole had written about the King's divorce. This document, which Cranmer, in accordance with the language of the period, calls a book, was probably a letter which Pole had written to Henry advising him not to proceed with the divorce. Pole's letter has not survived, but Cranmer's summary of it is obviously an accurate one, because Pole's arguments, as summarized by Cranmer, make out a very strong case against the divorce on grounds of political expediency. Cranmer did not fail to mention some of Pole's most effective points, such as the dubious methods by which the opinions of the Universities had been collected by Henry's agents, and he paid tribute to Pole's abilities. He wrote that Pole showed such wit and eloquence that he was worthy to be a member of the Privy Council, and he feared that if this document were read by the common people, it would be impossible to persuade them that Pole was wrong.[1]

In this letter to Wiltshire, which was written from Hampton Court, Cranmer mentioned that Anne and the King had ridden to Windsor together and had then returned to Hampton Court. Henry was now cohabiting with Anne. Cranmer probably resumed residence at Durham House with the Boleyns when he returned from Italy in October 1530, and then moved to Court as Anne's chaplain. Soon afterwards he became one of the King's chaplains, for he already held this post by January 1532.[2] This means that for at least six months Cranmer saw Henry and Anne day after day while they were cohabiting as man and wife. By this time, Cranmer had thoroughly convinced himself that Henry's marriage to Catherine was unlawful, and that Henry was acting virtuously in putting away his brother's relict and sending her to live at the palace of the Moor in Hertfordshire. But this did not make it permissible for Henry to commit fornication with Anne, and Cranmer must have known that they were doing this. We do not know whether he pretended not to notice, or whether he addressed some words of reprimand to the King and the lady; but he can hardly escape

[1] Cranmer to Wiltshire, 13 June 1531 (Cranmer's *Works*, ii. 229–31).
[2] Cranmer must have been a royal chaplain before he left for Ratisbon in January 1532, for he is referred to as the King's chaplain in a document drafted by Cranmer himself before his return to England; see Indenture between Cranmer and Hawkins, 19 November 1532 (Hist. MSS. Com., 7th Rep., p. 601).

the charge of having connived at this sin. He was not the only Catholic priest who was tolerantly overlooking the immorality of his patrons in 1531.

He continued to be a busy propagandist for the King's divorce. It was during this period that Cranmer was employed in an attempt to convince Sir Thomas More that Henry's marriage to Catherine was unlawful. More was still Lord Chancellor, and was dutifully serving the King in public, but he had not hesitated to tell him in private of his opposition to the divorce. Cranmer, Edward Lee, Fox and Nicholas de Burgo engaged in many arguments with More, but they did not succeed in convincing him that Henry's case was right. Cranmer was also engaged in translating into English a Latin treatise by Stokesley, Fox and de Burgo, in which the judgments of all the Universities which had held for Henry were examined and extolled. Cranmer made a number of alterations and additions to the text in the translation. It was probably about this time that he was appointed Archdeacon of Taunton. It is difficult to discover the date at which he obtained this preferment. One authority has stated that it was as early as 1525, but it is much more likely to have been in 1531. He was already Archdeacon of Taunton by January 1532, when he left on his second foreign mission. He was also granted some other benefice, which cannot be identified.[1]

We have one other glimpse of Cranmer between his visits to Italy and to Germany. He was present at the reconciliation between Gardiner and Barnes at Hampton Court, which must have taken place at the beginning of December 1531. Barnes, who had been the Prior of the Austin Friars at Cambridge, had been brought before Wolsey on a charge of heresy in 1526; but Gardiner had induced him to recant. This had

---

[1] More to Cromwell (February or March 1533/4) (More's *Works*, p. 1426). The book which Cranmer translated was published in London in 1531 under the title *The Determination of the most excellent Universities*; the Latin version was published (in incorrect sequence) by Burnet (iv. 136–44). See Stokesley to Cromwell, 17 July 1535 (*L.P.*, viii.1054). The original record of Cranmer's appointment as Archdeacon of Taunton has been lost; but see Le Neve, *Fasti*, i.168; Morice, (*Nar. Ref.*, p. 243); *L.P.*, iv. 6047 (p. 2698); Pollard, *Thomas Cranmer*, pp. 46–47 and n. Cranmer is referred to as Archdeacon of Taunton in all documents while he was Ambassador at Ratisbon during 1532, and he was probably made Archdeacon before this second foreign mission, and not, as Morice says, before his first; for Morice did not realize that Cranmer returned to England between his missions to Italy and Germany. Cranmer refers to 'my benefice' in his letter to Wiltshire of 13 June 1531 (Cranmer's *Works*, ii. 231).

saved Barnes' life; he was merely incarcerated in a monastery. But after he had escaped to the Lutherans in Germany, he denounced Gardiner for having persuaded him to renounce the truth. By 1531, Henry was interested in making contact with the German Lutherans, and he gave Barnes a safe-conduct to come to England, and invited him to Court. Soon after Barnes arrived, he had a talk with Gardiner at Hampton Court, at which Cranmer was present; and according to Gardiner, Barnes asked his forgiveness for having criticized him. This was some months before Cranmer first came into contact with Osiander and the Lutherans of Nuremberg, and it would be interesting to know the attitude which he adopted at this meeting between the pardoned heretic and the new Bishop of Winchester; but Gardiner did not give any indication of Cranmer's reactions when he revealed the incident to the world in his book against George Joye in 1545.[1] By that time, Barnes had been burned as a heretic, while Cranmer was still, to all appearances, Gardiner's fellow-Councillor and brother Bishop, though Gardiner had been secretly plotting to denounce him as a heretic. Gardiner's statement therefore tells us nothing beyond providing additional proof that Cranmer spent much time at Court in 1531.

[1] Gardiner, 'Declaration of such true Articles as George Joye hath gone about to confute as false' (Preface) in Muller, *Letters of Stephen Gardiner*, p. 167.

CHAPTER III

AMBASSADOR AT RATISBON

In January 1532, Cranmer was appointed as resident Ambassador at the Emperor's Court. Charles V resided in turn in different parts of his Empire, and was now travelling from Brussels to Ratisbon. Cranmer followed the Emperor, and had reached Ratisbon by 14th March. On his way, he passed through Nuremberg, and had his first experience of a town under Lutheran control. He noticed that they read a chapter of the New Testament in church every day. When he reached Ratisbon, he was able to compare impressions with Elyot, the retiring Ambassador, who had passed through Nuremberg with Charles' Court a short time before Cranmer. Elyot had been struck by the fact that they had eaten meat in Lent, though they had specially provided him with fish. He particularly noted that the priests were married, and that their wives were the most handsome women in Nuremberg.[1]

Elyot returned to England soon after Cranmer arrived, leaving his duties, his property and his financial difficulties to his successor. Elyot had been allowed one pound a day for his expenses, and Cranmer probably received the same allowance. This might seem generous enough at a time when the average daily wage of an unskilled labourer in England was fourpence, and the price of wheat was high at eight shillings a quarter. But an Ambassador abroad was obliged to incur considerable expenses in the way of travelling, and sending messengers in post, which cost a great deal, and he was also expected to maintain a household and state suitable to his station and the dignity of his King. This Cranmer found considerable difficulty in doing; and Hawkins, his successor as Ambassador to the Emperor, complained next year that like Cranmer he was forced to eat off pewter dishes, whereas all the other Ambassadors at Charles' Court had silver dishes at

---

[1] Vandenesse, 'Voyages de Charles-Quint' (in Gachard, *Collection des Voyages des Souverains des Pays-Bas*, ii. 101–2); Elyot to Norfolk, 14 March 1532 (Ellis, *Letters*, iii [ii] 191–3; *L.P.*, v. 869).

table.[1] If Cranmer made similar complaints, the documents have not survived.

Cranmer saw very little of the Emperor while he was at Ratisbon, for Charles was suffering from gout and spent most of his time at the neighbouring health resort of Abbach; but he carried on his negotiations with Charles' chief minister, Nicholas de Perrenot de Granvelle. The great question of the day was the Turkish danger. News had reached the West in the autumn of 1531 that Soleiman was preparing another invasion of Austria, and Charles was preparing to resist it. Every Englishman had been taught to be conscious of the Turkish menace, and knew that in theory the whole of Christendom ought to unite to assist the Emperor, its titular temporal head, to repel the infidel. But Henry was not at all anxious to incur any trouble or expense in order to help Charles, who was the chief obstacle in the way of his divorce. When Charles sent an envoy to England to make a formal appeal for military and financial assistance against the Turks, Henry made vague promises of support, but said that his definite answer would be communicated by Cranmer in due course. Cranmer's duty at Ratisbon was to play for time; he was to give Charles all moral support against the Turks, but to promise nothing more. He was also instructed to negotiate a new trade agreement with Charles in order to extend the opportunities for the English merchants' trade with Flanders; but he was unable to make much progress here, as the Emperor left the government of Flanders to his sister Mary of Hungary in Brussels.[2]

Cranmer made secret contacts with the German Lutherans. The Lutherans were engaged in protracted negotiations with Charles, who was prepared to compromise on religious controversies in order to obtain military assistance from the Lutherans against the Turks. The negotiations did not make much progress at first, and in May Cranmer seems to have thought that the Diet of Nuremberg would break up without any agreement being reached. On 18th May, he wrote to his government, and apparently told them that the Emperor was

---

[1] Elyot to Cromwell, 18 November 1532 (*L.P.*, v.1554); Hawkins to Cromwell, 24 December 1532 (*St. Pap.*, vii.406–7).

[2] Tyler, *Charles V*, p. 331; Chapuys to Charles V, 31 May 1532 (*Span. Cal.*, iv. [ii]. 954; *L.P.*, v.1058); Cranmer to Henry VIII, 4 September 1532 (Cranmer's *Works*, ii.231).

ill, that the Diet at Nuremberg had broken up in disorder, and that the Lutherans had made an alliance with King Sigismund of Poland, King Frederick of Denmark, John Zapolya of Hungary, and Albert of Brandenburg, the Grand Master of East Prussia, against Charles and his brother Ferdinand of Austria. This information was certainly incorrect, and it is perfectly possible that Cranmer never gave it; for we know about the contents of the letter only through a conversation between Eustace Chapuys, Charles' Ambassador in London, and the Duke of Norfolk, who was now Henry's chief adviser. When Chapuys said that Charles would soon have the Lutherans under control, Norfolk told him what Cranmer had written in his letter. But though Norfolk promised to send the letter to Chapuys, he later told him that he could not do so as he had left it with the King. This may have been because he had given Chapuys a misleading account of its contents.[1]

Cranmer was not entitled to play any part in the Diet at Ratisbon and Nuremberg; but he went to Nuremberg on at least two occasions to speak with the Lutheran leaders. On 14th July, he went there secretly and met John Frederick of Saxony and Spalatin and Pontanus, his advisers. He returned to Ratisbon next day, but went back to Nuremberg on the 20th, again travelling unobtrusively with only one servant attending him, and had a further talk with Spalatin. He could not openly urge the Lutheran Princes to refuse to help the Emperor against the Turks; but he tried to discourage them from voting for Charles' brother Ferdinand as King of the Romans, and he told them that both Henry and Francis I would assist them if they were attacked by the Emperor. But nothing that Cranmer could say was as powerful as the argument of Soleiman's mammoth army on the borders of Austria. Cranmer persuaded Spalatin to agree to continue the negotiations with Henry's envoy Paget; but by the time that Paget met John Frederick at Coburg at the beginning of August, the Lutherans had reached agreement with the Emperor.[2] Charles had suddenly made far greater concessions to the Lutherans than had hitherto seemed likely—doubtless far more than Cranmer had expected

---

[1] Chapuys to Charles V, 28 June 1532 (*Span. Cal.*, iv [ii]. 968; *L.P.*, v. 1131).

[2] Seckendorff, *Commentarius Historicus de Lutheranismo*, iii. 40–41; John Frederick of Saxony and others to Henry VIII (March 1538), *L.P.*, xiii [i]. 648; Höss, *Spalatin*, pp. 362-3.

on 18th May. He offered to permit the Lutheran Princes to maintain the religious practices in their territories until all religious differences were settled by a General Council of the Church; in return, the Lutheran Princes agreed to send forces to serve under Charles against the Turks.

There was also the question of the divorce. The case was slowly proceeding, subject to endless delays, in the Papal Court in Rome, where Carne, as Henry's excusator, was arguing that a Prince could not be summoned to appear before a Court outside his realm. In August 1532, Cranmer wrote from Ratisbon to Benet, the Ambassador in Rome, to inquire about the progress of the case, and was informed that in July the Pope had adjourned the proceedings until the beginning of November. Meanwhile Cranmer was concerning himself in Germany with the divorce. Within a week of his departure from London, Chapuys wrote to Charles that Cranmer had been instructed to make contact with the German Universities on his way to Ratisbon with a view to obtaining from them a judgment in Henry's favour with regard to the divorce, and he urged the Emperor to have Cranmer shadowed by his agents. But Chapuys seems to have been misinformed about this. As far as we know, Cranmer made no attempt to visit the German Universities; but he almost certainly discussed the divorce with the German Lutherans. Luther, who had no reason to love the persecuting King of England, had supported Catherine in the divorce case, on the grounds that the marriage of a man to his brother's widow was not prohibited by the divine law, though he thought that Henry might lawfully commit bigamy and marry a second wife; but it was worth while trying to persuade the Lutherans to reverse their attitude and to vex the Pope by declaring that Henry's marriage was invalid, as Calvin, Oecolampadius and Zwingli had done. Cranmer almost certainly discussed the divorce with Osiander at Nuremberg, though there is no contemporary evidence of this, and it may well have been due to Cranmer that Osiander, alone of all the German Lutherans, came out in support of Henry, though his book on the divorce was soon suppressed in Nuremberg in order to placate the Emperor.[1]

---

[1] Benet to Cranmer, 15 September 1532 (*St. Pap.*, vii. 378–9); Chapuys to Charles V, 30 January and 5 February 1532 (*Span. Cal.* iv. [ii]. 897, 898; *L.P.*, v. 762, 773); Osiander to Cranmer, 24 January 1538 (Pocock, ii. 483, where it is wrongly dated 1533).

Cranmer also discussed the divorce with several theologians at Ratisbon. He is said to have converted Cornelius Agrippa von Nettesheim, one of Charles' theologians, who admitted to Cranmer that Henry's marriage was void, but said that he dared not say this publicly for fear of the Emperor and the Pope. Dantiscus, the Polish Ambassador, maintained a position which Cranmer eight years later described as 'Papist', which doubtless means that he was supporting the validity of the Papal dispensation; but he listened to Cranmer with patience and courtesy, and actually agreed with him on a number of minor points.[1] Yet while Foxe and Morice tell us that Cranmer was converting the learned men at Charles' Court on the divorce issue, Cranmer himself was almost converted at Ratisbon to supporting Catherine. Before the end of his stay in Germany, Cranmer was telling Granvelle that he was shocked at Henry's conduct towards Catherine.

This remarkable fact has been completely ignored by Cranmer's biographers; but it is proved by the statement of Granvelle himself. On 26th September 1535, Granvelle wrote to Chapuys in London and told him how surprised he was at what Cranmer had done against Catherine and Mary, because when Cranmer was at Ratisbon he 'blamed admirably what the King of England his master and his other ministers were doing in the matter of the divorce against the said Queen and Princess'.[2] It is true that at the time when he wrote this letter, Granvelle was bitterly hostile to Cranmer; but this only makes it more likely that what he wrote to Chapuys was true. In September 1535, Cranmer was known throughout Europe as the man who was largely responsible for the divorce of Catherine, and Chapuys had been denouncing Cranmer in his letters to the Emperor and Granvelle. Granvelle would rather have been tempted to tell Chapuys that he had discovered Cranmer's evil intentions when he was Ambassador to the Emperor, than to mention that at that time Cranmer was expressing correct opinions about the divorce. Granvelle had no motive for lying, and was in the best possible position to know the facts.

[1] Anon. Biogr.; Morice (*Nar. Ref.*, pp. 221, 243); Cranmer to Wriothesley, 21 September 1540 (Cranmer's *Works*, ii. 401).
[2] Granvelle to Chapuys, 26 September 1535 (*Span. Cal.*, v [i]. 207; *L.P.*, ix. 449; Friedmann, *Anne Boleyn*, i. 179 n.)

Cranmer was not the only Ambassador who was betraying Henry in his talks with foreign rulers and ministers. Two years before, Richard Sampson, the Dean of the Chapel Royal, had told Charles V that his sympathies were on the side of Catherine. Sir Nicholas Carew went further, and offered to act as a spy for Charles. Benet repeatedly urged Charles and the Pope in private to reject the arguments which he himself was putting forward on Henry's behalf before the Papal Court, and was in secret communication with Catherine. Elyot also supported Catherine. It has been suggested that while Sampson, Carew, Benet, and Elyot were really betraying Henry, Cranmer was acting under instructions to deceive Granvelle by a pretence of sympathy for Catherine; but it is difficult to believe that Henry and Cranmer would have resorted to such a tactic in 1532. It is much more likely that Henry did not know what Cranmer was saying to Granvelle about his divorce; and far from informing Henry, Cranmer sent him the distinctly misleading information that he was certain that Charles would 'not forget to make mention unto the Pope of your Grace's great cause' when the Emperor met Clement at Bologna—a statement which certainly conveys the utterly false impression that Charles would use his influence with the Pope in favour of the divorce.[1]

As Cranmer cannot have spoken in this way to Granvelle from motives of personal advancement—he looked to Henry, not to Charles, for promotion—he must have been expressing his true opinion. Like Elyot, Carew, Benet, and Sampson, he had been won over during his foreign mission; and this is perhaps not really surprising. The situation looked very different from Ratisbon than from Durham House and Hampton Court. At Ratisbon, Cranmer was at the heart of Christendom, at the Court of Caesar with the infidel at the gate; this was not the time to defy the Holy Father, to disrupt the unity of the Church, to take the path which already was unmistakably leading towards schism. At Durham House and Hampton Court, everyone assumed, or pretended to assume, that the King was laudably repudiating an unlawful union because his conscience no longer permitted him to do what was prohibited

---

[1] Chapuys to Charles V, 4 January and 5 June 1532; Mai to Charles V, 29 February 1532 (*Span. Cal.*, iv [ii]. 880, 909, 957, where Mai's letter is wrongly dated 28 February; *L.P.*, v. 696, 834, 1077); Friedmann, *Anne Boleyn*, i. 150–1; Cranmer to Henry VIII, 20 October 1532 (Cranmer's *Works*, ii. 232–3).

by the word of God; but at Ratisbon, everyone thought that after twenty years of married life, Henry was trying to rid himself of a faithful wife, a scion of the royal house of Spain, because he was lusting for a young coquette of upstart stock.

Yet Cranmer was probably influenced more by the mood of Nuremberg than by the mood of Ratisbon. At Nuremberg too, for different reasons, Henry's conduct was condemned; and if Cranmer converted Osiander, Osiander and his colleagues may have exercised a counter-influence on Cranmer. They may have made Cranmer realize that something more was required than searching the Bible for texts to suit the convenience of Junker Harry, and that it was necessary, not merely that the validity of one marriage should be decided by theologians, but that the doctrine of the Church should be reformed. Both Ratisbon and Nuremberg, from their opposing angles, could have made Cranmer take a different view of his activities during the last three years—the lying and bribery in Italy, and the condonation of the immorality of his patrons in England. He not only admitted to Granvelle that he strongly condemned the conduct of his King towards his Queen, but even went so far as to act as a link between two of Henry's most active opponents. When he returned to England, he carried with him a letter from Cochlaeus to Robert Ridley. Cochlaeus, who was at Ratisbon in the embassy of Cardinal Campeggio, the Papal Nuncio, was one of the most active propagandists against the divorce, and Robert Ridley had been Catherine's proctor in the divorce proceedings at Blackfriars. It was no doubt in order to embarrass Cranmer that Cochlaeus published this fact two years later in the Preface to one of his books, and mentioned that he had held many discussions with Cranmer at Ratisbon; but Cranmer wrote to Henry to assure him that he could give a satisfactory explanation of the incident.[1]

The King's divorce was not the only matter on which Cranmer altered his opinion while he was in Germany. It was almost certainly at Nuremberg that he took at least the first steps towards becoming a Lutheran. There is no reason to believe that Cranmer showed any Lutheran tendencies before 1532, or any real deviations from orthodox doctrines, except for

---

[1] Cochlaeus, *Beati Isidori . . . de officiis Ecclesiasticis* (Preface, 1534 ed.); Cranmer to Henry VIII (July 1535), (Pocock, ii. 506–7.)

the importance which he attached to Scripture; but within a very short time of his visit to Nuremberg, he was giving clear indications of such deviations. He was certainly converted at Nuremberg to the Lutheran view as regards the celibacy of the clergy, for he was married—apparently by Osiander—to the niece of Osiander's wife. Cranmer was forty-three, but his wife cannot have been much more than twenty, for she married for the third time in 1564. In the records of Cranmer's trial, her name is given as Anne; but in fact it was almost certainly Margaret.[1]

Cranmer took a very hazardous step in marrying at Nuremberg. He did not, it is true, have any reason to believe that within four months he would be appointed Archbishop of Canterbury; but he was the Ambassador of his King to the greatest Prince in Europe, and his marriage, as a priest, was a crime by the laws of his own country and by those of the Court to which he was accredited. The authorities would have been far more tolerant if he had cohabited with a mistress, for this sin in a priest was regularly overlooked in practice; but the marriage ceremony showed that Cranmer was not merely a sinner, but a man who justified sin. If Cranmer's orthodox acquaintances knew of Margaret's existence, they obviously assumed that she was his mistress. We do not know whether Margaret remained at Nuremberg after the marriage, or whether she went with Cranmer to Ratisbon; but there is a passage in the letter which Dantiscus wrote to Cranmer in 1540 which—though it may very likely have a completely different meaning—may possibly be a veiled reference to the fact that Dantiscus knew about Margaret when he was at Ratisbon in 1532. 'For us,' he writes, 'nothing is more pleasant and delightful than celibacy and an undisturbed bed. I feel like joking; for as I write this I see myself talking to you, either at meals, as we used to do, or in the ship on the Danube to which you so kindly escorted me when I was leaving Ratisbon in those bygone years'.[2]

It has, indeed, occasionally been suggested that Cranmer did

---

[1] Morice (*Nar. Ref.*, p. 243); Foxe, viii. 34, 43; Parker, p. 388; 'Processus contra Thomam Cranmer' (Cranmer's *Works*, ii. 550, 557); Coll. Top. iii. 145. The only evidence that Osiander performed the ceremony at Cranmer's marriage is the statement made by Curtope at Cranmer's trial in 1555 that he had always heard that this was the case; but it is very probable.

[2] Dantiscus to Cranmer, 1 September 1540 (Cranmer's *Works*, ii. 403–4).

not marry Margaret, and that she was in fact his mistress, not his wife. This is not altogether impossible, for though in Mary's reign both Cranmer and the Papists were agreed that he had married Margaret, the Papists would have been as eager to accuse Cranmer of the graver offence of matrimony as he would have been to plead guilty to this rather than to fornication. It is, however, much more likely that he did go through a ceremony of marriage at Nuremberg, if only because Margaret, brought up in a pious Lutheran household, would probably have refused to live with Cranmer except as his wife, even if he had been prepared to cohabit in the more usual relationship. We may therefore assume that Cranmer was married in 1532, and it was an event of great significance. It has often been seen merely as a case of Cranmer succumbing to Margaret's charms; but it was also a gesture by which Cranmer secretly but unequivocally committed himself to Lutheranism. The priest who had been married by Osiander could not easily return to the ranks of orthodoxy.

By the end of August, Charles had assembled a large army in Austria, and was ready to take the field against Soleiman. He had still heard nothing from England since Henry's vague promise of help in May; but Paget had now arrived at Ratisbon with new instructions for Cranmer, and Cranmer was at last able to give a reply to the Emperor's request for assistance. At the end of August, Cranmer had an interview with Granvelle, and told him that Henry regretted that he was unable to send any help. He would have wished to send thirty thousand men from England, but they were not sufficiently well trained to be able to travel so far, or to fight in a climate so unlike their own; and history had shown that English soldiers fought much better against the infidel when they were commanded by their King in person. Henry was confident that Charles would defeat the Turks without his help, but if the Turks should in the future invade some country which was not able to defend itself, Henry would take command of his troops and come to its assistance. At Granvelle's request, Cranmer put his statement into writing so that it could be shown to the Emperor.[1]

---

[1] Cranmer to Henry VIII, 4 September 1532 (Cranmer's *Works*, ii. 232); Cranmer's Memorandum for Charles V, 28 August 1532 (*Span. Cal.*, iv [ii]. 987; *L.P.*, v. 1258).

Charles wrote a reply to Cranmer's statement which was dated 1st September, though it was only presented to Cranmer some time later, at Linz. He expressed his great disappointment at Henry's failure to send him aid, and said that if Henry was not intending to help, he should have told him earlier. He ridiculed the assertion that English troops would be too tired to fight after travelling as far as Austria, and wished that Henry had at least given some financial aid. Having drafted this protest, he set out against the Turks, and mustered his army at Linz, where he told the Ambassadors to meet him. Cranmer followed the Emperor by water down the Danube. His wife did not accompany him, and presumably stayed at Nuremberg; she later travelled to England to await Cranmer's return home.[1]

After pausing at Linz, Charles marched eastward against Soleiman, who on hearing of his advance retreated without giving battle into Hungary. Charles did not pursue him, but went to Vienna, and then to Italy. Cranmer was in Vienna at the beginning of October, and followed Charles by way of Innsbruck to Mantua. He did not know that Henry had already decided to recall him so as to appoint him Archbishop of Canterbury; but by 27th September, Henry had appointed Nicholas Hawkins, the Archdeacon of Ely, to succeed him as Ambassador to the Emperor. Cranmer did not hear the news until six weeks later; meanwhile, he was expecting to accompany Charles to Bologna, and then by sea to Spain.[2]

Austria had been saved from the Turkish hordes only to become the prey of her deliverers. Charles' Italian soldiers mutinied, and proceeded to ravage the country; and Cranmer, on his fortnight's journey from Vienna to Villach, encountered many inconveniences and dangers, and saw scenes of utter devastation and anarchy. The Turkish and Christian corpses were lying unburied on the battlefields. The mutineers had travelled ahead of Charles and the Court, and had robbed the villages on the road of food, stealing even the sacramental

---

[1] Cranmer to Henry VIII, 4 September 1532 (op. cit. ii. 232); Charles V's reply to Cranmer, 1 September 1532 (*L.P.*, v. 1277); Morice (*Nar. Ref.*, pp. 243–4).

[2] Cranmer to Henry VIII, 20 October 1532 (Cranmer's *Works*, ii. 232–4); Henry VIII to William and Louis of Bavaria, 27 September 1532; Henry VIII to Ferdinand of Austria, 1 October 1532 (Pocock, ii. 324, 327; *L.P.*, v. 1352); Vandenesse, 'Voyages de Charles-Quint' (in Gachard, *Voyages des Souverains des Pays-Bas*, ii. 103–4).

bread from the churches. What remained after they had passed was taken by Charles and his attendants, and Cranmer, following two days behind, found that all the inhabitants had fled from the unwalled towns and villages, leaving neither food nor bedding. He managed to find some straw to sleep on, and some fodder for his horses, among the deserted houses. Behind him came other bands of soldiers who completed the havoc. While the soldiers murdered, raped and burned, the countrymen formed themselves into bands, and harried the travellers, robbing and killing not only the soldiers, but the gentlemen of the Emperor's Court, including several of the foreign diplomats. The Emperor's household was attacked by plague, and Cranmer saw a comet in the sky. He thanked God for having spared his life. His chief fear was that the excesses of Charles' soldiers would provoke a revolution in Austria. When he wrote to Henry from Villach on 20th October, he mentioned the danger of insurrection, and commented: *'Deus omnia vertat in gloriam suam;* for hereof might follow such inconvenience as in many years after should be irreparable.' Throughout his life, he always had the greatest dread of popular revolution.[1]

Charles reached Mantua on 6th November, and about a week later Hawkins arrived from England to replace Cranmer as Ambassador. On 16th November, Cranmer had his farewell audience with Charles. On the 18th, Charles wrote to Henry accepting Hawkins as Ambassador in Cranmer's place, and informing him, in accordance with the usual diplomatic courtesies, of the ability with which Cranmer had represented Henry's interests while he was at his Court. On the 19th, Cranmer delivered his plate to Hawkins, making out inaccurately the receipt which Hawkins signed. This inaccuracy is surprising in a man who had so often acted as auditor at Cambridge; but it is typical of Cranmer that the mistake, which underestimated the quantity which he had delivered, was to his own disadvantage. On the same day, he left Mantua for England.[2]

[1] Cranmer to Henry VIII, 20 October 1532 (op. cit., ii. 232–6).
[2] Hawkins to Henry VIII, 21 November 1532 (*St. Pap.*, vii. 386); Charles V to Henry VIII, 18 November 1532 (*L.P.*, v. 1551); Indenture between Cranmer and Hawkins, 19 November 1532 (Hist. MSS. Com., 7th Rep., p. 601). Charles V's Chamberlain Vandenesse states that Charles had left Mantua on 7 November (Gachard, *Voyages des Souverains des Pays-Bas*, ii. 105); but this is evidently wrong, as his letter to Henry VIII on 18 November was written from Mantua.

CHAPTER IV

ARCHBISHOP OF CANTERBURY: THE DUNSTABLE JUDGMENT

WHEN the aged Warham died in August 1532, Henry decided to appoint Cranmer as Archbishop of Canterbury. The choice caused great surprise when it was known in London at the end of January 1533. Strype has suggested that Warham expected Cranmer to succeed him; but this is a quite unwarrantable deduction from the story told by Harpsfield. According to Harpsfield, Warham told his nephew twenty years before his death that at some time in the future there would be an Archbishop named Thomas who would ruin the see of Canterbury as surely as St. Thomas of Canterbury had glorified it. Whatever the truth of this story, Cranmer's appointment was no more expected in 1532 than it had been at the time of Warham's prophecy in 1512.[1]

It was not of course by any means a preposterous appointment. Cranmer was already esteemed as a learned royal chaplain; he had resided at Court, and held the important position of Ambassador to Caesar. But there were several other men who were much more eligible. Gardiner, who would probably have been appointed if Warham had died a year before, was temporarily out of favour owing to his defence of the clergy from the attacks made upon them in Parliament, and Tunstall of Durham had also offered some opposition to Henry; but Stokesley, Edward Lee of York, or even Longland of Lincoln were eminently suitable, while if Henry intended to appoint a Primate who was not already a Bishop for the first time since 1397, his brilliant Almoner Edward Fox was a more obvious choice than Cranmer. The fact that Cranmer was selected in preference to all these rivals at a time when he was far away in Austria and unable to compete with their intrigues, clearly proves that some powerful influence must have been working on his behalf at Court; and this can only have been the Boleyns.

---

[1] Chapuys to Charles V, 27–29 January 1533 (*Span. Cal.* iv. [ii]. 1043; *L.P.*, vi. 89); Harpsfield, *The Pretended Divorce*, p. 178. Strype (*Cranmer*, pp. 20–22), and Pollard (in *Thomas Cranmer*, p. 53), are very misleading on this point.

Henry was now very much under the influence of Anne and her family, and very anxious not to offend the lady's father. We need not believe the story of the Papist propagandists that when Cranmer thanked the King for having appointed him Archbishop, Henry told him to thank Anne Boleyn; but Wiltshire, Anne and Henry were obviously agreed that Cranmer was the most reliable man for Canterbury. They did not know what he had been saying to Granvelle.[1]

At Cranmer's trial in 1555, the royal proctor Martin put the matter brutally: Cranmer had said to the King, 'Give me the archbishopric of Canterbury and I will give you license to live in adultery.' Cranmer replied: 'You say not true.'[2] We can readily believe him, for things are not done as cynically as this. It was merely that the King and the Boleyns were sure that Cranmer would be reliable; and despite his vacillation in Germany, of which they knew nothing, they were right.

Cranmer told the Court at Oxford: 'I protest before you all, there was never man came more unwillingly to a bishopric than I did to that; insomuch that when King Henry did send for me in post, that I should come over, I prolonged my journey by seven weeks at the least, thinking that he would be forgetful of me in the mean time.'[3] Cranmer's admirers have attributed this reluctance to his innate modesty, while some of his critics have suggested that it was because of his illegal marriage; but neither explanation is satisfactory, for Cranmer had already accepted important positions, and Margaret would not be a much greater embarrassment to him as Primate than as Ambassador. The reason for Cranmer's reluctance is probably to be found in Granvelle's letter. Cranmer had serious doubts as to whether Henry's actions were right, and did not wish to be too closely associated with them. As a servant of the King, in a subordinate capacity, he had already been obliged to act in an unscrupulous way in Italy; as Archbishop, it might be worse. Cranmer's hesitation was due to a sound instinct that by accepting the archbishopric he might be placed in a position where he would be forced to violate his conscience in order to serve his King. Yet the offer of the highest position in Church and State

[1] Gardiner to Somerset, 6 June 1547 (Muller, p. 287); *Bishop Cranmer's Recantacyons*, p. 4; *Spanish Chronicle of King Henry VIII of England*, p. 19.
[2] Foxe, viii. 56.
[3] Foxe, viii. 55.

was tempting, and it was the duty of a subject to obey and serve his Prince. Cranmer's attitude was therefore contradictory.

He lost no time in starting on his journey. He left Mantua on 19th November, within a week of Hawkins' arrival there with the instructions for him to return. In view of the time which he would have had to spend in preparing his horses and making other arrangements for the journey, this shows a real haste in departure, and Hawkins wrote to Henry that Cranmer had left as soon as he had received his instructions.[1] But once on the road, Cranmer began to hesitate and to go slowly. He had hesitated and turned back eight years before on the road from Cambridge to Oxford when he preferred the quiet security of Jesus College to the venture of the Cardinal's foundation. He had much more reason to hesitate now; but he could not turn and go back to Mantua. He had had grave doubts as to the propriety of Henry's conduct; but he would not desert his Prince while on a foreign mission. He was not a Pole or a Pate.

He had one very good reason for travelling slowly—the weather and the state of the roads. In December 1532, France was in the grip of a great frost which made the roads very icy and dangerous. But an exceptionally good horseman such as Cranmer could have travelled from Mantua to London in less than seven weeks. Hawkins, who had not hurried, had taken six and a half weeks for the journey the other way; but a month later, Bonner prided himself on covering the distance from Bologna to Westminster, which was farther than the distance from Mantua, in sixteen days, and in February 1533 Chapuys' messenger riding in post travelled from London to Bologna in thirteen days. But Cranmer rode slowly along the frozen roads of south-eastern France at an average rate of fifteen miles a day. On 8th December, nearly three weeks after leaving Mantua, he was still thirty miles south of Lyons.[2]

Henry had meanwhile decided that Cranmer must travel home as quickly as possible. It was the usual practice to delay a year before filling vacant sees so that the King could meanwhile take the revenues; but in October Henry met Francis I

[1] Hawkins to Henry VIII, 21 November 1532 (*St. Pap.*, vii. 390–1).

[2] Hawkins to Henry VIII, 21 November 1532; Bonner to Benet, 31 January 1533 (*St. Pap.*, vii. 386, 410); Vaughan to Cromwell, 9 December 1532; Ortiz to the Empress Isabella, 22 February 1533 (*L.P.*, v. 1620; vi. 178; *Span. Cal.* iv [ii]. 1051).

at Calais, and obtained a promise of diplomatic support from Francis if he repudiated his marriage to Catherine and married Anne without waiting for the judgment of the Papal Court in the divorce case. He therefore needed a Primate immediately. His minister Thomas Cromwell sent Stephen Vaughan to France for the express purpose of hurrying Cranmer on his journey, and Vaughan is no doubt the messenger to whom Cranmer referred at his trial as having travelled to him in post. Vaughan found the roads in a most dangerous state; he wrote to Cromwell that he had had a fall from his horse at Amiens, and did not expect to get home without a broken leg. He told Cromwell that Cranmer wished to travel slowly, but that he would get him safely back to England, or die on the way, and he hoped that they would be home by Christmas. He met Cranmer just south of Lyons on 10th December; but he did not succeed in getting him home by Christmas, or in inducing him to quicken his progress by more than about two miles a day. It took them another month to travel home from Lyons, and they only reached London about 10th January.[1]

It was known in London within the next fortnight that Cranmer had been chosen as Archbishop of Canterbury. Harpsfield writes that Henry appointed Cranmer Archbishop at a bear baiting, and rumours which seem to refer to this incident were circulating in Kent next year.[2] Harpsfield is as biased a witness as could be found, but it would be a strange story to have invented if it were not true. Henry had been impatiently awaiting Cranmer's arrival, and if he happened to be watching a bear baiting when Cranmer at last arrived at Court, Cranmer might well have been led straight to the King's presence, and have been immediately appointed Archbishop of Canterbury. There was of course no kind of bargain made between King and subject at the bear baiting; but Cranmer knew what was expected of him.

About the time when Cranmer reached London, it became apparent that Anne Boleyn was pregnant. The possibility of the

---

[1] Vaughan to Cromwell, 9 December 1532 (*L.P.*, v. 1620). At his trial, Cranmer said that he took seven weeks over his journey home (Foxe, viii. 55). As he left Mantua on 19 November 1532, he must have reached London about 10 January 1533.

[2] Harpsfield, *The Pretended Divorce*, p. 290; Articles against Wynchelsey, (1534), (*L.P.*, vii. 1608).

birth of the long awaited male heir meant that there was
no time to be lost in appointing Cranmer as Archbishop, in
divorcing Catherine and in proclaiming Anne as Henry's wife
and Queen. About 25th January, Henry married Anne in secret.
Within a few weeks, rumours were circulating that they had
been secretly married by Cranmer, and when it was announced
at Easter that Anne was Henry's wife, everyone in the country
assumed that it was Cranmer who had married them; but in a
very frank and somewhat indiscreet letter which Cranmer wrote
to Hawkins in Barcelona on 17th June 1533, he told him that,
contrary to the general belief, he had not officiated at the
ceremony. He had not even known that they were married
until about a fortnight afterwards. The marriage was certainly
kept very secret for a short time if even Cranmer, who was so
much in Henry's confidence, was not made a party to the secret,
although he was at Greenwich, where the marriage took place,
within a day or so of the event—on 26th January, when Audley
was appointed Lord Chancellor.[1]

The next step was to expedite Cranmer's consecration. On
6th February, Henry ordered Cromwell, as Master of the Jewels,
to pay £1,000 to Cranmer as a loan to enable him to bear the
initial expenses of his office—a loan which Cranmer was unable
to repay for many years. Meanwhile Henry's agents exerted
themselves to obtain the necessary Papal bulls, for it was advantageous to Henry if England could go into schism with an
Archbishop whose consecration had been recognized by the
Pope. They threatened that unless Clement issued the bulls
without the usual charges of fifteen thousand florins, Henry
would bring into operation the Act of Parliament which
abolished the payment of all the annates to Rome. Chapuys was
repeatedly writing to Charles, urging him to persuade the
Pope, who was with Charles at Bologna, to refuse to issue the
bulls until after he had given judgment for Catherine in the
divorce suit in his Court in Rome, unless he inserted a condition
in the bulls that Cranmer was to swear an oath not to interfere
in the divorce case. He wrote to Charles that the Pope would
not be so eager to admit Cranmer as Archbishop if he knew

[1] Cranmer to Hawkins, 17 June 1533 (Cranmer's *Works*, ii. 246); Chapuys to
Charles V, 23 February and 10 April 1533 (*Span. Cal.* iv [ii]. 1053, 1058; *L.P.*,
vi. 180, 324); Memorandum of 26 January 1533 (Rymer, *Foedera*, xiv. 446–7).

that it was widely believed in London that Cranmer was a Lutheran. But by 3rd March Clement, acting with unusual speed and waiving all the charges, had issued eleven bulls authorizing Cranmer's consecration, and had sent the pall to Cranmer.[1]

Cranmer was consecrated in the Chapter House at West-minister on 30th March. Before the ceremony, he read out a protestation in a private room in the Chapter House in the presence of five officials and lawyers. It declared that he did not intend any oath to the Pope which he took at his consecration to be binding if it was against the law of God, or against our illustrious King of England or the Commonwealth, the laws or prerogatives of his realm of England, or to bind him to be any less free to advise and agree to the reformation of the Christian religion and of the government of the Church of England in any way which furthered the prerogative of the Crown. He then dressed in his consecration vestments, and proceeded to St. Stephen's Church, holding in his hand the paper on which his protestation was written. There he was con-secrated by Longland of Lincoln, with Veysey of Exeter and Standish of St. Asaph assisting. At the high altar, he took his consecration oath. He swore to be faithful and obedient to blessed Peter, to the Holy Roman Apostolic Church and to Pope Clement VII and his successors, to defend the Roman Papacy against all men, and to protect, defend, further and promote the honour, privileges and authority of the Roman Church and of the Pope. He also swore to persecute and denounce heretics, schismatics and rebels against the Pope. He stated that he swore this oath by God and the holy Evangelists, subject to the protestation contained in the document which he had read in the Chapter House. He then read out aloud his protestation. When he received the pall, he again took the oath in a somewhat short-ened form, and again read out his protestation.[2]

Cranmer also took the traditional oath of allegiance to the King in respect of his temporal lands and goods. He swore that he did 'renounce and utterly forsake all such clauses, words, sentences and grants which I have of the Pope's Holiness in

[1] Henry VIII's warrant, 6 February 1533; Chapuys to Charles V, 27–29 January and 9 and 23 February 1533 (*L.P.*, vi. 89, 131, 142, 180; *Span. Cal.* iv [ii]. 1043, 1047, 1053); Bonner to Benet, 31 January 1533 (*St. Pap.*, vii. 411); Collier, iv. 210.
[2] 'Processus contra Thomam Cranmer' (Cranmer's *Works*, ii. 559–62); for the protestation and the consecration oath, see also in Strype, *Cranmer*, pp. 683–5.

his bulls of the archbishopric of Canterbury, that in any manner was, is or may be hurtful or prejudicial to your Highness, your heirs, successors, estate or dignity royal; knowledging myself to take and hold the said archbishopric immediately and only of your Highness and of none other.'[1] The words of this oath are so strong that it seems almost unnecessary for Cranmer to have made the protestation; but this oath for the temporalities had been taken by Archbishops for more than four hundred years, and had for long been accepted by the Pope and everyone else as referring only to the temporalities of the see.

For four hundred years, historians have argued as to the morality of Cranmer's protestation. It was one of the chief accusations against him at his trial, while Pole declared that Cranmer, by his protestation, not only committed perjury, but declared in advance his intention of committing it. Others see it as a sign of Cranmer's outstanding scruple that instead of taking the oath and violating it, he insisted on declaring openly at the time that he only intended to keep the oath in certain circumstances. It cannot be denied that Cranmer took an oath having first made a protestation that he would only consider himself bound by the oath in so far as the oath did not conflict with something with which it obviously did conflict, though four years later Cranmer and his colleagues wrote in the Bishops' Book that it was a transgression of the Third Commandment if men 'swear to do that thing which they intended not to do'.[2] But it must remain a matter of argument as to whether Cranmer's action was more reprehensible than that of all his Papist predecessors who swore both the consecration oath and the oath for the temporalities, or than the action of Gardiner, who violated his consecration oath to the Pope, and of the Kings and others who obtained a dispensation from the Pope to break their oaths whenever it was politically expedient to do so.

But the point of the protestation seems to have been generally misunderstood. Cranmer probably made it, not because he wished to provide himself with a justification for violating his consecration oath, but because he had been ordered to do so by Henry as an act of policy. Foxe writes that Cranmer made

[1] The Oath for the Temporalities (Cranmer's *Works*, ii. 460).
[2] Pole to Cranmer, 6 November 1555; the Bishops' Book; the King's Book (Cranmer's *Works*, ii. 102, 538; Lloyd, *Formularies of Faith*, pp. 140, 304).

the protestation because his conscience did not permit him to take the consecration oath unless he did so; but Foxe's account of the incident is obviously wrong in almost every point. It is much more likely to have been a decision by Henry and his advisers. The consecration oath raised a problem for Henry. It was desirable that Cranmer should be consecrated with the Pope's consent in the traditional form without any omission which would invalidate the ceremony according to the Roman canon law; but Henry had denounced the consecration oath less than a year before. In May 1532, he had complained to the Speaker of the House of Commons that the Bishops' consecration oath conflicted with their oath to the King for their temporalities, and made the clergy only half his subjects.[1] This in itself would have been enough to make Cranmer reluctant to take the consecration oath; and the King was sufficiently aware of the logic of his own position for him to realize that it was desirable for Cranmer's consecration oath to be modified in some way. Moreover, while it was necessary that the Primate of the schismatic realm should have been properly consecrated, it was also desirable that he should, already at this stage, do some open act repudiating the supremacy of the Pope and strengthening that of the King, so that it would always be possible to declare in the future that he had taken his archiepiscopal see and all his powers from the King alone. In less than a year, the Pope will be the Bishop of Rome; soon he will be Antichrist. The Primate must not be too contaminated by his consecration oath.

There has been a great deal of argument as to whether the protestation was made secretly or publicly. On no occasion did either Pole or the judges at Cranmer's trial suggest that Cranmer had tried to keep his protestation secret; but he was accused of this by hostile historians three hundred years later.[2] The suggestion is not only false, but shows a complete failure

[1] For Foxe's story, see Foxe, viii. 66, which purports to be the account given by Cranmer himself at his trial; but the accuracy of the report is doubtful (see infra, Chap. XXIII). For Henry's complaint to the Speaker, see Lord Herbert, *The Life and Raigne of Henry VIII*, p. 335.

[2] The account which Watkyns the prothonotary gave at Cranmer's trial makes it clear that the protestation was read out publicly in the church (see 'Processus contra Thomam Cranmer', in Cranmer's *Works*, ii. 559–62). For the controversy between Todd and Lingard as to the secrecy of the protestation, see Lingard, *History of England*, v. 7 n.; Todd, *Vindication of Cranmer*, p. 41–49; Lingard, *Vindication of the 'History of England'*, pp. 75–78; Todd, *Reply to Lingard's Vindication*, pp. 19–40.

to understand the reason why the protestation was made. It would have been useless if it had been kept secret. Cranmer not only made the protestation in the Chapter House, but also read it out in full on two occasions in the church. If Henry had not wished it to be known that Cranmer had made the protestation, he would have told him not to make it at all, but to take the consecration oath and violate it later, as the other Bishops did. The idea of an oath as a most sacred commitment was far stronger in the sixteenth century than it is today; but it was rarely as strong as the arguments of political expediency.

By the beginning of February 1533, the Council had decided on an ingenious plan of campaign for the divorce, which would secure all the moral advantages of a legal judgment without the inconveniences of a real trial. Parliament was to pass a statute prohibiting appeals to Rome in ecclesiastical causes. Some selected canonists were to decide whether the depositions of the evidence given before Wolsey and Campeggio at Blackfriars in 1529 were sufficient to prove that the marriage of Catherine and Arthur had been consummated, while the Convocations of Canterbury and York were to pronounce, as a question of theology, whether, if the marriage had been consummated, the marriage of Henry and Catherine was lawful. Then Cranmer was to set up his Court to pronounce the sentence of nullity on the strength of the evidence of the depositions and the opinions of the canonists, of Convocation and of the Universities without the need for calling any witnesses. Two days after his consecration, Cranmer was present in the Upper House of Convocation when the House, after a keen debate between Stokesley and Fisher of Rochester, resolved that if Arthur and Catherine had consummated their marriage, Henry's marriage to Catherine was void. The Lower House did likewise, while the canonists decided that the marriage between Arthur and Catherine had been consummated. Cranmer then wrote to Henry petitioning to be permitted to sit in judgment on the validity of his marriage to Catherine. It is obvious that he would never have done this except on the King's instructions, and Cranmer virtually admitted this in his letter to Hawkins two months later.[1]

[1] Chapuys to Charles V, 9 February 1533 (*Span. Cal.* iv [ii]. 1047; *L.P.*, vi. 142); Records of Convocation, March–April 1533 (Wilkins iii. 756–7; Rymer, xiv. 454–5); Parker, p. 381; Cranmer to Hawkins, 17 June 1533 (Cranmer's *Works*, ii. 244).

Cranmer wrote to the King that the rude and ignorant common people were everywhere discussing the validity of his marriage and the consequent danger to the succession and the peace of the realm. It was the duty of the Archbishop of Canterbury, by the sufferance and grants of Henry and his predecessors, to judge ecclesiastical causes in accordance with the laws of God and holy Church, and to relieve the troubles of the people. 'Because I would be right loathe and also it shall not become me, for as much as your Grace is my Prince and Sovereign, to enterprise any part of my office in the said weighty cause without your Grace's favour obtained', Cranmer, 'beseeching your Highness most humbly upon my knees', asked permission to sit in judgment on the validity of Henry's marriage to Catherine.

Cranmer sent this draft to the King, who returned it with a number of amendments in his own handwriting which were designed to make the subservience of Cranmer's draft still more subservient. Cranmer was made to omit the statement that in exercising his jurisdiction as an ecclesiastical judge he was required to act in accordance with the laws of God and the Church and to relieve the wrongs of the people; and in the new draft he expressly asked for an actual license from the King permitting him to act as judge in the divorce case. Finally, where Cranmer had written 'Beseeching your Highness most humbly upon my knees to pardon me of these my bold and rude letters', Henry insisted that he should say: 'Eftsoons, as prostrate at the feet of your Majesty, beseeching the same to pardon me of these my bold and rude letters'.[1]

The opponents of Henry and Cranmer have naturally made great play with this picture of a cringing Archbishop and an arrogant King insisting on amendments because Cranmer was not abasing himself enough to please his insatiable vanity. But the wording of the petition was probably influenced more by considerations of policy than by Henry's personal pride. Henry thought it expedient that his marriage to Catherine should be pronounced a nullity by a court of law with Cranmer as the judge; but in the eyes of the people, a judge is higher than the litigants. The sight of Cranmer sitting as a judge over the King

[1] See Cranmer's *Works*, ii. 237–9, for both the original and the corrected drafts.

and Queen would greatly elevate the status of the Archbishop
of Canterbury at a time when Henry wished to strengthen his
royal supremacy. Cranmer must be degraded in order to
counteract his elevation. He must not only make it clear that
he was only acting as judge with Henry's permission, but must
do this in an utterly submissive manner. The phrase 'prostrate
at the feet of your Majesty' has often been cited as an example
of the vanity of Henry, who was not satisfied that Cranmer
should address him 'most humbly upon my knees'. But the
phrase was not thought out by Henry on this occasion; it was
the recognized expression used by a contrite subject in prison
or in disgrace when he was asking for mercy, and was used in
these circumstances by Wolsey, More, Mary and Cromwell.[1]
Its adoption here was a calculated attempt to abase Cranmer;
but the universal reaction to Dunstable showed the necessity of
this. It was not Cranmer prostrate at Henry's feet, but Cranmer
presiding as Henry's judge, that stirred the imagination of the
people, and it required some years of official propaganda before
the other and truer picture was generally accepted.

On the afternoon of 10th May, Cranmer opened his Court in
the priory at Dunstable, with Longland as an assistant judge
and Gardiner leading the counsel for the King. The proceedings
were open to the public, but there were very few spectators.
Dunstable had been chosen ostensibly to suit the convenience
of Catherine, who was living at Ampthill; but Chapuys was
probably right in thinking that it was really because Dunstable
was far enough from London to avoid the disturbances which
might otherwise have occurred, for there was widespread
popular support for Catherine. On Chapuys' advice, Catherine
did not appear at the trial either personally or by proxy. She
could not submit to Cranmer's jurisdiction without prejudicing
her appeal to Rome; and if she had appeared at Dunstable to
challenge the jurisdiction, she would have been guilty of a
praemunire under the recent statute prohibiting appeals to
Rome. Catherine's decision not to appear was very welcome to
Cranmer, for it would accelerate the proceedings, and as Anne's
coronation had been fixed for Whitsun, 1st June, the divorce case

---

[1] Wolsey to Henry VIII (August 1530); More to Henry VIII, 5 March 1534
(Ellis, *Letters*, i [ii] 50; ii [ii] 33; *L.P.*, iv. 6574); Mary to Henry VIII, (15 June
1536) (*St. Pap.*, i. 457); Cromwell to Henry VIII (12 June 1540) (Merriman,
Life and Letters of Thomas Cromwell, ii. 264, 267).

had to be completed without delay. This aspect had not been
overlooked by Chapuys; but he was convinced that whatever the
Queen might do, Cranmer would give judgment for Henry on
the day after Ascension.[1]

Yet even in Catherine's absence, the case proceeded more
slowly than Cranmer wished. When Catherine did not appear
at the opening session, Cranmer declared her contumacious;
but he could not proceed with the case in her absence unless he
could pronounce her to be truly and manifestly contumacious,
which he could only do on evidence that she had no intention of
appearing. When Catherine had been served with the citation
to appear, she had clearly stated that she would not do so; but
the witnesses who had heard her say this were not present in
Court at the first session. Thanks to this mismanagement by the
King's proctors, it was only at the second session that Cranmer,
after hearing these witnesses, could declare Catherine to be
truly and manifestly contumacious. At the fourth session of the
Court on 17th May, the King's proctors handed in the depositions
of the witnesses at the trial at Blackfriars, along with the
opinions of the Universities and the recent resolutions of the
Convocations of Canterbury and York as to the validity of
Henry's marriage and the dispensation of 1503.[2]

But though this was enough to enable Cranmer to give judgment, it was still necessary to waste five precious days. He
could not sit on a Sunday. The Monday, Tuesday, and Wednesday were the Rogation days, and it would have been as improper
for the Court to sit on Ascension Day as on any of the three
fast days. Friday the 23rd was therefore the earliest opportunity
for giving judgment, and Cranmer wrote to Cromwell that he
would be able to do so on that day; but he hoped that his intention would be kept secret until the Friday, because otherwise
Catherine might even now appear and delay proceedings,
especially if the news of the impending judgment led to agita-
tion among the people.[3]

Cranmer and Henry's other servants at Dunstable made very

---

[1] Cranmer to Hawkins, 17 June 1533 (Cranmer's *Works*, ii. 244); Bedyll to
Cromwell, 10 May 1533 (Pocock, ii. 473); Chapuys to Charles V, 27 April and
10 May 1533 (*Span. Cal.* iv [ii]. 1062, 1072; *L.P.*, vi. 391, 465).

[2] Bedyll to Cromwell, 10, 12, and 17 May 1533 (Pocock, ii. 473-5; *St. Pap.*,
i. 394-5); Cranmer to Henry VIII, 12 May 1533 (Cranmer's *Works*, ii. 241).

[3] Cranmer to Henry VIII; Cranmer to Cromwell, both 17 May 1533
(Cranmer's *Works*, ii. 242).

little attempt to maintain among themselves the public pretence that Cranmer was acting as an impartial judge. Bedyll, who was one of the King's proctors, wrote to Cromwell that Cranmer acted 'very well and very uprightly, without any evident cause of suspicion to be noted in him by the counsel of the said Lady Catherine, if she had had any present here'. Yet throughout the whole trial, he was regularly writing to the King and assuring him of the eagerness with which he was trying to carry out his wishes. The practice for a judge to be in private contact with one of the parties was by no means unknown even in cases between ordinary litigants; but Cranmer clearly considered himself to be serving his King, and not judging a case impartially, at Dunstable. On the first day of the trial he wrote a report to Henry. Two days later, on 12th May, he wrote to Henry again after the close of the second session, expressing the hope that Catherine's failure to appear would shorten the proceedings. On the 17th he wrote to the King again, explaining that because of the ferial days he could not give judgment before 23rd May. On the same day, he wrote to Cromwell—the letter has been somewhat mutilated—'I thank you for your two . . . and good advertisments by the same, which I have h . . . satisfied, according to such trust and expectation as the King. . . . Highness hath in me; for where I never yet went about to . . . willingly any man living, I would be loathe now to begin . . . my Prince, and defraud him of his trust in me.' This letter has not been sufficiently burned to hide the flagrant bias of the judge at Dunstable.[1]

Cranmer gave judgment on the morning of Friday 23rd May —the very day which Chapuys had foretold a fortnight before as the day on which judgment would be given. Post horses were waiting at St. Albans and Barnet to carry the news immediately to Cromwell and the King. Cranmer had apparently submitted a draft of his sentence to Cromwell or one of his agents, who amended it before Cranmer delivered it in open Court. On the day the sentence was delivered, Bedyll wrote to Cromwell: 'I think the sentence will please the King's Grace very well, for in very deed it is much better now than it was when it was first

---

[1] Bedyll to Cromwell, 12 May 1533 (*St. Pap.*, i. 395); Cranmer to Henry VIII, 10, 12, and 17 May 1533; Cranmer to Cromwell, 17 May 1533 (Cranmer's *Works*, ii. 241–3; *L.P.*, vi. 463).

devised, and ye know who amended it very singularly.' [1]

Cranmer as Papal Legate gave judgment that the marriage was against the law of God and invalid, that Henry and Catherine were forbidden to cohabit any longer, and that both were free to re-marry. In 1554, Pole wrote a public letter from Italy to Cranmer in his Oxford prison in which he referred to the fact that Cranmer had threatened to excommunicate Henry if he did not put away his brother's widow. No such threat appears in the Dunstable judgment; but it was referred to in a pamphlet published by order of the King and Council in the autumn of 1533, in which it is favourably contrasted with the unjust action of the Pope in excommunicating Henry without first giving him the customary warning—though in fact Clement had warned him on more than one occasion. Cranmer may have issued the threat in a separate document, though not in the judgment, or on some other occasion. 'Did you not in fact laugh yourself,' wrote Pole, 'when you made a pretence of all this severity and threatened the King in this way?' Pole added that he himself had wept when he read the Council's document and saw how they were making a mock of the King whom he so dearly loved. If Cranmer in fact threatened Henry with excommunication it was certainly laughable—as laughable as the protestations with which Pole denounced it in 1554.[2]

Already before he had given his judgment, Cranmer had received letters from Thirlby, the King's chaplain, instructing him to direct the King's proctors at Dunstable to be ready to argue the case as to the validity of Henry's marriage to Anne. Time was very short, as the matter had to be settled before Anne's coronation on 1st June. Cranmer and the King's proctors hurried back to London, and on 28th May, 'in a certain well known high gallery in our manor of Lambeth', in the presence of Cromwell, Thomas Legh and three other officials, Cranmer gave judgment that the marriage of Henry and Anne was lawful. Such a judgment was desirable, for it was now admitted that Henry had secretly married Anne before his marriage to

[1] Cranmer to Henry VIII, 23 May 1533 (Cranmer's *Works*, ii. 243); Tregonwell to Cromwell, 23 May 1533; Bedyll to Cromwell, two letters of 23 May 1533 (*L.P.*, vi. 525, 526; Pocock, ii. 476); Cranmer's judgment, 23 May 1533 (Burnet, iv. 189–91).

[2] 'Articles devisid by the holle consent of the Council' (autumn 1533) (Pocock, ii. 529); Pole, *Epistola ad T. Cranmer . . . de Sacramento Eucharistiae* (Le Grand, *Histoire du Divorce*, i. 298).

Catherine had been invalidated by Cranmer or any Court, and this seems to have caused widespread criticism throughout the country. We have no more knowledge of the reasons for Cranmer's decision than we have of the grounds on which he reversed it three years later. The authorities already realized that the marriage might be void under the canon law on two different grounds—because of Anne's alleged precontract of marriage with the Earl of Northumberland, and because her sister Mary had been Henry's mistress. But it seems unlikely that Cranmer inquired into either of these matters in 1533. According to Stokesley, who, though he was not present, would probably have known what had occurred at the hearing, Cranmer merely declared that as Henry's marriage to Catherine was unlawful, the King had never yet been married and had therefore been free to marry Anne.[1]

Cranmer's judicial processes were completed without a day to spare. Next day, Anne came in state from Greenwich to the Tower, and on 31st May Cranmer rode beside the French Ambassador in Anne's procession through London to Westminster, along the streets hung with tapestries and lined by the guilds and constables, past the pageants at Cheapside and Ludgate and the fountains flowing wine. Next morning, on Whitsunday, he anointed and crowned the Queen in Westminster Abbey. At the coronation dinner in Westminster Hall, Cranmer, alone of all the dignitaries present, was accorded the unusual distinction of being placed to sit with Anne and her ladies at her table. Edward Seymour and John Dudley—the future Dukes of Somerset and Northumberland—were his carver and cupbearer. The Bishops and the peers sat at lower tables, while the Duke of Suffolk rode around the hall on horseback, and Henry watched the proceedings through a hole in the wall. Hostile witnesses reported that during the coronation procession, men kept on their caps and remained silent when Anne passed; but for both Anne and Cranmer, that Whitsun was a day of earthly glory.[2]

[1] Cranmer to Henry VIII, 23 May 1533 (Cranmer's *Works*, ii. 243–4); Cranmer's judgment on Anne Boleyn's marriage (Rymer, xiv. 470–1); Stokesley to Bedyll, 4 January 1533/4 (*L.P.*, vii. 15).

[2] For the official plans and contemporary accounts of Anne's procession, coronation and banquet, see *L.P.* vi. 561, 562, 563, 585, 601; *Tudor Tracts*, pp. 9–19; Camusat, *Meslanges historiques*, ii. 17–18; Wriothesley, *Chronicle*, i. 18–22; Hall, *Chronicle*, pp. 798–805; Stow, *Annals*, pp. 563–8; Cranmer to Hawkins, 17 June 1533 (Cranmer's *Works*, ii. 245–6). One of these records names Clinton, not Dudley, as Cranmer's cupbearer.

CHAPTER V

THE ROYAL SUPREMACY

AFTER 1530, Henry VIII set out to crush the independence of the Church and to destroy all resistance to his autocracy. Obedience and adulation of the King was not only enforced by imprisonment, torture and death, but was fostered by an intensive propaganda campaign in print and sermon which must have reached almost everyone of the three million inhabitants of England. Cranmer was one of the principal ministers engaged in enforcing this policy.

We do not know when Cranmer first accepted the doctrine of unquestioning obedience to the Prince. His generation had been taught to obey the King and the temporal power, not merely from fear of punishment but from fear of God; but it was also taught to believe that restraints were imposed upon the King by the Pope and the Church, by the common law of the realm and the moral law of Christendom. The bidding prayer ordered the people to pray first for the Pope and the College of Cardinals, for the recovery of the Holy Land and the true Cross, for the Archbishop of Canterbury, the Bishops, Abbots and all the clergy, before they were also urged to pray for the King, that he might rule the realm in a manner pleasing to God. The General Sentence, which was read out in church four times a year, excommunicated those who had denied the rights of the Church, and had withheld rents and committed other offences against its privileges, before it also excommunicated those who challenged the rights of the King, and 'all those that war sustain against the King wrongfully'—for the possibility of a righteous war against the King was not excluded.[1] But by 1533, if not before, Cranmer believed in royal absolutism in its most extreme form. He was probably influenced, not so much by Marsiglio's *Defensor Pacis* and Tyndale's *Obedience of a Christian Man*, as by the political atmosphere in which he moved at Durham House and Hampton Court.

[1] The Bidding Prayer (Burnet, v. 149–52); Wynkyn de Worde, 'The Festival' (Strype, *Ecclesiastical Memorials*, i [ii]. 189).

Belief in royal supremacy became for Cranmer as fundamental a principle as his belief in the supremacy of Scripture. He acquiesced in every change of religious doctrine during the twenty years in which he, almost alone among the leading statesmen, survived every turn of official policy; on three occasions he granted Henry a divorce on very questionable grounds; he obeyed and glorified a cruel tyrant who repeatedly committed every one of the Seven Deadly Sins. This is often ascribed to weakness or cowardice; but there is no evidence that Cranmer was a coward. His statement to Morice that his schoolmaster had destroyed his natural audacity was only an expression of the usual criticism of brutality in schools by advanced educationalists. His recantations at Oxford are more likely to have been due to doubt than to fear. The evidence, on the contrary, proves that Cranmer was a brave man. His action in issuing his Declaration against the Mass in 1553 is alone sufficient to establish this. On several occasions, he intervened with Henry for men in disgrace or under sentence of death, and was as fearless in criticizing Henry to his face in private as he was loyal in praising him in public. Cranmer's aim was to promote royal absolutism, not to curry favour with Henry for his own benefit. He believed—as he and his colleagues wrote in the Bishops' Book[1]—that it was his duty as a loyal counsellor to tender the best advice to the King in Council, and he did not hesitate to do so even if the advice was unwelcome and he harmed himself by giving it. If his advice was rejected, he must obey the King like every other subject, and enforce in public the policy which he had opposed in private consultation. Cranmer was an agent of Henry's despotism, not through fear of his Prince, but through fear of damnation if he disobeyed his Prince.

Cranmer had need of all his courage in the summer of 1533. There was talk of civil war, and Chapuys, egged on by Fisher and some of the old nobility, was repeatedly urging the Emperor to declare war and invade. But for Cranmer, invasion was not the only thing to fear; he was in almost as great a danger if there were a reconciliation between Henry and Rome, for in such a situation he was the obvious man to be sacrificed

[1] The Bishops' Book; the King's Book (Lloyd, *Formularies of Faith*, pp. 154, 316).

as a scapegoat. Chapuys had always thought it better that the
Papal censures should be directed against Anne and Henry's
chief agents rather than against the King himself, so as to make
it easier for Henry to agree to a reconciliation with Rome; and
in August 1533 he recommended that if Henry made overtures
for a reconciliation, the Pope should refuse to receive the
English envoys unless Cranmer were handed over to him to
deal with. Cranmer's judgment at Dunstable had aroused the
greatest indignation among the Papists at home and abroad,
who were denouncing it as an act of rebellion against a spiritual
superior, and as heresy.[1]

Meanwhile Cranmer himself was dealing with a case of
heresy in June 1533—that of the young Cambridge scholar,
Frith. Frith not only denied the Real Presence and the existence
of Purgatory, but thought that it was unnecessary for salvation
to believe the truth on either point; of all the English martyrs
of the sixteenth century, he came nearest to advocating freedom
for doctrinal dissent. He was brought from the Tower to
Cranmer at Croydon, refusing an opportunity which was given
him by his guards to escape while they were passing through
Brixton woods. A modern writer has suggested that it was
Cranmer who ordered the guards to allow Frith to escape; but
there is no evidence of this, and it is very unlikely. Frith was
examined on several occasions by Cranmer and Gardiner and
other Commissioners, and as he refused to recant he was sent
to Stokesley, his Ordinary, for sentence. Foxe says that the
Commissioners were impressed by the skill with which Frith
defended his doctrines; but when Cranmer wrote to Hawkins
a few days later, he stated merely that Frith's doctrines were
'notably erroneous', and that Frith 'looketh every day to go
unto the fire'. He was burned with another sacramentary at
Smithfield on 4th July.

Foxe was afterwards told by Cranmer's chaplains about a
private conversation which they had overheard between Cranmer and his Cambridge colleague Nicholas Heath, soon after
Frith's trial. Heath developed Frith's arguments on certain
texts from Augustine with such skill that Cranmer commented

[1] Chapuys to Charles V, 9 February, 10 April, 18 and 29 May, 13 August,
10 October and 16 December 1533 (*Span. Cal.*, iv [ii]. 1047, 1058, 1073, 1077,
1108, 1133, 1161, where the letter is wrongly dated 3 August; *L.P.*, vi. 142, 324,
508, 975, 1249, 1528).

that Heath was obviously well on the way to becoming converted to Frith's doctrines himself. Foxe suggests that Frith
had almost persuaded both Cranmer and Heath to repudiate the
Real Presence; but it is more likely that Heath was indulging in
an intellectual exercise and that Cranmer was making a joke.
If this is so, it proves that Cranmer and Heath were very sure
of their position, and under no suspicion of unorthodoxy on the
Sacrament of the Altar.[1]

In July, Cranmer dealt with Elizabeth Barton, the nun of
Kent. Elizabeth Barton had begun having visions during an
illness in her native village of Courthope Street in Kent about
1526; her Lady of Courthope Street had cured her of the
disease, and had appeared whenever Elizabeth went into trances
before the inhabitants of the village, speaking in a hollow voice
as if from out of Elizabeth's stomach. At the bidding of the
Lady, Elizabeth entered the nunnery of St. Sepulchre's in
Canterbury, and chose Dr. Edward Bocking, a monk of Christ
Church, Canterbury, as her confessor. Thereafter Our Lady of
Courthope Street concerned herself chiefly with current
politics, including the King's divorce. The nun was told by an
angel to tell Henry to suppress heresy, to burn English translations of the Bible, and to respect the rights of the Pope; and she
also prophesied that if Henry married Anne, he would die within
a month, and that within six months the country would be struck
down by plague. She had made a favourable impression on
Warham and Fisher, and had been in contact with Wolsey and
More.

Such prophecies about the King were dangerous statements
to be emanating from a maid with a reputation for holiness.
Cromwell instructed Cranmer to examine the nun, and she was
brought to him at Otford at the end of July. After Cranmer had
questioned her, she asked to speak with him privately, and then
told him that she had had a revelation in her last trance that she
would receive, in her next trance at Courthope Street, a reply
from Henry and Anne to the warnings which she had given
them. At her request, Cranmer permitted her to go to Courthope Street, ordering her to return later to tell him what

[1] For Frith's case, see Foxe, v. 3–16; viii. 696–9; Cranmer to Hawkins, 17
June 1533 (Cranmer's *Works*, ii. 246); Judgment against Frith (Foxe, v. App.
Document xxii); Wriothesley, i. 22; Gairdner, *Lollardy and the Reformation*, iii.
74–75.

message she had received in her trance. Gwent, the Dean of the Arches, wrote to Cromwell on 11th August that Cranmer had let her go to Courthope Street in order to discover what story she would invent, and added that Cranmer 'doth yet but dally with her as he did believe her every word; and as soon as he hath all he can get of her, she shall be sent to you'.[1]

Cranmer's modern critics have expressed strong disapproval of his conduct towards Elizabeth Barton. They have drawn a picture of a wily man of affairs deceiving a weak-minded young woman, pretending to be her friend in order to lure her to destruction. But Cranmer had been appointed to investigate what was suspected of being a highly dangerous conspiracy in an age when all the people, and men as learned as Warham and Fisher, believed in prophecies and holy maids. Cranmer is not the only criminal investigator who has encouraged a loquacious suspect to talk in the hopes of obtaining useful information. But it should be noted that when Gwent wrote to Cromwell that Cranmer was dallying with the nun as if he believed everything she said, he was not praising Cranmer for his ingenuity, but criticizing him for his inactivity; for he told Cromwell—sycophantically perhaps—that no information would have been obtained from the nun had it not been for the interrogatories which Cromwell had drafted for Cranmer to put to her.[2]

In November, the nun was again examined at Lambeth by Cranmer, Cromwell and Latimer. Cranmer also examined Henry Gold, who had been Warham's chaplain and had acted as interpreter when Elizabeth had spoken with the Papal Nuncio. The conspirators were executed for high treason at Tyburn in April 1534. Fisher and More were accused of mis-prision of treason in failing to inform the authorities as to the revelations of the Holy Maid, and their names were included in the bill of attainder. At the beginning of March, More was examined by Cranmer, Norfolk, Audley and Cromwell. They treated him at first with great consideration, inviting him to

<hr />

[1] *Statutes of the Realm*, 25 Hen. VIII, c. 12; letter to Cromwell (November 1533); Goldwell to Cromwell (November 1533) (Wright, pp. 14–19); Cranmer to the Prioress of St. Sepulchre's (July 1533); Cranmer to Hawkins, 20 December 1533 (Cranmer's *Works*, ii. 252, 272–4); Gwent to Cromwell, 11 August 1533 (*L.P.*, vi. 967).

[2] Gwent to Cromwell, 11 August 1533, op. cit.

sit with them during the interrogation—a privilege which
More declined; but later they adopted a harsher attitude.
More's name was nevertheless struck out of the Bill of Attainder. According to More's son-in-law Roper, this was because Cranmer and his colleagues were convinced that the
bill would be defeated in the House of Lords if More were
included among its victims. They therefore implored Henry, on
their knees, to delete More's name from the bill.[1]

Anne Boleyn gave birth to Elizabeth on 7th September 1533.
Cranmer attended the christening at Greenwich three days
later. He was godfather when Elizabeth was baptized by
Stokesley at the font of silver, and he confirmed her immediately
afterwards. The birth of Elizabeth made any reconciliation with
Rome even more remote, and fortunately for Cranmer events
were now moving towards a final break. In July, the Pope
issued a bull excommunicating Henry, Anne and Cranmer,
and another depriving Cranmer of his see, though neither bull
was published. Henry decided to lodge an appeal against
Clement's sentence to a General Council of the Church—an act
of deliberate defiance of the Pope, who did not recognize any
right of appeal from his decrees to a General Council—and sent
Bonner to present his appeal to Clement at a stormy interview
at Marseilles. After deciding to appeal against his own excommunication, Henry came to the conclusion that it would be
advisable if Cranmer did the same. On 22nd November, Cranmer
wrote to Bonner in Marseilles, and asked him to present to the
Pope an appeal to a General Council. Cranmer was careful to
state that he was presenting his appeal at the King's command.[2]
Many years were to pass before Cranmer, in very different
circumstances, once again asked Bonner to present an appeal
to a General Council.

On 3rd December 1533, Cranmer was enthroned as Archbishop in his cathedral church at Canterbury. The ceremony was
preceded by a display of humility. Cranmer walked barefoot

[1] 25 Hen. VIII, c. 12; Cranmer to Cromwell, 5 January 1534 (Cranmer's
Works, ii. 277, where the date is wrongly given as 6 January; see *L.P.*, vii. 17);
Roper, *Life of More*, pp. 64–70.

[2] Hall, pp. 805–6; Wriothesley, i. 23; Cranmer to Bonner, 22 November 1533;
Cranmer to Hawkins, 20 December 1533 (Cranmer's *Works*, ii. 268–9, 274).
The date given by Cranmer for Elizabeth's birth is incorrect. Cranmer's letter to
Bonner is correctly printed in Cranmer's *Works*, and in Burnet, vi. 68, but in-
correctly in Strype, *Cranmer*, pp. 31–32, and *L.P.*, vi. 1454.

through the streets of Canterbury from the house of Christopher Hales, the Attorney-General, where he had changed into his enthronement vestments, to the cathedral; the streets had been covered with sand for him to walk on. After the enthronement came the worldly pomp and luxury—a great banquet. It may perhaps not have been as splendid as Warham's enthronement feast, but the monks of Christ Church, the city corporation, and Cranmer's officers were all called upon to supply meat and poultry. The Prior of Christ Church sent so many swans and partridges for the enthronement feast that he had none left to send to Cromwell as a Christmas present, and could only send a gift of apples. He was particularly anxious to placate both Cromwell and Cranmer, for Bocking and another brother of the priory had been implicated in the Holy Maid's conspiracy; and Cranmer discovered, while he was in Canterbury for his enthronement, that several novices had been contaminated by Bocking's teaching. Cranmer nevertheless intervened with the King on behalf of the monks. He told Henry that they were prepared, not only to pray on his behalf, but to offer him two or three hundred pounds.[1]

After his enthronement, Cranmer embarked on a visitation of his diocese. By now the realm was in schism. At the beginning of December 1533, the Council proclaimed that the Pope had no authority in England and was henceforth to be known as the Bishop of Rome. Four months later, Cranmer obtained a judgment from Convocation to the same effect. In the spring of 1534, Parliament abolished all the Papal powers in England, and transferred them to Cranmer. Henceforth the mandate for the consecration of Bishops was to be issued by the Archbishop of Canterbury on the receipt of the King's mandate, and the Pope's powers of granting licenses and dispensations were vested in him subject to an appeal to the Court of Chancery. Once again, as at Dunstable, it was Cranmer's newly granted powers, and not his subordination to the King in the exercise of them, which impressed observers. The Pope's supporters sneered at Cranmer as the 'new Pope', the 'English Pope', the

[1] Hist. MSS. Com., 9th Rep. (Pt. 1) p. 152; Cranmer to Bergavenny, 27 November 1533; Cranmer to Henry VIII, 13 December 1533 (Cranmer's *Works*, ii. 270-1); Goldwell to Cromwell, 10 December 1533 (Ellis, *Letters*, iii [ii]. 288); Christ Church Priory to Henry VIII (November 1533); Roland Lee and Bedyll to Cromwell, 10 December 1533 (Wright, pp. 22-25).

'Antipope', the 'patriarch Pope'. When in May 1534, in a conversation with Norfolk, the Scottish Ambassador's mention of
the Pope led Norfolk to ask angrily which Pope he meant,
Chapuys, who was told about the incident by his diplomatic
colleague, chose to interpret Norfolk's meaning as being an
inquiry as to whether the Scottish Ambassador had meant the
Pope of Rome or the Pope of Canterbury. Norfolk was of course
merely guarding himself against acknowledging the Bishop of
Rome to have the title of Pope.[1]

The government took steps to crush the supporters of the
Papacy by propaganda and repression. The right to preach was
restricted, and preachers were directed what to say in their
sermons. But the most far-reaching step was to require everyone
in the country to swear the oath of succession. In an age when
an oath was regarded with the utmost dread—at least in
theory—every man and woman was to be forced to swear, and
to commit themselves by a positive personal act, to support the
succession established by the divorce, and therewith the first
great act of defiance of Rome. Every person in authority, down
to the Justice of the Peace in every parish, was to administer the
oath to his inferiors. At the summit of the whole system were
Cranmer, Audley the Lord Chancellor, and the Dukes of
Norfolk and Suffolk. On 30th March 1534, they were appointed
as Commissioners to organize the swearing of the oath, and
themselves took the oath in the presence of the King in the
House of Lords before Parliament was prorogued.

The Act of Succession laid down that every subject should
take an oath, when required, to uphold the provisions of the
Act; those who refused to swear were to be guilty of mis-
prision of treason and punished by imprisonment during the
King's pleasure. The actual form of the oath was not laid down
in the Statute; but the Commissioners undoubtedly went beyond their powers with regard to the oaths which they administered. Cranmer and his colleagues first drafted a form of
oath which required the people to swear that they did not owe
allegiance to any 'foreign authority, Prince or potentate'; but

[1] Chronicle of monk of St. Augustine's (*Nar. Ref.*, p. 281); 25 Hen. VIII, c.20,
21; Chapuys to Charles V, 22 April, 14 May and 16 July 1534; anonymous
account of Anne Boleyn's coronation (June 1533); letter, probably to Lisle,
7 February 1535 (*L.P.*, vi. 585; vii. 530, 662, 980; viii. 185; *Span. Cal.*, v. [i].
45, 57, 71).

as there was nothing in the Act of Succession which contained any such provision, the oath was not within the terms of the Statute, and no one should have been imprisoned for refusing to swear it. This was remedied as soon as Parliament re-assembled in November; it was then enacted that this oath which the Commissioners had drafted and put to so many persons was the oath which Parliament had intended should be sworn. But Cranmer and his colleagues went further than this, and sometimes put the oath in a different form which expressly repudiated all allegiance to the Bishop of Rome. This oath, which was certainly not covered by the Act of Succession, was never retrospectively legalized by Parliament.[1]

On Monday 13th April 1534, Cranmer sat at Lambeth with Audley, Cromwell, and Benson the Abbot of Westminster to receive the oaths of the London clergy. Fisher and More were also summoned to take the oath that day. More has left a vivid description of the scene in his letter to his daughter Margaret Roper—of the Commissioners sitting on that very warm day as one by one the clergy were brought before them. More was the first to be called in, although others had arrived before him; but as he refused to take the oath, the Commissioners adjourned his case, and dealt with the clergy while he waited in the burned chamber. All the clergy subscribed except Wilson, Catherine of Aragon's confessor, who was sent to the Tower. Then More was brought back, and he resumed his brilliant equivocation. The Commissioners told him how many men had eagerly sworn since he had left them; but More replied that though he would blame no one for swearing, he would not swear himself. At this, Cranmer intervened. He said that if More did not blame those who had taken the oath, he could not be very sure that it was wrong to swear, but must consider it to be a doubtful matter; there was, however, no doubt that he ought to obey his Prince, so More should forget his unsure conscience on the propriety of taking the oath, and take the sure way of obeying his Prince by swearing it. This was the only argument which baffled More during the whole interview; he wrote to his daughter: 'This argument seemed me suddenly so subtle, and namely with such authority coming out of so noble a

[1] 25 Hen. VIII, c. 22; 26 Hen. VIII, c. 2; *House of Lords Journal*, 30 March 1534.

prelate's mouth, that I could again-answer nothing thereto, but only that I thought myself I might not well do so, because that in my conscience this was one of the cases in which I was bounden that I should not obey my Prince.' More had, in fact, found the answer; and he added that if Cranmer's argument were right, it would be an easy way out of every perplexity, for if there were any doubt on any issue dividing the doctors, a command from the King would settle it.

The Commissioners could get nothing from More but an undertaking that he would swear to the succession if he were allowed to draft the oath so as to make it reconcilable with his conscience. Fisher, who appeared before them on the same day, took the same attitude. More and Fisher were allowed to go free, but More was sent to the Tower four days later. Fisher seems to have been placed for a short time in Cranmer's custody before being transferred to the Tower. A few days before his arrest, Fisher was asked by representatives of St. John's College, Cambridge, of which he was Master, to promulgate new statutes for the College; but the old man said that he had no time to study them. The statutes were therefore issued by Cromwell and Cranmer.[1]

Four days after the first examination of Fisher and More, Cranmer wrote his famous letter to Cromwell on their behalf. He reminded Cromwell that Fisher and More had agreed to swear to the Act of Succession, and objected only to the preamble; and though they had refused to state their reasons for refusing to swear to the preamble, it was obviously either because the preamble repudiated the authority of the Pope, or because it condemned Henry's marriage to Catherine. He then proposed that they should be allowed to swear to the Act without the preamble, provided that they would swear to maintain the Act against all powers and potentates; for a submission to this extent by More and Fisher would have a great effect on Catherine and Mary, who thought that their souls would be

---

[1] For the examination of Fisher and More, see More to Margaret Roper (17 April 1534) (More's *Works*, pp. 1428–30); *Life of Fisher*, pp. 276, 279–82. There is considerable doubt as to Fisher's whereabouts for a few days after his first appearance before the Commissioners on 13 April. The authors of the *Life of Fisher*, who are unlikely to have minimized his sufferings, state that he was permitted to go to his house for a few days before being sent to the Tower (*Life of Fisher*, p. 280); but Husee wrote to Lisle on 17 April that Fisher was in Cranmer's custody (*L.P.*, vii. 502).

damned if they swore the oath, and also on the Emperor, who held the two men in such esteem. Cranmer was confident that if More and Fisher swore, everyone in the realm would do likewise. He suggested that the exact form of the oath which Fisher and More would take could be kept secret.[1] Cranmer's plea for the two men was thus made on grounds of expediency. On several other occasions, Cranmer was prepared to ask the King to pardon a Papist without raising the question of expediency, merely because it was a case where mercy might properly be shown; but in the case of More and Fisher, Cranmer was seeking to further the King's interests by a compromise under which More and Fisher would be spared, and their consciences satisfied, in return for a public announcement that they had capitulated on all points to Henry.

Henry rejected Cranmer's suggestion. Cromwell wrote to Cranmer that the King insisted that Fisher and More should swear to the preamble of the Act of Succession, as well as to the rest of the oath, as otherwise they would appear to be supporting the Papal authority and condemning Henry's marriage to Anne, and others would be encouraged to follow their example. Cromwell added that Henry 'specially trusteth that ye will in no wise suppose, attempt or move him to the contrary'.[2] There is here a difference of temperament between Henry and Cranmer, and not merely a different tactical appreciation. If Cranmer suggested mercy as a tactic, it was partly because a merciful policy was emotionally congenial to him; but while Cranmer wished to impress Catherine, Mary, and the Emperor by the sight of Fisher and More swearing to the Act of Succession, Henry preferred to impress them by the sight of the heads of two of his most eminent subjects stuck as high as London Bridge.

The letter in which Cromwell rejected Cranmer's suggestion is undated; but Cranmer had probably already received it by 21st April, four days after he wrote his letter to Cromwell. On that day, Fisher appeared again before the Commissioners at Lambeth. The authors of that biography of Fisher which was translated, though not written, by Richard Hall describe how Fisher was attempting to explain again that he would swear to

---

[1] Cranmer to Cromwell, 17 April 1534 (Cranmer's *Works*, ii. 285–6).
[2] Cromwell to Cranmer, (April 1534) (Merriman, i. 381).

certain parts of the Act of Succession, but not to other parts, when Cranmer demanded that Fisher tell them at once whether he would swear the required oath or no. Fisher then said that, confronted with this choice, he would refuse to swear, and he was thereupon committed to the Tower. This curt and almost brutal intervention by Cranmer is very different from the attitude which he had adopted in the case of More eight days before, and very different from Cranmer's usual conduct. We certainly cannot accept these biographers as a reliable authority in this matter. They wrote after the burning of Cranmer had been officially justified by their faction as retribution for Fisher's death, and went out of their way, in their book, to applaud the fact that Cranmer had been rightly burned.[1] But their account may well be correct on this point. If Cranmer had already received Cromwell's reply to his intercession for Fisher and More, he would probably have been eager to prove that he had loyally accepted Henry's decision, and was no longer prepared to allow Fisher to show the slightest equivocation with regard to the taking of the oath in the form in which it was originally submitted to him.

Catherine and Mary were also required to swear to the succession established by Parliament, and to acknowledge the invalidity of the marriage of Henry and Catherine and the royal supremacy over the Church. They both refused, despite blandishments and threats, until Mary eventually surrendered and acknowledged all this after Catherine's death in 1536. Henry subjected both mother and daughter to petty persecution, and according to Morice's story was only dissuaded from sending Mary to the Tower by the intercession of Cranmer. Morice writes that the Council, hearing of Henry's decision to send Mary to the Tower to suffer the penalties imposed on all his subjects, insisted on Cranmer protesting to the King, because he alone among them stood high enough in Henry's favour to venture to intercede for Mary. Henry granted Cranmer's re-

---

[1] *Life of Fisher*, pp. 284–5, 383. Of Cranmer's death, the authors write: 'At last in the reign of that blessed lady Queen Mary . . . he was called to a reckoning for many of his former ill doings. And lastly standing stiff in divers horrible and foul heresies, was most worthily burned with fire and consumed to ashes.' The *Life of Fisher* was not written by Hall, but by several theologians of Fisher's College of St. John's (one of whom was Thomas Watson, the Bishop of Lincoln under Mary), probably in about 1577 (see Van Ortroy's Preface to *Life of Fisher*, pp. 66–81).

quest, and spared Mary, but he told Cranmer that he would live to regret it.

The Protestant writers have often repeated this story of how Cranmer saved the Princess who afterwards burned him, to illustrate both Cranmer's kindness and Mary's ingratitude. It has been ignored, rather than challenged, by Cranmer's critics, though a Catholic gentleman, writing seventy years afterwards, stated that Cranmer's part in the story was invented by Foxe. But the story is confirmed by Morice, and as early as January 1556, two months before Cranmer was burned, the Protestant exiles had told Mary in a public letter that Cranmer had saved her life. Morice's story is very credible, except perhaps for the prophetic remark attributed to Henry. The King must certainly have contemplated imprisoning his obstinate daughter, whose resistance had exasperated him beyond measure, while the Council, and particularly Cranmer, would have shrunk from so drastic a measure against one so close to the King in blood, so popular among the people and so dear to the Emperor. Once again, Cranmer's inclination to mercy went hand in hand with his political caution. The only cause for surprise is that Henry did not overrule his Council.[1]

The Council knew that Chapuys was encouraging Catherine and Mary in their resistance, and they decided to try to persuade him to change his attitude, or at least to show him the solidarity of the dignitaries of Church and State. Chapuys came before the Lords of the Council, the Bishops and the Judges at Westminster at seven o'clock on a Saturday morning in May 1534, and was urged to use his influence to persuade Catherine and Mary to take the oath. Chapuys refused; he said that the Act of Succession was illegal, because it was against the natural law of Christendom, and as the people had only taken the oath

[1] Morice (*Nar. Ref.*, p. 259); Foxe, viii. 43; Tresham, 'Arguments why Queen Elizabeth better might make laws against the Catholics than for His Majesty to continue them' (Hist. MSS. Comm., *Various Collections*, iii. 132); *A Supplicacyon to the Quenes Maiestie*, p. 4. It is not clear, however, if the author of the *Supplicacyon to the Quenes Maiestie* refers to the same incident as that described by Morice and Foxe; for he writes: 'And here I may specially make mention to your Grace of that virtuous and learned man Thomas Cranmer Archbishop of Canterbury, who hath saved your Grace's life and put himself in jeopardy for your Grace's cause, as it is well known by some of his enemies that were of King Edward's Council; and I doubt not but that your Grace knoweth of it; and therefore I trust your Grace will requite him with mercy, and not suffer that wicked Bishop of Winchester to have his wicked will and purpose of him.'

under duress, they would be able to violate it as easily as the
Archbishop of Canterbury had violated his consecration oath to
the Pope. Cranmer remained silent during this discussion,
except for suggesting a few arguments to the speakers while
they were addressing Chapuys. It was more impressive if men
like Tunstall and Archbishop Lee, who were known to be
critical of Henry's policy, explained to the Emperor's Ambassador how enthusiastically they supported the King's position.
When Tunstall was speaking about the divorce, Cranmer
intervened to point out that they did not accept the Pope as an
impartial judge in the divorce case, both because he was afraid
of the Emperor, and because he could not be impartial where the
validity of his own dispensing power was in issue. This gave
Chapuys the opportunity to reply that he could give ten or
twelve reasons why Cranmer was not impartial in the divorce
case, and could therefore not be considered to have been an
impartial judge at Dunstable. We need not accept Chapuys'
account of Cranmer's inadequacy and discomfiture at the meeting; but the Ambassador was entitled to congratulate himself
on having scored two debating points at Cranmer's expense.
He had struck home with his remarks about Cranmer's consecration oath and his bias at Dunstable. It was what many of
Henry's subjects, without Chapuys' diplomatic immunity, were
thinking and whispering.[1]

[1] Chapuys to Charles V, 19 May 1534 (*Span. Cal.*, v [i]. 58; *L.P.*, vii. 690).

CHAPTER VI

THE FIRST STEPS TOWARDS REFORM

In April 1534, Cranmer began a visitation of his province. The purpose of the visitation was to assert the royal supremacy over the Bishops; but here again, as at Dunstable and in the Act of Dispensations, the emphasis was on Cranmer's authority as Archbishop. He acted under the royal mandate, but his inhibitions restraining the Bishops' jurisdiction and enforcing the authority of his visitors were issued in his own name as Metropolitan, Primate and Legate of the Apostolic See. The use of this title involved him in difficulties. When he came to St. Paul's on 30th April, and issued his Injunctions prohibiting Stokesley and his Ordinaries from exercising their jurisdiction for the next six months, Stokesley delivered a protestation to Cranmer, refusing to submit to the visitation on the grounds that Cranmer styled himself Legate of the Apostolic See, and stating that he would not comply with any act which Cranmer performed as Legate against the King's crown and the statutes and customs of the realm. Cranmer refused to enter this protestation in the Register. The visitation evoked similar protests from Longland of Lincoln, Repps of Norwich, Veysey of Exeter, and the President of Corpus Christi College in Oxford.[1]

These protests were occasioned by Cranmer's use of his title of Papal Legate. The title had been used for several centuries by Cranmer's predecessors, and was historically a mark of the independence of the see of Canterbury rather than of its subordination to Rome. The Archbishops of Canterbury, York, Pisa, Rheims and Metz were entitled, alone of all the Metropolitans in Christendom, to be Legates by virtue of their office, without having the title conferred on them personally by the Pope. But while the title of *Legatus Natus* might imply a relative

---

[1] Palsgrave to Cromwell (25 April 1534); Longland to Cranmer, 29 July 1534; Report of Visitation of Lincoln Cathedral, 4–7 August 1534; Longland's appeal, 2 March 1534/5; Claymonde to Cranmer, 2 March 1534/5; Courtenay to Cromwell, 9 March 1535 (*L.P.*, vii. 538, 1044 [i] and [iii]; viii. 312, 316, 359); Stokesley's appeal, (May 1534), (Strype, *Cranmer*, pp. 704–8); Strype, *Cranmer*, p. 41.

independence of Rome, it was hardly a suitable one for an Archbishop who denied that the Bishop of Rome had any authority at all in England, and it is remarkable that Cranmer was still using it six months after Papal supremacy had been cast off. He would obviously only have done so on Henry's instructions. He used the title of Legate in his visitation, as he had done in his judgment at Dunstable, for the same reason that he had sworn his consecration oath to the Pope—in a somewhat futile attempt to deceive the conservative elements in the country. The Archbishop's authority as Papal Legate was to be used to strengthen the royal supremacy at the same time as it was being loudly proclaimed that the potentate from whom the authority was derived had no such authority to delegate.

The ruse, however, turned out to be a blunder. While it is clear, from the form of the Bishops' protests, that they were partly motivated by their resentment against the interference of the see of Canterbury in their dioceses, the dominant factor was their fear of the consequences of submission to legatine authority. Five years before, the whole clergy had been held guilty of a *praemunire* because they had submitted to the exercise by Wolsey of his powers as Papal Legate, and the fact that the King had authorized Wolsey to exercise these powers was held to be no defence for the clergy. They had been forced to offer Henry a large subsidy as a gift in order to obtain his pardon. There is a real irony in the whole incident of Cranmer's visitation. Cranmer undertook it at the King's command in order to assert the royal supremacy in the name of the Pope whose power Henry was seeking to destroy, and he thereupon found himself accused of defying the King and upholding the Pope; while the Bishops, including such loyal supporters of Henry's policy as Stokesley and Longland, formed the only opposition to the visitation, and did so largely out of fear. They dared not submit to the King's will lest he should later punish them for having done so.

Cranmer conducted much of his visitation in person, going to Rochester in June and in the autumn to Gloucester, Worcester and Leicester, where he preached sermons against selfishness and avarice which greatly impressed a German Lutheran who heard them. This was the only time during his twenty years as Archbishop that he went to the northern parts of his province. He returned to Lambeth for the session of Parliament and Convocation, and on 11th November announced in Convocation that he would no longer style himself Legate of the Apostolic See. Henry obviously thought that there was nothing further to be gained by Cranmer's use of the title of Legate; but its renunciation did not save Cranmer from further difficulties when he extended his visitation to the diocese of Winchester in the spring of 1535. When Gardiner received Cranmer's orders for the visitation on the road as he was travelling up to London, he protested on the grounds that Cranmer's new title of Primate of all England derogated from the royal supremacy. Cranmer replied to Gardiner's criticisms in a letter to Cromwell which shows the friction which already existed between Cranmer and Gardiner, and the frankness with which Cranmer could write to Cromwell on the subject. He wrote that Gardiner was more concerned with his own interests than with the King's supremacy, 'against whose Highness he knoweth right well that I will maintain no cause, but give place, and lay both my cause and myself at my Prince's feet'. Cranmer argued that the Popes had never considered the Archbishop's title of Primate to be a derogation from the supreme Papal authority, and that if the Pope, as Supreme Head of the Church, could have a Primate under him, so could the King now as Supreme Head. He added that he personally would be very happy if all the Bishops abandoned their titles, and called themselves Apostles of Jesus Christ.[1]

Cranmer did not attempt to extend his visitation beyond the bounds of his province; but on several occasions he came into conflict with Archbishop Lee as a result of his intervention in the province of York. In the autumn of 1533, Cranmer intervened in the dispute between Lee and the Archdeacon of Doncaster as to their respective rights with regard to the ordination of clerics, though he ultimately used his influence to induce the Archdeacon to submit at least in part to Lee's demands. In the summer of 1535, Lee's reluctance to preach the royal supremacy led Cranmer to intervene in a more serious manner.

[1] Cranmer to Cromwell, 3 June 1534 and 12 May 1535 (Cranmer's *Works*, ii. 294, 304–6); Thalasius to Cromwell, 6 June 1535 (*L.P.*, viii. 831); Records of Convocation, November–December 1534 (Wilkins, iii. 769). Cranmer was at Gloucester on 30 August 1534, where he executed a deed in favour of Worcester priory (Hist. MSS. Com., 14th Rep., viii. 170).

Cromwell ordered Lee to preach in favour of the supremacy in his cathedral on St. Peter's Day, and sent Sir Francis Bigod to York to ensure that Lee complied with the command. Bigod was accompanied by his chaplain, who carried with him a license from Cranmer authorizing the chaplain to preach in the cathedral in Lee's place if Lee refused to obey; but Lee proved compliant, and suddenly showed a belated zeal in enforcing the supremacy. In the autumn of 1537, after the death of Kite, the Bishop of Carlisle, Lee complained to Cromwell that Cranmer had granted probate of Kite's will with regard to those chattels of Kite which were situated within the northern province; but Cromwell fully supported Cranmer in this matter. When Lee died, Cranmer demonstrated his primacy over the Archbishop of York by sending him a pall on the occasion of Holgate's consecration in 1545.[1]

In November 1534, Parliament enacted that the King was the Supreme Head of the Church of England, and that to deny any of his titles was high treason. In February 1535, Cranmer, along with all the other Bishops, took the oath renouncing all allegiance to the Bishop of Rome and accepting the King as Supreme Head; but the five Carthusians refused to swear. They were convicted of high treason on 29th April 1535. Cranmer intervened next day with an appeal for mercy for Webster, the Prior of the Charterhouse of the Isle of Axholme in Lincolnshire, and Raynold, a monk of Syon. He wrote to Cromwell that if their only crime was their refusal to take the oath, it would be better to persuade them to submit and to publish their submission, as this would be more likely to convert their supporters. He thought that if they were sent to him, he would be able to accomplish this. He did not, however, appeal for mercy on grounds of expediency alone. He also referred to Raynold's learning in divinity, and to the fact that Webster had previously promised him that he would not support Papal supremacy; and he lamented the fact that if they were executed, they would die in their error. We do not know why he appealed only for Webster and Raynold, and not for Houghton, Lawrence, and

---

[1] Archbishop Lee to Cromwell, 21 November 1533 and 6 August, 13 September, 7 October and 5 December 1537; Bigod to Cromwell, 11 June 1535 (*L.P.*, vi. 1451; viii. 854; xii [ii]. 459, 684, 851, 1175); *Gentleman's Magazine*, N.S. ix. 522-3 (November 1860); Wickham Legg, *Essays Liturgical and Historical*, pp. 114-6.

Haile; but this in itself suggests that expediency was not his chief object. Cranmer's proposal was rejected, and the Carthusians were executed—if their sympathizers' account was correct, with quite exceptional barbarity. At the beginning of June, More was once again brought before Cranmer and his colleagues; but Cranmer does not seem to have taken any part in the examination, which was conducted by Cromwell and Audley. More and Fisher were beheaded in July.[1]

The Charterhouse of London was then subjected to a merciless visitation. Cromwell installed an agent in the Charterhouse with instructions to enforce the strictest monastic discipline on the monks in the hopes that this would induce them to apply for a dispensation to leave the monastery. Two of the brothers were sent to Cranmer for instruction. One of them applied for a dispensation to discard his habit, which was eagerly granted to him; but the other, John Rochester, was sent back to the Charterhouse as Cranmer could make no progress with him. Rochester continued to be a loyal Papist until he was hanged in chains as a rebel in 1537.[2]

The authorities did not rely on terror alone, but also on propaganda. Gardiner, Fox and other leading churchmen published books in defence of the royal supremacy, all designed to prove, as Sampson expressed it, that 'the word of God is, to obey the King and not the Bishop of Rome'. It is surprising that Cranmer did not write any book on this subject. It was contemplated that he should write a reply to Cochlaeus' book on the divorce; in order to facilitate his task, all Fisher's writings against the divorce, which had been found among his papers when he was arrested, were sent to Cranmer. But there is little doubt that Cranmer never wrote any reply to Cochlaeus, or any book on the supremacy. This was probably because these books were primarily intended to be read by foreign Papists, who disapproved so greatly of Cranmer that they could never be influenced by a book published in his name. But Cranmer helped Gardiner to write his Answer to Pope Paul's denunciation of the execution of Fisher and More. On 26th September

<hr/>

[1] 26 Hen. VIII, c.1, 13; *L.P.*, viii. 190; Cranmer to Cromwell, 30 April 1535 (Cranmer's *Works*, ii. 303); More to Margaret Roper, (3 June 1535), (More's *Works*, pp. 1452–4).
[2] Fyllol to Cromwell, 5 September 1535 (Wright, pp. 67–70); Ortiz to the Empress Isabella, 21 August 1535 (*Span. Cal.* v [i]. 196; *L.P.*, ix. 143).

1535, Gardiner wrote to Cromwell that he had nearly completed his Answer, and would insert a substantial portion at the end, as Cranmer had suggested. He had probably discussed these passages with Cranmer when they were both at Winchester with the King a few days before. Gardiner's short treatise is as unpalatable as any defence of a political execution must always be; it contains a long and admittedly fictitious declaration which is put into Fisher's mouth, in which he holds the Pope responsible for his death through having sent him the Cardinal's hat. It is impossible to say how much the book owes to Cranmer's advice.[1]

As the repression of Papists got under way, Cranmer played an active part in denouncing suspects. His approaches to the King were not always in favour of leniency. He denounced the prior of the Black Friars at Cambridge, a monk of St. Augustine's in Canterbury, and the Vicar of St. Andrew's chapel at St. Albans—taking care, in this last case, to state that he was not claiming jurisdiction in the territory of the abbey of St. Albans, which was exempt from the authority of the Archbishop of Canterbury, but was merely denouncing the vicar as any other loyal subject might have done. The vicar and his curate had been making propaganda in the confessional and elsewhere against the divorce and the break with Rome. Cranmer's brother Edmund, whom he appointed Archdeacon of Canterbury in 1534 in succession to Warham's nephew, was also active as an informer. On St. Matthew's eve in September 1534, Edmund dined with Dr. Benger of Wingham near Canterbury, who told him that the Pope was the head of the Church and that these new laws would lead to broken heads. After Benger had been arrested six months later, Edmund told Cranmer what Benger had said, and Cranmer passed on the information to Cromwell. On several occasions, Cranmer took action against Phillips, the vicar of Croydon, where he so often resided. In January 1536, Cranmer discovered that the parson of Chevening in Kent had inserted into a book in the church a

---

[1] See Sampson's treatise (Strype, *Eccl. Mem.* i [ii]. 175); Bedyll to Cromwell, 28 July 1535 (Wright, pp. 44–45); Gardiner to Cromwell, 26 September 1535 (Muller, p. 68); Gardiner, 'Answer to Pope Paul III' (in Janelle, *Obedience in Church and State*, pp. 21–65). In 1691, Anthony à Wood had seen some writings by Cranmer on the royal supremacy (see Wood, *Athenae Oxonienses*, i. 578, sub. tit. William Knight).

piece of paper on which he had written in Latin: 'The King is like a tyrant who oppressed his people'. Cranmer hastened to inform the King, but he pointed out that the parson, who had been the victim of a financial fraud, had several times attempted to commit suicide, and was apparently hoping to be put to death for his offence. Cranmer obviously hoped that Henry would show mercy, though there was here no question of expediency. Few of the royal officers or the Bishops would have troubled to mention the mitigating factors in the case.[1]

One case of sedition involved Cranmer only indirectly, and in a somewhat curious context. The priest George Rowland was denounced to Cromwell for attempting to subvert a penitent in the confessional by urging him not to be influenced by a sermon of Latimer against Papal supremacy. Rowland was said to have told the penitent that on one occasion he had been examined by Cranmer on a charge of praying for the Pope, and that Cranmer had informed him that he might pray for the Pope as much as he wished in secret, but must not do so openly. It is impossible to believe this story of how Cranmer was prepared to permit freedom of thought, if not of speech, for he would obviously not have said this to Rowland; and as it is difficult to understand why Rowland should have told this story to his penitent, it is more likely that the report of Cromwell's agent was inaccurate on this point.[2]

The break with Rome had not yet led to any toleration of heresy in England; but though the realm was orthodox in doctrine, it had an Archbishop of Canterbury who had imbibed a great deal of Lutheran teaching in Germany, and this soon became well known. On 27th January 1533, when Chapuys wrote to the Emperor that Cranmer had been appointed Archbishop, he told him that Cranmer was a Lutheran. Chapuys had made no suggestion of this a year before, when he had warned Charles that Cranmer was going to approach the German Universities

[1] Cranmer to Cromwell, 7 June 1534, 14 March 1535 and 12 June 1538; Cranmer to Henry VIII, 17 January 1536; Examination of Rowland Phillips, 28–29 July 1537 (Cranmer's *Works*, ii. 295–6, 300–1, 319–20, 338–40, 369–71); Articles against Wynchelsey (1534); Skipwith to Cranmer, 18 March 1535; Skipwith and Waren to Cromwell (March 1535); Cranmer's articles against King, 14 April 1535; Waite to Lady Lisle, 10 October 1535 (*L.P.*, vii. 1608; viii. 406, 407, 589; ix. 583).
[2] Communication between Rowland and Stanton on 23 February 1535/6 (*L.P.*, x. 346).

about the divorce, or when he had told him in October 1532 that Cranmer was being replaced as Ambassador by Hawkins, though in this same letter he stated that Hawkins had been imprisoned as a Lutheran. Chapuys seems to have discovered Cranmer's Lutheranism during the course of the next four months. He had of course every motive for stressing this matter in January 1533, because he was urging Charles to prevent the Pope from issuing the bulls for Cranmer's consecration; and during the next few months he made every effort to persuade the Pope that Cranmer, along with Wiltshire and Anne, was a Lutheran and was encouraging Henry in schism and heresy. In April, Chapuys wrote that armed intervention was necessary to prevent England from becoming Lutheran, as Henry was encouraging this development, and Cranmer was even worse in this respect.[1]

In February 1534, Chapuys was holding Cranmer responsible for the *praemunire* proceedings against Nix, the aged Bishop of Norwich. Nix was heavily fined for having encroached on the privileges of the town of Thetford, and a subsidiary charge against him was that he had ordered the burning of Bilney in 1531 before the arrival of the King's writ, though the writ arrived before the execution. Chapuys told the Emperor that the real reason for the proceedings against Nix was that he had burned Bilney, who had been a bosom companion and brother to Cranmer; but it is very unlikely that there was any truth in this story.[2]

The hostile testimony of Chapuys is confirmed by a letter from a friendly source. On 29th April 1533, a month after Cranmer's consecration and a fortnight before he opened his Court at Dunstable, George Joye wrote to Latimer, urging him to write to Cranmer and animate him in his office, as he was in a dangerous place.[3] Evidently the rumours which had caused Chapuys to fear the worst had made Joye think that it was worth while for the reformers to encourage Cranmer.

Rumours that Cranmer was a heretic were spreading around

---

[1] Chapuys to Charles V, 30 January, 5 February and 1 October 1532, and 27–29 January, 9 February and 10 April 1533 (*Span. Cal.* iv [ii]. 897, 898, 1003, 1043, 1047, 1058; *L.P.*, v. 762, 773, 1377; vi. 89, 142, 324).

[2] Chapuys to Charles V, 11 February 1534 (*Span. Cal.* v [i]. 10; *L.P.*, vii. 171).

[3] Joye to Latimer, 29 April 1533 (*L.P.*, vi. 402).

the country. In the autumn of 1533, one of the chaplains of the Bishop of Bath and Wells said in the Bishop's palace that he hoped to see the day when Cranmer would be burned. A few months later, a Scottish friar said in a sermon at Newark that Cranmer was a heretic because of what he was doing against the Pope. The supporters of the Papacy considered it heresy to challenge the supremacy of the Pope, and the fact that Cranmer had pronounced sentence at Dunstable and supported the schism was in itself sufficient ground for them to call him a heretic. But Winchelsey, the monk of St Augustine's, Canterbury, whom Cranmer denounced in 1534, obviously thought that Cranmer was guilty of doctrinal heresy. Winchelsey was accused of saying that this new learning would set men together by the ears, and that Cranmer was the maintainer of it. More specifically, he had said that Cranmer had ordered a schoolmaster to ride twice in one week to Sandwich to read a heretical lecture there, and that he had promised to give a buck in summer and a doe in winter to the heretics of Sandwich.[1] This was not the last time that Cranmer was accused of heretical conduct in connexion with Sandwich, and while it is unlikely that these accusations were true—Winchelsey denied that he had made them—Cranmer may have maintained friendly personal relations with some advanced reformers at Sandwich.

During the first three years after Cranmer became Archbishop, he himself gave no indication of heresy; but on several occasions he extended his protection to persons who were suspected of being heretics. In the summer of 1533, he granted a license to Latimer authorizing him to preach anywhere in the province of Canterbury. Latimer was already well known as a heretic, and had been officially condemned for heresy in 1532. In the summer of 1533, he was engaged in his violent controversy at Bristol—he was attacking the invocation of Saints and the cult of the Virgin—and was again denounced as a heretic, and forbidden to preach by his Ordinary. After Cranmer had given him his license, it was impossible for any of the Bishops or lower ecclesiastical officials to prevent Latimer from preaching. Cranmer's action in granting him the license was interpreted as a sign that the Archbishop was supporting

[1] Erley to Cromwell (autumn 1533); Information against Letheraud (February 1534); Articles against Wynchelsey (1534) (L.P., vi. 1192; vii. 261, 1608).

heretics, and was strongly denounced, both in the reports of the Emperor's Ambassador and in the inns of Staffordshire.[1]

In 1534, Cranmer arranged for Latimer and Shaxton, who had also formerly been suspected of heresy, to preach some of the Lenten sermons to the King. Sampson, the Dean of the Chapel Royal, was most displeased. He reminded Cranmer that Latimer had been condemned by Convocation, and wrote that Cranmer must bear the sole responsibility for choosing Latimer to preach before the King, as he himself was no party to it except in so far as the King commanded this. Cranmer then warned Latimer to refrain from provocative attacks on his opponents when he preached before the King, though he encouraged him to condemn superstition in general terms on the basis of some Biblical text. He also urged him not to preach for more than an hour and a half, lest the King and Queen should grow bored. Soon afterwards, when new licenses were issued to all the preachers after April 1534, Cranmer employed Latimer to examine the preachers in order to decide which of them should be granted a new license. The entrusting to a notorious heretic of the task of ensuring that preachers were reliable was a remarkable gesture of defiance of the powerful forces of orthodoxy. Next year, he sent Latimer a book on theology for his advice as to whether a license should be granted for its publication.[2]

In March 1534, Cranmer used his influence in favour of Thomas Rose, who had been one of the men involved in stealing and burning the rood of Dovercourt in 1532, and was now the curate of Hadleigh in Suffolk, which was in Cranmer's peculiar jurisdiction. Rose was denounced to Cranmer for preaching that a man's soul could not be saved by good works. After examining Rose, Cranmer told the parishioners that Rose had merely said that a man could not be saved if he bequeathed his goods to be spent for the benefit of his soul without having charity; and he ordered them to cease attacking Rose. But Cranmer was careful to safeguard his own position by telling them not to

[1] Chapuys to Charles V, 10 October 1533; Examination of Mydnight, 10 October 1533 (*Span. Cal.*, iv [ii]. 1133; *L.P.*, vi. 1249, 1255).
[2] Cranmer to Latimer (January and May 1534); Cranmer to Sampson, 9 January 1534 (Cranmer's *Works*, ii. 296–7, 308–9, where Cranmer's letter to Sampson is wrongly dated 9 July, as it is in Cranmer's original letter); Sampson to Cranmer, 10 January 1534; Depositions of Revel, 29 February 1536 (*L.P.*, vii. 32; x. 371).

hesitate to report to him any offence which Rose might commit in future. When Rose 'was succeeded at Hadleigh by an ortho-dox curate, Cranmer continued to have trouble with the parish. The new curate, Payne, was summoned before Cranmer for having said that one Paternoster spoken at the orders of a priest was worth a million Paternosters spoken merely of a man's voluntary mind; but though Cranmer did no more than impose a penance upon Payne for his offence, Payne did not perform the penance, and Cranmer consequently excommuni-cated him, and in January 1537 asked Cromwell to sentence Payne to some further punishment.[1]

The case of the reformer Thomas-Patmore touched Cranmer closely, for it concerned the marriage of priests. This London parson was accused of having officiated at the marriage of another priest, and was imprisoned in the Bishop of London's prison. Patmore appealed from Stokesley to the King, but his appeal was suppressed by the jailers; and in due course he appeared before Stokesley's Court, where he recanted and carried his fagot. After his release, Patmore informed the authorities that his appeal to the King had been suppressed, and Cranmer was appointed, along with Cromwell and other Commissioners, to investigate the matter. The Commissioners do not appear to have taken any action in the case. On other occasions, Cranmer was again involved in conflicts with Stokesley, who was certainly his principal opponent at this time. Early in 1534, Lord Morley—who was himself a staunch conservative in religion—appealed to Cranmer in connexion with what appears to have been a case of religious persecution by Stokesley. In May 1535, when Cranmer appointed the reformer Hilsey to preach at Paul's Cross, Stokesley succeeded in preventing Hilsey from delivering the sermon. Two years later, Cranmer was involved in a similar dispute with Repps, the Bishop of Norwich, and complained to Cromwell that Repps did not permit any man of right judgment to preach in his diocese.[2]

---

[1] Cranmer to the Inhabitants of Hadleigh, 20 March 1534; Cranmer to Crom-well, 28 January 1537 (Cranmer's *Works*, ii. 280, 333–4); Foxe, viii. 582.
[2] Foxe, v. 34–37, App. Document xxiii; Morley to Morice (1534); Morice to Cranmer (1534); Hilsey to Cromwell (May 1535) (*L.P.*, vi. 1600, 1601; vii. 1643 (and see Errata)); Cranmer to Cromwell, 26 May 1537 (Cranmer's *Works*, ii. 336).

Cranmer's sympathy to the reformers was sufficiently well known for them to appeal to him, or at least to pretend that they had his support, when they found themselves persecuted by Bishops and by other officials. From every part of England came letters from monks who were being victimised in their monasteries for supporting the King's proceedings, and from priests who were suspected by their Ordinaries. They wrote to Cranmer for his protection, or merely told their persecutors that Cranmer had permitted them to act as they did. When Archbishop Lee suspended the preaching licenses of a number of preachers in his diocese whom he accused of preaching novelties and sowing dissension, the preachers nevertheless continued to preach, and claimed that Cranmer had granted them a license to do so. Cranmer's reputation as a favourer of reformers had spread overseas. Men who wished to obtain money from him wrote to him from Venice and told him that he and Latimer were inspiring a reformation of religion. In August 1535, Melanchthon wrote him a most friendly letter, declaring that if there were more Bishops like him, peace would be restored to the Church. It is also significant that when Cranmer's agent Theabold wrote to Cranmer from Antwerp on 31st July 1535, he clearly implied his disapproval of the arrest of Tyndale by the Emperor's officers.[1]

In the summer of 1534, unprecedented restrictions were imposed on preaching. Preaching without a license had always been prohibited; now all the licenses were withdrawn, and the Bishops were ordered only to issue new licenses to preachers whom they knew to be reliable. A royal directive to this effect was issued in the summer, after Cranmer, Gardiner, Stokesley and Longland had enforced the measure in their dioceses on their own initiative at Easter. The order was directed against heretics as well as Papists, and Cranmer stressed both these objects in his letter to the Bishops. He urged that those preachers to whom new licenses were issued should be ordered 'in no wise to touch or intermeddle themselves to preach or

---

[1] Morison to Cranmer, 30 December 1533; Wattes to Cromwell (April 1534); Indictment of Vaws (1535); Musarde to Henry VIII (August 1535) (*L.P.*, vi. 1582; vii. 577; viii. 20; ix. 52 [2] [ii]); Archbishop Lee to Cromwell, 23 April 1536 (Burnet, vi. 141); Melanchthon to Cranmer (August 1535) (*Corpus Reformatorum* ii. 930–1; Gorham, *Gleanings*, pp. 14–16); Theabold to Cranmer, 31 July 1535 (Demaus, *Tyndale*, p. 491).

teach any such thing that might slander or bring in doubt and opinion the Catholic and received doctrine of Christ's Church, or speak of such matters as touch the Prince, his laws or succession'. But when he wrote to Latimer about the instructions which Latimer was to give to the preachers to whom he granted licenses, he said nothing about preventing attacks on Catholic doctrine, and referred only to the need to prevent seditious preaching against the King's marriage and the Acts of Parliament. This was obviously the real purpose of the order.[1]

Apart from requiring the preachers to have new licenses, a proclamation of June 1534 prohibited them during the next year from either criticizing or defending the doctrines of Purgatory, the honouring of Saints, the marriage of priests, justification by faith alone, going on pilgrimages and the working of miracles. This order, while it prevented the reformers from spreading their beliefs, tended to favour them at the expense of their opponents. The preaching of heresy had always been punishable; but now for the first time, the adherents of the old learning were restrained from defending the old doctrines, and from reminding the people of the wickedness of these heresies. Chapuys told the Emperor that Cranmer was responsible for the order because he intended within a year to make new doctrinal declarations on the prohibited topics.[2] But Cranmer did not in fact make any such declarations within the year, and even if he was already considering the possibility of making some innovations in doctrine, it is unlikely that the ban on all discussion was a cunning manoeuvre on Cranmer's part with the object of furthering heresy. It was probably that Henry had not yet decided his policy on these issues, and thought that the prohibition would make it easier for him to move, in due course, as far as he wished to go, and no farther.

In January 1535, Cromwell was appointed as the King's Vicegerent in ecclesiastical affairs. Cranmer was now no longer the principal minister of the King's spiritual jurisdiction, as Henry had called him in April 1533;[3] this position was held

---

[1] Henry VIII to Cranmer, (May 1534), (*L.P.*, vii. 750); Cranmer to a Bishop (April 1534); Cranmer to Latimer (May 1534) (Cranmer's *Works*, ii. 283–4, 296–7).

[2] Order for Preaching, (June 1534) (Cranmer's *Works*, ii. 460–1); Chapuys to Charles V, 23 June 1534 (*Span. Cal.* v [i]. 68; *L.P.*, vii. 871).

[3] Henry VIII to Cranmer, (April 1533) (Cranmer's *Works*, ii. 238–9 n.).

by Cromwell, who had precedence over Cranmer and all the
Bishops. This enabled Cromwell to direct the expropriation of
the monastic lands, and was a striking gesture of the royal
supremacy over the Church. It also lowered the position of
Cranmer and his office in the public estimation, and counter-
acted the great impression which had been created by Cranmer's
mandates for the consecration of Bishops, by his provincial
visitation, and above all by the Dunstable judgment. The con-
ception of Cranmer as an English Pope had been useful in
undermining the allegiance of the people to the Roman Pope;
but it was now necessary to make it clear that the only English
Pope was the King. For the next five years, in administrative
matters, Cranmer was little more than a Bishop in his diocese.

Cranmer accepted his relegation without any open protest,
but he seems to have felt some resentment. When Cromwell
began to prepare for his visitation of the monasteries in the
summer of 1535, Cranmer came into conflict with Cromwell's
Visitors. Cranmer had not yet completed his own provincial
visitation, and despite the protests of Cromwell's Visitors the
Vicegerent's visitation was put off until the autumn. In July,
Layton, one of the Visitors, reported that Cranmer would be
very glad if Cromwell's visitation were abandoned altogether.
But when Cranmer received the mandate for Cromwell's visitation in September, neither he nor the Bishops uttered a word of
protest at the inhibition restraining them from exercising their
ecclesiastical jurisdiction. The Bishops who had protested
against Cranmer's visitation submitted with a display of real
enthusiasm to Cromwell's. A few weeks later, Cranmer and
the other Bishops were granted new commissions from Henry,
which made it clear that they exercised all their ecclesiastical
jurisdiction, including the right to ordain priests, by license of
the King and his Vicegerent.[1]

In September, the King summoned all the Bishops to Winchester, and ordered them to launch a new propaganda campaign in favour of the royal supremacy. Cranmer had certain
objections to the policy which was laid down. We do not know
the points to which he objected, but on the day before he left

[1] Layton to Cromwell (June 1535); Longland to Cromwell, 9 October 1535
(*L.P.*, viii. 955; ix. 569); Cranmer to Stokesley, 2 October 1535 (Cranmer's
Works, ii. 463); Wharton, *Specimen of Errors in Burnet's History*, pp. 52–53; and
see Burnet, iv. 410–13 and n.

Winchester, he drafted a document containing his criticisms for submission to the Council. About a month later, Cromwell told Latimer—who had just been consecrated by Cranmer as Bishop of Worcester—to write to Cranmer rebuking him for not having been sufficiently energetic in compelling the preachers in his diocese to preach the royal supremacy. This is the only recorded instance of Cranmer being officially censured during Henry's reign for his hesitancy in advancing the Reformation. It was perhaps no coincidence that the reproach came at a time when Cranmer had just been contesting the King's right to the lands of the deserted nunnery at Donnington. Cranmer, who was not in the least overawed, rejected Latimer's criticism as unjustified, and did not hesitate, in the same letter, to ask Cromwell to grant a favour to one of his friends.[1]

Cranmer was satisfied that in the country around Otford and Knoll, where he usually resided, the people had been properly indoctrinated with regard to the supremacy; but he was less happy about the position in the east of the county, and particularly in Canterbury. He therefore spent three months in East Kent, and preached two sermons in Canterbury Cathedral—the first at the end of October 1535, in the presence of Cromwell's Visitor Layton, and the second three weeks later. In these sermons, he attacked the Papal supremacy, and referred to the personal vices of some of the Popes; and he also emphasized that the canon law, though it contained some beneficial provisions and ought to be obeyed for the sake of order, was no more the word of God than was the common law of England, and men could not gain remission of sins by observing it. The Prior of the Black Friars in Canterbury preached a sermon soon afterwards in which he not only extolled the laws of the Church, but was unwise enough to cast doubt on some of Cranmer's allegations as to the personal vices of the Popes. Cranmer, after raising the matter with the Prior, eventually wrote to the King in August 1536, complaining that if the Prior were not dealt with, it would not only encourage Papists, but would render his own position intolerable and weaken the effect of his preaching in future. Cranmer's attitude in this case may appear

[1] Cranmer to Cromwell, 17 October and 2 November 1535; Cranmer to Henry VIII, 26 August 1536 (Cranmer's *Works*, ii. 312–5, 325–6); Certificate of Latimer's consecration, 23 September 1535 (*L.P.*, ix. 729 (7)); Latimer to Cromwell (25 October 1535) (Latimer's *Works*, ii. 370).

to conflict with Morice's statement that he always forgave
offences against himself while zealously punishing those which
touched the King. But Cranmer was probably alarmed at the
weakening of his personal position only because he wished to
maintain the prestige of the King's representative.[1]

In February 1536, Cranmer dealt with John Lambert, a
Cambridge Bachelor of Divinity, who had been charged with
heresy before Convocation in 1531. He had been imprisoned by
Warham in 1532 with forty-five accusations of heresy against
him; but according to Foxe, Warham died before the charges
could be proceeded with, and Lambert was quietly released
when Cranmer became Archbishop. He was now brought before Cranmer, Latimer and Shaxton at Lambeth, and accused
of heresy in having stated that it was sinful to pray to the
Saints. He could not have found three Bishops whose opinions
were nearer to his own on the subject of prayers to the Saints.
They told him that prayers to the Saints were unnecessary, but
not sinful, and offered to release him if he would agree that they
were merely unnecessary. Lambert refused to compromise.
Cranmer and his colleagues imprisoned him in the porter's
lodge at Lambeth; but they decided to release him surrepti-
ously. Four days later, he was told that he could go free.

But the martyr did not seek an easy escape. Next day, he
presented himself before the Bishops again, and asked to be
told officially whether he was free. The Bishops thereupon
argued with him again, and though they admitted that there
was no authority in Scripture for prayers to the Saints, they
finally lost all patience with him, and sent him to the Lord
Chancellor to deal with. At the second hearing, Latimer is said
to have been more bitter than his colleagues against Lambert.
Of the three Bishops, it was he who was the most outspoken
opponent of the excessive adoration of Saints; but he was
doubtless exasperated by the trivial nature of the differences on
which Lambert was compelling him to act as a defender of
orthodoxy, and he showed the usual hostility of extremists
towards those even more extreme than themselves. Some of
the reformers were indignant that Cranmer, Latimer, and
Shaxton had acted against Lambert. They attributed it to the

[1] Cranmer to Henry VIII, 26 August 1536 (Cranmer's *Works*, ii. 325–8);
Morice (*Nar. Ref.*, p. 247).

fact that Lambert had been denounced by Norfolk, Essex, and the Countess of Oxford, and considered that the three Bishops had done great hurt to the truth in order to curry favour with those members of the nobility. We have no information as to what happened to Lambert on this occasion, and he only re-appears in connexion with the more serious proceedings against him two years later.[1]

In February 1536, a bill for the suppression of all religious houses with an income of less than £200 a year was voted with great excitement and enthusiasm in Parliament, after the alleged immoralities of the monks had been disclosed to the indignant Lords and Commons. Cranmer did not play any part in the suppression of the smaller monasteries. His own priory of Christ Church, which in wealth was second only to West-minster among the English houses with an annual income of £2,349, was not due for suppression; but it was subjected, along with all the other surviving houses, to Cromwell's Injunctions, many of which were designed to weaken the whole monastic system. In November 1535, Cranmer was in Canter-bury concerning himself with the observance of the Injunctions in Christ Church, and was urging Cromwell to interpret them in such a way as to make it easier for the monks to leave the priory.[2]

Cranmer obviously approved, like all the reformers, of the suppression of the monasteries, for it struck a blow against one of the most firmly established institutions of the old religion, and indirectly at the doctrines of masses for souls, Purgatory, private masses and even the celibacy of the clergy, of which monastic life was the supreme example. The doctrinal reforma-tion which began in 1536 could hardly have occurred had it not been for the suppression of the monasteries and the desirability of accompanying this with propaganda against the doctrines peculiarly associated with the monks. The reformers believed that the revenues of the monasteries could be better applied for the relief of poverty and the provision of education for the people, rather than for prayers for souls; and this was one of

[1] Thomas Dorset to the Mayor of Plymouth and others, 13 March 1536 (Wright, p. 37); Foxe, v. 181, 225.
[2] 27 Hen. VIII, c. 28; Latimer's second sermon before Edward VI, 15 March 1549 (Latimer's *Works*, i. 123); *Valor Ecclesiasticus*, i. 16; Cranmer to Cromwell, 18 November 1535 (Cranmer's *Works*, ii. 317).

the reasons, along with the depravity of the monks, which was officially put forward to justify the dissolution of the lesser houses. But after the seizure of the monastic lands by the King, the reformers witnessed, to their disgust, the gifts and sales of the lands to favourites and speculators; and a few years later they were forced to admit that though matters had been bad under the monks, they were even worse under their successors.[1]

Cranmer's anonymous biographer states that Cranmer and the other Bishops of the new learning refused to agree to the grant of the monastic property to the King for his own use, and urged that it should be applied in financing hospitals and education. He states that this so angered the King that he succumbed to Gardiner's pressure and promulgated the Six Articles.[2] It was certainly not the opposition of Cranmer and his colleagues to the looting of the monastic lands which led Henry to introduce the Six Articles; but there is every reason to believe that Cranmer opposed the use to which the property of the monks was put. It was, moreover, thanks to the influence of the reformers—and probably to Cranmer's influence in particular —that at least a small part of the monastic assets were devoted to charitable and educational purposes, and not sold for profit by the King.

Yet Cranmer joined with the other dignitaries in making suits to obtain grants of the monastic property for his friends and relations. Within a month of the enactment of the statute suppressing the smaller houses, Cranmer had written to Cromwell to ask him to grant a lease of Shelford priory in Nottinghamshire to his brother-in-law, who was the clerk of his kitchen. In October 1536, Cranmer wrote again to Cromwell, asking him to grant the house of the Grey Friars in Canterbury to Thomas Cobham, Lord Cobham's brother, who was in Cranmer's service and had married his niece. In July 1538, he asked Cromwell to sell the freehold or grant a lease of the lands of the Charterhouse of Axholme to his friend Henry Stocketh, and he made a number of other applications to Cromwell for the grant of abbey lands to his friends and servants. Most of these suits were unsuccessful. Cranmer was no match for the more

[1] Brinkelow, *The Complaint of Roderick Mors*, chap. ii, pp. 8–9 (unpaginated).
[2] Anon. Biogr. (*Nar. Ref.*, p. 224).

enthusiastic landgrabbers when it came to using influence at Court.[1]

Cranmer's admirers have pointed out that he never made a suit for the grant of the monastic lands to himself, and certainly no record has been preserved of any such request. He received the lands of several of the suppressed houses under his exchanges with the King, but these were disadvantageous transactions to which Cranmer was compelled to agree against his will. Under these exchanges, Cranmer received the house and site of the monasteries of St. Radegund's near Dover and of Bilsington in Kent, of Malling Abbey, and of the nunnery of St. Sepulchre's-without-Canterbury, and also the lands which had belonged to these houses and to St. Augustine's Canterbury and other monasteries. He later exchanged the abbey of St. Radegund's for the priory of St. Gregory's in Canterbury. Apart from these exchanges, Cranmer was granted the freehold reversion of the monastery of Kirkstall and the nunnery of Arthington in Yorkshire for his personal use, and also the rectories of his native Aslockton and Whatton in Nottinghamshire, which had belonged to the abbey of Welbeck. Morice states that Dr. Butts, the King's physician, who had been one of Cranmer's fellow auditors at Cambridge, obtained for Cranmer a grant from the King of an abbey in Nottinghamshire—which was probably one of these properties mentioned—without Cranmer being aware of what was happening. Butts had pointed out to Henry that Cranmer had not obtained any of the monastic lands for himself. Cranmer accepted the gift, thinking no doubt that if the lands of the houses were to be divided, against his advice, among private purchasers, there was no reason why he himself should not benefit along with the others. In comparison with other prominent men—for example, Cromwell, Edward Seymour, and Anthony Browne—Cranmer's personal share in the loot was meagre.[2]

The propaganda campaign in favour of the royal supremacy culminated in London in February and March 1536, when on

[1] Cranmer to Cromwell, 25 March and 5 October 1536, 8 August and 6 December 1537 and 28 February, 22 June, 20 July, 3 and 23 August and 10 October 1538 (Cranmer's *Works*, ii. 321, 330, 337, 345, 358, 362-3, 372, 374, 379-80, 384, where the letter of 20 July 1538 is wrongly dated 1537; see *L.P.* xiii [i]. 1424 n.).

[2] Grants of 31 July 1538, 28 April 1540 and 7 June 1542 (*L.P.*, xiii [i]. 1519 [68]; xv. 613 [32]; xvii. 443 [15]); Morice (*Nar. Ref.*, p. 263).

seven successive Sundays a Bishop preached at Paul's Cross.
The first of these sermons was preached by Cranmer on 6th
February. He was still suffering from a bad cold and cough,
but he preached for two hours in the open air, and his sermon
attracted great attention in London. He not only argued that
the Pope had no authority in England and was a mere Bishop
of Rome, but went so far as to stigmatize him as Antichrist.
He referred to the prophecy that Antichrist would come when
the Empire was ruined, and said that this time had now arrived,
as the Lutherans had revolted against the Emperor in Germany,
and the Emperor exercised effective authority over only a small
part of his dominions. He also made some criticism of the
worship of images, the adoration of Saints, and Purgatory, and
attacked the monasteries. A few weeks later, Cranmer was
reported as having said that the King was intending to put down
all friars and chantry priests, and leave only those priests who
could preach; but it is very unlikely that Cranmer would have
said precisely this in a sermon.

It was probably this sermon of Cranmer on 6th February 1536
to which Harpsfield referred more than twenty years later in
his book on the *Pretended Divorce of Catherine of Aragon*.
Harpsfield stated that he was present about this time at a sermon
preached by Cranmer at Paul's Cross in which Cranmer stated
that the monasteries were 'places and dens of error and superstition', and that the commonwealth could not flourish unless
they were overthrown. Cranmer also said that it would greatly
benefit the people if the King seized the monasteries, because
this would make him so rich that he would not need to levy
new taxes. Harpsfield claims that no wise man in Cranmer's
audience believed him, and points out that in fact taxation
became even heavier after the suppression of the monasteries.
Cranmer was followed at Paul's Cross on the next two Sundays
by Hilsey and Longland, and at Quinquagesima Cranmer and
eight Bishops sat at the Cross to hear Tunstall prove to the
world that he had abandoned every trace of resistance to the
King's policy. The campaign was concluded with sermons on
the first three Sundays of Lent by Shaxton, Latimer, and
Salcott.[1]

[1] For these sermons at Paul's Cross, see Wriothesley, i. 33–35; Chapuys to
Charles V; Chapuys to Granvelle, both 10 February 1536 (*Span. Cal.* v [ii]. 21.

The English Reformation now entered on a new stage, largely as a result of Henry's tortuous foreign policy. In the face of the hostility of Catholic Europe, Henry entered into negotiations with the German Lutherans; but he had no wish to become too closely linked with them. He therefore refused their invitation to become a Lutheran, and adopted the attitude that doctrine and ceremonies should be regulated by every ruler in his own realm. This led him to appoint a Commission of Bishops and divines to draw up Articles of Religion, and they met at Lambeth, under Cranmer's presidency, in February 1536. It was virtually unavoidable that the meetings at Lambeth should lead to some alterations in orthodox doctrine, and this, together with the other recent developments, caused great alarm to the Papists. Chapuys wrote indignantly to Charles V about the Lambeth meetings, and Pole, in Venice, wrote in April that Cranmer had called the Pope Antichrist and that Parliament was intending to abolish Purgatory. It was in this situation—so favourable to the reformers—that Henry was informed of the adultery of Anne Boleyn.[1]

where the letter to Charles V is wrongly dated 17 February; *L.P.*, x. 282, 283); Harpsfield, *The Pretended Divorce*, p. 292; Thomas Dorset to the Mayor of Plymouth and others, 13 March 1536 (Wright, p. 38). For Cranmer's cold, see Cranmer to Henry VIII, 17 January 1536; Cranmer to Cromwell, 22 April 1536 (Cranmer's *Works*, ii. 320, 322).

[1] Chapuys to Charles V, 1 April 1536 (*Span. Cal.*, v [ii]. 43; *L.P.*, x. 601); Pole to Priolus, 24 March–3 April 1536 (*Epist. Poli*, i. 444).

CHAPTER VII

THE FALL OF ANNE BOLEYN

CRANMER's part in the fall of Anne Boleyn has been the subject of controversy. After Anne gave birth to a stillborn child in January 1536, Henry became attracted to Jane Seymour, who had been carefully taught how to achieve this result by a group of the old nobility which was in contact with Stokesley; while Cromwell was in favour of sacrificing Anne in order to improve relations with the Emperor. After the death of Catherine of Aragon, Chapuys told Cromwell that though the world would never recognize Anne as Henry's wife, it might be ready to recognize a new wife.[1] This sealed Anne's fate.

On 22nd April 1536, Cranmer, who was at Knoll, wrote to Cromwell asking for a favour for an acquaintance. At the end of the letter, he wrote: 'I was ever hitherto cold, but now I am in a heat with the cause of religion, which goeth all contrary to mine expectation, if it be as the fame goeth; wherein I would wonder fain break my mind unto you, and if you please, I will come to such place as you shall appoint for the same purpose'. These words have been interpreted by modern writers as showing that Cranmer was already in disgrace immediately before the fall of Anne Boleyn, and feared that the Reformation was in danger; but this interpretation is almost certainly wrong. Cranmer's reference to his being cold is certainly to the cough and cold from which he had been suffering since January. As regards the reference to the bad developments in religion, he was probably using the word 'religion', not in its modern meaning, but in the narrower contemporary sense of things appertaining to monasticism, and the rumours which he had heard probably concerned the plans for disposing of the monastic lands to courtiers and speculators instead of applying them to educational and charitable purposes. His reason for wishing to meet Cromwell was to persuade him and Henry to abandon these plans.[2]

---

[1] Chapuys to Charles V, 10 February and 1 and 29 April 1536 (*Span. Cal.*, v [ii]. 21, 43, 47, where the date is wrongly given as 17 February; *L.P.*, x. 282, 601, 752).
[2] Cranmer to Henry VIII, 17 January 1536; Cranmer to Cromwell, 22 April 1536 (Cranmer's *Works*, ii. 320, 322).

On 30th April and 1st May, Anne's brother Lord Rochford, her musician Smeaton, and Norris were arrested on a charge of high treason in having committed adultery with the Queen; on 2nd May, Anne herself was sent to the Tower. Cranmer had meanwhile received a letter from Cromwell, ordering him to come to Lambeth, but apparently telling him to stay there until he received further instructions. He travelled up from Knoll on 2nd May, and probably heard the news of Anne's arrest soon after he reached Lambeth. Next day, he wrote his famous letter to Henry, which has been interpreted on the one hand as a courageous plea for Anne, and on the other as a dastardly betrayal of his benefactress. After he had written the letter, but before he had dispatched it, he was summoned to come at once to the Star Chamber at Westminster. There he spoke with Audley, the Earls of Oxford and Sussex, and Lord Sandys, the King's Chamberlain, who gave him some information—what it was we do not know. He then wrote the last paragraph of his letter to the King. As Cranmer's actions can only be fairly judged on the basis of the text of the letter, it is here given in full.

'Pleaseth it your most noble Grace to be advertised, that at your Grace's commandment by Master Secretary his letters written in your Grace's name, I came to Lambeth yesterday, and do there remain to know your Grace's further pleasure. And forasmuch as without your Grace's commandment I dare not, contrary to the contents of the said letters, presume to come unto your Grace's presence; nevertheless, of my most bounden duty, I can do no less than most humbly to desire your Grace, by your great wisdom and by the assistance of God's help, somewhat to suppress the deep sorrows of your Grace's heart, and to take all adversities of God's hand both patiently and thankfully.

'I cannot deny but your Grace hath great causes many ways of lamentable heaviness; and also, that in the wrongful estimation of the world your Grace's honour of every part is so highly touched (whether the things that commonly be spoken of be true, or not) that I remember not that ever Almighty God sent unto your Grace any like occasion to try your Grace's constancy throughout, whether your Highness can be content to take of God's hand as well things displeasant as pleasant. And if He find in your noble heart such an obedience unto His will, that your Grace, without murmuration and overmuch heaviness, do accept all adversities, not less thanking Him than when all things succeeded after your Grace's will and pleasure, nor less procuring His glory and honour; then I suppose your Grace did never thing more acceptable unto Him, since your first governance of this your realm; and moreover, your Grace shall give unto Him occasion to multiply and increase His graces and benefits unto your Highness, as He did unto His most faithful servant Job; unto whom, after his great calamities and heaviness, for his obedient heart and willing acceptation of God's scourge and rod, "addidit ei Dominus cuncta duplicia".

'And if it be true, that is openly reported of the Queen's Grace; if men had a right estimation of things, they should not esteem any part of your Grace's honour to be touched thereby, but her honour only to be clearly disparaged. And I am in such a perplexity, that my mind is clean amazed; for I never had better opinion in woman than I had in her; which maketh me to think that she should not be culpable. And again, I think your Highness would not have gone so far, except she had surely been culpable. Now I think that your Grace best knoweth, that next unto your Grace I was most bound unto her of all creatures living. Wherefore I most humbly beseech your Grace to suffer me in that, which both God's law, nature, and also her kindness, bindeth me unto; that is, that I may with your Grace's favour wish and pray for her, that she may declare herself inculpable and innocent. And if she be found culpable, considering your Grace's goodness towards her, and from what condition your Grace of your only mere goodness took her and set the crown upon her head; I repute him not your Grace's faithful servant and subject, nor true unto the realm, that would not desire the offence without mercy to be punished to the example of all other. And as I loved her not a little for the love which I judged her to bear towards God and His Gospel; so, if she be proved culpable, there is not one that loveth God and His Gospel that ever will favour her, but must hate her above all other; and the more they favour the Gospel, the more they will hate her; for then there was never creature in our time that so much slandered the Gospel; and God hath sent her this punishment, for that she feignedly hath professed His Gospel in her mouth, and not in heart and deed.

'And though she have offended so, that she hath deserved never to be reconciled unto your Grace's favour; yet Almighty God hath manifoldly declared His goodness towards your Grace, and never offended you. But your Grace, I am sure, knowledgeth that you have offended Him. Wherefore I trust that your Grace will bear no less entire favour unto the truth of the Gospel than you did before; forsomuch as your Grace's favour to the Gospel was not led by affection unto her, but by zeal unto the truth. And thus I beseech Almighty God, whose Gospel He hath ordained your Grace to be defender of, ever to preserve your Grace from all evil, and give you at the end the promise of His Gospel. From Lambeth, the third day of May.

'After I had written this letter unto your Grace, my Lord Chancellor, my Lord of Oxford, my Lord of Sussex and my Lord Chamberlain of your Grace's house, sent for me to come unto the Star Chamber; and there declared unto me such things as your Grace's pleasure was they should make me privy unto. For the which I am most bounden unto your Grace. And what communication we had together, I doubt not but they will make the true report thereof unto your Grace. I am exceeding sorry that such faults can be proved by the Queen, as I heard of their relation. But I am, and ever shall be, your faithful subject.

'Your Grace's most humble subject and chaplain,

T. Cantuariensis.'[1]

Cranmer's critics have suggested that he was guilty of cowardice in writing this letter, because he did not make a stronger plea for Anne; but this view is quite unjustified. Almost every other courtier in his position would have hastened to denounce Anne, and to obscure the fact that it was to Anne that he owed his own promotion; but Cranmer made no attempt to do this, though he, who had actually crowned Anne, managed to insert a passage in his letter in which he mentioned that it was Henry alone who had 'set the crown upon her head'. His statement that if Anne were guilty she deserved punishment was the least which he could say; and if his exhortation to Henry to emulate Job was sadly out of place—according to Chapuys, 'you never saw Prince nor man who made greater show of his horns or bore them more lightheartedly'[2] —

[1] Cranmer to Henry VIII, 3 May 1536 (Cranmer's *Works*, ii. 323–4).
[2] Chapuys to Granvelle, 18–19 May 1536 (*Span. Cal.*, v [ii]. 54; *L.P.*, x. 909).

Cranmer did not know, when he wrote the letter, of the shameless rejoicing in which Henry would indulge during the next three weeks. It is, however, equally wrong to interpret the letter as an attempt to save Anne. Cranmer's aim was not to save the Queen, but to save the Reformation.

When Cranmer heard of Anne's arrest, it obviously occurred to him, as it did to almost everyone else, that it marked a reversal in Henry's policy—a repudiation of the Reformation with which Anne had been so closely associated. The news was received with joy by the Papists. The Pope and Pole suspended all their propaganda and intrigues against Henry while they hopefully awaited his approaches for a reunion with Rome. They confidently expected that Cranmer would fall with Anne. The Papal Nuncio in France had heard by 19th May that Henry had changed his religious policy and had called a halt to the suppression of the monasteries, while Cranmer was supposed to have fled from London but to have been brought back at Henry's orders. Chapuys wrote to Granvelle from London on the same day that the reforming Bishops were doomed, and mentioned the rumour—which even he stated might well be without foundation—that these Bishops had incited Anne to commit adultery by telling her that there was no need to go to confession, and that according to Lutheran doctrines she was entitled to commit incest if her husband could not satisfy her.[1] It is typical of Cranmer that at this hour he thought neither of saving himself nor of saving Anne, but only of the Reformation. He wrote to Henry to persuade him to adhere to the policy of Reformation even if he sacrificed the woman who had first led him to adopt this policy.

But Henry had no intention of abandoning the Reformation or of destroying Cranmer. Anne was sacrificed, not in order to end the schism from Rome, but in the interests of improved relations with the Emperor; and since the death of Catherine of Aragon, this no longer involved the repudiation of the divorce and of Cranmer's judgment at Dunstable. The foreign Papists were wrong in thinking that Cranmer was in danger. His modern biographers have stressed the danger in which Cranmer stood at this time; but the contemporary writers, Morice, Foxe,

[1] Pio to Ambrogio, 19 May 1536 (*L.P.*, x. 922); Chapuys to Granvelle, 18–19 May 1536, op. cit.

Parker, Aless and the anonymous biographer, do not mention the fall of Anne Boleyn as one of the occasions on which Cranmer was threatened. They refer to his perilous position at the time of the enactment of the Six Articles, at Cromwell's fall, at the time of the Prebendaries' plot in 1543 and the conspiracy against him in the Council; but none of them suggests that another such occasion was in May 1536. Cranmer remained in office and in favour, and Henry maintained the Reformation as Cranmer had urged him to do; but this meant that Cranmer had to play his part in the proceedings against Anne. He did this, not because he was afraid of the consequences to himself if he refused, or as the price of his own survival, but because as long as he was Archbishop of Canterbury the duty of acting in such matters fell to him, just as it was the duty of Norfolk and the other peers to perform their roles in the case.

On 15th May, Anne was convicted of high treason and sentenced to death; she strongly protested her innocence. Next day, Cranmer visited her in the Tower. The Constable of the Tower, Sir William Kingston, had been informed by Henry that Cranmer had been appointed as Anne's confessor, and was to have free access to her. On the day when Cranmer visited her, Anne told Kingston at dinner that she would be sent to a nunnery; she was very hopeful that her life would be spared. On the basis of this evidence, Cranmer's critics have often accused him of having promised Anne, at this interview, that she would not be executed if she provided the evidence necessary for him to declare that her marriage to Henry had been invalid, although he knew that he was deceiving her when he made this promise; but this is unlikely. Henry had no need to deceive Anne with false promises of life in order to gain her assistance, for as the sentence of the Court was that Anne should be either burned or beheaded at the King's pleasure, he had only to tell Cranmer to promise Anne the easier death if she complied with his wishes. In any case, it is rarely necessary for the authorities to make any promises to condemned prisoners in order to obtain their co-operation. Cranmer may have hinted to Anne that the divorce was the only chance of saving her life, but he is unlikely to have done more. Anne's mood alternated during her imprisonment between utter despair and the wildest hopes, and her optimism at dinner on 16th May cannot necessarily be attributed to what Cranmer had just told her. In fact, we cannot even be sure that she had already spoken with him, for we do not know whether Cranmer's visit to Anne on the 16th was in the morning or in the afternoon.[1]

The decision to divorce Anne twenty-four hours before beheading her, thereby sending her to her death with the knowledge that Elizabeth was bastardized, has been severely condemned by modern writers; but it was a shrewd political move for Henry to invalidate, for different reasons, a marriage which his enemies proclaimed to be invalid, and to bastardize a Princess who was regarded as a bastard by at least half the nation and nearly every foreign government. It is difficult to believe that Cranmer was able to convince himself that there was any other motive behind the divorce proceedings. At nine o'clock in the morning of 17th May, he opened his Court at Lambeth. No one was admitted except the proctors for Henry and Anne and a few of the Lords of the Council. The matter was urgent, as Anne's execution, which had been fixed for the 17th, was postponed for only forty-eight hours in order to enable Cranmer to pass his sentence before she was beheaded. The proceedings were completed by eleven o'clock. Cranmer gave judgment that the marriage between Henry and Anne was a nullity. His judgment gives no indication of the grounds for his decision, which is not surprising, for the reasons were never given in these formal judgments; but it is certainly remarkable that there is no surviving record of any kind as to the reasons for the divorce.[2]

There were three rumours circulating in London within a few days of the divorce. The first—which was certainly untrue —was that Cranmer had given judgment that Elizabeth was the child of Norris. The second was that he had pronounced the marriage to be void on account of Anne's precontract with the Earl of Northumberland; and the third, that he had done so on the grounds that Henry's adultery with Anne's sister was a bar to his marrying Anne, and invalidated the marriage. His-

---

[1] Kingston to Cromwell, 16 May 1536 (Ellis, *Letters*, i [ii]. 63, where, in the passage 'thys day at dyner the Quene sayd at she shuld go to a nunnery and ys in hope of lyf', the words 'a nunnery' are printed 'Anvures' and interpreted as meaning 'Antwerp'.

[2] Cranmer's sentence of divorce, 17 May 1536; Records of Convocation, June-July 1536 (Wilkins, iii. 803-4).

torians today are still divided as to whether the precontract with Northumberland or Henry's misconduct with Mary Boleyn was the grounds for Cranmer's decree; but it was almost certainly Henry's misconduct with Mary. It would obviously have been preferable to have chosen the precontract as the grounds, rather than find a reason which was so discreditable to the King; but there were difficulties about adopting this course. Four years before, Northumberland had sworn an oath before Warham—and had received the Sacrament before Norfolk—that he was not precontracted to Anne, and he now hastened to write to Cromwell on 13th May to remind him of this. Northumberland, having denied the existence of the precontract in 1532 in order to make it possible for Henry to marry Anne, could not now retract his denial without placing himself in an even more dangerous position than if he angered the King by refusing to retract it.[1]

There was another difficulty about basing the divorce on the grounds of the precontract. The purpose of annulling the marriage was to bastardize Elizabeth; but even if the marriage were unlawful, Elizabeth would be legitimate under the canon law if even one of her parents had believed that the marriage was valid, and had therefore been in good faith, at the time of her birth. It would have been difficult for Henry to deny that he had been in good faith as far as the precontract was concerned, for he could hardly have said that he had known about the precontract when he married Anne, in view of the fact that it had been officially declared before the marriage, after a public investigation, that there had been no precontract. It was far easier to hold that both Henry and Anne had known that Mary Boleyn had been Henry's mistress, and to base the absence of good faith, and Elizabeth's bastardy, on these grounds. The strongest evidence that Henry's misconduct was the grounds for the divorce is the fact that in the new Act of Succession of

[1] Chapuys to Granvelle, 18–19 May and 8 July 1536 (*Span. Cal.*, v [ii]. 54, 72; *L.P.*, x. 909; xi. 41); Wriothesley, i. 40–41; Northumberland to Cromwell, 13 May 1536 (Burnet, vi. 167). The chief evidence for the view that the precontract was the ground for the divorce is the statement in the Act of Succession of 1536 (28 Hen. VIII, c. 7) that the marriage was declared void because of certain impediments confessed by Anne to Cranmer when he was 'sitting judicially'. But apart from the obvious unreliability of the statement, it may have meant no more than that Anne, through her proctors, had admitted at the trial at Lambeth that Henry was entitled to a divorce.

July 1536, which recited the nullity of Henry's marriage to Anne, it was expressly enacted that a marriage of a man to the sister of his mistress was void as being within the prohibited degrees. This had not been included in the prohibited degrees laid down in the Act of Succession of 1533.

But in choosing this thoroughly undesirable reason for his decision, Cranmer faced another difficulty. In 1527, when Henry first decided that he wished to marry Anne, he had obtained from the Pope a dispensation permitting him to marry any woman in contravention of the bar of affinity, including the sister of his mistress, provided only that he might not marry his brother's widow. In marrying Anne, Henry had relied both on the invalidity of the Papal dispensation of 1503, which had permitted him to marry Catherine, and on the validity of the Papal dispensation of 1527. This position was only tenable on the grounds that in 1503 the Pope had wrongly purported to dispense with the divine law, whereas in 1527 he merely dispensed with a canonical bar. This dispensation of 1527 was now an obstacle to the divorce of Anne in 1536. It could have been surmounted by holding that a man's marriage to the sister of his mistress, as well as a marriage to the sister of his wife, was unlawful by divine law; but this had never been asserted by any theologian, and was expressly repudiated in one of the pamphlets written in connexion with Henry's divorce from Catherine—a pamphlet which may even have been written by Cranmer himself. Cranmer probably resolved the problem by holding that the Act of Dispensations of 1534 had invalidated all Papal dispensations retrospectively as well as for the future. It was obviously because this difficulty had arisen that a statute in July 1536 enacted that no dispensation which had at any time been granted by the Pope was valid unless it had been confirmed by the Lord Chancellor.[1]

Whatever the grounds for the divorce may have been, there were enough legal complexities to make it impossible to dispose of the case in two hours if there had been a fair and proper

[1] 25 Hen. VIII, c. 22; 28 Hen. VIII, c. 7, 16; Clement VII's dispensation, 23 December 1527 (Wilkins, iii. 707); and see Friedmann, *Anne Boleyn*, ii. 351–5. Burnet (iv. 146) published the document in which it is stated 'Carnalis copula affinitatem solo jure ecclesiastico repertam inducit'. Cranmer's name is written at the beginning of this document in his own hand; but Jenkyns (in *Remains of Thomas Cranmer*, i. viii–ix, n.) argues that this does not prove that Cranmer was the author.

trial. It is clear that Anne's proctors made no real attempt to argue against the divorce, and that Cranmer made short shrift of all the legal difficulties. It was obviously desirable to prevent it from being publicly known that the grounds for the divorce was Henry's misconduct with Mary Boleyn. Presumably no indication of the grounds was given to Convocation in June, when both Houses unanimously approved Cranmer's sentence of divorce; if the members present, who numbered more than a hundred, were informed as to the reasons, they preserved the secret surprisingly well. It is more likely that they were sufficiently servile to approve the divorce without knowing the grounds for the decision, relying merely on the assurance that when Cranmer gave his judgment, he had 'God alone before his eyes.'[1]

Cranmer was chosen to be Anne Boleyn's confessor. He did not take her confession when he visited her on 16th May. It has often been suggested that on this occasion he used his position as confessor to extract from Anne the admissions which he needed for the divorce proceedings next day; but it is very unlikely that he would have committed this grave impropriety, or that even Henry or Cromwell would have urged him to do so. On 18th May, Kingston wrote to Cromwell that he had not yet heard anything from Cranmer, and that the Queen greatly desired to be shriven. We may therefore presume that Cranmer visited Anne again late on the 18th to hear her confession. He was not present at her execution early next morning.[2]

If Cranmer heard Anne's last confession, he was in a position where he could form a better opinion than any other person as to her innocence or guilt. Anne was as religious as most of her contemporaries, and this aspect of her character had been accentuated during her imprisonment. Despite all the rumours which were circulating among their enemies, there is no reason to doubt that both Anne and Cranmer held the practice of confession in high esteem. If Anne affirmed her innocence in her final confession to Cranmer, he could be confident that she was speaking the truth. Cranmer was therefore the only surviving person with sure knowledge as to whether Anne had committed adultery and had wished to kill the King.

[1] 'Ac ipsum solum Deum prae oculis nostris habentes' (Cranmer's sentence of divorce, 17 May 1536 (Wilkins, iii. 804)).
[2] Kingston to Cromwell, 18 May 1536 (*L.P.*, x. 902).

It is this which gives such interest to the story which the Scottish reformer Aless told in his letter to Elizabeth I in 1559. Aless had come to England on the invitation of Cromwell and Cranmer, and was in London at the time of Anne's death. On the morning of 19th May 1536, he awoke from a dream at the first light between two and three o'clock, having dreamed that he had seen, in gruesome detail, the severed head of Anne Boleyn. As he was unable to sleep again after this experience, he rose, and crossed the river to Lambeth. On arriving there just before four o'clock, he found Cranmer walking in the garden, and told him about his horrible dream. Cranmer remained silent for a little while, and then asked: 'Do not you know what is to happen today?' Aless had not left his house for some days and had not heard any news. Cranmer then raised his eyes to Heaven, and said: 'She who has been the Queen of England upon earth will today become a Queen in Heaven'. He was too overcome with grief to say more, and burst into tears.[1]

The truth of this story has been doubted by many historians, and Cranmer's apologists have been particularly eager to deny it. It is of course to some extent suspect because it was written by Aless more than twenty-three years later to the daughter of Anne Boleyn soon after she had ascended the throne. But when full allowance has been made for Aless' lapses of memory and ulterior motives, the story is much more likely to be true than false—in substance, though doubtless not in every detail; for it is difficult to see why Aless, who had no favour to ask of Elizabeth, should have written to her from Germany to tell her a story which was untrue. In one set of circumstances, Aless' tale is very plausible. If Anne affirmed her innocence to Cranmer in their last talk on 18th May, it is not surprising that Cranmer could not sleep that night. He was not in any way responsible for her death, but he had not been able to make any attempt to save her, and he had invalidated her marriage and bastardized her child on grounds which he must have known were unsound in law and ethically disgraceful. We can imagine his feelings if he now became convinced of her innocence. He would henceforth be obliged to remain silent, to acquiesce in the official story of her guilt, while he alone knew that his benefactress, the

[1] Aless to Elizabeth I, 1 September 1559 (*Cal. For. Pap., Eliz.*, i. 1303 (p. 528)).

friend of the Reformation, had been wrongly condemned. The frustration, indignation and sense of guilt which such a situation would evoke in Cranmer might well have led him to burst out with his remark to Aless as he walked with him alone in the garden at dawn.

Cranmer had loyally obeyed the King with regard to Anne's divorce, but by so doing he had technically been guilty of high treason. The Act of Succession of 1534 had made it high treason to do anything to the 'prejudice, slander, disturbance or derogation' of Henry's marriage to Anne; and none of the Papists who had been executed for violating this statute had disturbed the marriage so effectively as Cranmer had done in his sentence of 17th May. A provision was therefore inserted for his benefit in the Act of Succession of 1536. It enacted that those who, from the best motives, had recently pointed out the invalidity of the King's marriage to Anne were not to be held guilty of high treason under the Act of 1534; but it also enacted that the invalidity of Anne's marriage did not remove the guilt of treason from anyone else who had said too early that the marriage was invalid. It was now to be high treason to dispute the validity of either of the two divorces which Cranmer had granted the King.[1]

Cranmer owed Anne £400 when she died; he was by far her highest debtor. The debts were duly noted by the King's officials, for they passed along with all Anne's assets to Henry by virtue of the forfeiture which resulted from her treason; but when a list of the King's debtors was compiled a few weeks later, the section containing the names of the debtors of the late Queen did not include Cranmer's name and debt along with those of the other debtors.[2] It is possible to draw almost any conclusion from this—that Cranmer was excused from paying the £400 on account of his services to Henry; that he hastened to pay the money to the King before the second list of debtors was compiled; or merely that his name was included in the first list, or omitted from the second, through an oversight.

On the day of Anne's death, Cranmer granted a dispensation permitting Henry to marry Jane Seymour despite the canonical

[1] 25 Hen. VIII, c. 22; 28 Hen. VIII, c. 7.
[2] 'Certain debts due to the late Queen Anne'; 'The late Queen's debts' (*L.P.*, x. 912, 1257 (ix)).

bar raised by their distant relationship—they were both descended from Edward III.[1] Cranmer was never required to find reasons for declaring that his dispensation was invalid, and that Henry's marriage to Jane was a nullity.

[1] Cranmer's dispensation, 19 May 1536 (*L.P.*, x. 915).

CHAPTER VIII

THE FORMULARIES OF FAITH
AND THE ENGLISH BIBLE

THE hopes of the Papists and reactionaries were quickly dashed after the execution of Anne Boleyn. Cranmer remained in favour, participating to the full in the public ceremonies which followed the proclamation of Jane Seymour as Queen, while the Convocation which assembled in June 1536 went farther than ever in the direction of a Reformation. The reactionary clergy in the Lower House ventured to present a petition to Cranmer protesting against sixty-seven heresies which had been propagated by various reforming sects; but nothing more was heard of this petition. By 11th July, Cranmer, along with Cromwell, the Bishops and Abbots, and fifty members of the Lower House of Convocation, had subscribed to the Ten Articles. The Ten Articles were the product of discussions between the Bishops which had been continuing since March. Strype seems to have thought that the Articles were drafted by Cranmer, but they are more likely to have been the work of Edward Fox, who presented them to Convocation on the King's behalf.[1]

For the first time, a statement of doctrine which was heretical at least by implication was officially promulgated in England. The Articles were designed to please all shades of opinion, including the German Lutherans, by condemning the doctrines which had inspired the traditional ceremonies while upholding the ceremonies themselves. Auricular confession was declared to be expedient and necessary. The Real Presence was affirmed, but the question of transubstantiation was ignored. It was stated that neither faith nor works were sufficient for salvation, but that 'our good works be necessarily required to the attaining of everlasting life'. Images in churches, prayers to the Saints and all the traditional ceremonies were approved, though their abuse

[1] Wriothesley, i. 44–48; Waite to Lady Lisle, 16 June 1536; Chapuys to Charles V, 1 April 1536 (*Span. Cal.*, v [ii]. 43; *L.P.*, x. 601, 1147); Protest against the Sixty-Seven Errors, 23 June 1536 (Fuller, *Church History*, ii. 81–86); Records of Convocation, June–July 1536 (Wilkins, iii. 808); Strype, *Cranmer*, pp. 57, 62–63.

for superstitious purposes was condemned; and while it was said to be uncertain whether there was any such place as Purgatory, prayers and masses for souls, and alms for mass-priests, were approved, as they could partly, though not wholly, relieve the souls of their pain.

The most remarkable fact about the Ten Articles is the omission of all mention of four of the seven Sacraments. Matrimony, Confirmation, Orders and Extreme Unction were ignored, as in the Lutheran Confession of Augsburg. There has been much controversy as to the significance of this omission as compared with the position adopted a year later in the Bishops' Book of 1537, when these four Sacraments were accepted as Sacraments, but stated to be inferior in status to Baptism, the Lord's Supper and Penance; but however this may be, there is no doubt as to Cranmer's attitude on this question. The omission of all mention of the four lesser Sacraments in 1536—which was obviously a political manoeuvre to placate the German Lutherans—cannot have been wholly satisfactory to Cranmer. Cranmer's views on the Sacraments about this time appear clearly from Aless' report of his speech to the Bishops in 1537, from his comments on the King's annotations to the Bishops' Book in 1538, and from his answers to the Seventeen Questions on the Sacraments in 1540. Cranmer believed that Baptism and the Lord's Supper were higher than the other Sacraments. Next in status came Penance. Matrimony was below Penance, but above the remaining Sacraments; while Confirmation, Orders and Extreme Unction were definitely placed in an inferior position, along with many other figures, to all of which Cranmer was quite prepared to accord the name of Sacrament. It is clear, from these documents, that whatever Cranmer may have thought in 1552, he did not believe in 1536 that Matrimony, Confirmation, Orders and Extreme Unction were unworthy of any mention at all in a formulary of faith.[1]

The policy of the Ten Articles was unity by ambiguity and silence. To achieve this, Henry sent a letter to Cranmer on 12th July—the day after the Articles were presented to Convocation—forbidding all preaching until Michaelmas except by the

[1] The Ten Articles (Burnet, iv. 272–85); Aless, *Of the auctorite of the word of God agaynst the bisshop of London*, pp. 11–14 (unpaginated); Cranmer's comments on Henry VIII's annotations on the Bishops' Book; Questions and Answers on the Sacraments (Cranmer's *Works*, ii. 99–100, 115–17).

Bishops or in their presence, and the ordinary sermons in cathedrals; anyone else who preached was to be arrested by the Bishops. The object of this order was to prevent persons from propounding the Articles 'after their fantastical appetites'; and when preaching was resumed after Michaelmas, all preachers were to be told not to interpret the Articles, but merely to read them out.[1]

At the beginning of October 1536, the revolt in Lincolnshire broke out. The rebels demanded that no more monasteries should be suppressed, and that the old religion be restored, as well as protesting against taxation and the Statute of Uses. From the beginning, Cranmer was a target for the rebels' attack. When two thousand of them first encountered the Justices of the Peace at Boston on 6th October, one of their four demands was that Cranmer, along with their diocesan Bishop Longland, Latimer, Bishop Hilsey of Rochester, Bishop Goodrich of Ely, Cromwell, Christopher Hales the Master of the Rolls, and Rich the Chancellor of the Augmentations, should either be handed over to them or banished from the realm. A few days later, they complained of Cranmer and other Bishops in a petition to the King. The men of Louth demanded that these Bishops, and also Cromwell, should be handed over to them; and we can well believe the statement of one of their leaders that they intended to murder them when they had them in their hold. The names of the King's evil counsellors whose dismissal or punishment was demanded varied on different occasions; but Cranmer and Latimer, alone of them all, were always included —for even Cromwell was occasionally omitted from the list.[2]

The rebels stressed their loyalty to the King, but demanded the dismissal of low born men from his Council. It was therefore natural that they should abuse, not only Cromwell as a shearman, but also Cranmer as a tavern keeper. The rumours about Cranmer having been an ostler, which originated at Cambridge at the time of his first marriage twenty years before, now found fertile soil. Cranmer had been accused of being an ostler by the curate of Kettering as early as September 1533; on one occasion, someone hung up a truss of hay outside his gate as a contemptuous

[1] Henry VIII to Cranmer, 12 July 1536 (Wilkins, iii. 807–8).
[2] Letter to Audley, 7 October 1536; Examination of Bradley, 3 November 1536; Pio to Dandino, 23 October 1536; Hudswell's Confession, undated (L.P., xi. 585, 828 [v], 848, 853).

allusion to the fact. He was now converted into a tavern keeper by these low born rebels to whom low birth was as great a disqualification as heresy where high office in the State was concerned.[1]

By 8th October, the revolt had spread to Yorkshire. Two emissaries were sent from Lincolnshire to Beverley to ask the Yorkshiremen for aid; they told them that in Lincolnshire every man cried out against Cromwell, Cranmer, Latimer, Audley and Rich and the King's Visitors. Soon everyone in Yorkshire knew that the men of Beverley were up, and a formidable rising had gained control throughout the county. The rebels under Aske made the same demands as the Lincolnshire men, though they extended them considerably; but the heretic Bishops, and particularly Cranmer and Latimer, were always singled out as responsible for all ills. In the rebels' song about 'Crim, Crame and Rich, With three Ls and the Lich', Cranmer is clearly identified, whoever may be meant by the 'three Ls'. The rebels demanded that the heretic Bishops should be burned.[2]

The attacks on Cranmer were not confined to the regions in the north where the people were in open revolt. Reports were sent to the authorities about persons in Essex and Suffolk who were speaking in favour of the rebels and abusing Cranmer as a heretic or an ostler, and making coarse rhymes about him. The Abbot of Colchester was heard to say that he would like to see Cranmer, Audley and Cromwell handed over to the rebels to deal with. When the Abbot gave a dinner after the December sessions in Colchester, some of the people present spoke openly in favour of the northern rebels, applauding their attacks on Cranmer and the others. Even government officials were suggesting that the King should promise the rebels that if they could prove that any of his advisers had subverted religion, he was ready to proceed against these heretics. Henry did not follow this advice; but he arrested a few heretics in order to appease the Yorkshire rebels. One of these was Marshall, who

[1] Morice (*Nar. Ref.*, p. 269); Chapuys' nephew to Mary of Hungary (October 1536) (Froude's Notes to William Thomas' *The Pilgrim*, p. 114); Depositions of Pynder and Lynne, 28 April 1534; Oath of the Yorkshire rebels (October 1536) (*L.P.*, vii. 559; xi. 705 [4]); Harrison, 'Description of Britaine' (in Holinshed, *Chronicles of England, Scotland and Ireland*, i. 256).

[2] The song of the Yorkshire rebels; their articles at Doncaster (October–November 1536); Examination of Hallam, 24 January 1537; Talbot's Deposition (April 1537); Document relating to the examination of Sennes and others (4 August 1537) (*L.P.*, xi. 786 [3], 902 [2]; xii [i]. 201 [pp. 89–90], 853; xii [ii]. 436; Speed's *History*, p. 775).

was placed in Cranmer's custody in Kent. Gostwick, the Treasurer of the First Fruits, who was no friend to the reformers or to Cranmer, suggested to Cromwell that Cranmer should be ordered to hand over Marshall to the rebels; but Marshall was allowed to remain in safety at Cranmer's house at Ford, near Herne, until the hour of danger had passed.[1]

The rebels were more certain that they hated Cranmer than they were of anything else, but their reasons for attacking him were far from clear. Usually they merely denounced Cranmer in the most general terms as a heretic. The men of Horncastle in Lincolnshire thought that Cranmer, along with Cromwell, Rich, Hilsey, Archbishop Brown of Dublin, and Longland, had made plans to seize the Church goods and pull down churches. At the conference at Pomfret on 27th November, the rebels seem to have asked that Cranmer and his colleagues be punished for having violated the Ten Articles. These accusations were of course ridiculous. Even Aske himself was not at all clear, when he was examined in the Tower in April 1537, as to why he thought that Cranmer and the other Bishops were heretics. At first he merely stated that it was because the Lincolnshire men had said that they were heretics; but later he added that it was because they had been the cause of the breach of unity in the Church, and were supposed to be supporters of the new learning and of the opinions of Luther and Tyndale. Aske referred to the illegality of Cranmer's judgment at Dunstable at a time when the divorce case was before the Court in Rome, and said that men thought that Cranmer had not been properly consecrated as Archbishop because he had not received a pall from Rome. This last allegation was untrue.[2]

[1] Gostwick to Cromwell, 1 December 1536; Pyrton and Sinclair to Cromwell (December 1536); Devices for appeasing the commons (December 1536); Bale to Cromwell (January 1537); Rogers' Confession, 12 February 1537; Examination of Myddleton (March 1537); Pickering's deposition (April 1537); Sayville to Cromwell, 25 July 1537; Trowman's deposition, 1 November 1539; Examination of Nuthake, 3 November 1539; Examination of Rouse, 4 November 1539 (*L.P.*, xi. 1220, 1319, 1410 [4]; xii [i]. 307, 407, 784, 1021 [9]; xii [ii]. 339; xiv [ii]. 439, 454, 458); Draft of Henry VIII's Answer to the demands of the Rebels in Yorkshire, (autumn 1536) (*St. Pap.*, i. 508). For criticisms of Cranmer at a later date, see Depositions of Baker and others, 17 August 1537; Roland Lee and others to Cranmer, Latimer and Hilsey, 8 April 1538 (*L.P.*, xii [ii]. 530; xiii [i]. 715).
[2] Proposals in the conference at Pomfret, 27 November 1536; Examination of Ledes (January 1537); Examination of Aske, 11 April 1537 (*L.P.*, xi. 1182 [2]; xii [i]. 70 [xii], 901 [p. 409]).

Immediately the revolt in Lincolnshire broke out at the beginning of October, the authorities drew up plans for raising troops to fight the rebels, and allocated various duties to the Lords and dignitaries of the realm. Cranmer was to supply three hundred men for service.. The original plan was for Henry to take the field in person, accompanied by Cromwell, Norfolk and other peers. Cranmer was chosen, along with Audley and other Lords of the Council, to attend on the Queen in London, and to be responsible for the safety of the city and the neighbourhood. Later Henry decided not to face the rebels himself, and the earlier arrangements were cancelled. Cranmer was then selected as one of the dignitaries who were to be responsible for the preservation of order in their counties; he was one of the nine chosen for Kent, and was in residence at Ford throughout that bitter winter. He was very active there in arresting and interrogating suspects, and discovered a seditious association among the monks of his priory of Christ Church in Canterbury.[1]

He stayed nearly all the winter at Ford, and returned to Lambeth at the beginning of March to play his part in drafting a complete formulary of faith to replace the brief statement in the Ten Articles. The work of drawing up the formulary had been referred to an assembly of Bishops and other divines under the presidency of Cromwell as Vicegerent which met frequently between February and July 1537. As well as holding meetings, they also adopted the method which was repeatedly used from this time onwards: a number of questions were drafted, probably by Cranmer, dealing with the essential issues in dispute, and all the selected Bishops and divines, including Cranmer himself, gave their answers. Here for the first time we find the divines, with a few exceptions, forming themselves into two groups, with all the members of each group adopting a common line against their opponents. This phenomenon is often repeated in the doctrinal arguments of the next fifteen years.[2]

Aless wrote a description of one of the meetings of these

---

[1] List of men to be supplied for service, and other documents (autumn 1536); Depositions of Stone and others, 28 January 1537 (*L.P.*, xi. 580 [3], [4], and [5]; xii [i]. 256); Cranmer to Cromwell, 28 January and 16 February 1537 (Cranmer's *Works*, ii. 333–4).

[2] Husee to Lisle, 18 February 1537 (*L.P.*, xii [i]. 457); Questions and Answers on Confirmation (Strype, *Eccl. Mem.* i [ii]. 340–63).

Bishops and divines in the Parliament House at Westminster. He states that it was in the year 1537. There are several indications that it may have been in 1536, in which case the discussions were those which preceded the promulgation of the Ten Articles and not the Bishops' Book; but these indications are not definite enough to counter the fact that Aless himself gives the year as 1537 in his account of the meeting, which was written in 1538. If Aless was using the English legal calendar when he gave the date as 1537, this places the meeting as having been held after 25th March; but he may have been using the ecclesiastical calendar under which the year began at Christmas. It must have been before the beginning of May 1537, when the question of the Sacraments was settled.[1]

Cromwell had happened to meet Aless in the street when he was on his way to the meeting, and he invited Aless to accompany him. In the Parliament House, they found the Bishops seated in order of precedence at a table covered with a cloth, with their priests standing behind them. When Cromwell entered with Aless, Cranmer and all his colleagues rose and bowed to Cromwell, who took his seat in the place of honour. Cromwell began by declaring that although the King had sufficient learning to solve all religious controversies himself, he did not wish to proclaim any formulary of faith without consulting his Bishops and Parliament. There followed a discussion about the number of Sacraments. Stokesley argued that there were seven Sacraments, and was supported by Archbishop Lee, Longland, Clerk, Sampson and Repps; Cranmer, Shaxton, Goodrich, Fox and Latimer opposed this view.

The summary of Cranmer's speech which is given by Aless is obviously not a verbatim report; but Aless was probably right as to its general tenor, for it is a lucid and moderate

---

[1] Aless, *Of the auctorite of the word of God agaynst the bisshop of London*, p. 7 (unpaginated); Husee to Lisle, 12 May 1537 (*L.P.*, xii [i]. 1187). Foxe (v. 378) correctly gave the date as given by Aless, i.e. 1537; but the editor of the 1877 edition tried to improve on Foxe by substituting 1536 as the year. The reasons for believing that it was 1536 are that Aless states that Fox had just returned from Germany at the time of the discussions, and Fox in fact returned in July 1536; and that he also states—incorrectly—that the meeting was held in the Convocation House. Convocation met in 1536, and not in 1537. But Aless' book, in which he gives the date as 1537, was written in 1538; see Gairdner, *Lollardy and the Reformation*, ii. 279 n., 321 n., where Gairdner revises his earlier opinion (expressed in his *English Church in the Sixteenth Century*, pp. 175, 192–3) and states that it was in 1537.

contribution to a heated discussion. Cranmer said that the question at issue was whether Confirmation, Orders and other
traditions which cannot be proved to have been instituted by
Christ should be called Sacraments and compared with
Baptism and the Lord's Supper; but they must strive for unity,
and not quarrel over words. They should define what a Sacrament is in Scripture, and what was meant when Baptism and
the Lord's Supper were called Sacraments; for though St.
Ambrose and other authors called the washing of the disciples'
feet, and other things, a Sacrament, no one now suggested that
these should be numbered among the Sacraments. Cranmer
adopted the same attitude in the discussions of 1540. Against
the traditional view of the conservative Bishops that there were
seven Sacraments, Cranmer showed that the Fathers had called
many more institutions Sacraments, and that all of them,
whether they were called Sacraments or by another name, were
inferior in status to Baptism and the Lord's Supper. He was not
concerned about the use of the word 'Sacrament'; but he raised
the washing of the feet to the level of Confirmation, Orders and
Extreme Unction in order to lower these last three Sacraments
below Baptism and the Lord's Supper. According to Aless, he
did not mention Penance and Matrimony in his speech, and he
seems to have been more doubtful, at least as regards Penance,
of their relation to Baptism and the Lord's Supper.

When Cranmer had finished his speech, Cromwell invited
Aless to address the Bishops. Aless supported Cranmer's case,
and became involved in angry exchanges with Stokesley, who
interrupted him. Aless argued for the supremacy of Scripture,
while Stokesley upheld the authority of unwritten verities;
according to Aless, Cromwell and Cranmer and the reforming
Bishops showed their amusement at Stokesley's arguments.
At twelve o'clock, Aless had not yet finished his speech, and he
offered to prove next day that Christian faith rested on the
Bible alone. But next day, as the session was about to begin,
Aless was visited by an Archdeacon who brought him a message
from Cranmer that his intervention on the previous day had
aroused great resentment among the Bishops; they felt that
Aless, as a foreigner, had no right to take part in their proceedings. Aless consulted Cromwell, who agreed that it would be
undesirable for Aless to attend the meeting, and he suggested

that Aless should give him his notes. Aless was certainly prepared to use strong language, for he had intended, if he had
spoken, to accuse the Bishop of London of 'shameful cavillation
and blasphemy'.[1]

This incident is a good illustration of the difference between
Cromwell and Cranmer. The layman to whom all the Bishops
bow as Vicegerent compels the Bishops to listen to a provocative harangue from a Protestant refugee; but Cranmer hears
the whispers of the Bishops when Cromwell is absent, and urges
Aless not to provoke them again. Aless' extremism would not
help Cranmer to achieve his aim of reaching the most favourable compromise by tact and finesse; but there was surely
another factor in Cranmer's attitude. Cranmer, with his great
belief in rank and position, resented the intervention of an
inferior as being a slur on the dignity of the Bishops. Cromwell,
relying on the King's authority, was prepared to humble the
Bishops and press forward with the Reformation. In these years
he was going much farther than Cranmer dared to go.

The Bishops and divines had reached agreement on all important points of difference by the beginning of May 1537; but
another two months was necessary to complete the drafting of
the book. On 21st July, Cranmer wrote to Cromwell that they
had reached agreement on all matters except some notes to the
Creed, which would be settled on Monday the 23rd. He asked
Cromwell for a license for the Bishops to leave London as soon
as they had done their work, as people were dying of plague
'almost everywhere in London, Westminster, and in Lambeth
they die at my gate even at the next house to me'. On the same
day, Latimer wrote to Cromwell that the greatest credit for
the work done in connexion with the book rested with Cranmer,
though he also referred to the great efforts of Fox.[2]

The *Institution of a Christian Man* was a lucid statement of
Henrician Christianity, and many convenient conclusions were
drawn from the Ten Commandments and the Paternoster. The
Fourth Commandment not to labour on the Sabbath day meant
that the holy days must be observed; but the people must not

---

[1] Aless, op. cit., pp. 7–28, 64 (unpaginated). See also in Cranmer's *Works*,
ii. 79, where the date is given as 1536.
[2] Husee to Lisle, 12 May 1537 (*L.P.*, xii [i]. 1187; Cranmer to Cromwell,
21 July 1537 (Cranmer's *Works*, ii. 337–8); Latimer to Cromwell (21 July 1537)
(*St. Pap.*, i. 563).

be 'over scrupulous, or rather superstitious', in abstaining from work on the holy day. 'Honour thy father and thy mother' was interpreted as meaning 'obey the King', who should be held in greater honour than parents; above all, this Commandment meant that the people must act as informers if they heard any-one plotting against the King. 'Thou shalt not steal' was directed against the sale of goods above the controlled price. 'Thou shalt not bear false witness against thy neighbour' was held to pro-hibit the preaching of heresy. It was explained that the Lord's Prayer begins with the words 'Our Father' because God permits us to call Him Father; and this called forth the comment: 'If our Sovereign Lord the King would say to any of us, Take me for your father and so call me, what joy in heart, what comfort, what confidence would we conceive of so favourable and gracious words'. There was hardly a passage in these sacred writings which Cranmer and his colleagues were not prepared to pervert for the greater glory of King Henry.

These passages were subscribed to with as much enthusiasm by Stokesley and the conservatives as by Cranmer and the reformers; but interspersed throughout the book were para-graphs and sentences, every word of which had been strenuously contested for many months in the meetings of the Bishops and divines. The book asserted that there were seven Sacraments, but stated that though Matrimony, Confirmation, Holy Orders and Extreme Unction had rightly been called Sacraments for so long, because they were holy and godly signs whereby certain gifts of the Holy Ghost were conferred, they were inferior to Baptism, Penance and the Sacrament of the Altar, as these three Sacraments were instituted by Christ as remedies necessary for our salvation. This distinction between the Sacraments, and other less important innovations, involved the authors of the book in deviations from the traditional teachings of the old Church; and Henry therefore decided not to issue the book in his own name, but to place the responsibility for it on the Bishops. At the same time, the Preface to the book made it clear that Cranmer and the Bishops who subscribed to it were not claiming to exercise any power independently of their 'dread and benign Sovereign Lord'. They asked the King for a license to publish the book, 'without the which power and license of your Majesty, we knowledge and confess that we have none authority either to assemble ourselves together for any pretence or purpose, or to publish anything, that might be by us agreed on or compiled'. They also asked the King to make any correction which he thought necessary to set forth his most virtuous desire, 'whereunto we shall in that case conform ourselves, as to our most bounden duties to God and to your Highness appertaineth'. The King's policy was successful; while the authority of the book was respected, it was the Bishops' Book—not the King's.[1]

But hardly had the book been published in September 1537 than the possibility of re-issuing it in the King's name was again under consideration. Henry revised the text of the book, and in January 1538 he sent his draft to Cranmer for him to comment on these revisions. Within a fortnight, Cranmer returned the draft with his comments, which throw a revealing light on Cranmer's relationship with the King. Far from flattering Henry, Cranmer was prepared to criticize his work very freely, and indeed on some points his criticism seems almost carping. 'I trust the King's Highness will pardon my presumption', he wrote when he sent his comments to Cromwell, 'that I have been so scrupulous, and as it were a picker of quarrels to his Grace's book, making a great matter of every light fault, or rather where no fault is at all; which I do only for this intent, that because the book now shall be set forth by his Grace's censure and judgment, I would have nothing therein that Momus could reprehend; and yet I refer all mine annotations again to his Grace's most exact judgment.'[2] Cranmer's devotion to royal absolutism, as well as the interests of the Reformation, required his utter subjection to the King in public on all occasions; but there was nothing inconsistent in tendering frank advice to Henry with a view to assisting him in pursuing the wisest policy.

Henry made nearly two hundred and fifty alterations in the Bishops' Book. Cranmer objected to eighty-two of these, and gave grudging approval only to four, though he wrote to Cromwell that he approved of all the King's alterations on which he

[1] The Bishops' Book and the Preface (Lloyd, *Formularies of Faith*, pp. 26–27, 128–9, 145, 148, 152–5, 163–5, 168, 181); Henry VIII's reply (August 1536) (Cranmer's *Works*, ii. 469–70).
[2] Cranmer to Cromwell, 14 and 25 January 1538 (Cranmer's *Works*, ii. 358–60).

had not commented. Most of Cranmer's objections did not deal with any point of controversy, but merely with the method of expression which Henry had adopted; on one occasion, he objected only to the King's grammar. Cranmer's comments emphasize the importance which he attached to the words of Scripture. He objected when Henry wished to delete the passage in the Bishops' Book referring to the stoning of the disobedient son prescribed in Deuteronomy. 'Of all the precepts there rehearsed,' wrote Cranmer, 'none ought rather to stand than this, for none of them doth express so largely the form of the punishment of an inobedient child.' Cranmer also objected to the verbal alterations which Henry proposed to insert into the text of the Ten Commandments and the Lord's Prayer as given in the Bishops' Book, though most of them merely made clearer the indisputable meaning of the words. 'We should not alter any word in the Scripture, which wholly is ministered unto us by the Ghost of God, 2 Pet. 1; although it shall appear to us in many places to signify much absurdity; but first the Scripture must be set out in God's own words, and if there be any ambiguity, absurdity or scruple, after it would be declared according to the true sense thereof.' On one occasion, at least, the amendment which Henry was proposing was remarkable. The Bishops' Book stated that men transgressed against the Tenth Commandment if they sought to take another man's wife, house or lands. Henry wished this to read that men transgressed the Commandment if they sought to take another man's wife, house or lands 'without due recompense'. To this, Cranmer made the comment: 'This addition agreeth not well with the coveting of another man's wife.'

One of Cranmer's comments is revealing. The commentary in the book on the commandment 'Thou shalt not kill' stated that no man might kill except Princes and those acting under their authority, and added that Princes might only kill in accordance with their laws. Henry suggested that this limitation on the power to kill should apply only to 'inferior rulers', and not to Princes; but Cranmer objected. He argued that Princes must also comply with their own laws, for though Princes could grant pardons and licenses to dispense with their ordinary laws, yet in doing so they were acting within their legal powers. Here Cranmer shows once again that he is not a servile flatterer; but he does not seek to weaken the royal absolutism. He is prepared to tell Henry that his power is subject to the law; but like all his contemporaries, he interprets the law as giving well-nigh absolute power to the King.

A few of Henry's revisions dealt with matters of fundamental importance. He proposed to delete the passage from the book which declared that images of the Father could be dispensed with if the people were able to conceive of Him without any bodily representation. The Bishops' Book also stated that those who could read would be well occupied on the holy day in reading out good books to those who could not read; but Henry wished to insert a more restrictive passage to the effect that they would be well occupied in reading out the books to 'such as they have charge of'. Cranmer opposed both these alterations.[1]

The summer of 1537 saw the publication of the English Bible. It has often been said that we are more indebted to Cranmer than to anyone else for the translation of the Bible into English; but Cranmer, though he strongly favoured the project, deserves far less credit than Cromwell for the English Bible. The official attitude to the translation of the Bible, which had been laid down by Henry in 1530, was that it was unnecessary for the people to read in the Bible what they could hear from preachers, and that the question as to whether to publish a translation was therefore a matter of expediency to be left to the authorities. Henry had added that while such a publication would be inexpedient at present because of the prevalence of heresy, he would cause a translation to be prepared in case it should be expedient to publish it at some later date. As this was the King's policy as early as 1530, there was nothing revolutionary in the proposal which Cranmer made in Convocation in December 1534 that a petition be sent to the King asking him to select good men to translate the Bible, especially as Cranmer had made a strong attack on heresy earlier in the session, and as this petition was accompanied by another which asked the King to confiscate all heretical books by Tyndale and others, and to punish anyone who argued on the meaning of Scripture. There is every reason to believe that Cranmer's

[1] For Henry VIII's proposed amendments to the Bishops' Book, and Cranmer's comments on them, see Cranmer's *Works*, ii. 83–114; for the passages cited, see pp. 101, 103–6.

suggestion had the support of many of the conservative prelates, who hoped that an authorized translation of the Bible
would stop the spread of Tyndale's illegal translation with its
provocative notes.[1]

It may have been Cranmer's zeal for the English Bible which
led to steps being taken at last to implement the decision of
1530, for nothing seems to have been done to prepare a translation until he took the initiative. He arranged for an English
translation of the New Testament to be copied out into notebooks, which he sent to some of the Bishops and other divines
for them to examine the adequacy of the translation. It has been
suggested that this translation which Cranmer sent to the
Bishops was Tyndale's translation, or Wyclif's. This is not
impossible, for Cranmer and the Bishops could have obtained a
license to read these heretical works; but it is more likely to
have been a new translation from the Latin Vulgate made by
one of Cranmer's chaplains, or by some other scholar.

Morice relates that all the Bishops and divines except
Stokesley returned the drafts of the translation, with their
corrections, to Lambeth by the day which Cranmer had named.
Gardiner corrected the translation of the Gospels of Luke and
John, and wrote to Cromwell on 10th June 1535 that he had done
a great deal of work on it. Stokesley had been asked to correct
the translation of the Acts, but he had not returned the corrected
translation by the appointed day. When Cranmer sent to Fulham
to inquire about this, Stokesley sent back the notebook with a
message that he would never collaborate in making it possible
for the people to read the Scriptures, as this would infect them
with heresies. On receiving this message, Cranmer expressed
surprise that Stokesley was not willing to do what the others
had done; but at this, Thomas Lawney—a priest who was
famed for his wit—remarked that Stokesley was not prepared
to spend any time on the New Testament since he had realized
that Christ had bequeathed him nothing in His testament, and
that he would have nothing to do with the Acts of the Apostles
because the Apostles were simple and poor. Morice tells us that
Cranmer laughed at this, as did the other persons present.[2]

[1] Henry VIII's proclamation, 24 May 1530; Records of Convocation, November–December 1534 (Wilkins, iii. 736, 769–70).

[2] Morice, 'Concerning Bishop Stokisley, bisshop of London' (Nar. Ref., pp.
277–8); Gardiner to Cromwell, 10 June 1535 (Muller, p. 66).

Although Morice states that Stokesley was the only divine who did not carry out the work which he had been given, it is certain that nothing more was done towards publishing the new translation after the Bishops and divines had returned their notebooks to Cranmer in the summer of 1535. Two years later, Cranmer wrote to Cromwell that he did not think that the Bishops' translation would be set forth until a day after Doomsday. It has sometimes been suggested that Cranmer's statement was grossly misleading, because all the New Testament had been translated except for Stokesley's Acts; but apart from the fact that this does not account for the Old Testament, Cranmer was not referring to delay in the completion of the translation, but to the opposition to the publication of the book. Cranmer was obviously distressed by this delay in publication, but he does not seem to have done anything to accelerate matters, and was probably alarmed at the extent of the opposition which he encountered. In his letter to Cromwell, he refers to the 'snubs', 'slanders, lies and reproaches' which Cromwell had suffered on account of his attempt to publish an English Bible.[1] This is more likely to have made Cranmer think of delay and compromise rather than of provoking a clash with powerful forces in the Church.

In October 1535, Miles Coverdale published at Zürich the first complete translation of the Bible in English. Ten months later, Cromwell's Injunctions ordered that a copy of the English translation of the Bible, when it was published, must be put in every parish church by 1st August 1537. This seems to have been entirely due to the initiative of Cromwell, and there is no indication that Cranmer played any part in it. Indeed, this paragraph of the Injunctions was omitted from the copy in Cranmer's Register, and was apparently added as an afterthought before the Injunctions were printed.[2] While the Bishops were delaying with their translation, the Vicegerent took the initiative of secretly negotiating for the publication of

---

[1] Cranmer to Cromwell, 4 August 1537 (Cranmer's *Works*, ii. 344).

[2] Cromwell's Injunctions of August 1536 were published by Burnet (iv. 308–13) and by Wilkins (iii. 813–15) from Cranmer's Register without the passage relating to the placing of the Bible in the churches; but this omitted passage is published in Burnet, vi. 216. These Injunctions must not be confused with Cromwell's Injunctions of September 1538, ordering the Bible 'of the largest volume in English' to be placed in the churches (Burnet, iv. 341–6), which Wilkins, who also published them (iii. 815–17) wrongly dated 1536.

another translation by an adherent of the new learning who had fled abroad. The preparations for the issue of Coverdale's Bible as the authorized translation were already far advanced when Grafton and Whitchurch the printers put forward the project of publishing Mathew's Bible in its place. This Bible was very largely the work of Tyndale himself. By the time of his arrest at Antwerp in 1535, Tyndale had translated the New Testament and the Old Testament as far as the Second Book of Chronicles; and the translation was completed by John Rogers under the pseudonym of Thomas Mathew. Coverdale also collaborated in the translation. Grafton and Whitchurch took the risk of printing the translation at Antwerp in 1537, and enlisted the support of Cranmer in an attempt to secure a license for its publication in England.

On 4th August 1537, Cranmer sent a copy of Mathew's Bible to Cromwell with a letter in which he said that he liked it better than any of the existing translations. He asked Cromwell to show it to the King, to whom it was dedicated, and to obtain from Henry a license permitting anyone to read it, without fear of persecution under any of the laws in force, until the Bishops' translation was issued. Cromwell promptly showed Mathew's Bible to Henry, and obtained his consent for it to be sold and read in the realm; and Cranmer wrote to Cromwell on 13th August declaring that this action had made him happier than if Cromwell had given him a thousand pounds. On 28th August, Cranmer wrote again to Cromwell, assuring him that his part in publishing the English Bible would be remembered on the day of Judgment.[1]

It was of course out of the question that the name of Tyndale should be used in connexion with the translation, for this would have branded Henry, in the eyes of his people and of foreign rulers, as an associate of this famous heretic. The translation was therefore published as the work of Thomas Mathew. The number of persons who knew that Tyndale had written more than half of it was very limited, but Cranmer was almost certainly one of them. It is clear from his letter to Cromwell of 4th August 1537 that he had examined several

[1] Cranmer to Cromwell, 4, 13 and 28 August 1537; Grafton to Cromwell, 28 August 1537 and undated (Cranmer's *Works*, ii. 344–7, 346 n.; Strype, *Cranmer*, pp. 731–2).

English translations of the Bible; and as we know from Foxe
that he was continually receiving the latest theological books
from abroad,[1] he had almost certainly read Tyndale's translation before August 1537, or at least those parts of it which
Tyndale had published—the Pentateuch and the New Testament. Cranmer would therefore have recognized the source
from which Mathew's Bible was derived, even if Grafton had
not told him.

Cranmer has not only been given the credit by his friends
for the English Bible, but has also been portrayed by his critics
as the organizer of a brilliantly successful conspiracy by which
Henry was deceived into licensing the translation by Tyndale,
and disseminating by his royal command the work of a heretic
whom he hated. This assumes that Henry was kept in ignorance
of Tyndale's authorship. It is difficult to believe that Cranmer,
who placed his devotion to his King before even his devotion to
Scripture, would have played any part in deceiving Henry as to
the authorship of the translation, or into taking a course of
action which might have had serious adverse repercussions. On
the other hand, it is perfectly possible that Henry was fully
aware of Tyndale's connexion with the translation. He was
never afraid to take bold decisions, and if Cromwell had convinced him of the advantages to be gained from publishing a
translation of the Bible which contained anti-Papist propaganda
in the notes, he may well have persuaded himself that even so
evil a man as Tyndale had been chosen as an instrument of a
godly purpose.

Cranmer had presumably also read Coverdale's translation
before the summer of 1537; but it would seem, from his letter
to Cromwell of 4th August, that he did not know that Cromwell
had been considering licensing it for publication in England.
Cranmer gave reasons in his letter as to why it was desirable
to license Mathew's Bible instead of waiting for the Bishops'
translation; but he did not even contemplate the possibility of
licensing a third translation. This suggests that Cromwell had
kept Cranmer in complete ignorance of the negotiations which
he had been pursuing with Coverdale, and that once again the
Vicegerent was in advance of the Primate in taking the revolutionary step of patronizing a translation of the Bible by a

[1] Foxe, viii. 13.

heretic. Altogether, there seems to be very little reason for Strype to give the credit for the English Bible to Cranmer. Cranmer was strongly in favour of an English Bible; he took steps to obtain the publication of a translation by the Bishops, but did not press forward with the plan when he encountered opposition; he was approached at the eleventh hour by the printers of a new translation, which he was very willing to recommend to Cromwell; and he rejoiced when Cromwell issued Mathew's Bible. As far as we know, this is Cranmer's total share in the publication of the first authorized translation of the Bible.

CHAPTER IX

THE DAILY LIFE
AND THE SECRET MARRIAGE

THANKS to Cranmer's secretary Morice and to John Foxe, we know something of Cranmer's private life as Archbishop of Canterbury. Foxe gives us a detailed account of his daily life, which was almost certainly based on information derived from Morice. Foxe says that Cranmer rose at the usual hour of five, as he had done at Cambridge; for though in his first edition of 1563 he had praised the industry and piety of Cranmer in rising at two or three o'clock in the morning, he altered this in his second edition of 1570 after he had been in touch with Morice. He then describes the rest of Cranmer's ordinary day—prayer and study till nine o'clock in the morning, then interviewing suitors or dealing with public affairs, and to bed at nine in the evening. Foxe mentions that Cranmer usually managed to find time to play or watch a game of chess in the afternoon, and that he used to go walking for at least an hour after supper. Presumably he walked in his gardens and parks; he would have acquired notoriety if, like Bishop Ferrar of St. David's, he had demeaned himself by walking instead of riding in public places. From Morice we know that he went hunting and hawking whenever possible after he had finished his studies for the day, thus resuming a pastime which he had learned as a boy but had not been permitted to indulge in as a Fellow at Jesus. Despite his short-sightedness, he shot deer both with the longbow, which he had been taught to use as a child, and with the cross-bow, the use of which had been restricted by statute to peers and wealthy landowners. Cranmer still excelled as a rider; he could ride the roughest horse in his stable better than any of his household.[1]

[1] Foxe, viii. 13, 41 (1st ed., p. 1476; 2nd ed., p. 2035); Morice (*Nar. Ref.*, pp. 239–40). For the impropriety of dignitaries walking in public, see the documents in Ferrar's case (Foxe, vii. 8, 15), and Heylin, *Ecclesia Restaurata*, i. 248. For shooting with the crossbow, see 19 Hen. VII, c. 4; 3 Hen. VIII, c. 13; 25 Hen. VIII, c. 17; Gray and Brittain, *Jesus College Cambridge*, p. 36. On 7 January 1535, Cranmer was granted a license which permitted one of his servants to kill deer with the crossbow for Cranmer's use (*L.P.*, viii. 149 [5]).

Cranmer was abstemious where the pleasures of the table were concerned. He often ate no supper, and on these occasions would wear gloves while he sat at the table with his household —'because,' writes Foxe, 'he would, as it were, thereby wean himself from eating of meat.' It is difficult to find any reason why Cranmer should have worn the gloves except to draw attention to the fact that he was indulging in this abstinence. Perhaps he thought that this was necessary in order to bring home to the people that the Bishops, under the new régime, despised worldly riches and good food; for soon after the break with Rome, Cromwell had been considering the desirability of adopting this policy. He had suggested that Cranmer should write to the clergy on this topic, in order to show the people that he was only concerned with proclaiming the truth and had no thought of promotion or pleasure.[1]

Morice writes that Cranmer, despite his onerous public duties, spent three-quarters of the day in study, as he had done when he was at Cambridge. Now he no longer sat, pen in hand, taking notes as he read, but usually pursued his studies standing up, dictating his books and letters to Morice. Foxe mentions that he spent an hour or two every day reading books which were always being sent to him from overseas. It was because of this time spent in study that he was able to furnish the King so rapidly with theological opinions and authorities. If Henry asked Cranmer overnight to provide him with a summary of the opinions of the theologians, both old and new, on some particular point of doctrine, Cranmer could always assemble by next day a summary of the opinions of some 'thirty, forty, sixty, or more somewhiles of authors'. None of Henry's chaplains or Bishops could provide such information so quickly.[2] Evidently Cranmer had an excellent memory, which had not been so badly injured by his schoolmaster as he supposed.

This concentration on his studies shows that Cranmer considered that the primary duty of an Archbishop of Canterbury was to be a divine and a theologian. He never became a purely political Bishop, like so many of his predecessors, abandoning both the study of theology and the administrative and pastoral

---

[1] Foxe, viii. 13; Draft by one of Cromwell's clerks (summer 1533) (Pocock, ii. 487–9).

[2] Morice (*Nar. Ref.*, pp. 249–50); Foxe, viii. 13.

duties of his office while he devoted himself to affairs of State, though he was naturally obliged to delegate much of the administrative business of his diocese to his Ordinaries. Apart from his small but populated diocese of Canterbury, the Archbishop had a peculiar jurisdiction over a number of districts within the geographical confines of other dioceses, and the Marches of Calais were within his diocesan jurisdiction. He was the Visitor of the great Benedictine monastery of Christ Church in Canterbury, which with seventy brothers was easily the largest monastery in England and was second only to Westminster in wealth. His various other duties and powers included the right to coin money in his private mint. Cranmer was the last Archbishop to possess this right, as the mint was closed in 1550.[1]

Much of his time was spent in dealing with judicial matters. His Court of Arches was the Court of Appeal from all the ecclesiastical Courts in the province of Canterbury, with a further appeal lying to the Lord Chancellor. The Court of Audience was a Court of first instance with concurrent jurisdiction in ecclesiastical causes throughout all the province of Canterbury with the diocesan Courts of the Bishops. In January 1542, Cranmer, like Warham before him, re-issued the old statute of Archbishop Winchelsey which limited the number of proctors in the Court of Arches to ten. The monopoly of these proctors—which carried with it the sole right to act as proctors in the Court of Audience and in the Bishop of London's Consistory Court—was unpopular, and Cranmer's order led to an unsuccessful protest being sent from an unknown writer to Parliament. The reasons given by this writer in favour of maintaining the number of proctors at twenty-four, and his account of the evils resulting from having only ten, are very convincing; he was probably right in his surmise that Cranmer had been persuaded by the proctors to make the order without fully appreciating its consequences.[2]

A few years after Cranmer became Archbishop, an attempt was made to abolish his Court of Audience. Strype published a document containing reasons for abolishing the Court which he says was written in 1536 (Old Style) and in the handwriting

[1] Oman, *The Coinage of England*, p. 262.
[2] Cranmer's Order, 12 January 1541/2 (Cranmer's *Works*, ii. 491–3); Protest against Cranmer's order, (1542) (Strype, *Cranmer*, pp. 717–28).

of the Registrar of the Lower House of Convocation. The writer of the document argued that the Archbishop's right to hold a Court of Audience was derived from his legatine power, which had been abolished by the Act of 1534, and that by holding the Court Cranmer was derogating from the authority of the Vicegerent. Cranmer replied that he now held his Court by the authority of the King as Supreme Head, and was legally entitled to do so—which was certainly a correct interpretation of the Act of 1534. The writer did not hesitate to indulge in a personal attack on Cranmer for having continued for so long to use his title of Legate, and this led Strype to suppose that Gardiner was responsible for the document; but if Strype is right in dating it in 1536–7, Gardiner can have had no hand in it, for he was Ambassador in France at the time. The references to the menace of the Court of Audience in the diocese of London and the malice displayed towards Cranmer suggest that it was inspired by Stokesley. The real objection to the Court was that it encroached on the jurisdiction of the Bishops' Courts, and as it sat in London it probably attracted more cases from Stokesley's Court than from any other. Standish of St. Asaph also protested against the Court of Audience. On this occasion, Cranmer was doubtless helped by the King's reluctance to make any unnecessary innovation. The Court of Audience continued in existence for more than two hundred years until it became obsolete.[1]

Cranmer often sat himself as a Judge in his Courts, and by contemporary standards at least was fair and impartial in the discharge of his judicial duties. His fairness is shown by his conduct on one occasion when he was serving on a Commission in 1535 to determine a dispute with regard to the payment of tithes in London, for he showed far more patience than Gardiner towards the witnesses. His impartiality is demonstrated by the case of Anthony Kingston. Anthony was the son of Sir William Kingston, the Constable of the Tower, who was related to Cranmer; but in July 1533, Cranmer wrote to Sir William to tell him that he could not grant his son's petition for the nullity of his marriage. Cranmer wrote: 'Except I can see some better

---

[1] 'A reply to the Archbishop against his Court of Audience' (Strype, *Cranmer*, pp. 714–16); Strype, *Cranmer*, pp. 55–56; Standish to Cromwell, 30 June 1535 (*L.P.*, viii. 953).

cause why they should not be man and wife than I do see yet, I shall never consent, that he shall live in adultery with another woman and she with another man. For if he were my son, I had rather that he begged all his life than to live in adultery; and so I think you had also.' These pious sentiments were written less than two months after Cranmer's Dunstable judgment, when he granted a decree of nullity to his King on very doubtful evidence, as he was to do on two further occasions within the next seven years. But for Cranmer, acting in a judicial capacity in a case between subjects was a very different matter from sitting as a judge in order to render a service to the King. Cranmer, unlike most judges of his time, was not prepared to show favour to the son of an influential relative, and was acting in accordance with his principles in adopting the attitude that justice must prevail over social position and friendship, but must yield to the interests, and even to the whim and lust, of the Prince. There was nothing hypocritical in the sentiments which he expressed in his letter to Kingston. Cranmer would have preferred his son to be a beggar rather than to commit adultery; but his son was not his King.[1]

Cranmer played an important part in collecting information from English spies abroad—a task which, along with all his other public duties, he had to perform at his own expense. In July 1533, the English merchants at Antwerp were approached by a man who said that he wished to arrange for letters to be taken to Henry or to Cranmer. The merchants thought that the man was an agent of the Emperor who was trying to obtain information from them. In the summer of 1535, Theabold was reporting to Cranmer from Antwerp that by posing as an opponent of Henry he had gained the friendship of Philipps, the English Papist refugee who had betrayed Tyndale to the Emperor's officers. Thanks to this, Theabold was able to tell Cranmer about the visit of a Papist agent to England, and that the authorities in Brussels had discovered the activities of some of Cromwell's agents in Flanders and Brabant. In January 1536, a servant of Cardinal Ghinucci approached Cranmer through an intermediary, giving him secret information about political and military matters in Italy. Cranmer accepted this

[1] Report to the Council, (February 1536), (*L.P.*, x. 248); Cranmer to Kingston. 19 July 1533 (Cranmer's *Works*, ii. 250–1).

man's offer of his services as a spy, and in November 1536 he
was able to pass on to Henry some information which he had
obtained from the spy about the plans for a General Council
and the activities of Pole. It was in connexion with Germany
that Cranmer's contacts abroad were most useful to Henry. It
was doubtless because of his knowledge of Germany and the
personal contacts which he had made there—and also perhaps
because of his sympathies towards Lutheranism—that Cranmer
was constantly used to instruct envoys who were sent by Henry
to the German Princes. He did this when Heath was sent to
Germany in January 1534, and when Barnes and Fox were sent
there in the summer and autumn of 1535. He also entertained
at Lambeth the envoys of the radical republics of Hamburg and
Lübeck who visited England in July 1534; and in the same
summer his knowledge enabled him to advise Cromwell that
greyhounds and mastiffs would be the most acceptable gift for
Henry to present to the Elector Palatine.[1]

Cranmer was much occupied with questions of patronage.
He had many preferments at his disposal, and was expected to
approach other dignitaries who had offices to dispose of on
behalf of his friends, his servants and other suitors. One of the
first to benefit from Cranmer's patronage was Erasmus. Cranmer continued to pay the pension which Warham had granted
to Erasmus, though Erasmus, on hearing that the new Archbishop was a Lutheran, had expected that the pension would be
stopped.[2] Cranmer not only intervened with his influential
colleagues in order to obtain positions and property for suitors,
but also, in accordance with the accepted practice, often asked
some Commissioner who was sitting as judge in a dispute to
show favour to one of the litigants if he could do so with right and
justice. It was considered improper to offer a bribe to a judge,
though this was often done in practice; but a private approach

[1] Lok to Cromwell, 26 July 1533; Gostwick to Cromwell, 11 August 1535;
Instructions to Fox (autumn 1535); letter of 15 January 1536; Cranmer to Lisle,
28 January 1537; Chapuys to Charles V, 16 and 27 July 1534 (*L.P.*, vi. 899; vii.
980, 1013; ix. 65, 213 [5]; x. 107; xii [1]. 258; *Span. Cal.*, v. [1]. 71, 75);
Theabold to Cranmer, 31 July 1535 (Demaus, *Tyndale*, pp. 490–2); Cranmer to
Cromwell, 5 January and 10 June 1534; Cranmer to Henry VIII, 18 November
1536 (Cranmer's *Works*, ii. 276, 296, 330–2); Cromwell to Cranmer, 5 January
1534 (Merriman, i. 372); Norfolk and Rochford to Cromwell, 19 July 1535
(Burnet, vi. 145).

[2] Erasmus to Schets, 5 February 1533; Erasmus to Vergara, 19 November
1533; Erasmus to Cognatus, 11 March 1536 (Erasmus, *Epist.* x. 151, 318; xi. 296).

on behalf of one of the parties was thought to be as legitimate, in the sixteenth century, as is the practice today by which Members of Parliament and local Councillors make approaches to executive officers on behalf of some uninfluential person. Cranmer's letters asking for favours show every sign of a sincere desire to help to do justice and to reward virtues and abilities.

But where positions in the Church were concerned, Cranmer was not prepared to allow influence to secure appointments for those without merit. This led him often to refuse requests from prominent personages to appoint men to ecclesiastical preferments. Soon after his consecration, he refused to collaborate in a project by which the Prior of St. Gregory's in Canterbury was to be persuaded to resign in order to make way for a nominee of Cromwell. He wrote to Cromwell: 'Ye do know what ambition and desire of promotion is in men of the Church, and what indirect means they do use and have used to obtain their purpose; which their unreasonable desires and appetites, I do trust that ye will be more ready to oppress and extinguish than to favour or further the same; and I remit to your wisdom and judgment, what an unreasonable thing it is for a man to labour for his own promotion spiritual.' Cranmer also refused requests for favours from the Duchess of Norfolk on two occasions.[1] He never hesitated, however, to make suits himself, including those on behalf of clerics seeking preferment in the Church. His attitude with regard to patronage seems to have been that although he would use his influence to obtain advancement for deserving persons, he would never permit it to operate so as to place unsuitable incumbents in office.

When Cranmer was appointed Archbishop, his see held many lands in Kent and Sussex and elsewhere. In the first few years after 1533, Cranmer had eleven residences—Lambeth, Croydon and Mortlake; Otford and Knoll in West Kent; and Canterbury, Maidstone, Charing, Ford, Wingham and Aldington in his diocese. During these years, he lived mostly at Lambeth, Croydon, Otford, and Knoll, all of which were within a day's ride of London and the Court. But by 1535, he began to be troubled by the matter of exchanges with the King, as a result of which he lost seven of his houses and much land, and received

[1] Cranmer to Cromwell, 6 May 1533; Cranmer to the Duchess of Norfolk, 23 July 1533 and undated (Cranmer's *Works*, ii. 240-1, 254-5, 294).

in exchange other lands, including a new residence. In March 1536 he granted Mortlake to the King along with his lands at Wimbledon and elsewhere in Surrey, and the King granted these lands to Cromwell when he created him Lord Cromwell of Oakham. Otford, Knoll, Maidstone, and Wingham were granted to Henry under the exchange of November 1537. Cranmer lost Aldington in another big exchange in March 1540, and Charing in 1545. His palace at Canterbury was burned down in December 1543, and was not rebuilt. He was granted Beakesbourne near Canterbury in 1538, but he exchanged it soon after, and he did not reside there until 1543, when he obtained it again. During his last ten years as Primate, Cranmer resided at Lambeth, Croydon, Beakesbourne and Ford.[1]

Morice describes at length the difficulties in which Cranmer was placed by Henry's insistence on these exchanges. The exchanges operated to Cranmer's disadvantage, if only because most of the lands which Cranmer received were leased to tenants under long leases at fixed rents, whereas the lands which Cranmer was forced to grant to the King were held by tenants on short leases, and could therefore be soon demised again at higher rents and for large fines payable on the granting of the lease. This was an important factor in a period of inflation. Morice was anxious, in his reminiscences of Cranmer which he wrote for Archbishop Parker, to defend Cranmer against the charge of having squandered the lands and revenues of his see. He states that before Cranmer was appointed Archbishop, he was required to agree to grant a ninety-nine years' lease of Wingham Barton to Anne Boleyn's Vice-Chamberlain, Sir Edward Baynton, but that after this he granted only short leases of twenty-one years or less, as this was more profitable to the see. He even went so far as to write to the Chapter of Christ Church Canterbury instructing them to refuse to confirm any lease which he might be compelled to grant for a term exceeding twenty-one years, which seems to have been a somewhat discreditable attempt to place the responsibility on the monks of Christ Church, who throughout the period from 1533

[1] 27 Hen. VIII, c. 34; 37 Hen. VIII, c. 16; Indentures and Grants of 31 July 1538 and 28 April 1540 (*L.P.*, xiii [i]. 1519 [68]; xv. 613 [32]; Stow, *Annals*, pp. 585–6; Hasted, *History of Kent*, vii. 434; ix. 227; Cranmer to Henry VIII, 18 February 1538 (Cranmer's *Works*, ii. 458, where it is wrongly dated 1541; see *L.P.*, xiii [i]. 310).

to the dissolution of the priory in 1540 were in any case in disfavour with the King.[1]

But the policy of granting short leases proved unsatisfactory for Cranmer, for by raising the value of the lands, it increased the desire of the King and his favourites to obtain them. Cranmer was therefore advised by James Hales and other barristers to grant leases for longer than twenty-one years in the hopes that it would make his lands less sought after. Thenceforth he deliberately granted long leases of many valuable lands in order to lower the value of the reversion; but this did not dissuade the greedy courtiers from inciting the King to make exchanges with Cranmer, and Henry continued to order Cranmer to make these exchanges until the end of his reign. Cranmer could hardly refuse to comply with Henry's wishes. It was Gardiner's refusal to agree to an exchange with Henry which led to his fall from power in 1546; and on the only occasion when Cranmer tried to oppose the King's claim to property, it immediately brought him a rebuke from Cromwell. In 1535, when all the nuns of Donnington, near Faversham, abandoned the nunnery, a dispute arose as to whether the lands of the nunnery were escheated to the Crown or to the see of Canterbury. Cromwell thereupon wrote to Cranmer that he would be sorry if the King should hear that Cranmer was opposing him in any matter. It was perhaps no coincidence that at the same time Cromwell instructed Latimer to write to Cranmer to reprimand him for his backwardness in preaching the royal supremacy in his diocese. Cranmer replied with dignity. 'And I am assured,' he wrote, 'the King's Grace's mind is, not to do wrong unto any subject he hath; and if I knew that it were his Grace's pleasure to have my title in the said lands, I would be more desirous to give it unto his Highness than he can be to have it. But for so much as I know not but his Grace would that I should have it, if my title be good, I must needs make my claim and declare my title; else I must lose it, be it never so just.' The property of the nunnery was escheated to the King, who eventually granted it to Sir Thomas Cheyney, the Lord Warden of the Five Ports.[2]

[1] Morice (*Nar. Ref.*, p. 264).
[2] Morice (*Nar. Ref.*, p. 265); Gardiner to Henry VIII; Gardiner to Paget, both 2 December 1546 (Muller, pp. 247–8); Cranmer to Cromwell, 17 October and 2 November 1535 (Cranmer's *Works*, ii. 312–4); Latimer to Cromwell, (25 October 1535) (Latimer's *Works*, ii. 370).

Morice, despite his respect for Henry VIII as a King, and his eagerness to show Henry's affection for Cranmer, does not conceal Henry's avarice and tyranny as regards the exchanges. He states that it was only thanks to Cranmer that any temporal revenues were retained by the see for the benefit of his successors. 'And I pray God,' wrote Morice to Parker about 1565, 'that they may maintain, in this mild and quiet time, that which he in a most dangerous world did uphold and left to his successors.' And Morice added: 'For as touching his exchanges men ought to consider with whom he had to do, specially with such a Prince as would not be bridled, nor be against said in any of his requests.' [1]

The secretary also tells of a conversation between Henry and Cranmer at which he was present, when Henry told Cranmer that he required his house at Knoll. As Cranmer wished to retain Knoll for himself, he suggested that it was too small, and that Henry might prefer to take his very large house at Otford, on which his predecessor Warham had spent the enormous sum of £30,000. Henry said that he preferred Knoll, because his health was affected when he was at Otford in low-lying ground; but as Knoll was small, he would have Otford as well as Knoll, so that his retinue could lodge in the unhealthy atmosphere of Otford when he himself stayed at Knoll. Cranmer consequently lost both these houses by the exchange of 30th November 1537. [2]

Cranmer was always in financial difficulties, and was obliged to sell some of his woods in order to pay his debts. When he was first appointed Archbishop, Henry granted him a loan of £1,000, and during the next few years Cranmer was periodically pressed by Cromwell to repay the money. In September 1535 Gostwick wrote 'sharp letters' to Cranmer on Cromwell's instructions demanding the immediate repayment of the money; but evidently both Cromwell and Henry viewed the matter leniently. In the summer of 1537, when the question of repayment was raised again, Cromwell persuaded Henry to give Cranmer a further period of grace. The debt was still unpaid in 1546; but by that time Cranmer, on his part, had lent Henry £1,000 as his contribution towards the forced loan for the French war, while Henry had paid over £2,000 to

---

[1] Morice (*Nar. Ref.*, pp. 264, 266).
[2] Morice (*Nar. Ref.*, p. 266); Collier, ix. 295.

Cranmer to compensate him for his losses in his exchanges.[1]

Cranmer's expenses as Archbishop were very great. In 1552, he wrote to Cecil that he found greater difficulty in living on his resources than he had done when he was a scholar at Cambridge, and in many of his letters he comments ruefully on his poverty. He was expected not only to entertain to dinner the members who sat with him on numerous Commissions, but also to provide alms and relief for a large number of dependents and licensed beggars. Owing to his financial difficulties, he may not have been able to do this on an appropriate scale, though Morice states that the rumour that Cranmer was parsimonious was maliciously circulated by covetous courtiers, who argued that Cranmer had more revenues than he required, and that more of his lands should be taken from him. Foxe says that they sometimes used the contrary argument that Cranmer's lavish entertainment showed that he had higher revenues than he required, and that the lands should be taken from him to curb his ostentation.[2]

Morice describes how Sir Thomas Seymour told Henry that Cranmer was failing to entertain in a manner befitting his station, because he was spending his revenues in providing for his wife and children. Seymour suggested that Cranmer and all the Bishops should be required to surrender their lands in return for a fixed salary—a proposal which was actually adopted in some cases under Edward VI. A month or so later—'whether it was of chance or of purpose it is unknown', writes Morice— Henry sent Seymour to Lambeth with a message for Cranmer at dinner time, and Seymour saw that Cranmer was entertaining a great number of people to dinner, providing four special courses for the chief officers of his household. When Seymour returned to Henry, he asked his pardon for having misinformed him as to Cranmer's style of living. Henry pointed out that if Parliament had been in session, or during the legal term,

---

[1] Morice (*Nar. Ref.*, p. 267); Warrants and payments, 6 February 1533, 20 March and 6 July 1541, 19 March 1542 and 25 July 1545; Gostwick to Cromwell, 11 and 27 September 1535; List of persons asked for money (summer 1544); List of the King's Debtors, (July 1546) (*L.P.*, vi. 131; ix. 341, 451; xvi. 745 (p. 361); xvii. 258 (p. 137, f. 51; p. 139, f. 56); xix [i]. 1032 [5]; xxi [i]. 643 (p. 319, f. 90), 1280 (p. 636); Record Office MSS., S.P. 1/96, p. 142; Cranmer to Cromwell, 31 August 1537 (Cranmer's *Works*, ii. 348).

[2] Cranmer to Cecil, 21 July 1552 (Cranmer's *Works*, ii. 437); Morice (*Nar. Ref.*, pp. 260, 267-8); Foxe, viii. 20.

Cranmer's entertainment would have been much more lavish, and he told Seymour that he had been used as a tool by unscrupulous courtiers who, having dissipated the revenues of the monastic lands which they had acquired, wished now to proceed to loot the lands of the Bishops. Henry said that he would never allow this to happen during his lifetime. Morice does not give the date of this episode, but it was probably at Easter 1538. He says that as a result, a project of introducing a bill in the next session of Parliament to seize the episcopal lands was abandoned.[1]

Despite all the disputes which have raged about Cranmer, it is universally agreed that he was pleasant and courteous in his conduct. Foxe credits Cranmer with the qualities which St. Paul prescribed as being necessary for a Bishop, and illustrates this with many examples. Even the author of *Bishop Cranmer's Recantacyons* gives him the credit for humility, gravity, and generosity, as well as courtesy, charm of manner, and a pleasant physical appearance. Osiander made almost exactly the same comment when he dedicated a book to Cranmer in 1537, and Bale also refers to his extraordinary charm. Apart from his habit of biting his lip when he was vexed, he never manifested anger or hatred. There was no trace of malice or desire for revenge in his character; and his friend Heath—who later became his opponent, and as Lord Chancellor issued the writ for the burning of Cranmer—once said that the way to win a favour at Cranmer's hands was by doing him an injury and then relenting a little. Cranmer, though not altogether pleased, admitted in effect that Heath's statement was true.[2]

Cranmer was on particularly friendly terms with the temporal lords and gentlemen with whom he had to do. The author of *Bishop Cranmer's Recantacyons* says that he secured his first appointment in the King's service by ingratiating himself with the nobility. This statement of a hostile writer is confirmed by

[1] Morice (*Nar. Ref.*, pp. 260–3); Foxe, viii. 20–22. The date of this incident can be fixed on the assumption that all the facts given by Morice are correct. It occurred after the first distribution of monastic lands, before Butts persuaded Henry to grant the Yorkshire estates to Cranmer, during a law vacation when Parliament was not in session, when the King was in the vicinity of London, when Seymour was at Court, and when Cranmer was in residence at Lambeth. It can therefore only have occurred during the Easter law vacation of 1538.

[2] Foxe, viii. 12–23; *Bishop Cranmer's Recantacyons*, pp. 3–4; Osiander, *Harmoniae Evangelicae*, Preface (1545 ed.) A. v; Bale's *Centuries*, f. 238 b.; Morice (*Nar. Ref.*, pp. 245–6); Warrant of 24 February 1556 (Burnet, v. 452–3).

a witness who at the time was far from hostile. In January 1533, Bonner wrote to Benet that Cranmer was 'a man, as ye know, of singular good learning, virtue, experience and all good parts', and added that he had been appointed Archbishop of Canterbury 'to the great comfort of the nobles of the realm, which favoureth him greatly'. We should expect that Cranmer, with his habitual courtesy and his respect for social rank, would show due deference to the nobles; but it is difficult to believe that he carried this to the point of subserviency, for there are too many instances of Cranmer refusing their suits. He raised objections to granting a divorce, not only to Kingston, but to Vaughan, who had escorted him through France in 1532, and to relieving a bar of consanguinity for an official for whom Cromwell intervened. He refused to grant dispensations to friends of powerful lords, and was well known for his troublesome scruples in this respect. He occasionally had disputes about property with important magnates, including Sir Christopher Hales, soon after he became Archbishop, and Sir Thomas Cheyney in 1552.[1]

Towards his social inferiors, Cranmer seems to have maintained the same courtesy and patience which he showed to his superiors and equals, though he would naturally take into account their difference of rank in his conduct. The only personal complaint against Cranmer from gentlemen and others who had to deal with him was his tendency to keep couriers waiting for several days for an interview or for a reply to letters, though once one of Cromwell's messengers complained of worse treatment at the hands of Cranmer and his servants. Morice says that Cranmer was greatly loved and respected by the servants of his household, and Foxe states that he never showed anger or called them 'fool' or 'knave', though this was a common practice among masters at the time.[2]

Among his equals and colleagues, Cranmer had many

[1] *Bishop Cranmer's Recantacyons*, p. 9; Bonner to Benet, 31 January 1533 (*St. Pap.*, vii. 411); Lord Herbert, *Henry VIII*, p. 347; Cranmer to Cromwell, 7 September 1536 and 14 March 1538; Cranmer to Cecil, 30 November 1552 (Cranmer's *Works*, ii. 328–9, 364, 441); Husee to Lisle, 30 April 1537; Vaughan to Paget, 7 March 1546 (*L.P.*, xii [i]. 1068; xxi [i]. 347); Morice (*Nar. Ref.*, p. 268).

[2] Worth to Lisle, 21 March 1534; Talbot to Cromwell, 14 October 1537; Husee to Lisle, 26 September 1538; Thistlethwaye to Sutton, 24 June 1539 (*L.P.*, vii. 350; xii [ii]. 906; xiii [ii]. 430; xiv [i]. 1153); Morice (*Nar. Ref.*, p. 268); Foxe, viii. 19.

friends, including some who were his religious opponents, such
as Thirlby. In 1534, Cranmer wrote a letter to Thirlby in which
he severely reprimanded him for his mismanagement in connexion with the submission of a document to the King, and made
aspersions on Thirlby's motives as well as on his efficiency; but
later Cranmer and Thirlby became intimate. Morice states that
if Thirlby admired some dish or other object which belonged to
Cranmer, Cranmer would always insist on giving it to him.
Foxe suggests that when Thirlby admired Cranmer's dishes, he
was deliberately seeking a gift; but when Foxe published this,
Thirlby, who was still living, had disgraced himself by participating, though with reluctance, in Cranmer's degradation
from holy orders.[1]

Cranmer was obviously on terms of close friendship with
Cromwell. Several of Cranmer's modern biographers, who
persist in portraying Cranmer as a subservient coward and
Cromwell as a ruthless chief of the secret police, have suggested that Cranmer was afraid of Cromwell, or even that
Cromwell was blackmailing Cranmer by threatening to reveal
his secret marriage. This is certainly wrong. Cranmer's letters
to Cromwell show not only a political collaboration, but friendship and intimacy. There is only one short period during the
autumn of 1535—soon after Cromwell had first begun to exercise his powers as Vicegerent—when there are signs of a certain
tension between them. It was during this period that Cromwell
told Latimer to write to Cranmer remonstrating at his slackness
in preaching the royal supremacy, that he reprimanded Cranmer
for claiming his rights with regard to the nunnery of Donnington, and that his subordinates were writing 'sharp letters'
to Cranmer demanding the immediate repayment of the money
which Cranmer owed the King. In 1539, Cromwell told Cranmer that he had sometimes complained to Henry about
Cranmer's conduct, but that Henry had refused to listen; he
was probably referring to the autumn of 1535. But the antagonism soon passed, and after the fall of Anne Boleyn in the
summer of 1536 their friendship seems to have been stronger
than ever. The clearest proof of their friendship, which com-

---

[1] Morice to Day the printer, 10 January (probably about 1565) (Ellis, *Letters
of Literary Men*, p. 26); Cranmer to Thirlby, 24 May 1534 (Cranmer's *Works*,
ii. 292–3); Foxe, viii. 71–72.

pletely disproves the theory that Cranmer was afraid of Cromwell, is the fact that the two men confided incriminating secrets to each other. In August 1538, Cranmer wrote a letter to Cromwell in which he expressed his doubts as to the truth of transubstantiation, which was a daring admission even in the heyday of the Henrician Reformation. According to Foxe, Cromwell was almost as communicative to Cranmer with regard to his disreputable youth.[1]

But Cranmer had other friends who were closer than Cromwell—friends with whom he removed the mask which he wore with everyone else. We know of their existence from Morice. 'It is to be noted,' wrote the secretary to Parker about Cranmer, 'that he was a man of such temperature of nature, or rather so mortified, that no manner of prosperity or adversity could alter or change his accustomed conditions; for being the storms never so terrible or odious, nor the prosperous estate of the time never so pleasant, joyous or acceptable, to the face of the world his countenance, diet or sleep commonly never altered or changed, so that they which were most nearest and conversant about him never or seldom perceived by no sign or token of countenance how the affairs of the Prince or the realm went. Notwithstanding, privately with his secret and special friends he would shed forth many bitter tears, lamenting the miseries and calamities of the world.'[2]

This is one of the most interesting passages in Morice's letter to Parker. Cranmer had secret and special friends to whom he confided his grief at public affairs—his grief, presumably, at such things as the proclamations against the marriage of priests, at the Six Articles, at the fall of Cromwell and the burning of Barnes, at the ban on the reading of the Bible. The secret has been preserved to the present time, and it is impossible to identify these friends, though obviously Morice himself was one of them. We cannot know which of the men with whom Cranmer collaborated closely were included among his secret friends, and which were among those nearest and conversant about him to whom he gave not the slightest sign of what he was thinking about public events. The secret

---

[1] Cranmer to Cromwell, 2 November 1535 and 15 August 1538 (Cranmer's *Works*, ii. 313–14, 375–6); Latimer to Cromwell (25 October 1535) (Latimer's *Works*, ii. 370); Morice (*Nar. Ref.*, pp. 258–9); Foxe, v. 365.

[2] Morice (*Nar. Ref.*, pp. 244–5).

friends perhaps included his brother Edmund, his Commissary Nevinson, his chaplains Champion, Nicholas Ridley, and Becon, and perhaps Heath, until he went over to the conservatives in 1540. In later years, they may have included his foreign guests Peter Martyr and Bucer when they were at Lambeth, though at that time Cranmer had less reason to shed bitter tears at the course of public affairs. But the only person, apart from Morice, whom we can definitely identify as one of the secret friends is the Scottish reformer Aless. In view of the statements in Aless' letter to Elizabeth in 1559, there is no doubt that Cranmer told him his most secret griefs about political and religious developments during the period when Aless was in England between 1536 and 1539.[1]

Perhaps the greatest of these griefs was the position of his wife. The secret of the marriage was extraordinarily well kept. It is remarkable that among all the accusations made against Cranmer by malicious rumour-mongers throughout the country, there is not a single reference to Margaret's existence—at least, not in any document which has been preserved. Neither Chapuys nor the Yorkshire or Lincolnshire rebels had heard a word about her; while the rebels were falsely accusing Cranmer of having been an ostler and not having received a pall, the damning truth of the second marriage was quite unknown to them. One of the rebels later confessed that he had made up a rhyme about Cranmer, to the effect that Cranmer would always be happy as long as he had an apple and a woman to play with; but the evidence against him showed plainly that his rhyme had in fact referred, not to Cranmer, but to the King. In 1539, the reformers were accusing Gardiner of taking two lewd women around with him disguised in men's clothes; but no counter-charges of immorality were made against Cranmer. It was only after 1549, when the marriage was made public, that there was talk about Cranmer's wife; and it seems to have been generally thought that he had only recently married her. Even a reformer like Stumphius did not know that he had married her seventeen years before; in June 1550, he wrote to Bullinger that Cranmer 'has lately married a wife'. Yet a number of persons knew about Margaret during Henry's reign. In Morice's story of Thomas Seymour's

[1] Aless to Elizabeth I, 1 September 1559 (*Cal. For. Pap. Eliz.*, i. 1303, pp. 528, 533).

allegations against Cranmer, he states that Cranmer's parsimony was attributed to the fact that he was saving money to buy lands for his wife and children; and if there is any truth at all in Harpsfield's story about Margaret in the chest and the fire at Canterbury, her existence must have been known to the gentlemen of Cranmer's household in 1543.[1]

Henry certainly knew about Cranmer's marriage, and although he always strongly condemned the marriage of the clergy, he permitted Cranmer to keep Margaret with him. It has been suggested that Cranmer told Henry that he had a wife when he was first made Archbishop of Canterbury; but it is very unlikely that he admitted to this indiscretion and breach of the canon law at that time. His obvious course was to keep silence on the reasonable assumption that if the authorities discovered about Margaret, they would think that she was his mistress, and extend to him the same indulgence which had been shown to Wolsey and to so many other prelates and priests.

But if this was the position in 1533, it was very different a few years later, when the celibacy of the clergy had become a real issue between the orthodox and the reformers. As soon as some of the sinners began to justify their sin, it was no longer possible for the authorities to overlook it. The first step against the married priests was taken in November 1536 to placate the rebels of the Pilgrimage of Grace. The King wrote a letter to all the Bishops in which he stated that he had heard that some priests had presumed to marry, and that all such priests who continued to exercise their priestly functions were either to be sent up to the Council or arrested by the Bishops. The rebel leaders rejoiced when Norfolk told them at Doncaster about this letter, particularly when he emphasized that it had been sent to Cranmer; though here again there is no indication that they even suspected that Cranmer himself was married. Two years later, Henry issued a more severe proclamation against married priests, punishing with imprisonment any who married after the date of the proclamation. In the summer of 1539 came the Act of the Six Articles, which imposed the punishment of

[1] Examination of Myddleton (March 1537) (*L.P.*, xii [i]. 784); Luther, Melanchthon and others to John Frederick of Saxony, 23 October 1539 (*Corpus Ref.*, iii. 799); Stumphius to Bullinger, 1 June 1550 (*Orig. Letters*, p. 466); Morice (*Nar. Ref.*, p. 260); Harpsfield, *The Pretended Divorce*, p. 275.

death by hanging on priests and their wives who continued to cohabit. A year later, an amending Act reduced the penalties to imprisonment and forfeiture of benefices and goods. After the Act of the Six Articles was passed, Cranmer sent his wife to her relations in Germany. Foxe states that Cranmer kept Margaret at his side throughout the whole time that the Six Articles were in force; but Parker, who was in as good a position to know as Foxe, is so categorical about Margaret's departure for Germany that it cannot be doubted. It would have been an enormous risk for Cranmer to keep Margaret with him after July 1539, when they were both liable to be hanged if they did not separate.[1]

In May 1543, the Prebendaries of Canterbury denounced Cranmer to the King as a heretic. It was on this occasion that Henry summoned Cranmer to his barge on the Thames, and in the course of the conversation asked him whether he considered that his bedchamber was exempt from the Six Articles. Cranmer then admitted that he had married when he was Ambassador in Germany, but explained that he had put away his wife and sent her back to Germany to comply with the Act of the Six Articles. Henry told Cranmer that he would not subject him to any punishment, and gave him a commission to examine and punish the Prebendaries who had denounced him.[2] It was probably as a result of what Henry said on this occasion that Cranmer decided that it was safe for Margaret to return to England. Apart from Foxe's statement that Margaret lived with Cranmer with Henry's permission while the Six Articles were in force, there is confirmation from other sources that they were cohabiting during the period after May 1543. All the evidence suggests that she was away in Germany for four years—from the summer of 1539 to the summer of 1543—and then resumed the hidden existence at Cranmer's side which she had led from 1533 to 1539. By this time, the provisions in the Act of the Six Articles against married priests were no longer being enforced.

The most famous thing about Cranmer's wife is the curious story of the chest. Within a few months of Cranmer's death,

[1] Henry VIII to the Bishops, 19 November 1536 (Wilkins, iii. 826); Proclamation of 16 November 1538 (Strype, *Cranmer*, p. 691); Darcy to Archbishop Lee, 18 December 1536 (*L.P.*, xi. 1336); 31 Hen. VIII, c. 14; 32 Hen. VIII, c. 10; Foxe, viii. 34, 44; Parker, pp. 390, 393.

[2] Parker, pp. 392–3. Morice (*Nar. Ref.*, p. 252) and Foxe (viii. 28–29) do not mention the conversation about Margaret in their accounts of the interview on the barge.

the author of *Bishop Cranmer's Recantacyons* was writing that
when Cranmer travelled from place to place, he carried with
him his wife hidden in a chest. About a year later, Nicholas
Harpsfield was giving more precise information about the chest
in his *Pretended Divorce of Catherine of Aragon*. 'The Archbishop
of Canterbury was married in King Henry's days, but kept his
woman very close, and sometime carried her about with him in
a great chest full of holes, that his pretty nobsey might take
breath at. In the meanwhile it so chanced that his palace at
Canterbury was set on fire; but Lord, what a stir and care was
there for this pretty nobsey, and for this chest; all other care in
a manner was set aside. He caused that chest with all speed to
be conveyed out of danger, and gave great charge of it, crying
out that his evidences and other writings which he esteemed
above any worldly treasure were in that chest; and this I heard
out of the mouth of a gentleman that was there present, and
knew of this holy mystery.'[1]

During the next fifty years, the story of Mrs. Cranmer in the
chest became part of the stock in trade of every Papist writer.
Sanders confined himself to a general reference to the chest in
his *Anglican Schism* in 1576; but in 1603 Parsons, in *Three
Conversions of England*, had a new story to tell. 'When he went
from London to Canterbury, it happened that at Gravesend,
where the Bishop [Cranmer] lay one night, his chests were
brought a land and put in a gallery. And this among other being
much recommended to the shipmen, as containing precious stuff,
belonging to my Lord's Grace, they severed it from the rest
and put it up end long against the wall in my Lord's chamber,
with the woman's head downward, which putting her in jeopardy to break her neck, she was forced at length to cry out.
And so the chamberlains, perceiving the error, took her forth
foully disfigured, and as good as half dead. This is a most
certain story, and testified at this day by Cranmer's son's
widow, yet living, to divers gentlemen, her friends, from whom
myself had it.'[2]

Thus Parsons states that he heard this story at second-hand
from Catherine Rogers, who married Cranmer's son Thomas

---

[1] *Bishop Cranmer's Recantacyons*, p. 8; Harpsfield, *The Pretended Divorce*,
p. 275.

[2] Sanders, *The Anglican Schism*, p. 181; Parsons, *Three Conversions of England*,
ii. 371.

as her second husband some time after 1576, when her first
husband died. It is very unlikely that she ever met Margaret,
who probably died about this date, and who for some years
prior to this had been on very bad terms with her son, with
whom she had engaged in litigation. Catherine might have
heard about the Gravesend incident, if it occurred, from her
husband, though he was probably not yet born at the time. But
Sir John Harington wrote in 1608 in his *Nugae Antiquae* that he
himself had questioned Catherine, who was related to his wife,
concerning the story which Parsons had told about her mother-
in-law in the chest, and she had sworn that she had never heard
the story or repeated it to anyone. This throws grave doubts
on the truth of Parsons' story.[1]

Harpsfield's story about the chest must be taken more
seriously. He recorded the Canterbury incident only fourteen
years after it was alleged to have taken place, for it was in
December 1543 that Cranmer's palace was burned. As this was
seven months after Cranmer's talk with Henry about his
marriage, Margaret had probably already returned from Germany. Harpsfield's story is repeated, not like Parsons' at fourth
hand, but only at second-hand, for he writes that he himself
heard it from a gentleman who was actually present. But though
Harpsfield makes a vague assertion that this gentleman knew
that Mrs. Cranmer was in the chest, the only concrete information which the gentleman gave Harpsfield was the words which
Cranmer spoke at the time of the fire. Cranmer insisted that the
chest be conveyed out of danger before anything else, and said
that 'his evidences and other writings which he esteemed above
any worldly treasure were in that chest'. The most likely explanation is that Cranmer was speaking the truth—that the
chest contained depositions in judicial cases, rare books and
manuscripts of Cranmer's writings which he was particularly
eager to save from the fire. But if some of the gentlemen who
were present knew about Margaret, they might well have made
jocular remarks to the effect that the treasure which Cranmer
valued above all else was his woman. This would be enough
to start the rumour that Margaret was carried about in a
chest, and to lead to the later inventions about the holes in the
chest and the porters at Gravesend. The whole story of the chest

---

[1] Waters, *Chesters of Chicheley*, p. 395; Harington, *Nugae Antiquae*, i. 3–4.

probably originated in Cranmer's solicitude for his papers during the fire at Canterbury.

But if Cranmer was never obliged to resort to the unpleasant procedure of putting his wife in a chest, he was certainly compelled to keep her existence a close secret for sixteen years; and Sanders may well be right in saying that this was Cranmer's greatest grief during Henry's reign. During all the long controversies and the threats to his position and safety, there was the continual anxiety that the fatal secret might leak out. It may have been something of a relief when this actually occurred in 1543, for having seen how Henry reacted to the situation, Cranmer could feel much safer in future. But it was not until 1549 that he could proclaim to the world that he was a married man, and that Margaret could openly sit as hostess at his table. The common people were as shocked by the marriage of priests as by any of the radical doctrinal changes of Edward VI; and the most striking illustration that Protestant England permitted the marriage of priests was the example set by the Archbishop of Canterbury in marrying himself, which made a great impression abroad as well as in England. After Mary's accession, the married priests were singled out from among the reformers for particularly harsh treatment. The people were now taught that Cranmer and Archbishop Holgate had 'led this holy harlot's dance', and Cranmer was vilified at his trial and in the official propaganda after his death as a monster of lust and concupiscence.[1]

He was at least spared the experience of seeing Margaret become a victim of Mary's government. She escaped to Germany, where she married Edward Whitchurch, the printer, with whom Cranmer had been in contact in connexion with the printing of the English Bible as early as 1537. They returned to England after Mary's death. Whitchurch died in 1561, and three years later Margaret married Bartholemew Scott, a Justice of the Peace for Surrey, at Camberwell. Margaret was still living in 1571, but she probably died soon after. She had no children by her last two husbands; but she bore a son and a daughter to Cranmer. The daughter, Margaret, was living in

---

[1] Sanders, *The Anglican Schism*, p. 181; 'Processus contra Thomam Cranmer' (Cranmer's *Works*, ii. 550); Barbaro's Report to the Venetian Senate, (May 1551) (*Ven. Cal.*, v. 703 [p. 348]); Harpsfield, *The Pretended Divorce*, p. 275.

1563, having married Thomas Norton, the lawyer, Member of Parliament and dramatist; but she had died childless before 1568, for by this year Norton was already married to Edmund Cranmer's daughter Alice, who was his second wife. The son, Thomas, was probably younger than his sister. Jewel referred to him as a 'boy' in 1559, while Foxe mentioned in the first edition of his *Book of Martyrs* in 1563 that the son was still young—a statement which he omitted from the second edition of 1570; and there is other evidence that Thomas was born after Margaret returned to England in 1543, and probably only a few years before Cranmer settled his Yorkshire estates in Thomas's favour in 1551. Cranmer is said to have had another daughter named Anne, but this is probably wrong, for though it is very possible that he had other children who died in infancy, it seems clear that only Thomas and Margaret survived to adult life.[1]

The Yorkshire estates were to cause friction and litigation between Margaret and her son. Cranmer settled the freehold reversion of his lands at Kirkstall in one of those complicated transactions which were rendered necessary by the existing state of English law. He granted the land to trustees to hold in trust for himself for his life, and thereafter to grant a lease for twenty years from his death to his Executors, who were to hold it on the trusts to be declared in his will. Subject to these grants, he devised the property to his son in tail. After Cranmer's conviction for high treason, the land was forfeited to the Crown; and in June 1557 Mary granted a lease of the property to two lessees. In December 1559, Elizabeth granted to Cranmer's son the right to receive the rent from these lessees, including the rent which they had already paid to the Crown;

---

[1] *Coll. Top.*, iii. 145 and n.; Strype, *Cranmer*, p. 600; Waters, *Chesters of Chicheley*, pp. 387, 389; Jewel to Peter Martyr, 26 January 1559 (*Zurich Letters*, English, p. 8, Latin p. 4) where 'Cranmerus puer' is certainly Cranmer's son; Foxe, viii. 43–44 (1st ed., p. 1478). Waters (op. cit., p. 387) states that Cranmer had a second daughter named Anne, who died young and unmarried during Cranmer's lifetime; and he is followed by Pollard (*Thomas Cranmer*, p. 327 n.). But the only authority for Waters' statement is the pedigree notes of Vincent the herald in the reign of James I (Vincent MS. (College of Arms) No. 105, f. 12), who states merely that Cranmer had two children, Thomas and Anne. As Thomas and Margaret were the only two surviving children of the Archbishop when the statute of 1563 was enacted, Waters apparently deduced that Anne had died before this date; but it is more likely that Vincent was mistaken as to the name of Cranmer's only daughter. It is probably no coincidence that this mistake is precisely the same as that which has arisen as to the name of Cranmer's wife.

but at about the same time, Margaret and her husband Whit-church acquired the property from the lessees. In 1571, Thomas the son brought an action for ejectment against his mother, the action being nominally fought between the lessees of the two parties in accordance with the usual legal fiction of the period. As Cranmer had been unable, as a convicted traitor, to make a will and appoint executors, the lease of twenty years from his death was void; but Margaret based her title on her purchase of the land from Mary's grantees. Her son was successful in his argument that the land had never lawfully been forfeited to the Crown as the legal estate had been vested in the trustees, and not in Cranmer, at the time of the forfeiture. It would appear that Thomas ejected his aged mother from the property by relying on a highly technical point of law, although there can be no doubt that Cranmer had intended Margaret to enjoy the benefit of the property for twenty years from his death; but it is impossible to ascertain the full truth behind the summary of the facts in the law reports. There is reason to believe that Thomas was a disreputable character. In 1571, he was summoned before the Ecclesiastical Court of the diocese of York to answer charges of fornication, and four years later he was charged before the same Court with having committed adultery with the wife of Thomas Bawick. He died without issue in 1598, and Cranmer's line became extinct.[1]

[1] For Cranmer's settlement of 10 June 1551 and the litigation, see *Cal. Pat. Rolls, Edw. VI*, iii. 321; *Ph. & Mary*, iii. 483–4; *Eliz.*, i. 417; Thomas Cranmer the son to Elizabeth I (undated) (Todd, *Archbishop Cranmer*, ii. 515–8); Cranmer's Case (1572) 2 Leo. 5; 3 Leo. 20; Dyer, 309a; Moore, 100; 1 And. 19; Waters, *Chesters of Chicheley*, pp. 384–5, 394–6; Pollard, *Thomas Cranmer*, p. 327 n. There seems to be no reason for Waters and Pollard to believe that Margaret Cranmer died about 1571.

CHAPTER X

THE NEGOTIATIONS WITH THE LUTHERANS

EVERY year, the greater feast of St. Thomas of Canterbury—whose martyrdom in the cathedral was still represented on Cranmer's seal—was celebrated on 7th July. The royal Injunctions of August 1536 had abrogated, with a few exceptions, all holy days falling in harvest time between 1st July and Michaelmas; and on 6th July 1537, Cranmer ate meat in his parlour with his household to make it known that he was not observing the usual fast on the eve of a holy day. A monk of St. Augustine's in Canterbury recorded in his chronicle that such a thing had never been seen before. When Cranmer went to his diocese at the end of July, after completing work on the Bishops' Book, he punished several persons who were still observing the suppressed holy days.[1]

As the suppression of these feast days was unpopular, Cranmer wrote to Cromwell suggesting that the duty of suppressing them should everywhere be left to the Bishops. 'I would fain that all the envy and grudge of the people in this matter should be put from the King and his Council; and that we, which be Ordinaries, should take it upon us; or else I fear lest a grudge against the Prince and his Council, in such causes of religion, should gender in many of the people's hearts a faint subjection and obedience.' He then mentioned that abrogated holy days and fast days were still being kept at Court.[2] He was as ready to point out that breaches of the law at Court were weakening respect for the King's laws as he was to take upon himself and his brother Bishops the odium of enforcing unpopular laws in order to safeguard the King's reputation.

In October 1537, Cranmer engaged in an acrimonious correspondence with a prominent dignitary of Kent who cannot be

[1] Resolution of Convocation, 19 July 1536; Henry VIII's proclamation, 11 August 1536 (Wilkins, iii. 823–4); Chronicle of monk of St. Augustine's (*Nar. Ref.*, p. 285); Strype, *Cranmer*, pp. 86–7; Cranmer to Cromwell, 28 August 1537 (Cranmer's *Works*, ii. 346–7).

[2] Cranmer to Cromwell, 28 August 1537, op. cit.

definitely identified. The man was certainly a Justice of the
Peace for Kent, and Cranmer appears to indicate, in one of his
letters, that he was a member of the Privy Council.[1] It has been
suggested that it was Sir Thomas Cheyney, the Lord Warden
of the Cinque Ports; Sir John Baker, the Attorney-General;
Sir Christopher Hales, the Master of the Rolls; Sir Thomas
Moyle, who later became Speaker of the House of Commons;
or Sir Anthony St. Leger, who became Lord Deputy of
Ireland. Both St. Leger and Moyle are excluded, for they
were serving on a Commission in Ireland in October 1537.
The identity of Cranmer's correspondent seems to be limited
to Cheyney, Baker or Hales. Baker is perhaps the more
likely.

Cranmer began the correspondence with a letter in stern
language, in which he accused the dignitary of failing to enforce
the King's ordinances for the suppression of Popery, of threatening the people in Kent with punishment if they read the Bible,
and of permitting his servants to say that the Bishops' Book had
put 'all the knaves of the new learning to silence'. Cranmer
wrote that these words were as seditious as the activities of the
rebels of Lincolnshire, and claimed that the Reformation was
restoring the old usage of the primitive Church: 'Truly you
and your sorts be so blinded, that you call old that is new and
new that is old.' He informed the dignitary that if it were not
for the favour which he bore him, he would proceed against his
servants as heretics if they would maintain either pilgrimages,
Purgatory, images or Saints, merits or works as they had been
taught and used in the last two or three hundred years. The
dignitary rejected Cranmer's accusations. Cranmer then wrote
a second letter in a more conciliatory tone, denying that he had
meant to compare the dignitary to the rebels of Lincolnshire.
This encouraged the dignitary to be more defiant, and his
second letter to Cranmer was harsher than the first. Here
Cranmer showed his lack of ability in dealing with a high-
ranking adherent of the old religion, imbued with all the self-
confidence derived from his social position and the orthodoxy

[1] Cranmer wrote to the dignitary that the King 'hath called you to so high
estimation as to be reputed one of his council' (Cranmer's *Works*, ii. 351). For the
correspondence, see Cranmer's *Works*, ii. 349–56. For the whereabouts of Hales,
St. Leger and Moyle, see *L.P.*, xii [ii]. 873; *St. Pap.*, ii. 452, sqq. For Baker's
activities against reformers, see *L.P.*, xviii [ii]. 546, p. 353.

of his opinions. After beginning on a note of high censure, and even threatening the dignitary's servants with a heresy trial, he ended on the defensive against the dignitary's denunciations. It was symptomatic of the weakness which Cranmer always showed towards the established order.

Cranmer was too merciful and too weak for the task of breaking the resistance of the Papists. He preferred to forgive rather than to punish, partly because forgiveness was a Christian duty and in accordance with his nature, and partly because he believed that appeasement was a better policy than intimidation. He adopted this attitude in the case of the Yorkshire parson which is related by Morice and Foxe. If Foxe's additions to Morice's story are correct, the incident probably occurred in the summer of 1538.[1] The parish priest, while drinking in an inn near Scarborough, persisted in declaring that Cranmer was an ostler who had no more learning than the goslings who were strutting on the green outside the inn. He was arrested and brought before the Council at a meeting which Cranmer did not attend, and was sent to the Fleet, where he lingered for two months. His uncle, who was a grocer in London and supplied the father of one of Cranmer's gentlemen with spices and fruit, interceded with Cranmer on behalf of the parson, who was brought before Cranmer under the vine tree in the garden at Lambeth. At first the parson asserted his innocence; but when Cranmer threatened to send him back to the Fleet if he persisted in this attitude, he confessed his guilt and asked for pardon. Cranmer then offered to prove that he was not ignorant by answering any question which the parson might put to him on divinity, philosophy or grammar, or on any of the other sciences. The parson, in great embarrassment, declined to do this; and Cranmer then said that as the parson would not test him, he would test the parson on his knowledge of the English Bible. But the parson did not know who was the father of either

---

[1] Morice (*Nar. Ref.*, pp. 269–72); Foxe, viii. 15–19. If Foxe is correct in stating that the conversation took place under the vine tree, it must have been during the summer. Both Morice and Foxe make it clear that it was after the publication of the English Bible and before the fall of Cromwell. This limits it to the summers of 1538 or 1539, or the early summer of 1540. The summer of 1538 is most likely, as neither Morice nor Foxe states that it was at the time of the Six Articles or the fall of Cromwell. For another case in which Cranmer intervened to ask pardon for a priest who had slandered him, see Cranmer to (probably) Audley, (April 1534) (Cranmer's *Works*, ii. 291–2).

David or Solomon, and was thus made aware of his ignorance and presumption. Cranmer pointed out that if he had had no more learning than a gosling, the King would not have sent him to argue before the Pope in the Rotta and as Ambassador to the Emperor. In the eyes of a man as loyal as Cranmer, there could be no better criterion of scholarship.

In view of the parson's submissive attitude, Cranmer ordered him to be released and sent back to his parish in Yorkshire. When Cromwell heard of the incident a few days later, he told Cranmer that he had been too lenient, and suggested that the parson should make a public recantation at Paul's Cross. Cranmer disagreed, and said that everyone who heard the recantation would think that the rumour about his being an ostler was true. Cromwell asked how many blockheads would believe this foolish story. 'Too many Papists,' said Cranmer. He then argued that the parson, who had been put to great expense during his imprisonment, should not also suffer the shame of a public recantation. Cromwell reluctantly agreed, but said: 'But I warrant you, one day, if they may, they will make you and me both as vile as ostlers.' It is clear that both mercy and timidity influenced Cranmer in this case. He took pity on the parson, but he also feared that 'too many Papists' would believe the slander. Cranmer seems always to have been restrained from taking bold measures by his awareness that there were 'too many Papists'.

He also, however, showed leniency towards the reformer Harridaunce, a Whitechapel bricklayer who had erected a tub in his garden from which he preached about Scripture to the passers-by. Harridaunce, who had no preaching license, was brought before Cranmer in the summer of 1538; but Cranmer, finding that Harridaunce had said nothing heretical, merely prohibited him from continuing to preach. Harridaunce was treated more harshly a few months later when, having resumed his preaching, he was tried for heresy and forced to carry his fagot at Paul's Cross.[1]

Cranmer spent most of the winter of 1537–8 at Ford, where he dealt with several cases of sedition, and during Lent gave a series of lectures at Canterbury on Paul's Epistle to the Hebrews; but he came to Court to participate in a number of

[1] Wriothesley, i. 82–83, 93.

public duties. He was present at the christening of Prince Edward at Hampton Court on 15th October, when he and Norfolk were godfathers at the font, with the Lady Mary as godmother. Queen Jane died twelve days after the birth of her son, and Cranmer played a leading part in the funeral solemnities, riding behind the corpse from Hampton Court to Windsor with his cross borne before him, side by side with Chapuys. In March, he was one of the English representatives who negotiated with Chapuys and Don Diego de Mendoza about the projected marriages of Henry to the Duchess of Milan and of Mary to Don Luis of Portugal; but Cranmer and his colleagues put forward such exhorbitant conditions for the marriages that the projects fell through.[1]

The breakdown of the marriage negotiations and the conclusion of peace between Charles V and Francis I led to the almost complete isolation of England, and the danger of war and a Crusade against England loomed large. Cranmer's role as a receiver of intelligence from abroad became even more important. He heard from his spy in Ghinucci's service that the Pope was attempting to organize a revolt in Ireland; he discovered that the cellarer of Christ Church priory, who had disappeared some eighteen months before, had been on a secret mission to Rome; he heard from Osiander about the diplomatic negotiations in Germany, and from Theabold in Italy about Pole's activities. In September 1538, Theabold made an unfortunate slip. He decided to send Cromwell some Italian verses which he had been shown vilifying the Pope and the Emperor, but in error he also enclosed some equally uncomplimentary verses about Cromwell himself. Theabold discovered his mistake, and hastily sought the assistance of Cranmer,

---

[1] Cranmer to Cromwell, 14 and 29 January 1538; Examinations of Bucke and others, (January 1538) (*L.P.*, xiii [i]. 76; Cranmer's *Works*, ii. 361; this letter of 14 January is not printed either by Jenkyns or the Parker Society, though both print another letter from Cranmer to Cromwell written on the same day); Chronicle of monk of St. Augustine's (*Nar. Ref.*, p. 286). For the description of the christening of Edward VI and the funeral of Jane Seymour, see 'The Christynnyng of Prince Edward' (Nichols, *Literary Remains of Edward VI*, pp. cclv–cclxii); *London Chronicle* (*Camden Misc. No. IV*, p. 11); Wriothesley, i. 70–71; Husee to Lisle; Husee to Lady Lisle, both 16 October 1537; 'Remembrance of the interment of Queen Jane' (*L.P.*, xii [ii]. 922, 923, 1060). For the royal marriage negotiations, see the Council to Gardiner, 31 March 1538; Instructions of March 1538; Chapuys to Mary of Hungary, 13 April 1538 (*L.P.*, xiii [i]. 628, 640, 756; xiii [ii]. App. 15; *Span. Cal.*, v [ii]. 223); Cromwell to Wyatt, 4 April 1538 (Merriman, ii. 133).

begging him to ask Cromwell to overlook the offence.[1]

Cranmer corresponded with foreign theologians. In the autumn of 1536, he wrote to Bucer, and received a reply which must have pleased him by its lavish praise of Henry. He also wrote a courteous letter to Vadian, though he would certainly have burned the Swiss reformer if he had advocated in England the opinions against the Real Presence which he expressed in the book which he sent to Cranmer. Cranmer told Vadian that he had read everything which Zwingli and Oecolampadius had written against the Real Presence, but that he would continue to believe in the doctrine unless he were shown far more persuasive authorities than any which they had produced, because there were far more passages from the Fathers in favour of the Real Presence than against it, and it was impossible to believe that Christ would have permitted His Church to remain for so long in error. About the same time, he wrote to Capito.[2]

Cranmer did not play an active part in the campaign against relics in 1538. The daring and provocative policy of publicly exhibiting the relics for ridicule and destruction was not in keeping with Cranmer's tactics, and it is not surprising to find Hilsey and Latimer being more prominent than Cranmer in the attack on superstition. But Cranmer certainly approved of the suppression of relics. In August 1538, he imparted to Cromwell his suspicions that the blood of St. Thomas in Christ Church, Canterbury, was really red ochre, and he urged Cromwell to investigate it. In September, to the indignation of Papist Europe, twenty carts carried away the loot from the shrine, and Becket's bones were burned.[3]

[1] Memorandum on information sent to Cranmer, undated; Theabold to Cranmer, 16 August and 1 October 1538; Theabold to Cromwell, 1 October 1538 (*L.P.*, xiii [i]. 77; xiii [ii]. 117, 507, 509); Cranmer to Cromwell, 16 February and 9 October 1537 and 3 and 15 August 1538 (Cranmer's *Works*, ii. 334, 356, 373–5); Osiander to Cranmer, 24 January 1538 (Pocock, ii. 483–6, where it is wrongly dated 1533).

[2] Bucer to Cranmer, 23 October 1537 (*Orig. Letters*, pp. 520–2, where it is wrongly dated 1538); Cranmer to Capito; Cranmer to Vadian (Cranmer's *Works*, ii. 340–4, where both letters are dated 1537). Gairdner (in *L.P.*, xv. 137) gives January 1540 as the date of the letter to Vadian; but he was wrong in believing that the book which Vadian sent to Cranmer was that which was published in 1539. The book in question was written in 1535–6; and Cranmer's letter to Vadian appears from the contents to have been written at the end of December 1537 (see Näf, *Vadian*, ii. 432, 441). His letter to Capito was probably written in August or September 1537.

[3] Cranmer to Cromwell, 18 August 1538 (Cranmer's *Works*, ii. 378); Payments to labourers demolishing Becket's tomb (September 1538); Mayor of Dover and others to Cheyney, 3 June 1539 (*L.P.*, xiii [ii]. 1280 [p. 534, f. 34 b.]; xiv [i]. 1073).

In the spring of 1538, Cranmer was concerned in a project for the revision of the Church service books. It has been suggested that it was at this time that he compiled his first great draft of the Liturgy; but there is no real evidence of this. We know only that Cromwell's chaplain Malet visited Cranmer at Ford, and remained there working on the draft of a new Liturgy after Cranmer had returned to Croydon in March. In April, Cranmer wrote to Cromwell that he wished to meet Malet again 'for further furtherance and final finishing of that we have begun'. It appears from Cranmer's letter that it was Cromwell who had instructed Malet to perform this work, and that once again it was Cromwell, not Cranmer, who was prepared to take another great step forward in the Reformation by initiating the idea of a revision of the Liturgy.[1]

In May 1538, the authorities took the novel step of proceeding against a Papist on a charge of heresy. The aged friar Forest, who had been Catherine of Aragon's confessor, had been convicted of high treason some years before for refusing to take the oath of supremacy; but he subsequently agreed to take the oath. Forest was neither executed nor pardoned, but was detained in prison, where he used his position of confessor to the other prisoners to urge them to remain true to the old faith. He could have been executed under the old sentence for treason; but it was decided to treat his offences as heresy, though four years before the official policy had been that the repudiation of Papal authority did not involve any doctrinal deviations from the faith of the Church of Rome.

Forest was tried for heresy at Lambeth on 8th May before Cranmer and other Commissioners. He was charged with believing that the Holy Catholic Church of the Creed was the Church of Rome, that Becket and Fisher had suffered for the Church, that he owed a double obedience both to the King and to the Pope, and with believing in the efficacy of Papal pardons and the old orthodox doctrine of Purgatory. Forest abjured all these heresies at his trial, and was sentenced to make a public recantation at Paul's Cross; but at the ceremony at Paul's Cross, he suddenly refused to recant. There is no record of any further proceedings against Forest, but presumably Cranmer sat again with his fellow Commissioners to pronounce the sen-

[1] Cranmer to Cromwell, 11 April 1538 (Cranmer's *Works*, ii. 366–7).

tence of excommunication which followed automatically from Forest's relapse into heresy, and was a necessary prelude to his execution as a heretic. On 22nd May, Forest was drawn to Smith-field, and hanged in chains over a fire which eventually roasted him to death. This exceptional cruelty was presumably in-flicted so that Forest should suffer some further punishment for his treason in addition to the penalty of burning for his heresy.[1]

Forest was the only adherent of the orthodox faith to be martyred as a heretic; all the other Papists suffered for treason. Within six months of Forest's death, the reaction had begun, and Henry, whilst as determined as ever to crush the Papists, did not wish to emphasize his deviations from the old orthodox doctrines, and directed the accusations of heresy only against the reformers. When the official religion changed under Edward VI, there was no King with the ruthlessness of Henry who was prepared to take such action against the orthodox.

The summer of 1538 saw the high water-mark of the Henrician Reformation. Not only did Henry's interest in the looting of the shrines lead him to encourage the assault on superstition throughout the realm, but the menace of joint action by Charles and Francis against him induced him to look to the German Princes as allies, and to contemplate doctrinal concessions to Lutheranism. Under the threat of the union of Papist Europe, the German envoys arrived in London in May 1538, and began a conference at Lambeth with Cranmer and the English Bishops with the object of reaching an agreement on a joint formulary of faith.[2] The chief difficulty was the Lutherans' objection to what they termed the three abuses in the practice of the Church of England—private masses, the administration of the Lord's Supper in one kind, and the prohibi-tion of the marriage of priests; but this was not an insuperable obstacle to an agreement, for these three negative points might properly be omitted from a formulary of faith, as they

[1] For Forest's case, see Lyst to Cromwell, 7 November 1532 and 4 and 18 February, 12 April and 20 May 1533 (Ellis, *Letters*, iii [ii]. 249–70); Bourchier, *Historia Ecclesiastica de Martyrio*, pp. 28–69; Cranmer to Cromwell, 6 April 1538 (Cranmer's *Works*, ii. 365–6); Cromwell's remembrances; Excerpts from Forest's Confession, (1538) (*L.P.*, xiii [i]. 877, 1043); Hall, pp. 825–6; Wriothesley, i. 78–80; *Greyfriars Chron.*, p. 42.

[2] Wriothesley, i. 81–82. The Germans arrived on 31 May, and not, as Wriothesley states, in June. The conference seems to have begun on 14 June (see Cranmer to Cromwell, 13 June 1538, Cranmer's *Works*, ii. 371).

had been from the Articles of Faith in the Confession of Augsburg. Yet despite all Cranmer's efforts to reach a settlement, the negotiations ultimately broke down. The Lutherans were not prepared to ignore the question of the three abuses, while in the last resort Henry did not really wish to commit himself to a doctrinal agreement with the Lutherans.

The delegates met two or three times a week from the middle of June until the middle of August. They began by attempting to draft an agreed formulary of faith, leaving the question of the three abuses, which would obviously be the main ground of disagreement, until afterwards. It was possible to make progress on the Articles of Faith, though as every word was liable to lead to some minor disagreement, the proceedings advanced very slowly. Cranmer thought that Stokesley, who was a bitter opponent of Lutheranism, was largely responsible for this. We know of a most significant incident in this connexion. Stokesley was informed by Richard Morison, the future Ambassador, that Cromwell required him to perform a certain duty; but he told Morison that he would be unable to do so unless he were given leave of absence from the meetings with the Germans. When Cranmer heard of this, he asked Morison to urge Cromwell not to take Stokesley away from the conference, because though they would certainly make much better progress if he were not there, nevertheless—as Morison expressed it to Cromwell—'men would talk, or at the least think evil, if he should be taken away from their assembly'.[1] Cranmer obviously feared that the people would say, or at least think, that there was disunity among the Bishops, and that it was only he and the other 'heretic Bishops' who were forcing the King into collaboration with Luther. He therefore wished for Stokesley, despite all his obstruction, to be present throughout every session of the conference. This was the same Cranmer who had sought to spare Fisher and More and to give out that they had conformed to the King's proceedings, and who had prevented Aless from haranguing the meeting of the Bishops. His policy was unsuccessful. Stokesley could attend every session of the conference with the Lutherans, but men would

---

[1] Morison to Cromwell, (summer 1538) (*L.P.*, xiii [i]. 1296). For the talks with the Lutherans, see also Sampson to Cromwell, 7 June 1540 (Strype, *Eccl. Mem.* i [ii]. 381–2).

continue to say that Cranmer and his collaborators were heretics.

Long though the negotiations were, the parties had been able to draft an agreed formulary of faith before the middle of August. In form it followed closely the Confession of Augsburg, but there were important modifications in doctrine. The Germans' doctrine of justification was modified by a declaration along the lines of the Ten Articles and the Bishops' Book that while men could only be justified by grace through Christian faith, true faith required good works to be performed. The question of transubstantiation was avoided by adopting the short statement on the Eucharist which had already been agreed between Fox and the Lutherans in the winter of 1535-6, and which merely asserted the Real Presence. The article on Penance was obviously the subject of lengthy discussion, not only with the Germans but among the English divines. Four different drafts of this article have been preserved; one of them contains corrections made by Cranmer, minimizing the importance of confession. Where the draft repeatedly stated that confession was necessary, Cranmer wished to replace the word 'necessary' by 'convenient'; and he also suggested the insertion of a phrase declaring that confession was not expressly, but only impliedly, authorized by Scripture. None of these amendments was incorporated into the article, which marked a clear victory for the orthodox English Bishops. The article on Civil Matters went far beyond the Confession of Augsburg in emphasizing the duty of obedience to Princes. It incorporated the doctrine of the Confession of Augsburg, which had barely been mentioned in the Bishops' Book, that Christians must not obey the magistrates if they were ordered to sin, as God must be obeyed rather than man; but this was swamped by lengthy declarations as to the obedience due to Princes, who must be obeyed, unless they ordered the subject to sin, even though they were unjust and wicked and used their power against the will of God.[1]

The agreement on the Articles of Faith was only the beginning, for there remained the question of the three abuses and

[1] For the draft agreement with the Germans, and draft articles on private masses, the worship of Saints, and images, see Cranmer's *Works*, ii. 472–84; but see *L.P.*, xiii [i]. 1307, as to whether the titles of the articles on the worship of Saints and images are written in Cranmer's hand. For the Confession of Augsburg, see Jenkyns, iv. 273–92 n.

the number of Sacraments. Both Cranmer and Cromwell wished to agree with the Lutherans in condemning the abuses; but Henry was strongly opposed to this, and decided that he himself would conduct the arguments on this matter in writing with the assistance of the orthodox Tunstall. By the middle of August, the Germans had still received no reply from Henry, and had not been able to hold any discussions about the abuses with the English representatives. They therefore decided to break off negotiations, or at least to force the issue by threatening to do so.

Cranmer and Cromwell made every effort to avoid a rupture. On Cromwell's instructions, Cranmer urged the Germans to postpone their departure, and though at first they insisted that they must leave England within eight days, he eventually persuaded them to agree to stay for another month on condition that the delegates proceeded immediately to a discussion on the abuses. The orthodox Bishops, however, refused to begin discussions about the abuses, arguing that as the King was writing to the Germans on the subject, it would be inadvisable for them to express an opinion which might differ from that of the King. They proposed instead to begin a discussion about the four lesser Sacraments which the Germans did not recognize as Sacraments. Cranmer wrote to Cromwell on 23rd August that the Bishops were merely seeking an excuse to disrupt the negotiations, as they knew that the Germans would never agree with them about any of these four Sacraments, with the possible exception of Matrimony. They would not discuss the abuses unless the King commanded them, 'for they manifestly see that they cannot defend the abuses, and yet they would in no wise grant unto them'. Cranmer also urged Cromwell to offer the Germans better living accommodation, as their present quarters were infected with rats and the smells of the kitchen penetrated to the parlour where they ate their meals. In fact, however, the Germans thought that their entertainment in England was lavish and expensive.[1]

Cranmer's letter of 23rd August makes it clear that both he and Cromwell agreed with the Germans about the three abuses,

---

[1] Cranmer to Cromwell, 18 and 23 August 1538 (Cranmer's *Works*, ii. 377–80); Seckendorff, iii. 180. For the letters of Henry VIII and the Lutherans on the three abuses, see Burnet, iv. 352–91.

Cranmer had approved of the marriage of priests as early as 1532, when he married Margaret, and by 1538 he had moved close to the Lutheran position, not only as regards the other abuses, but also—as we know from his letter concerning Damplip [1]—on transubstantiation. Next year he publicly proclaimed his belief in the administration of the cup to the laity at the time of the arguments over the Six Articles; but it is more surprising to discover his opinions in 1538 on private masses and transubstantiation, for he adopted an orthodox position on private masses, and presumably also on transubstantiation, during the discussions on the Six Articles.

The Germans remained in London for another month, as they had agreed to do, but it was impossible to make any progress. Henry absolutely refused to condemn the three abuses, and in view of this, the Lutherans were not prepared to be parties to any joint formulary of faith. The Articles which had been agreed were consequently never issued, and the Germans left at the end of September, having achieved no results at all. The failure to reach agreement with the Lutherans was to have disastrous consequences for the Reformation.

---

[1] Cranmer to Cromwell, 15 August 1538 (Cranmer's *Works*, ii. 375); and see infra, Chap. XI.

CHAPTER XI

THE TROUBLES IN CALAIS: THE CASE OF LAMBERT

THE diocese of Canterbury included the Marches of Calais, which comprised the town of Calais and a strip of territory some twenty-five miles long to a depth of about six miles from the coast. The Deputy of Calais was the aged Viscount Lisle, an illegitimate son of Edward IV, who adhered to the old doctrines in religion; his wife Honor was denounced by John Foxe as a bitter persecutor of the Gospel. Cranmer seems at first to have been almost on terms of friendship with Lisle. We know of one occasion when he asked Lisle to send him some wine for his cellars, and in the spring of 1534 he granted a preaching license, at Lisle's request, to the Warden of the Friars Observant in Canterbury, who was suspected of Papist sympathies. This action by Cranmer, at a time when the grant of preaching licenses was being subjected to a particularly careful scrutiny, shows how far he was prepared to go to please Lisle.[1]

When Cranmer first became Archbishop, his Commissary in Calais was William Peterson. Peterson was an orthodox official who took stern measures against heresy; but in the spring of 1534, Cranmer appointed John Butler to succeed Peterson. Butler was an ardent reformer, and he soon began to complain to Cranmer that the Council of Calais were refusing to administer the oath of supremacy in the Pale, and were persecuting reformers there. Lisle discharged a soldier from the garrison on a charge of reading heretical books, although the books were in fact those which had been published by the King's authority against Papal supremacy. Cranmer and Cromwell succeeded, after a great deal of difficulty, in forcing Lisle to reinstate the soldier in his post; but Cranmer continued to hear repeated complaints from Butler about the situation in Calais.[2]

[1] Cranmer to Lisle, 20 December 1535 (Cranmer's *Works*, ii. 318); Worth to Lisle, 21 March 1534; Palmer to Lisle (28 March) and 18 April 1534; Covert to Lady Lisle, 1 and 13 June 1534 (*L.P.*, vii. 350, 385, 510, 765, 837).

[2] Cranmer to Cromwell, 8 and 27 October 1535 (Cranmer's *Works*, ii. 310–11, 313); Wolfe Allarde to Henry VIII (April 1534); Husee to Lisle, 23 September 1534; Cranmer's draft of letter from Henry VIII to Lisle and others (4 November 1535); Butler to Cranmer, 11 February 1536 (*L.P.*, vii. 585, 1182; ix. 759; x. 292).

By 1537, Cranmer's friendly relations with Lisle had begun to deteriorate. On two occasions, Cranmer refused a request from Lisle that he should use his influence in favour of priests of Calais who had been denounced to the Council as Papists, and he also refused to grant a dispensation to enable a priest whom Lisle favoured to hold a benefice while he was under age. In the summer of 1537, he frankly told Lisle's representative in England that he had heard rumours that Lady Lisle was a little 'Papish'. But Cranmer was obviously reluctant to enter into open conflict with Lisle, who was a very influential noble and on friendly terms with Cromwell, and by January 1538 he seems to have become somewhat perturbed at Butler's activities in Calais.[1]

In the summer of 1538, Lisle's faction struck at Adam Damplip. Damplip had been chaplain to Fisher, and after Fisher's arrest he had fled to Pole in Rome; but there he became converted to extreme Protestant doctrines. Pole, after vainly trying to dissuade him, gave him, with typical generosity, some money to help him on his journey to England; and Damplip, passing through Calais on his way, was persuaded to remain there to help the reformers in the Pale. Damplip's activities led him into conflict with Dove, the Prior of the White Friars in Calais, for Damplip exposed a fraudulent miracle in Dove's priory by which the people were shown three Hosts covered with drops of blood. Dove thereupon denounced Damplip as a sacramentary for attacking the Real Presence.[2]

In July, Butler sent Damplip to Cranmer at Lambeth with a letter in which he denied the truth of the accusations against Damplip, and asked Cranmer to use his influence with Cromwell to obtain a cure for Damplip in Calais. After seeing Damplip, Cranmer formed the impression that he had very good knowledge and judgment, and he sent him to Cromwell with a letter in which he urged Cromwell to write to Lisle on Damplip's behalf. But Lisle had informed Cromwell that Damplip had been preaching heresies to the garrison at Calais, and Damplip was summoned before Cranmer and other Commissioners on a

---

[1] Cranmer to Lisle, 28 January 1537; Husee to Lisle, 15, 25 and 30 April 1537 and 6 February 1538; Husee to Lady Lisle, 3 August 1537; Richard Lee to Lady Lisle, 16 September 1537; Killigrew to Lisle, 5 June 1537; Butler to Cranmer, 19 January 1538 (*L.P.*, xii [i]. 258, 947, 1039, 1068; xii [ii]. 424, 705; xiii [i]. 108, 226; *L.P.* Addenda, 1226).

[2] Foxe, v. 498–500.

charge of heresy for denying the Real Presence.[1] Damplip
failed to appear, and went into hiding.

Foxe states that Cranmer connived at Damplip's flight. He
writes that Cranmer who was 'then yet but a Lutheran', was so
favourably impressed by Damplip's treatise on the Eucharist
that he stated that Scripture knew no such term as transubstantiation, and sent word to Damplip that if he appeared before the
Commissioners, he would be arrested and would probably not
escape a cruel death. This story is almost certainly untrue. An
illegal act of this kind could win the approval of Foxe in 1563,
but it is very unlikely that Cranmer would have been a party
to it in 1538. Cranmer would never at this time have placed
solidarity with a fellow reformer before loyalty to the King.
It is much more likely that he was speaking the truth when he
wrote to Cromwell that he greatly regretted that Damplip had
failed to appear to confound his accusers; for Cranmer wished
to remove Dove from his position as Prior or even to suppress
his priory altogether, and he was prepared to urge Cromwell to
do this even after Damplip had fled. Cromwell at first decided
to follow Cranmer's advice, but eventually Dove was only
required to make a public recantation in Calais. The project of
appointing Damplip as a curate in Calais had of course to be
abandoned after his flight.[2]

In his letter to Cromwell of 15th August 1538, when he informed him about Damplip's flight, Cranmer wrote: 'As concerning Adam Damplip of Calais, he utterly denieth that ever he
taught or said that the very body and blood of Christ was not
presently in the Sacrament of the Altar, and confesseth the same
to be there really; but he saith, that the controversy between
him and the Prior was because he confuted the opinion of the
transubstantiation, and therein I think he taught but the truth.'[3]

These words seem to indicate clearly that Cranmer had
ceased to believe in transubstantiation as early as 1538. One of
Cranmer's biographers has assumed that in this letter Cranmer
was referring only to the fraudulent miracle in Dove's priory,
and that when he wrote that 'he confuted the opinion of the

[1] Butler to Cranmer, 22 July 1538; Cranmer to Cromwell, 24 July 1538
(Cranmer's *Works*, ii. 372–3); Corbet to Lisle, 26 July 1538 (*L.P.*, xiii [i]. 1464).
[2] Foxe, v. 501; Cranmer to Cromwell, 15 and 18 August 1538 (Cranmer's
Works, ii. 375–7); Husee to Lisle, 3 October 1538 (*L.P.*, xiii [ii]. 523).
[3] Cranmer to Cromwell, 15 August 1538 (Cranmer's *Works*, ii. 375).

transubstantiation', he meant that Damplip had exposed the fraud of the three Hosts.[1] But it is curious that Cranmer should have used no stronger words than 'I think he taught but the truth' if he were referring to Damplip's teaching about the fraudulent miracle, for in 1538—at the height of the campaign against relics and forged miracles—he would almost certainly have written a great deal more on this subject in a letter to Cromwell. Moreover, it is not clear from Foxe's account of the incident that the miracle of the three Hosts was supposed to be connected with transubstantiation. Foxe does, however, state that Damplip preached against transubstantiation—and also against the Real Presence—in his sermons at Calais.

There are other reasons for believing that Cranmer had repudiated transubstantiation by 1538, for he certainly renounced the doctrine before he abandoned his belief in the Real Presence. In 1551, Cranmer wrote in his *Answer to Smith*: 'I confess of myself, that not long before I wrote the said Catechism [in 1548] I was in that error of the Real Presence, as I was many years past in divers other errors: as of transubstantiation, of the sacrifice propitiatory of the priests in the mass, of pilgrimages, Purgatory, pardons, and many other superstitions and errors that came from Rome.' This makes it clear that Cranmer renounced transubstantiation some years at least before he did the same with the Real Presence, and suggests that he abandoned all the doctrines to which he refers in this passage at about the same time. He had repudiated the doctrine of private masses by 1538, as we know from his letter to Cromwell about the discussions with the German Lutherans which he wrote on 23rd August, eight days after he wrote this letter about Damplip, and he had attacked the orthodox doctrine of Purgatory two years earlier than this. Foxe's account of the proceedings against Damplip is too inaccurate on other points to be reliable in this connexion, but he confirms that Cranmer had abandoned his belief in transubstantiation by this time, and states that Cranmer was then a Lutheran.[2]

Altogether, there is good reason to believe that by August 1538 Cranmer held those Lutheran doctrines on the Eucharist

---

[1] See Todd, *Archbishop Cranmer*, i. 176 n., 264 n.; Jenkyns, i. 257–8 n.

[2] Cranmer, *Answer to Smith*; Cranmer to Cromwell, 23 August 1538 (Cranmer's *Works*, i. 374; ii. 379); Foxe, v. 501.

which he appears to have advocated ten years later when he translated the Catechism of Justus Jonas, and that he had abandoned transubstantiation, while still adhering to the doctrine of the Real Presence. Compared to the Real Presence, transubstantiation was a subordinate issue. The Ten Articles and the Bishops' Book had laid down the doctrine of the Sacrament of the Altar in a manner which was compatible with a rejection of transubstantiation; it was only in 1539 that transubstantiation was expressly affirmed in the Six Articles. Even after 1539, it was the nature of the Presence, not the manner of the change in the elements, which was the real issue between the contending parties; and in the controversy between Cranmer and Gardiner in 1550-1, the issue of transubstantiation was treated as a separate and subordinate question to that of the Real Presence. It was therefore possible for Cranmer to say at his trial at Oxford that on the issue of the Presence he still maintained the Papist doctrine at the time of Lambert's trial— three months after he wrote his letter of 15th August 1538—and to insist that he had only held two different opinions, and not three, during his life on the question of the Presence.[1]

It has, however, been argued that Cranmer did not accept the Lutheran position when he abandoned transubstantiation, and that in 1538 he believed in the Real Presence, not by virtue of either transubstantiation or consubstantiation, but by impanation in the sense in which this was accepted by the medieval schoolmen. One of the reasons given in support of this view is Cranmer's attitude in the case of Atkinson, who was tried before Cranmer and Sampson in June 1538 for heresy concerning the Eucharist. Atkinson recanted, and was sentenced to carry his fagot at Paul's Cross. Burckhardt, the Vice-Chancellor of Saxony, who was in London at the head of the German Lutheran delegation, intervened on his behalf, and asked Cranmer to permit Atkinson to carry his fagot at his parish church instead of at Paul's Cross. Cranmer told Burckhardt that 'as that error of the Sacrament of the Altar was so greatly spread abroad in this realm, and daily increasing more and more', it was necessary that Atkinson should recant before the largest possible audience at Paul's Cross; but he nevertheless suggested to Cromwell that Burckhardt's request might be

[1] Foxe, viii. 56.

granted, as the Duke of Saxony had freed a man for whom Fox had interceded. It was probably during this same summer that Cranmer dealt with the Yorkshire parson who had called him an unlearned ostler. He had refused to make the parson recant at Paul's Cross because he wished to spare him the humiliation of a public recantation, and because he thought that 'too many Papists' would believe the story which the parson would be repudiating. He was far more reluctant to spare Atkinson from the same humiliation, and gave as his reason that too many persons believed the error about the Sacrament of the Altar. 'Too many Papists' was a reason for leniency; too many sacramentaries was a reason for severity. It was always so with Cranmer, for Morice says that he was far more severe towards Protestants than he was towards Papists.[1]

The fact that Burckhardt intervened in the case is strong evidence that Atkinson was a Lutheran, and from this it appears that in the summer of 1538 Cranmer was judicially condemning a man who believed in the Lutheran doctrine of the Eucharist; but we cannot definitely deduce from this that Cranmer rejected consubstantiation at this time. We can be sure that when Cranmer stated that the 'error of the Sacrament of the Altar was so greatly spread abroad', he was referring not to consubstantiation—which never took root in England—but to the sacramentarian denial of the Real Presence. We do not know the offence with which Atkinson was charged, but Cranmer probably feared that though Atkinson himself was a Lutheran, the effect of his activities had been to encourage sacramentarian beliefs in others. However this may be, we cannot be certain as to the opinions on the Eucharist which Cranmer held in the summer of 1538, apart from the fact that he believed in the Real Presence and was determined to punish any sacramentary who attacked the doctrine.

It was during the summer of 1538 that Cranmer had his first serious encounter with the adherents of the Swiss Zwinglian Bullinger, who were later, in the reign of Edward VI, to put such pressure on him to carry through a more vigorous Reformation. Bullinger had dedicated a book to Henry VIII, and he

[1] Smyth, *Cranmer and the Reformation under Edward VI*, pp. 56–59; Cranmer to Cromwell, 22 June 1538 (Cranmer's *Works*, ii. 371–2); Morice (*Nar. Ref.*, pp. 246, 272).

sent Partridge and some of his other English supporters to England to deliver a copy to the King and to other leading dignitaries. Partridge and his colleagues first visited Cranmer, and after giving him a copy of Bullinger's book asked him to present another copy to the King; but Cranmer, though courteous, was unenthusiastic. He at first refused to present the book to Henry, and suggested that Partridge should ask Cromwell to do this; but after supper, he agreed to present the book in two days' time, after he had read it himself. Partridge then visited Cromwell, and presented him with a copy of the book; and Cromwell, who was always ready to find any Protestant allies abroad, went to Court that same evening and showed Henry his own copy of the book. On hearing this, Cranmer promptly delivered the King's copy to the King without further delay, having as usual waited for Cromwell's initiative.

Cranmer also promised Partridge that he would write a reply to Bullinger's letter for Partridge to carry when he left England; but when the time arrived for Partridge's departure, Cranmer said that he had been unable to write to Bullinger, because he had left Bullinger's letter at his house in the country.[1] This was not the last occasion on which Cranmer showed his reluctance to respond to Bullinger's advances. The excuse was probably a genuine one, but we can hardly believe that it would have prevented Cranmer from writing to Bucer or Melanchthon. In March 1539, the English Zwinglians were again informing Bullinger that though Cranmer had promised to write to him, he was wholly employed in instructing the people and in drafting discourses in English to be used by the clergy instead of those in Latin which were in use—a statement which suggests that Cranmer had already begun work on some Homilies.[2]

In the autumn of 1538, the old nobility was struck down when the Marquis of Exeter and other Papists were beheaded. Cranmer followed the usual practice of staking a claim to the property of the accused men as soon as they were arrested on the

[1] Partridge to Bullinger, 17 September 1538 (*Orig. Letters*, pp. 611–2). Cranmer had previously had two short meetings with Partridge and the Swiss Zwinglian Gualter at Lambeth in the spring of 1537; see Gualter's Diary, 6 March and 22 April 1537 (*Zwingliana*, viii. 449, 454).

[2] Partridge, Traheron and others to Bullinger and others, 8 March 1539 (*Orig. Letters*, p. 626).

safe assumption that conviction for treason and forfeiture would follow in due course. On 14th November, he wrote to Cromwell to make suit on behalf of his chaplain Champion for a benefice held by a Papist 'being now in the Tower and like to be attainted of treason'. The Papist was duly executed in January. Sir Edward Neville, who was executed for saying that the King was worse than a beast, had been Master of the Game in Cranmer's parks. When the King appointed Cromwell to this forfeited office—and also to the post of High Steward of Cranmer's franchises, which had been held by Neville's brother Lord Bergavenny—Cranmer showed that strict sense of justice which rarely failed him when the King's interests were not involved. He refused to deliver the patents of the two offices to Cromwell until he had taken counsel's opinion as to whether the infant Lord Bergavenny and Sir Edward Neville's son had lawfully forfeited their interest in the offices; and in his letter to Cromwell, he expressed great sympathy for Neville's son and young Lord Bergavenny, and hinted that Cromwell might grant them some favour if the King agreed.[1]

Cranmer was engaged throughout the winter of 1538–9, first at Lambeth and later at Ford, in dealing with cases of treason and sedition by Papists, including one involving the circulation of Papist books in the Oxford Colleges. He also took action against a sailor who had spoken in praise of Becket in a private house after Cranmer had presented a play at his house at Ford about King John's struggle against the Pope. He was equally occupied, however, in suppressing the extreme wing of the Reformation. On 1st October, Cromwell appointed a Commission consisting of Cranmer and eight others to deal with Anabaptists. The reformers were in a majority on the Commission, on which such notable extremists as Barnes and Crome, who had faced charges of heresy themselves, sat together with Stokesley and Sampson. There are no records of the sessions of the Commission, but in November 1538 three Dutch Anabaptists were burned for heresy against the Sacrament of the Altar, and on 23rd December two English artisans were burned. There is little doubt that they were Anabaptists, and that like the three Dutch Anabaptists they had been condemned by Cranmer and his

---

[1] Cranmer to Cromwell, 14 November and 14 December 1538 and 21 January 1539 (Cranmer's *Works*, ii. 385–9).

colleagues; but it is significant that though they had doubtless been guilty of wilder heresies, it was for denying the Real Presence that the reformers on the Commission chose to send the Anabaptists to the fire.[1]

Cranmer's part in the trial of Lambert has caused more embarrassment to his admirers than anything else in his life. We do not know how Lambert fared after his first appearance before Cranmer and his colleagues in 1536, but in the autumn of 1538 he was at liberty in London, and attended a sermon preached by the reformer John Taylor. After the sermon, Lambert argued with Taylor against the Real Presence, and Taylor, having no time to discuss the matter, advised Lambert to send him his opinions in writing. On receiving Lambert's statement, Taylor showed it to Barnes, who persuaded Taylor to send it to Cranmer. Cranmer thereupon summoned Lambert before him on a charge of heresy.

There has been a lively controversy as to Cranmer's action at this hearing. His admirers deny that he condemned Lambert as a heretic, and argue that he would probably have adopted a lenient attitude with Lambert, had not Lambert been so foolish as to appeal from him to the King, thus taking the matter out of Cranmer's hands. To this, Cranmer's critics reply that Lambert would obviously not have appealed unless he had been condemned by Cranmer. But in fact it seems inaccurate to speak of an appeal at all. This is clear from a letter which Lambert wrote to Cromwell from prison before the trial at Westminster on 16th November, in which he told Cromwell that he had written to the King during the previous week, and had sent him a statement of his opinions on the Sacrament. He wrote that he had been partly forced to do this, but did not regret it at all, as he hoped that it would convert the King, or at least lead him to examine the matter further. Lambert told Cromwell that he would have wished to send him a copy of the treatise, but prisoners were not free agents in such things, and Cranmer was in possession of the only other copy of the document.

From the fact that Cranmer had examined Lambert, and was in possession of a copy of his treatise, it certainly seems as if it

[1] Cranmer to Cromwell, 8 and 10 October 1538 and 11 January 1539 (Cranmer's *Works*, ii. 381–4, 387–8, where the editor's suggestion that the play about King John was Bale's play is almost certainly wrong); Commission of 1 October 1538 (Wilkins, iii. 836–7); Wriothesley, i. 90; *Greyfriars Chron.*, p. 42.

was Cranmer who partly forced Lambert to send the treatise to the King, presumably because it had already been decided to stage a trial of the sacramentary before the Supreme Head in person. Cranmer did not condemn Lambert as a heretic, but he conducted all the preliminary investigations into the case, and far from wishing to keep the matter quiet, he put strong pressure on Lambert to appeal to the King, and to write the incriminating document on which he was tried and condemned.

Lambert was brought to trial at Whitehall on 16th November 1538. Henry presided, with Cranmer and the Bishops sitting on his right, and the nobles and Judges on his left. In his treatise, Lambert had given ten reasons for challenging the belief in the Real Presence, and on each of these points a different spokesman had been selected to argue with Lambert. The King having dealt with the first point—the words of Jesus—in the most crude and brutal manner, it was Cranmer's turn to argue against Lambert's second argument—that Christ, being in Heaven, could not be corporally present in the Sacrament, as He could not be in two places at once. Cranmer put forward the argument of Christ's appearance to St. Paul on earth, and Lambert replied with the answer which was later to be adopted by so many opponents of the Real Presence—that Christ had revealed himself to Paul on earth while remaining corporally in Heaven. Foxe says that Cranmer was so shaken by this reply that he was at a loss for an answer; but it is difficult to believe that Cranmer, who had read everything which Zwingli and Oecolampadius had written about the Eucharist, would have been taken aback at this familiar argument. Foxe states that both Cranmer and Henry were on the point of admitting the validity of Lambert's position when Gardiner intervened; but this is obviously wrong.

The proceedings lasted from noon till five o'clock in the afternoon. Lambert was a man of learning, and at first gave a good account of himself; but as the hall grew darker on that winter afternoon, he began to falter, and by the time they brought the lights he was unable to make any effective answer. Foxe says that he was tired, as he had, according to the usual practice, been compelled to stand throughout the whole five hours, and he was cowed by the brutality of the King. As he refused to recant, he was condemned, and burned at Smithfield.

The fire was deliberately withdrawn from him, and he was stuck on a pike and lifted out of the reach of the flames in order to prolong his sufferings.

Cranmer has naturally been criticized for his part in Lambert's case. It is untrue to suggest that he himself secretly agreed with Lambert's opinions at the time when he sat as one of his judges, for there is no doubt that at the time of Lambert's trial Cranmer believed in the Real Presence. But he cannot be exculpated from responsibility for the condemnation of Lambert. Foxe rightly makes no attempt to excuse him, and says that it was three reformers—John Taylor, Barnes and Cranmer—all of whom were to be victims of persecution in their turn, who were responsible for Lambert's martyrdom. The actions of Taylor smell unpleasantly like a provocation. He persuaded Lambert to set down in writing opinions which were well known to be punishable by death, and then sent the document to Cranmer at the instigation of Barnes, whom Foxe obviously considered to be primarily responsible for Lambert's fate. But Cranmer's conduct does not seem to have been particularly reprehensible. He was confronted with a heretical treatise written by a man whom he had tried for heresy two years before, and he had his duty to perform. He did no more than was to be expected from an Archbishop of Canterbury who believed that it was heresy to deny the Real Presence.[1]

On the day of Lambert's trial, a royal proclamation was issued which imposed a censorship on all books in English, expelled foreign Anabaptists and sacramentaries from the realm, and prohibited, on pain of death, all persons except learned divines from arguing about the Sacrament of the Altar in taverns and elsewhere. Married priests were prohibited from administering any Sacrament or holding any office, and priests who married after the date of the proclamation were to suffer imprisonment during the King's pleasure. The people were expressly commanded to observe all ceremonies which had not

[1] For Lambert's case, and the controversy as to Cranmer's part in it, see Foxe, v. 225–50; Lambert to Cromwell (autumn 1538); Husee to Lisle, 16 November 1538 (*L.P.*, xiii [ii]. 849 [2], 851); Cromwell to Wyatt, 28 November 1538 (Merriman, ii. 162); Elyot's *Dictionary* (Dedicatory Preface to Henry VIII) A. ii; Sampson's arguments against Lambert (Strype, *Cranmer*, pp. 736–40); Wriothesley, i. 88–89; *Greyfriars Chron.*, p. 42; Hall, pp. 826–7; Todd, *Vindication of Cranmer*, pp. 71–78; Lingard, *Vindication of the 'History of England'*, pp. 84–85; Todd, *Reply to Lingard's Vindication*, pp. 70–75.

been abrogated, such as holy bread, holy water and creeping to the Cross; while among all these measures directed against heresy, the only sop to the reformers was another denunciation of Thomas Becket. This proclamation was not generally recognized at the time as marking the beginning of the religious reaction; but the re-emphasis on the prohibition of the marriage of priests, so soon after the point had been argued between Henry and the German envoys, was a direct rebuff to the German Lutherans, and called forth a letter of protest from Melanchthon to Cranmer. There is no doubt that Cranmer was deeply distressed at the proclamation, and it would not be surprising if he had tried to prevent Henry from promulgating it; but there is no reason to believe that he was the author of a short document which set forth reasons against publishing a proclamation on the marriage of priests. Burnet and later writers believed that it was written by Cranmer, but Strype doubted this, and for various reasons it appears unlikely that Cranmer was the author.[1]

The reaction derived its strength from the inherent conservatism of the people. During the winter of 1538-9, Cranmer sent John Marshall to Nottinghamshire with instructions to report to Cromwell as to how the Reformation was being received in Cranmer's homeland. Marshall's report was written in optimistic tones, but it could not obscure the resentment of the people of Nottinghamshire and Lincolnshire. He tells of whispered opposition to the religious reforms, of resentment at the suppression of the monasteries, of slow progress in learning the Paternoster in English, of fear that 'Bishop Pole' would one day take vengeance for the execution of his brother, and of reluctance to work on holy days and to cease from playing shovelboard in ale houses.[2] With a King who was above all an opportunist, the hostility of the people, along with the international situation, tipped the scales in favour of reaction, and led to the promulgation of the Six Articles in May.

[1] Proclamation of 16 November 1538 (printed in part in Strype, *Cranmer*, pp. 685-91, and in part in Burnet, vi. 220-2); Melanchthon to Cranmer, 30 March 1539 (*Corpus Ref.*, iii. 676-9). For the document which Burnet entitled 'Some considerations offered to the King by Cranmer to induce him to proceed to a further Reformation', see Burnet, iv. 298-9, Cranmer's *Works*, ii. 466-7; but see Strype, 'Corrections of Burnet's History' (in Burnet, 1829 ed. iii [ii]. 544); and *L.P.*, xii [ii]. 409 n., where it is suggested that Heynes was the author.
[2] Marshall to Cromwell, 15 February 1539 (*L.P.*, xiv [i]. 295).

CHAPTER XII

THE SIX ARTICLES

O N 5th May 1539, Audley announced in the House of Lords that the King intended to abolish diversity in religion among his subjects, and directed the House to appoint a Committee to decide how to achieve this result. The Committee consisted of Cromwell, Cranmer, Archbishop Lee and six Bishops—Goodrich, Latimer, Salcott, Tunstall, Clerk, and Aldrich—and was almost equally divided between the reformers and the conservatives. On 16th May, Norfolk announced in the House of Lords that as the Committee had failed to agree on any articles, it was the King's wish that the House should consider six questions of doctrine—those six which were later dealt with in the Six Articles—with a view to an Act of Parliament being passed to enforce conformity to them.[1]

In fact, the Committee had had very little time in which to reach an agreement about the articles. They probably held their meetings in the morning, when the House of Lords was in session, for the members of the Committee had been given leave of absence from the House in order to attend the meetings of the Committee. All except two of them were absent from the House on 6th May. On Wednesday the 7th and 14th the House of Lords did not sit because of the meeting of Convocation which the members of the Committee presumably attended, unless they were also given leave of absence from Convocation. Four of the nine were present in the House of Lords on 8th May; on the 9th, they were all absent; all except one were present on the 10th and 13th May; and all were present on the 12th. It is unlikely that the Committee sat on Sunday the 11th or on the 15th, which was Ascension Day. This suggests that the Committee held only two or three meetings—on the 6th and 9th May, and possibly also on the 8th—and that when Cranmer and his colleagues returned to the House of Lords on 10th May they had already been told to abandon their discussions; for

[1] *House of Lords Journal*, 5 and 16 May 1539.

they held no further meetings on the 10th, 12th and 13th May.[1]

It is clear that the suggestion made by Norfolk that the Committee had failed to reach agreement after prolonged discussions has been much too readily accepted by later historians. In 1536 and 1537, the Bishops had been allowed to hold meetings over a period of five months while they were drafting the Ten Articles and the Bishops' Book; but now, as a Committee of the House of Lords, they were expected to produce results in time for a bill to be passed during the session. In any case, the setting up of the Committee was probably from the first intended only as a formality, so that the failure of the Bishops to agree would provide an excuse for dealing with the matter through the House of Lords; and this seems to be confirmed by the fact that Gardiner did not procure his own appointment as a member of the Committee.

Norfolk told the House of Lords, in his statement on 16th May, that the King required them to ascertain the truth with regard to six points—whether the Eucharist was truly the body of the Lord without transubstantiation; whether the Eucharist should be communicated to the laity in both kinds; whether, by the divine law, vows of chastity should be observed by men and women; whether private masses were to be observed by the divine law; whether by the divine law priests were permitted to marry; and whether auricular confession was necessary by the divine law. A disputation took place in the House of Lords on these six questions, though the articles eventually incorporated into the statute were drafted in a slightly different form. It is almost certain that the disputation began on Monday 19th May, and was continued on the 20th and 21st. Henry was present on the Monday and Wednesday. Foxe implies that Henry's intervention came at the end of the disputation, and it has generally been thought that he entered the House in order to coerce Cranmer and the reforming Bishops into abandoning the opposition which they had been maintaining, in his absence, for three days. But as Henry was present on the first, as well as on the last, day of the disputation, it is clear that Cranmer and his colleagues, on the first day at least, maintained their

[1] Ibid., 5, 6, 8, 9, 10, 12 and 13 May 1539. It is not easy to decipher the attendance records in the *House of Lords Journal*, but it seems that in this session those present were marked 'p', those marked 'pp' being present by proxy, and those with no mark against their name being also absent.

opposition to the Six Articles in the actual presence of the King.

Foxe states that Cranmer, 'then being married, as is supposed', opposed the Six Articles in the disputation for three days, but did so in a manner which was so respectful and obedient to the King that Henry could not be offended with him. He tells us nothing about the arguments which Cranmer used, except that he stated that they should be careful not to permit the majority opinion to triumph over the better opinion.[1] Foxe implies that he argued against all the six articles, but it is much more likely that he confined himself to defending the marriage of priests and opposing vows of celibacy—the two questions were not identical—to denying that confession was necessary by the divine law, and to supporting the administration of the Eucharist to the laity in both kinds.

More information as to Cranmer's attitude is provided in a letter of an unidentified peer. The peer, after praising the King's intervention in the disputation and acclaiming the Six Articles, wrote in his letter: 'And notwithstanding my Lord of Canterbury, my Lord of Ely, my Lord of Salisbury, my Lord of Worcester, Rochester and St. David's defended the contrary long time, yet finally his Highness confounded them all with God's learning. York, Durham, Winchester, London, Chichester, Norwich, and Carlisle have showed themselves honest and well learned men. We of the temporalty have be all of one opinion, and my Lord Chancellor and my Lord Privy Seal [Cromwell] as good as we can devise. My Lord of Canterbury and all these Bishops have given their opinion and came in to us, save Salisbury, who yet continueth a lewd fool.'[2]

The peers were enthusiastic for the Six Articles. On the second day of the disputation they agreed, at Norfolk's suggestion, that the King should be granted some recompense for his great labours in reforming religion, and next day they expedited a bill to seize the common lands of eleven parishes, without any compensation, to provide the King with a hunting

---

[1] H. L. Jo., 16, 19 and 21 May 1539; Foxe, v. 264–5. There is no record in the *House of Lords Journal* of the disputation being held; nor is there of the disputation of December 1548.

[2] Burnet, vi. 233. Gairdner (in *L.P.*, xiv [i]. 1040) gives 30 May 1539 as the probable date of the letter; but it is much more likely to have been written on 9 June.

ground a little nearer Hampton Court. On this issue, Cranmer voted with all the other peers; but on the Six Articles, he did not capitulate immediately—not even after Henry's intervention in the disputation in the House of Lords. He was still resisting when the Upper House of Convocation were asked to express their opinions on the Six Articles. There is no record of the date when these questions were submitted to the Upper House, but it was obviously after the end of the disputation in the House of Lords on 21st May and before the questions were submitted to the Lower House of Convocation on 2nd June. In reply to the questions, Cranmer stated that priests might lawfully marry and that it was necessary that the Sacrament of the Altar be administered to the laity in both kinds, being supported on this latter issue only by Barlow. On the question of auricular confession—which was the only one of the Six Articles in respect of which the reformers succeeded in defeating the conservatives—Cranmer was able to enlist the support of nine Bishops and two Abbots for his opinion that he could not find that confession was expressly enjoined by the word of God, but that its use was 'very requisite and expedient'. With regard to private masses, however, Cranmer agreed with all his colleagues that these might stand with the word of God, although nine months before he had written to Cromwell that private masses were indefensible. There is no record as to the answers given to the questions on transubstantiation and vows of chastity; but Gardiner was obviously speaking the truth when he wrote in 1550 that Convocation had approved of transubstantiation in 1539, and it is significant that Cranmer, though he pointed out in his *Answer to Gardiner* that some of the clergy had opposed transubstantiation at the time of the Six Articles, did not claim to have done so himself.[1]

Cranmer had hitherto shown great determination in opposing the Six Articles; but now he completely capitulated. It has generally been assumed that he merely abandoned his opposition to the Six Articles; but there is reason to believe that, together with his colleagues, he actually made some positive declaration in favour of them. The unknown peer used the

[1] *H. L. Jo.*, 20 and 21 May 1539; 31 Hen. VIII, c. 5; Acts of the Privy Council, 5 May 1548; Answers of Convocation on the Six Articles (*L.P.*, xiv [i]. 1065); Gardiner, *Explication and Assertion of the True Catholic Faith*; Cranmer, *Answer to Gardiner* (in Cranmer's *Works*, i. 239–40).

expression that Cranmer and the other reforming Bishops, except Shaxton, had 'given their opinion and come in to us', and there was a widespread belief in the country that the Bishops, including Cranmer, had been made to subscribe to the Articles.[1] This was apparently incorrect, but the fact that these rumours were circulating suggests that the reforming Bishops had made some definite declaration of support for the Six Articles. In view of the public display of disunity at the time of the disputation, and the resentment which this had aroused amongst the temporal peers, it was probably made clear to Cranmer and his colleagues that something more than mere silence was now required; and they probably expressed their agreement with the Six Articles when Parliament re-assembled on 30th May.

On that day, Cranmer was given the duty of considering the punishments to be imposed by the bill enforcing the Six Articles. The Lords adopted the unusual course of setting up two Committees for this purpose, one Committee consisting of three reforming Bishops, Cranmer, Goodrich, and Barlow, and the other of three orthodox Bishops, Archbishop Lee, Tunstall and Gardiner, with the addition in each case of one civil lawyer. The two Committees were directed to submit their recommendations to the King within two days. This procedure had the advantage of forcing Cranmer and the two other reforming Bishops to play an active part in enforcing the Six Articles, while ensuring that at least the other Committee would recommend that stern punishments be imposed.[2]

Cranmer, Goodrich, and Barlow were therefore obliged to propose suitable punishments for persons who should in future argue as they themselves had done during the disputation in the House of Lords; but they could not afford to appear to be tolerant of those who still refused to accept the Six Articles. There seems to be no evidence for Burnet's surmise that the proposals of the conservative Committee were accepted in preference to those of Cranmer and his colleagues, for we do not know what Cranmer's Committee recommended. Cranmer may have opposed the savage innovation by which heretics who opposed the Real Presence and transubstantiation were to be

[1] Letter from an unknown peer, (9 June 1539) (Burnet, vi. 233); Wriothesley, i. 101; Constantine's report to Cromwell, (October 1539) (*Archaeologia*, xxiii. 58); Aless to Elizabeth I, 1 September 1559 (*Cal. For. Pap. Eliz.*, i. 1303, p. 533).
[2] *H. L. Jo.*, 30 May 1539.

burned for the first offence, even if they recanted their heresy before excommunication, for here he could appeal to the traditions of the Church against a proposal which not only deprived a heretic of the right to save himself by a recantation, but also deprived the judges of the right to order him to carry his fagot in these circumstances. Cranmer's Committee may have recommended the other innovation by which the denial of the other five articles was to be felony, not heresy, and only punishable by death—by hanging, not burning—for the first offence if committed in a sermon or other public assembly, or before the judge at the trial; otherwise it was only to be punishable by death for the second offence, and was punishable for the first offence only by imprisonment during the King's pleasure. There can be no doubt as to the views which Cranmer held with regard to the penalty of death by hanging which was imposed on married priests and their wives who continued to cohabit; but it is far from certain that he expressed these views in the House of Lords Committee.[1]

On Saturday 7th June, Audley introduced the bill of the Six Articles in the House of Lords, and it was read for the first time. It passed the House with unusual speed, being read for the second time on Monday the 9th and for a third time on the 10th, after which it was immediately carried to the House of Commons. Cranmer may have spoken in favour of the bill, and certainly did not vote against it. Foxe states that the King desired Cranmer to withdraw from the House and go to the Council chamber or elsewhere 'whilst the Act should pass and be granted', but that Cranmer excused himself. It has generally been assumed that Foxe meant that the King ordered Cranmer to absent himself, but that the Archbishop insisted on attending and opposing the Six Articles; but if there is any truth in the story, it is much more likely that though Henry permitted Cranmer to be absent, Cranmer declined to avail himself of the privilege, and insisted on attending the House in order to assent to the bill; and this is almost certainly Foxe's meaning. Cranmer would never have opposed the Six Articles, either in the disputation or during the reading of the bill, if Henry had ordered him not to attend the House. Cranmer was present in the House of Lords at the first reading on 7th June, though both

[1] 31 Hen. VIII, c. 14.

Latimer and Shaxton, alone of all the Bishops, were absent. At the second reading on 9th June, Latimer was present along with Cranmer and the others, but Shaxton was still absent. At the third reading on the 10th, all the Bishops, including Shaxton, were present. This suggests that the Bishops were under strong pressure to attend and support the bill, that absence from the House was the only form of resistance now open to the opponents of the Six Articles, and that first Cranmer and the other reforming Bishops, then Latimer and finally Shaxton were persuaded to come to the House and set an example of unity and obedience.[1]

Latimer and Shaxton were not saved by their submission. As soon as Parliament had been prorogued on 28th June, Cromwell forced them to resign their bishoprics. The rumour spread throughout the country that they had resigned in protest against the Six Articles, and that Latimer had been caught at Rochester while attempting to escape abroad, and imprisoned in the Tower; but at the beginning of July, Latimer was seen with Cranmer at Lambeth, dressed in the garments of a simple priest, and he was not being followed by any government agent. Cranmer was not afraid to receive Latimer at Lambeth a few days after his disgrace. A few days later, both Latimer and Shaxton were placed in custody in the houses of the Bishops of Chichester and Bath and Wells.[2]

Cranmer had resisted the Six Articles for nearly as long as Latimer, if not as long as Shaxton; but he was treated very differently from his two colleagues. A few days after the Act of the Six Articles was passed, Henry sent Cromwell, Norfolk and Suffolk to Lambeth to inform Cranmer of the King's continued regard for him. The three Lords stayed to dinner with Cranmer, and praised him for his humility, which they contrasted with the pride and arrogance of Wolsey. This led to an unfortunate altercation between Cromwell and one of the Dukes as to Cromwell's attitude when he was Wolsey's servant,

---

[1] *H. L. Jo.*, 7, 9 and 10 June 1539; Foxe, v. 265; viii. 14. But see Foxe, viii. 23, where he states that Cranmer accepted Henry's offer and retired from the House of Lords while the Six Articles' bill passed; which is certainly wrong. These contradictory statements appeared in all the editions of the *Book of Martyrs* which were published during Foxe's lifetime.

[2] The Council to Petre, 14 May 1546 (*St. Pap.*, i. 849); Wriothesley, i. 101, 103; Warley to Lisle, 6 July 1539; Holland to Lisle, 7 July 1539 (*L.P.*, xiv [i]. 1219, 1228).

which Cranmer had some difficulty in appeasing.[1] Latimer's belated submission had not saved him; but Cranmer's was glorified as an act of obedience. Henry's attitude is a tribute, not so much to his generosity, as to his political sagacity. He was well acquainted with both Cranmer and Latimer, and knew which of the two men would be useful to him in the future in strengthening his tyranny.

It is not clear from Foxe whether it was on this occasion that Cromwell informed Cranmer that the King desired him to set down in writing his criticisms of the Six Articles for Henry's private use; but Foxe says that it was a few days after the Act was passed. Cranmer dictated a treatise to Morice, basing his argument on Scripture, patristic texts and reason. Morice then went to London to visit his father, carrying the treatise in his pocket. As he crossed the river, some soldiers who were in his wherry insisted on stopping to watch a bear baiting which was taking place in the water under the supervision of the Lady Elizabeth's bearward; but the bear broke loose and leaped into Morice's wherry, and in the ensuing panic Morice fell into the river, dropping Cranmer's treatise into the water. Before Morice could retrieve it, the bearward picked up the document, and passed it to a priest who was standing by. The priest explained to the bearward that the document was a heretical attack on the Six Articles, and when Morice came forward to claim it, and identified himself as Cranmer's secretary, the bearward declared that he had thought as much, and trusted that both Morice and Cranmer would be hanged—a reference no doubt to the new penalties provided by the Act. Morice persuaded a mutual acquaintance to invite the bearward to supper; but his friend failed to bribe the bearward to hand over the document. Morice then went to Cromwell for assistance; and when the bearward arrived at Hampton Court next morning —intending apparently to deliver the treatise to Gardiner or Sir Anthony Browne, the King's conservative favourite— Cromwell compelled the bearward to give him the document, and upbraided him for his conduct. When Cranmer heard of the incident, he could laugh and agree with Cromwell that as the bearward was ultimately forced to hand over the treatise, he would have been wiser to have accepted the bribe which

[1] Foxe, v. 265, 398; viii. 14; Parker, p. 390.

Morice had offered him for it; but the scene at the river-side shows the mood of the country in the summer of 1539. Conservatives in the most humble station actually dared to threaten the Archbishop in the presence of his secretary.[1]

It was probably in this summer of 1539 that Sir John Gostwick attacked Cranmer in a speech in the House of Commons. He complained that Cranmer had been preaching heretical sermons at Canterbury and Sandwich. Henry was indignant at Gostwick's conduct; he abused him as a varlet, and ordered him to ask Cranmer's pardon. Gostwick hurried to Lambeth and asked Cranmer for forgiveness, and Cranmer interceded for Gostwick with the King and persuaded him to pardon Gostwick. Morice explains the reason for Henry's anger: he was vexed that Gostwick should publicly criticize the Primate of the realm in Parliament, but above all he was incensed that he should criticize a man who was so high in favour with his Prince. As for Cranmer, he as usual wished to pardon those who had trespassed against him, and he obviously did not wish, at this time, to exacerbate public opinion by victimizing one of his critics.[2]

In opposing the Six Articles in the House of Lords, even in so humble a manner, Cranmer showed for the first time some measure of open resistance to the King's policy, for he had not been able to adopt his usual practice of confining his criticism to the privacy of Henry's closet. He argued openly against the Articles before some hundred Lords spiritual and temporal, and though the debates in the House were not held in public, and no report was published, Cranmer's attitude in the disputation was known everywhere almost immediately. It was probably only after considerable hesitation that Cranmer brought himself

[1] Foxe, v. 388–91.

[2] Morice (*Nar. Ref.*, pp. 251, 253–4); Foxe, viii. 27, where the date of 1544 which is given for this incident was inserted, not by Foxe, but by the editor of the 1839 edition. Parker (p. 392) dates it at the time of the Prebendaries' plot, i.e. 1543; but Gostwick was not a M.P. at this time. He was elected M.P. for Bedfordshire in December 1544, but it is unlikely that he took his seat in the House before he died on 15 April 1545 (see Gairdner, *Lollardy and the Reformation*, ii. 414–5). He may have sat in the Parliament of 1539–40, for which the records are lost. If the attempt to send Cranmer to the Tower was (as I believe) in 1543 (see infra, chap. XV), and Gostwick's speech, as Morice states, was before this, it must have been in the Parliament of 1539–40, as it could hardly have been earlier. It could have been either in the summer of 1539 or in the summer of 1540; but 1539 is perhaps more likely, as Morice and Foxe do not connect Gostwick's speech with the danger in which Cranmer was placed after the fall of Cromwell.

to argue as he did in the disputation; and it certainly required great courage to advocate, in the presence of the King and the indignant nobles, doctrines which had always been held to be heretical and which it was now proposed to punish by death. Morice was right when he wrote to Parker that it was very dangerous for Cranmer to oppose the Six Articles. He might have shared the fate of Latimer and Shaxton, and he expected something worse.[1] He aroused great hatred throughout the country. The plots to denounce him as a heretic a few years later were probably largely due to the notoriety which he had acquired through his opposition to the Six Articles in the House of Lords.

But after this splendid display of courage, Cranmer's surrender at the end of May was complete, and involved a betrayal of fundamental principles of his faith. It was a betrayal which was difficult to justify even on the basis of his doctrine of Christian obedience to the Prince. Cranmer believed, along with most of his contemporaries, that it was the duty of the subject to obey his Prince except when the Prince commanded him to sin; in that case, the subject—though not entitled to resist the Prince—was under a duty to disobey him and suffer martyrdom. To those who believed that the Six Articles were sinful, Cranmer's conduct was shameful, and many of the reformers thought that Cranmer had betrayed the Reformation. George Constantine discussed the Six Articles with Bishop Barlow's brother, the Dean of Westbury-on-Trim, on their four days' journey from Westbury to Carmarthenshire at the end of August 1539. The Dean told Constantine that Cranmer was to blame for the Six Articles, for if he had 'sticked', no man would have agreed to subscribe to the Articles. The fact that the Dean was apparently acting as a provocator, and denounced Constantine as a heretic the day after they reached their destination, does not alter the fact that he was, for his own purposes, expressing views about Cranmer's conduct which he thought were suitable views for a reformer to hold. Constantine replied that there was no reason to blame Cranmer more than Bishop Barlow, and said that he thought that Cranmer would not have subscribed unless Cromwell had forced him to do so.[2]

[1] Morice (*Nar. Ref.*, p. 248); Aless to Elizabeth I, 1 September 1559 (*Cal. For. Pap. Eliz.*, i. 1303, p. 533).

[2] Constantine's report to Cromwell (October 1539) (*Archaeologia*, xxiii. 56–78, especially p. 58).

Under the Act of the Six Articles, Cranmer and Margaret were both liable to be hanged if she remained with him after 12th July. He sent her to her relations in Germany. She had left the country before the visit of Norfolk, Suffolk, and Cromwell to Lambeth, for Cranmer knew that there was no time to lose. When he spoke to Aless during the last days of June, he strongly urged him to leave the country at once before a watch was placed on the ports, and he said that he wished that he himself could escape abroad. Perhaps he was thinking of Margaret when he spoke these words; but for someone in his position, flight would have been impossible, for even if Cranmer could have succeeded in escaping with some kind of false passport, or with none, he would not have wished to bring upon his King the disgrace which a flight of the Primate would have involved. Cranmer then discussed with Aless the dismissal of Shaxton and Latimer, who had not yet been placed in the custody of Sampson and Clerk. Cranmer said that if he had known that those Bishops who refused to accept the Six Articles would suffer nothing worse than dismissal from office, he would never have capitulated and subscribed to the Articles. It is probably incorrect to deduce from this that Cranmer only agreed to support the Six Articles through fear that he would otherwise be executed or imprisoned. If cowardice had in fact been his only motive, he would not have admitted this to Aless. Aless' story indicates rather that Cranmer was in a mood of bitter self-reproach for having surrendered over the Six Articles, and gave vent to his feelings with a statement which was very far from the truth.[1]

But probably this mood of self-reproach did not endure. Cranmer's Prince had ordered him to approve of private masses and the denial of the cup to the laity, to condemn the marriage of priests—including his own marriage—and to believe in transubstantiation; and Cranmer, who had rejected all these doctrines at least since the previous summer, had obeyed. He could only justify his conduct if these doctrines were not sinful,

---

[1] Parker, p. 390; Aless to Elizabeth I, 1 September 1559 (*Cal. For. Pap. Eliz.*, i. 1303, p. 533). Aless' talk with Cranmer cannot have taken place much later than the end of June, for Aless had reached Wittenberg by 9 July (Aless to Cromwell (summer 1539), *L.P.*, xiv [i]. 1353); but Latimer and Shaxton were not deprived until after the close of the Parliamentary session on 28 June (Wriothesley, i. 101).

and he may therefore have persuaded himself to believe in them. The man who could recant his opinions at Oxford in 1556 may have privately recanted in 1539; and certainly his conduct during the months which followed the Six Articles seems to show a strong reaction from his recent attitude of resistance, and almost a zeal to suppress heresy and enforce the Articles. Perhaps he even came to believe that the marriage of priests was wrong, and that his action in sending Margaret to Germany was a virtuous sacrifice.

The Act of the Six Articles was everywhere interpreted as a victory for reaction, and Lord Lisle and the authorities in Calais were not slow to take advantage of the situation. In May 1539 they wrote to Cranmer, complaining that Butler had encouraged heresy and had excommunicated a soldier for having placed a candle before the Host. They therefore informed Cranmer, in language which was almost peremptory, that they had asked Cromwell to remove the Commissary, and that if he did not do so they would write to the King himself. Butler was summoned to London, and the charges against him were investigated. The Council of Calais also sent William Smith, a priest of Calais, and Hare, a soldier of the garrison, to answer charges of heresy for having opposed confession, holy bread and holy water.[1]

Cranmer did not immediately surrender to this pressure from Lisle. He wrote to Lisle that there had been a procedural irregularity in the case against these men, and that he was so dissatisfied with the depositions that he proposed to take no further action. On 24th June Thistlethwaye, a friend of the accused reformers, wrote in a letter that Butler and William Smith would not be proceeded against and would soon return to Calais, while Prior Dove and Lady Lisle's chaplain would repent this business. He was also confident that Hare would not suffer. But it was perhaps no accident that Thistlethwaye had not been able to see Cranmer, who had been too busy to receive him; for within a fortnight Cranmer was in full retreat. On 26th June, Lisle wrote a firm letter to Cranmer, in which he said that the Council of Calais were fully satisfied with the evidence against the accused reformers to which Cranmer had

[1] The Council of Calais to Cranmer (May 1539), *L.P.*, xiv [i]. 1058; Foxe, v. 506.

objected. On 1st July, Lisle's agent Husee reported that the rumour that William Smith and Hare had been acquitted was not true; Cranmer was handling the accused very gently, but Hare would probably have to carry his fagot, and Smith the priest would not escape as easily as he expected. Husee's only regret was that no serious accusations were being brought against Butler; but by 9th July, he was able to write to Lisle that Butler too was facing his judges.[1]

The case of these Calais heretics was referred to a special Commission, with Cranmer presiding. Foxe's account of Hare's trial shows Gardiner as playing the leading part, and Cranmer a somewhat more reluctant one; but a very different impression is given in the letters written at the time by Lisle's agents. On 6th July, Warley wrote to Lisle an account of Hare's trial at Lambeth on the previous day which he had been given by John Leland the antiquary and another man who had been present. Warley reported that Cranmer had spoken very earnestly against Hare, and had ordered him to renounce his opinions.[2]

The change which had taken place in Cranmer's attitude to Hare in the course of a few days is striking. On 1st July, Husee was complaining to Lisle that Cranmer was handling Hare very gently; on the 6th, Warley, in a letter which is full of jubilation over the arrest of Latimer and other reformers, is satisfied that Cranmer had spoken very earnestly against Hare on the previous day. On the 5th, Cranmer and his fellow Commissioners wrote to Lisle, asking him to provide them with evidence that Hare had been guilty of heresy since the King's pardon to the Anabaptists and sacramentaries of February 1539, on which Hare was relying. A few days later, they were sitting as judges over Butler, William Smith and Thomas Broke, who represented Calais in the House of Commons and had opposed the Six Articles. Broke and Smith were charged with having uttered words in private conversation—in some cases, several years before—which implied disbelief in the Real Presence. The depositions in these cases revealed that two other men of Calais, who had not been sent to London, had been friends and supporters of Damplip. Cranmer asked why they were not before the

---

[1] Thistlethwaye to Sutton, 24 June 1539; Lisle to Cranmer, 26 June 1539; Husee to Lisle, 1 and 9 July 1539 (*L.P.*, xiv [i]. 1153, 1164, 1194, 1238).
[2] Foxe, v. 506–9; Warley to Lisle, 6 July 1539 (*L.P.*, xiv [i]. 1219)

Court, as there were charges for them to answer; and Long the soldier, whom Foxe lists among the 'persecutors' in Calais, duly saw to it that Lisle was informed as to what Cranmer had said. Here we see Cranmer taking the initiative in bringing these two other heretics to trial when even Lisle and his faction had not troubled to do so.[1]

Lisle knew to what extent Cranmer's position had been weakened by his opposition to the Six Articles, and he now wrote to Cranmer in an arrogant style very different from his courteous letters of the previous five years. On one occasion, he failed to address Cranmer as 'your Grace', which caused his ally Sampson to remonstrate with him on this false step, which had not passed unnoticed. But not for the first time, Cranmer reacted to arrogance from a powerful dignitary by becoming more conciliatory, and his letter to Lisle of 13th July marks a complete surrender. He promised to replace Butler as Commissary, and agreed to Lisle's request that he should impose restrictions on preaching in Calais. Lisle had complained that the people were defying the recent royal edict which prohibited them from reading the Bible in church during divine service and from arguing as to the meaning of the text; and Cranmer asked Lisle, in the absence of a Commissary, to enforce this order by his own authority in Calais. After dictating the letter, Cranmer added a note in his own hand in which he urged Lisle to try to find some new evidence against Hare and Broke which referred to words spoken by them since the date of the King's general pardon; 'for the more matters that be against them, the more it is to their condemnation'.[2]

Hare and Smith both recanted, and were sent back to Calais to perform their penance and carry their fagots there. Having been so active in the proceedings against them, Cranmer ventured to intervene with Lisle in their favour to the extent of writing on 28th July to request him not to imprison them or to inflict any other punishment upon them in addition to their penance. There was not sufficient evidence on which the Commissioners could condemn Broke; but he was sent to the Fleet for nearly four months while his case was further investigated. As

[1] Cranmer, Sampson and Gwent to Lisle, 5 July 1539 (Cranmer's *Works*, ii. 390); Foxe, v. 509–13; Husee to Lisle, 9 July 1539 (*L.P.*, xiv [i]. 1238).
[2] Sampson to Lisle, 20 July 1539 (*L.P.*, xiv [i]. 1290); Cranmer to Lisle, 13 July 1539 (Cranmer's *Works*, ii. 390–2).

for the Commissary, Cranmer appointed Harvey to succeed Butler in Calais. Harvey was so staunch a conservative that within two years he had been arrested and executed as a Papist traitor.[1]

At the end of July 1539, Cranmer examined a priest and a woman who had been caught in an act of immorality at Croydon. The woman had been the priest's mistress for three years, and though the priest declared that they had had no intercourse since Cranmer had ordered him not to associate with her, the woman confessed to an act of intimacy since 12th July, when the Six Articles came into force. Cranmer reported the case to Cromwell, and wrote: 'And forasmuch as there is no commission out as yet for the due correction and punishment of such offenders according to the Act in this behalf, I shall desire your Lordship to advertise me with convenient expedition of the King's Grace's pleasure, how and in what manner they shall be ordered'. The priest and the woman had not gone through any form of marriage ceremony—a fact which exempted them from the death penalty for the first offence—and as all the reformers were strongly opposed to illicit intercourse by priests, Cranmer was acting in accordance with his principles in taking steps to punish these culprits. But it is easy to imagine what the priest would have thought if he had known that the Archbishop himself had been cohabiting with a woman until a month before, for the majority of the English people, if they had known that Cranmer had married Margaret, would have thought that Cranmer's sin was far greater than that of the priest at Croydon. The eagerness with which Cranmer was seeking to enforce the Act of the Six Articles, before any Commission for executing the statute had been set up, shows how far he had gone since his great surrender at the end of May. But Cranmer had sent Margaret away, and having made the sacrifice for the cause of Christian obedience, he would not forgive a fornicating priest who had not done the same.[2]

But the triumph of the reaction, which had seemed complete in July, was short-lived. By September Henry had become alarmed at the growing friendship between Francis I and Charles V—

[1] Cranmer to Lisle, 28 July 1539 (Cranmer's *Works*, ii. 393); Foxe, v. 512–13, 523; *Chronicle of Calais*, p. 47; Wriothesley, i. 126. Peterson, Cranmer's first Commissary in Calais, was also executed as a Papist traitor in 1540.

[2] Cranmer to Cromwell, 30 July 1539 (Cranmer's *Works*, ii. 394–5); Examinations of Somer and Bayley, 28 July 1539 (*L.P.*, xiv [i]. 1333).

a friendship which culminated in the meeting at Loches in December 1539, about which Cranmer was informed in advance by one of his spies. Henry decided to adopt Cromwell's policy of forming an alliance with the German Lutherans by marrying Anne of Cleves. Cranmer was one of the English representatives who negotiated the marriage treaty with the delegates of Cleves and Saxony at Windsor. In this situation, Cromwell engaged in a fierce struggle for power with his opponents. Cranmer does not seem to have given Cromwell any assistance in this struggle. His attitude in July 1539 shows that he had passively accepted the reaction with all its consequences, and would never have struck back at the conservatives if Cromwell had not done so. He was, however, credited by the rumour-mongers with a part in the struggle for power between Cromwell and Tunstall which was supposed to be taking place. By November, the wildest stories were circulating. Tunstall's servants in his palace in Durham asserted that ten thousand citizens of London had risen and marched on Lambeth while Cranmer was sitting in judgment on an honest preacher who had been arrested for attacking heresy. Everyone believed that the reformers were once more in the ascendancy. The new situation saved the heretics of Calais who had not yet been dealt with. On 11th November, Cranmer and the other Commissioners reported to Cromwell that there was insufficient evidence on which they could convict the Calais men, and they were all discharged. Two days before, Husee had written to warn Lisle that Cromwell was now very hostile to him. It is not surprising that Lisle hastened to send some gifts of wine to Cranmer.[1]

The German Lutherans had been in despair over Henry's conservative religious policy and the Act of the Six Articles. Melanchthon wrote a letter of protest to Cranmer. On 23rd October, Luther, Justus Jonas, Bugenhagen and Melanchthon told the Duke of Saxony that it was useless to place any hopes

[1] Documents of the Cleves marriage negotiations (September–October 1539); Husee to Lisle, 9 November 1539; Swerder to Cranmer, 10 November 1539; Cranmer, Sampson and others to Cromwell, 11 November 1539; Depositions of Chaitour and others (December 1539 and 6 January 1540) (*L.P.*, xiv [ii]. 285, 286, 487, 492, 496, 750 (pp. 278, 280–1); xv. 31; Teschenmacher, *Codex Diplomatum*, pp. 144–9, in *Annales Cliviae*); Cranmer to Lisle, 17 November 1539 (Cranmer's *Works*, ii. 316, where it is wrongly dated 1535; see *L.P.* xiv [ii]. 537).

in Henry, as he was utterly unprincipled in religion, though for
opportunist reasons he had for long tolerated 'pious, learned
preachers like the deprived Bishop Latimer, Crome and others'.
They no longer mentioned Cranmer as one of the pious men of
England. On 29th October, Bucer wrote to Cranmer, enclosing a
letter from Grynaeus to Cranmer, which Grynaeus had asked
him to forward to Cranmer if he did not consider it to be too
harsh. Bucer told Cranmer that though it was very harsh, he
had nevertheless decided to forward it. Bucer's own letter was
very different from that which he had written to Cranmer two
years before. He had obviously been taken completely by surprise by the Six Articles, and was utterly disillusioned with
Henry. But when Burckhardt returned from England after
negotiating the Cleves marriage treaty, he was able to assuage
the fears of his colleagues. He explained to Melanchthon that
the Act of the Six Articles had not been put into force, that
Stokesley, who had instigated it, had now died, and that
Cromwell, Cranmer and Audley were excellent men who were
now more firmly in power than ever, as the attempts of their
enemies to oust them had failed. Burckhardt hoped that the Act
would be repealed when Henry married Anne of Cleves.[1]

In the autumn of 1539, Cranmer was concerned with the
publication of a new edition of the Bible. This edition, which
was published in April 1540, has become known as 'Cranmer's
Bible', though this name is sometimes inappropriately given to
the first edition of the Great Bible of April 1539. It is an irony
that Cranmer should have been more closely connected with
the third authorized translation of 1540 than with those of 1537
and 1539, because the edition of 1540 was the first which was
produced under the influence of the religious reaction, when
Cranmer's doctrines, including his belief in the importance of
reading Scripture, had begun to be threatened. In the summer of
1539, Henry issued a proclamation re-emphasizing that
although he was pleased to permit his subjects to read the
Bible, he was not compelled by God's word to do so, and prohibiting the reading of the Bible aloud to another. In a country
where the majority of the people were illiterate, this order was

[1] Burckhardt to Melanchthon (October 1539); Luther, Melanchthon and others to
John Frederick of Saxony, 23 October 1539 (*Corpus Ref.*, iii. 600–1, 796–800);
Bucer to Cranmer, 29 October 1539 (*Orig. Letters*, pp. 526–30); see also Aless to
Cromwell (summer 1539) (*L.P.*, xiv [i]. 1353).

a serious set-back to the spread of Scripture among the people. It was in these circumstances that Cranmer wrote his Preface to the new edition. On 14th November he wrote to Cromwell to inquire whether the King had approved his draft of the Preface, which must therefore have been written a few months earlier, at the height of the reaction which followed the enactment of the Six Articles.[1]

In the Preface, Cranmer explained that he had written it for the benefit of two different sorts of persons—'for truly some there are that be too slow and need the spur; some other seem too quick, and need more of the bridle'. There were those who refused to read Scripture, or even hindered others from reading it, and those 'which by their inordinate reading, undiscreet speaking, contentious disputing or otherwise by their licentious living, slander and hinder the word of God most of all other, whereof they would seem to be greatest furtherers'. Cranmer stated that he considered both groups to be equally reprehensible. He cited a long quotation from St. John Chrysostom to show the benefits to be derived from reading the Bible by all classes of persons, and then wrote that it was unnecessary to say more: it was sufficient that the reading of Scripture was approved of by Chrysostom and Henry VIII. 'This one place of John Chrysostom is enough and sufficient to persuade all them that be not frowardly and perversely set in their own wilful opinion; specially now that the King's Highness, being Supreme Head next under Christ of this Church of England, hath approved with his royal assent the setting forth hereof; which only to all true and obedient subjects ought to be a sufficient reason for the allowance of the same, without farther delay, reclamation or resistance, although there were no Preface, nor other reason herein expressed.

Cranmer then cited a lengthy passage from St. Gregory Nazianzene against presumptuous interpretation of Scripture by the unlearned. The object of reading the Bible was to reform oneself; he who otherwise intermeddled with the book would have to make account therefor. In his letter to Cromwell of 14th November 1539 he wrote that his purpose in the Preface was

[1] Proclamation against arguing on Scripture (Strype, *Eccl. Mem.*, i. [ii]. 434–7; the text of the proclamation shows that it was drafted during the Parliamentary session of April–June 1539); Cranmer to Cromwell, 14 November 1539 (Cranmer's *Works*, ii. 396, wrongly dated 1538 in *St. Pap.*, i. 590 n.).

to 'encourage many slow readers, and also stay the rash judgments of them that read therein'. He placed quite as much
emphasis on the latter as on the former object in the Preface.[1]

The surviving monasteries had been suppressed by statute in
the summer of 1539. Cranmer played a more active part in the
dissolution of the greater houses than in that of the smaller
monasteries in 1536, being concerned in the suppression of his
own priory of Christ Church in Canterbury and of the priory
at Rochester. In November 1539, Cromwell consulted Cranmer
with regard to the new establishment which was to be set up
at Christ Church to replace the priory. It was proposed to
appoint a Dean, twelve Prebendaries and six preachers, while
the establishment was to maintain ten students of divinity at
both Oxford and Cambridge, and sixty schoolboys in Canterbury. Cranmer made a number of criticisms of the scheme. He
objected to the appointment of twelve Prebendaries, who were
each to receive a salary of £40 a year, because Prebendaries
were prone to idleness and good living—'superfluous belly
cheer'—and were usually neither learners nor teachers, but
good vianders. He suggested that the office of Prebendary be
abolished, as Prebendaries were not mentioned by St. Paul as
being one of the estates of the Church, and proposed that the
money allotted for the salary of the Prebendaries should be
spent on maintaining twenty divines and forty students of
languages, the sciences and French in addition to the sixty
children learning grammar, logic, Hebrew, Greek and Latin.

The plan for Christ Church was typical of the age in allotting
£630 a year to the Dean and the twelve Prebendaries, while
only £200 a year was to be spent on maintaining twenty
divinity students at Oxford and Cambridge, and another £200
on the maintenance of sixty children at the school. The salary
of the Dean and Prebendaries amounted to one-third of the
total expenditure on the establishment of seventy-four persons,
on the repairs of the premises, on almsgiving, and on the wages
of six men to repair the highways in the vicinity. Cranmer had
no objection to this economic inequality; but his proposal to
spend £200 on twenty additional students rather than £480
for the Prebendaries to dissipate in good living, shows his con-

[1] Cranmer's Preface to the Bible of 1540; Cranmer to Cromwell, 14 November
1539 (Cranmer's *Works*, ii. 118–25, 396).

cern for education, as does his desire to enlarge the curriculum by the inclusion of the sciences and French along with the traditional subjects. Cranmer referred all his recommendations to the King to allow or disallow at his pleasure. They were all disallowed.[1]

After Cranmer's death, Morice wrote an account of Cranmer's discussions at about this time with Sir Anthony St. Leger, Rich, Hales and another Commissioner with regard to the education of poor children at Canterbury. Several of the Commissioners considered that only the sons of gentlemen should be admitted as scholars at the school, but Cranmer wished it to be open to children of all classes. He said that poor men's children were often endowed with gifts of nature, such as eloquence, memory, apt pronunciation and sobriety, which were the gifts of God, and they were frequently more studious than gentlemen's sons. His opponents said that a son should follow his father's vocation, and that only gentlemen's sons ought to learn the knowledge of government; for there was as much need of ploughmen as of any other class, and not every man could go to school. Cranmer replied that there was much truth in this argument; but to exclude poor men's children completely from the opportunity of receiving education would be to deny God's right to bestow His gifts wherever he would, and as presumptuous as setting up a Tower of Babylon. God would punish us for this by making our best born children dolts. Cranmer told his colleagues that though they were all gentlemen by birth, their families had originally sprung from low-class origins. If the gentleman's son was apt for learning, he should be admitted to the school; but if he were not, then a poor man's son should be chosen in his place.[2]

This conversation shows us Cranmer's ideas about social relationships. He believed that the lower classes must show respect and obedience to their social superiors, but thought that their gifted children should be permitted to rise in society, though he clearly implied that if a gentleman's son showed ability in learning, he should oust an equally intelligent child

---

[1] Commissions of 20 March 1540 (*L.P.*, xv. 378); Goldwell to Cromwell, 24 February 1540 (Ellis, *Letters*, iii [iii]. 277–8); Cranmer to Cromwell, 29 November 1539; Draft plan for Christ Church, Canterbury (Cranmer's *Works*, ii. 396–8).

[2] Morice's MS. for Foxe (*Nar. Ref.*, pp. 273–5).

THOMAS CRANMER

of humbler parentage. Here Cranmer did not go as far as Pole, who declared, when he was Archbishop, that though the children of the rich should not necessarily be excluded from the schools of the cathedral foundations, these were primarily intended for the education of poor men's sons;[1] but as the only churchman among the Commissioners, Cranmer maintained the viewpoint of the old Church on the question of educating the poor against the typical attitude of the gentry of the age.

[1] Pole's Constitution, 8 February 1556 (*Reform of England by Cardinal Pole*, p. 51).

CHAPTER XIII

THE FALL OF CROMWELL

ANNE of Cleves arrived at Dover on 29th December 1539. Cranmer and three Bishops received her in the wind and sleet on Barham Down, three miles from Canterbury, with an escort composed of the neighbouring gentlemen and Cranmer's own servants, whom he had hastily assembled in view of the breakdown in the official arrangements for Anne's reception. Cranmer accompanied Anne on her journey to Greenwich, and was present at the meeting of the Council on the evening of her arrival at which Henry, who had been disgusted by Anne's physical features, announced that he had doubts as to the validity of a marriage to Anne in view of Anne's precontract to Francis of Lorraine. The wedding was postponed for two days, while the Council re-opened discussions the same evening with Harff and Olisleger, the envoys of Cleves, who repeated the assurance which they had given at Windsor in October that the engagement between Francis of Lorraine and Anne had amounted only to espousals, and offered to obtain from Cleves a solemn declaration as to the absence of any precontract. The matter was then referred to Cranmer and Tunstall as canonists, and they decided that it appeared from the statement of the envoys of Cleves that there had been no precontract and no bar to Anne's marriage to the King. Henry and Anne were married by Cranmer on 6th January.[1]

Anne of Cleves was the third wife whom Henry married on the strength of a decision by Cranmer, and in her case, as in the case of Anne Boleyn, Cranmer was later obliged to rescind his original decision that the marriage was valid. On this occasion, Cranmer must have been fully aware of the implications of his

---

[1] Order for reception of Anne of Cleves (November 1539) (*Chronicle of Calais*, pp. 167–71); Suffolk and Cheyney to Cromwell, 29 December 1539; anonymous account of Anne of Cleves' journey; letter to Lady Lisle, 4 January 1540; Documents of the negotiations with Cleves, 5 January 1539/40 (*L.P.*, xiv [ii]. 754; xv. 14, 18, 861 [2] [1]); Cranmer to Cromwell, 29 December 1539 (Cranmer's *Works*, ii. 400); Wriothesley, i. 109–11; Hall, pp. 832–7; Depositions in Anne of Cleves' divorce (July 1540) (Strype, *Eccl. Mem.* i [ii]. 452–9); Cromwell to Henry VIII, two letters of 30 June 1540 (Merriman, ii. 268–76).

decision, and that a ruling that the marriage would be invalid, after Anne's state reception in England, would destroy all possibility of an alliance with the Lutherans and would involve the ruin of Cromwell. As Cranmer supported Cromwell and the German alliance, it cannot have been necessary to subject him to the pressure which Cromwell applied to Henry and possibly to Tunstall, who was supposed to be Cromwell's chief rival for power. The decision of Cranmer and Tunstall was indisputably correct on the point of canon law; the issue was one of fact as to the nature of the declarations which had been exchanged between Anne and Francis of Lorraine. On this point, the Bishops chose to accept the assurances of the envoys of Cleves; six months later, they chose not to accept them.

Henry's marriage to Anne of Cleves raised the hopes of the German Lutherans for an improvement in religious doctrines in England, and John Frederick of Saxony wrote to both Henry and Cranmer on this matter. On 10th May 1540, Cranmer replied to the Elector in a letter which was a eulogy of Henry. He compared Henry to a Hercules who had performed three great labours: he had expelled the Papal authority from England, he had suppressed idolatry—a reference, no doubt, to the suppression of the shrines—and he had destroyed the monasteries. If the German Lutherans wished to criticize any of the doctrines in force in England, they should remember that Henry was a most wise and pious Prince who had many wise and learned men to advise him. Perhaps Cranmer did not fully realize even now what his wise and pious Prince—the Prince who had decreed the Six Articles—was preparing to do; but when Cranmer returned to Lambeth from his diocese in April for the new session of Parliament, the situation was very ominous. Gardiner and Tunstall had been readmitted to the Council from which they had been excluded at the end of 1539; and in his Lenten sermons at Paul's Cross, Gardiner had attacked the Lutheran doctrine of justification which, as Bucer had pointed out, had hitherto survived the Six Articles and the attacks of the conservatives. Barnes' counter-attack on Gardiner had ended with Barnes, Jerome and Cranmer's chaplain Garrett being compelled to make a public recantation at Paul's Cross and imprisoned in the Tower. On 10th April, the French Ambassador Marillac wrote to Montmorency, the Constable of France, that

Cromwell was tottering, for the men who had seized the loot of the monasteries were now about to destroy the doctors whose preaching had incited them to the looting—including Cromwell and Cranmer, who 'do not know where they are'. But eight days later, Cromwell was created Earl of Essex and Lord Great Chamberlain of England, and he struck at his most highly-placed antagonists with unparalleled audacity. He sent Lord Lisle to the Tower on a charge of treason for plotting to deliver Calais to the French.[1]

At the end of May, Sampson, who two hours before had been appointed to be the first Bishop of the new diocese of Westminster, was arrested on a charge of treason. Sampson had been engaged in giving a series of lectures at St. Paul's, and Cranmer now took his place and lectured at St. Paul's in the first week of June. He presumably dealt with justification in these lectures, for he is said to have refuted the doctrines which Gardiner had put forward in his Lenten sermons during his controversy with Barnes; but it is unlikely that Cranmer went beyond the doctrine laid down in the Bishops' Book, which on the subject of justification gave full opportunity for a difference in emphasis between Cranmer and Gardiner.[2]

In the hour of triumph, the struggle for power ended in irrevocable defeat when Cromwell was arrested at the Council table on 10th June. It seems clear from Cranmer's letter to Henry that he was actually present at this meeting of the Council, and witnessed—no doubt in silence—the disgraceful scene when Norfolk tore the Cross of St. George from Cromwell's neck and all the Lords of the Council insulted him as he was hustled to the Tower. Marillac wrote to Montmorency that Cromwell's faction had been completely routed by Cromwell's arrest, for his only supporters were Cranmer, who did not dare to open his mouth, and Russell, the Lord Admiral, who had long since learned to bend to all winds.[3] Cranmer did, however, dare to open his mouth, and next day wrote the famous letter which survives only in the form in which it was published by Lord

[1] Seckendorff, iii. 261; Foxe, v. 430–4; Wriothesley, i. 114; *Greyfriars Chron.*, p. 43; Bucer to Cranmer, 29 October 1539 (*Orig. Letters*, p. 529); Marillac to Montmorency, 10 April 1540 (Ribier, *Lettres et Mémoires d'Estat*, i. 513).
[2] Marillac to Montmorency, 1 June 1540 (Kaulek, *Correspondance de Castillon et de Marillac*, pp. 187–8).
[3] Marillac to Montmorency, 11 and 23 June 1540 (Kaulek, pp. 190, 193–4).

Herbert in 1649. Lord Herbert states that he faithfully tran-
scribed the letter from the original, and though he obviously
omitted the formal words at the beginning and end of the letter,
it is not clear whether the text is otherwise complete.

Herbert writes that Cranmer intervened on Cromwell's behalf, 'for though (as is in his letter) he heard yesterday in his
Grace's Council that he is a traitor; yet he saith, who cannot be
sorrowful and amazed that he should be a traitor against your
Majesty, he that was so advanced by your Majesty, he whose
surety was only by your Majesty, he who loved your Majesty
(as I ever thought) no less than God; he who studied always to
set forwards whatsoever was your Majesty's will and pleasure;
he that cared for no man's displeasure to serve your Majesty; he
that was such a servant, in my judgment, in wisdom, diligence,
faithfulness and experience, as no Prince in this realm ever had;
he that was so vigilant to preserve your Majesty from all
treasons, that few could be so secretly conceived, but he de-
tected the same in the beginning? If the noble Princes of
memory, King John, Henry II and Richard II had had such a
councillor about them, I suppose they should never have been so
traitorously abandoned and overthrown as those good Princes
were; after which, he says again, I loved him as my friend, for
so I took him to be; but I chiefly loved him for the love which I
thought I saw him bear ever towards your Grace, singularly
above all other; but now, if he be a traitor, I am sorry that ever
I loved him, or trusted him, and I am very glad that his treason
is discovered in time; but yet again I am very sorrowful; for
who shall your Grace trust hereafter, if you might not trust him?
Alas! I bewail and lament your Grace's chance herein, I wot not
whom your Grace may trust. But I pray God continually night
and day to send such a counsellor in his place whom your Grace
may trust, and who for all his qualities can and will serve your
Grace like to him, and that will have so much solicitude and care
to preserve your Grace from all dangers as I ever thought he had.'[1]

This letter has often been compared to that which Cranmer
wrote after the arrest of Anne Boleyn, and both letters have

[1] Lord Herbert, *Henry VIII*, p. 457. The letter is printed in Cranmer's *Works*,
ii. 401, where the editor has transformed the opening passages of Herbert's text
into direct speech, and has dated it 14 June; but Cranmer wrote that he had heard
of Cromwell's arrest 'yesterday', thus clearly indicating that the letter was written
on 11 June.

been portrayed both as a courageous intercession and as a
cowardly betrayal of a fallen patron. The two letters were
written in very similar circumstances, though the two situations
were not identical. Anne Boleyn was accused of adultery, and
when Cranmer wrote his plea for her he could not have known
whether she was innocent or guilty; but Cromwell was charged
with treason in having attempted to force the King to further
the Reformation in which Cranmer himself believed. The
situation was far more dangerous for Cranmer in 1540 than in
1536, and this probably accounts for the fact that despite the
striking similarities there is one great difference between the
two letters. The chief purpose of Cranmer's letter about Anne
was to urge Henry not to abandon his support of the Reformation because of Anne's adultery; but he made no attempt, in his
letter of 1540, to dissuade Henry from pursuing the policy of
religious reaction which prevailed after the fall of Cromwell.

The letter of 1540 was nevertheless a courageous one to
write at a time when it was clear that Cromwell was lost, and
when Cranmer was expected to follow him to the Tower. To
appreciate it, we should compare it with the letter which
Henry received from his Ambassador to the Emperor. Two
months before, Pate had written to congratulate Cromwell on
being created Earl of Essex, assuring him that he did not have a
more faithful servant or truer bedesman in the world than Pate.
But now Pate wrote to Henry: 'O most noble and gracious
Prince, what complacency of himself, trust to his own wit and
judgment, what blindness, I say, and ingratitude is this of this
traitor, far passing Lucifer's, that by his example could not be
admonished to know himself, nor his Sovereign Lord, but
intending to pluck the sword out of his hand, hath deserved to
feel the power of the same to his confusion . . . but lauded be
our Lord God that hath delivered your Grace out of the bear's
claws, as not long before of a semblable danger of the lioness
that evermore thirsted the blood of your nobility.'[1]

Pate, it is true, had probably always been a secret opponent
of Cromwell, and Cranmer's letter may perhaps be more aptly
compared with one written by a conservative Bishop when it was
his turn to watch the downfall of his faction as Cranmer did in

[1] Pate to Cromwell, 27 April 1540; Pate to Henry VIII, 27 June 1540 (*St. Pap.*, viii. 338, 365).

1540. When Thirlby heard of the arrest of Norfolk and Surrey at Christmas 1546, he wrote to Paget, the King's Secretary: 'I would write unto you my heart, if I could, against those two ungracious, ingrate and inhuman *non homines*, the Duke of Norfolk and his son. The elder of whom I confess that I did love, for that I ever supposed him a true servant to his master; like as both his allegiance and the manifold benefits of the King's Majesty bound him to have been; but now when I should begin to write to you herein, before God I am so amazed at the matter, that I know not what to say; therefore I shall leave them to receive for their deeds as they have worthily deserved'.[1]

But Cranmer could not maintain his upright attitude without being involved in utter ruin. He was not required, as in the case of Anne Boleyn, to play a vital part in the proceedings against Cromwell; but he was present in the House of Lords on 19th June for the second and third readings of the Bill of Attainder which condemned Cromwell to death without permitting him to appear in his own defence. As the records state that the bill was carried with the consent of all who were present without a single dissentient voice, it is clear that Cranmer declared himself in favour of it, or at least allowed it to go through with unanimous approval, although the bill condemned Cromwell, not only as a traitor, but also as a heretic, and sentenced him to be hanged, drawn and quartered, or burned, at the King's pleasure. Cromwell's heresy was stated, in the statute, to consist of having encouraged Barnes and other heretics and disseminated heretical books; but Cranmer himself had done as much, both as regards doctrine and the protection of reformers, as his old colleague whom he was now, by his vote, sentencing to be burned for these offences.[2]

Cranmer was now required, for the third time, to play a leading part in divorcing Henry from his Queen. On this occasion, he did not sit alone as judge, for the case was tried by Convocation; but it is difficult to minimize Cranmer's role in the hurried and highly questionable divorce of Anne of Cleves, though Gardiner, who welcomed the divorce far more than Cranmer, certainly played a more important part. Cranmer was one of the

<hr />

[1] Thirlby to Paget, 25 December 1546 (Burnet, vi. 271).
[2] *H. L. Jo.*, 19 June 1540; Act of Attainder of Cromwell, 32 Hen. VIII, c. 60 (Burnet, iv. 415–23).

six members of the House of Lords who asked Henry to permit Convocation to determine the validity of his marriage. He presided at the sessions of the Committee of Convocation which examined the evidence, which reached the conclusion that the marriage was void, and which drafted the decree of divorce, though he was not a member of Gardiner's sub-committee which examined the witnesses; and he presided at the full sessions of Convocation when the decision and decree were approved. He afterwards, along with Archbishop Lee and Gardiner, announced the decision of Convocation, first to the House of Lords and then to the House of Commons. Cranmer was also one of the witnesses for the King. He signed a deposition, along with Audley, Norfolk, Suffolk, Southampton and Tunstall, dealing with the meeting of the Council and the negotiations with the envoys of Cleves at Greenwich on 3rd and 4th January, in order to show the doubts which had then arisen as to the validity of the marriage and the nature of Anne's commitment to Francis of Lorraine, and the reluctance with which Henry had consented to the marriage.[1]

The judgment declared the marriage void on three grounds—because of Anne's precontract with Francis of Lorraine, because the King had not freely entered into the marriage, and because he had not been able to consummate it. As regards the first grounds, Cranmer had formed the opinion in January, after hearing the statements of the envoys of Cleves, that the engagement between Anne and Francis of Lorraine was an espousal *de futuri*; in July, after reading the document which the envoys had sent, he reversed his opinion and decided that the engagement had been a precontract *de presenti*. There is nothing in the document which could justify such a conclusion. As for the second grounds, Cranmer knew that this was a fabrication, for he could not have believed that Cromwell, and he himself and his fellow-Councillors, had exerted such a degree of pressure on Henry to marry Anne that it invalidated the marriage through lack of free consent on Henry's part. Cranmer can perhaps hardly be blamed for accepting the evidence of non-consummation which was given by Henry and his courtiers and physicians, highly unsatisfactory though it is, in view of the fact that Anne

[1] *H. L. Jo.*, 6 and 10 July 1540; Records of Anne of Cleves' divorce, (July 1540) (Wilkins, iii. 851–5; Strype, *Eccl. Mem.* i [ii]. 452–3.

had been dissuaded by intimidation from defending the case; but his decision and that of Convocation was of course once again a political one.[1]

After assisting in the attainder of Cromwell and the divorce of a Protestant Queen on spurious grounds, Cranmer was next required to support the bill which declared Barnes, Jerome and his chaplain Garrett to be heretics, and sentenced them to be burned or to suffer any other kind of death which might please the King's Majesty. Cranmer voted in favour of the bill at the first and second readings on 17th and 19th July, though he was absent for the third reading on 21st July. It can have been little consolation to Cranmer that his old adversary Lisle and other prominent conservatives of Calais were included in the attainder, and sentenced to death for treason in the same bill which condemned the three reformers. Lisle was eventually pardoned, but promptly died of shock.

At the stake, Barnes declared that he had never been informed of what his heresy was alleged to consist. Parliament did not trouble to give any indication of this in the Act of Attainder; but in fact, Barnes was selected as the foremost representative in England of the Lutheran connexion.[2] He had no sympathy with sacramentaries, and had been most active in burning them. The only heretical opinions for which Barnes could have been condemned were his denial of transubstantiation—as opposed to the Real Presence—his doctrine of justification, his attacks on Purgatory and private masses in all their aspects, and his doctrine that priests could marry. Cranmer himself had been prepared, at least in private, to advocate the same views until a little over a year before. Cranmer has often been accused by his critics of concurring in the burning of men who believed in doctrines in which he himself believed; and this accusation, which is false as regards the cases of Frith and Lambert, appears to be justified of his action in voting for the attainder of Barnes. But in 1540, Cranmer was in grave danger, and was himself liable to be sentenced by the unanimous vote of his colleagues in the House of Lords and of the House of Commons to be burned for unspecified heresies.

[1] Records of Anne of Cleves' divorce (Burnet, iv. 431–9; L.P., xv. 861 [2] [iii]; Strype, Eccl. Mem. i. [ii]. 452–63).
[2] H. L. Jo., 17, 19 and 21 July 1540; Act of Attainder of Lisle, Barnes and others, 32 Hen. VIII, c. 58 (printed in part by Froude, iii. 333–4); Foxe, v. 435.

Cromwell was beheaded on 28th July. On the 30th, Barnes, Garrett and Jerome were burned at Smithfield, while simultaneously three priests were hanged, drawn and quartered at a few yards distance for denial of the royal supremacy. This grisly co-execution of Papists and heretics, after they had been dragged to Smithfield with one Papist and one heretic together on each hurdle, made a great impression on the people, and Foxe has given a remarkable explanation of it. He says that there was a division in the Council between what he calls the 'Protestants' and the 'Papists', with the Protestants demanding the execution of the three traitors, and the Papists demanding death for the three heretics. It was therefore agreed to execute them all. Foxe states that the Protestant Councillors were Cranmer, Suffolk, Edward Seymour, John Dudley, Russell, Paget, Sadler and Audley, and that the Papists were Gardiner, Tunstall, Norfolk, Southampton, Browne, Paulet, Baker, Rich and Wingfield. When Foxe wrote this passage, he can hardly have been in a good position to know about the discussions in the Council twenty-three years before, for he had not yet met Morice, who might have acquired the information as Cranmer's secretary. It is unlikely that this bloody compromise of executing all the six men was actually agreed between the two factions in the Council; but it was undoubtedly safer in 1540 for both sides to denounce Papists or heretics rather than to attempt to save their supporters, and as Cranmer would not have dared to make a plea for the three reformers, and Gardiner had no wish to save the three Papists, the decision in the Council to advise the King to execute them all was doubtless unanimous.[1]

In April 1540, Cromwell had announced the establishment of a Commission, consisting of the two Archbishops, six Bishops and twelve other divines, for the purpose of examining Christian institutions. At first the Commissioners sat on six days a week, but later they adopted the method of replying to questions in writing, and during the summer or autumn, Cranmer drafted the Seventeen Questions on the Sacraments for himself and his colleagues to answer. The Commissioners, after first giving their individual answers, held discussions amongst themselves,

---

[1] Marillac to Francis I, 6 August 1540 (Kaulek, pp. 208–9); Wriothesley, i. 120–1; Foxe, v. 438–9; Hilles to Bullinger (summer 1541) (*Orig. Letters*, pp. 209–11).

as a result of which many of them were able to agree on joint replies, though it was impossible to reach unanimity. A further document containing these revised and joint opinions was then submitted to the King. Cranmer, after originally giving his separate answers to his own questions, later wrote a second set of answers together with Barlow, the Bishop of St. Davids, which on some points gained the approval of some of the other Commissioners. The opinions which Cranmer expressed in this second document were strikingly different from those which he put forward on the first occasion.[1]

The Seventeen Questions dealt with three main issues—the number and origin of the Sacraments; the Prince's power to appoint and consecrate Bishops and priests; and the necessity for confession. On the question of the Sacraments, Cranmer in the first document stated his belief that the early authors spoke of far more than seven Sacraments, but that of all these Sacraments only Baptism, the Lord's Supper, Penance and Matrimony were instituted as Sacraments in Scripture. He adhered to this in his later answers, though he and Barlow altered the wording of his earlier answers so as to weaken the effect on nearly every point. With regard to confession, there was likewise no actual contradiction between Cranmer's first and second answers; but the second answers were so evasive as to give a completely different impression from the first answers. To the question as to whether a man was bound by Scripture to confess his sins to a priest, Cranmer at first replied: 'A man is not bound by the authority of this scripture "Quorum remiseritis" and such like to confess his secret deadly sins to a priest, although he may have him'. In the second document, Cranmer wrote: 'He that knoweth himself guilty of any secret deadly sins must, if he will obtain the benefit of absolution ministered by the priest, confess the same secret sins unto him'. This was nothing less than a cowardly evasion.

It was in connexion with the appointment and consecration of

[1] *H. L. Jo.*, 12 April 1540; for the Seventeen Questions and Answers, see Burnet, iv. 443–96; vi. 241–2, 246–8; Strype, *Cranmer*, pp. 744–51; Cranmer's *Works*, ii. 115–17. The answers were drafted after 12 April and before 29 December 1540, when Thirlby was consecrated Bishop of Westminster, for he is referred to as the Elect of Westminster in the document. This led Jenkyns (ii. 98 n.) to suppose that the answers were drafted after 17 September 1540, when Thirlby was elected by the Chapter; but Thirlby was referred to as the Elect of Westminster as early as July 1540, in connexion with the divorce of Anne of Cleves.

the clergy that Cranmer changed his attitude most conspicuously. In his first answer, Cranmer wrote: 'All Christian Princes have committed unto them immediately of God the whole cure of all their subjects, as well concerning the administration of God's word for the cure of souls as concerning the ministration of things political and civil governance.' He stated that the King could appoint Bishops and priests in the same way as he appointed the Lord Chancellor and the other temporal officers, and that the ceremonies which were used in making these appointments were not necessary, but merely convenient. Cranmer added somewhat gratuitously—for his question did not cover this point— 'And there is no more promise of God that grace is given in the committing of the ecclesiastical office than it is in the committing of the civil office'. He stated that the Apostles had chosen the Bishops in their time, not because they had been given authority by God to do so, but only because there were then no Christian Princes to choose them. With regard to priests, Cranmer replied at first: 'A Bishop may make a priest by the Scripture, and so may Princes and governors also, and that by the authority of God committed to them'; or the people could elect their priests if there were no Christian Princes. He was equally unequivocal in his original answer to the question as to whether, by the New Testament, it was necessary to consecrate a Bishop and priest, or whether appointment alone was sufficient: 'In the New Testament, he that is appointed to be a Bishop or a priest needeth no consecration by the Scripture, for election or appointing thereto is sufficient'.

All this was greatly changed in Cranmer's second set of answers. He now took the attitude that the making of Bishops and priests consisted of two parts—appointing and ordering. The appointing had been undertaken by the Apostles only because in their day there were no Christian Princes, and it now rested solely with Christian Princes. But apart from the appointing, ordering was necessary to confer grace. He now stated clearly, with Barlow, that 'Only appointment is not sufficient, but consecration, that is to say, imposition of hands with fasting and prayer is also required'; and he also wrote: 'We read not, that any other, not being a Bishop, hath since the beginning of Christ's Church ordered a priest'.

At the end of his first set of answers, Cranmer had written

his famous postscript: 'This is mine opinion and sentence at this present, which I do not temerariously define, and do remit the judgment thereof wholly unto your Majesty'. To Cranmer's critics, these words have been the final proof of his complete subserviency to Henry on fundamental questions of religious doctrine, while at least some of his admirers have quoted the words approvingly to show that Cranmer had doubts, even when he first formulated it, as to the validity of the extreme Erastian opinion on orders which he later revised. Neither of these conclusions is justified. The postscript, though it illustrates the subordination of the Church of England to Henry VIII, shows nothing as to Cranmer's character, as is clear from the fact that Bonner and Day—though not, as is often thought, all the divines who replied to the Seventeen Questions—added a similar statement in a postscript to their answers.[1] It had already been clearly laid down in 1536 and 1537 that the promulgation of religious doctrines was a matter for the Supreme Head, and that his Bishops and Commissioners were merely to offer advice which he might accept or reject as he pleased. The postscripts of Cranmer and his colleagues amount to nothing more than a statement that the opinions were being put forward as tentative suggestions for the King to consider. In view of the novelty and unorthodoxy of some of these opinions, this was a rudimentary precaution against an accusation of heresy.

After writing this postscript, Cranmer did in fact revise his opinion when he gave his second set of answers to the Seventeen Questions; but he did not do so in order to please the King, for it was his second opinion, not the first, which displeased Henry. Henry's marginal comments on the second document show that he was still inclined to believe that nothing more than appointment was necessary for the making of Bishops and priests.[2] Cranmer must have revised his first opinions under pressure,

[1] For the passages cited from Cranmer's answers, and the postscripts to the first answers, see Burnet, iv. 467–8, 475, 478, 487, 494–5; vi. 247–8; Strype, *Cranmer*, pp 749–51; Cranmer's *Works*, ii. 115–17. Burnet's marginal note to Cranmer's subscription has been widely interpreted as meaning that all the other Commissioners subscribed to Cranmer's statement that he remitted his temporary opinion to the King; but this is not correct. Only Cranmer, Bonner and Day made qualifying statements. Bonner wrote: 'Ita mihi Edmundo Londinensi Episcopo pro hoc tempore dicendum videtur, salvo judicio melius sentientis, cui me prompte et humiliter subjicio.' Day wrote: 'Opiniones non assertiones.'

[2] Answers to the Seventeen Questions, with Henry VIII's comments (Burnet, vi. 247).

not of the King, but of his fellow Commissioners; and the only thing for which he had to excuse himself to Henry was that he had not adhered to the extreme position which he had at first adopted. But we may be sure that Cranmer's motive throughout was conscientiously to serve his King.

It was obviously not the answers to the Seventeen Questions which led to the solitary resistance of Cranmer to the orthodox faction which is described by Morice and Foxe. This occurred in June or July 1540, when Cromwell was in prison awaiting execution. The members of the Commission for examining Christian institutions were meeting at Lambeth during those hot and dangerous days, when the heat was drying up the ponds, and the people in London were shouting in the streets against Cromwell and wagering 'thousands of pounds to hundreds' that Cranmer would be sent to join Cromwell in the Tower before the Commissioners at Lambeth had finished their discussions. In this situation, Heath, Day, Thirlby and Skyp, all of whom had hitherto been sympathetic to the reformers and close to Cranmer, deserted him and transferred themselves to Gardiner's faction; and in the discussions at Lambeth they opposed Cranmer on some point of doctrine which had arisen. As Cranmer alone maintained his position, Heath and Skyp took him aside and walked with him in the garden, urging him to submit to the King's wishes, as the King was entirely opposed to his position on this point. But Cranmer remained adamant, and warned Heath and Skyp that the King would never trust them again if he later discovered that merely in order to please him they had supported doctrines that were against the truth. When Henry heard of the incident, he supported Cranmer against all the other Commissioners, so that to everyone's astonishment it was Cranmer's view that prevailed; and 'the book altogether passed by his assertion against all their minds, more to be marvelled at, the time considered'.[1]

We do not know what question of doctrine was in issue on this occasion; but as the labours of the Commissioners eventually resulted in the publication of the King's Book of 1543, and as there is no record of any book of articles being issued in 1540, the dispute probably concerned a draft of a portion of the King's Book. The King's Book, however, did not represent a victory for

[1] Morice (*Nar. Ref.*, pp. 248–9); Foxe, viii. 23–24.

Cranmer over the reactionary Bishops, for it was a more orthodox document than the Bishops' Book of 1537 which it replaced. Nor was there any other point on which Cranmer persuaded Henry to make a further advance towards Reformation in the summer of 1540. It is therefore clear that Cranmer's victory was a defensive one, and that he persuaded Henry to reject a proposal of the other Commissioners to issue a document which took a backward step and repudiated some of the doctrines contained in the Bishops' Book—perhaps on the issue of justification. It was a great achievement for Cranmer to succeed in maintaining, during the crisis of 1540, so many of the gains of 1536 and 1537, and he had, as usual, performed his duty in giving his honest advice to the King even though the advice was unwelcome. On this occasion, his advice was accepted; if it had been rejected, Cranmer would have obeyed Henry's decision, and enforced it. For all his 'stiff standing to his tackle', to which Foxe refers in this context,[1] Cranmer subscribed to transubstantiation in the King's Book as he had subscribed to the Six Articles, and punished those who defied the book.

Cranmer survived the crisis of the summer of 1540 only because of the protection which Henry always extended to him. As with most other events in Cranmer's life, Henry's constant support has been interpreted both favourably and unfavourably to Cranmer. The critics have attributed it to Cranmer's complete subserviency, and suggest that, unlike Wolsey, More, Cromwell, Norfolk and Gardiner, Cranmer alone was never in disgrace because he alone was utterly submissive. The admirers believe that it was due to Cranmer's outstanding virtues, which compelled even Henry, for all his vices, to recognize that Cranmer was a better man than himself, and to love him in consequence. Both of these explanations must be rejected. Far from being subservient, Cranmer, for all his unquestioning loyalty to Henry and the principle of absolute monarchy, was less subservient than most of Henry's servants; but it is equally difficult to accept the alternative explanation of the sinful Henry being moved to appreciate the virtues in Cranmer. Some fifteen years before, when Henry had walked in the garden with Sir Thomas More with his arm around his neck, More told his friends that Henry would cut off his head without hesitation

[1] Foxe, viii. 24.

if this would win him a castle in France.[1] In 1540, Henry would have cut off Cranmer's head—or more probably have burned him—if he could have obtained any advantage by so doing. He retained Cranmer as Archbishop because, while he had no use for outspoken reformers like Barnes or Latimer, it was advantageous to have Cranmer in the Council and Convocation as a balance to the power of Gardiner and Norfolk, and as an advocate of moderate Reformation who would be useful if Henry should in future decide on a further advance in this direction. Cranmer remained in office, not because he was exceptionally subservient, but because he was a learned reformer who was sufficiently subservient to make it possible for Henry to retain his services.

[1] Roper, *Life of More*, p. 22.

CHAPTER XIV

KATHERINE HOWARD

CRANMER survived the fall of Cromwell without any loss of Henry's favour. Strype states that he was forced to retire for some months from public life, but Strype's reason for this conclusion is unconvincing. The rumours, however, that were circulating in England as to Cranmer's imminent peril had spread abroad, and reached Dantiscus at Heilsberg in his diocese in Poland. Dantiscus had been intimate with Cranmer when they were both Ambassadors at Ratisbon, and although as a Papist he obviously welcomed the recent developments in England, he took advantage of his personal friendship with Cranmer in order to fish in troubled waters. On 1st September 1540, he wrote a subtle letter to Cranmer, in which he expressed his joy at the falsehood of the rumour that Cranmer had been executed at Henry's orders, and proceeded to refer to the pillaging of Church property, the widespread punitive measures, and what he called 'so many marriages and so many divorces against all human, and even divine, law'. After mentioning their former friendship, he asked Cranmer to write to him about the situation in England and his own position, as the Polish merchants in London would always be willing to carry the letter.[1]

This was an embarrassing letter for Cranmer to receive in September 1540, for having with difficulty succeeded in extricating himself from a very dangerous situation, he had no wish to be discovered corresponding with a foreign Papist Bishop who sympathized with him in his predicament. Cranmer sent the letter to Wriothesley, the Secretary of State. 'Now since I received this letter', he wrote to Wriothesley, 'I have been much inquieted therewith, considering what heinous rumours by mischievous tongues be spread into so far countries of the King's Majesty, which would make any true and loving subject's heart bleed in his body to hear or read of his Prince'. He was at pains to draw Wriothesley's attention to these obnoxious passages

---

[1] Strype, *Cranmer*, pp. 122–3; Dantiscus to Cranmer, 1 September 1540 (Cranmer's *Works*, ii. 402–3).

by underlining them—though in no case had Dantiscus done more than criticize the King by implication—and asked Wriothesley to ascertain from Henry whether he should reply to the letter, and if so in what terms; 'for the matter is of such importance that I dare not presume to make a slender answer upon mine own head.'[1] Cranmer was too wise to fall into the trap of confiding in Dantiscus; his confidences were reserved for the secret friends at home. It was probably duty rather than fear that led him to send the incriminating letter to Wriothesley; but it was the safest and shrewdest course to adopt.

The divorce of Anne of Cleves, which had shocked even the cynical Francis I, was secretly denounced as a mockery by the reformers in England. One of them refused to believe that it was possible that the marriage had not been consummated after Anne had been alone in a room with Henry;[2] for this was the reputation which Cranmer's Prince had attained both at home and abroad. The reformers were particularly disgusted at Cranmer's part in the divorce. But the German Lutherans, who had been protesting against Henry's actions in their letters to Cranmer since the Act of the Six Articles, now became involved themselves in a sordid matrimonial scandal. In March 1540, Philip of Hesse was bigamously married, having been advised by Luther that he was justified, as an exceptional measure, in taking a second wife. Melanchthon, at Luther's insistence, attended the wedding as a bridesman.

This gave Cranmer the opportunity of censuring the German Lutherans who had so often criticized the improprieties of Henry. On 27th December 1540, he wrote to Osiander and severely condemned the marriage, which he complained had caused him embarrassment, for in England everyone was always eager to throw in his face any misconduct of which the German Lutherans had been guilty. He wrote that if the Lutherans attempted to justify the marriage of Philip of Hesse by referring to the polygamy of the men of the Old Testament, he would ask the 'introducers of novelties' whether they also wished to resort to the practice of Abraham and Ahasuerus in having concubines. As some of the Lutherans 'greatly and arrogantly condemn our Parliamentary statutes, disregarding, however, the very

[1] Cranmer to Wriothesley, 21 September 1540 (Cranmer's *Works*, ii. 401–2).
[2] Hilles to Bullinger (summer 1541) (*Orig. Letters*, pp. 205–6).

weighty and just causes for them', they ought to know how strongly their own conduct was condemned. 'What can you possibly say to excuse yourselves', asked Cranmer, 'when you allow a man after a divorce, with both spouses living, to contract a new marriage, and what is still worse, even without a divorce you allow one man to have several wives?' The judge of Dunstable, the President of the Convocation which divorced Anne of Cleves, had the effrontery to write this to Osiander.

This was not a propaganda statement; nor was it, as far as we know, shown to Henry for his approval or to anyone else. It was a private letter to an old and intimate friend, to his 'most beloved Osiander', in which Cranmer could safely express his true opinions about the marriage. But for Cranmer, it was a great opportunity to justify to himself his estrangement from Lutheranism. Not only did he call the Lutherans 'introducers of novelties'[1]—a phrase which was so often used by the orthodox faction when they referred to the reformers—but he ended his letter with a veiled threat of a complete breach with Lutheranism. He told Osiander that his acquaintance with the other Lutheran theologians had always been a slight one; 'and even of this, I confess, I should repent very much if I knew that these were the fruits of the new Gospel of which they boast so much, and which was also approved of by us, to some extent, until now, not without reason, as we thought'. The bigamous marriage in Hesse was a convenient excuse for a reformer who had turned his back on the Reformation and was supporting the Six Articles.

Cranmer now spent a great deal of time attending meetings of the Privy Council, which since the fall of Cromwell had played an increasing part in the detailed administration of the country. He dealt with fortifications in Calais and on the Scottish border, with the punishment of forgers and men who poached in the parks of great noblemen, and with payments from the royal treasury. The great machine interfered in every aspect of the life of the King's subjects, enforcing its authority with the savage punishments of the royal despotism in defiance of the old rules of the English common law. Cranmer and his colleagues sentenced criminals to have their ears nailed to the pillory—the responsibility for the execution of this punishment was on one

---

[1] Rerum novarum introductores'—Cranmer to Osiander, 27 December 1540 (Cranmer's *Works*, ii. 404–6).

occasion delegated to Cranmer—or to suffer other forms of
mutilation; and they sometimes resorted to the use of torture on
unconvicted prisoners, which was repugnant to the common law.
They ordered the deportation and execution of gipsies and the
punishment of thieves and vagabonds; according to a contemporary estimate, 72,000 persons were hanged during the
reign of Henry VIII—nearly two and a half per cent of the total
population of England. Cranmer's part in all these measures was
doubtless largely formal; but the man who ranked first among
all the Lords of the Council cannot avoid the moral responsibility
for the orders which were issued. On this point at least Cranmer's conscience was at ease, for he was serving his master, and
was enforcing in the executive sphere the absolute autocracy
which he advocated so zealously as a propagandist.[1]

In June 1541, Henry left London with his new Queen,
Katherine Howard, on a visit to Lincolnshire and Yorkshire,
being accompanied by Norfolk and Suffolk, and the Secretary
Wriothesley and other Councillors. As Gardiner was still
attending the Diet of Ratisbon, the government in London was
carried on by Cranmer, Lord Chancellor Audley and Edward
Seymour, Earl of Hertford, who reported all their decisions to
Wriothesley and the Council with the King, from whom they
received constant instructions. During Henry's absence, the
Council in London dealt with two Spanish priests who had
landed at Dartmouth on a private mission to effect the conversion of heretic England. Cranmer, Bonner and Thirlby examined the priests in an attempt to discover who had sent them,
and ordered them to renounce the Papal supremacy and recognize Henry as Supreme Head of the Church of England—a step
which was justified by the law of nations, especially as at this
very time, despite Henry's protests to the Emperor, English
merchants were in the prisons of the Inquisition in Spain because
they had refused to deny Henry's supremacy over the Church of
England. One of the priests submitted, and was placed in
Cranmer's custody; but the other refused, and was sent to the
Tower, though Cranmer warned him that if he refused to swear

---

[1] See Acts of the Privy Council, 10 August 1540–23 January 1546/7, especially
19 April and 17 June 1541 and 9 May 1543; Cranmer, Wriothesley and others to
the Council with the King, 9 September 1544 (*L.P.*, xix [ii]. 207). For the
number of executions, see Harrison, 'Description of Britaine' (in Holinshed, i.
313–4).

the oath of supremacy he would be executed, and pointed out in gruesome detail what was involved in being hanged, drawn and quartered. Cranmer was no doubt eager to save the man; but his attitude must have appeared in a different light to the Spanish priest, who declared that this law was evil and that he preferred to die ten such deaths rather than forsake the truth.[1]

The Papists were not the chief victims in 1541. During the spring and summer, there was a new wave of persecution of reformers under the Six Articles, though the extreme penalty was only imposed in a few cases. One of the victims was Mekins, a boy of 15, who was kept in rigorous imprisonment by Bonner, disowned by his frightened parents, induced to recant and eventually burned for words against the Sacrament of the Altar and for criticizing the execution of Barnes. The burning of Mekins on 30th July—a month after Henry had left for the north —caused at least one English reformer to reproach Cranmer with cowardice. The Zwinglian merchant Hilles took the opportunity of his visit to the Frankfort Fair to write to Bullinger in Zurich about events in England. He told Bullinger that during Henry's absence the government in London had been entrusted to Cranmer and Audley, who were supposed to be favourable to the reformers, but that Henry had no sooner departed than they ordered Mekins to be burned. This criticism was hardly justified, for Mekins had been convicted by a jury before Bonner as Bishop of London, and the act of the Council in London in issuing the writ for the execution was merely a routine administrative duty. Cranmer and his colleagues could not have pardoned Mekins without referring the matter to Henry, for when Henry was absent on another occasion three years later, they did not even venture to pardon a boy who had stolen from a lady of the Court without writing to the King to know his wishes. There is no reason, however, to believe that Cranmer made any attempt to persuade Henry to pardon Mekins or any of the other reformers who were martyred under the Six Articles. It was not a time when the authorities were likely to take the view that Mekins' criminal responsibility was diminished on account of his youth, for a few months later a

[1] Salcott and Bulkeley to the Council in London, 25 July 1541 (L.P., xvi. 1032); the Council in London to the Council with the King, 29 July and 2 September 1541 (St. Pap., i. 662-4, 682).

statute enacted that in cases of high treason the death sentence could be carried out on lunatics.[1]

Henry issued two orders during his visit to the north which showed that he had not completely abandoned a policy of reform. Soon after he left London he promulgated an order concerning holy days which had been drafted by Cranmer in July. It restored the feasts of St. Mark, St. Luke and Mary Magdalene, but abolished three other major holy days and prohibited the ceremony of the Boy Bishop and other celebrations with children on St. Nicholas' and Innocents' Day. On 12th October, Henry issued another order from Hull, requiring Cranmer to ascertain that no relics or shrines remained in any church, and that no candles were placed anywhere except before the Host. This order, which was probably drafted by Cranmer, made no innovation, for it had been contained in Cromwell's Injunctions of 1538; but the fact that Henry had once again authorized its enforcement was a warning to the conservatives that the Reformation had not died with Cromwell. Cranmer, whether or not he drafted the order, clearly approved of it, as he did of the order which he had drafted with regard to the holy days; but it would be wrong to imagine that Henry issued these orders because of the subtle machinations of Cranmer, who as a zealous reformer and a cunning tactician succeeded in gaining this great victory over the conservatives. Henry had personal motives for wishing to suppress and loot the shrines, and the abolition of relics facilitated this policy; while the suppression of additional holy days, which was the only new measure introduced by the orders, was counterbalanced by the restoration of the other three feast days. Cranmer knew that his duty was merely to advise his Prince, and he never sought to impose his will upon Henry; and indeed, when Henry issued the order of 12th October he had not seen Cranmer for three and a half months.[2]

It was during Henry's absence that John Lassels sought an interview with Cranmer, and informed him that he had been told by his sister Mary that Katherine Howard had committed

[1] Foxe, v. 441–2; Hall, p. 841; Wriothesley, i. 126; Hilles to Bullinger, 18–25 September 1541 (*Orig. Letters*, p. 221); Cranmer, Wriothesley and others to the Council with the King, 28 September 1544 (*L.P.*, xix [ii]. 324); 33 Hen. VIII, c. 20.

[2] The Council in London to the Council with the King, 8 and 24 July 1541 (*L.P.*, xvi. 978; *St. Pap.*, i. 661); Proclamation on holy days (summer 1541) (Wilkins, iii. 859–60); Henry VIII's order on shrines and images, and Cranmer's mandate, 4 and 15 October 1541 (Cranmer's *Works*, ii. 490–1).

acts of impropriety before her marriage with Derham and her lute player Mannox when she lived with Mary Lassels in the Duchess of Norfolk's establishment. Lassels may have acted from a sense of duty as a loyal subject, and was perhaps conscious of the risk involved in keeping the information to himself; but he was almost certainly a convinced reformer, for there is every indication that he was the same Lassels as the man who lamented the fall of Cromwell and denounced Norfolk in 1540, and as the gentleman of the King's household who was burned for heresy in 1546. The reformers attributed the fall of Cromwell to the wiles of Katherine Howard and the faction of Norfolk and Gardiner, and the exposure of the Queen might be very advantageous to the Reformation.[1]

Cranmer told Lassels not to repeat the story to anyone, and immediately communicated the information to Audley and Hertford. They decided to take no action until the King returned from the north. Audley and Hertford were afraid to tell the King, for Henry was passionately in love with Katherine, and they feared that he would vent his fury against the man who dared to accuse her of misconduct. They therefore suggested that Cranmer should inform Henry; and Cranmer, who was always ready to perform a painful duty, agreed to do so. Henry and Katherine reached Hampton Court on 29th October; but though Cranmer, Audley and Hertford were also at Hampton Court, they kept their secret, and said nothing for three days while they dealt in the Council with the report of the Commissioners of Sewers for Sussex and other routine questions. On All Saints Day, a Mass of thanksgiving was held at Hampton Court for the safe return of the King from the north and the happy life which he was leading with his Queen; but Cranmer still remained silent. He seems to have been postponing the ordeal for as long as possible; but further delay might be dangerous. He decided to write the information on paper rather than tell Henry to his face, and on All Souls Day he slipped the paper into Henry's hand during a Mass for the dead which was being celebrated by Bishop Longland of Lincoln.[2]

[1] The Council to Paget, 12 November 1541 (Nicolas, *Proceedings of the Privy Council*, vii. 353); Lassels' statement (September 1540) (*L.P.*, xvi. 101); Foxe, v. 550–2.

[2] The Council to Paget, 12 November 1541 (Nicolas, vii. 352–4); Acts of the Privy Council, 30 October 1541; Morice (*Nar. Ref.*, pp. 259–60); Marillac to Francis I, 22 November 1541 (Kaulek, p. 365).

We do not know the precise words which Cranmer used in his written message, but Morice states that he worded it with such circumspection that Henry suppressed his feelings and conducted the investigations in a most rational manner. The matter was kept a close secret while Lassels and his sister were examined, and Derham was arrested on the pretext that he had committed piracy. On 5th November, Cranmer and Wriothesley examined Mannox at Lambeth. Mannox was said by Mary Lassels to know a private mark on Katherine's body, and he now not only admitted to Cranmer and Wriothesley that he had been guilty of acts of familiarity with her, but confirmed Mary Lassels' accusations against Derham, who had supplanted him in Katherine's affections. Cranmer then returned to Hampton Court, and was present on the fateful Sunday 6th November, when Henry adopted the very unusual course of attending in person at a meeting of the Council which lasted all the morning. They obviously spent the whole time discussing the allegations against the Queen, though the clerk to the Council most prudently took no minutes of the meeting. The King left Hampton Court secretly during the afternoon, and Cranmer, together with Audley, Norfolk, Sussex and Gardiner, called at Katherine's apartments and accused her of premarital incontinence with Derham. Katherine strongly denied her guilt. Most of the Council then followed the King to Westminster, leaving Cranmer, Wriothesley and Sir John Gage at Hampton Court.[1]

The investigations had not so far revealed that Katherine had committed adultery, but merely that she had been the mistress of Derham, and perhaps also of Mannox, before her marriage, and had failed to disclose this before she married the King. Henry therefore decided to degrade her from the rank of Queen, and to confine her in custody, but not to proceed to harsher penalties; and Cranmer was ordered to tell Katherine how grievously she had offended, to expatiate on the punishment which she had deserved by law, and then to inform her that the King had been graciously pleased to pardon her and remit these punishments. He found her in a state of hysteria, and he feared that she was

[1] Morice (*Nar. Ref.*, p. 260); The Council to Paget, 12 November 1541 (Nicolas, vii. 353–5); Examination of Mannox, 5 November 1541; Chapuys to Mary of Hungary; Chapuys to Charles V, both 10 November 1541 (*L.P.*, xvi. 1321, 1328; *Span. Cal.*, vi [i]. 204; Gachard, *Analectes historiques*, i–iv. 235); Marillac to Francis I, 8–11 November 1541 (Kaulek, p. 352).

going out of her mind. 'I found her in such lamentation and heaviness', he wrote to Henry, 'as I never saw no creature; so that it would have pitied any man's heart in the world to have looked upon her'. In view of her state of mind, Cranmer departed from his instructions; he told her immediately that Henry had pardoned her. Katherine, thus reassured, made a statement in which she admitted her offence and bitterly reproached herself; but her statement indicated that though she did not appreciate the fact, the words exchanged between her and Derham amounted to a precontract, which still constituted a valid marriage if followed by intercourse. Her marriage to Henry was therefore void, and there was sufficient evidence for Cranmer to pronounce a decree of nullity.[1]

To judge from Cranmer's letter to Henry, this seems to have been his original intention after hearing Katherine's confession; but such a solution was unsatisfactory to Henry, for it made it impossible to punish Derham. If Derham was married to Katherine, it was no offence for him to lie with her; and though Parliament hastened to pass a statute which made it misprision of treason to fail to inform the King of the premarital incontinence of a woman whom he proposed to marry, it was doubtful if it could be held that this constituted an offence under the law in force in 1540. It was therefore necessary to charge Derham with treason in having attempted to commit adultery with Katherine after her marriage to Henry, the fact that he had acted as her secretary for a short time after she became Queen being treated as proof of the renewal of their former intercourse; but this was impossible if Derham were Katherine's husband. Cranmer was therefore told by the Council that the fact of the precontract must be suppressed, as it would assist the defence.[2]

On 12th November, the scandal was officially made public. Cranmer summoned Katherine's ladies and informed them about the Queen's misconduct with Derham before her marriage, but said nothing about the precontract. He then dismissed the household from the Queen's service after ensuring that they were provided for, and sent Katherine to Syon after depriving

[1] Cranmer to Henry VIII (6 or 7 November 1541) (Cranmer's *Works*, ii. 408–9); Examination of Katherine Howard (6 or 7 November) 1541 (Burnet, vi. 249–52).

[2] 33 Hen. VIII, c. 21; The Council to Cranmer and others, 11 November 1541; Sadler to Cranmer and others (12 November 1541) (*St. Pap.*, i. 692–4).

her of her more sumptuous dresses and all the paraphernalia of royalty. Meanwhile Katherine had made a further confession to Cranmer and the other Councillors which incriminated Culpepper, a courtier who was high in Henry's favour. He had not only been Katherine's lover before her marriage, but had visited her in her chamber during the night when she was in Lincoln with Henry on his recent progress; and though Henry had readily pardoned Culpepper when he had raped a park-keeper's wife, there was to be no pardon for him now. When Cranmer returned to London, he assisted in the examination of the suspects. No degree of torture could force Derham and Culpepper to admit that they had committed adultery with Katherine since her marriage to Henry; but they were convicted of high treason on the grounds that in view of their former connexion with Katherine, their visits to her since she was Queen was proof of adultery. Both men asked Cranmer and his colleagues to be granted the privilege of being beheaded instead of hanged, drawn and quartered, and the Councillors transmitted the request to the King. The boon of a painless death was granted to Culpepper, the adulterous courtier; but it was refused to Derham, who would confess to nothing more than that he had had intercourse with a woman to whom he was lawfully married before there had been any suggestion that she might marry the King.[1]

In January, when Parliament assembled, a Bill of Attainder was introduced condemning Katherine to death for high treason on the grounds of her adultery with Culpepper and Derham. Cranmer was one of the four members of the House of Lords who were appointed to examine Katherine before the bill was passed; but they could not make any favourable report to the House, which in any case had not waited to hear their report before passing the bill. Katherine was executed on 13th February 1542.[2]

[1] The Council to Cranmer and others, 11 November 1541; Sadler to Cranmer and others (12 November 1541); the Council in London to Browne and Sadler (6 December 1541), and undated; the Council with the King to the Council in London (7 December 1541); the Council in London to the Council with the King, 9 and 11 December 1541 and undated (*St. Pap.*, i. 691–9, 701–3, 705–7, 710–12); Examination of Katherine Howard, 12 November 1541 (Hist. MSS. Comm., Bath MSS. ii. 9–10); Trial of Derham and Culpepper, 1 December 1541 (*L.P.*, xvi. 1395); Acts of the Privy Council, 8, 9 and two meetings on 13 December 1541; Wriothesley, . 131–2, 134; Hilles to Bullinger, 10 May 1542 (*Orig. Letters*, pp. 226–7).

[2] 33 Hen. VIII, c. 21; *H. L. Jo.*, 21, 28 and 30 January and 6, 7, 8 and 11 February 1541/2.

Cranmer was involved in disgraceful transactions in the case of Katherine Howard. Apart from assisting in the illegal use of torture in the examinations, which was now so common as to be hardly an irregularity, he was responsible on 12th November at Hampton Court for suppressing all reference to the precontract on the grounds that it would assist the defence. In this matter, Cranmer acted on the direct orders of the Council. The criticism which has been most frequently levelled against Cranmer is that he deceived Katherine into making a confession by falsely promising her a pardon. In fact, however, Cranmer—who in this matter was also acting under instructions—offered the pardon unconditionally before the confession was made, and not as a reward for a confession. Nor was the pardon offered in bad faith, for at that time Henry had not discovered that Katherine had been unfaithful after her marriage as well as promiscuous before it, and the pardon was promised only in respect of her premarital incontinency. In any case, Katherine would ulti-mately have confessed even if she had not been granted a pardon, for her whole object was to save herself by throwing all the blame on her lovers.[1] Cranmer's actions followed inevitably from the fact of his position and of his belief in the doctrine of Christian obedience—his belief that it was his duty, as a Christian, to be a loyal servant of a King like Henry VIII.

Throughout the whole episode of Katherine Howard, Cran-mer was motivated solely by his duty to the King. Lassels may have acted from religious prejudice in denouncing Katherine; but this is certainly not true of Cranmer. Cranmer made no attempt to derive any advantage for the reformers from an exceptionally favourable situation. The adulterous Queen was Norfolk's niece, and had often met Henry, in the weeks before their marriage, at parties at Gardiner's house.[2] Her misconduct first came to light while Norfolk, Browne and Wriothesley were in the north with Henry, and Gardiner was travelling home from Ratisbon, and while Cranmer, Audley and Hertford, who were allegedly members of the Protestant faction in the Council, were the only Councillors of the first rank who remained in London. This was an opportunity for a daring and unscrupulous

[1] Katherine Howard to Henry VIII (12 November 1541) (Hist. MSS. Comm., 14th Rep., Bath MSS., ii. 8–9)
[2] Hilles to Bullinger (summer 1541) (Orig. Letters, pp. 201–2).

Protestant leader to induce some of the ladies of the Duchess of Norfolk's household to accuse the Duke and Gardiner, as well as the Duchess, of having known about Katherine's immoral life when they contrived for her to marry the King. But Cranmer obviously never even contemplated such a step. He prosecuted the case against Katherine Howard, not because she represented the conservative interest, but because it was his duty to God and the King to expose the adultery of his Sovereign's consort.

As soon as the rumours concerning Katherine leaked out in the second week of November 1541, the possibility occurred to both the French and the Emperor's Ambassadors that Henry was intending to divorce Katherine in order to remarry Anne of Cleves. Chapuys immediately urged the Emperor to use his influence to prevent it, while Marillac considered whether he could do anything to further it. At the same time a rumour began to circulate that Anne of Cleves was pregnant, and that Henry was the father of her child. The Council punished the men responsible for the rumour, and took steps to discourage any suggestion of a reconciliation with Anne; but Olisleger decided to make tentative approaches for the renewal of the marriage treaty with England. He wrote separate letters to Cranmer, Southampton and Hertford, which were presented by the Ambassador of Cleves in London in December 1541, urging the three Councillors, in the most general terms, to support the cause of Anne.[1]

Cranmer promptly wrote to Henry, enclosing Olisleger's letter and describing his talk with the Ambassador of Cleves. He told Henry that after reading Olisleger's letter, and noting the general terms in which Anne's cause was commended, he had suspected the real reason for the Ambassador's visit, and had pressed him to disclose it. The Ambassador had said that they hoped to see a reconciliation between Henry and Anne; 'Whereunto I answered, that I thought not a little strange, that

[1] Chapuys to Mary of Hungary; Chapuys to Charles V, both 10 November 1541 (*Span. Cal.*, vi. [i] 204; *L.P.*, xvi. 1328; Gachard, *Analectes historiques*, i–iv. 236); Marillac to Francis I, 8–11 November 1541 (Kaulek, p. 353); Acts of the Privy Council, 5 and 11 December 1541; the Council in London to Browne and Sadler (6 December 1541); the Council with the King to the Council in London, 7 December 1541; the Council in London to the Council with the King, 9 December 1541; Southampton to Henry VIII, 12 December 1541 (*St. Pap.*, i. 697–8, 701, 706–7, 714); Olisleger to Cranmer, 30 November 1541 (Cranmer's *Works*, ii. 410).

Oslynger should think it meet for me to move a reconciliation of that matrimony, of the which I, as much as any other person, knew most just causes of divorce'. Cranmer had told the Ambassador that out of his concern for the succession and the peace of the realm, he would never urge the King to receive in matrimony her from whom he had been rightly divorced; and when the Ambassador had wished to argue the matter further, Cranmer had said: 'Master Ambassador, this is a matter of great importance, wherein you shall pardon me; for I will have no communication with you therein, unless it please the King's Majesty to command me.'[1]

The account which Cranmer gave to Henry of his talk with the Ambassador of Cleves is almost certainly an accurate one; but even if it is not, the fact that he wrote this letter to Henry leaves no doubt as to his policy in December 1541, and how far he had changed his attitude to the German Lutherans since the summer of 1538. He was obviously anxious that no one should suspect him of having exposed the misconduct of Katherine in order to put back Anne in her place; and instead of responding to Olisleger's ambiguous message by an equally ambiguous assurance of goodwill, he forced the Ambassador of Cleves to commit himself so that he could firmly shut the door on any attempts to entangle him in the cause of Cleves and German Lutheranism. It would have been highly unwise to advocate a renewal of the Cleves marriage, for Henry found Anne repulsive; but Cranmer was probably actuated by his duty to the King and his concern for the succession if a child should be born of a marriage which had first been proclaimed valid, then annulled as void, and then once more proclaimed to be valid.

In January 1542, Cranmer presided at a new session of Convocation, crossing in his barge from Lambeth and walking in state from Paul's Wharf to St. Paul's with his cross borne before him. During the session, Cranmer tried in vain to check the gluttony of the clergy by issuing an order restricting the number of different dishes to be eaten at meals to ten in the case of the Archbishops, eight in the case of the Bishops, and less for the lower ranks of the clergy; but this order could only be enforced for a few months. The principal issue in Convocation was an

---

[1] Cranmer to Henry VIII, 13 December 1541, inadvertently dated 13 January by Cranmer (Cranmer's *Works*, ii. 409–10).

attack by the conservatives on the English Bible, a copy of which was still placed in every church of the Kingdom. When Cranmer formally asked the synod on 3rd February whether the Great Bible in English might be retained without scandal, the majority of Convocation replied that it might not, unless the translation were revised; and they selected certain Bishops and divines to examine the text. Cranmer was assigned the Gospel of St. Matthew, but most of the New Testament—though not the Old—was in the hands of his opponents. The conservatives wished above all to further the doctrine of salvation by works by altering 'Faith, Hope and Love' in the Great Bible to 'Faith, Hope and Charity'; but on 10 th March, Cranmer informed Convocation that it was the King's wish that the text of the English translation of the Bible should be referred to the Universities of Oxford and Cambridge for the doctors to examine whether any revision of the text was necessary. This led the orthodox majority to show the first signs of resistance to the King's will which had been shown in Convocation for several years. They stated that they considered it more suitable for the revision to be undertaken by Convocation than by the Universities, especially as the state of learning in the Universities had deteriorated so greatly in recent years; but Cranmer declared that whatever might be said about the state of the Universities, he would stick closer to the will and pleasure of the King his master. Goodrich and Barlow were the only members present who supported Cranmer; but these three were enough when they had the support of the King.[1]

It was probably Cranmer who persuaded Henry to refer the revision of the Great Bible to the Universities, and this has rightly been acclaimed as a triumph for Cranmer's tact and skill. It cannot have been difficult for Gardiner and his faction to persuade Henry in 1542 that Cromwell's Great Bible, which Henry had always disliked, ought to be revised, if not completely withdrawn; and it was certainly an achievement for Cranmer to succeed, without openly opposing the need for revision, in

---

[1] Fuller, *Church History*, ii. 122–5; Cranmer's Order (Cranmer's *Works*, ii. 491); Records of Convocation, January–March 1541/2 (Wilkins, iii. 860–2); Parker, p. 396. The order limiting the number of dishes for the clergy was first published by Strype (*Life of Parker*, iii. 117–18) who gives the date as 1541 (Old Style); it was undoubtedly issued during the session of Convocation of January–March 1542.

postponing any alteration for many months while the University doctors examined the text. Next year, in the persecuting atmosphere of 1543, Cranmer was unable to defeat a far more serious attack on the reading of the Bible; but this temporary triumph was one of the minor successes for the Reformation which Cranmer was able to win, at the cost of sacrificing his integrity, by remaining Archbishop of Canterbury after 1540. The reformers at the time did not think that the sacrifice was justified; but future historians, who were not subjected to the persecution of Henry's last years, have been more ready to justify Cranmer's policy.

CHAPTER XV

THE CRISIS OF 1543

THE year 1542 was an uneventful one in Cranmer's life and in the history of the English Reformation. Not a single heretic was burned during the year, and Cranmer was chiefly occupied with his executive duties in the Council—above all with the preparations for Henry's shameless aggression against Scotland. At Christmas 1542, a number of Scottish nobles, who had been taken prisoner at Solway Moss, were brought to London and entertained for a few weeks in the houses of great dignitaries until they were permitted to return to Scotland after giving their oath to further Henry's interests. The young Earl of Cassillis was entrusted to Cranmer's keeping. Cassillis became a Protestant some years later, as did so many of the Scottish nobles who opposed the Regent and the French alliance, and Strype suggested that he was converted by Cranmer during his fortnight's residence at Lambeth; but we may be sure that Cranmer uttered no heresy to Cassillis, and went no further than to denounce the Papal supremacy for which the Scots were fighting.[1]

Cranmer's continual attendance at the meetings of the Council prevented him from spending as much time in his diocese as in earlier years. While the government of the realm was in the hands of Cromwell, he had resided for about five months of the year at his manors in Kent; but after June 1540, he only went to his diocese infrequently for short visits of a few days. Cranmer's absence encouraged both the conspiracies of the conservatives and the ardour of the reformers in Canterbury. The reorganization of the Chapter of Canterbury after the dissolution of Christ Church Priory was completed in April 1541. Nicholas Wotton was appointed Dean, in spite of Cranmer's attempts to obtain the post for Crome or Thornden. Of the twelve Prebendaries, seven were former monks of the priory who were hostile to Cranmer; but three, Champion, Nicholas Ridley and Glazier, were sympathetic to the Reformation. Three of the six preachers

---

[1] Acts of the Privy Council, 21, 26 and 29 December 1542; Strype, *Cranmer*, pp. 140–1.

—Scory, Drum and Launcelot Ridley—were zealous reformers.[1]
This had already caused dissension when Cranmer visited
Canterbury at the beginning of June 1541, less than two months
after the foundation of the new establishment, for the orthodox
Prebendaries objected to the sermons which Scory and Launce-
lot Ridley had preached in Rogation Week.

On Trinity Sunday, Cranmer summoned a meeting of the
Prebendaries, and urged them to show Christian love towards
each other. Serles, who was the most outspoken of the orthodox
preachers, objected to having Launcelot Ridley and Scory
as preachers; but Cranmer told him that the King wished
the preachers to include three reformers along with three more
orthodox men. When Serles protested that this was a means to
set them at variance, Cranmer made the conclusive rejoinder:
'The King's pleasure is to have it so.' The conservative Prebendaries and preachers affected not to believe this statement;
but it was obviously true, for Cranmer would never have
ventured in 1541 to appoint three reformers to office without
first obtaining the King's express consent. Indeed, the idea is
much more likely to have emanated from Henry than from
Cranmer, for there were obvious advantages for Henry in
having both reformers and orthodox men in the cathedral who
would be very ready to denounce any heretical or Papist tendencies in the opposing faction.

But Serles was not to be deterred, and he turned to the
question of images. In the course of the conversation, Cranmer
told him that in Greek 'image' and 'idol' was the same word.
At this, William Gardiner, who was one of the orthodox
Canons, declared that he did not know Greek, but knew the
truth by St. Paul; and he emphasized his point by a text from the
Epistles to the Romans which he cited quite inaccurately.[2]
Cranmer was encountering the formidable barrier of unassailable
ignorance and prejudice. The conservative Canons and preachers
reiterated their complaints about Scory and Launcelot Ridley
when Cranmer paid two short visits to Canterbury in August

[1] Letters Patent for Christ Church, Canterbury, 22 March 1541 (*L.P.*, xvi.
779 [5]).
[2] For the meeting on Trinity Sunday, see the Depositions in the Prebendaries'
Case, September–November 1543 (*L.P.*, xviii [ii]. 546, pp. 321–2, 348, 352–3,
355, 361, 366–8); for complaints about Scory's preaching, see also ibid., pp. 304,
363.

and at the end of September 1541. On the second occasion, he entertained Gardiner, who was passing through Canterbury on his return from Ratisbon; and Gardiner was informed during his sojourn by Canon William Gardiner about the heretical sermons of the two reformers.[1]

The long and complicated story of the two years' faction fight at Canterbury which culminated in the Prebendaries' plot may be read at length in the depositions which Cranmer recorded when he investigated the matter in the autumn of 1543. The traditional Protestant view of the events as a conspiracy by the conservative Prebendaries to ruin Cranmer by lying evidence has been challenged by several modern historians, who have put forward a different explanation. They believe that Cranmer was secretly furthering the Reformation in his diocese by protecting reformers who had broken the law and framing the conservatives on false charges. It is impossible to discover the truth from the depositions, for a consistent picture can be drawn on the basis of either interpretation; but if we consider Cranmer's career in its entirety, it becomes evident that the accusations of the orthodox Prebendaries were far more false than true. Cranmer would never—and least of all in the years after 1540—have connived at breaches of the law by reformers, or urged his Commissary to exceed the King's Injunctions; nor would he have imprisoned orthodox divines who had not contravened the law. He was certainly innocent of the charges against him, which in the eyes of modern Protestants is perhaps less to his credit than if he had been guilty. The allegations of the Prebendaries against Cranmer, though probably made in good faith, were based on unsubstantiated stories and distortions of fact. The Prebendaries knew that Cranmer had opposed the Six Articles and was said to be a heretic, and they therefore put an unfavourable interpretation on all his utterances and believed every rumour which was circulated about him in the diocese. In fact, however, Cranmer, though determined to suppress any defiance of the King's decrees by the Papists, showed at least as much severity towards the reformers in his diocese as he did towards the Papists during these years.

In the late summer of 1541, Cranmer summoned Serles

[1] Depositions in the Prebendaries' Case, op. cit., pp. 323, 339; Gardiner to Cranmer (July 1547) (Muller, p. 356).

before his Court in connexion with Serles' sermons in Kent. There is no record as to what Serles had said, but it probably concerned images, for Serles did not accept the official doctrine that in certain circumstances images might be the subject of abuse; he had told Cranmer on Trinity Sunday that an image of the Virgin could never be the cause of idolatry. Serles did not appear before Cranmer, but travelled to the north to appeal to the Council with the King in Yorkshire. The matter was discussed at a meeting of the Council in York on 19th September, when the Councillors present included such conservatives as Norfolk, Tunstall, Southampton, Browne, Wriothesley and Rich, and Serles was ordered to report to Cranmer, taking with him—according to the usual practice in such cases—the sealed letter containing the instructions which would decide his fate. Cranmer sentenced Serles to a short term of imprisonment. When some of the conservative Prebendaries and preachers protested to Cranmer, he told them that it was at the orders of the Council that he had imprisoned Serles.[1] This was almost certainly the truth. Serles may have blundered in appealing from Cranmer to the Council, for if the case had been left to Cranmer he might have been more reluctant than the King and Council to punish an orthodox preacher who had contravened some Injunction.

Cranmer's Commissary in his diocese was Christopher Nevinson, who had married the daughter of Cranmer's sister. Nevinson was a far more ardent reformer than Cranmer, and had been one of the two members of the Lower House of Convocation who had voted against the Six Articles. As Commissary, he was over-zealous against the Papists and lenient to heretics. When Cranmer ordered him to remove certain images, in compliance with the King's Injunctions, Nevinson not only removed them, but broke them in pieces; and when Joan Bocher, a sacramentary and Anabaptist, was prosecuted before Nevinson in 1543, he raised objections to the proceedings and reminded Joan that she could rely on the King's pardon to Anabaptists and sacramentaries, as she had committed her offences before February 1539. But there is no reason to believe that Cranmer was responsible for Nevinson's actions in this respect, for he

---

[1] Depositions in the Prebendaries' Case, op. cit., pp. 339, 346, 376; Acts of the Privy Council, 19 September 1541.

was far more ready than Nevinson to take measures against reformers. When Cranmer learned that Chirden, a parson of Canterbury, had been attacking auricular confession—Chirden had said that the priests would have given absolution to Judas to free him from all guilt—he ordered Shether and William Gardiner, who were two of the most ardent conservatives in Canterbury Cathedral, to draft charges against Chirden. Cranmer ordered Chirden to appear before him at Lambeth; but Chirden had influential friends who rallied to his defence and obtained evidence from many witnesses that Chirden's sermons were innocent. It was only after he was confronted with this evidence that Cranmer stopped the proceedings against Chirden.[1]

Cranmer was equally firm in Scory's case. The conservative Prebendaries complained that Cranmer did not take proceedings against Scory and Launcelot Ridley; but it was not heretical for Scory and Launcelot Ridley to preach that Church services should be in English instead of Latin, though it was certainly unwise; while the more serious charges against Scory accused him of expressing opinions on matters such as Baptism which he would never have advocated even under Edward VI. As soon as Cranmer was informed that Scory had criticized the Real Presence, he lost no time in arresting him, though Scory was later released in the absence of any proof of his offence.[2]

The conservative Canons and clergy—and historians three centuries later—were ready to believe every rumour against Cranmer on quite insufficient evidence. Willoughby, who was a royal chaplain and a leading organizer of the plot against Cranmer, stated that Cranmer had on one occasion delivered a lecture, booted and spurred, in which he said that the Sacrament of the Altar was only a similitude. We can be certain that Cranmer had said no such thing, but Willoughby had heard this story from someone—he could no longer remember from whom—while they were gossiping at table. Canon Gardiner said that Cranmer had told his Chancellor Barbour, in the privacy of his room in Canterbury, that he would defend the doctrines which Scory and Launcelot Ridley had preached on the subject of

[1] Depositions in the Prebendaries' Case, op. cit, pp. 299, 309–10, 313–14, 329–30, 342, 359, 366.
[2] Ibid., pp. 304–5, 314–15, 317, 339, 341, 352, 361–7.

Baptism and original sin before any impartial judge, but that if they wished to find an impartial judge it would be necessary to fetch one from Germany. Cranmer might have said this in 1538, but not in 1541; and Canon Gardiner had only heard the story at third hand. Canon Gardiner also informed Bishop Gardiner that at least once a month Cranmer received letters from Germany, and wrote letters in reply, which passed through the hands of a man at the Fleur de Lys Inn at Canterbury, and the Prebendary was convinced that another man who visited Canterbury was a spy from Germany. The rumours did not spare Cranmer's family. His brother Edmund the Archdeacon was accused of improperly removing lights and breaking images, and Shether wrote to Bishop Gardiner that Cranmer's sister—the mother of Nevinson's wife—had two husbands living 'as it is of many thought'. As usual, none of these rumour-mongers suggested that Cranmer was married; but throughout these years Margaret was almost certainly in Germany, which may explain the monthly letters which were brought to the Fleur de Lys inn.[1]

The storm broke in March 1543. The Council, after beginning with some Portuguese Jews, began a new wave of persecution of heretics, and on 16th March Heynes, the Dean of Exeter, was questioned before the Council about his 'evil opinions'. Cranmer, who had always had a personal dislike for this eminent Cambridge reformer, presided at this meeting, and he and his colleagues sent Heynes to the Fleet. On the same day that Cranmer was imprisoning Heynes as a heretic, Serles and Willoughby were riding to London with articles in their pocket accusing Cranmer himself of heresy. During the next few days, the Council dealt with other heretics, including several members of the King's household—Philip Hoby, Weldon, and the musicians Sternhold and Marbeck—who were accused by Dr. London of heresy against the Sacrament of the Altar. They were all sent to the Fleet or the Marshalsea. On Palm Sunday, 18th March, Dr. London was visited by Serles and Willoughby, and a further step was taken in the plot against Cranmer. The plot was inspired by Bishop Gardiner, who was meeting Cranmer almost daily in the Council and in the Committee of Convocation where they were working, along with Thirlby and Heath, on the final

[1] Ibid., pp. 300, 329-31, 341, 359.

draft of the King's Book. On 8th April, they both attended a meeting of the Council and committed eight printers to prison, including two of Cranmer's old associates—Whitchurch, who later married Cranmer's widow, and Grafton—on a charge of printing illegal books. They also ordered the Lord Mayor to search every house in London in order to discover who had been eating meat in Lent.[1]

It was probably early in April that Henry was presented with the Prebendaries' articles against Cranmer. Morice and Foxe have described how Henry was passing Lambeth bridge in his barge in the evening, and summoned Cranmer, who had come out on to the bridge to salute him, to enter the barge. Henry was in a merry mood. 'Ah, my chaplain,' Morice says that he said, 'I have news for you. I know now who is the greatest heretic in Kent.' He then showed the articles of the Prebendaries to Cranmer, who asked only that a Commission be appointed to examine the truth of the charges; but Henry decided to appoint Cranmer himself as the Commissioner with the duty of investigating the action of the Prebendaries in making these accusations. Cranmer demurred, and pointed out that he would be considered a biased judge if he were to investigate the circumstances in which charges had been presented against himself. Cranmer had on a previous occasion raised the question of the impropriety of a man acting as judge in his own cause; but apart from this, he was probably reluctant to take proceedings against the orthodox Prebendaries and their associates, and would have preferred that the King should be served in this matter by some Commissioner who was orthodox in religion, and could not be suspected of acting out of sympathy with the Reformation. But Henry cared no more for the suspicions of the trouble-makers than for judicial impartiality, and he insisted that Cranmer and his diocesan officers should conduct the inquiry.[2]

Archbishop Parker adds some further information to that of Morice and Foxe concerning the conversation on the barge. His account of how Henry asked Cranmer whether he considered that his bedchamber was exempt from the Six Articles, and of

[1] Acts of the Privy Council, 9 and 16–19 March 1542/3 and 8 April 1543; Hawkins to Cranmer, 11 June 1533; Depositions in the Prebendaries' Case (L.P., vi. 623; xviii [ii]. 546, pp. 324–9, 331–2); Records of Convocation, 20–30 April 1543 (Wilkins, iii. 868).
[2] Morice (Nar. Ref., pp. 252–3); Foxe, viii. 28–29.

Cranmer's confession that he was a married man, relate to this
occasion.[1] Parker is wrong in a few details of his biography of
Cranmer, and his account of the words used by Henry and
Cranmer in this conversation is suspect in several particulars;
but like Foxe, he obtained his information from Morice, and
though this incident is not mentioned in the surviving account
which Morice wrote for Parker, or in Foxe's book, it is more
likely that Morice related it to Parker on some other occasion
rather than that Parker invented the whole story. We may
therefore believe that as Henry spoke with Cranmer on the
barge off Lambeth bridge on that April evening in the cold, wet
summer of 1543, he became more and more intimate, and
eventually mentioned the matter of Cranmer's wife; and it was
probably because of what Henry said or hinted on this occasion
that Margaret returned to Cranmer before the end of the year.

It was now that the conservatives made their famous attempt
to send Cranmer to the Tower. Some members of the Council
informed Henry that Cranmer was a heretic, and that though
no one dared to come forward and give evidence against him in
view of his high position, this evidence would be forthcoming
if Cranmer were imprisoned. Henry agreed that Cranmer
should be arrested at the Council table next day and sent to
the Tower; but that same night he sent his favourite Anthony
Denny, who was a friend of the Reformation, to summon
Cranmer from Lambeth. Cranmer rose from his bed and came to
Henry in the gallery at Whitehall. Henry told him that he had
agreed to the Council's proposal to arrest him, and asked Cranmer for his comments. It was more than twenty years later that
Morice recorded what Cranmer had told him about this
midnight talk; but his version of what was said, even if it is not
strictly accurate, gives a striking illustration of the impotent
Primate and of the King who understood so well the nature of
his own régime. Cranmer 'answered and most humbly thanked
the King that it would please his Highness to give him that
warning aforehand, saying that he was very well content to be
committed to the Tower for the trial of his doctrine, so that he
might be indifferently heard, as he doubted not but that his
Majesty would see him so to be used. "O Lord God!" quoth the
King, "what fond simplicity have you; so to permit yourself to

[1] Parker, pp. 392–3.

be imprisoned, that every enemy of yours may take vantage against you. Do not you think that if they have you once in prison, three or four false knaves will be soon procured to witness against you and to condemn you, which else now being at your liberty dare not once open their lips or appear before your face. No, not so, my Lord," quoth the King, "I have better regard unto you than to permit your enemies so to overthrow you".' He then gave Cranmer his ring, and told him that when he was arrested at the Council next day, he must produce the ring and appeal to be heard by the King in person; for it was well known that the royal ring was given to those persons to whom the King wished to grant this privilege of appeal.

Cranmer attended the meeting of the Council next day, but found the door closed against him. This was the calculated slight to the fallen Primate from the men who had kept on their caps in Cromwell's presence when they met him on the morning of his arrest. For three-quarters of an hour Cranmer was made to wait in the ante-room with the servants and suitors, while the clerks and officials walked in and out of the Council chamber through the ante-room without paying any attention to Cranmer. Morice then informed Dr. Butts, the King's physician, who was very close to Henry, and like Denny used his great influence on the side of the reformers. Butts immediately joined Cranmer in the ante-room, making a public demonstration of his friendship, and then went to Henry and told him of how Cranmer was being made to wait among lackeys; but though Henry was highly indignant, he allowed events to take their course. When Cranmer came before the Council, the colleagues with whom for many years he had worked and dined almost daily informed him that he was to be sent to the Tower to answer a charge of heresy; but Cranmer appealed to the King, and produced the ring. The Councillors knew at once that they had gravely blundered, and Russell declared that he had always said that the King would only allow them to send Cranmer to the Tower if it were a case of high treason—a statement which throws a revealing light on the discussions which had been taking place and on the sincerity of the accusers. The Councillors went with Cranmer to the King, who upbraided them for their conduct, while Norfolk asserted that they had only wished to charge Cranmer with heresy in order to give him the opportunity of vindicating himself; and Henry ordered them to shake hands with Cranmer, and warned them not to attempt to harm him again. He then ordered Cranmer to entertain the Councillors to dinner.

This story is so extraordinary that one might be inclined to reject it as an invention if it rested solely on the authority of Foxe, and in this instance we can sympathize with Parsons for doing so. But its truth is proved by Morice, who himself witnessed most of the incidents which he described, and was informed as to the rest by Cranmer. It is highly discreditable to Henry. If he intended to destroy Cranmer and then reversed his decision—which is a very likely explanation—his conduct was less reprehensible than if, as Morice naturally preferred to believe, he planned the whole affair, with its outcome, from the start. If Morice's explanation is correct, Henry's object can only have been to humiliate both Cranmer and his opponents in turn, and to sow mistrust and antagonism within his Council. In this he was certainly successful, for the incident had the effect of frightening both factions. Cranmer was henceforth even more anxious than before to avoid incurring the suspicion of heresy, and Morice assures us that after this experience Cranmer's enemies never again attempted anything against him as long as Henry lived.[1]

Neither Morice nor Foxe give the date of this episode, and there has been a great deal of speculation as to when it occurred. Most modern authorities are agreed that it was in 1545; but if all the facts which Morice gives are correct, it almost certainly took place between 23rd April and 4th May 1543, and it must have been on one of five days during this period. Even if Morice is wrong in stating that it was after the Prebendaries' plot, and Foxe is right in placing it before this other attempt against Cranmer, there are still only a few other dates on which it could have occurred. All these dates fall at periods when it is unlikely that there would have been an attempt to overthrow Cranmer; but in the spring of 1543 the situation was very favourable for his enemies to strike at him. We can therefore say with a high

---

[1] For the story of the attempt to send Cranmer to the Tower, see Morice (*Nar. Ref.*, pp. 254–8); for the versions of Foxe and Parker, see Foxe, viii. 24–26; Parker, pp. 393–5; and see Foxe, viii. 43, for the obviously incorrect version of the story published by Foxe in his first edition. For Parsons' comment, see Parsons, *Three Conversions of England*, ii. 384–5.

degree of probability that the attempt to send Cranmer to the
Tower occurred at the meeting of the Council on either 23rd,
26th or 29th April, or on 3rd or 4th May 1543; and of these dates,
26th April is much the most likely.[1]

At this very time, Cranmer was engaged, along with Gardiner, Thirlby, Heath, Salcott and Skyp, in correcting the final
draft of the King's Book. Gardiner played only a minor part in
this work; but Cranmer and the other four Bishops, all of whom
had been sympathetic to the Reformation until 1540, produced a
result which was virtually all that Gardiner could have desired.
The King's Book was for the most part a verbatim reproduction
of the Bishops' Book which it replaced; but the few alterations
mostly concerned important and controversial points, all of
which were settled in favour of orthodoxy. There was no longer
a distinction made between the three greater and the four lesser
Sacraments; and if the Sacrament of the Altar alone was elevated
above all the other six—including Baptism—this was on the

[1] If all the facts given by Morice are correct, the incident occurred after the
Prebendaries' plot in early April 1543, before the illness and death of Dr. Butts
in November 1545, at a time when the Court was at Westminster and when
Cranmer, Norfolk and Russell were present at the Council. There is no mention
of it in the Council minutes, which are lost for the period from 22 July 1543 to
10 May 1545; but it is very unlikely that so delicate a matter would have been
recorded in the minutes, in view of the outcome. The only period between 1 April
1543 and November 1545 when Cranmer, Norfolk and Russell were attending the
Council at Westminster was between 23 April and 4 May 1543, and also perhaps
in the spring of 1544, when the Council minutes are lost. All three are listed in
the minutes as being present at the meetings on 23 and 29 April, and 3 and 4 May
1543; but as Cranmer was not present when the meeting began, and was only
called in to be arrested, it is perhaps more likely that he would not be listed in
the minutes as being present. On 24, 25, 27 and 30 April, when Norfolk and
Russell were present, Cranmer was absent at Convocation (see Wilkins, iii. 868);
but the attempt to send Cranmer to the Tower may well have occurred on 26 April,
when the minutes record that Norfolk and Russell, but not Cranmer, were present
in the Council, and when Cranmer's absence is not accounted for by his presence
at Convocation (see Acts of the Privy Council, where there are a number of
obvious errors shown in the dates recorded in the minutes). Foxe (viii. 24, 27, 31)
places the incident before Gostwick's attack on Cranmer and the Prebendaries'
plot, but in this he departs from Morice's story; Parker (pp. 393, 395), states
that it was after Suffolk's death, which was in August 1545, but contradicts this
by clearly implying that it was at the same time as the Prebendaries' plot, which
is far more likely. Gairdner, after giving 1543 as the date in his *English Church
in the Sixteenth Century* (p. 233) revised his opinion in his *Lollardy and the
Reformation*, ii. 418–21, where he argued very plausibly that the incident took
place on 22 November 1545; but his theory depends on the highly unlikely assumption that Morice had confused Butts with Denny. Pollard (in *Thomas Cranmer*,
p. 154–5 n.) suggests somewhat cautiously that it was in 1545, before Butts died.
Apart from all other evidence, it is very unlikely that the Council would have
attempted to arrest Cranmer at any time in 1545, and the only time when such an
attempt might well have been made was in the summer of 1540, the spring of
1543 or the summer of 1546.

grounds that it contained both the body and blood of Christ in
the form of both bread and wine. Transubstantiation, as well as
the Real Presence, was now expressly affirmed. A new passage
explained at length that the doctrine that it was necessary to
receive the Sacrament in both kinds was 'pestiferous and
devilish', and the celibacy of the clergy was briefly upheld in the
course of the dissertation on Matrimony. The recent dispute
over the translation of certain words was introduced into the
commentary on the second article of the Apostles' Creed, which
was largely devoted to explaining that we must say 'Our Lord'
and not 'the Lord'; and the exposition of the meaning of 'holy
Catholic Church' in the Creed provided the opportunity of
stating that 'ecclesia' must be translated as 'Church'—that is to
say, not as 'congregation'. The King's Book also stressed the
importance of auricular confession, and stated that the Sacrament of Penance was the absolution pronounced by the priest,
though in cases of necessity a man could be saved by sincere
repentance without obtaining absolution. An exposition of two
different meanings of the word 'faith', which was probably
written by Cranmer, declared that though faith in its narrower
sense, as distinct from hope and charity, was a necessary requisite for salvation, it remained a sterile faith if it did not proceed
to hope and charity; but despite all Cranmer's efforts to persuade Henry to the contrary, the King's Book clearly stated that
works as well as faith was necessary for salvation.[1]

Cranmer was unable to repeat his success of the previous year
and defeat the new attack on the reading of Scripture. In the
Preface to the King's Book, Henry stated that though he had
formerly purged the realm of superstition by permitting the
reading of Scripture, the Devil was now causing a sinister
understanding of Scripture to enter the people's hearts. It was
necessary to stamp out arrogance and argument by issuing the
King's Book, which contained 'a perfect and sufficient doctrine
for the attainment of salvation'. Henry added that the reading of
the Bible was not so necessary for the people that they were
obliged to read it if this were inconvenient for the Prince and his
policy, and Parliament had therefore now decided to prohibit

[1] Records of Convocation, 20–30 April 1543 (Wilkins, iii. 868); Gardiner to
Ridley (February 1547) (Muller, p. 259); The King's Book (in Lloyd, *Formularies
of Faith*, pp. 221–5, 230, 244, 257–63, 265–6, 293, 368).

large sections of his subjects from reading Scripture. By the time that the book was published at the end of May, an Act of Parliament had prohibited anyone under the rank of gentleman or merchant from reading the Bible, even privately to himself. Cranmer was present at all the readings of this bill in the House of Lords when every member voted in favour of the bill. Presumably he managed to convince himself that even here his action was justifiable.[1]

Relations between England and France had reached the point of war after repeated incidents on the borders of the Pale at Calais—one of which had led Cranmer to deliver a strong protest to the French Ambassador in 1541. Henry was now the ally of the Emperor against a strange coalition of France, the Turks, the Northern Lutherans and the Pope, and Charles was eager that Henry, in view of his former connexion with Cleves, should give his moral support to Charles' attack on Cleves. On 19th May 1543, Henry spoke with Chapuys at Hampton Court, and undertook to declare war on France and to upbraid the Ambassador of Cleves because his master was daring to resist the Emperor; but Chapuys told Charles that when he met Cranmer and Gardiner and other Councillors after dinner they were prepared to commit themselves much further than Henry had done in the morning with regard to the declaration of war against France. The Archbishop who was suspected of Lutheranism and of receiving letters from Germany was eager to show that he supported Henry's foreign policy with enthusiasm and had no sympathy with the Protestants of Cleves who were being hanged by the soldiers of Henry's ally.[2]

Cranmer had delegated the duty of investigating the Prebendaries' plot to his Chancellor Cox, his Registrar Hussey, and Bellasis, a civil lawyer. They pursued the investigations at Canterbury while Cranmer remained at Court; but Cox and Hussey were not over eager, and after dallying for six weeks, they could find nothing incriminating against the orthodox Prebendaries and their associates. Morice was convinced that Cox and Hussey were secret supporters of the Papists, and he

[1] The King's Book (in Lloyd, pp. 215–19); 34 and 35 Hen. VIII, c. 1; *H. L. Jo.*, 8 and both sessions of 10 May 1543 (where it is wrongly dated 1542).
[2] Marillac to Francis I, 18 July 1541 (Kaulek, pp. 321–2); Chapuys to Mary of Hungary, 20 May 1543 (*Span. Cal.*, vi [ii]. 141, where it is wrongly stated to be written to Charles V; *L.P.*, xviii [i]. 570).

therefore wrote to Dr. Butts and Sir Anthony Denny, who contrived for Thomas Legh to be sent to Canterbury to replace Cox and Hussey. Legh had shown, as one of Cromwell's Visitors to the monasteries, that he possessed the necessary energy and harshness to discover the plot which that other Visitor of the monasteries, Dr. London, had hatched; and by organizing simultaneous raids on the houses of the suspected Prebendaries and gentlemen, he unearthed many incriminating documents. Twenty years later, Morice wrote: 'Insomuch that upon letters by me written unto Dr. Butts and Master Denny, Dr. Lee was sent down (after they had sat six weeks) by the King'; while Foxe, who had certainly heard the facts from Morice, states that the Papist sympathies of Cox and Hussey 'being well perceived by one of the Archbishop's servants, his secretary, he wrote incontinently unto Dr. Butts and Master Denny'. These passages suggest that Morice wrote to Butts and Denny on his own initiative, and not on Cranmer's orders. The credit of exposing the Prebendaries' plot belongs therefore to Legh, Butts, Denny and Morice, but not to Cranmer.[1]

But Cranmer showed no lack of energy when he went to his diocese in the middle of September 1543 to investigate the case in person. He pursued his inquiries at Canterbury, Beakesbourne and Faversham until the end of November, examining the Prebendaries and parsons and many other persons, and learning of lights before images, of fasting on the eve of abrogated holy days, of royal Injunctions defied and improper statements made in sermons, and of failure to expunge the name of the Bishop of Rome from prayer books. The notes which he made in the margin of the depositions which he wrote down show that he was not disposed to be lenient in this case. This is not surprising, for the conduct of the culprits amounted to defiance of the King's Injunctions, and Morice writes that although Cranmer was always ready to relent where his own interests were concerned, in matters which touched the Prince he was stout and inexorable. Cranmer wrote 'Seditious' opposite such statements as 'The people have not had hitherto the good wine of God's word, but a day would come that they should have good wine again', and 'As Christ was accused by two or three false knaves, so a man may be accused by two or three false knaves,

[1] Morice (*Nar. Ref.*, p. 253); Foxe, viii. 29.

and the judge as false a knave as the best, and so be condemned'. These statements had been made by Canon Gardiner in a sermon in the cathedral; but Cranmer was equally stern with reformers who had offended. He made a note that a statement that the mass and *dirige* were not laudable was 'offensive', and recorded that a man of Headcorn possessed books by Tyndale and Frith.[1]

Despite the defeat of the Prebendaries' plot, the conservatives were still in the ascendant. Several of the orthodox Prebendaries and their fellow conspirators were imprisoned for a time, and compelled to write letters of submission to Cranmer, entreating his forgiveness for having trespassed against him; but at the next session of Parliament in January 1544, a Statute of Pardons was passed of which they were able to take advantage. The reformers were more severely dealt with. In July, three sacramentaries were burned in the park at Windsor, though Henry pardoned the musicians of his household who had been associated with them; one reformer wryly commented that the King had burned these men in order to celebrate his marriage to Katherine Parr which had just taken place.[2] In the diocese of Canterbury, two priests were proceeded against for heresy at the Sessions of the Six Articles in September 1543, one of them being Richard Turner, whom Morice had appointed as curate in the parsonage of Chartham which Cranmer had granted him. Turner had been denounced some six months before by some of the orthodox Prebendaries for having preached against ceremonies, and was examined at Lambeth by Cranmer. The propriety of Turner's sermon was vouched for by Sir Thomas Moyle, the Speaker of the House of Commons, who was sufficiently orthodox for him to be approached by the Prebendaries when they were preparing to present the articles accusing Cranmer of heresy. In view of Moyle's attitude, Cranmer could hardly fail to discharge Turner.

The people of Chartham prepared a great reception for

---

[1] Depositions in the Prebendaries' Case (*L.P.*, xviii [ii]. 546, pp. 291–378, and especially pp. 292, 312). For the most lucid summary of this very complicated document, see the two accounts by Gairdner in his *Lollardy and the Reformation*, ii. 359–76, 393–400, and in his Preface to *L.P.*, xviii [ii], pp. xxxvi–xlix.

[2] See the letters of Hunt, Mills, William Gardiner, and Shether to Cranmer (in *L.P.*, xviii [ii]. 546, pp. 368–9, 373, 378; Strype, *Cranmer*, pp. 773–7); 35 Hen. VIII, c. 18; Hilles to Bullinger, 26 September 1543 (*Orig. Letters*, pp. 241–2).

Turner on his return from Lambeth; but Turner, realizing that this would be made the grounds of fresh complaint by the conservatives, left the highway and walked home eighteen miles through the woods in order to avoid a demonstration of sympathy. This did not prevent the conservatives from reporting that the demonstration had taken place, and Henry in anger ordered that Turner should again be brought before Cranmer, who was now in Canterbury investigating the Prebendaries' plot. Henry told Cranmer to have Turner whipped out of the county.

Morice intervened with Cranmer on Turner's behalf, but Cranmer refused his help because he feared that he would be accused of protecting heretics. Morice then asked Cranmer's permission to appear before the Council, along with other witnesses from Chartham, to prove that no public banquet had been held when Turner returned home; but Cranmer forbade him to do this, or to make any move to arrange for witnesses from Chartham to give evidence for Turner. All that Cranmer would permit was that Morice might make private approaches to his influential friends at Court, and on 2nd November 1543 Morice wrote to Denny and Butts about Turner. Morice was a loyal servant to Cranmer, and always found the most favourable explanation of his master's bias in favour of Papists and against Protestants; but he was unable to obscure the fact that Cranmer's conduct in the case was contemptible. 'As for my Lord of Canterbury', he wrote, 'he dare nothing do for the poor man's delivery, he hath done so much for him already. And his Grace hath told me plainly, that it is put into the King's head, that he is the maintainer and supporter of all the heretics within the realm; nor will he permit me or my neighbours to resort unto the Council for his purgation whilst he was at Chartham; saving only I have obtained this at his hand, that I may become a suitor in writing to my friends and good masters in the Court, for his delivery'. Butts chose an opportune moment when Henry was with his barber to mention the matter to him, and Henry ordered the proceedings against Turner to be quashed.[1] The physician thus succeeded where the Primate did not dare to tread. Cranmer, who had shown such courage in intervening for Henry's

---

[1] For Turner's case, see Morice to Denny and Butts, 2 November 1543 (Foxe, viii. 31–34, where it is wrongly dated 1544 by modern editors).

Papist daughter and for Fisher and More and the Carthusians, did not raise a hand to protect a reformer in his diocese when his own secretary could prove that the man was innocent; and if Morice's intervention at Court had been unsuccessful, Cranmer would undoubtedly have punished Turner in the full knowledge of his innocence. Cranmer had succeeded in retaining a few remnants of his integrity during the crisis of 1540; but he was forced to abandon them in the face of the perils of 1543.

CHAPTER XVI

THE NEW POLICY:
THE DEATH OF HENRY

ON 18th December 1543, Cranmer's palace at Canterbury was burned. Several persons lost their lives in the fire, including Cranmer's brother-in-law, who was probably the miller who had married that sister of Cranmer who was said to have committed bigamy. Cranmer was still in residence at the time, and Harpsfield's story of the chest relates to this occasion. According to Foxe, Cranmer alone remained calm during the fire, and bore the disaster with equanimity and an unchanging countenance. Owing to the fire, he was unable to entertain Gonzaga, the commander of the Emperor's armies in France, who was travelling to London for discussions on military operations, and he was therefore ordered by the Council to return immediately to Court in order that Lord Cobham, as the highest magnate remaining in Canterbury, should be free to receive Gonzaga. The Councillors did not consider it necessary, in their letter to Cranmer, to express any sympathy for the loss which he had suffered in the fire.[1]

1544 was a glorious year for English arms. Hertford was ravaging Scotland, fighting the war in such a way as to inflict the greatest possible suffering on the people, and burning the monasteries which he passed; for the war against Scotland was waged as a war against Popery. This did not prevent some of the reformers from being shocked at the English atrocities. John Hooper wrote to Bullinger that he shuddered at the devastation which Hertford had inflicted on the Scots. But Cranmer could only write letters with his fellow Councillors to Hertford, transmitting the King's order to him to put Edinburgh to fire and sword, 'without taking either the castle or town to mercy, though they would yield'. The Councillors did, however, suggest that as the Scottish prisoners of lower rank were starving in the English prisons, they might be granted

---

[1] Stow, *Annals*, pp. 585–6; Harpsfield, *The Pretended Divorce*, p. 275; Foxe, viii. 40–41; the Council to Cranmer, 20 December 1543 (*L.P.*, xviii. [ii]. 504).

some small relief 'if extreme necessity shall so require'.[1]

If the war against Scotland was a war against Popery, the war against France had begun as a war for the defence of Catholic Christianity against the ally of the Turk; but Charles' separate peace with Francis had altered the position, and this, though it had a disastrous effect on the military situation, was of great benefit to the Reformation in England. If Henry had been fighting as the ally of the Emperor, it is unlikely that he would have ordered prayers for the success of his campaign to be held in English instead of Latin, and have initiated the measures which were the beginning of a great new venture—the imposition of Church services in the English language. On 11th June 1544, Henry ordered that the Litany, or 'processions' as it was usually named—for it was sung by the priest and people as they walked in procession through the church or streets — should henceforth be sung in English. The English version, which had already been published before the end of May, introduced changes not only in the language, but also in the substance, of the Litany. The invocation of the fifty-eight Saints in the old pre-Reformation Litany had been replaced by the prayers to thirty-eight Saints in Bishop Hilsey's *Manual of Prayers* of 1539; and the English Litany now surreptitiously abolished the invocation of the Saints altogether by substituting a general appeal to Saints along with patriarchs and prophets. By October 1545 Cranmer had drafted a new Litany for festival days, and English verse translations of some of the Latin anthems, though he was not satisfied with the poetic quality of his verse. Meanwhile in May 1545 a Primer was published which contained a number of innovations, and included not only the Litany of 1544, but also a new version of the office of the Hours which was considerably shorter than the old version.[2]

[1] Hooper to Bullinger, 27 January 1546; Butler to Bullinger, 10 November 1542 (*Orig. Letters*, pp. 37, 634); the Council (Cranmer and others) to Hertford, 17 April 1544 (*Hamilton Papers*, ii. 341); Cranmer, Wriothesley and others to Paget, 20 July 1544 (*L.P.* xix. [i]. 943).
[2] Cranmer to Henry VIII, 7 October 1545; Orders of Henry VIII, the Council and Cranmer of 11 and 18 June 1544 and 10 and 11 August 1545 (Cranmer's *Works*, ii. 412, 494–6); Butterworth, *The English Primers 1529–1545*, pp. 247–50, 257–72; Dixon, *History of the Church of England*, ii. 349–50, 360–3. Cranmer's letter of 7 October is dated 1544 in Cranmer's *Works*, and 1543 in *St. Pap.*, i. 760–1; but the letter was written from Beakesbourne, and on 7 October 1544 Cranmer was at Otford with the Queen (see letters from the Council, in *St. Pap.* x. 96–97, 108; Lodge, *Illustrations of British History*, i. 73); while 1543 is out of the question. Collier, v. 147–8, dates it 1545, which is correct.

It has always been assumed that Cranmer was the author of all these publications, and though there is no evidence that he was connected with any of them except his Litany for festival days, it is highly probable that he was not only responsible for their publication, but also that he actually drafted them. We have no record that Cranmer had until now shown any interest in the question of prayers in the vernacular tongue; but this was an important tenet in the Lutheran doctrines, and in view of Cranmer's enthusiasm for the English Bible, there is very little doubt that for some years he had favoured services in English, and that he now won a victory for his beliefs in the only way in which he wished to win such victories—not by disobedience or surreptitious trickery, but by convincing his Prince in a private theological discussion that this was the course which God required him to pursue.

Cranmer was as active in the temporal government of the country as in drafting its liturgies. When Henry led his armies to the siege of Boulogne in July 1544, Cranmer, who entertained him to dinner at Ford on his last day in England, was appointed one of the members of the Council of Katherine Parr during Henry's absence. Cranmer was in constant attendance upon the Queen, travelling with her in her progress through Surrey and Kent, and staying with her for a time as a guest in his old palace at Otford. In the autumn of 1544, he was one of the Commissioners appointed to grant to various gentlemen and speculators the monastic lands which had not yet been disposed of, for it had been decided to sell these lands in order to raise money for the war. This was yet another instance in which Cranmer was employed in a transaction of which he had originally disapproved. Next summer, when the French were expected to land in Thanet, Cranmer played his part at Beakesbourne in the preparations against invasion in which the whole population of Kent was engaged. He urged the Council to place artillery on the cliffs, and his suggestion was duly referred to Sir Thomas Seymour, who was at Dover in command of the defence forces. He also provided shelter and medical and financial assistance for wounded soldiers who were travelling through Beakesbourne on their way home from Boulogne, which had been captured in the previous year, and added, along with a number of villages, to Cranmer's diocese.[1]

[1] Commissions of 26 June and 9 July 1544; Account of the campaign in France of

Cranmer had been regularly engaged since 1533 as a Commissioner for raising revenue, both from ecclesiastics and from laymen in Kent; and in Convocation he had played the foremost part, to the disgust of the more extreme reformers, in repeatedly offering voluntary gifts of money from the clergy to the King. Now that Henry had deliberately debased the currency in order to enrich himself at his subjects' expense, there was increasing reluctance to pay taxes; an Alderman of London who failed to pay was conscripted into the army, and another Alderman who criticized the tax was sent to the Fleet. Yet Cranmer, in his Litany, ordered the people to 'pray for our most dear and Sovereign Lord the King's Majesty, who doth not only study and care daily and hourly for our prosperity and wealth, but also spareth not to spend his sustenance and treasure, yea, ready at all times to endanger himself for the tender love and fatherly zeal that he beareth toward this his realm and the subjects of the same.'[1]

The taxation was particularly resented by those impoverished persons who had not yet been paid for the corn which they had provided for the army, but were nevertheless expected to pay taxes to the King. At the end of the war, in June 1546, Cranmer wrote to the Council with regard to the hardship of these persons, referring also to the resistance to taxation in the Cinque Ports, and the difficulties of the newly appointed clergy who were expected to pay their first fruits to the King as well as their special contribution for the war. Cranmer received a stern reply from Wriothesley and Norfolk: he must make the Cinque Ports pay; he must make the new incumbents pay both first fruits and contribution; and as for the unpaid suppliers of the army, he was told that 'such regard for the poor men's necessities was not expedient'.[2]

1544 (Rymer, xv. 39–40, 52); Things ordered at home, 7 July 1544; Report of measures to be taken for the defence of the Realm (May 1545) (St. Pap., i. 763–5, 786); Grants of monastic lands from 1 July 1544 to 14 April 1545; Presentations to benefices in Boulogne, 17 September 1546 (L.P. xix [i]. 812 [87], 1035; xix [ii]. 166, 527, 690, 800; xx [i]. 282, 621; xxi [ii]. 200 [25] and [26]); Foxe, viii. 22.

[1] Commissions of 30 January 1535, and undated (1544–5); Cobham to Cromwell, 14 March 1535; Cranmer to Hayman and Hales, 27 December 1544 (L.P., viii. 149 [40], 388; xix. [ii]. 782; xx. [i]. 623 [viii]. p. 325); Cranmer to Cromwell, 14 March 1535 (Cranmer's Works, ii. 301); Hilles to Bullinger (summer 1541) (Orig. Letters, p. 207); Wriothesley, i. 151; The Litany of 1544 (in Private Prayers of Queen Elizabeth, p. 567).

[2] Acts of the Privy Council, 11 June 1546.

At the beginning of October 1545, the citizens of Canterbury were terrorized by a band of soldiers who were on their way from Portsmouth to Boulogne. The soldiers stopped the people in the streets to demand change for a groat or an angel, and then made off with both the coin and the change; and they also forced their way into the cathedral and recited a coarse parody of the Book of Generations. Some of these soldiers were brought before Cranmer at ten o'clock one morning; but though Cranmer committed them to prison, he released them at two o'clock in the afternoon. Gardiner, who was passing through Canterbury on his way to the Emperor's Court at Brussels, was amused but indignant at the conduct of the soldiers and contemptuous of Cranmer's mildness. He wrote to Paget, the King's Secretary, that it seemed as if Cranmer dared not punish them. This may have been another case in which Cranmer's leniency was partly due to fear, for the Mayor had been afraid to take action against the soldiers, though Gardiner was convinced that he had jurisdiction to try them. Cranmer may likewise have hesitated to detain in prison for more than a few hours any man who had been ordered by superior authority to go to Boulogne to serve the King.[1]

Gardiner's mission to Brussels boded no good for Cranmer or the Reformation. It was probably the negotiations for a new alliance with the Emperor which was responsible for the introduction of a new bill against heresy in Parliament in November 1545. Cranmer naturally did not dare to oppose the bill; on the contrary, he presided in the Committee of the House of Lords which dealt with it. But the bill never passed the House of Commons, and was withdrawn after Cranmer and the peers had voted unanimously in favour of the persecuting measure. Henry did not exert pressure to force the bill through, but addressed the Lords and Commons on the need to put an end to religious strife in a speech which showed that he had made another change in policy. He was more interested in a bill for the seizure of the chantries—those endowments in the churches for a chantry priest to pray for the souls in Purgatory—which passed unanimously in both Houses of Parliament. Two years later, Cranmer, in the reign of Edward VI, voted against the second Chantries Act—an action which has often been cited in his

[1] Gardiner to Paget, 21 October 1545 (Muller, pp. 152-4).

favour; but in November 1545, Henry was still King, and Cranmer voted in favour of the Chantries Bill, as did all the Bishops, both reformers and conservatives.[1]

Henry was making approaches to the German Lutherans as well as to the Emperor. This made it difficult to persuade him to adopt any consistent policy in religion. After the promulgation of the new Litanies and the Primer, Cranmer worked together with Heath and Day, who were now Bishops of Worcester and Chichester, on a revision of the service books. Heath and Day had deserted Cranmer in 1540, but in the new situation they apparently agreed with Cranmer in putting forward radical proposals. They recommended the abolition of the covering of images and the veiling of the Cross in Lent, and of kneeling before the Cross on Palm Sunday, as well as of the vigil with the ringing of the church bells on the night of All Saints' Day, which was the sole survival of the obsolete vigils after holy days. Soon after Christmas 1545, Cranmer persuaded Henry, in an interview at Hampton Court, not only to enforce these recommendations, but also to abolish the most controversial of all the ceremonies—the creeping to the Cross on Good Friday. The day after his talk with Henry, Cranmer went to Kent, and from Beakesbourne sent to Henry a draft of the order effecting these decisions; but the order was not proclaimed. Henry decided not to promulgate it, because he had received a letter from Gardiner, who had strongly advised him not to make any innovations in religion while the negotiations for an alliance with the Emperor were proceeding in Brussels. Consequently, none of the recommendations of Cranmer, Heath and Day were put into effect.[2]

Cranmer stayed in his diocese—except for a visit to Greenwich at the end of February—for another six months. This was fortunate for his posthumous reputation, because his absence from Court prevented him from taking any part in the last persecution of Henry's reign. His admirers have acclaimed Cranmer's innocence of all share in the trial and death of Anne Askew and her companions; but there can be very little doubt

[1] *H.L.Jo.*, 27 and 28 November and 2, 3, 5 and 7 December 1545; Hall, pp. 864–6.

[2] Cranmer to Paget, 20 January 1546; Cranmer to Henry VIII, 23 January 1545/6 (Cranmer's *Works;* ii. 414–5, where this letter of 23 is wrongly dated 24 January, as it is in Burnet, v. 354; see *L.P.*, xxi. [i]. 109.); Foxe, v. 561–3.

that the only reason for this was his absence in Kent. Between the spring of 1545 and July 1546, Cranmer attended only seven meetings of the Council—six of these in November 1545, and one in February 1546.[1] Even when he was at Lambeth for the Parliamentary session of November and December 1545, he was absent from many of the Council meetings. It seems that after having for at least five years played an almost daily part in the executive business of the Council, he was now excused from this duty, probably in order that he could devote more time to his liturgical compositions and diocesan duties.

It was probably during this lengthy stay in his diocese at the beginning of 1546 that Cranmer held those discussions with Nicholas Ridley which led him to repudiate the Real Presence and adopt a position which was virtually a Zwinglian one. But the date of Cranmer's conversion on the most vital issue of his age is far from certain. He told his judges at Oxford in 1555 that he was converted by Ridley at some time after the trial of Lambert in November 1538. He was a little more specific in his *Answer to Smith*, where he stated that it was not long before he wrote the *Catechism* which was published in the summer of 1548. For the definite statement that it was in 1546 we must rely on the Preface to the Latin edition of Cranmer's book *The Defence of the True and Catholic Doctrine of the Sacrament*, which was published by the English exiles at Emden in 1557. This Preface is generally supposed to have been written by Sir John Cheke. If it was, it is reliable authority, for Cheke was an intimate personal friend of Cranmer; but Cheke may nevertheless have been mistaken as to the date, apart from the possibility that the Preface may not have been written by him at all. The only other evidence is that it seems probable—though not certain—that Ridley had been converted to the Zwinglian doctrine of the Presence by 1546 or earlier. It therefore seems probable that Cranmer was converted in 1546.[2]

[1] Acts of the Privy Council, 15–17, 22, 27 and 29 November 1545, and 21 February 1545/6.

[2] Cranmer, *Answer to Smith*; Cranmer, *Defensio Verae et Catholicae Doctrinae de Sacramento* (2nd Latin ed.), Preface (in Cranmer's *Works*, i. 374, App. p. 6). Ridley wrote in his 'Last Farewell' in 1555 that he was a debtor to Herne for his doctrine of the Lord's Supper, which suggests that he became converted while residing at Herne, i.e. before the end of 1546 (Ridley's *Works*, p. 407). Foxe (viii. 34–5) confirms that Ridley was partly responsible for converting Cranmer, but places it after the death of Henry VIII.

The conversion was remarkable. Cranmer was in his fifty-seventh year in 1546; he had believed in the Real Presence all his life, and for thirteen years had been opposing, with the greatest vigour, the sacramentaries who denied it. He had thought that their error was so widespread that the sternest measures were required to suppress it, and if the number of his victims fell short of the thirty-one heretics of whose death Stokesley had boasted on his death-bed, he had played at least some part in the execution of eleven of them.[1] Some nine years before, he had written to Vadian that he had read almost everything which Zwingli and Oecolampadius had written against the Real Presence, but that he rejected their arguments because of the weight of patristic texts in favour of the Real Presence, and because he believed that Christ would never have allowed His Church to remain in ignorance of the truth for so long.[2] It was therefore an extraordinary feat, even for a disputant as brilliant as Ridley, to persuade Cranmer to become a sacramentary at a time when the Act of the Six Articles was still on the statute roll, and a new wave of persecution had just begun. But it was one of those periods when, for no apparent reason, men are suddenly converted by the same arguments to which they have been impervious for so long. It was beginning to be realized that the denial of the Real Presence did not necessarily involve the mockery of the Host as a piece of bread, and that the Sacrament could be devoutly worshipped without believing that the Presence was corporal.

In these circumstances, the ideas of Zwingli and Oecolampadius

---

[1] See Foxe, iii. 104, for Stokesley's deathbed boast; elsewhere (v. 232) Foxe gives the number of Stokesley's victims as fifty, not thirty-one. By 1546, Cranmer had been responsible for burning eleven heretics—Frith, Lambert, the three Dutch Anabaptists in November 1538, Barnes, Jerome and Garrett (voting for the Bill of Attainder in the House of Lords) and the three Windsor heretics (being present at their examination before the Council). The two English artisans burned in December 1538 are not included in this total, though they were probably condemned by Cranmer and his fellow Commissioners. Joan Bocher and van Paris in Edward's reign bring up the number of martyrs whom Cranmer helped to burn to thirteen. There is no record that Cranmer played any part in the condemnation of the fourteen Dutch Anabaptists who were burned in June 1535, for it seems very unlikely that Gairdner was right in suggesting that Cranmer was the 'Doctor Chramuel' who, according to the Bishop of Faenza, tried to convert these Anabaptists (see Pio to Ambrogio, 8 June 1535, *L.P.*, viii. 846); for Pio would not have referred to the Archbishop of Canterbury by his name rather than by his office, and despite the inaccuracy of the description he was almost certainly referring to Cromwell.

[2] Cranmer to Vadian, (December 1537) (Cranmer's *Works*, ii. 342–3).

were able to penetrate even to the Primate of a Church which persecuted sacramentaries. His discussions with Ridley, which probably began as an intellectual exercise like his arguments with Heath at the time of Frith's trial, eventually led to the conversion of both Ridley and Cranmer. No doubt the conversion was only tentative. By May 1546, Ridley had returned to Court to play his part in examining Crome about his far milder heresies; and Cranmer stayed at Beakesbourne while Anne Askew was tortured, while Latimer and Shaxton, his old colleagues of the struggles of 1539, were once again brought within the shadow of the stake, and while the net which was to catch the heretics stretched out as far as the Queen herself. But Wriothesley did not try to bring Cranmer within the net. The man who had been given the King's ring was not troubled again by the Council, and after May 1543 Cranmer was the only subject in the realm who was safe from denunciation as a heretic.[1]

Cranmer had returned to Court by the beginning of July, when he was at Greenwich for the reception of the new French Ambassador who had arrived at the end of the war. Twelve days later, Anne Askew was burned, together with Lassels and two other reformers, while Shaxton recanted and proved his sincerity by preaching the sermon at the execution. Seven years before, Shaxton had shown more courage than any of the reforming Bishops; and perhaps Cranmer, who had set him the example in submission at the time of the Six Articles, had a heavy responsibility for the moral disintegration which led Shaxton to end his life as a minor persecutor under Mary. The burning of Anne Askew stirred the pity of the people, for there was a new spirit in the air when high-ranking ladies at Court sent gifts to a heretic in prison, and Wriothesley, the Lord Chancellor, was obliged to torture her with his own hands because the Lieutenant of the Tower refused to do so.[2]

This was the situation when d'Annebaut, the Admiral of France, was sent to England to cement the new friendship between Henry and Francis with a view to the formation of an alliance, embracing the German Lutherans, against the Emperor.

[1] The Council to Petre, 11 May 1546 (*St. Pap.*, i. 842–3); Foxe, v. 554–61; Morice (*Nar. Ref.*, p. 258).
[2] Selve to Francis I, 4 July 1546 (*Correspondance de Selve*, p. 5); Wriothesley, i. 167–70; *Greyfriars Chron.*, p. 51; Foxe, v. 547–8, 550–1.

The Admiral was entertained with lavish hospitality, and at Hampton Court, in place of the usual dinner at midday, the unusual attraction of evening banquets was provided in two temporary buildings which had been specially erected in the park. Henry was present at the first banquet on 24th August, and although he was now so ill and fat that he had to be carried in a special chair, he rose to his feet after the supper and stood talking, leaning on the shoulders of Cranmer and d'Annebaut. It was an excellent moment for the calculated indiscretion. Henry suggested that he and Francis might agree to abolish the mass in their realms and replace it with a communion service, while Francis repudiated the Papal supremacy, as a preliminary to requiring the Emperor to do the same in his territories under the threat of breaking off diplomatic relations. Henry then ordered Cranmer to draft a document setting out these proposals for Francis' consideration.

Cranmer was completely taken by surprise at this sensational proposal. It was not at his suggestion that Henry had made it, for even Cranmer, for all his courage in giving unwelcome advice to the King, would have hesitated to advise him to become a sacramentary—which was how any proposal to abolish the mass would be seen throughout England and Christendom. About a year later, Cranmer described the incident to Morice in words which Foxe long afterwards reported as follows: 'If I should tell what communication between the King's Highness and the said Ambassador was had, concerning the establishing of sincere religion then, a man would hardly have believed it; nor had I myself thought the King's Highness had been so forward in those matters as then appeared'. Cranmer told Morice that few men in England would have believed that Henry could have said such things. It is therefore not surprising that some modern historians have also refused to believe it. But it is perfectly possible for a despot to adopt a policy of which he has always disapproved, a month after he has had some of his subjects tortured to death for advocating the policy too soon.[1]

This incident may go far to explain why Cranmer renounced the Real Presence in 1546. There have been disagreements between historians as to whether the credit for Cranmer's

[1] Foxe v. 562–4; Wriothesley, i. 171–3; *Greyfriars Chron.*, pp. 51–52.

conversion on this question lies with Ridley or John à Lasco; but perhaps he was really converted by Henry and by the times. Cranmer himself stated clearly at his trial that he was converted by Ridley; but while this is doubtless true on the theoretical plane, Henry's attitude made it easier for Cranmer to follow Ridley's arguments to their logical conclusion. His discussions with Ridley on the Real Presence must have taken a very different form after 24th August 1546 from that which they had taken before Henry's talk with d'Annebaut in the pavilion in the park at Hampton Court.

The proposal which Henry had made to Francis was not accepted, and Henry did not raise the matter again. Next year, Cranmer told Morice that if Henry had not died, the project would have been carried out in England and France; but Cranmer was certainly mistaken in this. Henry's attitude was, however, a sign that in England a new policy was about to be launched. In November, Gardiner, who had chosen a most inopportune moment to refuse to agree to an exchange of lands with the King, was expelled from the Council. A month later, Norfolk, and Surrey his gallant, madcap son were sent to the Tower on a highly questionable charge of treason. Norfolk had been prominent in the plot against Cranmer in the Council, and his fall was a victory for the reformers' party; but it is certain that Cranmer, who spent very little time at Court during the autumn of 1546, played no part in the crushing of the Howards, though in due course he complied, as always, in executing Henry's policy. Cranmer voted for the Bill of Attainder which condemned Norfolk to death, and was present in the House of Lords when the King's assent to the bill was given by a Commission twenty-four hours before Henry died—late enough to save Norfolk's life.[1]

On the night of 27th January 1547, Cranmer was at Croydon while Henry lay dying at Whitehall. The physicians knew that there was no hope, but they dared not tell the patient, for six years before Lord Hungerford had been executed for foretelling the King's death. At last Denny ventured to tell Henry, who asked for Cranmer, but postponed sending to Croydon until it

---

[1] Gardiner to Henry VIII; Gardiner to Paget, both 2 December 1546 (Muller, pp. 246–9); Wriothesley, i. 176–7; *Greyfriars Chron.*, pp. 52–53; *H.L.Jo.*, 18, 19, 20, 24 and 27 January 1546/7.

was almost too late. The distance of some fifteen miles had to be travelled twice over on the winter roads at night, and by the time that Cranmer arrived at one o'clock in the morning, Henry had lost the power of speech; but he seized Cranmer's hand and would not release it. Cranmer urged him to call on Christ for mercy, and to give some sign with eye or hand that he trusted in the Lord; and Henry pressed Cranmer's hand before he died. We do not know whether Cranmer believed that this press of the hand was sufficient to atone for thirty-eight years of tyranny; but we may be sure that Cranmer rendered to Henry this last service as a priest as conscientiously as he had performed all his other duties to God and the King during the previous fourteen years. This phrase—'God and the King'—appears continually in Cranmer's letters, and it was rare indeed for Cranmer, except in his liturgical writings, to write the name of the Almighty without bracketing it with that of Henry VIII; for it never occurred to Cranmer—as it did to one of his contemporaries who was a more resolute anti-Papist than he—that 'thus was there no Reformation, but a deformation, in the time of that tyrant and lecherous monster'.[1]

---

[1] Foxe, v. 689; Gilby, 'An Admonition to England and Scotland' (in Knox's *Works*, iv. 563).

CHAPTER XVII

EDWARD VI:
THE BOOK OF HOMILIES

At Henry's death, power passed into the hands of Hertford. Hertford immediately rode to Hertford Castle to fetch the young King, and brought him on 31st January to the Tower, where Cranmer and Wriothesley were waiting at the head of the Lords of the Council to welcome him on the drawbridge. The Council then held a meeting in the Tower, at which it was decided to entrust the supreme authority and the office of Protector to Hertford, who was soon afterwards created Duke of Somerset, although Henry in his will had appointed all the Executors of the will to act as regents during Edward's infancy. Cranmer's name stood first in the list of the sixteen Executors; but as usual he had fared badly as compared with other courtiers as regards financial gain. Under the will, he received 500 marks— £333 6s 8d— which was a large legacy, but less than the £500 which Wriothesley, Somerset, Paulet, John Dudley Earl of Warwick and Russell each received.[1]

Thus England passed from the dangerous tempests of King Henry's time to the mild and halcyon days of King Edward VI. But though sixteen years later John Foxe described the transition in these terms, it was not seen in this light by Cranmer in 1547. One of Cranmer's modern biographers has suggested that he welcomed the death of Henry as a great opportunity, and that as he hastened from Croydon to Whitehall on the night of 27th January, he rejoiced that the chance for which he had been waiting had come at last.[2] But this is certainly wrong. The situation undoubtedly provided a great opportunity for a Protestant Archbishop who was determined to press forward with the Reformation, for Henry had lived long enough to set the

[1] Wriothesley, i. 179; Acts of the Privy Council, 31 January and 1 February 1546/7; Henry VIII's will, 30 December 1546 (Rymer, xv. 114-7).
[2] Foxe, v. 697; Belloc, *Cranmer*, pp. 211-2. Foxe's statement appeared in the first edition of 1563, but was omitted from later editions. Foxe had published a similar but differently worded statement in his Latin edition of 1559 (see 1st Engl. ed., p. 675, wrongly paginated, immediately preceding p. 685; Latin ed., p 200).

course for a reforming policy, and the new Protector had for some time supported the Reformation; but Cranmer was not the man to seize this opportunity. Any man who would have been capable of doing so would have been burned or would have fled abroad in 1540 or 1543. The man who was Archbishop of Canterbury when Henry died was a man who had always been sympathetic to reform and was almost a Lutheran by conviction; but he was a man who had spent sixteen years as a servile servant of a despot, and had lost whatever capacity for leadership he may once have possessed.

The death of Henry caused Cranmer great distress. He would of course in any case have been obliged to show the appropriate grief in public, for even if he had believed that the Reformation could now free itself from the shackles which Henry had imposed, he could not have taken this attitude openly, or expressed any criticism of Henry's policy. We can be sure that he agreed with Bale that it was sinful to criticize a King even when, like King John, he had been dead for more than three hundred years. But Cranmer expressed his grief at Henry's death even when speaking in the strictest privacy to his secret friends. He is said to have refused to shave after Henry died as a gesture of his sorrow, and he certainly grew a beard about this time, thus extending to the clergy the practice of wearing beards which had come into fashion at Court about twelve years before.[1]

Cranmer had no intention of using the opportunity of Henry's death to disturb the Henrician settlement, the Popery without the Pope that Henry had established with the help of Cranmer and his other ministers. Morice afterwards told Foxe how he had talked with Cranmer about the prospects of the Reformation in the summer of 1547, when the royal visitation was about to begin. Morice said that it would now be possible to introduce the measures which Cranmer had sought in vain to persuade Henry to promulgate, and which Gardiner's influence had always thwarted; but Cranmer replied that this was now much more difficult than if Henry had lived, and that Henry's death was a disaster for the Reformation. He said that if Henry had lived, he and Francis I would have overthrown the mass, but that now the Council shrank from enforcing those measures of reform which they knew to be desirable, because they feared

[1] Bale, *Kynge Johan*, pp. 85–86; Burnet, ii. 539.

as to how the people would receive reforms which were not sustained by Henry's authority. Cranmer was convinced that the deaths of Henry and Francis within a few months of each other was a punishment inflicted on the English for their sins. Perhaps he had really convinced himself of this when he officiated at the obsequies and requiem mass for Francis at St. Paul's in June despite the fact that less than two years before, Francis had authorized the butchery of thousands of his Protestant subjects. Cranmer was nearly as reluctant to think evil of a foreign Prince as of his own Sovereign.[1]

But if Cranmer was conscious, as is shown by his words to Morice, that there were practical disadvantages when the Supreme Head was only 9 years old, this was all the more reason for implanting in the people's minds that the King's power was unlimited, and that the royal supremacy over the Church could be exercised, as Scripture showed, by an infant Josias. The Council therefore surrendered all their patents of office which they had held from Henry, and accepted a new grant of them from Edward. Cranmer surrendered his see, and was re-appointed Archbishop of Canterbury by Edward on 7th February; but this was not, as is often thought, an isolated act by Cranmer, for all the Bishops did likewise, acting like Cranmer in compliance with a directive from the Council.[2] This was only a question of appointment, not of consecration, for Cranmer did not attempt to revive the opinion which he had held in 1540, and to deny the function of consecration in the ordering of Bishops.

The infant monarch was treated with the exaggerated respect which had been shown to Henry, and which caused surprise to foreign observers who were used to the etiquette of other Courts. When Cranmer and the Lords of the Council spoke to Edward, they did so on their knees. It was of course impossible to subject the royal person to punishment; but even in his father's reign Edward had been provided with Barnaby Fitzpatrick as a whipping boy. We do not know what Cranmer, with his modern views on education and his respect for royalty, thought about the propriety of punishing Barnaby for Edward's

---

[1] Foxe, v. 563–4; Wriothesley, i. 184; *Greyfriars Chron.*, p. 54.

[2] Commission of 7 February 1546/7 (Burnet, v. 127–9); Acts of the Privy Council, 31 January and 6 February 1546/7.

misdeeds; for though sixty years later the London audiences could see an actor in the part of Cranmer ordering Barnaby to be thrashed on the stage, there is no reason to believe that this uproarious scene from Samuel Rowley's play had the slightest basis in fact.[1]

To enforce the royal supremacy, to glorify the new Josias, to vest all real power in Somerset, and meanwhile to proceed slowly in the direction of Reformation provided that this could be done without arousing powerful opposition—this seems to have been Cranmer's policy, in so far as he had formulated any policy, in February 1547. But there were factors over which Cranmer had no control. The roof of St. Martin's Church in Ironmonger Lane in London was rotten with age, and it was necessary to repair it. While the work was being done, the crucifix and some of the images in the church crumbled into powder, and were removed; and the churchwardens, having spent so much money in repairing the roof, could not afford to replace the images. Incidents such as this can start a revolution. With Henry dead, and the prisoners pardoned, heresy was raising its head. The churchwardens removed the other images which had not been damaged at all, replaced the crucifix by the King's arms, and wrote passages from Scripture on the walls.

This was an unlawful act which could not be tolerated, and the churchwardens of St. Martin's were summoned before the Council on 10th February. The Council at first considered committing them to the Tower; but in view of the circumstances, and their humble apology, the churchwardens were merely ordered to replace the crucifix within two days. No order was given as regards the other images, which were perhaps more difficult to replace. Cranmer, who was present in the Council on this occasion, undoubtedly condemned the conduct of the churchwardens, for though he did not approve of images, he approved still less of disobedience. It was probably Somerset rather than Cranmer who was responsible for the fact that the churchwardens were treated with leniency.[2]

The coronation was held on Shrove Sunday, 20th February. The Council shortened the procedure by eliminating most of

---

[1] Ubaldini's M.S., cited in Raumer, *History of the Sixteenth and Seventeenth Centuries*, i. 71; Fuller, *Church History*, ii. 388; Rowley's play, *When you see me you know me*, lines 1771–1936.

[2] Acts of the Privy Council, 10 February 1546/7.

those parts of the traditional service which stressed the old, elective origin of the monarchy, on the grounds that the old ceremony was too long and tiring for the little King, and because parts of it were no longer permissible by law. The second reason was a more plausible one than the first, for the boy was subjected to all the long robing and anointing ceremony, and was afterwards required to wear the enormous crown throughout the long dinner which followed the coronation. It was only those ceremonies which weakened the royal authority which were thought to be too tiring for him.[1]

Cranmer did not preach a sermon at the coronation, but instead made a short address to the King. The text of the speech was first published 135 years later, and its authenticity has been questioned by some of Cranmer's modern admirers;[2] but it is unlikely that the speech is a forgery, and as Cranmer would certainly have agreed with the opinions expressed in it, there is no reason to doubt that he made this speech at the coronation. He explained that although the anointing and the other coronation ceremonies were good and useful, the King's title to the throne did not depend on them; if they were omitted, the 'King is yet a perfect monarch notwithstanding', for his election depended on God alone. There was reason for stressing this, for the people had always tended to attach too much importance to the coronation, and nine years before Cranmer had sent a man to the pillory for saying that Edward would not be a lawful King because his mother had never been crowned as Queen.[3]

'Your Majesty', said Cranmer to the boy of 9, 'is God's Vicegerent and Christ's Vicar within your own dominions, and to see, with your predecessor Josias, God truly worshipped and idolatry destroyed, the tyranny of the Bishops of Rome banished from your subjects, and images removed'. Edward ought to rule justly, because God favoured good Kings and punished bad

[1] Acts of the Privy Council, 13 February 1546/7; Milles, *The Catalogue of Honor*, pp. 54–59; Wriothesley, i. 182–3; *King Edward's Journal*, Year I.

[2] Cranmer's *Works*, ii. 126–7. The speech was first published in 1682 by Robert Ware in the second edition of *Foxes and Firebrands* (2nd ed. Pt. II, pp. 2–9). Ware stated that most of the documents which he published were found among Cecil's papers. Strype published the speech (in his *Cranmer*, pp. 205–7) in 1694, stating that it was found among Usher's papers. Pollard (in his *Thomas Cranmer*, p. 186 n.) expresses doubt as to the accuracy of the speech, and other modern writers have done likewise.

[3] Cranmer to Cromwell, 14 and 29 January 1538; Mone's examination (January 1538) (*L.P.*, xiii. [i]. 76; Cranmer's *Works*, ii. 361).

Kings; but 'being bound by my function to lay these things before your Royal Highness, the one as a reward if you fulfil, the other as a judgment from God if you neglect them; yet I openly declare before the living God and before these nobles of the land, that I have no commission to denounce your Majesty deprived if your Highness miss in part or in whole of these performances, much less to draw up indentures between God and your Majesty, or to say you forfeit your crown with a clause, for the Bishop of Rome, as have been done by your Majesty's predecessors, King John and his son Henry of this land'. Every Bishop and every man in public life would have agreed with these sentiments had it not been for the three words which Cranmer inserted so unobtrusively: 'and images removed'. This express reference to images was something more than the denunciation of idolatry in general terms which might have been expected; for Cranmer, though he had been conscious for some years that *idolus* and *imago* were the same word in Greek, would probably not have spoken of removing images if he had made the speech ten days earlier—before the case of the churchwardens of St. Martin's. Three days later, Ridley spoke at greater length about images in his Ash Wednesday sermon to the King, though he too was cautious.[1]

These hints were enough to let loose the first popular Protestant upsurge in England. The mass of the English people were deeply imbued with religious conservatism, but in London and the south-eastern counties there was a revolutionary minority, which was rapidly being reinforced by the returning exiles and alien refugees from abroad. Images were broken and thrown out of churches by apprentices and ardent young Protestants, who insulted priests in the streets. Many persons ate meat in Lent, and pamphlets were circulated telling the story of Anne Askew and of other martyrs who had been tortured and burned by the Bishops. The Sacrament of the Altar was ridiculed as a Round Robin; youths who had been encouraged to mock the miracles of the blood of Hayles and the rood of Boxley now mocked the miracle of a piece of bread which became Christ's body. Cranmer was undoubtedly shocked at these excesses;

[1] Cranmer's speech at the coronation, 20 February 1547 (Cranmer's *Works*, ii. 126–7); Depositions in the Prebendaries' Case (*L.P.*, xviii. [ii]. 546, pp. 321, 348, 352, 361, 366–8); Gardiner to Ridley (February 1547) (Muller, pp. 255–9).

when Thomas Dobb, a Cambridge Master of Arts, was brought
before Cranmer at this time on a charge of having interrupted
the mass at St. Paul's in order to denounce the adoration of the
Host, Cranmer imprisoned him in the Counter, where he died
before Somerset's pardon could reach him. But with the Protector attempting to pursue a policy of political liberalism and
religious toleration, the extremist movement spread and increased in violence. At such a time, the sermons of moderate
reformers were inevitably misunderstood. When Cranmer's
Commissary Glazier preached during Lent in March 1547 that
fasting in Lent, though meritorious, was not ordained by divine
law, this was interpreted on all sides as a heretical incitement to
the people to defy the fasting laws. Cranmer almost certainly
agreed with Glazier with regard to fasting in Lent, for Glazier's
views were endorsed in the Injunctions of the King's Visitors
six months later, and by implication in the royal proclamation
of January 1548. The statement of a distinguished modern
historian that Cranmer ate meat during Lent in 1547 is almost
certainly wrong.[1]

Gardiner made repeated protests against Somerset's weakness in repressing the attacks on images and the circulation
of heretical pamphlets. Gardiner had rightly become famous
during Henry's reign as the most able and ruthless of the orthodox leaders, and was bitterly hated by the reformers, who had
enthusiastically welcomed his fall from favour two months
before Henry died; but Cranmer had no more thought of
punishing Gardiner for having served Henry as a persecutor
than he had of revenging himself for the plots in which Gardiner
had engaged against him. Gardiner was permitted to play the
chief part in Henry's funeral at Windsor, with Cranmer and
the other Bishops assisting him, and he was given every opportunity of serving the new régime as faithfully as he had served

[1] Foxe, v. 705; Stow, *Annals*, p. 594; the Visitors' Injunctions (September
1547) (Burnet, v. 185); Proclamation of 16 January 1548 (Cranmer's *Works*, ii.
507–8). Froude (iv. 276) stated that an anonymous contemporary diary notes that
in 1547 'the Archbishop of Canterbury did eat meat openly in Lent, in the hall of
Lambeth, the like of which was never seen since England was a Christian country'.
But Froude gave no reference, and Gairdner, after forty years of extensive research,
was unable to discover the document to which Froude referred (Gairdner, *Lollardy
and the Reformation* iii. 23 n.) It is perhaps permissible to suggest that Froude was
somehow confusing this with the very similar entry in the diary of the monk of
St. Augustine's Canterbury (*Nar. Ref.*, p. 285) with regard to Cranmer eating
meat on the eve of Becket's feast day in July 1537.

the old. Cranmer was prepared to collaborate, not only with Gardiner, but even with Norfolk, who had escaped with his life when Henry died at two o'clock in the morning of the day on which Norfolk's execution was to take place. The Executors had merely to take no action and allow the sentence to be carried out; but Norfolk's life was spared, though Somerset excepted him from the royal pardon and held him imprisoned in the Tower. Norfolk had played an important part in the attempt to send Cranmer to the Tower in 1543; but this exceptionally unscrupulous politician knew who was the easiest person to dupe. In March or April 1547, he asked Cranmer to visit him in the Tower, and apparently persuaded Cranmer to forgive him, after a talk lasting more than two hours in which tears of emotion were shed on both sides; but the Emperor's Ambassador van der Delft realized that Cranmer would not succeed in obtaining Norfolk's release, as he had so little influence with the Protector and the Council, and Norfolk remained in prison throughout Edward's reign.[1]

Cranmer clearly showed his attitude to Gardiner, and his whole policy in 1547, when he drafted the Homilies. Cranmer had prepared a Book of Homilies as early as 1542, and Convocation had been on the point of issuing the book when Henry had decided that it was undesirable to publish any statement of doctrine which might conflict with the King's Book, which was then in the course of preparation. It was probably Cranmer who suggested in the spring of 1547 that a Book of Homilies should now be officially promulgated; but he had no intention of utilizing the opportunity by entrusting the work of preparing the Homilies exclusively to reformers. He invited Gardiner to assist in drafting the Homilies. He had adopted the same attitude in 1538, when he had been so eager to prevent Stokesley from leaving the conference with the German Lutherans, even though Stokesley obstructed the progress of the negotiations; and now, with Gardiner in disgrace, with Somerset in power and the Protestant artisans demonstrating against priests, Cranmer preferred to bring back Gardiner into the circle of power and to issue homilies to which Gardiner was prepared to subscribe.

---

[1] Funeral ceremonies of Henry VIII (February 1547) (Strype, *Eccl. Mem.* ii [ii]. 291–2, 300, 305–9); Van der Delft to Charles V, 27 April 1547 (*Span. Cal.* ix, p. 85).

He adopted the same policy successfully with Tunstall, who remained in favour despite his orthodox religious opinions, and collaborated in the issue of the Book of Homilies; but Gardiner objected to Cranmer's Homilies before he had even read them. He objected to the issue of any homilies at all, on the grounds that they had been rendered superfluous by the issue of the King's Book in 1543, and argued that it was the duty of Henry's Executors to uphold the Henrician religious settlement until Edward was old enough to decide his policy himself. He also argued that not even the royal authority could overrule an Act of Parliament, and that by Act of Parliament it was heresy to challenge the doctrine of the King's Book.[1]

The Homilies do not appear to have been approved by any Commission of Bishops and divines, and the opinions expressed in them may be assumed to be those of Cranmer, who for the first time in his life was able to issue a theological declaration precisely as he desired it. His contemporaries believed that while Cranmer approved and authorized all the twelve Homilies, he himself was the author of three of them— of the Homilies of Salvation, of True, Lively and Christian Faith, and of Good Works annexed unto Faith, all of which are really part of one continuous declaration of the doctrine of justification.[2] This doctrine fell a good way short of the new Protestant theology of justification by faith in its Lutheran and Calvinist form. Cranmer went to St. Hilary and St. Ambrose for the plain statements that 'faith alone justifieth' and that 'he which believeth in Christ should be saved without works, by faith alone', and commented: 'What can be spoken more plainly than to say that freely, without works, by faith only, we obtain remission of our sins?' But he immediately qualified this position by explaining that the faith which was necessary for salvation was a true and lively faith, which manifested itself in good living and good works. A man who professed to believe in

[1] Gardiner to Somerset, 6, 10, and undated June 1547; Gardiner to Cranmer, (June 1547); Gardiner to the Council (30 August 1547) (Muller, p. 292, 296–8, 302–3, 310–5, 369–71); Records of Convocation, February 1542/3 (Wilkins, iii. 863); Morison to Cromwell (summer 1538) (*L.P.*, xiii [i]. 1296); 32 Hen. VIII, c. 26; 34 & 35 Hen. VIII, c. 1.

[2] *Certayne Sermons or Homelies* (edition of 31 July 1547) contains all the Homilies. Gardiner obviously thought that Cranmer was the author of the *Homily of Salvation* (see Gardiner to Somerset, 14 and 27 October, and 12 November 1547 (Muller, pp. 397, 403, 406, 408, 413)); see also Woolton's *Christian Manual* of 1576 (p. 31), and Foxe, viii. 35.

Christ and in the words of Scripture nevertheless lacked faith if he lived ungodly, though a man could in exceptional circumstances be saved by true faith alone without works if, like the thief who was hanged with Christ, he had no time in which to perform any. Cranmer agreed with Augustine that if a Jew or pagan clothed the naked and fed the poor, he would receive no heavenly reward for this, and he quoted from Chrysostom: 'I can show a man that by faith without works lived and came to Heaven; but without faith never man had life'.[1]

In emphasizing, on the one hand, the necessity for good works, and on the other that no man could attain salvation by his own good works without relying on God's mercy and Christ's merits, Cranmer was adhering to the King's Book. But he had expounded this doctrine in the Homilies by proceeding from the basic premise that man was justified only by faith, without works, whereas the King's Book had stated equally clearly: 'It is plain that not only faith, as it is a distinct virtue or gift by itself, is required to our justification, but also the other gifts of the grace of God, with a desire to do good works'. Cranmer made further departures from orthodox doctrine in the Homily of Good Works, where he compared the existing traditions to those which the Jews had exalted above God's commandments, and included among 'Papistical superstitions and abuses' not only St. Agatha's letters, beads, shoes, girdles and other relics, but also holy bread, holy water, palms and candles. The use of these ceremonies had been expressly approved in royal proclamations in Henry's reign, and they were not suppressed until February 1548.[2]

When Gardiner wrote to Cranmer at the beginning of June 1547, he had not yet read the Homilies, which were first published on 31st July; but Cranmer knew that it would be impossible to deny these contradictions between the Homilies and the King's Book. He consequently replied to Gardiner's argument that the King's Book had removed the need for homilies by claiming that it was necessary to issue the Homilies because Henry had

---

[1] 'The Homily of Salvation', 'The Homily of Faith', and 'The Homily of Good Works' (Cranmer's *Works*, ii. 128–49; for the passages cited, see pp. 130–1, 143).
[2] The King's Book (in Lloyd, *Formularies of Faith*, p. 368); 'The Homily of Good Works' (Cranmer's *Works*, ii. 146–8); Proclamations of 16 November 1538 and 26 February 1539 (Strype, *Cranmer*, p. 690; Wilkins, iii. 842) ; and see also *The Rationale of Ceremonies, 1540–1543*.

been seduced into promulgating the King's Book. By relying on the King's Book against the Homilies, Gardiner forced Cranmer to repudiate the Henrician formulary to which he had subscribed in 1543, and to find someone other than a King who could be blamed for it; and when Cranmer wrote to Gardiner that Henry knew full well who had seduced him, the hint was unmistakable that this was Gardiner himself. The Protestant pamphleteers had already begun to propagate the myth of Gardiner as the wicked genius who was responsible whenever Henry had done wrong.

Gardiner, however, considered that it was an affront to the honour of Princes to suggest that any Prince, particularly their late master, could ever be seduced into doing wrong, and he wrote to Cranmer in great indignation. Cranmer had mentioned in his letter to Gardiner that despite his opposition to the King's Book he had enforced it in his diocese, and had forbidden the reformer Joseph to preach against the book. Presumably Cranmer hoped that this would encourage Gardiner to follow his example of obedience; but Gardiner used the incident against Cranmer. He asked Cranmer how he could say that the King's Book was wrong when he had formerly forced Joseph to adhere to it, and he pointed out that if Cranmer had thought that the King's Book was wrong, he should have opposed it, for God should be served rather than man. Gardiner, unlike many of Cranmer's modern biographers, knew that Cranmer's principles did not permit him to obey his King when he was given an order to sin; and Gardiner was right when he implied that Cranmer should have offered himself for martyrdom in 1543—odious though the argument was in the mouth of the man who would have been the first to have ensured that Cranmer had suffered that martyrdom.[1] Cranmer could only reply that he had earnestly endeavoured in 1543 to persuade Henry that the doctrines in the King's Book were wrong, and that he had finally submitted to Henry's arguments.

Gardiner wrote again to Cranmer at the beginning of July. He strongly criticized Cranmer's doctrine of justification, and appealed to him to stand together with his brother Bishops against the extremists and the mob, 'especially when you see religion so beset that, once the door is open, you cannot with-

[1] Gardiner to Cranmer, (June 1547) and (July 1547) (Muller, pp. 299–316 318–22). Cranmer's letters to Gardiner are lost.

stand the attack of those bursting in'. This appeal to episcopal solidarity was backed by the thinly-veiled threat: the King's ministers were mortal men, and in the present unsettled state of the realm anything might happen to them. 'Whatever will be tried in religion, it will be at your peril, and to the misfortune of all, if anything shall turn out unhappily'.[1]

The Homily of Good Works shows that Cranmer, in the summer of 1547, was already in favour of abolishing holy bread and holy water, and the ceremonies on Palm Sunday and candles at Candlemas; but the Injunctions to the Visitors which were issued for the royal visitation in May 1547 did not suppress any of these abuses. The Visitors were ordered to remove any images to which pilgrimages or offerings had been made; but images were not suppressed, and the doctrine laid down—that the images were to be only a representation and not an object of veneration—did not go beyond the doctrines of the King's Book. The provisions concerning the English Litany and the English Primer were only an extension of the policy of 1544 and 1545; and though it was now not only laudable to work on holy days, but sinful not to work, no more holy days were suppressed. The only innovation was the reversal of the policy of 1543 by the order requiring the clergy to read the New Testament and Erasmus' Paraphrase on it, and prescribing that a chapter from the English Bible was to be read at matins and evensong on every Sunday and holy day. But there was nothing in the Injunctions to encourage the Protestant extremists. The people were forbidden to remove images or insult priests, to make any alteration in the fasting days or in any part of the common prayer, or to break the established ceremonies of the Church until the King abolished them. In September the Council actually told Paulet, the Lord Great Master, to replace images which had been improperly removed by the people, though the order was later countermanded.[2]

We know from Morice that Cranmer was not entirely satis-fied with the Injunctions. It was in this connexion that he told Morice that the Council would have preferred to have gone farther, but that now that they had an infant King instead of

[1] Gardiner to Cranmer (July 1547) (Muller, pp. 316–60. The passages cited are on p. 334 and p. 348, in Latin, though most of Gardiner's letter is in English).
[2] Edward VI's Injunctions, (May 1547) (Cranmer's *Works*, ii. 498–504); Privy Council Documents, 26 September 1547 (Dasent, *Acts of the Privy Council*, ii. 518).

Henry, they feared to arouse opposition.[1] Cranmer was probably referring to the failure to condemn holy bread and holy water and the ceremonies which he had criticized in his Homily of Good Works. But if the Injunctions did not go very far, they went far enough, along with the Homilies, to arouse the resistance of Gardiner and Bonner. When the Visitors arrived at St. Paul's, Bonner protested against the Injunctions, and declared that he accepted them in so far as they were lawful; and Gardiner also resisted the visitation, though in a more surreptitious manner than Bonner. The Council committed Bonner and Gardiner to the Fleet, but Bonner was released after a few days in view of his submission.

Somerset was with the army in Scotland when Bonner and Gardiner were imprisoned, and it has been suggested that Cranmer was responsible for the decision. There is no record of the attendance at the Council meetings of 12th and 25th September, at which Bonner and Gardiner were sent to the Fleet. The minutes of both meetings were signed by Somerset, Cranmer, Paulet, Northampton, Browne, Wingfield and North; but this is no proof of the presence of these Councillors, for the minutes were often signed a long time later, and Somerset was in fact absent on both occasions. But Cranmer was probably present, for he had been attending nearly every meeting of the Council since Henry's death, and the Emperor's Ambassador reported that Cranmer was one of the chief members of the Council to whom the government of the country had been delegated during Somerset's absence.[2] It is also probable that Cranmer was in favour of committing Bonner and Gardiner to prison, for this was a quarrel which touched the Prince. Cranmer had no wish to revenge himself on Gardiner for his plots, or to punish the two Bishops for the blood of the Protestant martyrs which they had spilt at Henry's orders; but their refusal to submit now, as he himself had submitted in the past, was for Cranmer a serious offence, and to argue that an infant King and his Protector need not be obeyed was nothing less than sedition.

Cranmer treated Gardiner as he would have treated any other man who had disobeyed the royal authority. On 7th October,

[1] Foxe, v. 563.
[2] Acts of the Privy Council, 12, 21 and 25 September 1547 (where the minutes of the meeting of 12 September dealing with Bonner's case are wrongly dated 12 August); van der Delft to Charles V, 25 August 1547 (*Span. Cal.* ix, p. 141).

after Gardiner had been nearly a fortnight in the Fleet, he was brought before Cranmer, who sat with Ridley—the new Bishop of Rochester—and Cox the King's Almoner and others to hear the case. Cranmer argued with Gardiner about the Homily of Salvation in a conciliatory, and even defensive, manner; but he told him that the whole realm had accepted the Homilies, and that he alone was obdurate. He then told Gardiner that if he would submit, he would be reinstated in the King's Council to work together with his old colleagues under the Protector, but that if he were defiant, he would be sent back to the Fleet. Gardiner indignantly rejected the proposal, and in his account of the interview—which is the only account which we have—he interpreted it as an attempt to bribe him;[1] but Cranmer had done nothing improper or unusual in offering Gardiner the opportunity of purging his contempt by submission, and thereafter of rendering further services to his King to the best of his great abilities. The only novelty was Gardiner's attitude. The author of *De Vera Obedientia*, the great executive of Henry's despotism, announced that neither offers of advancement nor orders of the government would induce him to betray his faith; for though Gardiner drew a distinction between an adult King and a Protector, he had in effect been driven by the victory of heresy to reject the royal supremacy, and to set up against the King's authority the orthodoxy of an authoritarian Church.

[1] Gardiner to Somerset, 14 and 27 October 1547 (Muller, pp. 397–8, 403–4, 408).

CHAPTER XVIII

THE BOOK OF COMMON PRAYER

THE Parliament and Convocation of November 1547 marked the
first real attempt to overthrow the orthodox religion and trans-
form England into a Protestant state. Under the pressure of
events, Cranmer had advanced a considerable distance since the
summer, when he had adopted the attitude that with an infant
King it was necessary to move more slowly than if Henry were
still alive; by November, he was prepared, under Somerset's
leadership, to take a step which Henry had always opposed, and
to abolish the three abuses which had featured in the discussions
with the German Lutherans in 1538—the denial of the cup to
the laity, private masses and the celibacy of the clergy. When
Convocation met on 5th November, Cranmer promptly obtained
a license from the King pardoning the members of Convocation
for any offence which they might commit under the Act of the
Six Articles by expressing their opinion on the three abuses;
and the clergy, thus reassured, proceeded to pass a resolution in
favour of permitting the marriage of priests, and another which
approved of the administration of the communion to the laity in
both kinds.[1] The latter resolution did not deny that both the
body and blood are present in both the bread and wine; but it
urged the adoption of a practice which, though strictly speaking
not heretical, had come to be considered as heretical by implication.

Somerset and Cranmer were moving slowly forward. They
introduced a bill to permit the marriage of priests so late in the
session that there was no time for it to pass into law; but there
was no delay in proceeding with a bill permitting the Sacrament
of the Altar to be administered to the laity in both kinds. The
situation had been transformed by the death of the great auto-
crat whom Cranmer had served for so long, and by the liberal
spirit in the air. Cranmer was now prepared to support measures
which he knew that Henry had condemned; and in a Parliament

[1] Records of Convocation, November–December 1547 (Wilkins, iv. 15–16);
Parker, p. 398.

which abolished all the statutes for the burning of heretics, and greatly reduced the terror of the treason laws, he found the courage to vote against the official policy of Somerset's government when he joined the conservative Bishops in the House of Lords in opposing the second Chantries Bill, which completed the seizure of the chantries which Henry had begun in 1545. We do not know the grounds of Cranmer's opposition to the seizure of the chantries in 1547, but five years later he was arguing that the sale of the chantries should be postponed in order that the assets should be available for Edward's use when he came of age. Probably his real motive, both in 1547 and in 1552, was the same which had led him to oppose the distribution of the monastic lands, for though he condemned chantries as much as monasteries, he objected in both cases to the suppression of these obnoxious institutions being made the excuse for the enrichment of courtiers. He had not, of course, voted openly in Parliament against the seizure of the monasteries, and he would no more have voted against the second Chantries Act if Henry had been alive than would the orthodox Bishops who had supported him in his opposition, and who had set him the example of Parliamentary independence by voting against the bill for the administration of the Sacrament in both kinds.[1]

No action was taken in Parliament or Convocation with regard to private masses; but Cranmer dealt with this immediately after the session had ended at Christmas, when he formulated some questions to be answered by himself and other Bishops and divines as to whether the Sacrament of the Altar benefited anyone other than the communicants, and as to the origin and desirability of the practice by which the priest alone communicated.[2] Other questions dealt with masses for souls and

---

[1] H.L.Jo., 10 and 15 December 1547; Morice (Nar. Ref., p. 247); Foxe, viii. 15. Morice states that Cranmer argued 'for the steying of the chauntries untyll his highnes hadd come unto lawfull age' against the Duke of Northumberland. He was therefore not referring to the occasion of the Chantries Act of 1547, before Northumberland had come to power, but obviously to the time when the Commission for the sale of the chantries was set up in July 1552 (see Writ of 7 July 1552, in Lit. Rem. Edw. VI, p. 414 n.). Burnet, ii. 101, gives this as Cranmer's reason for opposing the Chantries bill in 1547.

[2] For the Questions and Answers on the Mass, see Burnet, v. 197–217; for the passages cited, see pp. 198, 201, 212. Cranmer's answers are printed in Cranmer's Works, ii. 150–1, where they are wrongly stated to be the answers of several Bishops. The date of the Questions and Answers is disputed; but it was probably between 20 December 1547 and 3 February 1548 (see Gasquet and Bishop, Edward VI and the Book of Common Prayer, pp. 82–85). Dixon (ii. 476–8 n.),

with the language in which the mass should be celebrated. On the question of private masses, Cranmer and John Taylor adopted an unequivocally Lutheran position which was in advance of all their colleagues, for neither Ridley, Barlow, Cox, Goodrich nor Holbeach was prepared to join Cranmer in stating without qualification: 'The receiving of the said Sacrament by one man doth avail and profit only him that receiveth the same'. The other reformers agreed with him that it was desirable to revert to the practice of the primitive Church whereby the people received the Sacrament with the priest, and that masses for the dead should be abolished. On the question of language, Cranmer said: 'I think it convenient to use the vulgar tongue in the mass, except in certain secret mysteries, whereof I doubt'— a position in which the other reformers more or less concurred. The orthodox Bishops objected to the mass being said in English, and asserted that, though it was always better if there were other communicants, it was not unlawful for the priest to celebrate mass alone.   The sharpest division of opinion came in reply to the question: 'What is the oblation and sacrifice of Christ in the mass?' Cranmer answered: 'The oblation and sacrifice of Christ in the mass is so called not because Christ indeed is there offered and sacrificed by the priest and the people (for that was done but once by Himself upon the Cross); but it is so called because it is a memory and representation of that very true sacrifice and immolation which before was made upon the Cross'. His position was clearly adopted by Holbeach, Goodrich, Barlow and Taylor, and a little more ambiguously by Ridley and Cox. The orthodox Bishops took the traditional attitude that the mass was a sacrifice.

In November and December 1547, the Protector took action against the extremists. He was conscious that the extremists were a menace to authority, and he feared the Emperor, who had warned the English government not to proceed further with the Reformation, and had obtained an assurance from Somerset that he had no intention of doing so. A royal proclamation was issued, threatening to punish any apprentice who

though wrong in believing that it must have been prior to the enactment of the Chantries Act, may well be right in suggesting that it was when the northern Bishops were in London for the session of Parliament and Convocation. The most likely date is immediately after the bill for Communion in both kinds was passed on 20 December 1547.

manhandled or insulted a priest, and an Act of Parliament made any insult to the Sacrament of the Altar an offence punishable by imprisonment during the King's pleasure. On 27th December, a royal proclamation, of which Cranmer must certainly have approved, even if he did not draft it, prohibited all discussion about the nature of the Presence except by learned men in private. The people must believe that the body and blood of Christ is there; but no one must discuss, either in the pulpit or in the alehouse, whether it is there really or figuratively, whether with legs, arms, toes and nails, and whether both flesh and blood were in both the bread and wine. This was the old policy of Henry's reign of imposing a complete prohibition on both criticism and defence of the established doctrines.[1]

During the first half of 1548, Somerset and Cranmer were moving slowly forward; but they were determined to prevent the Reformation from developing too fast. In January 1548, candles at Candlemas, ashes on Ash Wednesday and palms on Palm Sunday were suppressed, and on 21st February the Council ordered Cranmer to remove all remaining images. Before the end of the year, all the ceremonies had been abolished except the sepulchre at Easter and the two lights before the high altar, and in the leading places of worship, like the Chapel Royal and St. Paul's, more and more of the service was being conducted in English. But fasting in Lent and on the fast days was enforced. The proclamation of 6th February, which announced that no one would be punished for failing to creep to the Cross on Good Friday or for refusing to use holy bread or holy water, threatened to punish with imprisonment anyone who did not use all the other ceremonies which had not yet been suppressed. All unlicensed preaching was forbidden, and steps were taken to restrain the reformers who had been granted a preaching license. On 13th May, Somerset wrote to the preachers and told them that 'it is not a preacher's part to bring that into contempt and hatred which the Prince doth either allow or is content to suffer . . . Why should a private man, or a preacher, take this royal and kingly office upon him; and not rather, as his duty is, obediently follow himself and teach likewise others to follow and

[1] Pole to Soto, 6 April 1547 (*Poli Epist.*, iv. 44); van der Delft to Charles V, 15 November and 5 December 1547 (*Span. Cal.* ix, pp. 205–6, 218–21); 1 Edw. VI, c. 1; Proclamations of 12 November and 27 December 1547 (Dasent, *Acts of the Privy Council*, ii. 521–2; Cranmer's *Works*, ii. 505–7).

observe that which is commanded? . . . it is the part of a godly man, not to think himself wiser than the King's Majesty and his Council, but patiently to expect and to conform himself'.[1] Cranmer was certainly in full agreement with these sentiments.

This cautious policy did not succeed in appeasing the conservatives. In January 1548, the Council released Gardiner from prison, though he had made only a very qualified submission with regard to the Homilies; but he continued his opposition by devious means in his diocese. In June, he defied an order from the Protector prohibiting him from dealing with controversial issues concerning the Sacrament when he preached before the King on St. Peter's Day; he spoke about the Real Presence and transubstantiation in his sermon. Next day, the Council committed Gardiner to the Tower. The minutes of this meeting of the Council were signed by Somerset, Cranmer, Paulet, Cheyney and Russell—the same Russell who five years before had been present at the meeting of the Council when Gardiner's faction had decided to send Cranmer to the Tower. Gardiner believed that he had been imprisoned for defending the Real Presence; but for Cranmer, it was a case of punishing a most wilful disobedience to royal authority.[2]

Cranmer and Somerset had shown six months earlier that they would not overlook disobedience in their friends any more than in their opponents. The Marquis of Northampton, the brother of Katherine Parr, wished to divorce his wife, who had committed adultery, and marry Elizabeth Brooke, the daughter of Lord Cobham. Elizabeth's uncle was in Cranmer's service, and had married his niece. In April 1547, a Commission was established to decide whether, after a divorce for adultery, the spouses were free to remarry. Cranmer presided over the Commission, and made an exhaustive analysis of the conflicting opinions of the early Fathers and the decisions of the General Councils with regard to the remarriage of one or both parties after a divorce for adultery. While the Commissioners delayed

[1] Cranmer to Bonner, 27 January and 24 February 1547/8; Proclamations of 16 January and 6 February 1548; Somerset to the preachers, 13 May 1548 (Wilkins, iv. 22; Cranmer's *Works*, ii. 507–13); Wriothesley, ii. 2–3; *Greyfriars Chron.*, p. 55.
[2] Acts of the Privy Council, 8 January 1547/8 and 30 June 1548; Somerset to Gardiner, 28 June 1548; Udall's report of Gardiner's sermon (Foxe, vi. 86–93).

giving judgment, Northampton grew impatient, and cohabited with Elizabeth Brooke. But he was unfortunate in being confronted with Somerset and Cranmer, who were perhaps the only two men in authority who were not prepared to tolerate illegality in influential peers; and Northampton, the brother of the Queen Dowager and one of the members of the inner Council which ruled the realm under the Protector, was forced to appear before his colleagues to explain his conduct, and to separate from Elizabeth Brooke, who was ordered to reside in the house of Katherine Parr.

Three months later, in April 1548, Cranmer and the Commissioners, acting on the advice of a group of lawyers, gave judgment that where a spouse committed adultery, both spouses were free to remarry, as the adultery had terminated the marriage.[1] Four years later, Cranmer's Code of Ecclesiastical Law allowed only the innocent spouse to remarry after divorce, and Burnet suggested that in Northampton's case some of the Commissioners disagreed with the decision. But even if this is true—and there is no real evidence of it—it is very unlikely that the Commission would have given a judgment to which Cranmer was seriously opposed; and it is therefore clear that Cranmer had altered his opinion since 1540, when he had written to Osiander, in connexion with the bigamous marriage of Philip of Hesse, that marriage after divorce was never lawful. In Northampton's case, Cranmer was not granting a decree of nullity for reasons of state, but was determining the important theological question as to whether the parties to a valid marriage could in any circumstances remarry during the lifetime of their spouse. He reached a decision which was satisfactory to Northampton, and extended to the wife of this great nobleman a privilege which was later refused to other guilty wives; but we need not assume that Cranmer was affected by improper considerations. When Kings were not involved, Cranmer did not allow anyone, however powerful, to influence him in the exercise of his judicial duties. He had certainly given proof of this in Northampton's case.

In the summer of 1548, Cranmer conducted a visitation of

[1] Commissions of 19 April and 7 May 1547 (*Cal. Pat. Rolls, Edw. VI*, i. 137, 261); Acts of the Privy Council, 28 January 1547/8; Answers on the Northampton divorce, (1548) (Burnet, v. 183–4). In Burnet (ii. 118–22 and n.) Cranmer's notes on the Church's attitude to divorce are inaccurately summarized.

his diocese. His purpose was to ensure that the Reformation in Kent had gone as far as the Protector had ordered, and no farther. He drafted a list of eighty-six matters which his Visitors were to investigate concerning the obedience of the clergy to the King's Injunctions and the conduct of the people. One of these matters to be investigated was whether the Sacrament was placed in the sepulchre on Good Friday. From this it has been deduced that Cranmer was going ahead of the Council and suppressing in his diocese one of the two remaining ceremonies which had not yet been abolished; but it is much more likely that he was dutifully seeking to enforce obedience, and to compel the extremists to comply with the order of 6th February by observing the ceremonies which had not yet been suppressed. Cranmer did not, however, inquire as to whether any priest was secretly married, but on the contrary asked whether anyone was criticizing married priests and refusing to take communion from them.[1] The bill permitting priests to marry had not been reached in the House of Lords; but evidently Cranmer and the government treated it as being law already.

The drafting of a new communion service in which both the bread and wine would be administered to the communicants was probably entrusted to a Commission of thirteen Bishops and divines. There can be very little doubt that Cranmer presided over their meetings at Windsor, and played the leading part in drafting the Order of the Communion which was issued on 8th March 1548. The document was very short, though the form of service contained in it was considerably longer than the one which it replaced. It did not interfere in any way with the mass, which was still conducted according to the old Sarum Use, but merely added to it a communion service for the benefit of those few members of the congregation who had come to mass in order to communicate, and not only to gossip with their neighbours and pursue their debtors. But the Order of the Communion contained some innovations. The General Confession which preceded the communion expressly told the people that though it was proper to confess their sins to a priest, they must not condemn those who did not choose to do so, but preferred to confess direct to God; and the priest was directed

[1] Articles for the visitation of Canterbury diocese (1548) (Cranmer's *Works*, ii. 154-9).

that in the event of it being necessary to consecrate more bread during the administration of the communion, he was not to elevate the Host. This was enough to alarm the conservatives, who interpreted the Order of the Communion as abolishing the mass, although in fact it not only did not interfere with the mass, but expressly forbade anyone to do so. But the King's Preface to the book clearly hinted that alterations would be made in the mass in the near future, and this, combined with the opposition of the conservatives, led the reformers to welcome the Order of the Communion. It has been suggested that some of the words and phrases used in the Order of the Communion indicate that the men who drafted it did not believe in the Real Presence; but there are other words which indicate exactly the opposite, and it is unlikely that Cranmer intended to make any great innovation with the new communion service. He and Somerset seem to have become alarmed that they had done so much, especially when disorders broke out in the churches, and they did not attempt to enforce the prohibition on the elevation of the Host. In June, van der Delft told Prince Philip of Spain that the mass was once more said in all the churches.[1]

There is, however, considerable doubt as to the opinions with regard to the Eucharist which Cranmer held at this time. We know that in 1550 he believed in the doctrine which he expressed in his books on the Sacrament. This doctrine fell short of the extreme sacramentarian position, and of that of Zwingli, and it may even have fallen short of the modified Zwinglianism of Bullinger and Hooper and their followers; but it went as far as the doctrines of Peter Martyr, farther than those of Bucer, and far beyond Lutheranism. Despite all the many variations of opinion on the Eucharist, the burning issue was whether Christ was really present in the Sacrament, not only in

[1] Foxe, v. 716; Order of the Communion (*Liturgies of Edward VI*, pp. 2, 4, 8); van der Delft to Charles V, 16 May 1548; van der Delft to Philip of Spain, 15 June 1548 (*Span. Cal.*, ix, pp. 265–6, 273); Burcher to Bullinger, 29 October 1548 (*Orig. Letters*, p. 643); Selve to Henry II, 30 September 1548 (*Correspondance de Selve*, p. 453); and see Gasquet and Bishop, pp. 89–96. There is no evidence other than that of the unreliable Heylin in 1661 (Heylin, *Ecclesia Restaurata*, i. 118–19) that the Order of the Communion was drafted by the same Commissioners as drafted the Prayer Book of 1548; nor is there any evidence earlier than 1655 of the names of the Commissioners who drafted the Prayer Book (see infra); but it is not unlikely that the Order of the Communion was drafted by the thirteen Commissioners named by Fuller (*Church History*, ii. 354) as having drafted the Prayer Book.

a spiritual sense, but corporally, in substance. In this sense, Cranmer did not believe in the Real Presence in 1550, and according to the writer who perhaps was Cheke, he had ceased to believe in it in 1546; but two years later, Cranmer was acting as if he still believed in the Real Presence, and everyone was convinced that he did. As late as the autumn of 1547, Cranmer was sitting in judgment on a sacramentary. When a gentleman and his wife at Wressel in Yorkshire discovered that their servant did not believe in the Real Presence, they sent him to Cranmer—not to Archbishop Holgate—for punishment. Cranmer committed the man to prison, and though we do not know how he ultimately dealt with the case, it is clear that the master and mistress had no doubt of Cranmer's orthodoxy on the Sacrament of the Altar. In view of Cranmer's attitude during the first two years of Edward's reign, it has often been suggested that Cranmer was converted on the question of the Eucharist, not by Ridley in 1546, but by John à Lasco in 1548.[1]

The true explanation is probably that Cranmer's conversion was a gradual and irregular process. In the light of all the facts, we can form a conjecture as to the development of his opinions on the Eucharist—that by 1538, he had ceased to believe in transubstantiation and had accepted the Lutheran doctrine; that after June 1539, he repudiated his opinion under duress, and conformed to the old orthodox doctrine in the Six Articles and the King's Book; that in 1546 he was persuaded by Ridley to renounce the Real Presence, at a time when Henry himself was suggesting that the mass should be suppressed. But when Henry died, Cranmer abandoned all his hopes of rapid progress, believing that the repudiation of the Real Presence could only be proclaimed by an adult King; and during 1547, the popular attacks on the Sacrament must have caused a reaction in Cranmer's attitude. Cranmer believed that men should not come to the Lord's table as they came to other common meats and drinks, but with great fear and dread, because there 'is not only represented, but also spiritually given unto us, very Christ Himself'. This was very different from talk about a Round Robin, a Jack-in-the-Box, a vile cake, a God made of fine flour.

---

[1] Preface to Cranmer's *Defensio Verae et Catholicae Doctrinae de Sacramento* (2nd Latin ed.) (in Cranmer's *Works*, i. App., p. 6); see Chap. xvi, p. 252, supra; Foxe, v. 705; Parsons, *Three Conversions of England*, i. 609.

That kind of language probably revived all Cranmer's old horror of sacramentaries. It led his mentor Ridley to forget his quarrels with Gardiner. 'Why, my Lord', said Ridley when Gardiner was arguing about justification, 'what make you so great a matter herein? You see many Anabaptists rise against the Sacrament of the Altar; I pray you, my Lord, be diligent in confounding of them'. The immediate task was to be diligent in confounding these Anabaptists, not to sow doubts by denying the Real Presence.[1]

So at the beginning of 1548, Cranmer did not advance beyond Lutheranism in his Questions and Answers on the mass, and in the Order of the Communion. When Gardiner was brought before the council on 8th January in order to be released from prison, Cranmer told him that he fully agreed with the doctrine of the Presence which Gardiner had expressed in his book on the Sacrament in 1546. In June, when Prince Philip was being reassured as to the worship of the mass in England, Cranmer issued a catechism for the instruction of English youth which plainly asserted the Real Presence. This was the catechism of the Lutheran churches in Nuremberg, which Cranmer translated into English from a Latin translation by Justus Jonas of the original German. At his trial, Cranmer agreed that he had translated it, and referred to the English edition as 'my book', and it is thus clear that even if he did not undertake the translation work himself, he accepted full responsibility for the English edition. The Preface consisted of a letter from Cranmer to the King. In other ages, an Archbishop dedicating a children's catechism to a 10-year-old King might have made some reference to the fact that the King was himself a child; but Cranmer did nothing so derogatory of royal dignity, and wrote that as the King had decided on a gracious reformation of all ungodliness, he petitioned him to permit the Catechism to be read by the children of his most loving subjects.[2]

[1] Cranmer, *Defence of the true and Catholic doctrine of the Sacrament* (Jenkyns, ii. 402); *Greyfriars Chron.*, p. 55; Report of Ridley's trial (Foxe, vii. 523); Gilby, *An answer to the develish detection of Gardiner*, f. xvi ; Brinkelow, *Lamentacyon against the Citye of London*, p. 43 (unpaginated).
[2] Gardiner's unpublished Preface to his *Explication and Assertion of the True Catholic Faith* (Muller, p. 448); Cranmer's Preface to *A Short Instruction into Christian Religion* (the Catechism of 1548), pp. xxxi–xxxv; Cranmer's *Works*, ii. 418–20. See also the statement as to the Catechism by Cranmer's chaplain Rowland Taylor in his account of his examination in 1555 (Foxe, vi. 685).

The Catechism, both in the original and in Cranmer's translation, was completely Lutheran. It taught that there were three
Sacraments—Baptism, Penance and the Sacrament of the Altar
—and numbered the Ten Commandments so that the condemnation of graven images was not a separate commandment.
There was the usual emphasis on obedience to parents and to
magistrates; and though Cranmer omitted, in his translation, a
passage in the Latin which censured magistrates who forced the
people to swear unnecessary oaths, he allowed the statement
that magistrates should be disobeyed when they ordered men
to sin to remain in its full Lutheran vigour. The only major
alteration from the Latin text in Cranmer's translation was the
addition of a lengthy and entirely new passage, denouncing
images in the strongest language as idols. On the issue of
images at least, Cranmer and the realm had gone farther than
the Lutherans.[1]

On the subject of the Sacrament of the Altar, Cranmer gave
the children the full force of Jonas' anti-sacramentarian propaganda. 'Christ saith of the bread, This is my body, and of the
cup he saith, This is my blood. Wherefor we ought to believe
that in the Sacrament we receive truly the body and blood of
Christ . . . And whereas in this perilous time, certain deceitful
persons be found in many places, who of very frowardness will
not grant that there is the body and blood of Christ, but deny
the same, for none other cause but that they cannot compass by
man's blind reason how this thing should be brought to pass,
ye good children shall with all diligence beware of such persons,
that ye suffer not yourselves to be deceived by them. For such
men surely are not true Christians. . . . Wherefore, good
children, doubt not but there is the body and blood of our Lord
which we receive in the Lord's Supper. For He hath said so,
and by the power of His word hath caused it so to be. Wherefore
seeing Christ saith, Do this as often as ye do it, in remembrance
of me, it is evident hereby that Christ causeth, even at this time,
His body and blood to be in the Sacrament after that manner and
fashion as it was at that time, when He made his maundy with
His disciples'. It is not surprising that the Zwinglains did not like
the Catechism, though it was not true to say that in it Cranmer

approved 'that foul and sacrilegious transubstantiation of the Papists'.[1]

It is extraordinary that Cranmer should have denied in 1551, in his books against Gardiner and Smith, that he taught the doctrine of the Real Presence in this Catechism. He admitted that shortly before he translated the Catechism he had believed in the Real Presence, but he insisted that in the Catechism itself he had taught the doctrine of the Presence which he held in 1551. In fact the Catechism, in Cranmer's translation, asserted the truth of the Real Presence in the strongest terms. It may perhaps be possible, by a feat of casuistry, to reconcile the words of the Catechism with a denial of the Real Presence; but this was certainly not the impression which the book was meant to convey to its child or adult readers. If Cranmer translated the Catechism in such a manner that in its hidden meaning it denied the Real Presence, he was guilty of gross deception on his readers; but it is much more likely that he was deceiving himself in 1551 rather than that he was deliberately deceiving the children in 1548, and that in later years he chose to forget how, under pressure of political developments, he had repudiated this new doctrine of the Presence in 1548.[2]

Further information as to Cranmer's opinions on the Eucharist is provided in the letters of the Zwinglians in England. John ab Ulmis, a hot-headed young German student at Oxford, and the English Zwinglians Traheron and Burcher, were in touch with Cranmer, and wrote regularly to their leader Bullinger in Zurich, who was anxious to convert Cranmer and to influence religious developments in England. Bullinger sent a letter to Cranmer by the Zwinglian merchant Hilles, in which, after a general exhortation to Cranmer to act as a diligent Bishop, he discreetly turned to the question of the Eucharist. When Cranmer received the letter in the middle of August 1548, he expressed his satisfaction with the exhortation; but the Zwinglians who were with him had no illusions that he would be

[1] Ibid., English pp. 207–9; cf. Latin pp. 176–8; Ulmis to Bullinger, 18 August 1548 (*Orig. Letters*, p. 381).

[2] Cranmer, *Answer to Gardiner*; Cranmer, *Answer to Smith* (Cranmer's *Works*, i. 226–7, 374); see also Cranmer's remarks at the deprivation proceedings against Bonner (Foxe, v. 765) which certainly refer to the Catechism of 1548, and his statement in his *Defence of the true and Catholic doctrine of the Sacrament* (Jenkyns, ii. 440–1). For a somewhat far-fetched interpretation of the Catechism in a Zwinglian sense, see Gasquet and Bishop, pp. 129–31; and see Constant, *The Reformation in England*, ii. 259–60 n.

influenced by Bullinger's arguments about the Presence. Ulmis and Burcher were disgusted with Cranmer's attitude to the Eucharist and with his Lutheran Catechism, and the shrewder and more reliable Traheron was equally pessimistic. He wrote to Bullinger on 1st August 1548 that Cranmer was a kind and good-hearted man in other respects, but that on the question of the Eucharist, he and Latimer were among the small number of learned men who were not making any progress at all towards the Zwinglian position. Traheron obviously did not despair of Latimer; but he held out no hopes at all of Cranmer's conversion and had been told by the nobility that Cranmer was 'lukewarm'. [1]

In August, John à Lasco came to Lambeth on Cranmer's invitation from his exile home at Emden. This Polish nobleman, who had been expelled from his Hungarian bishopric on account of his marriage, held Zwinglian opinions on the Eucharist. About a month after à Lasco arrived in England, Traheron wrote again to Bullinger on 28th September, and told him that Cranmer and Latimer and other Bishops, who had hitherto seemed to be Lutherans, had been converted to the Zwinglian view of the Eucharist. On 29th October, Burcher was still complaining to Bullinger about Cranmer's Lutheran Catechism; but on 27th November, Ulmis wrote to Bullinger that 'even that Thomas himself'—he meant Cranmer—'by the goodness of God and the instrumentality of that most upright and judicious man Master John à Lasco is in a great measure recovered from his dangerous lethargy'.[2] Within three weeks, Cranmer had made his first public declaration against the Real Presence in the disputation in the House of Lords.

Ulmis' letter is the only evidence to support the theory that Cranmer's conversion was due to John à Lasco, and it is not of great value. Ulmis spent much of his time travelling to London to hear gossip about current politics when he ought to have been studying at Oxford; but his information was often wrong, and he was not in a good position to know the facts about the change in Cranmer's opinions. But we do not have to rely on

[1] Hilles to Bullinger, 18 June 1548; Traheron to Bullinger, 1 August 1548; Ulmis to Bullinger, 18 August 1548; Burcher to Bullinger, 24 August and 29 October 1548 (*Orig. Letters*, pp. 262, 320, 380–1, 641–3.)

[2] Traheron to Bullinger, 28 September 1548; Ulmis to Bullinger, 27 November 1548; Burcher to Bullinger, 29 October 1548 (*Orig. Letters*, pp. 322, 383, 642–3).

any Zwinglian letter-writer to realize that the opinions on the
Presence which Cranmer put forward in the House of Lords in
December 1548 were very different from those which he had
expressed in the Catechism in June. Something had led him to
change his attitude during the autumn of 1548, and to express
openly the doctrine of the Eucharist to which Ridley had converted him two years before. The arguments of à Lasco may
have played their part, but the clue to the true explanation is
probably to be found in Traheron's letters. Traheron wrote that
the nobility had become Zwinglian, and were regarding Cranmer as lukewarm. It would be a great over-simplification to state
that Cranmer changed his opinions on the Presence in order to
please the nobles, who had instinctively realized that they
would be the beneficiaries of any doctrine which weakened the
authority of the Church and the priesthood; but when Somerset,
Warwick, Dorset and Northampton were prepared to denounce
the Real Presence, Cranmer could follow suit without fearing
that he was encouraging heretical artisans.[1]

The time had come to prepare the new Prayer Book. We
cannot be sure that the book was submitted to the thirteen
divines who a hundred years later were supposed to have drafted
the first Book of Common Prayer; but it is certain that in
September and October 1548 Cranmer presided over an
assembly of Bishops and divines who met at Windsor Castle
and at Chertsey to examine a draft which Cranmer himself had
prepared.[2] Cranmer had for some years been engaged in work
on a new liturgy. As early as 1538, he had entertained Malet at
Ford while Malet was drafting some liturgical project on

[1] Traheron to Bullinger, 1 August 1548; for Ulmis' neglect of his studies at
Oxford, see Hooper to Bullinger, 7 November 1549; Ulmis to Bullinger, 30 April
1550 (*Orig. Letters*, pp. 70, 320, 403–4).
[2] In 1655 Fuller (in his *Church History*, ii. 354) stated that the first Book of
Common Prayer was drafted by Cranmer, Day, Goodrich, Skyp, Holbeach, Ridley,
Thirlby, May, John Taylor, Heynes, Robertson, Redman and Cox. For the
meetings at Windsor and Chertsey in September and October 1548, and Cranmer's
presence there, see Cranmer to Mary I (September 1555) (Cranmer's *Works*, ii.
450); *K.Edw.Jo.*, Year II; Selve to Henry II, 30 September 1548 (*Correspondance
de Selve*, p. 453), where certainly Chertsey, not Chelsea, is meant; *Greyfriars
Chron.*, p. 56; Coverdale to Fagius, 21 October 1548 (*Orig. Letters*, p. 32). For
the submission of the Prayer Book to an assembly of Bishops, apparently early in
October 1548, see the Disputation in the House of Lords, 15 and 17 December
1548 (in Gasquet and Bishop, pp. 403–4); Burcher to Bullinger, 29 October 1548
(*Orig. Letters*, p. 643). For Cranmer's part in drafting the Prayer Book, see 2 &3
Edw. VI, c. 1; Anon. Biogr. (*Nar. Ref.*, p. 225); and see Gasquet and Bishop,
pp. 134–46.

Cromwell's instructions; but Cranmer's two great drafts of the liturgy probably date from after 1543, when Convocation had decided to complete Henrician uniformity by abolishing the small divergencies between the five Uses in force in various parts of England and substituting a common service, based on the Sarum Use, for the whole realm. There was nothing very radical about Cranmer's first draft. It was based on the reformed breviary which the Spanish Cardinal Quignon had produced for Pope Paul III in 1535, but was more conservative than Quignon's work, and differed less from the old Sarum Use. The whole service was to be in Latin. Cranmer probably drafted this document in the reactionary days of 1543; but it was not adopted, and a year or so later it was easier to put forward more revolutionary proposals. It was probably about 1545 that Cranmer drafted his second liturgy. In this draft, the eight traditional Hours into which the day's service was divided— maintaining the splendid fiction that the devout Englishman went to church eight times a day—were replaced by morning and evening prayers; the Lord's Prayer and some other parts of the services were to be in English; and the traditional Sarum calendar of Saints' Days, by which everyone regulated their lives and dated their letters, was to be replaced by a new calendar of Cranmer's invention in which Biblical personages from the Old Testament were commemorated along with many obscure martyrs and other characters of the post-Biblical legends.[1]

Cranmer abandoned both these drafts in the autumn of 1548, and produced a third for examination by his brethren at Windsor and Chertsey. This too was based on Quignon, on Cranmer's earlier drafts, and on the old Greek liturgies, and even apparently in one point on the Mozarabic ritual of ancient Spain, as well as on the Sarum Use; but it also showed an unmistakable connexion with Luther's liturgies, and the Communion service

[1] See Cranmer's first two drafts of the Prayer Book, in *Cranmer's Liturgical Projects*, pp. 3–165, where Part II of the document (pp. 115–65) is the earlier draft, and Part I (pp. 3–112) the later; see Wickham Legg's Introduction, pp. xvii–lxviii, and Gasquet and Bishop, pp. 16–39, 311–96. But see Smyth, *Cranmer and the Reformation under Edward VI*, pp. 74–77, for the suggestion that Wickham Legg and Gasquet and Bishop have mistaken the sequence in which Cranmer's first two drafts were composed, and that Part I was written in 1538—before Part II. and see Ratcliff, 'The Liturgical Work of Cranmer' (in *Thomas Cranmer: Three Commemoration Lectures*, pp. 26–40). See also Cranmer to Cromwell, 11 April 1538 (Cranmer's *Works*, ii. 366–7).

was concerned throughout with eliminating as far as possible the idea of the mass as a sacrifice. The Offertory and the accompanying prayers, during which the people gave money to purchase the bread and wine, and which contained words relating to the sacrifice, were replaced by a collection for alms for the poor; in the Canon, the prayers before consecration were changed so as to omit all reference to sacrifice; after the words of consecration, there was no longer mention of the sacrifices of Abel, Abraham, and Melchisadek; and now it was their prayers— no longer the elements on the altar—which the people prayed should be carried on high by angels. All this was Lutheran; but there were a few points in which the eager searcher could perhaps detect signs of something worse. The words of consecration of the Sarum Use prayed that the elements 'may be made unto us the body and blood of Thy most dearly beloved Son our Lord Jesus Christ'. Cranmer changed this to a prayer that the elements 'may be unto us the body and blood of Thy most dearly beloved son Jesus Christ'. The omission of the word 'made' was thought to be very significant, as was the suppression of the elevation of the Host. The Order of the Communion had forbidden elevation during the communion service; but now it was prohibited in the mass itself at the moment of consecration.[1]

Yet it seems clear that the popular indignation against the Book of Common Prayer was not caused by any of these changes, but by the provision that the whole of the mass was to be in English instead of in Latin. Cranmer later told Queen Mary that the divines who examined the draft of the Prayer Book were unanimous in approving the proposal that the mass should be in English. If this is true—and it is confirmed by Ridley—it shows that the orthodox Bishops and divines were prepared to give way on this point in order to fight for more essential matters.[2] But to the ordinary Englishman, this question of the language was the most essential point of all. He did not notice if the word 'made' was left out of the Canon; but he knew that his Latin

[1] The First Book of Common Prayer (*Liturgies of Edward VI*, pp. 76–99; see p. 88 for the passage cited); for the service in the Sarum Use, see Wickham Legg, *The Sarum Missal*, pp. 216–29; see also Gasquet and Bishop, pp. 184–228; Constant, *The Reformation in England*, ii. 70–84.

[2] Cranmer to Mary I (September 1555) (Cranmer's *Works*, ii. 450); Ridley to West, 8 April 1554 (Ridley's *Works*, pp. 340–1).

mass had been abolished. His indignation was perhaps caused
by the fact that he did not wish to have the hidden mystery of
the Latin mass replaced by a service in a language which he
could understand, and which therefore required a more active
mental participation on his part. But whatever the reason, the
alteration in the language of the mass outraged all the conservative instincts of the people.

Cranmer's draft did not meet with the unanimous approval of
the Commissioners at Windsor and Chertsey, as was falsely
claimed in the recitals of the Act of Uniformity. Thirlby opposed
the innovations, particularly the abolition of the elevation of
the Host. Eventually all the Commissioners seem to have
accepted the draft, except Day, who refused to agree chiefly
because of the omission of the references to oblation and the
deletion of the words 'may be made unto us' from the Canon.
But the opposition was of no avail, for the nobility had turned
Zwinglian; and when the proposed Prayer Book was the subject
of a disputation in the House of Lords in the middle of December, Cranmer and the reforming Bishops came out with a public
repudiation of the Real Presence.[1]

The issue in the disputation was whether the bread remained
in the Sacrament after consecration. Cranmer, Ridley, Holbeach
and Goodrich, supported by the able if untheological advocacy
of Sir Thomas Smith, the Secretary of State, asserted against the
arguments of Heath, Day, Repps and Tunstall that the bread
remained bread; but Cranmer did not limit himself to a denial
of transubstantiation, which was the only question actually in
dispute. He was not as lucid and outspoken as Ridley, but he
stated his position unequivocally. He asserted that evil men did
not receive the body when they ate the bread; that Christ is in
Heaven, not in the bread and wine; that the bread was a sign of
the body; and that the bread and wine are not changed out-
wardly but inwardly. 'The change is inward, not in the bread
but in the receiver . . . Christ is in the world in His divinity,
but not in His humanity. The property of His Godhead is

[1] 2 & 3 Edw. VI, c. 1; Report of the Disputation in the House of Lords, 15–19
December 1548 (Gasquet and Bishop, pp. 397–443; for Cranmer's arguments, see
pp. 398–402, 418–20, 425, 427–31, 434, 440–2; the passage from Cranmer's
argument cited here is on p. 440; for Bonner's statement, see pp. 406–7);
Traheron to Bullinger, 31 December 1548; Peter Martyr to Bucer, 26 December
1548; Burcher to Bullinger, 22 January 1549 (*Orig. Letters*, pp. 322–3, 469–70,
645–6); Constant, *The Reformation in England*, ii. 78–9.

everywhere, but His manhood is in one place only'. Bonner intervened to state roundly that the new Prayer Book contained the same heresy which had been condemned in Lambert's case, because the last rubric of the communion service referred to the 'Sacrament of the bread' and the 'Sacrament of the wine'. Even now the government was prepared to make concessions, and the passage was altered—perhaps at Cranmer's suggestion—to read 'Sacrament of the body' and 'Sacrament of the blood'. This was quite reconcilable with the manner in which Cranmer interpreted his doctrine of the Presence.

In Parliament, the Act of Uniformity was carried against the votes of the orthodox Bishops in the House of Lords, as was a bill permitting priests to marry. But the resistance of the Bishops encouraged the resistance throughout the country, which had already led to riots and executions when images had been suppressed in the previous year. A very dangerous situation was developing, and the people were saying that it was time that the Emperor's armies came. Yet Cranmer seems to have been taken by surprise by the extent of the opposition of the Bishops in Parliament. Peter Martyr wrote to Bucer at Christmas 1548 that no one had expected this, and as Martyr had spent a great deal of time with Cranmer during the previous year, it is obvious that Cranmer had not expected it.[1] Cranmer presumably still hoped, with all his concessions and moderation, to win over all men of goodwill, if not obstinate malefactors like Gardiner. In Cranmer's eyes, his Book of Common Prayer merely purged the services of the innovations which had crept in during recent centuries, and returned to the old practices of the primitive Church, while the translation of the mass into the vernacular enabled the people to understand its meaning. But Cranmer was now encountering outraged conservatism in all its fury.

[1] *H.L.Jo.*, 15 January and 19 February 1548/9; Selve to Henry II, 30 September 1548 (*Correspondance de Selve*, p. 453); Peter Martyr to Bucer, 26 December 1548 and 22 January 1549; Burcher to Bullinger, 29 October 1548 (*Orig. Letters*, pp. 469, 477, 643).

CHAPTER XIX

THE REVOLTS OF 1549

IN March 1549, Thomas Seymour, the Lord Admiral, who was alleged to have plotted to overthrow his brother the Protector, was beheaded for high treason under the provisions of an Act of Attainder. It has been suggested that there was something new and improper in the fact that Cranmer, as a priest, signed Seymour's death warrant; but the ecclesiastical members of the Council had often joined in authorizing executions in the days of Henry VIII, and Cranmer had less to do with Seymour's execution than might have been expected. He signed the minutes of the meeting of the Council when the first accusation of treason was made against Seymour in January 1549; but he had nothing more to do with the case until two months later, when he again signed the minutes—along with Somerset and twelve other Councillors—at the meeting where it was decided that Seymour should be beheaded three days later after Goodrich had visited him to give him final spiritual assistance. Cranmer was expressly excepted from the rest of the Council when they entrusted themselves with the duty of interrogating Seymour in the Tower; and there is no record of his denouncing Seymour in violent sermons of the kind which Latimer preached. Peter Martyr, who was residing in Oxford but was in constant communication with Cranmer, wrote to Bucer in January that it was a tragedy that a man as friendly to the Reformation as Seymour should have fallen into such misfortune, though he was sure that his offence was grave. Cranmer probably held the same opinion.[1]

Cranmer now turned to deal with Anabaptists. In December 1548, he had compelled a Lincolnshire parson who denied the Trinity and the divinity of Christ to recant and do public penance, and in April and May 1549 he presided over a Commission which dealt with other heretics. Champneis of Stratford

---

[1] Burnet, ii. 187–8; Acts of the Privy Council, 17 January, 22 February and 15 and 17 March 1548/9; Peter Martyr to Bucer, 22 January 1549 (*Orig. Letters*, p. 477).

had preached that some men were the elect of God, who were unable to sin once they had received the Spirit, and were entitled to seize all things necessary for their bodily requirements. Putto, the Colchester tanner, believed that Christ had not descended into Hell. Thombe, a London butcher, believed that Christ took no flesh of the Virgin, and denied the value of Baptism; and Joan Bocher, who was probably Thombe's wife, asserted the same heresy, and said that Christ was the spiritual seed, but not the natural seed, of the Virgin. All the men recanted, and carried their fagots at Paul's Cross, though Putto and Thombe, who were insufficiently penitent, were brought before Cranmer again, and made to do their penance a second time. Joan Bocher refused to recant, and on 30th April Cranmer excommunicated the woman whom he had falsely been accused of shielding by the Prebendaries of Canterbury six years before. The heresy statutes had been repealed in 1547, and there was more than a year's delay before the Council, having assured themselves of the legality of burning heretics independently of statute under the common law, sent Joan to the fire at Smithfield on 2nd May 1550.[1]

Foxe attributed to Cranmer the direct responsibility for the burning of Joan Bocher. He described the reluctance of the young King to sign the warrant for her execution, both on account of his natural kindness and because he did not wish to send Joan to the Devil by burning her before she had repented. As the Council could not induce Edward to sign, they sent Cranmer to persuade him, and Cranmer eventually succeeded, after Edward had said that before God he would place the responsibility for his action on Cranmer. Cranmer later said that he had never in his life had a more difficult task than persuading Edward to agree to burn Joan Bocher. It was not until the nineteenth century that Cranmer's admirers thought it

---

[1] Judgments against Champneis, Ashton, Joan Bocher and Thombe, 28 December 1548 and 27 and 30 April and 11 May 1549 (Wilkins, iv. 39–44, where, following Cranmer's Register, the date of the proceedings against Champneis is given as 1548; but see Wriothesley, ii. 10–11); *Greyfriars Chron.*, pp. 58–9; Wriothesley, ii. 10–13; Examination of Philpot, 6 November 1555 (Foxe, vii. 631); Micronius to Bullinger, 20 May 1550 (*Orig. Letters*, p. 560); Hutchinson, *The Image of God* (Hutchinson's *Works*, pp. 145–7); Parsons, *Three Conversions of England*, ii. 'Note of Sundry Heretikes and Sectaries', g. 2; Depositions in the Prebendaries' Case (*L.P.*, xviii [ii]. 546, pp. 291, 313–4, 331, 353–4, 359, 366). Cranmer was concerned in further proceedings against Putto a year later (see Acts of the Privy Council, 28 April 1550).

necessary to deny the truth of Foxe's story; but when public opinion had come to prefer a martyr who was not also a persecutor, it was strenuously argued that whatever Cranmer may have done in the case of Frith and Lambert, he was not responsible for persuading Edward to burn Joan Bocher. Three arguments are put forward to prove this—the first, that Edward expressed no regret at Joan's execution when he recorded the fact in his Journal; the second, that the warrant for the execution was signed by the Council, and not by Edward; and thirdly, that Cranmer was not present at the Council meeting of 27th April 1550 when the decision was taken to burn Joan.[1]

The fact that Edward showed no sign of regret in his Journal is not surprising, for apart from the fact that all his entries are very brief, his reference to Joan Bocher is entered under 2nd May 1550—the date of her execution—which, according to Foxe's story, was after he had been persuaded to consent to her death. The other points are more weighty, and seem to prove that Foxe, on this occasion as on many others, was wrong on points of detail; but it is unlikely that he invented the whole incident, even though he was one of the few persons in the sixteenth century who had doubts as to the propriety of burning even Anabaptists, and probably intended his story of Edward's reluctance to burn Joan Bocher to serve as propaganda against burning heretics. The story, moreover, first appeared in the second edition of the *Book of Martyrs*, after Foxe had met Morice and learned from him a great deal about Cranmer. It was obviously unnecessary for Cranmer to persuade Edward to sign the warrant, which was issued by the Council; but Edward may well have been disturbed when he heard that the burnings at Smithfield, which he had been taught to view with horror, were about to start again; and if Edward was objecting to burning Joan Bocher, the Council would certainly have been anxious to persuade him that her death was necessary. Cranmer was by far the most suitable counsellor to be chosen to explain to Edward that while it was evil of Papists to burn Christians

---

[1] Foxe, v. 699; *K. Edw. Jo.*, 2 May 1550; Acts of the Privy Council, 27 April 1550. For criticism of Foxe's story, see especially Bruce in Introduction to Hutchinson's *Works*, pp. iii–v; Dixon, iii. 238 n.; Pollard, *Thomas Cranmer*, pp. 261–3. For Foxe's attitude to the persecution of Anabaptists, see Foxe to Elizabeth I (summer 1575) (Fuller, *Church History*, ii. 576–7).

whom they falsely accused of heresy, it was the duty of a Christian King to punish offences against God as resolutely as he punished offences against himself, and to send those who in fact were heretics to the flames. In view of Foxe's story, there is every reason to believe that Cranmer persuaded Edward that the burning of Joan Bocher was justified.

The Book of Common Prayer came into force at Whitsun. Next day the disorders broke out in Devonshire, and within a month the Council were confronted with a conservative religious revolt in the west, with an agrarian insurrection in Norfolk, and with riots against enclosures all over the south-east of England. Cranmer played an active part in directing the measures to be taken for the suppression of the disturbances, and along with Somerset, Paulet, Rich, and the Secretaries Petre and Thomas Smith, signed the constant instructions sent to Russell in Devonshire, promising to send him more German mercenaries and urging him to use severity.[1] Cranmer also wrote a reply to the western rebels' petition to the King, as did Somerset—in the King's name—and Nicholas Udall, the disgraced headmaster of Eton. Udall and Somerset pointed out the foolishness of the rebels' demands, and that the consequence of granting them would be harmful to the interests of the rebels themselves; but Cranmer took a much higher tone, and denounced the wickedness of rebellion. His reply is marked throughout by a passionate indignation which is largely absent from the answers of Somerset and Udall.[2]

The rebels' petition began by stating: 'We will have all the General Councils and holy decrees of our forefathers observed, kept and performed; and whosoever shall againsay them, we hold them as heretics'. Cranmer was incensed at this language. 'Is this', he asked, 'the fashion of subjects to speak unto their Prince, "We will have"? Was this manner of speech at any time used of the subjects to their Prince since the beginning of the world? Have not all true subjects ever used to their Sovereign

[1] See the Council to Russell, 18, 24, 25 and two letters of 27 July, 19, 21, 22 and 27 August, and 10 and 12 September 1549 (*Troubles connected with the Prayer Book*, pp. 29–30, 35–42, 60–73).

[2] For the petition of the Western rebels, and Cranmer's answer, see Cranmer's *Works*, ii. 163–87; for the passages cited, see pp. 164, 168, 176, 185–6. For Somerset's two answers (in the King's name), see Foxe, v. 732–6; Tytler, *England under Edward VI and Mary*, i. 178–82. For Udall's answer, see *Troubles connected with the Prayer Book*, pp. 141–93.

Lord and King this form of speaking, "Most humbly beseecheth your faithful and obedient subjects"?' He then told them that the 'holy decrees of our forefathers' were Papist, and that if they believed them they were heretics and traitors.

The rebels demanded the restoration of the Six Articles. Cranmer replied that the Six Articles were introduced by the evil counsel of Papists, and were so far from the truth that they would never have passed in Parliament if Henry had not come in person to the House of Lords. It is strange that Cranmer should have gone even as far as this in blaming Henry for the Six Articles, though he hastened to add that within little more than a year, 'the same most noble Prince' moderated the statute, so that the Act of the Six Articles remained in force for little more than a year. This last statement, as Cranmer knew well, was untrue; but the rest of his reply to the rebels on this point shows that for Cranmer the Six Articles meant primarily the persecution of married priests, which had not continued for long after 1539. Cranmer certainly did not intend that his reference to Henry's presence in Parliament during the debates on the Six Articles should be cited, as it was in 1681 by the opponents of royal power, as if Cranmer, in this polemic against rebellion, had been protesting against the overawing of Parliament by the King.[1]

The rebels wished to have the mass in Latin, with only the priest communicating, and communion only at Easter, and then only in one kind. Cranmer told them that they should wish to understand what was said in the mass, and favour frequent communion of all the people. They demanded that the Sacrament be hung over the altar, and that all who refused to worship it should die like heretics; but Cranmer wrote that this practice had only been introduced since the thirteenth century. As for their demand that Baptism be celebrated every day and not only on Sundays, Cranmer pointed out this could always be done in cases of necessity, and that in the early Church children were only baptized at Easter and Whitsun. Cranmer denounced as superstition and idolatry the rebels' demand for holy bread, holy water, palms, ashes, images and all the old ceremonies. He lamented that when they were offered the heavenly bread of

[1] Report of Winnington's speech in the House of Commons on 7 January 1681 (Hist. MSS. Com., Beaufort MSS., p. 110).

life in the Sacrament, they refused it except at Easter, and the cup of the most holy blood they refused to drink at any time; yet they wished to eat and drink holy bread and holy water, which were the poisoned bread and stinking puddles of the Bishop of Rome. The rebels objected to the new liturgy in English because some of the Cornishmen could not understand English; but Cranmer was sure that even fewer of them understood Latin. Cranmer also rejected the rebels' demands for prayers for souls in Purgatory, for the suppression of the English Bible as leading to the spread of heresies, and for the release of their leaders, which Cranmer compared to the Jews' demand for the release of Barabas. They asked for Pole to be pardoned and made a member of the Council because he was of royal blood; but Cranmer thought Pole was unworthy to live, for he had incited the Emperor and the French King to invade the realm.

Cranmer ended by dealing with the rebels' social demands. They had asked that a gentleman should only be allowed one servant for every hundred marks' worth of land that he owned. Somerset and Udall had dealt with this demand by pointing out that it would cause unemployment; but Cranmer preferred the high moral tone. 'Was it ever seen in any country since the world began that the commons did appoint the nobles and gentlemen the number of their servants? Standeth it with any reason to turn upside down the good order of the whole world, that is everywhere and ever hath been, that is to say, the commoners to be governed by the nobles, and the servants by their masters? Will you have now the subjects to govern their King, the villains to rule the gentlemen, and the servants their masters? If men would suffer this, God will not; but will take vengeance of all them that will break His order, as He did of Dathan and Abiram'.

The rebels also demanded that half the abbey lands be taken from their present owners and used for building new abbeys. Cranmer had once objected to the distribution of the abbey and chantry spoils to speculators; but he did not choose to refer to this when confronted with rebellion. He was indignant that the Western men should wish to seize, not only the property of their Prince, 'but also against all right and reason to take from all other men such lands as they came to by most just title, by gift, by sale, by exchange, or otherwise. . . . And do you not tremble for fear that the vengeance of God shall fall upon you before you have grace to repent?'

By the middle of July, the situation was very grave, and the Council were expecting the Western men to march on London. Stage plays were banned, and a censorship of books was imposed. On 18th July, martial law was proclaimed in London, and two days later the citizens began a permanent watch on the city gates. On Sunday the 21st, Cranmer came to St. Paul's, wearing an alb and cope and a silk cap, but no vestments or mitre, and addressed the Lord Mayor and Aldermen and the people in the quire. He said that these revolts were a punishment sent by God for our evil living, and urged the congregation to fast and pray and set aside good living and rich apparel. He then conducted the service in English, singing a new prayer against rebellion which he had composed, and celebrated mass, administering the communion to the Dean and seven other communicants. He preached again in the quire at St. Paul's on Saturday 10th August, and gave thanks for Russell's victory before Exeter. He was expected to come again on 31st August, after news had reached London that Warwick had defeated Ket at Norwich; but he sent Joseph to preach in his place. Burnet tells us that Cranmer also preached at Court on the fast day which the Council proclaimed.[1]

We can form a clear impression of the text of these sermons from the account of contemporary chroniclers, and from two documents which have survived among Archbishop Parker's papers. One is a discourse for a sermon containing insertions written in Cranmer's hand, which was apparently based on a sermon by Peter Martyr. The other is a short collection of notes on rebellion written in Cranmer's hand—presumably as notes for a sermon. These documents show clearly the lines along which Cranmer was preaching at this time, though he does not seem to have used them for his sermon of 21st July. In the notes, Cranmer refers, under the heading 'How God hath plagued sedition in time past', to the swallowing up of Dathan and Abiram by the earth, and to other cases of men punished for sedition in the Book of Kings and the Acts. The notes continue:

'Tumults in England. Jack Cade. Jack Straw.

[1] Acts of the Privy Council, 13 August 1549; Proclamation of 6 August 1549 (Fuller, *Church History*, ii. 359); Wriothesley, ii. 15–18, 20; *Greyfriars Chron.*, pp. 60–62; Burnet, ii. 213–4.

'In Germany for their sedition were slain almost in one month about two hundred thousand.

'The sword by God's word pertaineth not to subjects, but only to magistrates.

'Though the magistrates be evil, and very tyrants against the commonwealth, and enemies to Christ's religion; yet the subjects must obey in all worldly things, as the Christians do under the Turk, and ought so to do, so long as he commandeth them not do against God'.[1]

The other document deals at greater length with the evils of rebellion. It is not clear whether this document, in the form in which it has survived, was drafted by Cranmer or by Peter Martyr; but it is clear from the insertions in Cranmer's own hand that he approved of the contents even if he did not write it or use it as the basis for a sermon. This document shows that Cranmer's attitude differed from that of Latimer and Lever and the great radical preachers. Latimer preached that the rebellion, in itself a sin, was a punishment on the nobles for their covetousness and their oppression of the poor; but Cranmer's document states that it was a punishment on the rulers for their laxity in punishing the blasphemy, adultery and gluttony of the people, and for their leniency towards vagabonds. Apparently he did not consider that the Act of 1547, by which vagabonds and their children were to be made slaves and ruled by whip and chain and fed only on refuse meat, was harsh enough. The document places far greater emphasis on the sins of the people than on those of the gentlemen, and states that though the commons may claim that they are rebelling to correct the covetousness of the gentry, in fact it is the people rather than the gentry who must be censured for covetousness.[2]

As soon as the revolts had been suppressed, the government took action against Bonner, who was thought to be responsible for the illegal celebration of the old mass in several London churches. The Council ordered Bonner to preach at Paul's Cross on 1st September, where he was to denounce the sin of rebellion and to state that the authority of an infant King was as great as that of a King of full age. Bonner denounced rebellion, but said

---

[1] Cranmer, *Notes for a Homily against Rebellion* (Cranmer's *Works*, ii. 188–9).

[2] Cranmer, *A Sermon concerning the time of Rebellion* (Cranmer's *Works*, ii. 190–202, especially pp. 191, 193, 196). Cf. Latimer, in his last sermon before Edward VI, (Lent 1550) (Latimer's *Works*, i. 247–9); and see 1 Edw. VI, c. 3.

nothing in his sermon about the authority of an infant King; and the Council thereupon appointed a Commission, consisting of Cranmer, Ridley, May the Dean of St. Paul's, Sir Thomas Smith and Petre to inquire as to whether Bonner ought to be deprived of his bishopric. When the proceedings opened at Lambeth on 10th September 1549, Bonner immediately adopted the insolent attitude of a conservative Bishop who was convinced in his heart that his function was to sit in judgment on heretics, and not to be judged by them. The official policy was to deprive him, not for his doctrinal opinions, but for his disobedience in refusing to obey an order to preach on the power of an infant King; but Bonner's tactic was to make it appear that he was to be deprived for believing in the Real Presence.[1]

Cranmer adopted a firm attitude towards Bonner, for this was a quarrel which concerned the Prince. He was indignant at Bonner's insolence, and complained at one point that Bonner was treating him with a disrespect which would have been improper even if he had been sitting in his capacity as Archbishop, but which was utterly unpardonable in view of the fact that he was sitting as the King's Commissioner. Cranmer did not, however, handle the proceedings well on the first day. When Bonner objected to Hooper being called as a witness against him on the grounds that Hooper was a detestable heretic who denied the Real Presence, Cranmer was unwise enough to become involved in an argument with Bonner about the Real Presence. In the course of the argument, Cranmer asked Bonner whether he believed that Christ's nose, mouth and eyes were separately present in the Sacrament, for Cranmer had by now moved sufficiently far on the subject of the Presence to be prepared to resort to this well-known Zwinglian argument. It is not surprising that Petre stared at Cranmer in an attempt to catch his eye, for Cranmer had fallen right into Bonner's trap. At last Cranmer told Bonner that he was not there to dispute about the Sacrament, but to execute the commission of his Prince.

Smith was present at the second session, and thereafter he took charge of the trial. He was more successful than Cranmer in restraining Bonner, but Bonner repeatedly reverted to the

[1] For the proceedings against Bonner, see Foxe, v. 741–98, and especially pp. 752–3, 765, 775, 787, 795; Micronius to Bullinger, 30 September 1549 (*Orig. Letters*, pp. 557–8); Wriothesley, ii. 24; *Greyfriars Chron.*, pp. 63–64.

question of the Sacrament. He accused Cranmer of contradicting himself as regards the Eucharist, and referred to the fact that Cranmer had upheld the Real Presence in one of his books. Bonner was obviously referring to Cranmer's Catechism, which was doubtless the reason why Cranmer replied that a boy of ten would understand the doctrine better than Bonner. On one occasion, Cranmer ordered the commission to be read out again, to show the audience that Bonner was not being proceeded against because of his opinions on the Eucharist.

At the fifth session, Smith ordered the marshal to arrest Bonner for contempt, and to take him to the Marshalsea. Bonner promptly pointed out that it was impertinent of Smith to give the order when Cranmer, his superior, was present; but Cranmer had allowed Smith to take over the conduct of the trial. It was Cranmer, however, who pronounced the judgment on 1st October which deprived Bonner of his bishopric. Bonner remained in prison for his contempt for nearly four years.

A few days after Bonner was deprived, the Lords of the Council issued their proclamation against Somerset, accusing him of inciting the people to rise against the nobles and gentlemen. In reply, Somerset called on the people to rise to protect him and the King against the designs of the Lords and gentlemen who had always oppressed the people. In response to a summons from Somerset, Cranmer came to Hampton Court on 6th October with sixty horsemen whom he had assembled to help to protect the King from the rebellious Lords. Paget, Smith and Somerset's secretary Cecil were also at Hampton Court; Warwick, Paulet and all the rest of the Council were in London, where they invited Arundel and Wriothesley, who were prominent conservatives in religion, to join them. It was widely believed that they were intending to appoint Mary as Regent.[1]

On the evening of 6th October, a large band of people from the neighbouring villages assembled at Hampton Court, ready to fight for King and Protector against the gentry. By the light of the torches, they crowded into the outer courtyard of the palace, while Somerset brought out the King to them, taking him to the gate to greet the crowds who had not been able to enter the

---

[1] Proclamation of 1 October 1549; Papers distributed in October 1549 (Tytler, i. 205, 208–11); Acts of the Privy Council, 6 October 1549; anonymous eyewitness account (in *Engl. Hist. Rev.*, lxx. 605–6); van der Delft to Charles V, 8 October 1549 (*Span. Cal.*, ix, p. 459).

courtyard. The Protector harangued them in a stirring speech; but a few hours later, fearing an attack upon Hampton Court, he decided to occupy the Tower of London. He immediately left for London with the King and Cranmer and all the Court; but on the road to Kingston they met an officer of the royal household, who informed them that the Tower was in the hands of the rebel Lords. Turning their horses' heads, they rode to Windsor. They had covered the twenty miles, and had reached Windsor, by midnight.[1]

But Somerset had already begun to regret the bold course which he had adopted, and on reaching Windsor he wrote to the Lords in London offering to make any reasonable agreement with them. On the same day, 7th October, the Lords sent Sir Philip Hoby to Windsor with a letter to the King, and with another which was addressed to Cranmer and Paget. In this letter, the Lords stressed their loyalty to the King, and explained that they had only assembled their forces because they feared that Somerset was intending to attack them. They stated that if Somerset would leave the Court and disband his men, they would be pleased to discuss with Cranmer and Paget what steps should be taken to protect the King's interests; but if Cranmer and Paget were more concerned to support one man's cause than the King, law and order, they would be responsible for all the ills which would follow, and the Lords would make other account of them.[2]

Next day, Cranmer and Paget replied to the Lords' letter. Here was an opportunity for Cranmer to anathematize rebellion, and to denounce the Lords for their disobedience in language such as that which he had used in his answer to the Western rebels. But he wrote to the Lords in a very different vein. The Lords had defied the authority of the King's Protector as blatantly as the Devon men and Ket, even if they had not made any 'demand' of the King, but had throughout used proper language as humble petitioners to his Highness; but in July the rebels were commoners, and in October they were Lords. Cran-

---

[1] Cranmer, Paget and Wingfield to the Lords in London, 11 October 1549; the Lords in London to Mary and Elizabeth, 9 October 1549 (Tytler, i. 242, 249); *K.Edw.Jo.*, Year III; anonymous eye-witness account (in *Engl. Hist. Rev.*, lxx. 606–7.

[2] Somerset to the Lords in London, 7 October 1549 (Tytler, i. 215); the Lords in London to Edward VI, 7 October 1549; Somerset's articles, 8 October 1549 (Burnet, v. 273–6); Acts of the Privy Council, 7 October 1549.

mer therefore signed the letter to the Lords, which was probably
drafted by Paget, and which stated that though Somerset, like
the Lords, had taken up arms because he feared for his own
safety, they had now succeeded in persuading him, out of his
devotion to duty, to resign his office as Protector; but he could
not be expected to submit to force, or to yield without conditions
when he thought that the Lords sought his life, for 'life is sweet,
my Lords'. This letter, unlike Cranmer's reply to the Western
rebels, was full of such mundane considerations. It was signed
by Smith, as well as by Cranmer and Paget, although the Lords
had not written to Smith and had no intention of accepting
his support.[1]

When the Lords received this letter, they wrote again to
Cranmer and Paget on 9th October, ordering them to protect the
King's person and to prevent his removal from Windsor, 'as you
will answer for the contrary at your uttermost perils'. They
wrote that they thought it strange that Cranmer and Paget
should allow the King to remain in the charge of Somerset's
servants at Windsor, and that they looked to them to set this
matter right. By this time, Russell and Herbert, who had
reached Wilton on their journey home from their victorious
campaign in Devonshire, had placed their mercenaries at the
disposal of the Lords in London. On the 10th, Cranmer and
Paget wrote a short letter to the Lords, which was again signed
by Smith, in which they tried to suggest that they had only
supported Somerset under duress. They also removed Somerset's adherents from attendance on the King. The Lords then
sent the Vice-Chamberlain Wingfield to Windsor, to complete
the overthrow of Somerset's power. In Wingfield's report to the
Lords, which was signed by Cranmer and Paget, he described
how Somerset had been placed in custody in a very high tower in
the castle, as his old apartments had been too near to the King, and
how Somerset's sons had been sent to confinement in Somerset's
house. They took the opportunity of telling the Lords that
Edward had caught a cold during his night ride from Hampton
Court—a useful item for addition to the Lords' propaganda.[2]

---

[1] Cranmer, Paget and Smith to the Lords in London, 8 October 1549 (Tytler, i.
223–7, Cranmer's *Works*, ii. 520–2).
[2] Acts of the Privy Council, 9 and 10 October 1549; Cranmer, Paget and Wingfield
to the Lords in London, 11 October 1549 (Tytler, i. 241–3); Cranmer, Paget and
Smith to the Lords in London, 10 October 1549 (Cranmer's *Works*, ii. 522).

On 12th October, Warwick and the Lords arrived at Windsor, and on the 13th Cranmer presided at the full meeting of the Council, with all the rebel Lords sitting with him. They sent Smith and Somerset's other followers to the Tower, accusing them of being the chief instruments of Somerset's misgovernment. Next day, Cranmer again presided at the meeting of the Council at which Somerset was sent to the Tower.[1]

Cranmer's action in October 1549 is yet another case where his conduct has been differently assessed by his friends and foes. While the critics have accused him of betraying Somerset, his admirers have praised his loyalty in remaining at Hampton Court and Windsor and in refusing to join the Lords until further resistance was impossible. One of the most eminent of these admirers has actually suggested that the only step which Cranmer took against Somerset was the purely executive act of changing the members of the royal household after Somerset had submitted.[2] But in fact Cranmer's conduct amounted to a betrayal, not so much of Somerset as of his own principles. We cannot say that he betrayed Somerset because he acted openly without deception, and did not make any approach to the Lords until after he had persuaded Somerset to surrender; but he was unfaithful to the principles of Christian obedience and to the interests of the Reformation.

The significance of Cranmer's conduct in October 1549 has been obscured by the fact that the overthrow of Somerset did not involve the defeat of the Reformation; for Cranmer surrendered to rebels who he had every reason to believe were intending to undo the liturgical and doctrinal reforms which he had introduced in the past two years. The Book of Common Prayer, the Lord's Supper as a communion instead of a sacrifice, the marriage of priests, justification by faith—all were threatened by a movement which was led by Wriothesley and watched with hope by the Emperor and Mary and by Gardiner from his prison. Cranmer could not have known, when he signed the letter to the Lords of 8th October, that Warwick was about to trick his conservative supporters. That very morning, the Lords in London called the Mayor and Aldermen to the Guildhall, and denied

[1] Acts of the Privy Council, 12, 13, and 14 (wrongly recorded as 13) October 1549.
[2] Pollard, *Thomas Cranmer*, p. 254 n., who calls it 'a natural and necessary measure.'

that they wished to overthrow the recent religious innovations and revert to the old unreformed religion; but it is unlikely that news of this declaration had reached Windsor when Cranmer signed the letter the same day. Yet on 8th October, Cranmer, following Somerset's own example, decided to capitulate before a treasonable conspiracy of religious conservatism. He had not, moreover, any reason to believe at this time that resistance was impossible, for it was only twenty-four hours later that he learned that the army leaders at Wilton had decided to support the revolt.[1]

Cranmer's conduct was almost certainly motivated by his dread of popular revolution. He preferred to see a successful defiance of the King's government and the overthrow of the Reformation rather than a rising of the people in arms to defend the King's government against the Lords. When Russell and Herbert read the Protector's appeal to the commons, they wrote to Somerset: 'Your Grace's proclamations and billets sent abroad for the raising of the commons we mislike very much'. We may be sure that Cranmer shared these sentiments, and much misliked the sight of the armed yeomen at Hampton Court on the evening of 6th October. He therefore joined with Paget in urging Somerset to submit, as he told the Lords that he had done, while at the same time he tried to save his friends as far as possible.[2] He appealed to the Lords to show mercy to Somerset, and he and Paget allowed Smith to sign their letters to the Lords in a vain attempt to lift Smith on to the bandwagon with them. But when the Lords had taken charge at Windsor, Cranmer sat at the Council board while Somerset and Smith were sent to the Tower, for he could do nothing to save them, and would only have endangered himself and the future of the Reformation by refusing to collaborate with the new rulers. This was not the first time that Cranmer had rendered a service to the Reformation by submitting to forces which appeared to be intent on its destruction.

[1] See Acts of the Privy Council, 8 October 1549; Cranmer, Paget and Smith to the Lords in London, 8 October 1549 (Tytler, i. 223–7; Cranmer's Works, ii. 520–2). For the Papist support for the Lords' coup d'état, see Ponet, Short Treatise of Politic Power, pp. 133–4; Gardiner to Warwick, 18 October 1549 (Muller, pp. 440–1); van der Delft to Charles V, 8 October 1549 (Span. Cal., IX, pp. 458–9).

[2] Russell and Herbert to Somerset, 8 October 1549; Cranmer, Paget and Smith to the Lords in London, 8 October 1549 (Tytler, i 219, 225–6; Cranmer's Works, ii. 521).

The reformers were in despair after the fall of the Protector. Hooper, who was Somerset's chaplain, was expecting to be handed over to the vengeance of Bonner, who had threatened him when he gave evidence against Bonner at the deprivation proceedings. Abroad, the wildest rumours were circulating; the Protestants in Switzerland had heard that Bucer and the other foreign Protestant theologians had been arrested, and that all was lost. The Emperor's Ambassador wrote to Charles that though the new government had not yet shown its hand, it was about to re-establish the Catholic faith, and that Cranmer would be expelled from the Council before the end of the month.[1]

The Reformation was perhaps saved by international developments. It was an ominous sign when Cranmer and his colleagues in the Council, within a week of the overthrow of Somerset, sent Cheyney and Hoby to the Emperor to inform him of the changes which had occurred in the government in England, and to request his assistance in the defence of Boulogne against the French. But Charles refused his help, and Warwick, who was more interested in ousting Wriothesley than in saving Boulogne, did not conclude the alliance with the Empire which had so often heralded a conservative religious policy at home. So it was Wriothesley, not Cranmer, who was expelled from the Council before the end of October; and when the Spanish reformer Dryander saw Cranmer and Bucer at Lambeth on 5th November, they were in the best of health and spirits. On 17th November, the merchant Hilles—always one of the shrewdest of the Zwinglian political forecasters—wrote to Bullinger that the situation in England was much better than it had seemed a month ago. By this time, the Council had issued a royal proclamation announcing that, far from undoing the Reformation, there would be further measures of religious reform; and on Christmas Day a letter was sent to the Bishops, which was signed by Cranmer and other Lords of the Council, informing them that there would be no return to the Latin service and the old superstitious ceremonies. The letter repudiated the idea which had spread abroad that Somerset alone had been responsible for the reform of religion, and that this policy would now

[1] Hooper to Bullinger, 7 November and 27 December 1549; Dryander to Bullinger, 3 December 1549; Stumphius to Bullinger, 28 February 1550 (*Orig. Letters*, pp. 69–71, 353, 464–5); van der Delft to Charles V, 17 October 1549 (*Span. Cal.* ix, p. 462).

be reversed, and ordered that all the old service books of the
Sarum Use, and of any other service which conflicted with the
Book of Common Prayer, must be brought in and destroyed. By
April 1550, Somerset had been released from the Tower and
restored to the Council, and the reformers were satisfied that
the development of the Reformation would not be impeded by
the unfortunate incident of October 1549.[1]

[1] Acts of the Privy Council, 19 (wrongly dated 18) October 1549; van der
Delft to Charles V, 26 November 1549 (Span. Cal. ix, p. 477); Hilles to Bullinger,
17 November 1549; Dryander to Bullinger, 3 December 1549 (Orig. Letters, pp.
268, 353–4); the Council to the Bishops, 25 December 1549 (Burnet, v. 287–8;
Troubles connected with the Prayer Book, pp. 127–9); Cranmer to Edmund Cranmer,
14 February 1549/50 (Cranmer's Works, ii. 522–4). The proclamation announcing
that there would be no change in religion, to which Dryander referred in his letter
of 3 December 1549, has not survived, but must have been issued before Dryander
left England in the middle of November; it must not be confused with the letter to
the Bishops on Christmas Day.

CHAPTER XX

THE CONFLICT WITH HOOPER

By Christmas 1549, it was clear that the Reformation would
advance even further under Warwick than it had gone under
Somerset, and Cranmer henceforth became increasingly concerned with the growing influence of the Protestant extremists.
On the question of the Real Presence, however, he was prepared
to move forward with his more radical colleagues and to take
steps to eradicate belief in the doctrine among the clergy and the
people. The Council had taken the unprecedented step of forbidding even the Bishops to preach in their own dioceses without
a licence from Cranmer, and before the end of 1549 Cranmer
was requiring any preacher who applied for a license to subscribe to some articles which he had drafted. These articles
have not been preserved, but we know that they compelled the
preachers to accept a doctrine of the Eucharist which was
sufficiently near to Zwinglianism to win the approval of Hooper.[1]

The new doctrine of the Eucharist made it advisable to change
the existing ordinal, with its emphasis on the sacrificial functions
of the priest. Cranmer was almost certainly responsible for the
form of the new ordinal of February 1550, which in many respects, though not in all, followed the recommendations of
Bucer. The new ordinal sought to dispense with the later
traditions, and to revert to the simpler ceremony of the primitive
Church; but its main purpose was to delete the references to
sacrifice. The lesser orders of sub-deacons, acolytes, exorcists,
lectors, and ostiaries were abolished, and the members of the
remaining orders—Bishops, priests and deacons—were seen
primarily as ministers who were to preach the word of God. The
ordinal, while retaining many ceremonies in addition to the
imposition of hands and the consecrating prayer, abolished the
anointing of the hands of the priest, for the hands were no
longer to perform a sacrifice; and when the priest received the

[1] Hooper to Bullinger, 27 December 1549 and 5 February 1550 (*Orig. Letters*,
pp. 71–72, 76); Licenses to Scory and John Taylor, 4 and 10 June 1552 (Lemon,
Cal. St. Pap., i. 40–41); Strype, *Eccl. Mem.* ii [i]. 142.

Eucharistic vessels, the accompanying words 'Receive power to offer sacrifice to God and celebrate the mass for the living and the dead' were omitted, as were other references to sacrifices in the ordering of Bishops, priests and deacons. These changes were logical, and of fundamental significance; but they naturally did not attract the public attention as did the alteration of the form and language of the common service. Even the Venetian Ambassador could so far misunderstand the position as to inform his government that the only difference between the new English ordinal and their own was the omission of the oath of obedience to the Pope. Cranmer would have been surprised if he had known that of all his liturgies, formularies and books, the ordinal would remain as the most controversial after four hundred years.[1]

Cranmer presided over the Commission of six Bishops and six other divines who were appointed to draft the ordinal, which was given statutory authority in advance. The Commissioners had completed their work within a week of the passing of the statute which authorized their appointment, which suggests that they were merely expected to approve a draft which Cranmer had already prepared. Heath alone refused to agree. The Council were no longer prepared to tolerate opposition such as that which the orthodox Bishops had shown to the Book of Common Prayer; and on 8th February Heath was summoned to the Council to explain his conduct. On the 28th, he was called again, and directly ordered to subscribe to the new ordinal; as he refused, the Council sent him to the Fleet on 4th March. Cranmer was present at these last two meetings, and though he was probably more patient with Heath than most of the other Councillors, he could obviously not oppose the proposal to punish Heath for his disobedience.[2]

---

[1] The Ordinal of 1549/50 (*Liturgies of Edward VI*, pp. 159–86); Bucer, *De Ordinatione Legitima Ministrorum Ecclesiae Revocanda* (in Bucer, *Scripta Anglicana*, pp. 238–59); Barbaro's Report to the Venetian Senate, (May 1551) (*Ven. Cal.*, v. 703 (p. 349)); for the old Pontifical and Ordinal, see Maskell, *Monumenta Ritualia Ecclesiae Anglicanae*, iii. 154–225, 241–80.

[2] 3 & 4 Edw. VI, c. 12; *H.L.Jo.*, 31 January 1549/50 (afternoon session); Acts of the Privy Council, 8 and 28 February and 4 March 1549/50. Heylin (*Ecclesia Restaurata*, i. 173) states that the twelve Commissioners who drafted the Ordinal were the same as the thirteen who drafted the first Prayer Book with the exception of Day; but this surmise is certainly wrong if the Prayer Book was drafted by the thirteen Commissioners named by Fuller (and by Heylin himself, in op. cit., i. 119); for Heath was not one of these thirteen Commissioners.

The ordinal also aroused opposition from another quarter, for it did not go far enough to be acceptable to Hooper. At Christmas 1549, Cranmer was showing great friendship to Hooper, though he was still unenthusiastic about Bullinger and the Swiss Zwinglians. Hooper, for his part, was favourably impressed with Cranmer's doctrine, and wrote to Bullinger: 'We desire nothing more from him than a firm and manly spirit. Like all the other Bishops in this country, he is too fearful about what may happen to him'. Six months later, he told Bullinger again: 'Canterbury has relaxed much of his Lutheranism, whether all of it I cannot say; he is not so decided as I could wish, and dares not, I fear, assert his opinion in all respects'. Hooper had acquired great influence and was intimate with both Warwick and Somerset. The Council could not afford to ignore a popular Protestant preacher who attracted great crowds in London, and who considered that his chief mission was to save the people from Anabaptism. In February 1550, Cranmer ordered Hooper to preach the Lenten sermons to the King. Hooper took the opportunity to denounce the vestments of the clergy as sinful, arguing that while all vestments were the mark of the suppressed priesthood of Aaron, the existing vestments of the clergy were Papist in addition, and imparted the idea of a sacrificing priest. He also condemned as blasphemous the oath of supremacy which the Bishops swore at their consecration, because it was sworn 'by God, all Saints and the holy Evangelists.'[1]

Cranmer reacted at once to Hooper's sermon; he complained to the Council, protesting particularly against Hooper's criticism of the oath. For fifteen years, Cranmer had been enforcing the oath of supremacy, and he probably considered it to be almost seditious for Hooper to criticize it from any aspect. Cranmer spoke with great violence against Hooper when Hooper was called before the Council four days after he had preached the sermon; but the Council sympathized with Hooper's position with regard to the oath, and decided to appoint him Bishop of the vacant see of Gloucester, though Hooper refused to wear the

[1] Hooper to Bullinger, 31 May, 25 June and 27 December 1549, and 5 February, 27 March and 29 June 1550; Micronius to Bullinger, 30 September 1549; Burcher to Bullinger, 16 October 1549 and 20 April 1550 (*Orig. Letters*, pp. 64–65, 71–72, 75, 77, 79, 82, 87, 89, 557, 659, 662); for the oath of supremacy, see Burnet, vi. 290–1.

tonsure, or the vestments prescribed by the new ordinal, or to swear the oath of supremacy by the Saints and Evangelists.[1]

This gave Cranmer and Ridley the pretext to begin their struggle with Hooper. It was undoubtedly a pretext, because their conduct throughout the controversy proves that the real issue was neither the oath nor vestments, but whether extremism should be represented on the episcopal bench. Hooper was in no way a rebel, for he continued to the end of his life to believe in non-resistance to authority. But Cranmer must instinctively have realized that Hooper would one day be called the father of Nonconformity; and though he and Ridley were prepared to have Hooper as an individual taking his place as a Bishop amongst them, it was only on condition that he ceased being a Nonconformist. As the tonsure was not prescribed in the ordinal, and was worn only as a matter of custom, this could not be set up as a serious obstacle to Hooper's consecration. Cranmer therefore took his stand in the first place on the question of the oath; but when Hooper persuaded the Council to change the oath, and the King struck out the reference to the Saints and the Evangelists, Cranmer fell back on the vestments issue, arguing that as vestments were prescribed in the ordinal, he would be guilty of a *praemunire* if he consecrated Hooper without them. Warwick thereupon informed Cranmer that he would be granted a royal pardon for any *praemunire* which he might incur; and as Cranmer was evidently still not satisfied, he was granted a formal pardon under the King's own hand. This should have removed all Cranmer's objections, for he certainly never questioned the King's power of pardon, or even Edward's right to alter the wording of the oath of supremacy without the sanction of Parliament.[2]

The doctrine of Cranmer and Ridley with regard to vestments did not in itself exclude a solution which was acceptable to Hooper. They considered that vestments were inessentials which the magistrates were free to order at their discretion,

[1] Hooper to Bullinger, 27 March and 29 June 1550; Hales to Gualter, 24 May 1550; Ulmis to Bullinger, 28 May 1550; Stumphius to Bullinger, 1 June 1550; Micronius to Bullinger, 20 May, 4 June and 28–31 August 1550 (*Orig. Letters*, pp. 81, 87, 187, 410, 466–7, 559–60, 565–6); Acts of the Privy Council, 15 May 1550.

[2] Ulmis to Bullinger, 22 August 1550; Micronius to Bullinger, 28–31 August 1550 (*Orig. Letters*, pp. 415–6, 566–7); Warwick to Cranmer, 23 July 1550; the Council to Cranmer, 5 August 1550 (Foxe, vi. 640–1).

from which it followed that if the magistrates saw fit to pre-scribe them, it was the duty of the subject to obey. The dispute with Hooper could therefore have been solved by ordering Hooper to be consecrated without vestments, which the King and Warwick would certainly have been prepared to do. More-over, in this same summer of 1550, Cranmer and Ridley—acting on their own authority without any order or pardon from the King—had ordained Thomas Sampson as a priest without his wearing vestments, to which he objected on the same grounds as Hooper.[1] But Sampson was an obscure candidate for the priesthood, and not the leader of the extremists in London.

In July, Cranmer left London for his diocese, where he re-mained for about four months. In September, he was at Canter-bury, conducting a visitation of his cathedral church which was primarily concerned with the morals of the clergy and the care of ecclesiastical property at Canterbury. While he was in Kent, he was entrusted with the duty of guarding and converting Hugh Weston, who in Mary's reign was to preside at the great dis-putation at Oxford. Weston had been imprisoned for his orthodox doctrines, and was now released on recognisances and ordered to reside with Cranmer until All Saints Day in order to receive instruction from him. By November, Cranmer had returned to Court in response to a summons from the Council, and was concerned with the case of Barlow and the Dean of Wells.[2]

Barlow, who had been translated from St. David's to Bath and Wells three years before, was one of Cranmer's oldest collaborators, having faithfully supported him in the doctrinal controversies of Cromwell's time. He now removed Goodman, the Dean of Wells, who was an opponent of the Reformation, in order to give the preferment to Somerset's physician, the reformer William Turner—for it was the accepted practice for laymen to hold certain offices in the Church. Goodman began proceedings in the Court of King's Bench, claiming that Barlow, in evicting him, had been guilty of a *praemunire* in having

---

[1] Strype, *Cranmer*, p. 273, where the date of Sampson's ordination is wrongly given as 1549.

[2] Articles for the visitation of Canterbury Cathedral, 10 September 1550; Cranmer's Injunctions, 29 October 1550 (Cranmer's *Works*, ii. 159–62); Acts of the Privy Council, 11 September 1549 and 15 July, 18 October and 11 November 1550.

usurped the royal prerogative; but the Council, who supported Barlow, ordered the Judges not to take cognizance of the case, and when the Judges objected, they were summoned before the Council to explain their conduct.

Cranmer was consulted with regard to the case. His personal sympathies were with Turner and Barlow; but as usual he placed law and duty above personal friendship, and referred the question to the lawyers of the Court of Arches for legal advice. After hearing their opinion, he felt obliged to tell Turner that though Goodman deserved to be deprived, Barlow had no power to deprive him, as Goodman had been appointed Dean by the King and not by the Bishop. Cranmer thought that the correct procedure was for the King to appoint Commissioners who could deprive Goodman. The Council preferred a simpler remedy; they pardoned Barlow for his *praemunire*, sent Goodman to the Fleet, and browbeat the Judges into holding that the deprivation of Goodman by Barlow had been lawful. But Cranmer had stood for the law and the King's authority over the Bishops, even if it meant, in this case, supporting an opponent against his friends.[1]

The rejection of the doctrine of the Eucharist as a sacrifice led to the removal of altars and their replacement by the communion tables of the Lord's Supper. Ridley had taken the lead in suppressing altars in his diocese of London in the summer of 1550; but Day, though he had now accepted the Book of Common Prayer and renounced the Real Presence, had preached against the removal of altars in his diocese of Chichester. The Council had been obliged to send Cox to the diocese to preach against Day's sermons, and early in November 1550 they ordered Day to submit. On 23rd November, the Council sent a letter to all the Bishops ordering them to remove all the altars in their dioceses; but Day informed the Council that though he would not actively resist the suppression of altars, his conscience would not allow him to be a party to it. He cited a text from Isaiah in support of altars, which was refuted by Cranmer and Ridley; but as Day remained obstinate, he was ordered by the Council to report to Cranmer, Goodrich or Ridley for

[1] Acts of the Privy Council, 11 October and 22 and 26 November 1550 and 12 and 18 February 1550/1; Turner to Cecil, 5 January 1550/1 (*Troubles connected with the Prayer Book*, p. 133).

instruction about his error. Day immediately arranged to visit Cranmer at Lambeth; but Cranmer went to Court that day, and though he returned to Lambeth earlier than usual in order to talk with Day, he arrived late, and Day, who was feeling unwell, had already departed. Day was summoned again before the Council, and Cranmer and Goodrich tried vainly to convince him that he was wrongly interpreting a text from Paul's Epistle to the Hebrews. The Council ordered Day to submit by 7th December, and when he refused, they gave him another forty-eight hours in which to do so. It was not until 11th December that they sent him to the Fleet.[1]

Cranmer does not seem to have been responsible for the policy of the Council with regard to altars and the arrest of Day, though he was present at the meeting when Day was committed to prison. As early as 1549, Cranmer's Visitors had removed altars when they conducted a visitation of the diocese of Norwich during the vacancy in the see before Thirlby was translated there; but this does not seem to have been done under a directive from Cranmer. The demand for the suppression of altars came from Hooper. Cranmer was one of the Councillors who signed the order for the general suppression of altars on 23rd November; but if the attendance records in the Council minutes are correct, he was not present at the meeting of the Council on that date. He seems therefore to have had no part in the decision to issue the order, and merely added his signature later, as was frequently done. In view of his new doctrine of the Eucharist, Cranmer obviously approved of the suppression of altars, and though he might have hesitated to initiate the policy or to enforce it with the vigour of Ridley, he was ready to justify it by theological arguments, as he did in the case of Day. This seems to have been his chief activity in Day's case.[2]

Cranmer was obviously equally ready—and perhaps indeed more ready—to punish disobedience with imprisonment in the

[1] Acts of the Privy Council, 7 October, 8 and 30 (wrongly dated 31) November and 1, 4, 7 and 11 December 1550; the Council to Ridley, 23 November 1550 (Foxe, vi. 5).
[2] Thirlby to the Archdeacons of the diocese of Norwich, 3 December 1550 (Norfolk Archaeology, vii. 72–73 n.); Hooper's fourth sermon on Jonah, 5 March 1550 (Hooper's Works, i. 488). According to the attendance records (in the Acts of the Privy Council) Cranmer was absent from all the meetings of the Council at which Day's case was discussed, except for the meeting on 11 December; but this is certainly wrong, as the records themselves show that Cranmer was present at least at the meetings on 1 and 4 December.

case of Hooper as in the case of Day. Hooper was still refusing to be consecrated in vestments, and argued that he was justified in his disobedience because the order which he had been given to wear vestments was an order to sin. Cranmer wrote to Bucer in Cambridge in order to obtain his opinion as to whether vestments were sinful; but Bucer replied that vestments, though undesirable, were not sinful, and might therefore be prescribed by the magistrates—a view which was shared by all the foreign theologians in England except à Lasco. Cranmer does not seem to have been as bitter as Ridley in his criticism of Hooper during the controversy; but no one is more likely than Cranmer to have been impressed by Ridley's arguments that Hooper's attitude was seditious, and there is little doubt that when the Zwinglians in England complained of the conduct of 'the Bishops', they included Cranmer in this category. The political gossip which young Ulmis at Oxford was telling his friends was as usual incorrect; he wrote to Bullinger on 31st December 1550 that Hooper would have been arrested had it not been for the fact that Cranmer and the Marquis of Dorset had petitioned for him in Parliament. In fact, Parliament was not in session at any time during the vestments controversy, and though Cranmer may have urged the Council to be patient with Hooper, he was obviously prepared if necessary to use stern measures.[1]

Hooper was ordered to keep to his house and not to preach; but he defied this order, and issued a pamphlet which displeased the authorities, though it was primarily concerned with emphasizing the duty of Christian obedience to the magistrates. The Council, on 13th January 1551, ordered Hooper to be confined in Cranmer's house, with a clear intimation that worse would befall him if he did not prove amenable to Cranmer's arguments. Cranmer undoubtedly agreed with this decision. It is significant that Cranmer, who was engaged throughout this

[1] Cranmer to Bucer, 2 December 1550 (*Troubles connected with the Prayer Book*, pp. 130–1; Cranmer's *Works*, ii. 428); Hooper to Bullinger, 1 August 1551; Ulmis to Bullinger, 31 December 1550; Peter Martyr to Bullinger, 28 January 1551; Micronius to Bullinger, 13–20 October 1550; Utenhovius to Bullinger, 9 April 1551; Burcher to Bullinger, 28 December 1550 (*Orig. Letters*, pp. 91, 95, 426, 486–7, 571, 573, 585–6, 674–5, where the date of Ulmis' letter is wrongly given as 1551 in the text, and correctly in the headnote); Bucer to Cranmer, 8 December 1550 (Bucer, *Scripta Anglicana*, pp. 681–4; Gorham, *Gleanings*, pp. 214–20); Bucer to à Lasco (December 1550) (Strype, *Eccl. Mem.* ii [ii]. 444–55); à Lasco to Cranmer (1550) (Gabbema, *Illustrium et Clarorum Virorum Epistolae*, pp. 500–17).

period in the deprivation proceedings against Gardiner, did not attend any other meeting of the Council between 16th December and 8th February. Yet he came to this one meeting on 13th January when Hooper's case was dealt with. [1]

Hooper remained for a fortnight at Lambeth with Cranmer. Cranmer was engaged in the daily proceedings against Gardiner, but found time to transfer his attention from the disobedience of the orthodox Bishop in 1548 to that of the Zwinglian Bishop elect in 1551. One morning Peter Martyr was nearly successful in persuading Hooper to submit; but someone whom Martyr described as the 'leader of the farce'—he probably meant à Lasco—visited Hooper after dinner, and Hooper became more adamant than ever. Cranmer therefore wrote to the Council that 'Master Hooper cannot be brought to any conformity, but rather persevering in his obstinacy coveteth to prescribe orders and necessary laws of his head'. On 27th January the Council sent Hooper to the Fleet, where he remained for three weeks. From his prison, he wrote to Cranmer that he had submitted to the Council's orders; but as he repeated in the letter some of his old arguments against vestments, he was informed that this was not enough. He thereupon wrote a second letter to Cranmer which was sufficiently submissive, though it did not reach the depths of self-abasement. He stated clearly that he did not consider it sinful to wear vestments, as his objection to them was the same as that of Bucer and Martyr, and that he now realized that it was more worthy of Christian humility for him to accept the judgment of Cranmer and the laws rather than to trust in his own judgment. [2]

Hooper was released from prison, and on 8th March he was consecrated in vestments at Lambeth by Cranmer, with Ridley assisting. Cranmer, true to his nature and his principles, was very ready to forgive a penitent Hooper; and when Hooper wrote to Bullinger from his diocese in August, he referred to Cranmer in the warmest terms. He commented on Cranmer's admiration for Bullinger, and mentioned that Cranmer had been

[1] Strype, *Cranmer*, p. 308; Hooper, *A Godly Confession and Protestation of the Christian Faith* (Hooper's *Works*, ii. 65–92); Acts of the Privy Council, 13 January 1550/1.
[2] Peter Martyr to Bucer (February 1551); Hooper to Cranmer, 15 February 1551 (Hooper's *Works*, ii. pp. xv–xvi; Gorham, *Gleanings*, pp. 232–5); Acts of the Privy Council, 27 January 1550/1.

gratified by the praise which Bullinger had bestowed on King Edward in his last letter. Hooper did not write all that he would have wished in his letter to Bullinger for fear lest the letter should be intercepted; but it is unlikely that he desired to write anything hostile to Cranmer. When Hooper came to London in January 1552 for the Parliamentary session, he stayed with Cranmer at Lambeth for three months; and when Bullinger wrote to Cranmer, interceding on Hooper's behalf in connexion with the vestments controversy, Cranmer could reply that Bullinger need have no fear, as Hooper was now his guest and the vestments controversy was forgotten.[1]

In June 1550, Somerset had proposed in the Council that another attempt should be made to induce Gardiner to conform with a view to releasing him from prison. Some of the reformers did not relish this prospect, and thought, like the Duchess of Suffolk, that it was merry with the lambs now the wolf was shut up; but Cranmer, who was present in the Council when Somerset's proposal was accepted, was probably in favour of the decision. Cranmer went to his diocese soon after Somerset paid his first visit to Gardiner in the Tower, and was absent from the Council during the negotiations in July 1550, when the authorities so nearly reached an agreement with Gardiner; but the talks broke down on a minor point, and Gardiner retracted the concessions which he had made.[2] The Council then abandoned their plan of releasing Gardiner, and in December 1550 Cranmer presided over a tribunal which was to determine whether Gardiner should be deprived of his bishopric for disobedience.

The trial lasted for twenty-two sessions, extending over two months. The Council and the Commissioners were careful to comply with legal formalities and to show consideration to Gardiner. They allowed him to be represented by counsel, though it was doubtful if he were legally entitled to this, and they gave facilities for his witnesses, bringing Heath and Day from prison and some sixty witnesses from Winchester and elsewhere. Though half the members of the Council gave

[1] Wilkins, iv. 67 (where the oath taken by Hooper is given as including the oath by the Saints); Strype, *Cranmer*, p. 364; Hooper to Bullinger, 1 August 1551; Anne Hooper to Bullinger, 3 April 1551 (*Orig. Letters*, pp. 91–3, 95, 108); Cranmer to Bullinger, 20 March 1552 (Cranmer's *Works*, ii. 430–1).

[2] Whalley to Cecil, 26 June 1551 (Tytler, ii. 21–4); Holinshed, iv. 105; Acts of the Privy Council, 8, 10 and 13 June, and 8, 10, 11, 13, 15 and 19 July 1550; Foxe, vi. 73–75, 79–85.

evidence against Gardiner in an attempt to prove that Henry VIII had always doubted Gardiner's loyalty, the chief accusation against him was that he had disobeyed the royal proclamation and Somerset's order by referring to the Real Presence in his sermon on St. Peter's Day in 1548. In reply, Gardiner maintained that it was not illegal in June 1548 to defend the Real Presence, and like Bonner attempted to show that he was being penalized for upholding the Sacrament of the Altar. Cranmer did not repeat the mistake which he had committed at Bonner's deprivation proceedings; he refused to dispute with Gardiner on the Real Presence, and quietly but firmly persisted until he forced Gardiner to reply—in the negative—to the question as to whether he had disobeyed an order when he preached his sermon on St. Peter's Day.

Cranmer treated Gardiner with the greatest courtesy, addressing him as 'my Lord', and smiling at him pleasantly. This is vouched for by so bitter an opponent of the Reformation as the Emperor's new Ambassador Scheyvfe, though he attributed it to the hypocrisy of the Commissioners. Scheyvfe reported that they were pressing Gardiner to confess that he had done wrong and to ask for the King's pardon, but that as they knew that he would never agree to do so, they had already decided to deprive him and to continue to hold him in prison. It was probably true that Warwick and the Council had at last decided to deprive Gardiner, and that the result of the trial was virtually predetermined; but Cranmer's attitude at the hearing suggests that he at least was still clinging to his hope of four years before that it would be possible to induce Gardiner to co-operate with the Reformation. It was only towards the end of the proceedings that he changed his attitude. In Scheyvfe's last report of the trial, he stated that Cranmer and Ridley had engaged in bitter discussions with Gardiner about the Sacrament—presumably because they were attempting to prevent Gardiner from raising this issue. Gardiner accused them of being heretics, and challenged them to a public disputation; and when they refused, he handed them the manuscript of a book which he had written in prison against Cranmer's book on the Eucharist. On 14th February, Cranmer gave judgment depriving Gardiner, who returned to the Tower for the rest of Edward's reign.[1]

[1] For the proceedings against Gardiner, see Foxe, vi. 93-266; Scheyvfe's

Gardiner was succeeded as Bishop of Winchester by John Ponet, who was translated from Rochester. Ponet had formerly been Cranmer's chaplain. This brilliant reformer of 35 years of age, who was as gifted a clock-maker as he was a theologian, was involved in a scandal, being accused, like Archbishop Holgate of York, of cohabiting with the wife of another man. In July 1551, Ponet was divorced from a woman who was apparently the wife of a butcher of Nottingham after a hearing in St. Paul's at which he was ordered to make an annual maintenance payment to the butcher. Three months later, he married another woman at a ceremony at Croydon at which Cranmer was present. It is difficult to disentangle the true facts of Ponet's divorce case; but though a hostile diarist commented that Ponet's conduct in the affair was shameful, it is very unlikely that Cranmer would have attended Ponet's wedding if Ponet had so recently been guilty of a matrimonial offence involving moral turpitude. Cranmer was the last man to be tolerant of immorality if the offender was a reformer.[1]

It was possible to deprive and imprison the conservative Bishops, but Mary was still able to defy the law with impunity. She could rely on the friendship of the Emperor, who bullied the English government on her behalf. Henry had forced Mary to renounce the Papal supremacy; but she took her stand, like Gardiner, on Henry's religious settlement, which she claimed could only be reversed by an adult King in person. In the dangerous summer of 1549, Charles V extorted a promise from Somerset that Mary should be allowed to hold mass in her house in Norfolk in defiance of the Act of Uniformity; but in December 1550, the Council decided on sterner measures; and took action against Mary's chaplains. Strype does not seem to have had any reason for his belief that Cranmer was the author of the letter which the Council wrote to Mary on Christmas Day 1550, in which they justified their attitude; but Cranmer may well have drafted the theological parts of the letter. Mary refused to submit, relying on Somerset's promise to the Emperor. It was thought advisable that she should receive her

advices (January 1551); Scheyvfe to Charles V, 1 March 1551 (*Span. Cal.* x, pp. 214, 226); Acts of the Privy Council 14 and 16 December 1550 and 19 January and 15 February 1550/1; Wriothesley, ii. 45–46; *Greyfriars Chron.*, p. 68.

[1] Machyn, *Diary*, p. 8; *Greyfriars Chron.*, p. 70; *Coll. Top.*, iv. 91.

orders from the 13-year-old King himself. On 18th March 1551 she came to Court at Westminster, riding through London with a great escort of gentlemen and cheered by all the conservative elements in the city. Edward received her with brotherly solicitude in the presence of the whole Council, but told her that her license to hear mass was withdrawn. Next day Scheyvfe had an interview with Edward, in which he succeeded in conveying the impression that if Mary's mass was prohibited the Emperor would declare war, though according to his own report to Charles he said very much less than this.[1]

The Council decided to yield for the time being, at least until a consignment of gunpowder which was held up at Antwerp had been allowed to leave for England. Cranmer, Ridley and Ponet were ordered to satisfy the King's conscience and to convince him that he was justified in licensing the sinful mass. The Bishops told Edward that though it was a sin to license sin, it might be winked at for a time if necessity required it, and that it was now necessary to wink at Mary's mass in order to safeguard peace, the security of the realm and the trade of the King's subjects. Cranmer probably played the chief part in the discussion, for he knew the King better than did the other two Bishops, and he would have found it more congenial to advise retreat than would Ridley and Ponet, who were two of the most forceful leaders among the reformers. They were unable to convince Edward. They left him in tears, and reported their failure to the Council, while Cranmer congratulated Edward's tutor Cheke on the King's piety and intelligence. The Council eventually succeeded in persuading Edward that their policy was necessary.[2]

Soon after this incident, in the spring of 1551, Cranmer virtually withdrew from active participation in the government of the Kingdom, and only occasionally attended a meeting of the Council, being primarily engaged in theological and liturgical writings. It was the summer of the great earthquake which caused much destruction at Croydon; but though the tremor broke Cranmer's windows and threw down the books in his

---

[1] The Council to Mary, 25 December 1550 (Cranmer's *Works*, ii. 526-30); Strype, *Eccl. Mem.* ii [i]. 450; Machyn, pp. 4-5; *K. Edw. Jo.*, 18 and 19 March 1551; Scheyvfe to Charles V, 6 April 1551 (*Span. Cal.* x, pp. 251-61).

[2] *K. Edw. Jo.*, 20, 23 and 25 March 1551; *Moryson's Discourse* (*Lit. Rem. Edw. VI*, pp. ccxxv-ccxxx); Foxe, v. 700-1.

THE CONFLICT WITH HOOPER

library, it did not injure him or damage his house. It was also the summer of the sweating sickness, which struck the country in the worst outbreak since 1517, killing 872 persons in London in twelve days in July, including several nobles. Cranmer, though he fell ill in May, did not catch the sweat. He was probably old enough to be immune, because it mostly attacked males between 30 and 40; but Mrs. à Lasco, who was staying with Cranmer at Croydon, caught the disease, and in accordance with the usual custom Cranmer was ordered not to come to Court for fear lest he should carry the infection to the King. He was summoned, however, along with all the other Lords of the Council to a special meeting at Richmond on 9th August 1551 to deal with a matter of great importance. It was the question of Mary's mass. The Council decided to defy the Emperor's threats and to order the officers of Mary's household to prevent the celebration of the mass in her house.[1]

Mary's officers came before the Council a few days later, and as they refused to be the instrument of the suppression of her mass, they were sent to the Tower. Before the end of the month, Lord Chancellor Rich had been to Coggeshall to arrest Mary's chaplain and to tell Mary, as she showered abuse at him from her window, that the King no longer permitted her to celebrate mass. But Cranmer was not present at any of these other Council meetings after the first meeting on 9th August, when everyone had been required to come, presumably with the intention of identifying them all with the hazardous policy. This new attitude of firmness was not long maintained. Mary's officers and chaplains were released from prison in the following spring, and were allowed to return to Mary, who was henceforth able to hold a secret mass in her house while the official policy of winking at it was resumed. Mary continued to be treated with deference and honour as the King's sister, though she had told the Council that she would never be intimidated by such mild and lenient laws. The Council paid large sums of public money for the upkeep of her household, and on one occasion Cranmer and his colleagues

---

[1] A Lasco to Hardenberg, 31 May and 23 August 1551 (Gerdes, *Scrinium Antiquarium*, i–ii. 676, 679; Gorham, *Gleanings*, pp. 263–4, 273); Scheyvfe to Charles V, 25 July 1551 (*Span. Cal.* x, pp. 332–3); Machyn, pp. 7–8; Caius, *A Boke or Counseill against the Sweate* (in Hecker, *The Epidemics of the Middle Ages*, pp. 366–7); Acts of the Privy Council, 2 and 9 August 1551; *K. Edw. Jo.*, 9 August 1551.

in the Council gave orders to torture two men who were suspected of stealing her hawks.[1] When Edward died, they reaped the harvest of their weakness in permitting Mary to impress herself on the people's minds as a Princess to be loved and respected; but the man who had saved Mary from Henry's rage in 1534 must have approved of Warwick's mildness towards her.

Cranmer was prepared to be merciful towards less powerful Papists than Mary. At some time during Edward's reign, he dealt with the case of Henry Moore, the former Abbot of Tower Hill, who had become vicar of Stepney. Whenever a reformer preached in Moore's church in Stepney, Moore caused the bells to be rung so that no one could hear the sermon; and he was consequently arrested by Underhill, an army officer, and brought before Cranmer at Croydon. Cranmer rebuked him a little, but apparently not very strongly, and ordered him not to repeat the offence. Underhill, who was an ardent reformer, told Cranmer that he had been too lenient and that he should have deprived or punished Moore; but Cranmer replied that there was no law by which Moore could be punished—a statement which Underhill rightly denied, for no Court would have held that Cranmer had acted illegally if he had imprisoned a man for disturbing divine service. Underhill disclosed the incident in the reign of Elizabeth in order to show the folly of being lenient to Papists. He said to Cranmer: 'If ever it come to their turn, they will show you no such favour'. 'Well', said Cranmer, 'if God so provide, we must abide it.' 'Surely,' said Underhill, 'God will never cone you thank for this, but rather take the sword from such as will not use it upon His enemies.' The Papists, when it came to their turn, showed no such mercy to Cranmer, though by a strange irony they showed mercy to Underhill himself.[2]

Cranmer adopted a very different attitude in the case of the Anabaptist George van Paris. Van Paris was a Dutch surgeon who had fled from Flanders to Paris to escape persecution, but finding that Henry II was as savage a persecutor as Charles V, he joined the Dutch colony in London, where à Lasco's congregation denounced him to the English authorities as a heretic.

[1] Acts of the Privy Council, 10, 14, 22, 23 and 29 August 1551, 18 March 1551/2, 14 April and 7 December 1552, 7 March 1552/3 and 3 and 14 June 1553; the Council to Sussex, 3 June 1553 (Ellis, *Letters*, iii [iii]. 308–9).
[2] Underhill's Autobiography (*Nar. Ref.*, p. 157).

He was tried before Cranmer and other Commissioners in April 1551, with Coverdale acting as an interpreter, on a charge of denying the divinity of Christ. As he refused to recant, Cranmer passed the sentence of excommunication which sent van Paris to the fire.[1]

It was always the same with Cranmer, and even his loyal secretary could not refrain from criticism. 'One thing he commonly used wherein many did discommend him, which was this: he always bare a good face and countenance unto the Papists, and would both in word and deed do very much for them, pardoning their offences; and on the other side, somewhat over severe against the Protestants'. Morice's brother once raised the matter with Cranmer, and pointed out how this attitude encouraged the Papists and discouraged the Protestants. Cranmer answered that Papists should not be deterred by harshness from embracing the truth of the Gospel which they had not yet learned; in dealing with Papists, the reformers should remember that it was a rule of Christ to do good for evil. But those who had already accepted the Gospel were obliged to set a good example, and it would be wrong to wink at their faults, for Christ had said: 'The servant, knowing his lord and master's pleasure and commandment, if he regardeth not the same is worthy of many plagues'.[2] It is not uncommon for leaders of reforming movements to be more hostile towards their own extremists than to the adherents of the old order; but few of them have been prepared to justify their attitude with such cogent arguments as Cranmer.

[1] Judgment against van Paris, 6 April 1551 (Wilkins, iv. 44–45); Foxe, Latin ed., p. 202.
[2] Morice (*Nar. Ref.*, pp. 246–7).

CHAPTER XXI

THE LAST YEARS OF EDWARD

DURING the last three years of Edward's reign, Cranmer largely withdrew from the work of government and devoted himself to five great projects—the propagation of his new doctrine of the Eucharist, the reform of the Prayer Book, the promulgation of a new formulary of faith and a code of ecclesiastical law, and the unification of the Protestant movements of Europe. He accomplished the first of these tasks by the publication of a book about the Eucharist which was everywhere accepted as the leading exposition of the official doctrine which had replaced the Real Presence. Cranmer had not written a book since he became Archbishop, which may explain why his enemies were able to spread the rumour that Cranmer was not learned, and why even some reformers thought of him as an administrator rather than as a theologian; but they revised their opinion after the publication of his *Defence of the True and Catholic Doctrine of the Sacrament of the Body and Blood of Christ*. At his trial in September 1555, Cranmer said that he had written the book seven years before, and he may have begun to write it as early as the autumn of 1548, when he first publicly repudiated the Real Presence. It had been published before the end of July 1550.[1]

Dividing the book into five parts, Cranmer dealt in turn with the true use of the Lord's Supper, the error of transubstantiation, the nature of Christ's Presence in the elements, the reception of the body and blood of Christ, and the nature of the sacrifice. He cited freely from Scripture and patristic texts, but concentrated chiefly on the arguments of reason, stating his case with great lucidity. There is considerable difference of opinion today as to the nature of Cranmer's doctrine of the Eucharist; but it is difficult to believe, after reading his *Defence of the True and Catholic Doctrine of the Sacrament*, that it was as high as is often suggested. He certainly condemned the view that the elements were no more worthy of honour than ordinary bread and wine;

---

[1] Peter Martyr to Bucer, 26 December 1548 (*Orig. Letters*, p. 470); Foxe, viii. 52, 60.

but he repeatedly emphasized that they derived their efficiency from the receiving, and apart from their reception in communion, he denied to the elements not only a corporal, but even a spiritual Presence. 'Figuratively He is in the bread and wine, and spiritually He is in them that worthily eat and drink the bread and wine; but really, carnally and corporally He is only in Heaven, from whence He shall come to judge the quick and dead. This brief answer will suffice for all that the Papists can bring for their purpose, if it be aptly applied.' 'All that love and believe Christ Himself, let them not think that Christ is corporally in the bread, but let them lift up their hearts unto Heaven and worship Him sitting there at the right hand of His Father . . . in no wise let them worship Him as being corporally in the bread, for He is not in it, neither spiritually as He is in man, nor corporally as He is in Heaven, but only sacramentally, as a thing may be said to be in the figure whereby it is signified.' Cranmer also criticized the doctrine of transubstantiation, attempting to reduce it to absurdity, and argued that evil men do not receive the body and blood of Christ when they receive the Sacrament, though good men feed on Him spiritually when they do so.[1]

In the course of his book, Cranmer made two hostile references to the book on the Eucharist which Gardiner had written in 1546. This gave Gardiner the pretext to write a reply to Cranmer's book in the Tower during the summer and autumn of 1550, and he presented it to Cranmer and the Commissioners at the concluding session of his trial in February 1551.[2] In this lengthy work, Gardiner subjected all Cranmer's arguments to penetrating criticism, and though Cranmer later denounced the book as legalistic quibbling, such comment conceals a grudging recognition of its merit. With his respect for authority, Gardiner obviously felt obliged to exercise discretion in attacking a book written by the Archbishop of Canterbury. He therefore began

---

[1] Cranmer's *Defence of the True and Catholic Doctrine of the Sacrament* is published in Jenkyns, ii. 275–463; for the passages cited, see pp. 401, 446; see also Cranmer, *Answer to Gardiner* (in Cranmer's *Works*, i. 140–1).

[2] For Cranmer's references to Gardiner's *Detection of the Devil's Sophistry*, see Jenkyns, ii. 339, 376. Gardiner's *Explication and Assertion of the True and Catholic Faith touching the most Blessed Sacrament of the Altar* is printed, along with Cranmer's *Answer unto a Crafty and Sophistical Cavillation devised by Stephen Gardiner*, in Cranmer's *Works*, i. 10–365. See also Scheyvfe to Charles V, 1 March 1551 (*Span. Cal.* x, p. 226); Cranmer, *Answer to Gardiner* (Cranmer's *Works*, i. 10).

by stating that he hoped that Cranmer was not the author of the
book which had been published in his name, and that he would
refer to 'the author', and not to Cranmer by name, out of his
respect for Cranmer's position; but he made it clear that he
believed that Cranmer was in fact 'the author' whom he was
attacking. Gardiner also adopted the tactic of citing Luther and
Melanchthon and other Lutheran writers in defence of the
Real Presence, as well as Cranmer's Catechism and the Book of
Common Prayer. In other circumstances, Gardiner would have
searched the Book of Common Prayer to find passages which
proved that its authors were heretics who did not believe in the
Real Presence; but shortly before he wrote his book, Gardiner
had gone so far as to agree to accept the Book of Common
Prayer as a condition of his release from prison, and he now
argued that the Book of Common Prayer contained words which
implied belief, not only in the Real Presence, but also in transubstantiation.[1] This transparent tactic has actually succeeded
in causing certain modern writers to cite Gardiner's support in
order to prove the orthodoxy of the Prayer Book of 1549.

During the spring and summer of 1551, Cranmer wrote an
answer to Gardiner's 'crafty and sophistical cavillation', and at
Michaelmas he applied for, and received, a license permitting
his printer to publish the book. He made no attempt to suppress
the manuscript which Gardiner had handed to him at the trial,
but published the complete text, replying to it paragraph by
paragraph. This massive tome lacks the quality of Cranmer's
first book on the Eucharist. It was written in an even more
abusive style than Gardiner's book, and there is hardly a paragraph in which Cranmer does not apply some insulting epithet to
Gardiner; but it lacks the grandeur which distinguishes the
invective of writers like Ridley and Pole, and which Cranmer
himself attained in his reply to the Western rebels, and reads
merely like a petty outburst of ill-temper. There is no evidence
to support the suggestion of a modern historian that the *Answer
to Gardiner* was drafted by Ponet; but it is certainly not written
in Cranmer's usual style, though Cranmer may have thought
that this was an appropriate way in which to address a prisoner

---

[1] Gardiner, *Explication and Assertion of the True and Catholic Faith* (Cranmer's
Works, i. 10–365, especially pp. 10, 13, 19–20, 51, 55, 62, 83–84, 92, 137, 149,
159, 162, 178, 184, 223, 229, 239, 325, 334–5); Foxe, vi. 81.

who had been deprived of his see for disobedience to the King.[1]

Cranmer also entered into controversy with Richard Smith, who as early as May 1547 had been brought before Cranmer and forced to make a public recantation for having uttered, in a sermon at Paul's Cross, some ill-chosen words which could be interpreted as supporting Papal supremacy. Smith had fled to Louvain after opposing Peter Martyr in the disputation on the Real Presence at Oxford, and at the end of 1550 he wrote a reply to Cranmer's book on the Sacrament. By March 1551, the Council were taking action against men who had been smuggling Smith's book into England. Cranmer dealt with Smith's criticism in several passages in his *Answer to Gardiner*, and concluded with a short answer against the 'false calumniations' of Smith, which was written in a bitterly sarcastic style which at times achieves real wit. It is here that Cranmer, after denying that he had defended the Real Presence in his Catechism of 1548, stated that until shortly before he wrote the Catechism he believed in the Real Presence.[2]

The day after Gardiner had presented his book to Cranmer at his trial and had been deprived of his bishopric, the Council ordered that he should no longer be permitted to have pen and paper in the Tower. We do not know how long this order remained in force; but in 1552, Gardiner succeeded in writing a second reply to Cranmer's *Answer*. He probably wrote the book secretly, without the knowledge of the authorities, for after the manuscript had been smuggled to Paris, it was published there anonymously under the pseudonym of 'Marcus Antonius Constantius, theologian of Louvain.' By this time, Tunstall had been placed under house arrest, where he likewise occupied himself in writing a book in defence of the Real Presence.[3] It was not until Cranmer in his turn was in prison that he wrote a reply to these two works.

---

[1] Cranmer, *Answer to Gardiner*; Cranmer to Cecil or Cheke, 29 September 1551 (Cranmer's *Works*, i. 3–4, 9–367; ii. 429–30); Acts of the Privy Council, 1 October 1551; Hudson, *John Ponet*, pp. 31–32.

[2] Wriothesley, i. 184; Smith, *Confutation of a certain Book called The Defence of the True and Catholic Doctrine of the Sacrament set forth in the name of Thomas Archbishop of Canterbury*; Acts of the Privy Council, 8 March 1550/1; Cranmer, *Answer against the false calumniations of Dr. Richard Smith* (Cranmer's *Works*, i. 368–79, especially p. 374).

[3] See M. A. Constantius, *Confutatio Cavillationum quibus sacrosanctum Eucharistiae Sacramentum ab impiis Capernaitis, impeti solet*; Tunstall, *De Veritate Corporis et Sanguinis Domini nostri Jesu Christi in Eucharistia*.

The Book of Common Prayer had been criticized by reformers as soon as it was issued. Calvin and the Zwinglians, while hailing it as a great advance, pointed out its imperfections, and as early as April 1549 the reformers were hoping that changes would be made in it as soon as possible. By January 1551, the question of revising the Prayer Book had been discussed amongst the Bishops, and between Cranmer and Peter Martyr. Martyr urged Cranmer to make more radical alterations than had been contemplated by the Bishops, and Cranmer was sympathetic, though he showed less resolution than Cheke in overcoming the opposition of his more conservative colleagues. The authorship of the second Prayer Book is even more uncertain than the authorship of the first book, but the primary responsibility for it almost certainly rests with Cranmer. He probably consulted many theologians, both English and foreign, about the alterations, and his chief inspiration seems to have come from Bucer. Bucer died at Cambridge in February 1551; but two months before his death, he published his *Censura*, in which he made a detailed criticism of the Prayer Book in all its aspects, and the matters to which he objected were in most cases removed in the second Book of Common Prayer.

The second book differed further from the first Prayer Book than the first had differed from the Sarum Use. Every part of the first book, except the marriage service, was considerably changed in 1552. The baptism and confirmation services were completely revised, while the alterations in the funeral service, which were particularly extensive, abolished prayers for the deceased and everything which implied that the future of his soul in Purgatory could be affected by the suffrages of the living. Extreme unction was abolished in the visitation of the sick, as was the reservation of the Host for the sick, which had been criticized by Martyr, though not by Bucer. The ordinal of 1550 was amended by the omission of the delivery of the chalice and paten to the priest, and the suppression of all vestments except the rochet went far towards satisfying Hooper. In the communion service, all traces of the old mass were swept away, along with every prayer or rubric which indicated a belief in the Real Presence. The controversy of 1548 as to whether the bread and wine should 'be unto us', or 'be made unto us', the body and blood, was now quite eclipsed by the prayer that 'we, receiving these Thy creatures of bread and wine . . . may be partakers of His most blessed body and blood'.[1]

The role of the foreign theologians—particularly Bucer and Martyr—in the preparation of the second liturgy of the Church of England is a tribute to Cranmer's foresight in attempting to draw around him an association of international Protestant theologians. Cranmer's contacts with Lutheran Germany, his old friendship with Osiander, his systematic reading of foreign theological books, perhaps even his German wife, all served to unite him with the Protestants of Europe. When Charles V proclaimed the Interim in 1548 and terrorized the free cities of Germany into ousting the Lutherans from office, Cranmer hastened to offer asylum in England to the leading Lutheran pastors. He was convinced that Charles would be victorious in his campaign against the Lutherans and that Lutheranism would be eradicated in Germany, and he was eager that the leading Lutheran divines should come to England to assist in teaching in the universities and in advising him in compiling liturgies and formularies. The Italians Peter Martyr and Ochino had arrived before the end of 1547; but it was not until the spring of 1549 that Cranmer, after urging them for many months, was able to persuade Bucer and Fagius to abandon all hope of saving the situation in Strasburg. Cranmer made all the arrangements and paid the expenses of their journey, and warmly welcomed them at Lambeth in April 1549. He took them with him when he moved to Croydon for the summer, and presented them to the King at Court. Bucer was appointed Regius Professor of Divinity at Cambridge, and Martyr was given the same post at Oxford. Fagius also went to Cambridge. Ochino was made a Prebendary of Canterbury, and Fagius' son was educated at the school there.[2]

---

[1] Bucer and Fagius to the ministers at Strasburg, 26 April 1549 (*Orig. Letters*, pp. 535–6); Peter Martyr to Bucer, 10 January and (February) 1551 (Strype, *Cranmer*, pp. 898–9; Gorham, *Gleanings*, pp. 227–9, 232); Calvin to Cranmer (1551) (*Calvini Epistolae*, pp. 61–62, in *Calvini Opera* vol. ix; Gorham, *Gleanings*, pp. 277–80). See the Second Book of Common Prayer in *Liturgies of Edward VI*, pp. 187–355; the passage cited is on p. 279. For Bucer's *Censura*, see in his *Scripta Anglicana*, pp. 456–503; and see Constant, *The Reformation in England*, ii. 182–205, for the effect of his recommendations. There is no evidence as to who drafted the second Prayer Book, beyond the fact that it appears from Cranmer's letter to the Council of 7 October 1552 (in Lorimer, *John Knox and the Church of England*, p. 103) that Cranmer, Ridley and Martyr had some part in it.

[2] Cranmer to à Lasco, 4 July 1548; Cranmer to Hardenberg, 28 July 1548; Cranmer to Bucer, 2 October 1548 (Cranmer's *Works*, ii. 420–4); Coverdale to Fagius, 21 October 1548; Peter Alexander to Fagius, 24 March 1549; Fagius to

Both Martyr and Bucer encountered a good deal of opposition in the Universities, for repeated purges and visitations had not succeeded in eradicating Popery and superstition from among the Fellows and undergraduates, and Oxford especially was becoming the centre of conservatism in England. But the distinguished aliens, though conscious of the blindness and ignorance around them, and longing for their German stoves in the cold climate of Cambridge, realized that they were performing useful work in England, while Cranmer could congratulate himself on having to some extent supplied the deficiency of gardeners in the Lord's vineyard. Bucer may even have learned to speak English; Martyr did not, but Latin was all that was necessary in the Universities and in Cranmer's company. Cranmer was on terms of intimate friendship with Bucer and Martyr, and when Bucer died in February 1551, Cranmer arranged for the King to pay a pension to Mrs. Bucer, and together with Matthew Parker acted as Bucer's executor in England.[1]

Apart from these eminent theologians, many other foreign Protestants came to England as refugees from the persecution in the Netherlands and France. More than five thousand of them settled in London—nearly ten per cent of the total population of the city—where they came into conflict with Ridley on account of their Church services, which differed from those prescribed in the Book of Common Prayer. It was almost certainly thanks to Cranmer's influence that the foreign Protestants were permitted to have their own church in London, and to worship there after

Ullstetter, 18 and 28 April 1549; Fagius to Conrad Hubert, 7 May 1549; Ochino to Musculus, 17 July and 23 December 1548; Dryander to Vadian, 5 June 1549; Peter Martyr to Bucer, 22 January 1549; Bucer to Cranmer (3 September) and 23 December 1548; Bucer and Fagius to the ministers at Strasburg, 26 April 1549; Bucer to Sturmius, 30 May 1549; Bucer to Hardenberg, 14 August 1549 (*Orig. Letters*, pp. 32–33, 329–36, 352, 476, 531–7, 539); Peter Alexander to Bucer, 24 March 1549; Fagius to Marbach, 26 April 1549 (Bucer, *Scripta Anglicana*, p. 191; Gorham, *Gleanings*, pp. 75–76, 78); van der Delft to Charles V, 27 December 1547 (*Span. Cal.* ix, p. 238).

[1] Mrs. Bucer to Cranmer (February 1552); Bucer to Brenz, 15 May 1550; Bucer to Calvin, 25 May 1550; Bucer to the ministers at Strasburg, 26 December 1550 (*Orig. Letters*, pp. 363–4, 542–51); Cranmer to Mrs. Bucer; Cranmer to Conrad Hubert and others, both 20 April 1552 (Cranmer's *Works*, ii. 434–5); Acts of the Privy Council, 31 March 1551. For Martyr's ignorance of English, see Martyr to Bucer, 10 January and (February) 1551 (Strype, *Cranmer*, p. 898; Gorham, *Gleanings*, pp. 227, 232). Bucer may have learned English, for in his *Censura* he seems to have translated passages of the Prayer Book direct from the original English edition; see Dixon, iii. 280 n.

their own fashion. In July 1550, they were organized in a congregation under the supervision of John à Lasco, and were
granted a license from the King to contravene the Act of
Uniformity; but Paulet, the Lord Treasurer, placed every
obstacle in their way, and as late as November 1552 they were
being harassed by local officials. Authoritarian Bishops like
Ridley and Goodrich considered that any departure from
uniformity in religion was potentially subversive; but Cranmer
apparently thought that à Lasco and his deputies, who knew
their congregation and spoke their language, would be more
likely than the English authorities to detect signs of heresy and
Anabaptism among the foreign colony. His judgment was
vindicated when the foreigners denounced van Paris. Micronius,
the pastor of the Flemish section, considered Cranmer to be the
chief supporter of the strangers' church, which would probably
not have survived without his friendship and protection.[1]

In March 1552, Cranmer decided to convene an international
Protestant congress. He hoped that the various Protestant
groups would unite and compose their differences, particularly
on the subject of the Eucharist, in view of the fact that the
Council of Trent were now issuing decrees about the adoration
of the Host. Cranmer wrote to Bullinger, Calvin and Melanchthon, suggesting that they should organize a conference in
England or elsewhere. He could not claim that this assembly
would be a General Council of the Church, because since 1536 he
and all Henry's Bishops had been strenuously propagating the
view that a General Council could only be convened with the
consent of all Christian Princes, and that any Christian Prince
holding sovereign power could veto the convening of a General
Council; but it could be called a 'godly synod'. He did not insist
that it should be held in England, but he told Melanchthon that
King Edward had agreed to give official support for a conference
in England, and that this would make it possible to claim that
the synod had been convened with the consent of Princes.
Cranmer wished all Protestant parties to be represented at the

[1] Letters Patent for the German congregation, 24 July 1550 (Burnet, v. 305–8);
Ochino to Musculus, 23 December 1548; Micronius to Bullinger, 20 May, 28–31
August and 13–20 October 1550, 14 August and 7 November 1551, and 18
February 1553; Utenhovius to Bullinger, 9 April 1551 (*Orig. Letters*, pp. 336,
560, 567–71, 573, 575, 577–8, 581, 586–7); Fagius to Marbach, 26 April 1549
(Gorham, *Gleanings*, p. 78); à Lasco to Cecil (November 1552) (Strype, *Cranmer*,
pp. 880–1); Acts of the Privy Council, 4 November 1552.

conference, and was eager that Brenz should come, although he knew that Brenz's opinion on the Eucharist was Lutheran, and opposed now to his own. But neither Bullinger, Calvin nor Melanchthon were enthusiastic, and the conference was never held. It could not in any case have been successful, for not even Cranmer's tact and patience could have reconciled the Lutherans' doctrine of the Eucharist with the position of Calvin and the Zwinglians. Cranmer again showed his concern with the Protestant movement abroad in October 1552, when he proposed that à Lasco should be sent to Poland as the English Ambassador, so that he might work for the Reformation in his native country under the protection of diplomatic immunity.[1]

Cranmer also encountered failure in another of his great objectives—the suppression of the growing immorality in the country. The people were as ready as ever to indulge in vice—particularly in the national vice of gluttony, for the Englishman was renowned throughout Europe for his appetite for food. Before the Reformation, vice was to some extent held in check by the canon law and the ecclesiastical Courts; but when the Roman canon law and the prestige of the Bishops fell into disrepute after the break with Rome, this check was removed. The repudiation of the old traditions, the continuous changes in doctrine, and the weakening of respect for authority led to a degeneration in private and public morals. The Lords who were the strongest supporters of the Reformation were among the worst offenders, for though they were continually arguing about justification by faith, their morals were deplorable.[2]

Cranmer and the reformers consequently favoured the promulgation of a new code of ecclesiastical law, the re-establishment of the authority of the Bishops' Courts, and above all the renewal of the power of excommunication, which apart from heresy cases had fallen into complete disuse in the last fifteen years, though it had never been abolished. But neither

[1] Cranmer to Bullinger; Cranmer to Calvin, both 20 March 1552; Cranmer to Melanchthon, 27 March 1552; Calvin to Cranmer (summer 1552); Utenhovius to Bullinger, 12 October 1552 (Cranmer's *Works*, ii. 430-4, 432 n.; *Orig. Letters*, pp. 592, 711-4); à Lasco to Bullinger, 10 April 1551 (Gorham, *Gleanings*, p. 246); Declaration of Convocation on General Councils, 20 July 1536 (Burnet, iv. 302). See also Cranmer to Calvin, 4 October 1552 (*Corpus Ref.* xlii. 370).

[2] Becon, *Jewel of Joy* (Becon's *Works*, ii. 415-6); Scory to Edward VI (spring 1550) (Strype, *Eccl. Mem.* ii [ii]. 481); Latimer's last sermon to Edward VI, Lent 1550 (Latimer's *Works*, i. 256-8); Bucer to Calvin, 25 May 1550; Burcher to Bullinger, 28 January 1549 (*Orig. Letters*, pp. 545-8, 647).

the nobles, the gentry nor the people had any desire to see the re-establishment of ecclesiastical discipline. The proposal to establish a Commission to draft a new code of ecclesiastical law was therefore accepted in principle, but not acted upon, in 1534 and again in 1536 and in 1544. Cranmer apparently played a leading part during Henry's reign in working for the promulgation of a new code of ecclesiastical law. He made a collection of the most obnoxious passages from the *Corpus Juris* in favour of Papal supremacy in order to show the necessity of replacing it by a new code; but though he persuaded Henry in January 1546 to call for the report of the Commissioners who had been appointed to draft the code, no further action was taken.[1]

In November 1549, Cranmer and the Bishops again raised the matter in Parliament. The whole of the episcopal bench, both reformer and orthodox, united on this issue. They denounced the immorality of the nation, and introduced a bill giving power to the Bishops and their Ordinaries to excommunicate and imprison; but the bill was defeated, and other less drastic bills were introduced. Eventually a statute was passed which authorized the King to appoint thirty-two Commissioners within three years to draft a new code of ecclesiastical law. This was the course which had been adopted in 1534 and 1536 and 1544, and had become the accepted method of shelving the whole project. Cranmer and the Bishops voted against the bill, presumably as a protest against its inadequacy and hypocrisy.[2]

On this occasion, however, the Act led to some result. Before the three years had expired, Commissioners were appointed in October 1551; but Cranmer realized that the traditional number of thirty-two prescribed by the Act—eight Bishops, eight other divines, eight civil lawyers and eight common lawyers—was too large to be convenient. The work of drafting the code of ecclesiastical law was therefore entrusted to a sub-committee of eight of the thirty-two Commissioners, the four groups being

[1] 25 Hen. VIII, c. 19; 27 Hen. VIII, c. 15; 35 Hen. VIII, c. 16; Strype, *Cranmer*, pp. 189–91; Burnet, i. 520–1; Cranmer, *A Collection of Tenets from the Canon Law;* Cranmer to Henry VIII, 23 January 1545/6 (Cranmer's *Works*, ii. 68–75, 415, where the letter is wrongly dated 24 January).

[2] *H. L. Jo.*, 14 and 18 November, 5, 10, 11, 17, 23 and 24 December 1549, and 25 (morning session) and 31 (afternoon session) January 1549/50; *House of Commons Journal*, 14 and 18 November and 3 December 1549 and 8, 21, 22 and 31 January and 1 February 1549/50; 3 & 4 Edw. VI, c. 11.

represented by two members each; these were to 'rough hew' the code, while the full Commission would later examine and approve the draft of the eight. The credit for this belated start is almost certainly due to Cranmer. Cranmer was a member of the Committee of eight, and it seems clear that he and Peter Martyr were chiefly responsible for drafting the code; but it should not be assumed that Cranmer approved of all the provisions of the *Reformatio Legum Ecclesiasticarum*. The larger body of thirty-two obviously did not accept the recommendations of the eight without careful consideration, for there were prolonged discussions and disagreements at meetings of the full Commission in February and March 1552; and we know that in at least one matter Cranmer disagreed with their final recommendations; for the code directed that communicants should receive the Sacrament sitting down, though Cranmer believed that they should receive it on their knees.[1]

It was of course essential, in the view of Cranmer and his colleagues, that the code should be promulgated, not by the Bishops themselves, but by the King, from whom the Bishops' new powers to suppress immorality must be derived. The new code was therefore issued in the King's name, and worded throughout as if written by Edward himself in the first person. It laid down the principles of the Christian faith, dealing with the usual points of doctrine from the new official Zwinglian standpoint, and dealt with moral offences, with the duties of the Bishops and the clergy, and the organization of the Church. Divorce was permitted for adultery and desertion and on other grounds, and the innocent, though not the guilty, spouse was allowed to remarry; adultery was punished by banishment or imprisonment for life. The code gave the Bishops the power which they had been demanding in order to suppress immorality. As a last resort, if ecclesiastical censures failed, they could impose a sentence of excommunication, which deprived the ex-

[1] Acts of the Privy Council, 6 October and 9 November 1551 and 2 February 1551/2; Commissions of 4 and 11 November 1551 and 12 February 1552 (*Cal. Pat. Rolls, Edw. VI*, iv. 114, 354; *Reformation of the Ecclesiastical laws*, pp. xxx–xxxii); *K. Edw. Jo.*, 10 February 1552; Skinner to Bullinger, 5 January 1552; Ulmis to Bullinger, 10 January and 5 February 1552; Peter Martyr to Bullinger, 8 March 1552; Micronius to Bullinger, 9 March 1552; Utenhovius to Bullinger, 9 March 1552 (*Orig. Letters*, pp. 314, 444, 447, 503–4, 580, 589–90, where Skinner's letter is wrongly dated 1550); *Reformation of Ecclesiastical Laws*, p. 31; Cranmer to the Council, 7 October 1552 (Lorimer, *John Knox and the Church of England*, pp. 103–5).

communicated man of all legal rights and subjected him to complete social ostracism. No one was permitted to speak to him, and if he did not do public penance within forty days he was to be imprisoned. Thus the old power of excommunication was to be restored, though the code repeatedly emphasized that it was only to be used in extreme cases, and included the novel provision that a Justice of the Peace was to be present when the sentence was pronounced.[1]

The Code of Ecclesiastical Law naturally contained provisions about the punishment of heretics, and there has been a great deal of controversy as to the effect of these provisions. The wording of this part of the code is far from clear, and it has been interpreted in two completely different ways. The third title of the code lays down the procedure for the trial of the heretic by the Bishop, with a right of appeal to the Archbishop, and a further right of appeal to the King in person. If the heretic is obdurate, he is to be excommunicated; but if he publicly repents and recants within sixteen days, the excommunication is reversed. The heretic who despises excommunication is to be handed over to the secular power for 'punishment'. The doubt arises as to what was meant by punishment, in view of the fact that the first title stipulates that those who oppose the Christian religion are to forfeit their life and property, while a later provision in the third title states that persons convicted of heresy who are unrepentant are to be accounted 'infamous', and suffer the prescribed penalties, which involve the loss of all legal rights. This has made it possible for Burnet to claim that the Code of Ecclesiastical Law abolished the burning of heretics other than those who denied the truths of the Christian religion —that is to say, of the Creeds—whereas Collier interpreted the code as retaining burning as the penalty for all unrepentant heretics. The later Roman Catholic writers accepted the latter interpretation, and proceeded to argue that as other parts of the code laid down that it was heresy to deny the reformers' doctrines of the Eucharist and justification and the other doctrines mentioned in the code, the effect of the code was to provide that those who believed in the traditional Catholic doctrines should suffer death as heretics. They therefore accuse Cranmer of preparing to burn Catholics.

[1] *Reformation of Ecclesiastical Laws*, especially pp. 49–58, 167–88.

It appears, however, that though the code retained the death penalty—and this obviously meant death by burning—for certain kinds of obstinate heretics, its object was to make the law of heresy more lenient. The heretic was granted the privilege of a further opportunity, even after he had been excommunicated, to repent and recant before he was delivered to the secular power, though it was already the practice to give heretics an almost indefinite number of opportunities to save themselves by a recantation until the moment when the fagots were lit. The fact that the code provided that a heretic could be declared to be infamous envisaged that some persons who were convicted of heresy and refused to recant would not be put to death. It is not so clear whether the 'punishment' provided for obstinate heretics in general was a different kind of punishment from the death penalty expressly reserved for those who denied the truths of Christianity. One of the drafts of the code contains a note that the punishment for these other heretics was to be only banishment or imprisonment for life; but it is doubtful if this note was actually incorporated as part of the code. It is, however, unlikely that Cranmer intended to make any drastic change in the law of heresy, or in the existing practice in enforcing it. If he had intended either to put an end to the burning of Anabaptists or to initiate the policy of burning Papists and conservatives, it would have aroused a great deal of comment in the letters of the reformers and their opponents, and in the polemical pamphlets of the contemporary writers. There is little doubt that Cranmer still regarded burning, in the last resort, as the punishment for Anabaptists, while the adherents of the old religion were to be punished with the censures and imprisonment laid down in the second Act of Uniformity of 1552.[1]

October 1551 saw the downfall of Somerset and his adherents. Cranmer was apparently made to play his part in the proceedings against Somerset, for though he had only attended one meeting of the Council during the previous four months, he sat comparatively regularly in the Council in October and November, being present when Somerset's supporters were sent to the Tower and

[1] For the provisions of the Code as to the punishment of heretics, see *Reformation of Ecclesiastical Laws*, pp. 7, 23–28; and see note by Cardwell at p. 330: Collier, v. 479–80; Burnet, ii. 333; Lingard, *History of England*, v. 462–4 and n.; Dixon, iii. 376 n.; Todd, *Archbishop Cranmer*, ii. 329–34; Belloc, *Cranmer*, p. 253 and n. See also 5 & 6 Edw. VI, c. 1.

when the decision was taken to torture them. But he made an unsuccessful attempt to save Somerset's life, despite the fact that he himself may have been in some danger at this time. Scheyvfe, who thought that Cranmer would soon be arrested, reported that he had earnestly intervened for Somerset, and this is confirmed by a somewhat cryptic passage which Ridley wrote in prison in 1555. Cranmer made a more public intervention on behalf of Tunstall. After Tunstall had been arrested in December 1551 and charged with complicity in Somerset's so-called plot, a bill was introduced in the House of Lords to deprive him of his see of Durham. The bill passed the House of Lords against the two dissentient votes of Cranmer and the conservative Lord Stourton, but was defeated in the House of Commons —probably because of the unpopularity of Warwick, who was now Duke of Northumberland. Tunstall was then deprived by a Commission of lawyers.[1]

We have no knowledge as to why Cranmer, alone of all the reforming Bishops, opposed the deprivation of Tunstall. It has sometimes been assumed that it was because of personal friendship; but there is no other reason to believe that Cranmer was a friend of Tunstall, as he was of that other conservative Bishop, Thirlby. There are other possible explanations of his action. Apart from his usual predilection towards leniency, Cranmer probably believed that a Bishop should only be deprived by order of the King for disobedience. It was for disobedience, not for their doctrinal opinions, that Cranmer had passed sentence of deprivation on Bonner and Gardiner, and that a Commission of lawyers had deprived Heath and Day. But Tunstall, though he had voted against all the measures of reform in the House of Lords, had not done so in disobedience to an order, and he was not now being accused of disobedience. Cranmer may also have disapproved of a Bishop being deprived by an Act of Parliament, for though he could justify a deprivation after a legal investigation by Commissioners appointed by the King, it was another

[1] Acts of the Privy Council, 19 October, 5 and 21 November and 19 December 1551, and 24 January 1551/2; Scheyvfe to Charles V, 26 October 1551; Scheyvfe's advices, 12 February 1552 (*Span. Cal.* x, pp. 389, 453); Machyn, p. 26; *Greyfriars Chron.*, p. 75; *H. L. Jo.*, 31 March 1552. Ridley wrote in his *Piteous Lamentation*: 'I have heard that Cranmer, and another whom I will not name, were both in high displeasure, the one for showing his conscience secretly, but plainly and fully, in the Duke of Somerset's cause, and both of late, but specially Cranmer, for repugning as they might against the late spoil of the Church goods' (Ridley's *Works*, p. 59).

matter if temporal peers and the House of Commons could deprive, by their votes, any Bishop to whom they were opposed. If
Cranmer had already discovered that Northumberland wished
to deprive Tunstall in order to seize a large part of the lands
and revenues of the vacant see for himself, he would have had
another motive for opposing the bill. Cranmer also voted, in
this Parliamentary session of 1552, together with a number of
other Bishops, against the Act restraining the sale of benefices.[1]
Presumably he opposed this measure because it did not go far
enough to suppress the evil.

In the autumn of 1552, Cranmer again came into conflict
with the extremists. This time it was not Hooper or the Anabaptists, but a 'runagate Scot' who was stirring up his congregation
in the north against the covetousness of the nobility and the
remnants of Popery in England. Northumberland had entered
into a strange alliance with John Knox. Knox not only attacked
covetous Lords, but had even by implication denounced the
execution of Somerset in a public sermon; but Northumberland
apparently hoped to use Knox as a weapon against Cranmer.
He suggested that Knox should be appointed a Bishop in order
to separate him from his congregation in the north, and to
enable him to serve as a 'whetstone to quicken and sharp the
Bishop of Canterbury.' Knox refused to be a party to this tactic,
and when Northumberland offered him the see of Rochester, he
proceeded to harangue Northumberland on the evils of covetousness. Yet Northumberland continued to help and encourage
Knox.[2]

Cranmer and Knox came into conflict on the issue of kneeling
at communion. Knox had taught his congregation at Newcastle
not to receive on their knees, because kneeling implied adoration
of the Host. Knox's view was irreconcilable with Cranmer's
high estimation of the reception of the Eucharist, and the
practice of kneeling to receive, which had always been adopted
in the days of the Sarum Use and under the Prayer Book of
1549, was now expressly prescribed by a rubric in the second

[1] H. L. Jo., 20 February 1551/2.
[2] Knox, *Admonition to the Professors of God's Truth in England* (Knox's *Works*,
iii. 277–8); Northumberland to Cecil, 28 October and 7 December 1552 and 9
January 1552/3 (Tytler, ii. 142, 148, 158–60). The phrase 'a runagate Scot' as
applied to Knox (not to Aless) is Weston's, in Latimer's disputation at Oxford in
1554 (Foxe, vi. 510).

Book of Common Prayer—probably because of Knox's activities at Newcastle. At the end of September 1552—less than five weeks before All Saints Day, when the new Prayer Book was to come into force—Knox preached before the King and stated that it was idolatrous to kneel to the bread and wine at communion. The Council wrote to Cranmer, who had just been ordered to investigate the activities of an extremist sect in Kent, and told him to postpone his departure to his diocese until the issue raised by Knox had been settled. On 7th October, Cranmer wrote to the Council from Croydon, defending the practice of kneeling at communion, and in the course of the next few days he discussed the matter with Ridley and Martyr, who almost certainly agreed with Cranmer that kneeling must be retained. On 11th October, Cranmer for the first time for three months attended a meeting of the Council to which he had been specially summoned; and though there is no record in the minutes of the question being discussed, there is little doubt that he was called in order to deal with the kneeling issue.

The Council decided to make no change in the Book of Common Prayer except to insert the black rubric. On 27th October, five days before All Saints, the Council ordered the publication of the rubric; the printers, in their hurry, inserted the new slips at random places in the copies of the Prayer Book. The rubric stated that the fact that the congregation were to receive the communion on their knees did not imply adoration of the Host, which was idolatrous because Christ was in Heaven and could not be in two places at the same time. Cranmer, who could have no objection to the rubric and may actually have drafted it, had gained the victory on this point, and Knox reluctantly ordered his congregation in the north to submit.[1]

The issue of kneeling arose again in connexion with the Articles of Religion. Cranmer had been engaged in preparing the Articles since 1551, and in that year he submitted a draft to some kind of assembly of Bishops. In May 1552, the Council wrote to Cranmer for a copy of the Articles, and asked him what the Bishops had decided; but evidently Cranmer was still working

---

[1] Second Book of Common Prayer (*Liturgies of Edward VI*, pp. 279, 283); Utenhovius to Bullinger, 12 October 1552 (*Orig. Letters*, pp. 591–2); Acts of the Privy Council, 27 September and 8, 11 and 27 October 1552; Cranmer to the Council, 7 October 1552; Knox, *Epistle to the Congregation of Berwick* (autumn 1552) (Lorimer, *John Knox and the Church of England*, pp. 103–5, 259–63).

on the Articles, because it was not until 19th September that he
sent them to the Council, though this delay may have been
partly due to the fact that he fell ill during the summer. At the
end of October, the Council sent the Articles to the four royal
chaplains and two other divines for their opinion. One of these
divines was Knox, who objected to the article which stated that
all the ceremonies prescribed in the second Book of Common
Prayer were holy and godly and could be proved by Scripture,
because the ceremonies in question included kneeling at communion. Knox and his colleagues insisted on the deletion of the
statement that the ceremonies could be proved by Scripture,
and agreed to accept another article which gave a more modified
approval to the ceremonies in the Prayer Book. The Articles
were then sent back to Cranmer on 23rd November, and Cranmer
returned them to the Council next day. In their final form, the
Articles approved the Book of Common Prayer in stronger
terms than had been used in the draft which Knox and the King's
chaplains had accepted; but the statement that the ceremonies
could be proved by Scripture was not reinserted.

When the Articles were sent to the royal chaplains, they were
in the form of forty-five Articles. In June 1553, they were
eventually issued as forty-two Articles. This change was
brought about by compressing four Articles into one; but a
number of other changes were made, all of which tended to
modify the vigour of the doctrines asserted. It is usually supposed that these changes were made by Cranmer after Knox and
his colleagues had completed their work on the document; but
the changes could certainly not all have been made during the
twenty-four hours during which Cranmer had the Articles in his
possession in November 1552. Cranmer may perhaps have been
responsible for some of the changes which were made between
November and the following June; but here again we cannot
assume that he was in complete agreement with the forty-two
Articles in their final form. He can hardly have approved of the
fact that there was no reference to any of the Sacraments except
Baptism and the Lord's Supper, even though it may have been
thanks to him that the final draft no longer expressly declared
that these were the only two Sacraments, as had been stated in
the original forty-five Articles. Cranmer may also have been
responsible for the declaration that the Sacraments were effectual

signs of grace, and not merely tokens of Christian men's professions; but it is very unlikely that it was Cranmer who modified the language in which the royal supremacy over the Church was expressed.[1]

The Articles asserted the reformers' doctrines on all the old controversies; but they also dealt with issues which had not previously been mentioned in an official English formulary of faith. Along with royal supremacy, obedience to magistrates, the Real Presence, justification by faith, and Anabaptism, the Articles dealt with predestination and freewill, and condemned Millenarianism and other sectarian heresies which were being raised by new sects of extremists. Henry Hart and his Freewillers had been causing trouble in Kent and Essex since the beginning of 1550; and when Cranmer was at Ford during the winter of 1552-3, he dealt with the activities of David Joris' Family of Love. Joris had been persecuted and mutilated in Flanders, and later died peacefully in Basel, leaving only his dead body to be burned for heresy by the reformers. His Family of Love were not revolutionary Anabaptists, but a wholly exclusive pacifist sect.[2]

Foxe tells of one case which Cranmer investigated at this time, in which the local Papists and conservatives, seizing the opportunity provided by a drive against heretical sects, accused a man and woman of Ashford of being supporters of these sects, though the only evidence against them was apparently the fact that they were alleged to have committed adultery together in the woman's house. This offence would ordinarily have been dealt with as a case of immorality by Cranmer, or more probably by his Ordinary; but the local gentry were obviously eager to

[1] Acts of the Privy Council, 2 May, 21 October and 20 November 1552; Cranmer to Cecil, 25 August, 19 September and 24 November 1552 (Cranmer's Works, ii. 438-41); the Forty-Five Articles (Hardwicke, History of the Articles of Religion, pp. 279-88); the Forty-Two Articles (in English and Latin) (Liturgies of Edward VI, p. 526-37, 572-82); Lorimer, John Knox and the Church of England, pp. 108-28; Gairdner, Lollardy and the Reformation, iii. 357-61; Dixon, iii. 480-4 and n. The Council sent the Articles to Cranmer on 20 November 1552, but he only received them on the 23. As to whether Knox was a royal chaplain, see Dixon, iii. 325-7 n., 478-9 n.; Gairdner, Lollardy and the Reformation, iii. 340-1.

[2] The Forty-Two Articles (Liturgies of Edward VI, p. 526-37); Acts of the Privy Council, 8 March 1549/50, 27 January and 3 February 1550/1 and 27 September 1552; Cranmer to Cecil, 20 November 1552 (Cranmer's Works, ii. 440); Scheyvfe to Granvelle, 20 November 1552 (Span. Cal. x, p. 593); Rogers, The Displaying of the Family of Love, pp. 15-18 (unpaginated); Blesdike, Historia vitae Davidis Georgii, pp. 15-16; Dixon, iii. 207-10 n.

connect it with the Family of Love, perhaps because the name of Joris' sect had confirmed them in their belief that Anabaptists held women in common. Cranmer tried the case with other Commissioners at Ashford. Many witnesses gave evidence against the defendants, and persisted, despite an intensive cross-examination by Cranmer, in saying that they had seen the defendants committing adultery by the light of the moon when they peered into the woman's hovel, through the half-open door. The other Commissioners urged Cranmer to pass a severe sentence on the accused; but Cranmer adjourned the case for dinner. On their way to dinner, he asked his colleagues to lead him past the house of the accused woman; and as they passed the house, Cranmer examined the door through which the witnesses claimed to have seen the offence committed, and exclaimed: 'Surely, they be false harlots, I see very well now; for I perfectly understand the matter'. One of the Commissioners pointed out that he had already urged Cranmer to punish them; but Cranmer explained that it was not the defendants, but the witnesses for the prosecution, who were the false harlots. Cranmer had realized from his inspection of the door and from his calculation of the position of the moon on the night in question, that the witnesses could not have seen what was happening inside the house; and he therefore acquitted the defendants. The truth of this story can hardly be doubted, despite the fact that Foxe omitted it from the second edition of his *Book of Martyrs*; for in the first edition, he states that he had heard the story from a man who had been told it by Cranmer, and that it could be confirmed by the accused woman herself.[1]

Cranmer had returned to London before the end of February, and participated in the difficult Parliamentary session of March 1553, when the rising opposition to Northumberland in the country was reflected in the House of Commons. Northumberland had lost patience with the reforming clergy and preachers, and his attempt to use Knox and the extremists against Cranmer and the Bishops having failed, he now tried a new tactic. When Cranmer spoke in the House of Lords in favour of the promulgation of the Code of Ecclesiastical Law, Northumberland intervened in the debate to say that the clergy would do well, instead of preaching about the immorality of the people, to look

[1] Foxe, viii. 41–43 (1st ed., p. 1476–8).

to their own conduct. He complained that some of the preachers were attacking the nobility and the leaders of the State in a manner which was openly seditious, and he blamed the Bishops for their failure to prevent the preachers from doing this.

Northumberland's new policy was more successful than the old. He had failed to bribe Knox and the extremists to become his pawns in the struggle against Cranmer; but he succeeded in frightening Cranmer into joining him against the extremists and Knox. Cranmer immediately reacted to Northumberland's speech by adopting an apologetic tone, protesting that he and the Bishops were not to blame, as they knew nothing about the sermons of which Northumberland had complained. A few weeks later, Knox was summoned before the Council, and reprimanded for his opposition to kneeling at communion, for his refusal to accept a cure in London, and in general for his defiance of authority. Cranmer was present at the Council, and apparently played an active part in this discussion with Knox. However much he might disapprove of Northumberland and the spoil of Church goods, Cranmer was always prepared, in the last resort, to unite with a covetous Duke against a radical agitator.[1]

In view of the opposition of Northumberland, of the nobles and of the people, the Code of Ecclesiastical Law was never promulgated; but the publication of formularies of faith and works of religious instruction did not interfere with the pleasures of the laity, and there was never so much activity in this respect as in the last few weeks of Edward's reign. Three more editions of the Bible were published, bringing the total since Edward's accession to twenty-five; in March, a new Primer was issued; and on 21st May, the Forty-Two Articles were published by the King's printer, together with a catechism. It has been suggested that the Catechism was written by Cranmer; but though Cranmer accepted full responsibility in Mary's reign for having issued it, there seems to be no doubt that Ponet was the author. The title page of this publication untruthfully described the Articles as having been agreed to by the Convocation of London in 1552—that is to say, by the Convocation which had sat in March 1553, and which under the

---

[1] Scheyfve's notes, 10 April 1553 (in Gairdner, *Lollardy and the Reformation* iii. 400–1); Calderwood, *History of the Kirk of Scotland*, i. 280–1.

English legal calendar had been in the year 1552—though in fact the Articles had not been approved in Convocation any more than had the two editions of the Prayer Book. Cranmer was not responsible for this falsehood. When he saw it, he objected, and pointed out the error to the Council; but he was told that the Articles were described as having been agreed to by the Convocation of London in the year 1552 because they had been issued during the time when Convocation was in session. This extraordinary explanation would have been ridiculous even if it had been true; but in fact the Articles were set forth when Convocation was not in session, and in the year 1553—that is to say, after 25th March.[1]

The authorities, however, were eager that the Articles should appear to have been approved by the clergy, and it was decided that the priests throughout the country should subscribe to the Articles. On 26th May, Cranmer sat to receive the subscriptions of some of the London clergy; and a fortnight later, the King ordered that any priest who refused to subscribe, and who agitated against the Articles, was to be reported to the Council. On 23rd June, Cranmer sat again at Lambeth, and more priests came before him and subscribed to the Articles.[2] By this time, Cranmer himself had subscribed to an even more controversial document.

[1] The Primer of 1553; The Catechism and the Forty-Two Articles (*Liturgies of Edward VI*, pp. 357–540); Report of the Disputations of October 1553 and April 1554 (Foxe, vi. 396, 468); Cheke to Bullinger, 7 June 1553 (*Orig. Letters*, p. 142); *Greyfriars Chron.*, p. 77; Dixon, iii. 170–1 n.; Gairdner, *Lollardy and the Reformation*, iii. 375–83. Gairdner (p. 373 n.) suggests that Cranmer wrote the so-called Little Catechism which was included in the Primer of March 1553; but this is based on a misunderstanding of Cranmer's remarks in his disputation at Oxford (Foxe, vi. 468), which certainly refer to Ponet's Catechism which was published together with the Articles in May 1553.

[2] *Greyfriars Chron.*, p. 77; Edward VI's mandates, 9 and 19 June 1553 (Burnet, vi. 295–300); Utenhovius to Bullinger, 7 June 1553 (*Orig. Letters*, p. 594).

CHAPTER XXII

THE TRAITOR

In June 1553, Edward VI, who knew that he was dying, decided with Northumberland to oust Mary from the succession and vest the Crown in his cousin Jane Grey. Cranmer had been in residence at Greenwich, after a long absence from Court, at the beginning of June; but he had already returned to Lambeth by the middle of the month when the project for the succession was first disclosed to the Council. Northumberland persuaded all the Lords of the Council who were present at Court to consent, and then turned his attention to the Judges. The Judges were particularly reluctant to agree, because Henry VIII had provided in his will that Mary was to succeed to the throne if Edward died childless; and under a statute of 1545, it was high treason to dispute the succession which Henry had established in his will. But all the Judges agreed, and signed Edward's devise of the Crown to Jane, except for Justice Hales, who was nevertheless afterwards singled out for persecution by Mary. Chief Justice Montague later wrote that they had only been persuaded to agree by a promise that the devise would subsequently be ratified by Parliament.[1]

When Cranmer was summoned to Greenwich, he was informed about the devise, and was asked to sign the Engagement by which the Lords of the Council undertook to support the devise and to uphold it with their lives. He disliked the plan, and despite the protests of Northumberland asked for a private audience with the King, hoping to dissuade Edward from making the devise; but he was not permitted to see Edward alone, and Northampton and Lord Darcy, the Lord Chamberlain, were present throughout the interview. Cranmer strongly urged Edward to abandon the project, but Northampton and Darcy argued against him, and the King remained adamant. Cranmer then questioned the legality of the devise in view of the provisions of the Act of Parliament of 1545; but Edward and the

---

[1] Acts of the Privy Council, 2, 3, 5 and 8 June,1553; Montague's statement (Fuller, *Church History*, ii. 419–23); 35 Hen. VIII, c. 1.

Council assured him that the Judges had advised that the statute did not bar a King who was in possession of the Crown from devising it to whomsoever he wished. Cranmer was astonished, but thought that in view of the opinion of the Judges and King's Counsel he, being no lawyer, should not oppose the King on this point. Edward then said that he regretted that Cranmer, alone of all his Council, should refuse to do his will in this matter; and Cranmer was so grieved at these words that he agreed to subscribe.[1]

This is the story that Cranmer wrote to Queen Mary some five or six months later, when he was beseeching her to pardon him for his share in Jane Grey's usurpation. There are two other accounts of the events at Greenwich in June 1553. The one was written by Cecil a few months afterwards in order to gain his pardon from Mary, and he adhered to the same story in 1573, when he was serving Elizabeth, who had also been excluded by Edward's devise. The other is that of Chief Justice Montague, which was written for the same purpose between September 1553 and June 1554. Montague's account conflicts with Cranmer's on certain points, but this does not prove that either account is untrue, as the contradictions are probably explained by the fact that Northumberland and the Lords of the Council told a different story to Cranmer and to Montague. Cranmer's story is the most plausible of the three, for while Montague's account gives the impression of being somewhat over-dramatized, and Cecil's is obviously the invention of a man whose sole concern was to be on the winning side, Cranmer's account of his actions corresponds exactly with what we should have expected of him in such circumstances.[2]

The devise of the Crown to Jane Grey, with its exclusion of Elizabeth as well as of Mary, was in later years condemned by the Protestants as severely as by the Catholics. If for Catholics it was a treasonable confederation of heretics, the Protestants of the future saw it as a plot by the unscrupulous Northumberland, who, though he made a pretence of being a Protestant, confessed on the scaffold that he was in fact a Papist; and they were eager to claim that honest Protestants had no part in the enterprise. They were therefore obliged to apologize for Cranmer's

[1] Cranmer to Mary I (December 1553) (Cranmer's *Works*, ii. 443–4).
[2] Cranmer to Mary I (December 1553), ibid.; Cecil's statement (Tytler, ii. 192–5); Alford to Cecil, 4 October 1573 (Strype, *Annals of the Reformation*, iv. 485); Montague's statement (Fuller, *Church History*, ii. 419–25).

part in it. Of all the questionable actions which Cranmer committed during his life, this was the most difficult to reconcile with the seventeenth century ideology of the Church of England. But it cannot have been so clear to Cranmer in June 1553 which course of action was dictated by the principles of Christian obedience. Mary and Elizabeth had no hereditary claim to the Crown, for, as Edward's devise pointed out, they were both bastards. Cranmer himself had bastardized them by his judgments at Dunstable and Lambeth, which had not been reversed by the statute which made it possible for them to succeed to the Crown. Their right to the Crown depended solely on an Act of Parliament; and once Cranmer had been persuaded that the Judges had disposed of the purely legal objections, he would have had no hesitation in violating an Act of Parliament at the command of his Prince. Cranmer's doctrine of Christian obedience did not rest on respect for either hereditary or statutory title, but on the duty of obedience to the elect of the Lord. This obedience was due to Saul as well as to David, irrespective of how they had won their throne, and meant in practice submission to any *de facto* King—a highly convenient doctrine for cynical courtiers, but one which could raise difficult problems for men like Cranmer who sincerely believed in it.

Cranmer could therefore support Edward's devise with a clear conscience, and it may indeed appear strange that he had any hesitation in doing so, in view of the fact that however much he disliked Northumberland's government, he must have realized that Mary's accession would involve the overthrow of the Reformation. But Cranmer and the reformers had never contemplated taking action to prevent the accession of a Papist Princess. Apart from Cranmer and Goodrich in the Council, Ridley and Sandys, the Vice-Chancellor of Cambridge University, were the only leaders among the Protestant clergy who gave active support to Jane. Ridley was unique in justifying the exclusion of Mary from the throne, in his sermon at Paul's Cross, by the fact that she was a Papist. Of the others, not even Knox supported Jane, while Hooper gave active support to Mary during the struggle.[1] Within seven years, Protestantism

---

[1] Foxe, vi. 389–90; viii. 590–2; Hooper, *An Apology against the untrue and slanderous reports* (Hooper's *Works*, ii. 556–7); Knox, *Admonition to the Professors of God's Truth in England* (Knox's *Works*, iii. 307–9).

would have chosen the path of armed revolt in France and
Scotland; but the English reformers of 1553 were still loyal to
the doctrine of Christian obedience.

It was perhaps precisely because Mary was a Papist that
Cranmer was eager to dissuade Edward from making his devise,
lest it should be thought that the reformers were responsible for
excluding Mary because of her religious opinions; but when his
advice was rejected, Cranmer obeyed his Prince, and signed the
Engagement by which he and the other Lords of the Council
agreed to defend the devise to Jane, and never to swerve from it,
and to do their utmost to punish anyone who did so. On 21st
June, he also signed first at the head of the witnesses to the
formal Limitation of the Crown to Jane.[1]

Edward died on 6th July. On the 10th, Jane was proclaimed in
London, and during the next nine days Cranmer was in attendance upon her, and present at the Council meetings, in the
Tower. His name stands first among the signatures of the letter
to Mary in which the Council informed her that she could not
succeed to the throne on account of her illegitimacy, and ordered
her to be an obedient subject of Queen Jane. He was presumably
present at the meeting of the Council on 13th July, when Northumberland, before marching to crush Mary's revolt in Norfolk,
told the Councillors that he trusted in their loyalty because they
could expect no mercy from Mary. Cranmer remained in London with the Council, behind the strong defences of the Tower,
where they heard of the desertion of the Earl of Oxford to
Mary, of the rising in Buckinghamshire, of the mutiny of the
fleet at Yarmouth, and of the demonstration against Ridley at
Paul's Cross. He signed the letters of the Council to the officers
and noblemen of all the shires, urging them to stand fast for
Jane.[2]

On 19th July, the Council wrote to Rich in Essex, ordering him
'to remain in that promise and steadfastness to our Sovereign
Lady Queen Jane's service, as ye shall find us ready and firm

[1] Engagement to observe the Succession (June 1553); Letters Patent for the
Limitation of the Crown, (21 June 1553) (*Chronicle of Queen Jane*, pp. 90–91, 99).
[2] Wriothesley, ii. 85–88; Machyn, p. 35; *Greyfriars Chron.*, pp. 78–79 (where
Ridley's sermon is wrongly dated 9 July); Stow, *Annals*, p. 610; the Council to
Mary, 11 July 1553 (Foxe, vi. 385–6, where it is wrongly dated 9 July); Stow's
MS. (*Chron. of Queen Jane*, pp. 6–7); Jane's Council to the Sheriff, etc., of
Nottinghamshire and Derbyshire, and of Wiltshire, 12 and 15 July 1553 (*Retro-
spective Review*, 2nd Series, i. 504–5 (1827); Hoare, *Modern Wiltshire*, vi. 266–7).

with all our force to the same. Which neither with honour nor with safety nor yet with duty we may now forsake'. This letter was signed by Cranmer, Shrewsbury, Herbert, Paget, Arundel and eleven other Lords of the Council. Later in the day, Shrewsbury, Herbert, Paget and Arundel won over the Mayor and the city for Mary, and proclaimed Mary as Queen in Cheapside amid scenes of great enthusiasm. Cranmer played no part in this decisive event which placed Mary on the throne and in power, for he and Cheke and Jane's father Suffolk were the only Lords of the Council who were not present at the proclamation and at the *Te Deum* in St. Paul's; they had obviously not been invited to participate in the *coup* on Mary's behalf. Nor did Cranmer accompany Suffolk when the Duke, hearing of what had occurred, told his daughter that she was no longer Queen, and went out to Tower Hill and proclaimed Mary there.[1]

During the night, while all London cheered and drank around the bonfires in the streets, the Council met at Baynards Castle and wrote to Mary, describing themselves as 'We, your most humble, faithful and obedient subjects, having always (God we take to witness) remained your Highness' true and humble subjects in our hearts, ever since the death of our late Sovereign Lord and master your Highness' brother', and informing her that although they had hitherto been compelled to dissemble their true feelings, they had now proclaimed her as Queen in her city of London. We do not know whether Cranmer was one of the Lords who signed this letter, for our knowledge of it is derived, not from the letter that was sent to Mary, but from the copy which Cecil made and retained, which does not contain the signatures; but the letter was probably signed by the same Councillors who signed the letter to Northumberland, for both letters were almost certainly drafted at the same meeting of the Council. Cranmer certainly signed the letter to Northumberland at Cambridge, ordering him to submit at once to Queen Mary, his lawful Sovereign, and declaring that Cranmer and his colleagues would proclaim him a traitor and fight against him if he did not do so. It is clear that the Lords, after confronting Cranmer and Suffolk with a *fait accompli*, had

---

[1] The Council to Rich, 19 July 1553 (Strype, *Cranmer*, p. 913); Wriothesley, ii. 88–89; anonymous letter (July 1553) (*Chron. of Queen Jane*, pp. 11–12); Machyn, p. 37; *Greyfriars Chron.*, p. 80.

invited them to join in adhering to Mary. Next day, with the
church bells still ringing and the Londoners taking a holiday,
Cranmer went with all the Lords of the Council to dinner with
the Lord Mayor to celebrate Mary's accession. He also signed
a document, together with Goodrich and Paulet, advising Mary
of certain urgent administrative matters which had arisen in
connexion with Edward's death and her accession, and sent
Cecil to deliver it to the new Queen in Suffolk.[1]

Cranmer remained at liberty for another fifty-six days.
Before the end of July, Northumberland, Jane, Ridley and many
others had been imprisoned. Suffolk and Cheke, who like
Cranmer had played no part in the desertion to Mary of 19th
July, were also arrested, though Suffolk was released after a few
days. On 3rd August, Mary rode into London, releasing Gardiner
and Norfolk when she came to the Tower, and appointing them
to the Council. On the 5th, Bonner was freed from the Marshalsea, to be escorted in triumph by his supporters to the Bishop of
London's palace while Cox was put in the empty cell which
Bonner had vacated. But Cranmer remained free, and there is no
contemporary evidence for Strype's statement that he was
ordered to remain in his house at Lambeth. The only action
taken against him was the confiscation of some equipment which
he had apparently supplied to Northumberland's forces. At the
beginning of August, he was ordered to perform one of his
duties as Archbishop in transmitting the mandate for the sum-
moning of Convocation in October—that Convocation which
had been called in order to condemn all the measures which the
reformers had introduced in Edward's reign.[2]

[1] The Council to Mary I (Strype, *Cranmer*, p. 915); the Council to Northumber-
land (Stow, *Annals*, p. 612); Wriothesley, ii. 89–90; anonymous letter, (July
1553) (*Chron. of Queen Jane*, pp. 11–12); Machyn, p. 37; *Greyfrairs Chron.*, p. 80;
'Certain articles wherein the quenes hyghnes pleasure is to be knowen' (Record
Office, S.P. 11/1, f. 6); Alford to Cecil, 4 October 1573 (Strype, *Annals*, iv. 489);
and see Conyers Read, *Mr. Secretary Cecil and Queen Elizabeth*, p. 101. The
Council's letter to Mary is endorsed with the date 20 July in the copy retained by
Cecil, but the writers state in the letter that they have proclaimed Mary as Queen
'this day', i.e., 19 July. Froude (v. 208) is probably right in thinking that it was
written at a meeting of the Council held during the night of 19–20 July. The
Council's letter to Northumberland, which is also dated 20 July, was almost
certainly written at the same meeting; it had been delivered to Northumberland at
Cambridge early on the morning of 20 July (see Stow's MS., in *Chron. of Queen
Jane*, p. 10).

[2] Wriothesley, ii. 90–96; Machyn, pp. 37–39; *Greyfriars Chron.*, pp. 81–82;
Acts of the Privy Council, 31 July 1553; Records of Convocation, October–
December 1553 (Wilkins, iv. 88).

A few days later, Cranmer played at least some part in Edward's funeral. The funeral rites were performed according to the Book of Common Prayer, which was still the law of the land, for the Emperor had with difficulty persuaded Mary to agree to this by pointing out that as Edward had died a heretic, he was not entitled to the benefit of an orthodox Catholic funeral. Cranmer brought Edward's body from Greenwich to Whitehall; but it is not certain whether he officiated in any way at the funeral service. Three months later, the Italian reformer Terentianus, who was in England at the time, wrote to Ulmis that Cranmer had performed the ceremony 'with many tears', and this is confirmed by the French Protestant Poullain, who had been the head of the colony of foreign Protestants at Glastonbury. After he had left England, Poullain printed a Latin translation of Cranmer's Declaration against the Mass, and inserted a marginal note to the effect that Cranmer had officiated at Edward's funeral; but Poullain may merely have been repeating the story which Terentianus had told the reformers in Europe. If Cranmer officiated, it is surprising that this is not mentioned by any of the diarists who described the funeral, for though they all recorded that Day preached the sermon, they made no mention of Cranmer except to state that he brought the body to Whitehall.[1]

About the same time, Cranmer went to Court—presumably to the Tower, where Mary was residing. He would obviously not have gone to Court unless he had been summoned, and Strype may well be right in suggesting that the Council wished to question him about his part in supporting Jane. The anonymous biographer states that he requested an audience of the Queen, but that Mary refused the request. On the occasion of this visit to Court, he saw Cecil, but he did not speak to him, because—as he explained in a letter to Cecil on 14th August—he thought that it would be unwise for them to be seen talking

[1] Scheyvfe, Renard and others to Mary I, 24 July 1553; Scheyvfe, Renard and others to Charles V, 2 and 8 August 1553 (Gachard, *Voyages des Souverains des Pays-Bas*, iv. 84, 86; *Span. Cal.* xi, pp. 134, 156); Charles V to Scheyvfe, Renard and others 29 July 1553 (Weiss, *Papiers d'Etat de Granvelle*, iv. 60); Terentianus to Ulmis, 20 November 1553 (Fuessli, *Epistolae ad Ecclesiae Helveticae Reformatoribus*, p. 310; *Orig. Letters*, pp. 367–8); *Vera Expositio Disputationis Institutae mandato D. Mariae Reginae*, unpaginated following p. 29 (for Poullain's marginal note) (in Burnet, v. 375); *Greyfriars Chron.*, pp. 82–83; Machyn, pp. 39–40; Wriothesley, ii. 96–97; Foxe, vi. 537; 'A note of the Kyng's funerall', 8 August 1553 (Record Office, S.P. 1/11, f. 10–13).

together. In this letter, he also mentioned his concern that Cheke had been indicted for treason.[1]

At the end of August, the authorities decided to legalize the return to office of Bonner, who for the previous three weeks had been acting as if he were Bishop of London. Notices were duly served on Cranmer and the other Commissioners who had deprived Bonner to appear at St. Paul's on 27th August before the Commissioners who had been appointed to deal with the matter; but apart from this summons to the respondents, there was hardly even a pretence of a judicial process. The Queen's commission to the Commissioners ordered them to invalidate the illegal deprivation of Bonner and to reinstate him as Bishop of London in Ridley's place, as the Commissioners had merely to pronounce sentence in an issue which had already been prejudged as notorious. Cranmer appeared by proxy, and evidently submitted without resistance to the Commissioners' inevitable decree.[2]

The government was still in some doubt as to how to deal with Cranmer. Mary had proclaimed a policy of religious toleration; but she had already begun to arrest reformers, and by the beginning of September the Council had imprisoned Bradford, Becon and Hooper, had confined Rogers under house arrest, and had summoned Coverdale, Saunders and Latimer to appear before them. None of these reformers had given any support to Jane, and they were imprisoned solely for their religious beliefs, though different pretexts were found in each case. But Cranmer was still free. Foxe later wrote that he had heard that Heath had said that the Council had decided to dismiss Cranmer from his archbishopric, and permit him to retire on a pension, provided that he remained confined to his house and made no public statement about religion. If this is true—and Foxe does not vouch for its truth—there must have been disagreement in the government as to whether Cranmer's submissive attitude had earned him the right to be treated leniently; for Bonner was not so ready as Heath to forgive the man who

[1] Cranmer to Cecil, 14 August 1553 (Cranmer's *Works*, ii. 441–2); Anon. Biogr. (*Nar. Ref.*, pp. 226–7); Foxe, viii. 37; Strype, *Cranmer*, p. 439. Mary moved from the Tower to Richmond on 12 August, but the Council remained at the Tower (Wriothesley, ii. 97; Acts of the Privy Council, 13, 14 and 16 August 1553).
[2] Commission of 22 August 1553 (*Cal. Pat. Rolls, Ph & Mary*, i. 74–75); Strype, *Eccl. Mem.* iii [i]. 35–36; *Greyfriars Chron.*, p. 83.

had committed them both to prison. Bonner seems to have conducted some kind of inquiry into the case of the Protestant leaders, and to have had discussions with them. On 1st September, a man in London mentioned in a letter that Cranmer, Hooper and Lever had been engaged in lengthy talks with Bonner at their houses. On the day that this letter was written, Hooper was sent to the Fleet; and on 6th September, Bonner wrote to his steward: 'This day is looked that Master Canterbury must be placed where is meet for him; he is become very humble and ready to submit himself in all things, but that will not serve'. But Cranmer remained at liberty.[1]

Cranmer's freedom from arrest, combined with his presence at the celebration banquet at the Guildhall and at Edward's funeral and his visit to Court, would be sufficient, even without the humility and readiness to submit to which Bonner referred, to account for the rumour which spread among the people. It was rumoured that Cranmer had offered to say mass at Edward's funeral, and before the Queen in St. Paul's, and that it was on Cranmer's instructions that Thornden, his Suffragan Bishop of Dover—a former monk who owed his subsequent preferments to Cranmer—had celebrated mass in Canterbury Cathedral. Cranmer was incensed, and decided to make a public statement against the mass. He wrote out a declaration in which he did not mince his words. He stated that the allegations that he had offered to say mass at the funeral and before the Queen were lies spread by Satan, Christ's adversary, in order to overthrow the Lord's holy supper and restore his Latin satisfactory mass which he—Satan himself—had invented. He wrote that the mass had been set up in Canterbury by 'a false, flattering and lying monk', without his advice, and issued a challenge to his opponents: if the Queen would consent, he and Peter Martyr and four or five others whom he would choose would dispute with their opponents, not only on the merits of the Book of Common Prayer, but also that the doctrine in force in England under Edward VI was purer than any that had been known for a thousand years. He decided to attach his archiepiscopal seal to the declaration

---

[1] Acts of the Privy Council, 22, 29 and 31 August, and 1, 2 and 4 September 1553; Foxe, vi. 392–3; viii. 38; Dalby's letter, 1 September 1553 (Harleian MS. No. 353, f. 143); Bonner to Shirley and others, 6 September 1553 (Burnet, v. 373).

and to affix it to the door of St. Paul's and to every church door in London.[1]

Thus Cranmer not only took a step which sealed his fate at the very moment when it rested in the balance, but stretched to its extreme limits the doctrine of Christian obedience. He did not go beyond the limit, for there was nothing illegal in his action. It was not yet illegal to criticize the mass; on the contrary, the mass itself was still illegal, though the Queen was refusing to enforce the law which suppressed it, and was punishing any magistrate who did so. Nor had Cranmer violated the Queen's proclamation of 18th August, which prohibited all preaching and made it an offence to call anyone a heretic or a Papist.[2] Cranmer was merely offering to defend the established service and doctrines of the Church of England, and this only provided that the Queen gave her consent; and he used words of censure only of an institution which was condemned by law and of a Suffragan who had broken the law. Yet his plan of publicly displaying his declaration on the doors of the churches could easily be interpreted as seditious by his opponents. It was an action which Cranmer himself might well have denounced as seditious a few years before, for it was in effect an appeal to the people against the policy which the Queen was intending to pursue. Events had led Henry VIII's Archbishop, at the age of 64, to take one short step in the direction in which the younger generation was moving. Two years later, Ponet and Knox would issue a call for revolution.

Cranmer did not immediately publish his declaration, and obviously could not do so before consulting Martyr. Martyr had been imprisoned in his house at Oxford—where the University had given vent to all its Papist enthusiasm since Mary's accession—and was petitioning the Council to be allowed to leave the country, or at least to be permitted to come to London to petition for this in person. Cranmer had offered to stand bail for Martyr if he were allowed to come to London; but though

[1] Foxe, vi. 539; viii. 37–38; Scheyvfe, Renard and others to Charles V, 4 and 19 September 1553 (*Span. Cal.* xi, p. 198; Gachard, *Voyages des Souverains des Pays-Bas*, iv. 126); Anon. Biogr. (*Nar. Ref.*, p. 227); Peter Martyr to Bullinger, 3 November 1553 (*Orig. Letters*, p. 505). For Cranmer's *Declaration against the Mass*, see Cranmer's *Works*, i. 428–9; and cf. the version (from Poullain) in Burnet, v. 374–7.
[2] Mary I's proclamation of 18 August 1553 (Foxe, vi. 390–1); Acts of the Privy Council, 13 August 1553.

Martyr's friends had spent two days waiting in the Council ante-room at the appointed time, they had been sent away without being seen or given any information. While Cranmer was awaiting Martyr's arrival, he was visited by Scory, who had been ousted from his bishopric of Chichester when Day's deprivation had been set aside as illegal. Scory saw Cranmer's declaration against the mass lying on the window sill, and after reading it, he asked and obtained permission from Cranmer to take a copy of it. Scory then arranged for hundreds of copies to be made, and within a few days Cranmer's declaration was on sale in every scrivener's shop in London. Cranmer later told the Council that he had not authorized Scory to publish the statement.[1] Both these men were cowardly in turn at the expense of the other. In 1543, Cranmer imprisoned Scory for preaching a sermon against the Real Presence at a time when Cranmer was eagerly participating in the persecution of heretics; in 1553, Scory took heroic action which led to Cranmer's ruin, and then saved himself by a recantation while Cranmer went to a dreadful death because of what Scory had done. It would be wrong, however, to hold Scory solely responsible for Cranmer's fate, or to give him the sole credit for Cranmer's courageous action; for if Cranmer had carried out his intention of fixing the declaration to the doors of the churches, the consequences would have been the same.

Soon afterwards—within a day or two at the most—Peter Martyr arrived at Lambeth, having at last obtained permission to leave Oxford, and was warmly welcomed by Cranmer. Martyr was pleased to learn about Cranmer's declaration on the mass, with its challenge to their opponents to dispute, as he himself had been contemplating issuing such a challenge. He stayed with Cranmer at Lambeth while they discussed the arguments which they would put forward in the disputation. But Cranmer was expecting the worst, and had already paid all his creditors in order to prevent them from suffering loss through the forfeiture of his goods if he were attainted of treason.[2]

Cranmer was summoned to come before the Council at

[1] Terentianus to Ulmis, 20 November 1553 (Fuessli, pp. 313–4; *Orig. Letters*, pp. 369–71); Foxe, viii. 38
[2] Terentianus to Ulmis, 20 November 1553 (Fuessli, pp. 314–5; *Orig. Letters*, pp. 369–71); Foxe, vi. 393; viii. 19–20, 44.

Westminster on 13th September. Latimer appeared before the Council on the same day, and was sent to the Tower. According to Foxe, the Council began by asking Cranmer about the inventory of his goods which he had been ordered to prepare with a view to his being granted a pension; but they soon turned to the declaration against the mass, and said that it was seditious. Foxe states that Heath attempted to help Cranmer by suggesting that he must be sorry that such a statement had been published in his name, and this may be so, though according to the Council minutes Heath was not present at the meeting. But Cranmer would not repudiate his declaration. He said that he had written the statement, and that though he regretted that Scory had published it, this was only because he had wished to enlarge it before affixing it to the doors of the churches. They let him go, and told him to come again next day in the afternoon.[1]

Cranmer returned to Lambeth and dined with Martyr and the members of his household. He gave them no indication as to what had occurred; but after dinner, he invited Martyr to his private chamber, and told him everything, explaining that it was now certain that he would be arrested and brought to trial, and would never see Martyr again. He advised Martyr to try to leave the country illegally without a passport if the Council did not grant him one without delay, for he was sure that Martyr would be in great danger if he remained in England, and could not hope for any justice. Martyr obtained his passport, and reached Strasburg in safety. Cranmer sent his wife—and probably his children too—to Germany, as he had done in 1539; they went secretly and illegally. He made no attempt to escape himself, for though a year or so later he was urging the rank and file of the Protestants to fly, he thought in September 1553 that if he fled himself he would be accused of betraying the cause, and would demoralize the reformers. He thought that he could do far more as a martyr in England than as a refugee abroad. Next day, in the afternoon of 14th September, he appeared again before the Council in the Star Chamber, where he found several of his old friends and enemies. Gardiner was presiding, and Tunstall and Norfolk were present, along with Paulet, Paget

---

[1] Acts of the Privy Council, 13 September 1553; Foxe, vi. 394; viii. 38. Heath had been appointed a member of the Privy Council on 4 September (see Acts of the Privy Council, 4 September 1553).

and Petre, who had served on Jane's Council, and Cranmer's old collaborator Rich. They told him that his action in circulating seditious bills had revived the guilt of his treason in supporting Jane, and after a long discussion he was sent to the Tower.[1]

He remained a prisoner for two months, confined in the tower next to the watergate, which was later known as the Bloody Tower, where Northumberland had been imprisoned until his execution four weeks before. Meanwhile the government had decided to make Cranmer the scapegoat for all the disasters of the last twenty years. By issuing his declaration against the mass, Cranmer had tipped the scales against those of the Queen's advisers who were urging her to show mercy to him; he had shown, as a man in London wrote to a friend, that 'the Bishop of Canterbury is the old man he was.' Bonner and Mary could now indulge their hatred of Cranmer to the full. The Lords of the Council who had signed Edward's devise and denounced Mary as a bastard were forgiven as completely as were Gardiner and Bonner and the other men who had worked for the overthrow of Papal supremacy and the divorce of Mary's mother; Cranmer alone was to be held responsible for these evils.[2]

At the beginning of October, Mary's first Parliament met, and with great enthusiasm voted support for Mary's policy. They passed a statute which invalidated Cranmer's sentence of divorce at Dunstable, after reciting that that most excellent Prince of most worthy memory King Henry VIII had been induced to seek a divorce from Queen Catherine, to whom he was lawfully married. God had given that marriage 'godly fruit (your Highness' most noble person)'; but 'Thomas Cranmer, then newly made Archbishop of Canterbury, most ungodly and against all laws, equity and conscience prosecuting the said wicked devise of divorce. . . . and taking his foundation partly upon his own unadvised judgment of the Scripture' and the pretended judgment of the said Universities, 'and partly upon bare and most untrue conjectures gathered and admitted by him upon matters of no strength or effect', without admitting or hearing

[1] Terentianus to Ulmis, 20 November 1553; Peter Martyr to Bullinger, 3 November 1553 (Fuessli, p. 315; *Orig. Letters*, pp. 371–2, 505–6); Parker, pp. 400–1; Acts of the Privy Council, 14 September 1553; Foxe, vi. 394; Wriothesley, ii. 103; *Greyfriars Chron.*, p. 84; Stow's MS., (*Chron. of Queen Jane*, p. 27).

[2] Stow's MS., ibid. (p. 27); letter from London, 8 September 1553 (Harleian MS. No. 353, f. 143).

anything that could be said on Catherine's behalf, gave sentence of divorce 'by unlawful and corrupt means and ways'.[1]

At the end of October, a great disputation on the Real Presence was held in Convocation. The reformers felt that they were at a great disadvantage because their leaders were in prison, and they asked that Ridley and Rogers and some others should be brought from custody and allowed to take part in the disputation. They did not apparently suggest that Cranmer should come, although the Archbishop of Canterbury—the author of the two great books on the Eucharist—was by far their most eminent leader. They probably did not dare to ask for Cranmer, in view of the intensity of the official propaganda against him. The authorities did not allow any of the imprisoned men to take part, and the doctrine of the Real Presence was approved by the whole of Convocation except for six reformers in the Lower House.[2]

On 13th November, Cranmer was brought to trial on a charge of high treason, along with Lady Jane and her husband Guilford Dudley, and Dudley's two brothers Ambrose and Henry. They were taken from the Tower to the Guildhall on foot in procession, led by a man carrying the axe aloft, with Cranmer coming next, followed by Guilford Dudley, and then by Jane dressed all in black, with Ambrose and Henry Dudley at the rear. At the Guildhall, they were tried before a special Commission consisting of Norfolk and other peers as well as the common law Judges. Cranmer was charged with high treason on two counts: the first, that on 10th July he entered the Tower of London with other traitors and there proclaimed Lady Jane Dudley to be Queen; the second, that when the Duke of Northumberland was levying war against the Queen at Cambridge, he and other traitors sent more than twenty men in arms as reinforcements for Northumberland. It probably caused considerable surprise when Cranmer pleaded not guilty, for Northumberland and his accomplices had all pleaded guilty at their trial in August. A Middlesex jury was impanelled and presented with evidence of Cranmer's treason. Cranmer argued that he was not guilty because he had acted in obedience to King Edward's orders; but this argument did not impress the common

[1] 1 Mary st. 2, c. 1; *H. C. Jo.*, 26, 27 and 28 October 1553.
[2] Report of the Disputation in Convocation, October 1553 (Foxe, vi. 396).

law Judges on the tribunal, and Chief Justice Morgan told him that no one, not even the King himself, could authorize a man to break the law. After the jury had retired, Cranmer withdrew his plea of not guilty and pleaded guilty before the jury had returned their verdict. If Mary was the lawful Queen, Cranmer was undoubtedly guilty in law; but two years later, at his trial for heresy, he said that he thought that he had admitted too much at his trial for treason. Jane and the Dudleys were then arraigned, and all immediately pleaded guilty, and the whole proceedings were concluded in a few hours. Morgan pronounced the sentence required by law on all the five defendants—Cranmer and the men to be hanged, drawn and quartered at Tyburn, and Jane to be burned or beheaded at the Queen's pleasure.[1]

The traitors were taken back to the Tower to await execution. There was considerable speculation as to whether the sentences would be carried out, for Mary was pursuing a lenient policy. On the day after the trial, Noailles, the French Ambassador, thought that all the five traitors would be executed; but the Emperor's Ambassador Renard reported that Jane would be pardoned, and that Cranmer would suffer. This seems to have been the general opinion. Ever since Cranmer's arrest, the people had expected that he would be put to death, which is not surprising in view of the vitriolic denunciations which the authorities were launching against him. Peter Martyr in Strasburg seems to have thought in December that whereas the Dudleys' sentence would be commuted to beheading, the full cruel sentence of hanging, drawing and quartering would be carried out on Cranmer. A Lasco at Emden had heard a rumour that Cranmer had actually been put to death on 8th December, and that a riot had only been averted because Cranmer had appealed to the people to be patient and obedient as he was led through the streets on his way to the place of execution.[2]

[1] Stow's MS. (*Chron. of Queen Jane*, p. 32); Wriothesley, ii. 104; Machyn, p. 48; *Greyfriars Chron.*, p. 85; Foxe, vi. 413; Report of Cranmer's trial (in 4th Rep. of Deputy-Keeper of Records, App. ii. 237–8); Ponet, *Short Treatise of Politic Power*, p. 62; Grafton, *Chronicle*, ii. 536, 538.
[2] Noailles to Henry II (22 September) and 14 November 1553 (*Ambassades de Noailles*, ii. 161–2, 256–7); Renard to Charles V, 14 and 17 November 1553 (Gachard, *Voyages des Souverains des Pays-Bas*, iv. 204, 209); Peter Martyr to Calvin, 3 November 1553; à Lasco to Hardenberg, 12 December 1553 (Peter Martyr, *Loci Communes*, pp. 1091–2; Gerdes, *Scrinium Antiquarium*, i–ii. 695; Gorham, *Gleanings*, pp. 305–7); Peter Martyr to Bullinger, 15 December 1553 (*Orig. Letters*, pp. 507–8).

For at least a month after the trial—apart from the two months before it—Cranmer was confined to a cell, without air or exercise, expecting shortly to be hanged, cut down while still alive, disembowelled and finally killed by beheading after his limbs had been amputated. He was not being called upon to suffer this agony as a martyr for the truth of the Gospel, but as a punishment for the crime of treason—the crime which Cranmer abhorred more than any other, and of which he had been forced to confess himself guilty. At the beginning of December, Cranmer was declared to be a traitor by Parliament in an Act of Attainder which confirmed the judicial convictions of Cranmer and Jane and of Northumberland and the other traitors.[1] It was after this statute was passed that Cranmer wrote to Mary beseeching her pardon. After twenty years in high politics, Cranmer knew the manner in which traitors in the Tower were expected to write to their Sovereign, and he began in the appropriate style.

'Most lamentably mourning and moaning himself unto your Highness, Thomas Cranmer, although unworthy either to write or speak unto your Highness, yet having no person that I know to be mediator for me, and knowing your pitiful ears ready to hear all pitiful complaints, and seeing so many before to have felt your abundant clemency in like case, am now constrained most lamentably, and with most penitent and sorrowful heart, to ask mercy and pardon for my heinous folly and offence in consenting and following the testament and last will of our late Sovereign Lord King Edward VI, your Grace's brother.' He then explained how he had been induced to sign the devise, after he had failed to persuade Edward to abandon the project, and added that when he finally signed, he did so unfeignedly and without dissimulation. The fact that Cranmer mentioned this, instead of claiming, like Cecil and all the other Councillors, that he had only signed in order to trick Northumberland, suggests that Cranmer was speaking the truth in the letter, as does the fact that he made no attempt to throw all the blame on the dead Northumberland, which was both the official line and the excuse of all the other members of Jane's Council. Cranmer wrote to Mary that the Act of Parliament which blamed him and Northumberland for conspiring against her was false, not only

[1] 1 Mary, st. 2, c. 16; *H. C. Jo.*, 27 and 28 November and 4 December 1553.

because Northumberland had been seeking his destruction for some time, and would never have trusted him as a fellow conspirator, but also because he had never had any private talk with Northumberland about the devise. It was Edward himself who had persuaded him to sign when Northumberland was not present; and in another passage, he named Northampton and Darcy, who were both now members of Mary's Council, as having been present at his interview with the King, implying that it was they who had urged him to sign and who had persuaded the King to adhere to his plan for the devise.

Then Cranmer passed to the question of religion, and made a lucid summary for Mary's benefit of the doctrine of Christian obedience. 'Now as concerning the estate of religion, as it is used in this realm of England at this present, if it please your Highness to license me I would gladly write my mind unto your Majesty. I will never, God willing, be author of sedition, to move subjects from the obedience of their heads and rulers; which is an offence most detestable. If I have uttered my mind to your Majesty, being a Christian Queen and governor of this realm (of whom I am most assuredly persuaded, that your gracious intent is, above all other regards, to prefer God's true word, His honour and glory) if I have uttered, I say, my mind unto your Majesty, then I shall think myself discharged. For it lieth not in me, but in your Grace only, to see the reformation of things that be amiss. To private subjects it apperaineth not to reform things, but quietly to suffer that they cannot amend. Yet nevertheless to show your Majesty my mind in things pertaining unto God, methink it my duty, knowing that I do, and considering the place which in times past I have occupied. Yet will I not presume thereunto without your Grace's pleasure first known and your license obtained; whereof I most humbly prostrate to the ground do beseech your Majesty'.[1] Cranmer had reverted to the doctrine of Christian obedience in all its purity, after having come so close to abandoning it at the time of his declaration against the mass.

On 17th December, the Council ordered that Cranmer, Lady Jane and the Dudleys were to be permitted to walk in the garden of the Tower because the lack of fresh air in their prisons was causing injury to their health. To be granted the liberty of

[1] Cranmer to Mary I, (December 1553) (Cranmer's *Works*, ii. 442–4).

the Tower was not only a privilege, but a mark of favour, and an indication that they would be treated leniently. It soon became known that Cranmer was not to be executed for treason, but would be allowed to suffer as a heretic. Mary had rejected the advice which Charles V had given her to proceed against her enemies for treason, for she would not punish men for treason against herself when they had been guilty of the far more heinous offence of heresy against God. We can well believe Foxe's statement that Cranmer was profoundly happy when he heard of her decision. Cranmer was to be granted the public disputation which he had asked for—on his opponents' terms and conditions. The people were saying that the reformers had been worsted in the disputation in Convocation in October 1553 because they had not been represented by their most learned men; and the authorities therefore decided to hold another disputation in which Cranmer and Ridley, the reformers' foremost champions, should be utterly discredited. It was decided to hold the disputation at Oxford, as a reward to the University for the orthodox loyalty which it had shown throughout Edward's reign.[1]

At the end of January 1554, the men of Kent rose in arms under Sir Thomas Wyatt. They marched on London, and occupied Southwark, where they were well within range of the cannon in the Tower. The rebels claimed that they had risen to prevent the marriage of Mary to Philip of Spain; but in fact it was a rebellion of heretics from the dioceses of Canterbury and Rochester, from the county where the extremist sects had been troubling Cranmer a year before. Ponet was with them, while the Duke of Suffolk tried to raise a revolt in the Midlands. But though Wyatt's victory was the only political development which could save Cranmer from Tyburn or the stake, we may be sure that during these critical days Cranmer was praying for the defeat of the rebellion. He would strongly have approved of the conduct of those zealous Protestants who took up arms to fight for Mary, for this was a popular rebellion which could not be excused by any argument such as those which had been put forward in the previous summer by the supporters of Edward's devise to Jane Grey. Cranmer must have been deeply apprehensive at the prospect that at the moment when he was expecting to have the opportunity of suffering martyrdom for religion, he

[1] Acts of the Privy Council, 17 December 1553; Foxe, vi. 413; viii. 38.

might be set free by the sinful act of misguided reformers who were disgracing the true religion in which they professed to believe.

But by the beginning of February the revolt had been defeated. Many rebels were being brought as prisoners to the Tower, while the officers of the garrison stood at the watergate immediately below Cranmer's prison insulting and manhandling them as they entered. Before the end of the month, Elizabeth had been sent to the Tower, and Jane Grey and her husband, along with Suffolk, had been beheaded. With so many new prisoners arriving at the Tower, it was no longer possible to keep the prisoners in separate dungeons, and in the middle of February Cranmer was put in the same cell together with Ridley, Latimer and Bradford. Bradford had been arrested in August 1553 for being involved in the Protestant riot against Bourn's sermon at Paul's Cross, though in fact it was he and the reformer Rogers who had appeased the riot and saved Bourn's life. During the next eighteen months, Bradford was to assume the leadership of the Protestants in the prisons, and do more for his cause than he had ever been able to do when he was at liberty. The four men read the New Testament together, and discussed the texts which they would cite against the Real Presence in the forthcoming disputation.[1]

Cranmer probably benefited greatly from being forced to share a cell with Ridley, Latimer and Bradford. His three companions were in a fighting spirit, and though they all believed in the duty of Christian obedience, they do not seem to have been inhibited by the doctrine in their resistance to persecution to the same extent as Cranmer. Cranmer had been through a greater ordeal than the others in the previous five months, for he alone had been sentenced to death for a crime of which he was ashamed. The revival of his morale in the next few weeks was probably due to the encouragement which he derived from the dogged determination of Latimer, the intellectual confidence of Ridley and the intolerant piety of Bradford.

[1] Stow's MS. (*Chron. of Queen Jane*, pp. 51–52); Ridley to Grindal (June 1555) (Ridley's *Works*, p. 390); Latimer's protestation, 20 April 1554 (Strype, *Eccl. Mem.* iii [ii]. 292–3); Foxe, viii. 593.

CHAPTER XXIII

THE HERETIC

ON 12th March 1554, Cranmer, Ridley and Latimer left the Tower on their journey to Oxford. It was widely believed both in England and abroad that Hooper had accompanied them; but Hooper was not selected to take part in the disputation, probably because his presence was required in London in connexion with the proceedings to deprive him of his bishopric. Cranmer and his companions were taken to Brentford, where they were handed over to Sir John Williams, the Sheriff of Oxfordshire, who two years before had been sent to the Fleet by Cranmer and the Council for irregularities in his handling of government funds. From Brentford they were taken to Oxford, and imprisoned in the common jail of Bocardo—probably in separate cells—where they were held for a month before the disputation. At first they were allowed to walk together on the roof of the prison, which was part of the parapet on the northern wall of Oxford; but this was soon forbidden, after there had been complaints that they were able to get into contact with the people there.[1]

The disputation was arranged in a manner which was grossly unfair to Cranmer, Ridley and Latimer. They suffered from a lack of books, having only been allowed to bring with them from the Tower as much as they could carry on their horses, and though they were provided with books to enable them to prepare for the disputation, they only had possession of the books for a few days. Each reformer was forced to argue against thirty-three opponents, consisting of the most learned divines of

[1] Acts of the Privy Council, 8 April 1552 and 8 March 1553/4; Stow's MS. (*Chron. of Queen Jane*, p. 68); Machyn, p. 57; Lever to Bullinger, 11 April 1554; Peter Martyr to Bullinger, 3 April 1554 (*Orig. Letters*, pp. 154, 515); Renard to Charles V, 9 March 1554 (*Span. Cal.* xii, p. 146); Ridley to Bradford (April 1554); Ridley to Grindal (June 1555) (Ridley's *Works*, pp. 359–60, 390); Foxe, vi. 439. Foxe is certainly wrong in giving the date of the departure of Cranmer, Ridley and Latimer from the Tower as 10 April. Machyn says it was 8 March; but the Council's order for their removal was only given on 8 March. Renard, writing on 9 March, says that they left on that day; but as the writer of the MS. which Stow used was obviously stationed in the Tower, the date which he gives—Monday 12 March—is probably correct, the departure being for some reason delayed for three days after the 9, when Renard had expected it.

Convocation and the two Universities, to say nothing of nearly a thousand ardent Papists demonstrating their hostility in the audience. The rules of disputation were violated, for while Cranmer, Ridley and Latimer had each to act as respondents and defend their thesis from the criticism of their opponents,they were deprived of the opportunity of opposing in their turn while their opponents acted as respondents. They were under an even greater disadvantage in that, although they had nothing to gain except an intellectual victory, it was generally understood that if they were condemned as wrong they would be burned as heretics.[1]

On 13th April, while their opponents were participating in the formalities and banquets which preceded the disputation, Ridley and Latimer were removed from Bocardo to the houses of the town officials in Oxford; but Cranmer remained in the jail. On Saturday the 14th, the three Protestant leaders were brought in turn before the Commissioners in St. Mary's Church. Cranmer was respectful and humble, and appeared completely composed; he refused an offer of a stool, and stood leaning on his staff throughout the proceedings. He was now for the first time given the precise terms of the three questions to be debated —the Real Presence, transubstantiation and the mass as a sacrifice—and was ordered to submit a written statement of his beliefs. Two days later, on the Monday, Cranmer began the disputation in the Divinity Schools, standing from about half past eight in the morning till nearly two o'clock in the afternoon confronting the Commissioners and disputants and the Prolocutor Weston. Weston, who had achieved a great success as Prolocutor in the disputation in Convocation in October, was to ruin his career a few years later by his lewd conduct with women; and he now indulged his sensual appetite by arranging for himself and the disputants to be supplied with beer throughout the disputation. He offered some drink to Cranmer, who refused with thanks. Cranmer also refused Weston's offer of an interval of half an hour during the six-hour disputation, though he was continually engaged in argument while his opponents rested in turn. The disputation was conducted throughout in Latin; but this at least was no disadvantage to Cranmer.

When the proceedings opened, Weston announced the purpose

[1] Foxe, vi. 441-3; Ridley to Grindal (June 1555) (Rjdley's *Works*, p. 390).

for which they had assembled. 'You are assembled today, my brethren, to overthrow that detestable heresy of the truth of the body of Christ in the Sacrament.' This was a slip of the tongue, which was immediately submerged in the laughter of a confident and carefree audience; what was more significant, though it caused no laughter nor any comment from anyone except Cranmer, was the frank admission that they had met to confound a doctrine which they had already dubbed as heresy, and not impartially to ascertain the truth. Cranmer did not weaken in his arguments with Weston, with his old adversary Richard Smith, with Cole and the other disputants, but held his own despite the jeers of the Oxford audience. He made a favourable impression on at least one observer; but the argument did not reach a very high level, as both sides did little more than reassert their position. Cranmer did not put his case as strongly as he had done in his books on the Eucharist. He refused to admit that he opposed the Real Presence, and said that the Presence was real, though Christ was not present in a natural and organic body; but when his opponents stated that by the Real Presence they meant that Christ was present in the flesh that He took from the Virgin, Cranmer unequivocally denied it, and adhered to his opinion: 'His true body is truly present to them that truly receive Him, but spiritually.' Eventually Weston closed the disputation by proclaiming his slogan of *Vicit Veritas* which he had launched in Convocation in October.[1]

Cranmer was led back to Bocardo. Next day, it was the turn of Ridley, who put his case much more forcibly than Cranmer and was subjected to loud abuse from Weston and the audience. They became almost as angry on the Wednesday, when Latimer admitted his weakness in disputation but refused to accept the Real Presence. The proceedings were then adjourned until the Friday. On the Thursday John Harpsfield, who was one of the disputants arguing against the three heretics in the disputation, took his examination for his degree as Doctor of Divinity. The examination consisted of Harpsfield maintaining the truth of the Real Presence as respondent in a disputation; and though

[1] For the disputation, see the report in Foxe, vi. 439–69 (the passages cited are on pp. 444, 445 and 468), and in Cranmer's *Works*, i. 393–423; Cranmer to the Council, 23 April 1554 (Cranmer's *Works*, ii. 445–6); Anon. Biogr. (*Nar. Ref*,. p. 228); and see the anonymous account published in Foxe's first edition (Foxe, vi. App. Document iii; 1st ed., pp. 932–5).

Weston himself argued the case against the Real Presence in order to test Harpsfield's ability, it was decided to bring Cranmer from prison to dispute against Harpsfield. As the object of the disputation was to test Harpsfield, and not to make public propaganda against sacramentaries, Cranmer was allowed to develop his arguments without interruption. He appears to have argued with greater ability than he had shown in the disputation on the Monday, and one Oxford scholar who heard him was deeply impressed by his skill. Cranmer even ventured to raise the pertinent but provocative question as to how long Christ's body was alleged to remain in the bread as it passed through the body of the eater; but this, which would have aroused a storm of indignation if he had put it forward on the Monday, now evoked only a mild protest from Harpsfield. After Weston had argued on Cranmer's side against Harpsfield, he thanked Cranmer for his kindness in assisting them and for his courtesy and ability in argument; and all those present saluted Cranmer by raising their caps to him. Then Cranmer returned to Bocardo, while Weston made a declaration that he had only opposed the doctrine of the Real Presence for the sake of argument.[1]

Next day the grimmer proceedings were resumed. On Friday, 20th April, Cranmer, Ridley and Latimer were brought in turn before Weston and the Commissioners in St. Mary's Church. They were not allowed to argue, but were told that they had been proved wrong in the disputation and were now offered an opportunity of recanting and expressing their belief in the Real Presence. They each in turn refused, Cranmer protesting that he had not been able to do himself justice in the disputation, because having to argue against four or five persons at once, and with the interruptions of the audience, he could only have stated his case by shouting down his opponents. Then the three heretics were all brought back together, and Weston read the sentence of condemnation, after giving them one more opportunity to recant. They were told that they were condemned as heretics and were no members of the Church. They each made a short statement which showed that they were all expecting death in the near future. Cranmer said: 'From this your

[1] Reports of the Disputations (Foxe, vi. 470–520, especially pp. 516–8, 520; vi. App. Document iii; also in Cranmer's *Works*, i. 423–7).

judgment and sentence, I appeal to the just judgment of God Almighty, trusting to be present with Him in Heaven, for whose Presence in the altar I am thus condemned.' Then he was taken back to Bocardo, while the authorities prepared to spread the news throughout England and Europe that Cranmer, Ridley and Latimer had stumbled and faltered in the disputation and had exposed themselves as ignorant and unlearned heretics.[1]

Next day the proceedings were completed with a procession through the streets of Oxford, in which Weston walked holding the Host in his hands while the people knelt and adored it. The three heretics were forced to watch the procession, which passed Bocardo and the house where Ridley was a prisoner, while Latimer was taken to Carfax to see it. Latimer ran into a shop and refused to look at the idolatrous worship; but there is no record that Cranmer made any gesture of protest as he watched, from the gate of the prison, the procession which symbolized the ruin of the Reformation. From henceforth the authorities would spare him nothing in the way of humiliation and mental suffering.[2]

On 23rd April, Cranmer wrote a letter to the Council, protesting against the unfair manner in which the disputation had been conducted. He gave the letter to Weston to carry with him when he returned to London. Foxe tells us that Weston opened it on the journey, read it, and refused to deliver it to the Council; but it is unlikely that even Weston would have ventured to break the seals of a letter written to the Council. Cranmer prefaced this letter with a short appeal for a pardon for his treason, reminding the Lords that some of them knew how unwillingly he had supported Edward's devise. But the brevity of this appeal suggests that it was inserted more or less as a formality, and Cranmer was obviously expecting to be executed as a heretic and not as a traitor. Everyone, both at home and abroad, was expecting him to be burned in the near future, and a bill had been introduced in Parliament to re-enact the statutes for burning heretics which had been repealed in 1547. But on 1st May, the bill was defeated in the House of Lords, thanks largely to the machinations of Paget, who was playing an involved political game for his own purposes with the aim of

[1] Foxe, vi. 533–4.
[2] Foxe, vi. 534.

supplanting Gardiner. This made it politically difficult for Mary to burn Cranmer, Ridley and Latimer, even though it had been decided in Joan Bocher's case that it was legal to burn an excommunicated heretic under the common law without relying on statutory powers; while there was also doubt as to whether Weston's sentence against Cranmer and his colleagues at Oxford amounted in law to a formal sentence of excommunication. On 3rd May, the Council asked the Judges and Queen's Counsel for legal advice as to the position of Cranmer, Ridley and Latimer who had been condemned as heretics by both the Universities, Cranmer having also been convicted of high treason. There is no record of the reply which the lawyers gave, but it was decided not to burn the Oxford heretics for the time being. Nor was there any intention of executing Cranmer as a traitor, though he was never pardoned, and his conviction for treason remained in force until it was set aside by statute in 1563.[1]

In the autumn of 1554, Mary at last felt able to acknowledge Papal supremacy and to reunite the realm with Rome. It was therefore decided that heretics should be tried in the Courts of the Papal Legate, and burned for denying Papal supremacy as well as for heresy against the Sacrament of the Altar. By December, Pole was ensconced in Lambeth Palace as Papal Legate, the realm was reunited with Rome, and a new Parliament had re-enacted the heresy statutes at the price of a Papal bull confirming the title of the purchasers of the former monastic lands. But though the burnings began in February 1555, Cranmer, Ridley and Latimer were kept alive throughout the summer of that dreadful year. In Cranmer's case, a specially elaborate procedure was necessary to excommunicate and degrade a man who had been consecrated Archbishop with the consent of the Pope. The see of Canterbury had been declared

---

[1] Cranmer to the Council, 23 April 1554 (Cranmer's *Works*, ii. 445–6); Foxe, vi. 535; *H. L. Jo.*, 1 May 1554; Renard to Charles V, 1 and 6 May 1554 (*Span. Cal.* xii, pp. 230–1, 238–40); Acts of the Privy Council, 3 May 1554; 5 Eliz., c. 45. For the general expectation that Cranmer, Ridley and Latimer would be burned immediately, see Lever to Bullinger, 11 April 1554; Peter Martyr to Bullinger, 3 April 1554; Bullinger to Calvin, 9 September 1554 (*Orig. Letters*, pp. 154, 515–6, 750); Peter Martyr to Calvin, 9 May 1554 (Peter Martyr, *Loci Communes*, p. 1092; Gorham, *Gleanings*, pp. 316–7); Renard to Charles V, 9 March 1554 (*Span. Cal.* xii, p. 146); Ridley to Cranmer (April 1554) (Ridley's *Works*, p. 363); Bradford, *Paraphrase of 79th Psalm* (Bradford's *Works*, i. 290). Latimer was expecting to be burned on 21 April 1554 (Foxe, vi. 534).

vacant in December 1553 after Cranmer's conviction for treason, and the diocese was being administered by Nicholas Harpsfield, the Archdeacon of Canterbury, while Bonner as Bishop of London was carrying out the duties of Metropolitan in the province.[1] But this was not effective in the eyes of the Pope and Pole to degrade Cranmer from the archiepiscopal rank which had been conferred upon him under the Pope's authority and from which only the Pope could deprive him. As Mary would not execute a priest until he had been degraded from his orders, she could not yet execute Cranmer. These various factors explain why Cranmer was not proceeded against until September 1555.

For seventeen months after the disputation of April 1554, Cranmer remained almost completely isolated in Bocardo. The reformers in the prisons and the refugees abroad regarded him with devotion as the Primate of the Church of England to whom they looked for guidance on all points of doctrine and conduct. Even the extremists had come to respect him, having convinced themselves that Cranmer had been intending to draft a third Book of Common Prayer which would have been much more radical than any of his previous liturgies. In the disputes among the English colony at Strasburg about the services in the Prayer Book, it was considered a powerful argument to state that the Archbishop of Canterbury approved of them. But Cranmer probably knew nothing of this, as he seems to have largely lost contact with his friends. He wrote very few letters from prison. At one time at least he was deprived of pen and paper, and we do not hear of him writing secret letters like Ridley with window leads or other primitive substitutes for a pencil. Immediately after the disputation in April 1554, Ridley wrote to Cranmer, urging him to obtain writing materials by bribing his servant; but apart from the problem of writing materials, there was the difficulty of communication. Ridley complained in his letter that his servant was unable to gain access to Cranmer, although the servant could see Latimer and Cranmer's servant was allowed to speak to Ridley.[2]

---

[1] 1 Ph. & Mary, c. 6, c. 8; Wharton, *Specimen of Errors in Burnet's History*, pp. 127–8.
[2] *The Troubles at Frankfort*, p. 50; Sampson to Calvin, 23 February 1555 (*Orig. Letters*, pp. 170–1); Cranmer to Mary I (September 1555) (Cranmer's *Works*, ii. 454); Foxe, viii. 35; Ridley to Cranmer and Latimer (April 1554) (Ridley's *Works*, p. 363).

Apart from a few letters which he wrote to the Queen and the authorities, only three letters written by Cranmer from Bocardo have been preserved. One was written after his trial to a lawyer in the University in connexion with his appeal to the General Council. Of the other two, one was a short letter to Peter Martyr, which according to Bullinger was written in 1555. Cranmer sent it to Martyr by an intermediary whom he did not identify in the letter, and wrote that as the intermediary was completely trustworthy, he had decided to send his information to Martyr verbally through the intermediary rather than risk putting it into writing in the letter. The other letter was written to the reformer Mrs. Wilkinson, urging her to fly from England to escape persecution, as Christ and Paul and others had fled before oppressors. Cranmer explained that if a Christian were captured and confronted with the choice of recantation or death, he must bravely face death, but that it was tempting God to seek martyrdom unnecessarily and to refuse to seek safety in flight. Foxe and the Protestant propagandists glorified the courage of Latimer and Hooper and other reformers who refused to flee from persecution; but Cranmer, though he had refused to flee himself, had never considered that flight was incompatible with Christian obedience, for he had urged Aless to flee in 1539, and now, along with Ridley, he was advocating flight as a general policy to be pursued whenever possible. Many Protestants had fled abroad, including Morice, who had escaped from prison, leaving some important correspondence between Cranmer and Edward VI and other valuable documents to be seized by the officers who searched his house and lost for ever to posterity.[1]

Foxe says that Cranmer sent a message and a token from Bocardo to the woman whom he had acquitted of the charge of adultery at Ashford in the winter of 1552–3; but we know of no other letters, and in his letter to Martyr, Cranmer stated that this was the only time that he had tried to write to anyone. Bradford wrote to Cranmer, as well as to Ridley and Latimer, to ask his advice about the bitter controversy which he was

[1] Cranmer to Mrs. Wilkinson (1554 or 1555); Cranmer to a lawyer (November 1555); Cranmer to Peter Martyr (1555) (Cranmer's *Works*, ii. 444–5, 455–8; Foxe, vi. 645; vii. 464; Aless to Elizabeth I, 1 September 1559 (*Cal. For. Pap., Eliz.*, i. 1303 (p. 533); Ridley, *Piteous Lamentation* (Ridley's *Works*, pp. 62–66); Morice to Day the printer, 10 January (probably about 1565) (Ellis, *Letters of Literary Men*, p. 25).

waging with his fellow-prisoners the Freewillers in the King's
Bench prison in London; but as far as we know, Ridley was the
only one of the three leaders in Oxford who replied to Bradford's
letters. Rowland Taylor and Saunders wrote from prison to
Cranmer, Ridley and Latimer, and Ridley wrote two letters to
Cranmer; but if Cranmer replied, his letters have not been preserved. It is possible that Cranmer never received any of these
letters, and in fact, if the messenger was unable to deliver them,
it is easier to understand why Coverdale was able to publish
them ten years later, and why we are able to read their contents
today.[1]

While Cranmer was in Bocardo, he attempted to pursue his
old controversy with Gardiner about the Eucharist by replying
to Gardiner's second book against him which had been published
under a pseudonym in Paris in 1552. Cranmer also studied in
Bocardo the book on the Eucharist which Tunstall had written
when he had been in prison. Soon after the disputation of April
1554, Cranmer asked to speak with Tunstall about the Eucharist;
but Tunstall refused to come. He was over 80, and felt too old
to travel from Durham to Oxford; and he was probably right in
thinking that Cranmer had asked to see him, not because Cranmer was thinking of recanting, but because he wished to convert
Tunstall. Cranmer was writing his reply to Gardiner under very
difficult conditions, and feared that he would be unable to
complete the book before he was burned. Two sections of the
book were apparently seized and destroyed by the authorities at
Oxford, and though the third section somehow reached Foxe's
hands, it was never published and was later lost. It was left to
Peter Martyr to pursue the controversy from Zurich on Cranmer's behalf. Cranmer also wrote a short treatise in which
he drew attention to eighteen places in Gardiner's writings
where Gardiner had formulated the case in favour of the Real
Presence in a different way from Smith and Tunstall, and thus
could be said to have disagreed with his two colleagues, and
sixteen places where Gardiner contradicted himself, or at least
appeared to do so. The reformers could console themselves, at
this grim moment, with the thought that they had discovered the

---

[1] Foxe, vi. 620–1; viii. 43, 100–1; Ferrar, Bradford and others to Cranmer,
Ridley and Latimer (January 1555) (Bradford's *Works*, ii. 169–71); Ridley to
Cranmer (April 1554); Ridley to Cranmer and Latimer (autumn 1554) (Ridley's
Works, pp. 361–3); Coverdale, *Letters of the Martyrs*.

inconsistencies of their opponents. Cranmer had the word, even though his adversaries had the sword.[1]

On 7th September 1555, Cranmer was served with notice to appear on a charge of heresy before the Pope's Commissioners, being informed that if dissatisfied he could appear in Rome before the Papal Court within eighty days.[2] The rank and file heretics were now being dealt with in the Court of their Ordinary under the old procedure of the canon law, while the leaders were tried before special Commissions appointed by Pole as Papal Legate. But a special procedure was adopted for Cranmer, who as a properly consecrated Archbishop and Metropolitan was theoretically to be tried by the Pope himself. Paul IV delegated the conduct of the trial to Cardinal de Puteo, and Puteo, from Rome, appointed Brooks, the Bishop of Gloucester, to act as judge. Cranmer was denounced before Brooks by Philip and Mary, who were represented by their proctors Martin and Story, on sixteen charges of blasphemy, incontinency, heresy and perjury, the principal accusations being his first marriage to Black Joan of the Dolphin, his second marriage while in holy orders, his perjury in his consecration oath, his disobedience to the Pope his superior, and his heresy as regards the Sacrament of the Altar.[3]

The trial began at eight o'clock in the morning of 12th September in St. Mary's Church in Oxford. Brooks sat on a high scaffold under the Sacrament, with Story and Martin on a lower level. When Cranmer entered, he refused to take off his cap to Brooks, as he did not recognize the authority of the Pope's Commissioner; but he took off his cap and knelt to Story and Martin because they represented the King and Queen. The proceedings

---

[1] *Bishop Cranmer's Recantacyons*, pp. 23–24; Cranmer, *Matters wherein the Bishop of Winchester varied from other Papists; Matters wherein the Bishop varied from himself*, etc. (in Cranmer's *Works*, i. 380–8, and in Foxe, vii. 597–602, who thought that Ridley wrote this treatise; but it is attributed to Cranmer in the 1580 edition of Cranmer's *Answer to Gardiner*, and this is more likely); Peter Martyr, *Defensio doctrinae veteris et Apostolicae de sacrosancto Eucharistiae Sacramento*; Cranmer to a lawyer (November 1555); Pole to Cranmer, 6 November 1555 (Cranmer's *Works*, ii. 455–6, 537); Foxe, viii. 35. The phrase 'You have the word and we have the sword' is attributed by Holinshed (iv. 9) to Weston in the disputation in Convocation in October 1553; but it does not appear in the transcript of the disputation which Foxe published.

[2] Cranmer to Mary I (September 1555) (Cranmer's *Works*, ii. 447).

[3] For the report of Cranmer's trial, see *Processus contra Thomam Cranmer*, and Foxe's report (Cranmer's *Works*, ii. 212–24, 541–62; Foxe, viii. 44–68); for the passages cited, see Foxe, viii. 54–57.

lasted two days. Several witnesses were called to give evidence that they knew or had heard say that Cranmer was guilty of the offences with which he was charged—witnesses who had returned to confront Cranmer with his past. There was Croke, who had worked so closely with him in Italy in 1530; Serles, the Canon of Canterbury, who already in 1543 had denounced Cranmer as a heretic; his literary antagonist Richard Smith; and other doctors who had argued against him in the disputation of the previous year.

To judge by the official report of the trial, Cranmer completely failed to do himself justice, and his answers during his examination by Martin were so unfortunate that Foxe later suggested that the report of the trial was not altogether accurate. Martin was very successful in exposing the contradictions in Cranmer's position. When Cranmer protested against the Papal encroachment on the royal authority and asserted the supremacy of the Prince in his realm, Martin pointed out that Cranmer had been convicted of treason against his Prince. When Cranmer said that he had sworn an oath to accept the royal supremacy and would be guilty of perjury if he broke that oath by admitting the Pope, Martin referred to the oath of obedience to the Pope which Cranmer had sworn at his consecration. When Cranmer adhered to his doctrine of the Lord's Supper, Martin reminded him that he had been responsible for burning Lambert, who had held the same opinion which Cranmer was now defending.

Martin's questions and Cranmer's answers read like a model cross-examination from an advocate's text-book, with Cranmer in the part of the wretched victim in the witness box.

'*Martin*. You say that you have sworn once to King Henry VIII against the Pope's jurisdiction, and therefore you may never forswear the same; and so ye make a great matter of conscience in the breach of the said oath. Here will I ask you a question or two. What if ye made an oath to a harlot, to live with her in continual adultery, ought you to keep it?

'*Cranmer*. I think no.

'*Martin*. What if you did swear never to lend a poor man one penny, ought you to keep it?

'*Cranmer*. I think not.

'*Martin*. Herod did swear whatsoever his harlot asked of

him he would give her, and he gave her John Baptist's head. Did he well in keeping his oath?

'*Cranmer*. I think not.

'*Martin*. Jephtha, one of the judges of Israel, did swear unto God that if he would give him victory over his enemies he would offer unto God the first soul that came forth of his house. It happened that his own daughter came first, and he slew her to save his oath. Did he well?

'*Cranmer*. I think not.

'*Martin*. So saith St. Ambrose, *De Officiis*: "It is a miserable necessity which is paid with parracide." Then, Master Cranmer, you can no less confess, by the premises, but that you ought not to have conscience of every oath, but if it be just, lawful and advisedly taken.

'*Cranmer*. So was that oath.

'*Martin*. That is not so. For first it was unjust, for it tended to the taking away of another man's right. It was not lawful, for the laws of God and the Church were against it. Besides, it was not voluntary; for every man and woman were compelled to take it.

'*Cranmer*. It pleaseth you to say so.

'*Martin*. Let all the world be judge. But, sir, you that pretend to have such a conscience to break an oath, I pray you, did you never swear, and break the same?

'*Cranmer*. I remember not.

'*Martin*. I will help your memory. Did you never swear obedience to the see of Rome?

'*Cranmer*. Indeed I did once swear unto the same.

'*Martin*. Yea, that you did twice, as appeareth by records and writings here ready to be showed.

'*Cranmer*. But I remember I saved all by protestation that I made by the counsel of the best learned men I could get at that time.

'*Martin*. Hearken, good people, what this man saith. He made a protestation one day to keep never a whit of that which he would swear the next day. Was this the part of a Christian man?'

And Martin went on to say that Cranmer 'letted not to make two solemn oaths quite contrary; and why? For otherwise, by the laws and canons of this realm, he could not aspire to the

Archbishopric of Canterbury.' When Cranmer said that never man came more unwillingly to a bishopric than he did, and referred to his delay on his journey home from Mantua, Martin remarked: 'What may we conjecture hereby, but that there was a compact between you, being then Queen Anne's chaplain, and the King: Give me the archbishopric of Canterbury, and I will give you licence to live in adultery.'

Martin was as effective on the question of the Real Presence.

'*Martin.* You, Master Cranmer, have taught in this high Sacrament of the Altar three contrary doctrines, and yet you pretended in every one *verbum Domini*.

'*Cranmer.* Nay, I taught but two contrary doctrines in the same.

'*Martin.* What doctrine taught you when you condemned Lambert the sacramentary in the King's presence in Whitehall?

'*Cranmer.* I maintained then the Papists' doctrine.

'*Martin.* That is to say, the catholic and universal doctrine of Christ's Church. And how when King Henry died? Did not you translate Justus Jonas' book?

'*Cranmer.* I did so.

'*Martin.* Then there you defended another doctrine touching the Sacrament, by the same token that you sent to Lynn your printer; that whereas in the first print there was an affirmative, that is to say, Christ's body really in the Sacrament, you sent then to your printer to put in a "not", whereby it came miraculously to pass that Christ's body was clean conveyed out of the Sacrament.

'*Cranmer.* I remember there were two prints of my said book; but where the same "not" was put in, I cannot tell.'

Martin had misrepresented the facts on this point. His statement was certainly untrue, because nowhere in the text of the Catechism is there a sentence whose meaning in expounding the nature of the Presence could be altered by the insertion of the word 'not'. But Cranmer was quite incapable of exposing Martin's falsehood; and even had he done so, it would only have proved that he had never tried to change those passages in the Catechism which so plainly asserted that the Presence was corporal. Martin therefore continued:

'*Martin.* Then from a Lutheran, ye became a Zwinglian, which is the vilest heresy of all in the high mystery of the Sacrament; and for the same heresy you did help to burn Lambert the sacramentary, which you now call the Catholic faith and God's word.

'*Cranmer*. I grant that then I believed otherwise than I do now; and so I did until my Lord of London, Dr. Ridley, did confer with me, and by sundry persuasions and authorities of doctors drew me quite from my opinion.

'*Martin*. Now sir, as touching the last part of your oration, you denied that the Pope's Holiness was Supreme Head of the Church of Christ.

'*Cranmer*. I did so.

'*Martin*. Who say you then is Supreme Head?

'*Cranmer*. Christ.

'*Martin*. But whom hath Christ left here in earth His vicar and head of His Church?

'*Cranmer*. Nobody.

'*Martin*. Ah! Why told you not King Henry this when you made him Supreme Head? And now nobody is! This is treason against his own person as you then made him.

'*Cranmer*. I mean not but every King in his own realm and dominion is Supreme Head, and so was he Supreme Head of the Church of Christ in England.

'*Martin*. Is this always true? And was it ever so in Christ's Church?

'*Cranmer*. It was so.

'*Martin*. Then what say you by Nero? He was the mightiest Prince of the earth after Christ was ascended. Was he head of Christ's Church?

'*Cranmer*. Nero was Peter's head.'

This evasive answer encouraged Martin to lay a trap for Cranmer, who fell straight into it.

'*Martin*. I ask whether Nero was head of the Church or no. If he were not, it is false that you said before, that all Princes be, and ever were, heads of the Church within their realms.

'*Cranmer*. Nay, it is true, for Nero was head of the Church, that is, in worldly respect of the temporal bodies of men, of whom the Church consisteth; for so he beheaded Peter and the Apostles. And the Turk too is head of the Church in Turkey.

'*Martin*. Then he that beheaded the heads of the Church, and crucified the Apostles, was head of Christ's Church; and he that was never member of the Church is head of the Church, by your new found understanding of God's word.'

It is not surprising that Foxe thought that the notary must have falsified Cranmer's answers on this point. Cranmer undoubtedly believed that though the duty of Christian obedience was owed to all Princes, whether Christian or pagan, it was only Christian Princes who were head of the Church in their realms. But though it is certainly possible, as Foxe suggests, that some further explanation or qualification which Cranmer made was not reported, the whole examination, as reported by the notary, shows that Cranmer had great difficulty in formulating his real opinion during this withering examination. It is unlikely that the whole report of the trial was an invention, for though there was no limit to the unscrupulousness of the authorities where Cranmer was concerned, the official reports of other trials do not distort the highly effective replies given by some of the reformers to their judges.

Foxe also gives a summary of a speech which Cranmer made to the Court on the subject of his appointment as Archbishop of Canterbury, which was not included in the official report, but was given to Foxe by someone who was present at the trial. According to this report, Cranmer said that after Warham died, Henry sent a message to him at Ratisbon to return home, and he was informed by his friends that he was being recalled in order to be made Archbishop. He did not desire the archbishopric, because he wished to pursue his studies and was reluctant to take his consecration oath to the Pope; and he consequently pretended that some very important matter had arisen at Ratisbon which made it imperative for him to remain there as Ambassador. He stayed at Charles's Court for another six months; but when Henry realized that this important matter had not developed, he sent another summons to Cranmer to return home, and Cranmer was obliged to go. This story was untrue. Cranmer did not dally for six months at Ratisbon, for he had reached London and had been appointed Archbishop within five months of Warham's death; and apart from this, there would have been no time for a courier to have been sent from London to Charles's Court, to return home with Cranmer's answer, and for a second messenger to have been sent, in the three months which elapsed between Warham's death and Cranmer's departure from

Mantua. Presumably the basis of truth in the story was the fact that Cromwell had been obliged to send a second messenger —Vaughan—to escort Cranmer through France after the original summons to return home had been sent to Cranmer by Hawkins; but Cranmer's account of the events of twenty-three years before was virtually a fabrication—if indeed Foxe's report of Cranmer's statement is accurate.

Cranmer succeeded, however, in exposing the weakness of certain aspects of his opponent's case. He pointed out that it was under Warham, before he became Archbishop, that the clergy first acknowledged the King to be Supreme Head of the Church of England, and that Brooks, who was sitting as the Pope's sub-delegate, had sworn the oath repudiating Papal supremacy in the days of Henry VIII. With regard to the charge that he had cohabited for many years with his second wife, at first secretly and later openly, and had had children by her, he admitted that this was true, but added that it was better for him to have his own wife than to be like other priests and have other men's wives. Then Martin reminded him that his children were bondmen of the see of Canterbury. This was a reference to the decree of the Synod of Pavia in 1018 that the children of married priests should become slaves of the Church and never be en-franchised;[1] but it had not been enforced for many years where the bastards of priests were concerned. Cranmer smiled, and asked whether, when some parish priest had children by a concubine, his bastards were to be made bondmen of his bene-fice; and he hoped that his own children would not be put in any worse a position than such bastards.

Brooks was not authorized to condemn and excommunicate Cranmer, for he was merely presiding at the trial on behalf of Cardinal de Puteo, and after the conclusion of the hearing he sent the transcript and the documents to Rome. No further action could be taken until the expiry of the eighty days which Cranmer had been granted on 7th September in which to appeal and appear in Rome in person; but this was a hypocritical formality, as Cranmer was behind bars in Bocardo, and Mary had no intention of permitting him to go to Rome within the

---

[1] For the decree of the Synod of Pavia (and that of the Synod of Malfi of 1189 extending it to the wives and concubines of priests) see *Catholic Encyclopaedia*, iii. 486, sub. tit. 'Celibacy.'

eighty days. But the eighty days' delay, and the time required for travel between Rome and England, along with the degradation proceedings and the necessary formalities, gave Cranmer about six months of life in which to try to finish his book against Gardiner on the Eucharist; but he seems at this time to have been deprived of pen and paper except when it was given to him for the purpose of writing to the authorities.[1]

Immediately after the trial, Cranmer wrote a long letter to the Queen, in which he showed the extent and the sincerity of his belief in royal supremacy by criticizing Mary for having prosecuted him before a Papal Court instead of putting him to death under her own royal power. 'Alas, it cannot but grieve the heart of any natural subject to be accused of the King and Queen of his own realm, and specially before an outward judge, or by authority coming from any person out of this realm; where the King and Queen, as if they were subjects within their own realm, shall complain and require justice at a stranger's hands against their own subject, being already condemned to death by their own laws. As though the King and Queen could not do or have justice within their own realms against their own subjects, but they must seek it at a stranger's hands in a strange land; the like whereof, I think, was never seen. I would have wished to have had some meaner adversaries; and I think that death shall not grieve me much more than to have my most dread and most gracious Sovereign Lord and Lady (to whom under God I do owe all obedience) to be mine accusers in judgment within their own realm, before any stranger and outward power.' He then went on to explain at great length his objections to Papal supremacy, from which he passed into an equally lengthy criticism of the Pope for prohibiting the service in the common tongue and the administration of the Sacrament in both kinds and for believing in the Real Presence.[2]

Cranmer mentioned in the letter that he was presuming to write to Mary because he wished her to judge his opinions from what he wrote himself and not from what she heard about him from others; but his hope was not fulfilled. It was one of Mary's boasts that she would never read or listen to the arguments of

[1] Cranmer to Mary I (September 1555) (Cranmer's *Works*, ii. 454).
[2] Cranmer to Mary I (September 1555) (Cranmer's *Works*, ii. 447–54; the passage cited is on p. 447).

the Protestants, and when Martin delivered Cranmer's letter to her, she asked whether it was lawful for her to read, or even to receive, a letter from a heretic. She gave the letter to Pole, and entrusted him with the duty of replying to Cranmer.[1]

About the same time, Cranmer wrote another letter to the Queen, in which he told her that he had heard that she had sworn an oath of obedience to the Pope at her coronation, and that if this were true—which in fact it was not—this oath conflicted with her other oath at her coronation to uphold the laws of her realm. At the end of this letter, Cranmer mentioned that he had been summoned to appear in Rome on the eightieth day after 7th September, and offered to go there to defend God's truth in Rome; but he left the decision as to whether he should go entirely to Mary's pleasure. He can hardly have made this offer in the hope of prolonging his life, nor is it likely that he declared his readiness to go to Rome in order that his supporters could claim—as they rightly did—that he had been forcibly prevented from complying with the formal summons to appear there. He probably acted merely out of a sense of duty. Having been chosen by his Prince in 1530 to oppose the Pope's prerogative in the Rotta in Rome, this devoted royal servant was again offering in 1555 to serve his Sovereign in the same capacity, conscious that he had thus discharged his duty, and that if Mary refused his offer the responsibility before God rested with her. Mary had no intention that Cranmer should go to Rome. She wrote to the Pope urging him to pass sentence on Cranmer as soon as possible, so that she could appoint Pole as Archbishop of Canterbury without any further delay.[2]

On 1st October, Ridley and Latimer were excommunicated after a trial for heresy; but before they were burned, a last attempt was made to persuade the two men, and Cranmer, to recant. They were visited by the Emperor's confessor, the Spanish friar Soto. Latimer refused to see Soto, and though Soto spoke with Ridley he could not shake him at all; but Cranmer was less intractable. He told Soto that he wished to speak with Pole, and though he refused to recant, Soto formed the impression

[1] Ibid., ii. 447; *Bishop Cranmer's Recantacyons*, p. 35. For other examples of Mary's refusal to read heretical writings, see Foxe, vi. 354; the Council to Mary, 25 December 1550 (Cranmer's *Works*, ii. 528).
[2] Cranmer to Mary I (September 1555) (Cranmer's *Works*, ii. 454); Michiel to the Doge and Senate of Venice, 1 October 1555 (*Ven. Cal.* vi. 231).

that he might soon be persuaded to do so. Pole did not grant Cranmer an interview; but on hearing of Soto's success, he wrote to King Philip that it might after all prove possible to avoid burning Cranmer if Soto succeeded in persuading him to recant in the next few days.[1]

On 16th October, Ridley and Latimer were burned in the town ditch just outside the northern walls of Oxford. On the way to execution, they were led past Bocardo, and looked up in the hope of seeing Cranmer and exchanging a few last words with him; but Cranmer was not at the window. Foxe states that this was because he was engaged in disputation with Soto, and it is very likely that Soto was with him at this time. It had, however, been arranged that Cranmer should watch the execution from the roof of the prison on the parapet of the northern wall. The authorities presumably hoped that this would encourage him to recant. They may have realized that he was not a man who would enjoy a burning, for as far as we know he had never, like other Bishops, attended the burning of a heretic on any previous occasion during his years of power. He was seen and recognized by the onlookers as he stood on the walls, and attracted a great deal of attention. Even with the burning of Ridley and Latimer to watch, there was no doubt a real subsidiary interest in observing the reaction of Cranmer to the burning of his friends.

It was a horrible burning. Latimer was quickly suffocated by the smoke; but Ridley's pile burned slowly, and when his brother-in-law tried to shorten the agony by adding more fuel, he only succeeded in still further slowing down the fire. Ridley was still alive and screaming after his legs had been burned away. Cranmer afterwards told Woodson, the Keeper of Bocardo, that Ridley's execution had been badly mismanaged. Woodson apparently took the official attitude that the sole responsibility for Ridley's long agony rested on his blundering brother-in-law; but whoever was to blame, Cranmer had seen for himself what a burning might involve.[2]

If the Papists thought that this experience would persuade Cranmer to recant, they had made a miscalculation. When Soto returned for another talk with Cranmer after that first hopeful

[1] Pole to King Philip (October 1555) (*Poli Epist.*, v. 47).
[2] Foxe, vii. 547–8, 550–1; *Bishop Cranmer's Recantacyons*, pp. 48–50; Parker, pp. 402–3; Bullinger to Calvin (winter 1555–6) (*Orig. Letters*, p. 751).

interview, he found that the heretic had become much more obstinate. Soto persevered, and came day after day to Bocardo; but Cranmer grew more and more difficult, and when Soto visited him for the last time about 23rd October, Cranmer was very hostile, and Soto withdrew in disgust, convinced that it was useless to attempt to save Cranmer. Cranmer had never been in a more determined mood. If fear of death alone could have led him to recant, he would have done so during these last talks with Soto after his ordeal of 16th October; but a week after he had witnessed Ridley's torments, Cranmer was firmly resolved to die in the flames rather than admit Papal supremacy and the Real Presence.[1]

[1] *Bishop Cranmer's Recantacyons*, p. 43; Pole to Muzzarelli, 26 October 1555 (*Ven. Cal.* vi. 255), where Pole wrote that he had sent the document to Cranmer on 23 October, but would not have sent it if he had already heard about the obstinacy which Cranmer had shown in his talks with Soto. This fixes the date of Cranmer's last talk with Soto as either 22, 23, 24 or 25 October.

CHAPTER XXIV

THE RECANTATIONS

In the summer of 1554, when Pole was waiting on the shores of Lake Garda for the summons to return to England as Papal Legate, he wrote a pamphlet, in the form of an open letter to Cranmer, in which he attacked Cranmer's heresy concerning the Eucharist and all his acts of misconduct since the days of the divorce of Catherine of Aragon. No one had troubled to show the pamphlet to the prisoner to whom it was ostensibly addressed; but when Pole heard from Soto that there was a possibility that Cranmer might recant, he sent Cranmer a copy of the document on 23rd October 1555. By the time that Cranmer received it, he must already have held his final meeting with Soto, and Pole, having heard about Cranmer's intransigeance, was regretting that he had troubled to send him the pamphlet. The pamphlet was written in Pole's most brilliant style, striking mercilessly at all the weak points in Cranmer's armour. Cranmer commented that the pamphlet was very impressive, but that Pole had been too bitter, and that his allegations were untrue.[1]

A few weeks later, Cranmer received another and more recent polemic from Pole. On 6th November 1555, Pole wrote a reply to Cranmer's letter to the Queen about Papal supremacy. Having appealed to his Sovereign to assert her royal authority, even at the cost of his own life, against a foreign power, Cranmer received a reply from the Legate of that foreign power to whom the Queen had handed the letter without reading it. Pole's letter had all the venom, but none of the brilliance, of his pamphlet on the Eucharist of eighteen months before. It informed Cranmer that he was wicked, blind and ignorant, and was about to receive his well-deserved punishment; for Pole,

---

[1] Pole, *Epistola ad T. Cranmer . . . de Sacramento Eucharistiae;* for a French translation, see Le Grand, *Histoire du Divorce,* i. 289–368. For the date at which it was written, see Strype, *Cranmer,* p. 549. Froude (v. 578–83) wrongly states that it is a letter which Pole wrote to Cranmer after Cranmer's degradation in February 1556. See also Pole to Muzzarelli, 26 October 1555 (*Ven. Cal.* vi. 255), and supra, p. 381., n.; *Bishop Cranmer's Recantacyons,* pp. 42–43.

who had once been a man of integrity and culture, had now sunk to writing insults to a fallen opponent who was awaiting a dreadful death. The most significant thing about this letter is the absence of any real attempt to persuade Cranmer to recant. Pole inserted a few passing references to the fact that Cranmer could only save his soul by repentance, and did not fail to mention the penitent thief on the Cross, and to sign the letter 'Your very true comforter in God, you not refusing His grace, R. Pole, Car. Leg.' But this necessary minimum fell far short of the stirring exhortations to repent which had marked Pole's pamphlet about the Eucharist in 1554, and which were usually addressed to heretics. Pole even went so far as to write that he had no doubt that Cranmer would not repent.[1]

There is every indication that Pole and Mary did not wish to obtain a recantation from Cranmer. They wished to burn him. The authorities displayed such bitter hostility towards Cranmer that Foxe and the Protestants were convinced that Mary was motivated by a desire for personal revenge against Cranmer for having pronounced the sentence at Dunstable which had bastardized her;[2] but this is unlikely, in view of the readiness with which Mary forgave Gardiner and Bonner and the other men who had done as much as Cranmer with regard to the divorce. Cranmer was the victim of something far more terrible than the vengeance of a woman; he was the victim of the cold, calculating power politics of a Queen and a Papal Legate. They had decided to make the leader of the Reformation the scapegoat for all the sins of schism and heresy. It was essential to find a scapegoat for Henry VIII in order to defend the reputation of a Prince, and convenient also to produce one for the benefit of all the nobles and officials who had served Henry as faithfully as had Cranmer, but could now be usefully employed in the service of a tyrant of a different hue. In any case, it was desirable that the leader of the Reformation should be burned, in order to impress upon the people that he was as low and ignorant a heretic as the artisans and peasants who had been burned as sacramentaries. By burning Cranmer, they would put the Reformation beyond the bounds of decency.

[1] Pole to Cranmer, 6 November 1555 (Cranmer's *Works*, ii. 534–41). Parts of Pole's letter are missing, and some of the missing parts are summarized in *Bishop Cranmer's Recantacyons*, pp. 44–45.

[2] Foxe, viii. 37; Anon. Biogr. (*Nar. Ref.*, pp. 226–7).

It was politically much easier for Mary and Pole to burn Cranmer if he did not recant. It was possible in law to burn a heretic who had recanted, for after the sentence of excommunication had been pronounced, the law could take its course unless the Queen chose to exercise her prerogative of mercy; but it was very unusual to burn a repentant heretic, who was usually made to carry his fagot and perform some lesser penance, unless he was a relapsed heretic who had recanted once, then relapsed into heresy, and then recanted again. A priest had been burned at Canterbury in 1498 after he had recanted, but he may perhaps have been a relapsed heretic. According to Sir Thomas More, Bilney, who was burned in 1531, recanted before he died, and though this seems to be wrong, it is at least clear that More was prepared to justify the burning of a repentant heretic in Bilney's case; but Bilney was certainly a relapsed heretic. The Act of the Six Articles expressly enacted that sacramentaries who denied the Real Presence or transubstantiation were to be burned even if they recanted, and several repentant heretics were burned under the Act; but this was a statutory and Henrician innovation which contravened the established practice under the old Roman canon law.

When the burnings started in Mary's reign, it was only unrepentant heretics who suffered. The choice, in Ridley's vivid phrase, was Turn or Burn, and every heretic was offered his life at the stake on condition that he recanted. It was not until January 1556 that the Council gave orders that in view of the contempt with which the heretics at the stake treated the Queen's offer of pardon, they were in future to be burned immediately without being offered their lives at the stake if they recanted.[1]

There is abundant evidence that Pole did not wish to obtain a recantation from Cranmer because it would be easier to burn him if he did not recant. Such an attitude was of course inconsistent with Pole's duty to attempt to save the soul of every heretic by persuading him to recant, rather than to send him to his death unrepentant. But Pole had always shown a skill in reconciling religious doctrine with political expediency. When he was formulating a policy towards the divorce of Catherine of

[1] Foxe, iv. 7, 643–52; More, *The Confutation of Tyndale's Answer* (More's *Works*, p. 350); Collier, iv. 71; Jewel's controversy with Cole (Jewel's *Works*, p. 59); 31 Hen. VIII. c. 14; Ridley to Cranmer (April 1554) (Ridley's *Works*, p. 363); Acts of the Privy Council, 19 January 1555/6; Burnet, iii. 440–1.

Aragon, he had begun by searching Scripture to discover the divine law; but in view of the conflict of Biblical texts, he felt free to oppose the divorce on the grounds that an alliance with the Emperor was more advantageous for England than an alliance with France.[1] He seems likewise to have succeeded in 1555 in reconciling his duty as a Cardinal with the interests of the State. He knew that Cranmer had remained a heretic after reading the books of Gardiner and Tunstall on the Eucharist, and had refused to recant at the disputation in 1554 and at his trial before the Pope's sub-delegate. Pole had nevertheless sent Soto to argue with Cranmer, but as Cranmer had been particularly obstinate, he doubtless felt that he had done enough to satisfy his conscience, and could take the politically expedient course of burning Cranmer as an unrepentant heretic.

Cranmer decided to follow Luther's example and appeal to a General Council. There was no possibility of his appeal being heard, for the Popes had been proclaiming for nearly a hundred years that it was heresy to state that a General Council had any authority over them; but it was important that the appeal should be drafted in proper legal form. Cranmer was not permitted to consult with any lawyer, but at the beginning of November he wrote to a member of Oxford University who was learned in the law, and asked him for assistance in drafting the appeal. We do not know the identity of this lawyer to whom Cranmer could write in very friendly and confidential terms in November 1555. There are indications in the letter that Cranmer was losing his composure. He told the lawyer to make haste in drafting the appeal, because his case was due to be heard in Rome on 16th November at the expiry of the eighty days, whereas in fact the eighty days expired on 26th November. Cranmer recognized the probability that his appeal would not be allowed, but he nevertheless clung to the illusion that he might be able to postpone his fate by this appeal, at the same time emphasizing that he only wished to do this in order to have time to finish writing his book against Gardiner on the Eucharist, and that otherwise he would prefer to die in Christ's quarrel rather than remain in prison. He ought to have realized that there was no possibility whatever that his appeal would be admitted.[2]

---

[1] Cranmer to Wiltshire, 13 June 1531 (Cranmer's *Works*, ii. 229–31).
[2] Cranmer to a lawyer, (November 1555) (Cranmer's *Works*, ii. 455–6).

One of Cranmer's sisters now came to his assistance. We do not know if this was his sister Alice, who as an expelled Prioress would have been in the best position to help him. The author of *Bishop Cranmer's Recantacyons* calls this sister 'the Catholic sister', as opposed to the Protestant one; but Alice's name does not appear in Pole's list of nuns in receipt of a pension in February 1556, although she had been allotted a pension of £14 a year when her priory was dissolved in 1536; so she had presumably died, unless the explanation is that Pole deprived her of her pension because of her efforts on her brother's behalf. However this may be, Cranmer's Catholic sister came to Oxford to see him, and made repeated approaches to Pole and Mary, endeavouring to obtain for Cranmer all the rights to which he was entitled under the canon law as an Archbishop who had not yet been degraded by the Pope's authority. It was apparently as a result of her activity that Cranmer was removed from Bocardo and taken to the house of Marshal, the Dean of Christ Church College. This was probably about the beginning of December 1555. Foxe states that it was after Cranmer's degradation in the middle of February 1556, and this has generally been accepted by later historians; but Foxe was not in a good position to know the details with regard to Cranmer's last weeks, which he learned from refugees abroad, whereas the author of *Bishop Cranmer's Recantacyons*, who almost certainly obtained his information direct from the Spanish friars and wrote it in his book within a few months, makes it clear that Cranmer went to Christ Church before New Year's Day.[1]

Cranmer was kindly treated in Christ Church, where the air and living conditions were much better than in Bocardo. Foxe states that he was permitted to walk and play bowls in the College grounds. One of the Canons of Christ Church, Henry Sidall, who presumably did not realize that the official line was that Cranmer was irredeemable, was anxious to persuade him to recant; and his efforts seem to have met with some success. The soft treatment at Christ Church may have had the effect of softening Cranmer, who must also have been conscious that his time was drawing near. The eighty days which he had been granted to appear in Rome had expired on 26th November, and

---

[1] *Bishop Cranmer's Recantacyons*, pp. 51, 53, 93; Baskerville, 'A Sister of Archbishop Cranmer' (*Engl. Hist. Rev.*, li. 288–9); Foxe, viii. 80.

three days later Cardinal de Puteo presented his report on
Cranmer's trial to Paul IV in the Consistory. On 4th December,
after Cranmer had been called upon and pronounced contumacious for his absence, the Pope excommunicated him for heresy,
and ordered him to be degraded from holy orders and delivered
to the secular power for punishment. There was great rejoicing
in the streets of Rome, where Cranmer was burned in effigy.[1]

Cranmer asked to have further discussions with learned men
about religion. Marshal, who was highly gratified, approached
Brother John de Garcina, a brilliant young friar from Valladolid
University, who had just been appointed, before he was 30, to
be Regius Professor of Divinity at Oxford. Garcina was very
reluctant to speak with Cranmer, for he was convinced that as
Cranmer had not been converted by the public disputation or
by his talk with Soto, he himself would be equally unsuccessful.
But Sidall and Soto strongly urged Garcina to make a further
attempt to save Cranmer's soul, and told him that even if he
failed, he would at least expose the falsity of the story which
the Protestants were spreading that the Papist theologians
were too unsure of themselves to venture to argue with Cranmer. Eventually Garcina agreed, and he spoke with Cranmer at
Christ Church on New Year's Eve. He asked Cranmer what
question he wished to discuss with him, and Cranmer replied
that it was Papal supremacy. Garcina referred to *Tu es Petrus*
and other texts, and then asked Cranmer if he wished to discuss
any other point. Cranmer said that he wished to discuss Purgatory, and Garcina explained the orthodox doctrine. In due
course, Garcina left, having achieved no results.[2]

But Cranmer's action in asking for discussions with orthodox
divines was highly significant; and so was his choice of topics.
Papal supremacy and Purgatory were the first doctrines of the
old Church which Cranmer had repudiated; he had denounced
them both for twenty years. He asked Garcina to argue on the
two points on which his opposition to Popery was most firmly
established. The inference is that Cranmer was eager to recant

---

[1] *Bishop Cranmer's Recantacyons*, p. 69; Foxe, viii. 80; Jewel's controversy
with Harding (Jewel's *Works*, p. 629); Paul IV's sentence, 4 December 1555 (in
Poli Epist., v. 139–42); Navagero to the Doge and Senate of Venice, 30 November
1555 (*Ven. Cal.* vi. 295); Carne to the Council, 30 November 1555 (Tytler, ii.
486).

[2] *Bishop Cranmer's Recantacyons*, pp. 51–65.

in order to save his life, and wished to be helped by Garcina's arguments to surmount the two greatest obstacles for his conscience. Cranmer was hopefully waiting to be persuaded by opponents who did not really wish to persuade him.

In January, Cranmer was taken back to Bocardo. This was probably because the Papal decree of excommunication had now officially reached Oxford, and it was no longer proper for Christians to have social contact with Cranmer, though they could speak with him in order to try to convert him and whenever it was strictly necessary for official reasons. It must have been a further shock to the wretched old man to be taken back to the common jail, where he had been almost completely isolated for twenty months before they had taken him to Christ Church. In his loneliness, Cranmer made what is now recognized by the experts of psychological warfare as being a fatal blunder for a prisoner: he made a friend of his jailer. He had come to be absolutely dependent on the friendship of the Governor of the prison.

Woodson had spent a great deal of time with Cranmer, and had endeavoured to convert him in his simple layman's way. He had high hopes of success, for Cranmer had shown signs of wavering; but as the weeks passed by, and Cranmer still could not bring himself to recant, Woodson began to lose patience. He eventually decided that Cranmer was a hardened heretic, and ceased visiting him. On 28th January, Cranmer requested to see the Keeper, and when Woodson arrived, Cranmer asked him why he had not visited him for so long. Woodson said that he would not listen any more to this pretence of friendship from Cranmer, because it was now plain that Cranmer was deceiving him, and had no real intention of returning to the Christian fold. Cranmer said that they could discuss this matter at some other time, but he greatly desired to talk to Woodson that day. Woodson agreed to stay on condition that Cranmer took control of himself, and showed that he wished to belong to the Christian community; and Cranmer, who was obviously trying to put off the decision as long as possible, promised that if Woodson would stay with him, he would give proof of his repentance after supper. Woodson spent the whole day with Cranmer, and after supper asked him if he was now prepared to recant; but Cranmer said that he was unable to decide, and asked to be allowed to postpone his decision to another day. At this,

Woodson left the room in disgust, declaring that this was typical of Cranmer's dishonesty and insincerity. Cranmer fainted. When he came to himself, he lay on his bed in despair, and in the middle of the night his attendant, who slept in the next room, heard him sobbing and moaning. The attendant hurried through the silent prison and woke the Keeper, who came at once to Cranmer; but the only comfort which Woodson would give him was to tell him that this was a divine punishment for his obstinacy. Cranmer thereupon wrote out his first recantation. He had remained firm after witnessing the burning of Ridley; but he could not endure the social ostracism and the contempt of the Keeper of Bocardo.[1]

To explain why Cranmer recanted, and then retracted his recantations, we should have to know many facts about his personality which could only have been known to his most intimate friends. If there was any person—his wife, or Morice, or someone else—who knew the real truth, the knowledge has died with them. Only the official Protestant and Catholic explanations have survived. The Protestants, after originally claiming that the recantations were forged, later admitted that they were genuine, and said that Cranmer had been induced to recant by a promise that his life would be spared if he did so. The Catholic theory is that his recantations were utterly insincere, and made with the calculated motive of saving his life. These are the simple explanations which serve propagandist purposes; but it is very unlikely that either of them is true.

We know in considerable detail the exact circumstances in which Cranmer recanted, and this makes it possible at least to speculate about his motives, and to realize that the usual explanations do not fit the facts. These facts could not be known to Foxe and the other Protestant refugees abroad, or to the secret sympathizers in Oxford; they could only be known to the enemies who surrounded Cranmer in Bocardo. Alan Cope—or whoever wrote *Bishop Cranmer's Recantacyons*—probably obtained his information direct from Garcina and the other friars. He was violently hostile to Cranmer, and some of his statements are certainly wrong; but most of the information which he gives about the last six months of Cranmer's life is probably true, for it is not the sort of story which an enemy propagandist would

[1] Ibid., pp. 65–67.

invent. In the hundred years since his manuscript was redis-
covered, only three authors appear to have made any use of it,
because both Cranmer's admirers and his critics prefer to adhere
to the old propaganda versions.[1] But though the Protestants do
not like *Bishop Cranmer's Recantacyons*, which shows Cranmer
neither as a hero nor as a victim who was forced to confess by
ill-treatment, the book is nevertheless a terrible indictment of
Mary's government and of the men whom its author so greatly
admired. It shows a systematic application of mental cruelty
towards a defeated and lonely old man who had been marked
down for burning whatever he might do.

Cranmer must often have thought about the possible weakness in his position and of possible grounds for recantation.
When he decided to recant in the middle of the night, he groped
at once for the bridge which could take him back from royal
supremacy to Rome. In his first recantation, he wrote: 'Forasmuch as the King and Queen's Majesties, by consent of their
Parliament, have received the Pope's authority within this
realm, I am content to submit myself to their laws herein, and to
take the Pope for chief head of this Church of England, so far as
God's laws and the laws and customs of this realm will permit.—
Thomas Cranmer.' This was of course quite insufficient, as was
doubtless pointed out to him, for it recognized the authority of
the Pope for the wrong reason, as an indirect consequence of
royal supremacy. Next day Cranmer wrote out another recantation, which has not survived, but was apparently very similar to
the first. Within a few days he had gone much further, and produced an unqualified submission to the Pope: 'I, Thomas
Cranmer, Doctor in Divinity, do submit myself to the Catholic
Church of Christ, and to the Pope, Supreme Head of the same
Church, and unto the King and the Queen's Majesties, and unto
all their laws and ordinances.—Thomas Cranmer.' Cranmer
was now slipping fast. He asked, and was granted, permission to
attend mass and to carry a candle at Candlemas.[2]

---

[1] For the authorship of *Bishop Cranmer's Recantacyons*, see Gairdner's Preface
to *Bishop Cranmer's Recantacyons*, pp. v–xiii. Dixon, Gairdner and Mason seem to
be the only authors to have made any use of the information in it. Pollard (in
Thomas Cranmer, pp. 361–2 n.) virtually rejects the whole document as untrue
because of its author's prejudice and a few minor inaccuracies.

[2] Cranmer's First and Second Submissions, in *All the Submissions and Recantations of Thomas Cranmer* (Cranmer's *Works*, ii. 563); *Bishop Cranmer's Recantacyons*, pp. 63, 68–9.

The news of Cranmer's recantations must have come as an unwelcome surprise to Mary and Pole. They could not admit to themselves that they were displeased, but it obviously upset their calculations. Having hitherto adopted the attitude that Cranmer would never recant, their new line was that his recantation was insincere; for they had decided that Cranmer would be burned whatever occurred. Before burning him, it was necessary to degrade him from all his orders in the Church, and Bonner and Thirlby were sent to Oxford to officiate at the ceremony. No one could be relied upon to perform this duty more offensively than Bonner, who had probably been selected for the purpose because he was acting as Metropolitan during the vacancy in the archiepiscopal see. Thirlby, who had been Cranmer's friend for many years, assisted Bonner half-heartedly and shamefacedly. Cranmer had been a generous host to Thirlby, and had probably been responsible, in Edward's reign, for Thirlby's translation to Norwich when his diocese of Westminster was abolished, despite the opposition which Thirlby had shown to the Book of Common Prayer. It is unlikely that the choice of either Thirlby or Bonner was made with the deliberate design of hurting Cranmer; but it was turning the knife in the wound to select his most brutal enemy and his most ungrateful friend to inflict this public humiliation upon him.

The degradation took place in the church of Christ Church College on 14th February 1556.[1] After the sentence of the Pope had been read out, Bonner denounced Cranmer with savage invective, exulting over his downfall, declaring that this was the man who had despised the Pope and was now being sentenced by the Pope, that this was the man who had condemned the Sacrament of the Altar and had now come to be judged with the Sacrament hanging over the altar, and beginning each sentence with the words 'This is the man'. He referred to the curious incident—which has never been satisfactorily explained —of how Cranmer had once sat upon an altar when he was acting as a judge. Cranmer intervened to explain that the incident to which Bonner was alluding was an occasion when he had sat as a Commissioner in St. Paul's; if there was an altar

[1] For the proceedings at Cranmer's degradation, see Foxe, viii. 71–80; the text of Cranmer's appeal to the General Council is at pp. 73–76 (in Cranmer's *Works*, ii. 224–7).

concealed under the platform upon which Cranmer and his colleagues had sat, he had known nothing about it; Bonner, as the diocesan Bishop, and his officers had been responsible for erecting the seating accommodation in the cathedral.

When Bonner had finished, they began the ceremony of degrading Cranmer from all his orders in the Church. They forced him to put on the vestments of an Archbishop in order to strip them off him; but Cranmer fought back. He presented to Bonner his appeal to the next General Council, protesting against the jurisdiction of the Pope to try him on the grounds that the Pope had no authority in England, that he was not an impartial judge in an issue which concerned his own supremacy, and protesting against being condemned in his absence when he had not been permitted to go to Rome. This vigorous denunciation of the usurped power of Rome was in absolute contradiction to the three recantations which Cranmer had signed a fortnight before. It was obviously the document which the lawyer had drafted for him, and it must have been in his possession for some time. He had probably put it aside when he signed his recantations; but as the authorities showed no interest in his recantations, he hesitated, and took the appeal to the General Council with him when he went to the degradation ceremony. Perhaps he was still uncertain whether he would present it until Bonner's insults goaded him into defiance.

Thirlby told Cranmer that he had no right of appeal, and proceeded with the degradation; but Cranmer's spirit had revived, and when Bonner and Thirlby removed his Archbishop's pall, he asked which of them had a pall to remove his pall. They pointed out that though as Bishops they were inferior to Cranmer as an Archbishop, they were delegates of the Pope, and as such had authority to degrade an Archbishop from his archiepiscopal rank. Cranmer was then dressed in priest's vestments and degraded from the priesthood, his hair being shaved to remove the tonsure which he had worn for nearly forty years, and his fingers scraped to remove the unction from the hands that had been anointed to celebrate the Sacrament of the Altar. Foxe tells us that though Thirlby scraped Cranmer's fingers as gently as possible, Bonner did it roughly; but here we can hardly take Foxe's report too seriously, whether it emanated from the rumours of the English Protestant colony in Switzerland or the subsequent reports of the bystanders. After being successively degraded from the five minor ecclesiastical orders, Cranmer was dressed in a townsman's cloak and cap and delivered to the secular power. The Bishops presumably ended the ceremony by repeating the usual formula: 'My Lord Judge, we ask you with all the earnestness which we can that for the love of God, for piety, for considerations of mercy and because of our intercession, you bring upon this most wretched man no peril of death or mutilation.'[1] But Foxe states merely that when the degradation was completed, Bonner said to Cranmer: 'Now are you no lord any more.' He had perhaps been infuriated by the fact that Thirlby had addressed Cranmer as 'my Lord' during the proceedings.

As Cranmer returned to Bocardo in the townsman's cloak in which they had dressed him, one of the officials took pity on him. He had been handed Cranmer's own cloak when it was removed for the degradation ceremony, and he now followed Cranmer on his way to the prison and gave him back the cloak. He tried to comfort Cranmer by reminding him of the kindness which Thirlby had shown him during the proceedings; but Cranmer could not refrain from commenting that Thirlby might have shown him far greater kindness in view of all that he had done for Thirlby. When they reached Bocardo, the official offered to buy some wine for Cranmer. Cranmer said that he would prefer some fish, as he had eaten very little in his anxiety before the degradation; and the official was about to give him the money for the fish, when he remembered that in the reign of Henry VIII a man had forfeited all his lands for having given money to a priest who was imprisoned in the Tower. He therefore gave the money for the fish to the jailers. This precaution did not prevent him from being summoned before Bonner and Thirlby, who threatened to send him to the Council; for as Foxe wrote a few years later, 'such was the cruelty and iniquity of the time, that men could not do good without punishment'.[2]

[1] This was the regular formula at the conclusion of the degradation ceremony (see Paul IV's bull of 14 December 1555, in Foxe, viii. 79).

[2] Foxe, viii. 80. Foxe's story is confirmed by the accounts of the bailiffs of Oxford, which show that salmon was purchased for Cranmer's dinner on 14 February (The Costs and Charges paid by the Bailiffs of Oxford, in *Oxford City Records*, p. 234).

CHAPTER XXV

THE CHOICE

Two days after the degradation, Bonner visited Cranmer in Bocardo. The purpose of his visit is not clear, but he presumably did not go merely to mock and gloat, and was probably sent to elucidate the contradiction between Cranmer's recantations and his appeal to the General Council. If Cranmer adhered to the anti-Papal statements in his appeal, he could be stigmatized as a relapsed heretic, and burned; but Cranmer presented Bonner with a new recantation. It was an attempted compromise between the submission to Papal authority in the second recantation and the rejection of it in the appeal to the General Council. It returned to the anomalous position which Cranmer had adopted in the first recantation of 28th January—that he would obey the Pope because he was ordered to do so by Philip and Mary. 'I am content to submit myself to the King and Queen's Majesties, and to all their laws and ordinances, as well concerning the Pope's supremacy as others. And I shall from time to time move and stir all other to do the like, to the uttermost of my power, and to live in quietness and obedience unto Their Majesties, most humbly, without murmur or grudging against any of their godly proceedings. And for my book which I have written, I am contented to submit me to the judgment of the Catholic Church, and of the next General Council.—Thomas Cranmer.'

Bonner rejected this recantation as worthless. He was particularly incensed at the reference to the General Council. Cranmer thereupon wrote out another recantation which, though it appeared superficially to be a complete submission, was so ambiguously worded that it was almost capable of being interpreted as not being a recantation at all. 'Be it known by these presents that I, Thomas Cranmer, Doctor of Divinity, and late Archbishop of Canterbury, do firmly, steadfastly and assuredly believe in all articles and points of the Christian religion and Catholic faith, as the Catholic Church doth believe and hath ever believed from the beginning. Moreover, as concerning the

Sacraments of the Church, I believe unfeignedly in all points as the said Catholic Church doth and hath believed from the beginning of Christian religion. In witness whereof I have humbly subscribed my hand unto these presents the 16th day of February 1555. [1555/6].—Thomas Cranmer.'[1]

The unsatisfactory nature of these recantations was perhaps satisfactory for Mary and Pole. On 24th February, the Council ordered Heath, as Lord Chancellor, to issue a writ to the Mayor of Oxford ordering him to burn Cranmer, though the date of the execution was not yet fixed. But in Oxford, the Spanish friars, realizing that they had been mistaken in their belief that Cranmer would never recant, and finding him half repentant and half defiant, made strenuous efforts to save Cranmer's soul. They obviously did not know the political decisions which had been taken at Court, for Pole could not openly admit that he did not wish Cranmer to recant. Cranmer was now for the first time subjected to intensive pressure to recant, and this completely overcame the new resistance which had arisen in his mind. Garcina wrote out another recantation, and persuaded Cranmer to sign it on 26th February. It was as complete a recantation as could have been desired. Cranmer repudiated all Lutheran and Zwinglian heresy, and declared his belief in the Real Presence and transubstantiation, in all the other six Sacraments, in Purgatory, in all the doctrines of the Church of Rome, and in Papal supremacy. This document was witnessed by Garcina and Sidall, the Canon of Christ Church, who had shown such interest in Cranmer's repentance ever since Cranmer had stayed at the College.[2]

At the beginning of March, this fifth recantation was published in London by Riddall and Copland, the printers. They were not the official government printers. The official printer was Cawood, who had a patent entitling him to print all government publications. As soon as the document was circulated, the Protestants denounced it as a forgery, and pointed out that it

[1] The Third and Fourth Submissions, in *All the Submissions and Recantations of Thomas Cranmer* (Cranmer's *Works*, ii. 563); *Bishop Cranmer's Recantacyons*, pp. 73–74.

[2] Warrant of 24 February 1556 (Burnet, v. 452–3); Foxe, viii. 80; *Bishop Cranmer's Recantacyons*, pp. 75–78; the Fifth Submission, in *All the Submissions and Recantations of Thomas Cranmer*, where it is undated; but the date of the fifth recantation is given as 5th Kal. Mar. in Bonner's Register (1556 being a leap year); see Cranmer's *Works*, ii. 563–4; Foxe, viii. App. Document ii.

was witnessed by one of the hated Spaniards. On 12th March, Noailles informed Henry II that two or three days before, Cranmer had petitioned Pole to respite his execution for some days because he was on the point of recanting his heresies, and that the execution had been postponed at the last moment. The Ambassador wrote that Mary and Pole were very pleased that there was a possibility that Cranmer might recant. On 13th March, Riddall and Copland were summoned before the Council and ordered to surrender all copies of Cranmer's recantation to Cawood to be burned, and to undertake not to print any more copies of it, or any other book which had already been condemned, or which had been published within the last forty years; nor were they to print any book in the future until it had been read and approved by the Council or by the diocesan Bishop. About ten days later—within a day or two after Cranmer's death on 21st March—Cawood had published an official pamphlet containing all Cranmer's recantations, including the fifth recantation.[1]

We have no definite knowledge as to why the Council banned the publication of the fifth recantation. The Venetian Ambassador wrote to his government on 24th March that the recantation was suppressed because it was witnessed by two Spaniards—Soto and his colleague—and that this had made the people, who hated Spaniards, suspect that it was a forgery. This information was inaccurate, for the recantation was not witnessed by Soto and another Spaniard, but by Garcina and Sidall—by one Spaniard and one Englishman. No contemporary observer seems to have suggested the explanation which was put forward in the nineteenth century and is generally accepted today—that the fifth recantation was suppressed because Riddall and Copland had printed it without a licence in violation of Cawood's monopoly. Yet neither of these explanations seems quite sufficient to account for so strange a fact as the suppression by Mary's government of the recantation of the leader of the Protestant Reformation. If the Council had approved of the publication, they would have disregarded the lies of the heretics about the forgery by the Spanish witnesses, and Cawood would have been

[1] Michiel to the Doge and Senate of Venice, 24 March 1556 (*Ven. Cal.* vi. 434); Noailles to Henry II, 12 March 1555/6 (*Ambassades de Noailles*, v. 319); Acts of the Privy Council, 13 and 16 March 1555/6.

told that on this occasion he must waive his objection to the violation of his monopoly. The fact that the printers were prohibited from printing any other banned book, and were required to submit their future publications to the censorship of their Ordinary, also suggests that the Council were concerned in this case with questions of heresy rather than of patents.[1]

The true explanation is probably that when Garcina persuaded Cranmer to sign the fifth recantation, it was not at all to the liking of Mary and Pole, who had no intention of publishing it. Garcina, unaware of Pole's policy, and believing perhaps that the delay in printing the recantation was due to the negligence of Cawood or to some other incompetent official, took matters into his own hands and arranged for Riddall and Copland to print it. We know that Garcina was a man of some independence of spirit, for three years later, in Spain, he was imprisoned by the Inquisition as a suspected heretic.[2]

The publication of the fifth recantation aroused great interest and controversy in London. Mary and Pole had obviously been very successful in preventing any news of Cranmer's earlier recantations from leaking out, for even Noailles did not suspect that Cranmer had signed five other recantations during the past six weeks. It came as a complete surprise to everyone; and this, along with the Spanish witness, assisted the whispered Protestant allegation that it was a forgery. The first reaction of the Council was to seize and burn all copies of it; but the thought must have occurred to them that they would have difficulty in explaining their conduct, as they ought to have rejoiced that Cranmer had recanted, and probably would not admit even to themselves that they were displeased. They could justify the suppression of the fifth recantation on the grounds that it was witnessed by a Spaniard—it was government policy

[1] Michiel to the Doge and Senate of Venice, 24 March 1556 (*Ven. Cal.* vi. 434). It was apparently Lingard (in his *History of England*, v. 478 n.) who first suggested that the Fifth Recantation was suppressed because it infringed Cawood's patent. Pollard (in *Thomas Cranmer*, pp. 371-2 n.) suggests that the Fifth Recantation was originally witnessed, not by Garcina and Sidall, but by Garcina and Soto, as Michiel wrote, and points out that the Fifth Recantation has not been preserved in the edition which Copland published; but if the authorities decided to obtain new witnesses to the Fifth Recantation before Cawood published it, it seems very unlikely that they would have chosen even one Spaniard for this purpose; so it is much more likely that the fifth recantation was republished by Cawood with the same witnesses.

[2] Llorente, *History of the Inquisition of Spain*, p. 316.

to prevent the Spaniards from openly meddling in English affairs—and this explanation of why they had suppressed the fifth recantation reached the Venetian Ambassador. Meanwhile the Council were pretending that they were pleased that Cranmer had recanted, but that they doubted his sincerity. This would explain why Noailles heard that Cranmer had petitioned Pole to postpone his execution, and that Pole had willingly granted this in order to give him an opportunity to recant.[1]

Once the fifth recantation had been published and so widely discussed, it was almost impossible for Mary and Pole to adhere to their old line. Some time between 13th and 17th March they must have decided on a new policy—to make the fullest use of Cranmer's recantations, but nevertheless to send him to the fire. Instructions were obviously sent to Oxford to obtain new and better recantations from Cranmer with a view to their being published by the official printer along with all the other recantations. Meanwhile the local officials had been ordered on 9th March to make all preparations for the execution, and Lord Williams and other gentlemen of the neighbourhood had been instructed to bring their servants into the town to be available if necessary to suppress any attempt to rescue Cranmer or any heretical demonstration at his burning. The Council had no illusions that these burnings were popular. They knew, to their disgust, that what ought to have been a salutary lesson as to the fate of heretics was often made an occasion for a tribute to the martyrs and a demonstration against the Queen, and they had issued instructions to the authorities to arrest anyone who showed sympathy for a heretic at an execution.[2]

Once Cranmer had gone so far as to sign the fifth recantation, the gates of his defences were broken. He was visited by Soto, Marshal, Sidall and Roscius, another Spanish friar, as well as by Garcina, and they all welcomed him with enthusiasm as a repentant sinner. Cranmer must of course have been asking himself whether he would be burned, or whether in view of his recantations he would be pardoned and condemned to some lesser penance; but he did not give any indication of this to the friars. He would not have done so even if in fact his object in recanting

[1] Noailles to Henry II, 12 March 1555/6 (*Ambassades de Noailles*, v. 319); Michiel to the Doge and Senate of Venice, 24 March 1556 (*Ven. Cal.* vi. 434).
[2] *Bishop Cranmer's Recantacyons*, p. 75; Foxe, viii. 83; Acts of the Privy Council, 14 January 1555/6.

had been to save his life, as this would have proved his insincerity; but it is very unlikely that Cranmer recanted merely
to save himself from being burned. His repentance was almost
certainly sincere, even if it was the kind of repentance which
only appears at the prospect of punishment. Soon after he had
signed the fifth recantation, he had a dream in which he saw two
Kings contending together for his soul. One of the Kings was
Jesus, and the other was Henry VIII. It had at last occurred to
Cranmer, at least in his sleep, that service to Henry had not
always been compatible with service to Christ. He asked to be
allowed to attend mass and to be present during communion,
and this was apparently permitted. Friar Roscius had succeeded
Garcina as Cranmer's chief spiritual attendant, and he visited
Cranmer day after day in Bocardo, and subjected him to an
elementary catechism on the mass—a chastening experience for
a man who had been Primate for twenty years and had written
learned books on the Eucharist.[1]

In the *Book of Martyrs*, Foxe wrote that Cranmer was not
informed that he was to be burned until the day of his death;
and it has usually been assumed that he learned of his terrible
fate either at the ceremony which preceded the burning, or at
the earliest only shortly before he left the prison on the same
morning. But the author of *Bishop Cranmer's Recantacyons*
states that Cranmer was told that he would be burned before he
signed the sixth recantation three days before his death. This is
strong evidence, for it would have suited this writer very well if
he could have said that Cranmer only signed the sixth recantation because he still hoped to save his life, and as other facts
confirm his statement, there is no reason to doubt it. It was
certainly on 17th or 18th March that Dr. Cole, the Provost of
Eton, arrived in Oxford, having been sent by the Queen to preach
the usual sermon at Cranmer's burning. He visited Cranmer in
Bocardo, and informed him that he was to be burned on the
morning of Saturday the 21st. Cranmer received the news
calmly, and said that he was not afraid to die, but that the load
of his sin lay heavy on his conscience. He then told Cole that he
was anxious about his son, for owing to his conviction for
treason, all his property had been forfeited and his son could
inherit nothing from him. Cranmer asked Cole to intercede with

[1] *Bishop Cranmer's Recantacyons*, pp. 79–82, 84.

the Queen to permit his son to have part of the property. He should not have expected any favour to be shown to the son of a priest at a time when the authorities were punishing a priest who had been seen carrying his child in his arms. Cole told Cranmer that he should concentrate on showing that he was a true Catholic, and not concern himself with other matters.[1]

On 18th March, Cranmer signed his sixth recantation. When he had told the friars about his dream of the two Kings, they said that sins as horrible as those which he had committed could not be atoned for by private repentance alone, and that he would have to make yet another public recantation. Cranmer agreed, and wrote out his sixth recantation in his own hand, though it had apparently been composed by Roscius. In this document, Cranmer recanted in abject terms, and vilified himself. He declared that he had committed grave offences against the realm of England and the Church of Christ; that he had been a worse persecutor than Paul; that he had been responsible for Henry VIII's divorce from Queen Catherine, which had been the source of all the evils which had fallen on the country; and that he had blasphemed against the holy Eucharist by denying the Real Presence. He implored forgiveness from the King and Queen, from the nation and from God. He referred to the penitent thief on the cross, and mentioned that despite the sincerity of the thief's repentance, he had nevertheless been compelled to suffer crucifixion.[2]

Cranmer had three more days of life remaining to him. On the Thursday and Friday, he discussed with Cole and the friars what he should say at the ceremony at the stake on Saturday, for it had been decided that Cawood should publish the text of Cranmer's statement at the stake along with the six recantations. He must have written a transcript of his speech, because

---

[1] Foxe, viii. 83; *Bishop Cranmer's Recantacyons*, pp. 83–85; Report on the diocese of Lincoln, Easter 1556 (Strype, *Eccl. Mem.* iii [ii]. 392.)

[2] *Bishop Cranmer's Recantacyons*, pp. 84–90; the Sixth Recantation, in *All the Submissions and Recantations of Thomas Cranmer* (Cranmer's *Works*, ii. 564–5), where it is dated 18 March. In *Bishop Cranmer's Recantacyons* (p. 90) it is dated 9 March, which is certainly wrong; and the author of *Bishop Cranmer's Recantacyons* himself implies in another place (p. 84) that Cranmer wrote the sixth recantation three days before his death, i.e., 18 March. It has often been suggested that Pole wrote the draft of the sixth recantation; but there is no evidence whatever of this, and it is very unlikely. The author of *Bishop Cranmer's Recantacyons* (p. 85) implies that it was drafted by the friars at Oxford—most probably by Roscius.

it was published by Cawood a few days later; and though it did not bear his signature, this is perhaps not surprising, as it was to be issued not as a written recantation but as the report of a speech. It is unlikely that the speech was written by the Spanish friars, for it was in English, not in Latin, and Cranmer almost certainly wrote it himself. In it, he stated that he was a wretched caitiff and miserable sinner who had committed sins, many without number and great above measure, one of which burdened his conscience most of all, about which he would speak more hereafter. Then came the Lord's Prayer, and four exhortations to the people—not to love the pleasures of this world; to 'obey your King and Queen willingly and gladly, without murmuring or grudging, not for fear of them, but much more for fear of God, knowing that they be God's ministers, appointed by God for to govern and rule you; and therefore they that resist them resist God's ordinance'; to love their neighbour; and to give to the poor, which had never been as necessary as now, when the price of food was so high. Then, after declaring the Queen's just title to the Crown, Cranmer concluded:

'And now, forasmuch as I am come to the last end of my life, whereupon hangeth all my life past, and all my life to come, either to live with my Saviour Christ for ever in joy, or else to be in pains ever with the wicked devils in Hell; and I see before mine eyes presently either Heaven ready to receive me, or else Hell ready to swallow me up; I shall therefore declare unto you my very faith, without colour or dissimulation; for now is no time to dissemble, whatsoever I have said, preached or written in time past.

'First, I believe in God the Father Almighty, Maker of Heaven and earth'—and here he was to recite the Creed. 'And I believe every article of the Catholic faith, every clause, word and sentence taught by our Saviour Jesus Christ, His Apostles, and prophets, in the New and Old Testament, and all articles explicate and set forth in the General Councils.

'And now I come to the great thing that so much troubleth my conscience, more than any other thing that ever I did; and that is, setting abroad untrue books and writings, contrary to the truth of God's word; which now I renounce and condemn, and refuse them utterly as erroneous, and for none of mine. But you must know also what books they were, that you may beware of them, or else my conscience is not discharged; for they be the books which I wrote against the Sacrament of the Altar sith the death of King Henry VIII. But whatsoever I wrote then, now is time and place to say truth; wherefore, renouncing all those books, and whatsoever in them is contained, I say and believe that our Saviour Christ Jesu is really and substantially contained in the blessed Sacrament of the Altar, under the forms of bread and wine.'[1]

But it is clear that Cranmer was beginning to doubt once more. He knew now that recantation would not save his life, and the friars were pressing him too hard. They suggested that in this final speech he should insert the *Ave Maria* after the Lord's Prayer; but Cranmer refused. They had to accept the transcript of his speech, as it stood, and send it to the printers without the *Ave Maria*; but they continued to urge him after the transcript had been sent to Cawood. Cranmer eventually promised that he would say the *Ave Maria*; but the friars continued to worry him, urging him to sign more copies of the fifth recantation, presumably because they required copies which had not been witnessed by a Spaniard. On Friday the 20th, Cranmer signed more copies, but he told the friars that nothing would induce him to sign any other paper. They wished him to sign still more copies; but he would not do so, and they left the copies with him as he prepared for his last night on earth. He recited part of the statement that he was to read out next day, and retired to bed.[2]

It was probably during the night that he wrote out a very different version—a Protestant version—of his last speech. It was the same, without the *Ave*, until the last paragraph; but the last paragraph read:

'And now I come to the great thing which so much troubleth my conscience, more than any thing that ever I did or said in my whole life. And that is setting abroad of a writing contrary to the truth; which now here I renounce and refuse as things

---

[1] 'The Prayer and Saying of Thomas Cranmer a little before his Death', in *All the Submissions and Recantations of Thomas Cranmer* (Cranmer's *Works*, ii. 565–6).

[2] *Bishop Cranmer's Recantacyons*, pp. 90–92, 99–100. The author of *Bishop Cranmer's Recantacyons* seems to have been surprised that Cranmer omitted the *Ave Maria* in St. Mary's Church; but the *Ave Maria* is omitted from the version of the speech which Cawood published. This suggests that Cranmer, after refusing to include the *Ave* in the draft which he prepared for Cawood, later promised the friars that he would include it in his speech.

written with my hand contrary to the truth which I thought in
my heart, and written for fear of death, and to save my life if it
might be. And that is all such bills and papers which I have
written or signed with my hand since my degradation, wherein
I have written many things untrue. And forasmuch as my hand
offended, writing contrary to my heart, my hand shall first be
punished therefor; for, may I come to the fire, it shall be first
burned. And as for the Pope, I refuse him as Christ's enemy and
Antichrist, with all his false doctrine. And as for the Sacrament,
I believe as I have taught in my book against the Bishop of
Winchester, the which my book teacheth so true a doctrine of
the Sacrament that it shall stand at the last day before the judgment of God, where the Papistical doctrine contrary thereto
shall be ashamed to show her face.'[1] Thus he repudiated the
recantations which he had written since his degradation, for-
getting his earlier recantations, which were quite incompatible
with the present declaration, and doing himself less than
justice, in his remorse, by attributing the recantations to fear of
death alone. This was no more true than when he had told Aless
that it was only fear which had led him to subscribe to the Six
Articles.[2]

But he obviously still could not decide which of the two
versions of the document he would read out at the stake next
morning, and was in an agony of indecision. At five o'clock in
the morning, Cranmer signed the remaining copies of the fifth
recantation which he had refused to sign the previous evening.

[1] This is the text of the last paragraph of Cranmer's final speech as given by
Foxe (viii. 88). There are minor divergencies between the text of the full
speech as given in *All the Submissions and Recantations of Thomas Cranmer*, by
'J.A.', by the anonymous biographer and by Foxe; for an analysis of them, see
Dixon, iv. 535–9 n., 541–2 n. Great significance has been attached to the fact that
according to these texts Cranmer did not refer, in the Protestant version of the
speech, to 'whatsoever I have said, preached or written in time past', but only to
'whatsoever I have written in time past', or to 'whatsoever I have said or written
in time past'; but when we take into account Cranmer's state of mind, and the
possibility of errors in transcription, the significance of this distinction may be
wholly imaginary. The last thirty-eight words of the speech, as cited here, are to
be found only in Foxe, and it has therefore been suggested that Foxe invented
them; but as Foxe, though inaccurate in other matters, was scrupulous in copying
documents, it is more likely that the words were written by Cranmer, but that he
was prevented from uttering them in St. Mary's Church, as stated by 'J.A.' (see
Strype, *Cranmer*, p. 557); for Cranmer's original draft of the Protestant version of
the speech may have come into the hands of some other person, as well as of
'J.A.'
[2] Aless to Elizabeth I, 1 September 1559 (*Cal. For. Pap. Eliz.*, i. 1303 (p. 533)).

This was four hours before he was due to be taken from Bocardo to the stake.[1]

An event occurred during those four hours which according to the Oxford Papists had a profound effect on Cranmer. A man came to Bocardo with a message for Cranmer, and said that he had been sent by Cranmer's sister. This was not the Catholic sister, but the other one; perhaps it was the sister who had married the miller and had been denounced by the Canons of Canterbury in 1543. Her messenger 'brought him a ring', writes the author of *Bishop Cranmer's Recantacyons*, 'but I do not know with what instructions. This ring seemed to be the first sign of evil.' There is material here for the dramatist and the fiction writer which has never yet been utilized. The ring may indeed have had some personal significance for Cranmer, stirring up private memories too deep for a historian to fathom, and rousing a spirit of defiance and resistance to persecution; but it is more likely that the story was a piece of Papist melo-drama, like the tales of the attempts to rescue Cranmer during the night. In any case, Cranmer did not reach an irrevocable decision when he received the ring, for he was obviously still undecided when he left his prison for the last time at nine o'clock. As he said farewell to Woodson on leaving Bocardo, he assured him that he would not retract his recantations. He handed him fourteen copies of the fifth recantation which he had signed, and said that if anyone denied that he had recanted, this document would provide the proof that he had reverted to the Catholic faith.[2] But he had hidden in his bosom the Protestant version of his final speech, as well as the other version.

He still did not know whether he was going to recant, and which paper he would read out. But this was not, as is usually thought, because he was in doubt as to whether he would be

[1] *Bishop Cranmer's Recantacyons*, p. 93. Pollard (in *Thomas Cranmer*, p. 377 n.) assumes that the document which the author of *Bishop Cranmer's Recantacyons* states that Cranmer signed was the Catholic version of the final speech, i.e., the seventh recantation. Pollard doubts the truth of this, because he believes that the authorities would not have published an unsigned copy of it in *All the Submissions and Recantations of Thomas Cranmer* if Cranmer had signed it. But the draft of the unsigned version of the seventh recantation must already have been sent to Cawood for publication before 21 March, and it would then have been too late to replace it by any signed version. Moreover, *Bishop Cranmer's Recantacyons* clearly implies that the documents which Cranmer signed on 21 March were fourteen copies of a revised version of the fifth recantation.
[2] *Bishop Cranmer's Recantacyons*, pp. 93–94.

pardoned or burned. It is much more likely that the only question for Cranmer was whether to live with his Saviour Christ for ever in joy, or whether to be in pains ever with the wicked devils in Hell; seeing before his eyes either Heaven ready to receive him or Hell ready to swallow him up, he did not know which was the truth which would save him, and which was the falsehood which would damn him.

It was raining that morning, as it had so often rained during the wet spring of 1556; and this made it necessary to hold all the preliminary proceedings, which would normally have been held at the stake, in the shelter of St. Mary's Church.[1] The rain might also dampen the hundred and fifty fagots of wood and furze, and cause a slow fire, and the kind of death which Hooper and Ridley had suffered; but perhaps this thought did not occur to Cranmer in his concern for the fate of his soul. Cranmer walked through the rain between Garcina and Roscius in the procession from Bocardo to the church, where Lord Williams and the officers of the secular power were waiting along with the divines. Cranmer wore a ragged gown and an old square cap which covered the bald head which had been shaved at his degradation, and his beard reached nearly to his waist. They exhibited him on a raised platform, where he stood, looking the very picture of shame and remorse, with the tears rolling down his cheeks, as was thought proper in the sixteenth century for a man who was undergoing an emotional experience.

Cole preached the sermon, and spoke of Cranmer's crimes, of the infinite mercy of God, and of the penitent thief. He stated that Cranmer died reconciled to the Christian Church, and that in every church in Oxford masses satisfactory would be celebrated for his soul. But the events of the last ten days had made it necessary to give some explanation as to why this repentant heretic was going to be burned; and Cole explained that Cranmer's heresies had been so evil that even after his repentance it was necessary for him to be punished for them in the fire. Then Cole made an extraordinary statement. He said that Sir Thomas More and Cardinal Fisher of Rochester had been

---

[1] For the proceedings in St. Mary's Church and at the stake, see Foxe, viii. 84–90; *Bishop Cranmer's Recantacyons*, pp. 94–108; Anon. Biogr. (*Nar. Ref.*, pp. 228–33); J.A.'s letter, 23 March 1556 (Strype, *Cranmer*, pp. 551–9); Parker, p. 403. For the fagots used, see 'The Costs and Charges paid by the Bailiffs of Oxford' (in *Oxford City Records*, p. 240).

martyred for the word of Christ, and that their deaths demanded retribution. The execution of the Duke of Northumberland, a layman, was retribution for the death of the layman More, but the death of Fisher the cleric would have to be atoned for by the death of the cleric Cranmer. This is the version given by the author of *Bishop Cranmer's Recantacyons*. Foxe's report makes the statement even worse. According to Foxe, Cole said that More's death was atoned for by Northumberland's, but that it was still necessary to atone for the death of Fisher, because the deaths of three wretches like Hooper, Ridley and Ferrar were insufficient to balance that of so good a man as Fisher; so Cranmer's life must also be thrown into the scales to make the balance. It is right to give Cole the benefit of the doubt, and accept the more moderate version. We will therefore assume that he merely demanded an eye for an eye, and not four eyes for an eye, and judge him, not on the statements of his enemies, but on the eulogies of his friends. There remains no doubt that the almost unprecedented act of burning a repentant heretic was officially justified in the execution sermon as an act of vengeance.[1]

Cranmer was the only man in public life who had interceded for the lives of More and Fisher; and the authorities were aware of this, for Cranmer had recently had occasion to point out the fact to the friars.[2] It was a flagrant injustice to select Cranmer to atone for the death of Fisher when Gardiner, who had been the chief apologist for his execution, had died as Mary's Lord Chancellor, and had been granted all the honours of a great state funeral, and while Rich, whose evidence had condemned both Fisher and More, was burning heretics in Essex and was in great favour with Mary. Cranmer had always tried to conform to the exhortation to forgive his enemies, and had never indulged in revenge. It is not surprising that he recoiled from the religion for which Cole was the spokesman—from a religion which stood for revenge and injustice—and decided that this was not the faith in which to go to Heaven. Perhaps this passage in Cole's sermon was responsible for Cranmer's last decision.

When Cole had finished, he called on Cranmer to speak to the people and give proof that he believed in the true Catholic

[1] *Bishop Cranmer's Recantacyons*, pp. 96–97; Foxe, viii. 85.
[2] *Bishop Cranmer's Recantacyons*, pp. 80–81.

faith. But Cranmer read out the speech which he had written on that other paper which he had secreted in his bosom. When he left out the *Ave Maria* after the Lord's Prayer, Garcina and the friars began to fear the worst. Cranmer also failed to declare the Queen's title to the Crown, though he read out the passage on the duty of obedience to the King and Queen, bowing his knee as he mentioned their name. When he came to the end of his statement, it was the recantations that he repudiated—'all such bills which I have written or signed with mine own hand since my degradation, wherein I have written many things untrue. And forasmuch as my hand offended in writing contrary to my heart, therefore my hand shall first be punished; for if I may come to the fire, it shall be first burned'. By now the uproar had begun; but Cranmer had time to say: 'And as for the Pope, I refuse him as Christ's enemy and Antichrist, with all his false doctrine. And as for the Sacrament, I believe as I have taught in my book against the Bishop of Winchester.' Then they stopped him and pulled him down from the stage; but he had said enough.

Lord Williams told him that he must be out of his mind. But Cranmer went eagerly out of the church and ran towards the stake, with Garcina and Roscius running beside him, trying desperately to persuade him to recant again before he died. Garcina reproached him for his insincerity, and said that he would have admitted the supremacy of the Pope if the Pope had spared his life. Cranmer agreed that this was true. Garcina said that at least Cranmer had confessed this sin to a priest. 'Well,' said Cranmer, 'is not confession a good thing?' Cranmer had no more pride or deceit left in him, and was prepared to confess the truth to his bitterest enemies. His words to Garcina on the way to the stake were probably nearer the truth than the statement which he had just made in the church that he had recanted through fear of death. If the Pope had spared his life he would not have revoked his recantations, because although he had not recanted only to save his life, he took the ultimate decision to die a Protestant out of disgust with a Church which was prepared to burn a repentant heretic.

At the stake, he said farewell to a number of his acquaintances in the University, and offered them his hand. Ely of Brazenose College refused to shake hands with Cranmer; but several of the others took Cranmer's hand, defying the insults of Ely, the rules of the canon law and the latest royal edicts. Cranmer had still in his possession the transcripts of his final speech in both versions. The author of *Bishop Cranmer's Recantacyons* states that he handed a copy of his recantation to Lord Williams at the stake, and this can only have been the Catholic version of his final speech. He must have handed the Protestant version—the speech which he had in fact delivered—to someone as he stood at the stake, or perhaps he dropped it on the ground. A Papist whose initials were J.A. obtained it, and made a copy of it a few days later; and so in due course it was possible for Foxe and future generations to read it. J.A. must certainly have obtained a copy of the Protestant speech, for he could not have remembered so long a discourse if he had not had a copy of it; nor is it possible that he invented or paraphrased the words, because they resemble much too closely the text of the Catholic version which Cawood published. According to the Venetian Ambassador, Cranmer threw his fifth recantation into the flames, declaring that he had only signed it in order that he might live to serve the Protestant cause, but no one who was present confirms this story, and it is unlikely that Cranmer was carrying yet another document when he went to the stake.[1]

When the fagots were lit, Cranmer held his right hand steadily in the fire. Once he withdrew it to wipe his face—or perhaps it was because of the pain; but he promptly replaced it in the fire, and he did not move it again. He called out: 'I see Heaven open and Jesus on the right hand of God.' The Papists were horrified at his presumption and blasphemy, and at his mendacity when in fact he was on the road to Hell; but Cranmer knew at last that he had taken the right decision, and that it was Heaven ready to receive him, not Hell ready to swallow him up. He did not utter a cry, but held his hand in the flames until he collapsed and died in the fire and smoke. Despite the rain, the end came quickly. His enemies found something among the ashes which they thought was Cranmer's heart, and believed that it could not burn because of its wickedness.[2]

---

[1] Michiel to the Doge and Senate of Venice, 24 March 1556 (*Ven. Cal.* vi. 434); *Bishop Cranmer's Recantacyons*, p. 107; J.A.'s letter, 23 March 1556 (Strype, *Cranmer*, pp. 551–9); 'The Prayer and Saying of Thomas Cranmer a little before his Death', in *All the Submissions and Recantations of Thomas Cranmer* (Cranmer's *Works*, ii. 565–6).

[2] *Bishop Cranmer's Recantacyons*, pp. 108–9.

Thus Cranmer died an unrepentant heretic. Perhaps if he had lived for another hour, he would have recanted again; but he died at a moment when he was a Protestant, and by holding his hand in the flames till the end he proved to all the onlookers that he did not turn again before he died. His show of spirit and his courage in holding his hand in the fire impressed many of those who saw it, including the Papist J.A.; for an act such as this cannot be effaced by the glib official line that there was nothing heroic in Cranmer holding his hand to be burned in view of the fact that it would soon have been burned in any case.[1]

Before this last half-hour, Cranmer's conduct was far from heroic; but by his vacillation he embarrassed his persecutors far more than he could have done by heroism. Within a day or so of his death, Cawood had printed *All the Submissions and Recantations of Thomas Cranmer*, which ended with Cranmer's final statement in the form in which it was not delivered. The people were told that the heretic leader had recanted and died repentant. But a scene which has been witnessed by hundreds of people cannot be kept secret for long, and within three days it was known in London that Cranmer had repudiated his recantations before he died. The government then admitted this, and reverting to their old line of a fortnight earlier argued that Cranmer had never been sincere in his repentance, and that they had consequently been right in deciding to burn him despite the recantations. But this naturally led the people to question the authenticity of all the recantations. The Protestants spread the story of what had occurred at Oxford in an improved version, and said that Cranmer had denied at the stake that he had ever signed any recantation. Coming at a time when public opinion was turning sharply against the Queen and the old religion, the official change of policy with regard to Cranmer's recantations brought discredit on Mary and the Church of Rome. On 24th March, the Venetian Ambassador wrote to the Doge and Senate about Cranmer's fifth recantation with its Spanish witness, and stated that this incident, together with the execution, would cause even more unrest, as could be seen every day from the way in which the preachers were

---

[1] J.A.'s letter, 23 March 1556 (Strype, *Cranmer*, p. 559); Harpsfield, *Dialogi Sex*, pp. 743–4.

treated, and by the hostile demonstrations in the churches.[1]

This was not the first occasion on which Cranmer had done more for his cause by his weakness than he could ever have done by his resolution. Three hundred years later, Merle d'Aubigné wrote that Cranmer was a reed which bent before the axe rather than an oak which was felled by it.[2] If Cranmer had been a man of greater integrity and principle, he would never have become Henry's Archbishop, and would not then have been able to perform the work which he accomplished between 1533 and 1540. A man of principle would certainly not have collaborated with Henry after 1539 and 1540; but if Cranmer had not done so, there would have been no Archbishop of Canterbury in 1547 who favoured the Reformation and who could provide, not indeed the driving force, but the theological guidance and direction, of the Reformation under Edward VI. These facts are undeniable, whether we choose to see in them the hand of Providence, the laws of history, or pure chance.

Cranmer was an agent of Tudor despotism. He glorified the King, denounced enemies of the régime to the Council, punished political opposition, applied torture to suspects and sent heretics to the stake. Yet he was not a cruel man; and if he was sometimes influenced, usually unconsciously, by selfish motives, he tried far harder than most of his contemporaries to adhere to the principles in which he believed. He was not, as is often said, a coward, and showed many examples of his courage apart from his decision to issue his declaration against the mass in 1553 and that act of endurance when he held his hand in the fire. As a man, he was superior to most of his contemporaries in public life. His evil actions were nearly all the result of his fidelity to the doctrine of Christian obedience to the Prince.

This fact cannot altogether relieve Cranmer of the moral

[1] Michiel to the Doge and Senate of Venice, 24 March 1556 (*Ven Cal.* vi. 434); Sampson to Bullinger, 6 April 1556 (*Orig. Letters*, pp. 173–4); Zanchy to Bullinger, 6 April 1556 (*Hieronymi Zanchii Epist.* pp. 280–1, in Zanchius, *Opera Theologica*, vol. viii; Gorham, *Gleanings*, pp. 355–6). For the official attitude, see Vannes' talk with the Queen of Poland (Vannes to Mary I, 25 April 1556 (*Cal. For. Pap., Mary*, p. 224)); Mason to Devonshire, 29 March 1556 (Lemon, *Cal. St. Pap.* i. 77); Lalaing to King Philip, 11 April 1556 (*Span. Cal.* xiii. 266); *Bishop Cranmer's Recantacyons*, pp. 110–13; Parsons, *Three Conversions of England*, ii. 378; Harpsfield, *The Pretended Divorce*, pp. 293–4; Sanders, *The Anglican Schism*, pp. 222–3. See also the report of Cranmer's degradation and death in Bonner's Register (printed in Foxe, viii. App. Document ii).

[2] Merle d'Aubigné, *Vindication of Cranmer's Character from the attack of Mr. Macaulay*, p. 10.

responsibility for his actions. We are often told that it is unfair
to judge him by present standards, and that we must take into
account the century in which he lived; but though some future
historian may seek to excuse the acts of Hitler's followers by
pointing out that they lived in the twentieth century and must
be judged by the standard of their age, this argument does not
dispose of the problem. There was no necessity for Cranmer to
believe in Christian obedience and to serve Henry VIII in high
office. He might have remained faithful to the Church of Rome
and died with More and Fisher, or have rejected the Real
Presence when only a brave handful were doing so, and suffered
with Frith and Lambert. He might even have become an Anabaptist, or an atheist like the old professor at the Sorbonne,[1] or have
denounced all religious persecution as an adherent of the Family
of Love. He might have been a careerist like Norfolk and Rich,
and an instrument of royal absolutism under Mary as well as
under Henry; while he could easily have chosen to give an
unwelcome opinion about the King's great matter in 1529, and
spent the rest of his life in peace at Cambridge. Cranmer deserves both the credit and the blame for having chosen the path
which led him to become the persecutor of Frith and Lambert,
the author of the Prayer Book and the martyr at Oxford.

John Foxe made many mistakes with regard to facts, but he
is entitled to have the last word on the subject of Cranmer. It is
impossible to agree with Foxe that Cranmer should have been
called St. Thomas of Canterbury, while his reference to Master
Allen appears to be a clerical error, as there is no record of such
a man being numbered among Cranmer's victims. But the rest
of Foxe's passage will serve as an epitaph for Cranmer. 'Lest
he should have lived longer with shame and reproof, it pleased
God rather to take him away, to the glory of His name and
profit of His Church. So good was the Lord both to His Church,
in fortifying the same with the testimony and blood of such a
martyr; and so good also to the man, with this cross of tribu-
lation to purge his offences in this world, not only of his recantation, but also of his standing against John Lambert and Master
Allen, or if there were any other, with whose burning and blood
his hands had been before anything polluted. But especially he
had to rejoice, that dying in such a cause, he was to be numbered
amongst Christ's martyrs.'[2]

[1] Wriothesley, i. 107–8.   [2] Foxe, viii. 90.

BIBLIOGRAPHY

Most of the existing manuscripts concerning Thomas Cranmer had been published by the end of the nineteenth century. The most important of the unpublished sources are:

1. Cranmer's Register, at Lambeth Palace. Apart from the important entries which were printed by Strype, Burnet and Wilkins, the Register relates almost entirely to formal administrative matters which have little to do with Cranmer personally.

2. The Harleian MS. No. 353 in the British Museum contains interesting references to Cranmer in connexion with the events in September 1553.

3. The State Papers, volumes 1–11 in the Public Record Office contain a number of documents concerning Cranmer which have never been published or calendared.

Information as to Cranmer's family is to be found in *Pedigrees. Vincent No. 105 F*, and other of the Vincent Manuscripts in the College of Arms. These volumes are not ordinarily open to public inspection, and I am grateful to Windsor Herald and the College of Arms for permission to view them.

The following Bibliography contains the names of books cited as references, and of the more important printed works relating to Cranmer.

CONTEMPORARY SOURCES

Books written (or consisting chiefly of documents written) before
1600

Acts of the Privy Council. See Dasent; Nicolas.
—References to *Acts of the Privy Council* dated before 22 April 1542 are to Nicolas, *Proceedings and Ordinances of the Privy Council of England*, vol. vii; references to *Acts of the Privy Council* dated after this date are to Dasent, *Acts of the Privy Council of England* (New Series), vols. i–v.
ALESS, A. *Of the auctorite of the word of god agaynst the bisshop of london* (probably Leipzig, 1540).
ALLEN, W. *A true sincere and modest defence of English Catholiques that suffer for their Faith both at home and abrode: against a false, seditious and slaunderous libel intituled: The Execution of Justice in England* (Ingoldstadt, 1584).

BIBLIOGRAPHY 413

ANDERSON, E. *Les Reports du Treserudite Edmund Anderson, Chivalier, Nadgairs Seigniour Chief Justice del Common-Bank* (London, 1664).

BALE, J. *Illustrium majoris Britanniae scriptorum* (Wesel, 1548) (referred to as *Bale's Centuries*).

—*Kynge Johan: a play* (Camden Society) (London, 1838).

BATESON, M. 'Aske's Examination' (*English Historical Review*, vol. v) (London, 1890).

BECCADELLI, L. *Vita Reginaldi Poli Cardinalis ac Cantuariensis Archiepiscopi* (Venice, 1563).

BECON, T. *The Works of Thomas Becon, S.T.P.* (Parker Society) (Cambridge, 1843–4).

BÉMONT, C. *Le Premier Divorce de Henri VIII et le Schisme d'Angleterre* (Paris, 1917). See also under Modern Secondary Sources.

Bishop Cranmer's Recantacyons (*Miscellanies of the Philobiblon Society*, vol. xv) (London, 1877–84).

The Bishop's Book—The Institution of a Christian Man—see Lloyd, *Formularies of Faith.*

BLESDIKE, N. *Historia vitae Davidis Georgii* (Deventer, 1642).

BOESCH, P. 'Rudolph Gwalthers Reise nach England im Jahr 1537' (*Zwingliana*, vol. viii) (Zurich, 1947).

BOURCHIER, T. *Historia Ecclesiastica de Martyrio Fratrvm Ordinis Divi Francisci, dictorum de Observantia* (Paris, 1582).

BRADFORD, J. *The Writings of John Bradford, M.A.* (Parker Society) (Cambridge, 1848–53).

BRADFORD, W. *The Correspondence of the Emperor Charles V and his Ambassadors at the Courts of England and France* (London, 1850).

A Brief London Chronicle 1547–1564. See *Two London Chronicles.*

BRIEGERUS, J. *Flores Calvinistici Decerpti ex vita Roberti Dudlei Comitis Lecestriae in Anglia: Hollandiae ac Zelandiae pro Elizabetha Angliae Reginae Gubernatoris. Ioannis Calvini, Thomae Cranmeri, Ioannis Knoxij: aliorumque Protectorum et Apostolarum sectae Zwinglianae in Anglia, Scotia, Gallia, Belgio et Germania* (Naples, 1585).

BRINKELOW, H. *The cõplaint of Roderyck Mors, sometyme a gray Fryre, unto the parlament house of England hys naturall countrey, for the redresse of certain wycked lawes, evell custumes ãd cruell decrees* (1548 ed.)

—*Lamentacyon of a Christẽ agaist the Citye of London for some certaine greate vyces used theri* (1548 ed.)

BUCER, M. *Scripta Anglicana* (Basle, 1577).

BURNET, G. *The History of the Reformation of the Church of England* (ed. Pocock, Oxford, 1865) (vols. iv–vi for original documents; see also old Secondary Sources).

BURTON, E. *Three Primers put forth in the Reign of Henry VIII* (Oxford, 1834).

CAIUS, J. *A Boke or Counseill against the Disease commonly called the Sweate.*—See Hecker, *The Epidemics of the Middle Ages* (under Modern Secondary Sources).

Calendar of Letters, Documents and State Papers relating to the Negotiations between England and Spain in Simancas and elsewhere (ed. P. de Goyangos, G. Mattingly, R. Tyler, etc.) (London, 1862–1954) (referred to as *Spanish Calendar*).

Calendar of State Papers and Manuscripts relating to English Affairs in the Archives of Venice and other Libraries in Northern Italy (ed. Rawdon Brown, Cavendish Bentinck, etc.) (London, 1864–1947) (referred to as *Venetian Calendar*).

Calendar of State Papers (Domestic Series) of the reigns of Edward VI, Mary, Elizabeth, 1547–1580.—See Lemon (under Modern Secondary Sources).

Calendar of State Papers (Domestic Series) of the reign of Elizabeth 1601–1603, with Addenda 1547–1565, preserved in the State Paper Department of Her Majesty's Public Record Office (ed. H. A. F. Green) (London, 1870).

Calendar of State Papers (Foreign Series) of the reign of Edward VI 1547–1553 preserved in the State Paper Department of Her Majesty's Public Record Office (ed. W. B. Turnbull) (London, 1861).

Calendar of State Papers (Foreign Series) of the reign of Elizabeth, 1558–1589, preserved in the State Paper Department of Her Majesty's Public Record Office (ed. J. Stevenson, etc.) (London, 1863–1950).

Calendar of State Papers (Foreign Series) of the reign of Mary, 1553–1558, preserved in the State Paper Department of Her Majesty's Public Record Office (ed. W. B. Turnbull) (London, 1861).

Calendar of the Patent Rolls preserved in the Public Record Office, Edward VI, 1547–1553 (London, 1924–7).

Calendar of the Patent Rolls preserved in the Public Record Office, Philip and Mary, 1553–1558 (London, 1936–9).

Calendar of the Patent Rolls preserved in the Public Record Office, Elizabeth, 1558–1563 (London, 1939–48).

CALVIN, J. *Calvini Opera.* See *Corpus Reformatorum.*

—*Ioannis Calvini Noviodunensis Opera Omnia* (Amsterdam, 1667 (1671) ed.) (cited as *Calvini Opera*).

Cambridge University Grace Book B (ed. M. Bateson) (Cambridge, 1903–05).

Cambridge University Grace Book Γ (ed. W. G. Searle) (Cambridge, 1908).

CAMUSAT, N. *Meslanges historiqves, ou Recevil de Plvsievrs Actes, Traictez, Lettres missiues et autres memoires qui peuuent seruir en la deduction de l'histoire depuis l'an 1390 jusques a l'an 1580* (Troyes, 1619).

CARDWELL, E. *The Reformation of the Ecclesiastical Laws as attempted in the Reigns of King Henry VIII, King Edward VI, and Queen Elizabeth* (Oxford, 1850).

CAVENDISH, G. *The Life and Death of Thomas Wolsey* (London, 1899 ed.)

Chronicle of Calais in the reigns of Henry VII and Henry VIII (ed. J. G. Nichols) (Camden Society) (London, 1846).

Chronicle of Queen Jane and of Two Years of Queen Mary and especially of the Rebellion of Sir Thomas Wyat (ed. J. G. Nichols) (Camden Society) (London, 1850).

Chronicle of the Years 1532–1537, written by a Monk of St. Augustine's Canterbury. See Nichols, *Narratives of the Reformation.*

CHRYSOSTOM, Saint John. *Homilies on the Epistles of St. Paul the Apostle to Timothy, Titus and Philemon* (Oxford, 1843).

COCHLAEUS, J. *Beati Isidori Hispalensis quondam Archiepiscopi de Officiis Ecclesiasticis libri Duo ante annos DCCCC ab eo editi* (Leipzig and Antwerp, 1534).

CONSTANTINE, G. Narrative—*(Archaeologia,* vol. xxiii (London, 1831)).

Corpus Reformatorum (ed. C. G. Bretschneider and H. E. Bindseil) (Halle and Brunswick, 1834–1900).

COUSIN, HUGHES. See Bémont (under Modern Secondary Sources).

COVERDALE M. *Certain most godly, fruitful and comfortable letters of such true Saintes and holy martyrs of God as in the late bloodye persecution here within this Realme gaue their lyues for the defence of Christes holy gospel* (London, 1564).

CRANMER, T. *A Defence of the true and Catholike doctrine of the sacrament of the body and bloud of our saviour Christ* (London, 1550).

—*An Answer of the Most Reverend Father in God Thomas Archebyshop of Canterburye, Primate of all Englande and Metropolitane unto A crafty and sophisticall cavillation devised by Stephen Gardiner doctour of law, late byshop of Winchester, agaynst the trewe and godly doctrine of the moste holy Sacrament of the body and bloud of our Saviour Iesu Christe* (London, 1551).

—The same (London, 1580 ed.).

—*A Short Instruction into Christian Religion, being a Catechism set forth by Archbishop Cranmer in MDXLVIII together with the same in Latin, translated from the German by Justus Jonas in MDXXXIX* (Oxford, 1829).

—*Catechismus, That is to say, a shorte Instruction into Christian Religion for the synguler commoditie and profyte of childrē and yong people. Set forth by the mooste reverende father in God Thomas Archbyshop of Canterbury, Primate of all England and Metropolitane* (London, 1548).

—The same (2nd ed.) (London, 1548).

—*The Remains of Thomas Cranmer*. See Jenkyns.

—*The Works of Thomas Cranmer, Archbishop of Canterbury, Martyr, 1556* (ed. J. E. Cox) (Parker Society) (Cambridge, 1844–6) (referred to as *Cranmer's Works*).

Cranmer's Liturgical Projects. See Legg, J. Wickham.

CROMWELL, T. *Letters*. See Merriman.

DASENT. J. R. *Acts of the Privy Council of England (New Series)* (London, 1890–1907).

Deputy-Keeper of Public Records, Reports of (London, 1840–1902).

DYER, J. *Reports of Cases in the Reigns of Hen. VIII, Edw. VI, Q. Mary, and Q. Eliz. taken and collected by Sir James Dyer, Knt., some time Chief Justice of the Common Pleas* (London, 1794).

EDWARD VI. *Journal*. See Burnet, *History of the Reformation*.

—*Literary Remains*. See Nichols, J. G., *Literary Remains of King Edward VI*.

EHSES, S. *Römische Dokumente zur Geschichte der Ehescheidung Heinrichs VIII von England 1527–1534* (Paderborn, 1893).

ELLIS. H. *Original Letters illustrative of English History* (London, 1824–46) (referred to as 'Ellis, *Letters*').

—*Original Letters of Eminent Literary Men of the Sixteenth, Seventeenth and Eighteenth Centuries* (Camden Society) (London, 1843).

ELYOT, T. *The Boke named the Gouernour* (Everyman ed.) (London, 1907).

—*The Dictionary of syr Thomas Eliot knyght* (London, 1538).

ERASMUS, D. *De Pueris Statim ac Liberaliter Instituendis Libellus*. See Woodward, *Desiderius Erasmus concerning the Aim and Method of Education* (under Modern Secondary Sources).

—*Opus Epistolarvm Des. Erasmi Roterodami* (ed. P. S. Allen) (Oxford, 1906–58).

FABYAN, R. *The New Chronicles of England and France* (London, 1811 ed.).

FECHT, J. *Historiae Ecclesiasticae Seculia A.N.C. XVI. Supplementum* (Frankfort and Speier, 1684).

FOXE. J. *The Book of Martyrs*.—

Latin ed.: *Commentarii rerum in ecclesia gestarum, maximarumq. per totam Europam, persecutionum, à Vuicleui temporibus ad hanc usq. aetatē descriptio* (Strasburg, 1554).

2nd Latin ed.: *Rerum in Ecclesia gestarum, quae postremis & periculosis his temporibus euenerunt, maximarumq. per Europam persecutionum, ac Sanctorum Dei Martyrum, caeterumq.* (Basle, 1559) (referred to as 'Latin edition').

1st English ed.: *Actes and Monuments of these latter and perillous dayes touching matters of the Church* (London, 1563).

2nd English ed.: *The Ecclesiasticall History, contayning the Actes and Monuments of thynges passed in every kynges tyme in this realm, especially in the Church of England* (London, 1570).

The Acts and Monuments of John Foxe (ed. S. R. Cattley) (London, 1837–41).

The Acts and Monuments of John Foxe (ed. J. Pratt, London, 1877). See also editions of 1576, 1583, 1596, 1610, 1632 and 1641. (Except where otherwise stated, all references to 'Foxe' are to the 1877 edition).

FUESSLI, J. C. *Epistolae ad ecclesiae Helveticae Reformatoribus vel ad eos scriptae* (Zürich, 1742).

GABBEMA, S. A. *Illustrium et Clarorum Virorum Epistolae* (2nd ed., Harlingen, 1669).

GACHARD, L. P., *Analectes Historiques* (Brussels, 1856–71).

—*Collection des Voyages des Souverains des Pays-Bas* (Brussels, 1876–82).

GARDINER, S. *Answer to Pope Paul III.* See Janelle, *Obedience in Church and State.*

—*Confutatio Cavillationum, quibus sacrosanctum Eucharistiae Sacramentum, ab impiis Capernaitis, impeti solet, Authore Marco Antonio Constantio, Theologo Lovaniensi* (Paris, 1552).

—*Explication and Assertion of the True Catholic Faith touching the most blessed Sacrament of the Altar with Confutation of a book Written against the Same.* See *Cranmer's Works.*

—*Letters.* See Muller, *Letters of Stephen Gardiner.*

GERDES, D. *Scrinium Antiquarium, sive Miscellanea Groningana nova, ad historiam Reformationis ecclesiasticam praecipue spectantia* (Groningen and Bremen, 1749–65).

GILBY. A. *An Admonition to England and Scotland to bring them to repentance.* See *Knox's Works.*

—*An Answer to the devillish detection of Stephane Gardiner Bishoppe of Wynchester* (London, 1547/8).

GORHAM, G. C. *Gleanings of a few scattered ears during the period of the Reformation in England* (London, 1857).

GRAFTON, R. *Grafton's Chronicle, or History of England* (London, 1809 ed.).

Greyfriars Chronicle—Chronicle of the Greyfriars of London (ed. J. G. Nichols) (Camden Society) (London, 1852).

GUALTER, R. *Diary.* See Boesch.

HALL, E. *Hall's Chronicle* (London, 1809 ed.).

Hamilton Papers—Letters and Papers illustrating the Political Relations of England and Scotland in the XVIth Century (ed. J. Bain) (Edinburgh, 1890–2).

HANCOCK, T. *Autobiography*. See Nichols, *Narratives of the Days of the Reformation*.

HARPSFIELD, N. *A treatise on the Pretended Divorce between Henry VIII and Catherine of Aragon* (Camden Society) (London, 1878).

—*Dialogi Sex contra summi Pontificatus, Monasticae vitae, Sanctorum, Sacrarum Imaginum Oppugnatores et Pseudomartyres* (Antwerp, 1566).

—*The life and death of Sr Thomas Moore, knight, sometymes Lord high Chancellor of England, written in the tyme of Queene Marie by Nicholas Harpsfield* (ed. E. V. Hitchcock and R. W. Chambers) (Early English Text Society) (Oxford, 1932).

—See also Bémont, *Le Premier Divorce de Henri VIII*.

HARRISON, W. *Description of Britaine*. See Holinshed.

Historia von Thoma Cranmero dem Ertzbischoff zu Cantuaria inn Engelland (Weissenfels, 1561).

Historical Manuscripts, Reports of the Royal Commission on (London, 1870–1942).

HOLINSHED, R. *Chronicles of England, Scotland and Ireland* (London, 1807–8 ed.)

Homilies—Certayne Sermons, or Homelies, appoynted by the kynges Maiestie, to be declared and redde, by all persones, Vicars, or Curates, every Sondaye in their churches, where they have cure (1st ed., London, 31 July 1547).

HOOPER. J. *The Works of John Hooper* (Parker Society) (Cambridge, 1843–52).

Household Book of Henry VIII. See *Trevelyan Papers*.

House of Commons Journal (vol. i. 1547–1628).

House of Lords Journal (vol. i., 1509–78).

HUTCHINSON, R. *The Works of Roger Hutchinson* (ed. J. Bruce) (Parker Society) (Cambridge, 1842).

JANELLE, P. *Obedience in Church and State* (Cambridge, 1930).

JENKYNS, H. *The Remains of Thomas Cranmer, D.D., Archbishop of Canterbury* (Oxford, 1833).

JEROME, SAINT. *Sancti Eusebii Hieronymi Stridonensis Prebyteri Opera Omnia* (in Migne, *Patrologiae Cursus Completus* (Latin Series), vols. 22–30) (Paris, 1845–6).

JEWEL, J. *The Works of John Jewel, Bishop of Salisbury* (Parker Society) (Cambridge, 1845–50).

KAULEK, J. *Correspondance politique de M.M. de Castillon et de Marillac 1537–1542* (Paris, 1885).

King's Book.—A Necessary doctrine and erudition for any Christian Man; set forth by the King's Majesty of England. See Lloyd, *Formularies of Faith*.

KNOX, J. *The Works of John Knox* (Wodrow Society) (Edinburgh, 1846–64).

LAMB, J. *A Collection of Letters, Statutes and other documents from the Manuscript Library of Corpus Christi College illustrative of the History of the University of Cambridge during the period of the Reformation from A.D. MD to A.D. MDLXXII* (London, 1838).

LATIMER, H. *The Works of Hugh Latimer* (Parker Society) (Cambridge, 1844–45).

LEGG, J. WICKHAM. *Cranmer's Liturgical Projects* (Henry Bradshaw Society) (London, 1915).

—*The Sarum Missal* (Oxford, 1916).

LEONARD, W. *Reports and Cases of Law argued and Adjudged in the Courts at Westminster, In the Times of the late Queen Elizabeth and King James* (London, 1687).

Letters and Papers (Foreign and Domestic) of the Reign of King Henry VIII (ed. J. Brewer and J. Gairdner) (London, 1862–1910). (Referred to as 'L.P.'.)

Life of Fisher. See *Vie du bienheureux martyr Jean Fisher.*

Liturgies of Edward VI. The Two Liturgies, A.D. 1549, and A.D. 1552: with other Documents set forth by authority in the reign of King Edward VI (ed. J. Ketley) (Parker Society) (Cambridge, 1844).

LLOYD, C. *Formularies of Faith put forth by authority during the reign of Henry VIII* (Oxford, 1856 ed.).

LODGE, E. *Illustrations of British History, Biography and Manners in the reigns of Henry VIII, Edward VI, Mary, Elizabeth and James I* (London, 1838).

London Chronicle in the times of Henry VII and Henry VIII (ed. C. Hopper) (Camden Miscellany No. IV) (Camden Society) (London, 1859).

A London Chronicle 1523–1555. See *Two London Chronicles.*

The Lyfe and Death of Thomas Cranmer, late Archebushope of Caunterbury. See Nichols, *Narratives of the Days of the Reformation.*

MACHYN, H. *The Diary of Henry Machyn, Citizen and Merchant-Taylor of London, from A.D. 1550 to A.D. 1563* (ed. J. G. Nichols) (Camden Society) (London, 1848).

MALAKIEWICZ, A. J. A. 'An Eye-witness's Account of the Coup d'Etat of October 1549' (*English Historical Review*, vol. lxx.) (London, 1955).

MARTYR, PETER. *Defensio Doctrinae veteris et Apostolicae de sacrosancto Eucharistiae Sacramento* (Zürich, 1559).

—*Loci Communes D. Petri Martyris Vermilii* (London, 1583).

MASKELL, W. *Monumenta Ritualia Ecclesiae Anglicanae* (London, 1847).

MERRIMAN, R. B. *Life and Letters of Thomas Cromwell* (Oxford, 1902).

MOORE, F. *Cases Collect & Report per Sir Fra. Moore Chevalier, Serjeant del Ley* (2nd ed., London, 1688).

MORE, T. *Workes of Sir Thomas More wrytten by him in the Englishe tonge* (London, 1557).

MORICE, R. *A declaration concernyng the Progeny, with the maner and trade of the lif and bryngyng upp, of that most Reverent Father in God, Thomas Cranmer, late archebisshopp of Canterbury, and by what order and meanes he came to his prefermente and dignitie.* See Nichols, *Narratives of the Days of the Reformation.*

—*Concerning Bishop Stokisley, bisshop of London.* See Nichols, *Narratives of the Days of the Reformation.*

—*Cranmer and Canterbury School.* See Nichols, *Narratives of the Days of the Reformation.*

MORS. R. See Brinkelow.

MULLER, J. A. *The Letters of Stephen Gardiner* (Cambridge, 1933). (Referred to as 'Muller').

NICHOLS, J. G. *Literary Remains of King Edward VI* (Roxburghe Club) (London, 1857).

—*Narratives of the Days of the Reformation, chiefly from the Manuscripts of John Foxe the Martyrologist; with two contemporary biographies of Archbishop Cranmer* (Camden Society) (London, 1859).

—See also *Chronicle of Calais; Chronicle of Queen Jane; Greyfriars Chronicle; Machyn's Diary.*

NICOLAS, H. *Proceedings and Ordinances of the Privy Council of England* (London, 1834–37).

NOAILLES, A. DE. *Ambassades de M.M. de Noailles en Angleterre* (ed. Vertot) (Leyden, 1763).

Original Letters relative to the English Reformation written during the reigns of King Henry VIII, King Edward VI and Queen Mary: chiefly from the Archives of Zurich (ed. H. Robinson) (Parker Society) (Cambridge, 1846–7).

OSIANDER, A. *Harmoniae Evangelicae Libri IIII* (Paris, 1545).

Oxford City Records.—Selections from the Records of the City of Oxford 1509–1583 (Oxford and London, 1880).

PARKER, M. *Correspondence of Matthew Parker, Archbishop of Canterbury* (Parker Society) (Cambridge, 1853).

—*De Antiqvitate Britannicae Ecclesiae & Priuilegiis Ecclesiae Cantuariensis, cum Archiepiscopis eiusdem* 70 (1572) (referred to as 'Parker').

PILKINGTON, J. *The Works of John Pilkington, Bishop of Durham* (Parker Society) (Cambridge, 1842).

Plumpton Correspondence—a series of letters chiefly domestic written in the reigns of Edward IV, Richard III, Henry VII and Henry VIII (ed. T. Stapleton) (Camden Society) (London, 1839).

POCOCK, N. 'Papers of Archbishop Holgate 1547' (*English Historical Review*, vol. ix.) (London, 1894).

—*Records of the Reformation: The Divorce 1527–1533* (Oxford, 1870).

—See also Burnet, *History of the Reformation; Troubles connected with the Prayer Book of 1549;* and Pocock (under Modern Secondary Sources).

POLE, R. *Epistolarum Reginaldi Poli S.R.E. Cardinalis et aliorum ad ipsum* (ed. A. M. Quirini) (Brixen, 1744–57).

—*Reg. Card. Legati Apostolici Epistola ad T. Cranmer qui archiepiscopalem sedem Cantuariensis ecclesiae tenens novam de Sacramento Eucharistiae Doctrinam contra perpetuum Catholicae Ecclesiae consensum professus est ac tradidit.* See Le Grand, *Histoire du Divorce* (under Old Secondary Sources); and see Pole, *Epistolarum Reginaldi Poli.*

—*The Reform of England by the Decrees of Cardinal Pole* (ed. H. Raikes) (Chester, 1839).

PONET, J. *A shorte treatise of Politicke Power.* See Hudson (under Modern Secondary Sources).

POULLAIN, V. *Vera Expositio Disputationis Institutae mandato D. Mariae Reginae Angl. Franc. & Hibern, etc. in Synodo Ecclesiastica, Londini, in Comitijs regni ad 18 Octob. Anno 1553. His accessit Reverendiss. in Christo patris ac Domini D. Archiepiscopi Cantuariens. epistola apologetica ex Anglio autographa Latina facta* (1554).

Private Prayers of the reign of Queen Elizabeth (Parker Society) (Cambridge, 1851).

PROCTER, F., and WORDSWORTH, C. *Breviarum ad Usum Insignis Ecclesiae Sarum* (Cambridge, 1892).

The Rationale of Ceremonies 1540–1543, with Notes and Appendices and an Essay on the Regulation of Ceremonial during the reign of King Henry VIII (ed. C. S. Cobb) (Alcuin Club) (London, 1910).

Reformatio Legum Ecclesiasticarum. See Cardwell.

RIBIER, G. *Lettres et Mémoires d'Estat des Roys, Princes et Ambassadeurs sous les Regnes de François Ier, Henri II et François II, 1537–1559* (Paris, 1666).

RIDLEY, N. *The Works of Bishop Ridley* (Parker Society) (Cambridge, 1841).

RO.-BA. *The Life of Syr Thomas More, sometymes Lord Chancellour of England* (ed. E. V. Hitchcock and P. E. Hallett) (Early English Text Society) (Oxford, 1957).

ROGERS, J. *The Displaying of an horrible Secte of grosse and wicked Heretiques, naming themselves the Family of Love: newly set forth by I.R.* (2nd ed., London, 1579).

ROPER, W. *The Mirrour of Vertue in Worldly Greatnes (The Life of Sir Thomas More)* (London, 1903 ed.).

RYMER, T. W. *Foedera, Conventiones, Literae, Et Cujuscunque Generis Acta Publica inter Reges Angliae* (London, 1704–17).

SANDERS, N. *The Rise and Growth of the Anglican Schism* (London, 1877 ed.).

SELVE, O. DE. *Correspondance politique de Odet de Selve* (ed. G. Lefèvre-Pontalis) (Paris, 1888).

SLEIDAN, J. *The General History of the Reformation of the Church from the Errors and Corruptions of the Church of Rome* (1517–56, continued to 1563 by F. Bohun) (London, 1689 ed.).

SMITH, R. *A Confutation of a certen booke called a defence of the true, and Catholike doctrine of the sacramēt etc. sette fourth of late in the name of Thomas Archebysshoppe of Canterburye* (Louvain, 1550).

Spanish Calendar. See *Calendar of Letters, Documents and State Papers relating to the Negotiations between England and Spain.*

Spanish Chronicle.—*Chronicle of King Henry VIII of England, being a contemporary record of some of the principal events of the reigns of Henry VIII and Edward VI; written in Spanish by an unknown hand* (ed. M. A. S. Hume) (London, 1889).

State Papers during the reign of Henry VIII (London, 1831–52).

Statutes of the Realm (London, 1810–24).

STOW, J. *Annales, or A Generall Chronicle of England, begun by Iohn Stow; continued and augmented by Edmund Howes* (London, 1631).

STRYPE, J. *Annals of the Reformation; Ecclesiastical Memorials; Life of Parker; Memorials of Cranmer* (for the documents published in the Appendices). See Strype (under Old Secondary Sources.)

A Supplicacyō to the quenes maiestie (1555).

SZTÁRAI, M. *Historia Cranmerus Thamas Erseknek az igaz hitben való alhatatoságáról ki mikor az Papa tudomaniat hami solnaia Angliaban Maria Kiralne Asszony altal szörniů halalt szeniedet* (Debrecen, 1582).

TESCHENMACHER, W. *Annales Cliviae, Juliae, Montium, Marcae, Westphalicae, Ravensbergae, Geldriae et Zutphaniae* (Frankfort and Leipzig, 1721 ed.).

THOMAS, W. *The Pilgrim: a dialogue of the life and actions of King Henry VIII* (ed. J. A. Froude) (London, 1861).

Trevelyan Papers prior to A.D. 1558 (Camden Society) (London, 1857).

The Troubles at Frankfort.—*A Brieff discours of the troubles begonne at Franckford in Germany Anno Domini 1554 Abowte the Booke off common prayer and Ceremonies, and continued by the Englishe men theyre to thende off Q. Maries Raigne* (Zürich, 1575).

Troubles connected with the Prayer Book of 1549 (ed. N. Pocock) (Camden Society) (London, 1884).

Tudor Tracts 1532–1588 (ed. A. F. Pollard) (Westminster, 1903).

TUNSTALL, C. *De veritate Corporis et Sanguinis Domini Nostri Iesu Christi in Eucharistia* (Paris, 1554).

Two London Chronicles from the Collections of John Stow (ed. C. L. Kingsford) (Camden Miscellany No. XII) (Royal Historical Society) (London, 1910).

TYTLER, P. F. *England under the Reigns of Edward VI and Mary* (London, 1839) (for documents published)—see also under Modern Secondary Sources.

UNDERHILL, E. *A Note off the examynacyon and impresonmentt off Edwarde Underehylle.* See Nichols, *Narratives of the Days of the Reformation.*

Valor Ecclesiasticus temporis Regi Henrici Octavi (London, 1810–34).

VANDENESSE, J. *Sommaire des voyaiges faictz par Charles cincquiesme de ce nom.* See Gachard, *Collection des Voyages des Souverains des Pays-Bas.*

Venetian Calendar. See *Calendar of State Papers and Manuscripts relating to English Affairs in the Archives of Venice.*

Vera Expositio Disputationis Institutae mandato D.Mariae Reginae. See Poullain.

Vie du bienheureux martyr Jean Fisher Cardinal, Évêque de Rochester † 1535: texte anglais et traduction latine du XVI. siècle (ed. Fr. van Ortroy) (Brussels, 1893).

Visitation Articles and Injunctions of the Period of the Reformation (ed. W. H. Frere) (Alcuin Club) (London, 1910).

WEISS, C. H. *Papiers d'état du Cardinal de Granvelle* (Paris, 1841–52).

WHITTINGHAM, W. See *The Troubles at Frankfort.*

WILKINS, D. *Concilia Magnae Britanniae et Hiberniae a Synodo Verolamiensi A.D. CCCCXLVI ad Londinensem A.D. MDCCXVII* (London, 1737).

WILSON, J. M. 'Wolsey's and Cranmer's Visitations of the Priory of Worcester' (*English Historical Review,* vol. xli.) (London, 1926).

WOOLTON, J. *The Christian Manual* (Parker Society) (Cambridge, 1851).

WRIGHT, T. *Three chapters of Letters relating to the Suppression of the Monasteries* (Camden Society) (London, 1843).

WRIOTHESLEY, C. *A Chronicle of England during the reigns of the Tudors from A.D. 1485 to 1559* (ed. W. D. Hamilton) (Camden Society) (London, 1875–7).

ZANCHY, H. *Operum Theologicarum D. Hieronymi Zanchii* (Heidelberg, 1613).

Zurich Letters, comprising the correspondence of several English Bishops and others with some of the Helvetian Reformers during the reign of Queen Elizabeth (Parker Society) (Cambridge, 1852–5).

OLD SECONDARY SOURCES

(Works written between 1600 and 1800)

BOSSUET, J. B. *Histoire des Variations des Églises Protestantes* (Paris, 1688).

—English translation: *History of the Variations of the Protestant churches* (Dublin, 1836).

BURNET, G. *The History of the Reformation of the Church of England* (Oxford, 1829 ed.)

—*The History of the Reformation of the Church of England* (ed. N. Pocock) (Oxford, 1865). See also Burnet, under Contemporary Sources.

Unless otherwise stated, references to 'Burnet' are to the 1865 edition).

CALDERWOOD, D. *The History of the Kirk of Scotland* (Wodrow Society) (Edinburgh, 1842 ed.).

COLLIER, J. *The Ecclesiastical History of Great Britain* (London, 1840 ed.).

DUCAREL, A. C. *Some Account of the Town, Church and Archiepiscopal Palace of Croydon* (London, 1783).

—*The History and Antiquities of the Archiepiscopal Palace of Lambeth* (London, 1785).

FULLER, T. *Abel Redevivus, or The Dead yet speaking* (London, 1867 ed.).

—*Church History of Britain from the birth of Jesus Christ until the year MDCXLVIII* (London, 1868 ed.).

—*The University of Cambridge* (ed. Prickett and Wright) (Cambridge, 1840).

GILPIN, W. *Life of Thomas Cranmer, Archbishop of Canterbury* (London, 1784).

GODWIN, F. *De Praesulibus Angliae commentarius omnium Episcoporum nencnon et Cardinalium ejusdem gentis Nomina, Tempora, Seriem atque actiones maxima memorabiles* (ed. W. Richardson) (Cambridge, 1743).

—*Annales of England containing the Reignes of Henry the Eighth, Edward the Sixt, Queene Mary* (London, 1630).

HARINGTON, J. *Nugae Antiquae* (London, 1779 ed.).

HASTED, E. *The History and Topographical Survey of the County of Kent* (Canterbury, 1797–1801).

HAYWARD, J. *The Life and Reign of King Edward VI*. See Kennet.

HERBERT OF CHERBURY, LORD. *The Life and Raigne of King Henry the Eighth* (London, 1649). See also Kennet.

HEYLYN, P. *Ecclesia Restaurata* (Cambridge, 1849 ed.).

KENNET, W. *A Complete History of England with the lives of all the Kings and Queens thereof* (London, 1706).

LE GRAND, J. *Histoire du Divorce de Henry VIII Roy d'Angleterre et de Catherine d'Arragon, avec la Défense de Sandérus* (Paris, 1688).

—*Lettres de Mr Le Grand a Mr Burnet tovchant l'histoire des Variations, l'Histoire de la Reformation & l'Histoire du Divorce de Henry VIII et de Catherine d'Arragon* (Paris, 1691).

LE NEVE, J. *Fasti ecclesiae Anglicanae* (Oxford, 1854 ed.).

MILLES, T. *The Catalogve of Honor or Tresvry of Trve Nobility Pecvliar and Proper to the Isle of Great Britaine* (London, 1610).

PARSONS, R. *A Treatise of Three Conversions of England from Paganisme to Christian Religion* (1603–4).

PRYNNE, W. *The Antipathie of the English Lordly Prelacie both to Regall Monarchy and Civill Unity* (London, 1641).

ROWLEY, S. *When you see me you know me, Or, The famous Chronicle Historie of king Henry the eight* (Marlowe Society) (Oxford, 1952).

SECKENDORFF, V. L. *Commentarius Historicus et Apologeticus de Lutheranismo* (Leipzig, 1694).

SPEED, J. *The History of Great Britaine under the Conquests of the Romans, Saxons, Danes and Normans* (London, 1611).

STEPHENS, E. *The Liturgy of the Ancients represented As near as well may be, in English Forms: Positions concerning the Differences between the True English Liturgy, and the deformed disordered Cranmerian Changeling, by which it was Supplanted: The Cranmerian Liturgy, Or, The Subtility of the Serpent, In corrupting the True English Liturgy, by Cranmer and a Faction of Calvinists* (London, 1696).

STRYPE, J. *Annals of the Reformation and establishment of religion and other various occurrences in the Church of England during Queen Elizabeth's happy reign* (Oxford, 1824 ed.).

—*Corrections of Burnet's History.* See Burnet, *History of the Reformation of the Church of England* (1829 ed.).

—*Ecclesiastical Memorials relating chiefly to religion and the reformation of it and the emergencies of the Church of England under King Henry VIII, King Edward VI and Queen Mary I* (Oxford, 1822 ed.).

—*The Life and Acts of Matthew Parker, the first Archbishop of Canterbury in the reign of Queen Elizabeth* (Oxford, 1821 ed.).

—*Memorials of the Most Reverend Father in God Thomas Cranmer, Sometime Lord Archbishop of Canterbury* (Oxford, 1840 ed.).

See also Strype (under Contemporary Sources) for original documents published in Appendices.

WARE, R. (*sub. nom.* PHILIRENES). *Foxes and Firebrands* (2nd ed., Dublin, 1682).

WHARTON, H. (*sub nom.* A. HARMER). *Specimen of Errors and Defects in the History of the Reformation by G. Burnet* (London, 1693).

WHISTON, W. *An Enquiry into the evidence of Archbishop Cranmer's Recantation, or Reasons for a Suspicion that the pretended Copy of it is not genuine* (London, 1736).

WOOD, A. *Athenae Oxonienses: An Exact History of all the Writers and Bishops who have had their Education in the most ancient and famous University of Oxford from the Fifteenth year of King Henry VII Dom. 1500 to the end of the year 1690* (London, 1691/2).

MODERN SECONDARY SOURCES
(Works written after 1800)

ALLEN, J. W. *A History of Political Thought in the Sixteenth Century* (London, 1928).

ANDERSON, C. *The Annals of the English Bible* (London, 1845).

ASHTON, J. *The Father of the English Reformation* (London, 1925).

AUBIGNÉ, J. H. MERLE D' *Histoire de la Réformation du Seizième Siècle* (Paris, 1835–53).

—English translation: *History of the Reformation of the Sixteenth Century* (Edinburgh, 1846–53).

—*Histoire de la Réformation en Europe au temps de Calvin* (Paris, 1863–78).

—English translation: *The Reformation in Europe in the time of Calvin* (London, 1863–78).

—*Vindication of Cranmer's character from the attack of Mr. Macaulay: a letter to the Most Noble the Marquis of Cholmondeley* (London, 1849).

BAILEY, A. 'A legal view of Cranmer's Execution' (*English Historical Review*, vol. vii.) (London, 1892).

BASKERVILLE, G. 'A Sister of Archbishop Cranmer' (*English Historical Review*, vol. li.) (London, 1936).

—*English Monks and the Suppression of the Monasteries* (London, 1937).

BELLOC, H. *Cranmer* (London, 1931).

BÉMONT, C. *Les Revolutions d'Angleterre en 1553 et 1554 racontées par un fourier de l'Empereur Charles-Quint* (*Revue Historique*, vol. 110) (Paris, 1912). See also under Contemporary Sources.

BENRATH, K. *Bernardino Ochino von Siena: ein Beitrag zur Geschichte der Reformation* (Leipzig, 1875).

—Translation: *Bernardino Ochino of Siena: a Contribution towards the History of the Reformation* (London, 1876).

BLIGH, J. *The Ordination of the Priesthood* (London and New York, 1956).

BLUNT, J. H. *The Reformation of the Church of England 1514–1662* (London, 1869–81).

BRIDGETT, T. E. *Life of Blessed John Fisher, Bishop of Rochester, Cardinal of the Holy Roman Church and Martyr under Henry VIII* (London, 1890 ed.)

—*The Life and Writings of Blessed Thomas More, Lord Chancellor of England and Martyr under Henry VIII* (London, 1924 ed.).

BRIGHTMAN, F. E. *The English Rite: being a synopsis of the sources and revisions of the Book of Common Prayer* (London, 1915).

—'The Litany under Henry VIII' (*English Historical Review*, vol. xxiv.) (London, 1909).

BROMILEY, G. W. *Baptism and the Anglican Reformers* (London, 1953).

—*Thomas Cranmer, Archbishop and Martyr* (London, 1956).

—*Thomas Cranmer, Theologian* (London, 1956).

BROWNE, E. H. *An Exposition of the Thirty-Nine Articles* (London, 1882 ed.).

BURBRIDGE, E. *Liturgies and Offices of the Church* (London, 1885).

BUTLER, C. *The Book of the Roman-Catholic Church: in a series of letters addressed to Robert Southey* (London, 1825).

BUTTERWORTH, C. C. *The English Primers 1529–1545* (Philadelphia, 1953).

Catholic Encyclopaedia (ed. C. G. Hubermann, etc.) (London, 1907–13).

CHAMBERS, R. W. *Thomas More* (London, 1935).

CHENEY, D. 'The Holy Maid of Kent' (*Transactions of the Royal Historical Society*, New Series, vol. xviii.) (London, 1904).

CHESTER, H. *Hugh Latimer, Apostle to the English* (Philadelphia, 1954).

COBBETT, W. *A History of the Protestant Reformation in England and Ireland* (London, 1829).

Collectanea Topographica et Genealogica (London, 1834–43).

COLLETTE, C. H. *The Life, Times and Writings of Thomas Cranmer D.D., the first reforming Archbishop of Canterbury* (London, 1887).

CONSTANT, G. 'La Chute de Somerset et l'Élévation de Warwick: leurs conséquences pour la Réforme en Angleterre' (*Revue Historique*, vol. 172) (Paris, 1933).

—*La Réforme en Angleterre* (Paris, 1930–9).

—English translation, *The Reformation in England* (London, 1934–41) (references are to the English translation).

—'La Transformation du culte anglican sous Edouard VI' (*Revue d'Histoire Ecclésiastique*, vol. xii.) (Louvain, 1911).

—'Le Changement Doctrinal dans l'Église Anglicane sous Edouard VI 1547–1553' (*Revue d'Histoire Ecclésiastique*, vols. xxxi–xxxii.) (Louvain, 1935–6).

—'Politique et Dogme dans les Confessions de Foi d'Henri VIII Roi d'Angleterre' (*Revue Historique*, vol. 155) (Paris, 1927).

COOPER, C. H. *Annals of Cambridge* (Cambridge, 1843).

—*Athenae Cantabrigienses* (Cambridge, 1858–61).

'Cranmer's Martyrdom' (*Notes and Queries* [1st Series], vol. ix.) (London, 1854).

DEANE, A. C. *The Life of Thomas Cranmer* (London, 1927).

DEMAUS, R. *The Life of William Tyndale* (ed. R. Lovett) (Manchester, 1922).

DIMOCK, N. *Papers on the Doctrine of the English Church concerning the Eucharistic Presence* (London, 1911).

DIX, G. *Dixit Cranmer et non timuit: a Supplement to Mr. Timms* (London, 1948).

—*The Shape of the Liturgy* (Westminster, 1945).

DIXON, R. W. *History of the Church of England from the Abolition of the Roman Jurisdiction* (London, 1878–1902).

DODDS, M. H. and R. *The Pilgrimage of Grace 1536–1537 and the Exeter Conspiracy 1538* (Cambridge, 1915).

DU BOULAY, F. R. H. 'Archbishop Cranmer and the Canterbury Temporalities' (*English Historical Review*, vol. lxvii.) (London, 1952).

DUGMORE, C. W. *Eucharistic Doctrine in England from Hooker to Waterland* (London, 1942).

—*The Mass and the English Reformers* (London, 1959).

DUNLOP, C., and SMYTH, C. *Thomas Cranmer: Two Studies* (London, 1956).

EADIE, J. *The English Bible* (London, 1876).

ELTON, G. R. *The Tudor Revolution in Government: Administrative changes in the reign of Henry VIII* (Cambridge, 1953).

FRIEDMANN, P. *Anne Boleyn: a chapter of English History 1527–1536* (London, 1884).

FROUDE, J. A. *The Divorce of Catherine of Aragon* (London, 1891).

—*The History of England from the fall of Wolsey to the death of Elizabeth* (London, 1870 ed.) (referred to as 'Froude').

GAIRDNER, J. 'Cranmer and the Boleyn Family' (*Notes and Queries*, 10th Series, vol. iv) (London, 1905).

—'Henry VIII's English Litanies' (*English Historical Review*, vol. xxiii) (London, 1908).

—*Lollardy and the Reformation in England* (London, 1908–13).

—*The English Church in the Sixteenth Century from the Accession of Henry VIII to the death of Mary* (London, 1902).

—'The Fall of Cardinal Wolsey' (*Transactions of the Royal Historical Society*, New Series, vol. xiii) (London, 1899).

—See also Gairdner's Prefaces to *Letters and Papers of Henry VIII*, vols. v–xxi (ii) : and his Preface to *Bishop Cranmer's Recantacyons*.

GARRETT, C. H. *The Marian Exiles: a Study in the Origins of Elizabethan Puritanism* (Cambridge, 1938).

GASQUET, F. A. *Henry VIII and the English Monasteries* (3rd ed., London, 1888–9).

GASQUET, F. A., and BISHOP, E. *Edward VI and the Book of Common Prayer* (London, 1890).

GOODE, W. *An unpublished letter of Peter Martyr, Reg. Div. Prof. Oxford, to Henry Bullinger* (London, 1850).

GRAY, A., and BRITTAIN, F. *A History of Jesus College, Cambridge* (London, 1960).

HALLAM, H. *Constitutional History of England: Henry VII to George II* (Everyman ed.) (London, 1913).

HARDWICKE, C. *A History of the Articles of Religion* (London, 1884).

HECKER, J. C. F. *The Epidemics of the Middle Ages* (Sydenham Society) (London, 1844).

HOARE, R. C. *The History of Modern Wiltshire* (London, 1822–43).

HOOK, W. F. *The Lives of the Archbishops of Canterbury* (London, 1860–75).

HOPF, C. *Martin Bucer and the English Reformation* (Oxford, 1946).

HÖSS, I. *Georg Spalatin 1484–1545* (Weimar, 1956).

HUDSON, W. S. *John Ponet: Advocate of limited monarchy* (Chicago, 1942).

HUGHES, P. *The Reformation in England* (London, 1950–4).

HUTCHINSON, F. E. *Cranmer and the English Reformation* (London, 1951).

'Impossibilities of History' (*Notes and Queries* [1st Series], vol. ix) (London, 1854).

INNES, A. D. *Cranmer and the Reformation in England* (Edinburgh, 1900).
—*Ten Tudor Statesmen* (London, 1906).

JANELLE, P. *L'Angleterre catholique à la veille du schisme* (Paris, 1935). See also under Contemporary Sources.

LEBAS, C. W. *The Life of Archbishop Cranmer* (London, 1833).

LEE, HANNAH FARNHAM, *The Life and Times of Thomas Cranmer* (Boston, Mass., 1841).

LEGG, J. WICKHAM. *Essays Liturgical and Historical* (London, 1917). See also under Contemporary Sources.

LEMON, R. *Calendar of State Papers (Domestic Series) of the reigns of Edward VI, Mary, Elizabeth, 1547–1580, preserved in the State Paper Department of Her Majesty's Public Record Office* (London, 1856).

The Life of Thomas Cranmer (London, 1856).

LINGARD, J. *A Vindication of certain passages in the fourth and fifth volumes of the History of England* (1st ed., London, 1826).
—*History of England from the first invasion by the Romans to the Accession of William and Mary in 1688* (5th ed., London, 1849).

LITTLEDALE, R. F. *Innovations: a lecture delivered in the Assembly Rooms, Liverpool, April 23rd 1868* (Oxford and London, 1868).

LLORENTE, J. A. *The History of the Inquisition of Spain from the time of its establishment to the reign of Ferdinand VII* (London, 1826).

LOANE, M. L. *Masters of the English Reformation* (London, 1954).

LORIMER, P. *John Knox and the Church of England* (London, 1875).

MACAULAY, THOMAS, LORD. *The Works of Lord Macaulay* (Albany ed.) (London, 1898).

MACLURE, M. *The Paul's Cross Sermons 1534–1642* (Toronto, 1958).

MAITLAND, S. R. *Essays on Subjects connected with the Reformation in England* (London, 1899 ed.).

MARSHALL, W. *The Story of Cranmer Archbishop of Canterbury* (Edinburgh, 1876).

MASON, A. J. *Thomas Cranmer* (London, 1898).

MAYNARD, T. *The Life of Thomas Cranmer* (London, 1956).

MENTZ, G. *Die Wittenberger Artikel von 1536* (Leipzig, 1905).

MESSENGER, E. C. *The Lutheran Origin of the Anglican Ordinal* (London, 1934).

—*The Reformation, the Mass and the Priesthood* (London, 1936–7).

MORTIMER, C. G., and BARBER, S. C. *The English Bishops and the Reformation 1530–1560: with a Table of Descent* (London, 1936).

MOZLEY, J. F. *John Foxe and his book* (New York, 1940).

—*William Tyndale* (New York, 1937).

MULLER, J. A. *Stephen Gardiner and the Tudor Reaction* (London, 1926). See also Muller (under Contemporary Sources).

MULLINGER, J. B. *The University of Cambridge* (Cambridge, 1873–1911).

NÄF, W. *Vadian und seine Stadt St. Gallen* (St. Gallen, 1944–57).

NEILL, S. *Anglicanism* (Pelican ed.) (Harmondsworth, 1960).

OMAN, C. W. *The Coinage of England* (Oxford, 1931).

OSBORN, R. R. *Holy Communion in the Church of England* (London, 1949).

OXONIENSIS. 'The Band which fastened Archbishop Cranmer to the Stake' (*Gentleman's Magazine*, New Series, vol. 3) (London, 1857).

PICKTHORN, K. *Early Tudor Government: Henry VIII* (Cambridge, 1934).

POCOCK, N. 'The Condition of Morals and Religious Belief in the Reign of Edward VI' (*English Historical Review*, vol. x) (London, 1895).

See also Pocock (under Contemporary Sources).

POLLARD, A. F. 'Council, Star Chamber and Privy Council under the Tudors' (*English Historical Review*, vols. xxxvii–xxxviii) (London, 1922–3).

—'Cranmer, Thomas' (*Encyclopaedia Britannica* 13th ed., London and New York, 1926).

—*Factors in Modern History* (London, 1907).

—*Henry VIII* (London, 1905 ed.)

—*Thomas Cranmer and the English Reformation 1489–1556* (London, 1926 ed.).

See also *Tudor Tracts* (under Contemporary Sources).

PORTER, H. C. *Reformation and Reaction in Tudor Cambridge* (Cambridge, 1958).

POWICKE, F. M. *The Reformation in England* (Oxford 1941).

PROCTER, F., and FRERE, W. H. *New History of the Book of Common Prayer with a Rationale of its Offices* (London, 1905 ed.)

See also Procter and Wordsworth (under Contemporary Sources).

RATCLIFF, E. C. *The Liturgical Work of Cranmer.* See *Thomas Cranmer: Three Commemorative Lectures.*

RAUMER, F. L. G. VON. *Briefe aus Paris zur Erläuterung der Geschichte des sechzehnten und siebzehnten Jahrhunderts* (Leipzig, 1831).

—English translation: *History of the Sixteenth and Seventeenth Centuries* (London, 1835).

READ, CONYERS. *Mr. Secretary Cecil and Queen Elizabeth* (London, 1955).

ROSE-TROUP. *The Western Rebellion of 1549* (London, 1913).

RUPP, E. G. *Studies in the making of the English Protestant Tradition* (Cambridge, 1947).

SARGANT, J. A. *The Life of Archbishop Cranmer* (London, 1829).

SMITH, H. MAYNARD. *Henry VIII and the Reformation* (London, 1948).

—*Pre-Reformation England* (London, 1938).

SMITH, L. B. *Tudor Prelates and Politics* (Princeton, N.J., 1953).

SMYTH, C. H. *Cranmer and the Reformation under Edward VI* (Cambridge, 1926).

See also Dunlop.

SOAMES, H. *The History of the Reformation of the Church of England* (London, 1826–8).

SOUTHEY, R. *The Book of the Church* (2nd ed., London, 1824).

STEVENSON, J. *Cranmer and Anne Boleyn* (London, 1892).

STONE, D. *History of the Doctrine of the Holy Eucharist* (London, 1909).

STONE, J. M. *The History of Mary I, Queen of England* (London, 1901).

STUBBS, W. 'Archbishop Holdegate's Pall' (*Gentleman's Magazine*, New Series, vol. ix) (London, 1860).

STURGE, C. *Cuthbert Tunstal: Churchman, Scholar, Statesman, Administrator* (London, 1938).

TANNER, L. E. 'The Nature and Use of the Westminster Abbey Muniments.' (*Transactions of the Royal Historical Society*, 4th Series, vol. xix) (London, 1936).

Thomas Cranmer 1489–1556: Three Commemorative Lectures delivered in Lambeth Palace (Westminster, 1956).

TIMS, G. B. *Dixit Cranmer: a reply to Dom Gregory* (London, 1946).

TODD, H. J. *A reply to Dr. Lingard's Vindication of his History of England as far as respects Archbishop Cranmer* (London, 1827).

—*A Vindication of the Most Reverend Thomas Cranmer, Lord Archbishop of Canterbury, and therewith of the Reformation in England against some of the allegations which have been recently made by the Reverend Dr. Lingard, the Reverend Dr. Milner and Charles Butler, Esq.* (2nd ed., London, 1826).

—*The Life of Archbishop Cranmer* (London, 1831).

TYLER, R. *The Emperor Charles the Fifth* (London, 1956).

TYTLER, P. F. *England under the Reigns of Edward VI and Mary* (London, 1839). See also under Contemporary Sources.

Victoria History of the Counties of England: Kent (London, 1908–32).

WATERS, R. E. CHESTER. *Genealogical Memoirs of the extinct family of Chester of Chicheley* (London, 1878 ed.).

WILLOUGHBY, H. R. *The First Authorized English Bible and the Cranmer Preface* (Chicago, 1942).

WINTERS, W. 'Notices of the Ministers of the Church of Waltham Holy Cross' (*Transactions of the Royal Historical Society* (Old Series, vol. viii) (London, 1880).

WOODWARD, W. H. *Desiderius Erasmus concerning the Aim and Method of Education* (Cambridge, 1904).

INDEX

Burckhardt, George. *See* Spalatin

Burghley, William Cecil, Lord. *See* Cecil

Burgo, Nicholas de, 37

Burnet, Gilbert, Bishop of Salisbury, 1, 6–7, 177, 182, 277, 296, 333

Butler, John, Commissary of Calais, 166–7, 189–92

Butts, Sir William, 97, 237, 239 n., 242, 244

Cade, Jack, 296

Calvin, John, 9, 11, 42, 326, 329–30

Campeggio, Lorenzo, Cardinal, 25, 45, 58

Capito, Wolfgang, 159

Capon, John. *See* Salcott

Capon, William, 23

Carew, Mary. *See* Boleyn

Carew, Sir Nicholas, 44

Carne, Sir Edward, 42

Casale, Sir Gregory de, 35

Cassillis, Gilbert Kennedy, Earl of, 229

Catherine of Aragon, Queen of England, her divorce from Henry VIII, 25, 28, 30, 37, 42–45, 53–54, 58–64, 108, 355–6, 382–5, 400; protests against Cranmer being her judge, 35; sent to The Moor, 36; refuses to attend trial at Dunstable, 60–61; and the Oath of Succession, 74–77; her death, 100, 104; mentioned, 73, 160

Catherine Howard. *See* Katherine

Catherine Parr. *See* Katherine

Cawood, John, 395–7, 397 n., 400, 402, 404 n., 408–9

Cecil, William, Lord Burghley, 3, 141, 299, 344, 347–9, 358

Champion, Richard, 146, 173, 229

Champneis, John, 290–1

Chapuys, Eustace, the Emperor's Ambassador, his conversations with Norfolk, 41, 72; his reports to Charles V and Granvelle, 42–43, 52, 54, 66–67, 85–86, 88, 91, 99, 103–4, 146, 225; and the trial at Dunstable, 60–62; his interview with the Coun-

cil, 77–78; his part in Anne Boleyn's fall, 100; at Jane Seymour's funeral, 158; his interview with Cranmer and Gardiner, 241

Charles V, Holy Roman Emperor, Wiltshire's embassy to him, 29–30; and Henry VIII's divorce, 31, 34, 42–44; Cranmer at his Court, 39–40, 49, 376; and the Turkish invasion, 40–42, 47–48; Chapuys' reports to him, 42, 54, 66, 85–86, 91, 99; urged to invade England, 66, 289, 295; his peace negotiations with Francis I, 158, 161, 192; and Englishmen imprisoned in Spain, 217; his alliance with Henry VIII, 241, 246–7, 250–1; Henry VIII and Francis I unite against him, 254–5; warns Somerset not to proceed with the Reformation, 274; and Warwick's *coup* against Somerset, 302, 304; and Mary's mass, 317–19; proclaims the Interim, 327; his advice to Queen Mary, 349, 360; mentioned, 49 n., 75, 78, 98, 100, 104, 135, 320, 379, 385

Cheke, Sir John, 252, 280, 326, 347–8, 350

Cheyney, Sir Thomas, 139, 143, 155, 276, 304

Chirden, Humphrey, 233

Cholmondeley, George Horatio Cholmondeley, 2nd Marquis of, 9

Chrysostom, Saint John, 18–19, 195, 267

Claymonde, John, President of Corpus Christi College, Oxford, 79

Clement VII, Pope (Giulio de Medici), and Henry VIII's divorce, 25, 29, 32–33, 35, 42–44, 78; appoints Cranmer Grand Penitentiary, 30–31; and Cranmer's consecration, 54–55, 86; excommunicates Henry VIII, 63, 70; his dispensation to Henry VIII, 108; mentioned, 67, 72

Clerk, John, Bishop of Bath and Wells, 87, 119, 178, 184, 188

Clinton and Saye, Edward Fiennes, 9th Baron, Earl of Lincoln, 64 n.

his anger with Gostwick, 186; his marriage to Anne of Cleves, 193, 199–200; and the fall of Cromwell, 201–4; his divorce from Anne of Cleves, 204–5, 215; and the Seventeen Questions on the Sacraments, 210; supports Cranmer's views against the other Bishops, 211–12; his visit to the north, 217–19; and Katherine Howard, 220–5; and Cranmer's talk with Olisleger, 225–6; his war against Scotland, 229, 246; and the Prebendaries of Canterbury, 230, 235; and the attempt to send Cranmer to the Tower, 236–8; and the King's Book, 240, 267–8; his alliance with Charles V, 241, 247, 250–1; and the Windsor heretics, 243; and Turner's case, 244; his order for the English Litany, 247; at the siege of Boulogne, 248; debases the currency, 249; his speech to Parliament, 250; and the chantries, 250, 273; refuses to abolish certain ceremonies, 251; and d'Annebaut's visit, 254–6; his death, 256–7, 265; his will, 258, 343; his funeral, 264; and the Homilies, 265; and the Code of Ecclesiastical Law, 331; Cranmer's dream of him, 399; mentioned, 1, 5, 22 n., 65–67, 85–86, 88, 91, 93, 119, 132, 134–6, 144, 154, 158–9, 173, 185, 189–90, 195, 197, 206–8, 214, 216, 232, 259–61, 270, 272–3, 280, 316–17, 372, 375, 383

Henry II, King of France, 320, 396

Herbert of Cherbury, Edward, Lord, 6, 202

Herbert, Sir William, Earl of Pembroke, 301, 303, 347

Hertford, Edward Seymour, Earl of. *See* Somerset.

Heylin, Peter, 6

Heynes, Simon, 23, 234, 285 n.

Hilary, Saint, 266

Hilles, Richard, 218, 283, 304

Hilsey, John, Bishop of Rochester, prevented by Stokesley from preaching, 89; preaches at Paul's Cross, 98; and the revolts of 1536, 115, 117; attacks relics, 159; and the Six Articles, 180; his *Manual of Prayers*, 247

Hoby, Sir Philip, 234, 300, 304

Holbeach, Henry (Rands), Bishop of Rochester, and of Lincoln, 274, 285 n., 288

Holgate, Robert, Archbishop of York, 82, 151, 280, 317

Hooper, John, Bishop of Gloucester and Worcester, and the war against Scotland, 246; a witness against Bonner, 298, 304; and the overthrow of Somerset, 304; approves of Cranmer's articles on the Eucharist, 306; and the vestments controversy, 308–10, 313–15, 326; and the suppression of altars, 312; supports Mary against Jane Grey, 345; imprisoned, 350–1; his deprivation, 362; refuses to flee, 369; his execution, 405–6; mentioned, 279, 336

Houghton, John, Prior of the Charterhouse, 82–83

Hungerford, Walter, Lord, 256

Husee, John, 190,193

Hussey, Anthony, 241–2

'J.A.', 408–9

Jane Grey, Queen of England (Jane Dudley), 5, 343–8, 356–9, 361

Jane Seymour, Queen of England, 100, 111–13, 118, 158, 262

Jerome, Saint, 18

Jerome, William, 200, 206–7, 253 n.

Jewel, John, Bishop of Salisbury, 152

John, King of England, 173, 202, 259, 263

John Frederick, Duke of Saxony, 41, 171, 193, 200

John Zapolya, King of Hungary, 41

Jonas, Justus, 170, 193, 281–2, 374

Joris, David, 339–40

Joseph, John, 268, 296

Joye, George, 38, 86

Katherine of Aragon. *See* Catherine.